W9-DJK-584

THE LISZT COMPANION

Edited by Ben Arnold

GREENWOOD PRESS
Westport, CT • London

Library of Congress Cataloging-in-Publication Data

The Liszt companion / edited by Ben Arnold.
  p. cm.
  Includes bibliographical references (p.) and indexes.
  ISBN 0–313–30689–3 (alk. paper)
  1. Liszt, Franz, 1811–1886—Criticism and interpretation. I. Arnold, Ben, 1955–
ML410.L7L565 2002
780′.92—dc21   2001040558
 [B]

British Library Cataloguing in Publication Data is available.

Library of Congress Catalog Card Number: 2001040558
ISBN: 0–313–30689–3

First published in 2002

Greenwood Press, 88 Post Road West, Westport, CT 06881
An imprint of Greenwood Publishing Group, Inc.
www.greenwood.com

Printed in the United States of America

The paper used in this book complies with the
Permanent Paper Standard issued by the National
Information Standards Organization (Z39.48–1984).

10 9 8 7 6 5 4 3 2 1

To Elizabeth and William Arnold
With my love and devotion

Contents

Editorial Note

The following abbreviations are used:

JALS   *Journal of the American Liszt Society* (1977–).

LSJ   *Liszt Society Journal* (London, 1975–).

LSP   *Liszt Society Publications* (London, 1950–).

LW   Rena Charnin Mueller and Maria Eckhardt, "Franz Liszt: Works" in *The New Grove Dictionary of Music and Musicians* 2d ed. Stanley Sadie (London: Macmillan, 2001), 14:786–872.

MW   *Grossherzog Carl Alexander Ausgabe: Der Musikalische Werke Franz Liszts*. Ed. Ferruccio Busoni, Peter Raabe, P. Wolfrum and others (Leipzig: Breitkopf & Härtel, 1907–1936. Reprint. London: Gregg Press, 1966).

NLE   *Franz Liszt: Neue Ausgabe sämtlicher Werke/New Edition of the Complete works*, 1st ser. ed. Zoltán Gárdonyi, Imre Sulyok, István Szelényi, and others. 2d ser. ed. Imre Sulyok, and Imre Mező (Kassel and Budapest: Editio Musica Budapest, 1970–).

S   Humphrey Searle, "Franz Liszt: Works" in *The New Grove: Early Romantic Masters: Chopin, Schumann, Liszt*, rev. Sharon Winklhofer. Vol. 1. London: Papermac, 1985. Even though the new catalog in the second edition of the *New Grove Dictionary* appeared during the final editing of the *Companion*, we have continued to use "S" numbers to identify Liszt's works since the recordings and secondary literature on Liszt currently use these familiar numbers.

Preface

With each passing decade the significance of Franz Liszt's contributions to the nineteenth century and his immense impact on twentieth-century music have become better recognized. His transformation of themes and his harmonic innovations are celebrated today, as is his role in using octatonic and whole-tone scales, tritones, augmented chords, and other dissonances that led to the dissolution of tonality near his century's end. His formal combination of multi-movements within sonata form have intrigued numerous musicians, and his virtuosic excesses and performing capabilities refocused the entire era of nineteenth-century virtuosi. His role as leader of the New German School and of *Zukunftsmusik,* with its emphasis on the symphonic poem and programmatic music, greatly influenced immediate generations.

The Liszt Companion provides a scholarly overview and investigation into the main body of Liszt's music with brief discussions of his life, letters, writings, and reception in the German press during his lifetime. The focus of the companion is on Liszt's music, because scholars have turned their attention in book form more to Liszt's life than they have to his compositional output in the past quarter century.

The format for the book is similar to the first Liszt compilation, *Franz Liszt: The Man and His Music,* edited by Alan Walker over thirty years ago. It is not intended to replace Walker's volume, which offers insights into Liszt's music primarily through the eyes of performers, but to update and re-evaluate Liszt's music and to synthesize the immense amount of secondary literature on Liszt into a manageable and readable survey. Throughout the discussions, we have intended *The Liszt Companion* to be accessible to the educated general reader and, at the same time, indicative of the significant research in the field of Liszt scholarship today.

Many people have brought their talents and industry to this project, and I would like to thank all of the authors for their generous contributions and their conscientious work in preparing their individual chapters. I would particularly like to acknowledge the many hours of conversation and guidance Michael Saffle has offered throughout the process. Joyce Clinkscales, head of the Music and Media Library at Emory University, has been a great asset to the research, as have the outstanding and efficient interlibrary-loan personnel at Emory. I also want to thank Emory University for allowing me a sabbatical leave during spring semester 2000 to work on this book.

Finally, I want to express my deepest appreciation to my wife who has supported and encouraged me throughout the research, writing, and editing of this volume. I especially want to thank her for the pleasure of performing Liszt's songs with her over the years and for her assistance with the chapter on Liszt's songs and melodramas.

Ben Arnold
Emory University
Atlanta, Georgia

I

Life, Writings, and Reception

1

Franz Liszt: 1811–1886

Klára Hamburger

Dear Liszt, through the mist, beyond the rivers, above the cities where pianos sing your glory, where the printing-press translates your wisdom, wherever you may be, in the splendors of the Eternal City or in the haze of dreamy countries consoled by Gambrinus, improvising songs of delectation or of ineffable sorrow, or confiding to paper your abstruse meditations, singer of everlasting Delight and Anguish, philosopher, poet and artist, I greet you in immortality! (Charles Baudelaire: *Le Thyrse,* 1863).[1]

Baudelaire's description of Franz Liszt is among the most beautiful a great contemporary artist ever wrote about him. Liszt was certainly worthy of these words. He was an outstanding figure of his time: a bright, unique, tolerant, liberal European spirit (member of several Masonic lodges) in the "wicked nineteenth century," as Thomas Mann called it. He was without any kind of ill will and hatred (neither of nationalistic, religious, social, or personal kind), unselfish, and ready to help anyone. He was a phenomenon, a captivating personality of magnetic emanation, and a man of particular beauty, attractiveness, and sex appeal. Liszt was a witty and most cultivated and brilliant *causeur,* with a kind of sarcastic humor and manners of a *grandseigneur.* He spoke several languages: above all French, his favorite, German, and certainly a little Italian; he knew some English and a minimal amount of Hungarian. He was a worshipped, *non plus ultra* performer: a pianist, improviser, and musician—the greatest reformer of piano playing—and an outstanding conductor and pedagogue. And, last but not least, he was one of the most significant composers of the nineteenth century and one of the great romantic masters who had enormous influence on his younger contemporaries all over Europe, preparing in many ways the formation of different trends of twentieth-century Western music. He did not belong to those few geniuses who composed only masterpieces, but Liszt certainly produced numerous masterpieces among his piano compositions from his youth to his latest works. He remained faithful to his motto taken from his "noble compatriot," the great reformer, the Anglophile Hungarian Count István Széchenyi: "Pure soul, pure intention—whether successful or not."[2]

He was a contradictory, typical romantic personality, and full of ambivalent features; he was a demoniac artist, "Mephisto disguised as an abbé," as he was called, and "half Franciscan, half Gypsy," as defined by himself.[3] Cardinal Giacomo Antonelli referred to Liszt as "the Hungarian sorcerer."[4] The ambitious and confident young virtuoso genius became a more and more modest composer, when, still in his thirties, he ended his performer career, enduring with patience all kind of attacks against his works. He often said: "We can wait." He wrote to Richard Wagner on 29 December 1853: "You can be assured that I harbor not the slightest vanity concerning my works, and even if I produced nothing good and beautiful in my entire life, I would rejoice no less truly and intimately at the good and beautiful that I recognize in others."[5]

He never became fond of money and never accepted any fee from his pupils, except in his early youth when he had to support his mother and himself. He donated large sums to all kinds of charitable and cultural purposes, although he lived in a most modest way especially when he became old and lonely. He supported the appreciation of his predecessors, contemporaries, and younger colleagues, and was ready to concede his time freely, giving advice to anyone and reading and criticizing the innumerable scores he received. Yet, he was not free from vanity. Many people were horrified at his habit of wearing his decorations, medals, and different draperies or accepting veneration and hand-kisses in public from his pupils and admirers of both sexes in his declining years. Sometimes he wore a national costume of a Hungarian noblemen with the sword of honor—an object of constant mockery, especially in France—or later his long abbé cassock. Always longing for solitude and asceticism in order to work, he was not able to live without social success, and, to an increasing degree, without alcohol. A faithful and sincere-minded Catholic and father to three children, he never married, but took minor orders in the Catholic Church in 1865. Nevertheless, this most attractive man was never able to resist feminine seduction. Besides being a conscientious, plebeian artist whose idea was *Génie oblige* (instead of *noblesse oblige* as he wrote at the end of his essay on Paganini), he was not free from snobbism. He felt most comfortable in the society of aristocrats and prelates and had a foible for highborn ladies. His long lasting partners Countess Marie d'Agoult, mother of Liszt's three children, and Princess Carolyne von Sayn-Wittgenstein, as well as many others, belonged to that class.

Liszt was a noble-hearted and most generous artist, who professed that art, and music above all, was a task of higher order that ennobled mankind. It was in this sense that he consciously took upon himself the mission of an apostle of art and always remained faithful to it. In his essay fragment "On the Future of Church Music" in 1834, he proclaimed the necessity of creating a *musique humanitaire*, and he was a genuine *musicien humanitaire* himself all his life. His notions remained the same as those he had claimed as a young man of twenty-four in his essay "On the Position of Artists." He wrote: "The two classes which, by virtue of their office, their authority, are capable [of] reconciling every class . . . and of leading mankind, in mutual love towards the great humanitarian aim, are the priests and artists."[6] In spite of all his romantic, theatrical attitudes, and posing, he considerably improved the social circumstances of artists, in word and deed. In addition to writing these essays, he established a foundation for pensioned orchestra members in Hamburg in October 1840, and more than two decades later in 1861 he founded the General Association of German Musicians. In 1873 he also established a scholarship for young pianists in the capital of his native land. Wherever he stayed for a considerable time—in Weimar, Rome, or Budapest[7]—he contributed in an unselfish way to the development of their musical life.

CHILDHOOD IN THE HABSBURG EMPIRE, 1811–1823

Franz (or Ferenc in Hungarian) was born in Western Hungary on 22 October 1811. His native village, Doborján (or Raiding in German), belongs today to Austria. Both of his parents—Adam (1776–1827), an employee in charge of sheep farming of Hungary's richest and most powerful magnate Prince Miklós Esterházy, and Maria Anna Lager (1788–1866), orphan to an Austrian master baker—were of German origin. At the time, the whole of Hungary belonged to Austria. Since 1687 and the expulsion of the Turks, the Habsburg Emperors of Austria were the crowned kings of Hungary. The official language was German, and the people of higher classes could not speak Hungarian. Neither did a large number of people who lived like the Liszts on the western border of the country near Austria. The legitimization of the Hungarian language and national culture was to be one of the main aims of the so-called Reform period in the coming decades. It was quite natural, therefore, that Liszt could not speak Hungarian and did not take lessons in this Finno-Ugric language—very different from the Indo-Germanic ones—before he returned to Hungary later in life. Nonetheless, he always declared himself to be a Hungarian, and this was evident for his father and mother as well.

His parents, especially Adam who had not been able to become a career musician himself, were delighted to notice that their only child was undoubtedly a prodigy. The young Liszt possessed an extraordinary musical talent, playing the piano, sight-reading, and improvising in a most brilliant way at an early age. He progressed at a phenomenal speed, leading Adam, his first teacher, to show his fragile son off, fascinating all acquaintances and relatives who heard him. In 1819 Adam took his son to Vienna—at the moment the music center of Europe where Ludwig van Beethoven and Franz Schubert were still living. Liszt's father presented the boy to the famous piano teacher and Beethoven pupil, Carl Czerny, who was much impressed. As a result Adam decided to go to Vienna so that his son would have the opportunity to study with the best teachers. Since Prince Esterházy was not willing to give Adam a job in Vienna, he asked for a year's leave of absence and moved there with his wife Anna and Franz in the spring of 1822. Before leaving, the child gave some concerts in the nearest towns of his native land, Sopron (Ödenburg) and Pozsony (Pressburg or today, Bratislava, Slovakia).

In Vienna, the capital of the despotic, art-detesting Emperor Francis I, the Liszt family, without any income, had serious financial problems. Fortunately, Czerny and an aging Antonio Salieri, Liszt's music theory teacher, undertook the brilliant boy's training without charge. As Liszt's name became known, he played in various private palaces, and from 1 December 1822 performed several times in public with great success.

His ambitious father wanted his son to continue his studies at the Conservatoire in Paris so that he might become a celebrated artist with a brilliant career in Paris and London, as he himself would have liked to have done. Adam likely anticipated considerable earnings in Western Europe as well. Consequently, he requested that Prince Esterházy extend his leave of absence for two more years, but the prince refused. Adam, therefore, had to make a serious final decision: he would either give up his home and all kind of safe harbor or sell everything he possessed. The example of Leopold and Wolfgang Amadeus Mozart who, five or six decades earlier, had toured Western Europe was still vivid at the time and most certainly a contributing factor to Adam's decision. Before leaving the Austrian Empire he received permission from Prince Esterházy to allow Franz perform in Pest, capital of Hungary. Before his first concert on 1 May 1823 in the Hotel of the Seven Electors, Adam, in the name of his son, announced the event in German: "I am a Hungarian, and I know of no greater joy than to respectfully present to my dear mother country before my departure to France and England the first fruits of my education and training, as the first offering of the most intimate affection."[8]

PARIS: THE YOUNG VIRTUOSO AND CHILDE HAROLD'S PILGRIMAGE, 1823–1839

Was Adam right to take the child prodigy to the leading metropolis of Europe and take him on concert tours instead of letting him study and develop in peace? Master Czerny, who found Liszt's playing undisciplined some years later, actually disapproved of it. From Liszt's letters, written to his own children, we can see that he always felt handicapped because of his lack of formal education. In his essay "Lettres d'un bachelier ès musique" published on 12 February 1837 in the *Revue et Gazette musicale,* he (or Marie d'Agoult, who generally worked out his ideas at the time) formulated it with more bitterness, mentioning that his father cast him "into the midst of a glittering society," exposed him to the stigmatizing "humiliation of artistic dependency," where he was "patronized and remunerated by" the aristocracy "like a juggler, or like Munito the performing dog."[9]

Many years later Liszt became much more tolerant of his father and highly appreciated his self-sacrifice. All things considered, Adam, in spite of several negative points, created unique opportunities for his son in his formative years.

Thanks to his father, Liszt the prodigy became able to share in the most valuable double heritage of European culture of his time. The future master of romantic music grew up in Paris at the dawn of romanticism and received his education from the great poets, thinkers, and painters of the most important artistic movement of the nineteenth century. This development happened to a young boy whose musical training, artistic taste, and approach to music had been based in Vienna—the best possible place of his time in Central Europe. In this metropolis lived the greatest masters of classicism: Franz Joseph Haydn, Mozart, Beethoven, and Schubert. Especially the two latter masters had a definitive influence on Liszt's own art. Beethoven's kiss, which Liszt supposedly received in Vienna in 1823, was only a legend. The story, nonetheless, had a symbolic meaning for Liszt. Beethoven remained his idol. In the preface to Liszt's piano transcriptions of Beethoven's symphonies (1863–1865), he wrote, "The name of Beethoven is a name sacred in art." In addition, Liszt donated large amounts for the Beethoven monument and festival in Bonn in 1845 and composed two cantatas in his honor. His composing art is deeply rooted in that of Beethoven's. As a performer, his Beethoven interpretations were mentioned as sublime by Wagner and nearly everyone who had the chance to hear them. Liszt had a special predilection for the much less appreciated Schubert; he became one of Schubert's first proponents, performing his own arrangements of Schubert's songs throughout Europe. On the other hand, Liszt's own style became fertilized to a high degree by the innovations of the great Austrian composer in the field of form and harmony.

Leaders of the Romantic Movement played a tremendous influence on Liszt. In Paris he met and knew many of these leaders: Victor Hugo, Alphonse de Lamartine, Alfred de Vigny, Alfred de Musset, George Sand, Prosper Mérimée, Heinrich Heine, and many others. Paris became his mental homeland and French, which he learned as a teenager, became his favorite language. Liszt became obsessed with French society and his self-study of ancient and contemporary French philosophers and writers. He shared their new aesthetic principles, breaking with the old traditions. Their idolized personalities—Dante Alighieri, William Shakespeare, Jean-Jacques Rousseau, Count Claude Henri de Saint-Simon, Vicomte François-Auguste-René de Chateaubriand, and Lord Byron—became his own. Byron, in particular, influenced Liszt both in substance and appearance. These figures had a significant impact on his life and artistic development. Liszt was clearly drawn to the Christian socialist utopian theory of his "paternal friend and benefactor," the Abbé Félicité de Lamennais who soon broke with the Catholic Church. Lamennais had a decisive influence on Liszt, particularly concerning his ideas on the artist's, especially the musician's, mission and the ennoblement of mankind.

Even in the domain of music, Liszt's training was not serious in Paris. Barred from becoming a student of the Conservatoire because he was "non-French" and consequently "a foreigner," Liszt had to find his teachers outside of the Conservatoire. His father chose two teachers for him in music theory: the conductor and composer Ferdinando Paër, who probably orchestrated the thirteen-year-old's only opera *Don Sanche* (1824–1825), and the Czech composer Antonín Reicha, who was an excellent teacher, as Hector Berlioz tells us. The young virtuoso's career, however, made serious work nearly impossible.

Liszt hardly experienced any normal childhood. From age twelve he supported his parents who had given up everything for his sake. In December 1823 the family with their minimal savings arrived in Paris, the glittering and expensive Western metropolis. The child prodigy, *le petit Litz* as he was called, began giving concerts in the capital in private palaces as well as in public. By 1826 he was performing outside of Paris in the French provinces. On 17 October 1825 the première of his opera *Don Sanche* took place at the Paris Opéra. In May and June 1824, 1825, and 1827, he toured England with his father, and at the end of 1826 and beginning of 1827 he performed in Switzerland. His mother Anna returned to Austria to her relatives in the fall of 1825. In August 1827, while having a short rest with his son at Boulogne-sur-Mer, Adam suddenly fell seriously ill and died after a few days on 28 August. At this time Liszt asked his mother to come to France, and they lived together in Paris—Liszt returning home to her at their little Paris flat after his tours.

Developing into a most handsome, elegant, and attractive young man with good manners, Liszt gave piano lessons mainly to distinguished young girls in additions to his concerts in order to support his mother and himself. Admired by his pupils, at seventeen he fell in love with one of them, Countess Caroline de Saint-Cricq. Some months later, however, her father put an end to this relationship with this young "nobody," triggering in Liszt an acute mental crisis. He retired completely from playing in public and wanted to join the church. His mother, however, prevented him from joining, as had his father not long before his death. Liszt revived during the three glorious days of the Paris revolution in 1830—a time in which he sketched his never-completed "Revolutionary" symphony.

About 1830 Liszt met three great musicians in Paris whose art and personalities produced a great effect and influence on his own evolution: Berlioz, the French composer and father to "program music" and "idée fixe"; Niccolò Paganini, the demoniac Italian violinist who produced fantastic, never-before-heard effects on his instrument thanks to his unimaginable, transcendental virtuosity; and Frédéric Chopin, the Polish composer who created a new kind of a brilliant yet personal and poetic piano style based on improvisation, and rooted in the folk music of his dear, faraway, and oppressed *patrie*.

Around 1834 Liszt composed his first important piano works: the solo piece *Harmonies poétiques et religieuses* (S 150), the cycle *Apparitions* (S 155), and the unfinished piano concerto *De profundis* (S 691). He dedicated the concerto to Lamennais with whom he spent some wonderful weeks on the Abbé's estate in La Chênaie, Brittany. At the time Liszt was in love with the Countess Marie d'Agoult, née de Flavigny (1805–1876)—a beautiful, cultured, dazzling, spiritual, distinguished young lady, fired by literary ambitions and living in an unhappy marriage with an older husband. In May 1835 the already pregnant Countess and Liszt left Paris and rendezvoused in Geneva. The coming years were those of "pilgrimage" where the couple lived and traveled in Switzerland (until August 1837) and Italy (from August 1837). Liszt's pilgrimage was influenced to a large degree by his model, Lord Byron and his hero, Childe Harold. Liszt made some triumphant returns to Paris during this time as well. He had developed into the most brilliant, incredible virtuoso genius of his time. It was a highly important period for him as a composer as well, creating his own, special musical idiom inspired by literature, nature, and the fine arts. His first cycle *Album d'un voyageur* (S 156, first version of the Swiss volume of *Années de pèlerinage*, S 160) as well as many sketches or early versions of later works (*Années*, vol. II: *Italie*, S 161, piano concertos, and *Grandes études* S 137) were born in these years. His essays entitled "Lettres d'un bachelier ès musique" appeared regularly in the *Gazette Musicale de Paris*, although Marie had actually written the essays based upon drafts Liszt gave her.

Marie gave birth to their three children: Blandine (1835–1862), Cosima (1837–1930), and Daniel (1839–1859). This period of Liszt's life ends with his second concert tour to Vienna in November 1839. The first triumphal tour had been given there in April 1838 to benefit his Hungarian compatriots after the flood of the Danube in Pest. By this time, Liszt and Marie had fallen out of love, and in October 1839 Marie returned alone to Paris with the two little girls who were to live with Liszt's mother. Their baby brother joined them a little later.

THE VIRTUOSO TOURS, 1839–1847

The years between 1839 and 1847 were unprecedented triumphs for Liszt the virtuoso and creator of modern solo recital. In a few years with dazzling speed, he traveled over nearly the whole of Europe, with the exceptions of Scandinavia and the area south of the Balkan peninsula. From examining the map of his tours,[10] we can see the incredible number of places he toured, including some he visited several times in Germany, Hungary, the Austrian Empire, France, Great Britain, Ireland, the Netherlands, Belgium, Denmark, Spain, Portugal, the Ukraine, Russia, Turkey, and the principality of Romania. These tours included cities outlining the vast regions he traveled: Glasgow, Copenhagen, Riga, St. Petersburg, Moscow, Kiev, Odessa, Bucharest, Constantinople (Istanbul), Gibraltar, Lisbon, Limerick, and Dublin. Almost impossible to imagine, he toured for the most part in horse-drawn coaches and jolting post-chaises as well as, upon occasion, by ship. He also traveled in numerous regions where public security did not exist during those times.

Never before had an instrumental performer enjoyed such boundless celebration, approaching the star quality and cult following of popular musicians today. The "Liszt-mania" surpassed even that of the Baroque castrato singers a century before. This most attractive young man—a famous Don Juan—became the craze of the entire European continent. The press even suggested that "this man is obviously Satan himself, otherwise he would not be able to accomplish on a piece of wood . . . what he accomplishes."[11] Serious musicians, like Robert Schumann, reported as well: "yesterday again he [Liszt] played in his concert like a God, and the furor is not to be described."[12] Liszt surpassed all the well-known piano virtuosos of his time, including Ferdinand von Hiller, Johann Pixis,

Alexander Dreyschock, Johann Baptist Cramer, Friedrich Kalkbrenner, Heinrich Herz, Ignaz Moscheles, and Sigismond Thalberg. Liszt was a genial performer, musician, and improviser who produced miracles on his instrument that no other pianist could duplicate. The piano itself had to be reformed to suit his new orchestral and pianistic effects and colors, not to mention his incredible passages of octaves, chords, trills, staccato notes, and fast repeated notes. He would at times fall into ecstasy when playing, being demoniac or seraphic or thousands of emotions in between. He placed the piano with its open lid on the podium parallel to the public in order to get a reverberate sound. As early as 1839, he established the idea of the solo recital, "musical soliloquies," as he wrote to Princess Cristina Belgiojoso: "I have devised [them] specially for the Romans, and which I am quite capable of importing to Paris, so boundlessly impudent do I become! Imagine that, failing to concoct a programme which would have any kind of sense, I dared, for the sake of peace and quiet, to give a series of concerts entirely alone, affecting the style of Louis XIV and saying cavalierly to the public, 'Le Concert—c'est moi.' "[13] Because of his exuberant style of playing, he was called in the English musical world, a "giant," "tiger-tamer," "Aurora Borealis of musical refulgence," and a "Niagara of thundering harmonies."[14]

The music he performed contained, in great part, concessions to public taste and included pieces of many insignificant composers. Among his own new works were brilliant fantasias on popular songs of several nations and tunes of well-known operas, as well as popular works like the *Grand galop chromatique.* He played, nonetheless, Preludes and Fugues from Bach's *Das Wohltemperierte Klavier,* the *Goldberg Variations,* as well as his own transcriptions of Bach's organ works. In the 1830s when Beethoven was not popular in Paris, Liszt performed Beethoven's sonatas, concerti, and chamber works in addition to his own transcriptions of Schubert's Lieder, and works by Domenico Scarlatti, George Frideric Handel, Carl Maria von Weber, Felix Mendelssohn, Berlioz, Chopin, and Schumann.

During his glorious tours across Europe, he—in addition to giving concerts and taking part in soirées, balls, and receptions arranged in his honor—found time for composing. Beside many new transcriptions, arrangements, opera fantasias, and his first series of Hungarian national works, he turned to new forms in vocal and orchestral genres. During these eight hectic years he composed the so-called *Malédiction* piano concerto with string accompaniment (S 121), his first secular and sacred choral works, his first *Beethoven Cantata* (S 67), and a great number of Lieder.

In this period of his career, Liszt visited numerous countries and cities where he met, in two instances, people who were to become important in his future life. The first was Carl Friedrich, Grand Duke of Weimar in whose court he gave his first concerts at the end of November 1841, and where, a year later, he was appointed as court conductor in extraordinary service. The second was Princess Carolyne von Sayn-Wittgenstein (1819–1887), an ultra-rich, Polish, fanatic Catholic landowner in the Ukraine, who was separated from her husband. The princess first heard Liszt in Kiev in February 1847. Liszt, tired of his virtuoso life, had for years sought a companion to settle down with, and longed for quiet work as a composer. The princess—quite different from the beautiful and elegant Parisian Countess d'Agoult—would not be his ideal partner. Her influence turned out to be injurious in many respects, including his relationship to his mother and children as well as his writings and essays. The princess actually wrote large portions of his essays from this period based upon his ideas. Yet, at the moment they met, it was this exceptionally literate, cultured woman of high intellect who succeeded to settle him down and encourage him to compose. It would be with the princess during their twelve years together in Weimar that Liszt composed the greatest part of his well-known, mature works.

LISZT AND HUNGARIAN MUSIC

Liszt's visits to his native country between 1839 and 1840 and in 1846 were important for the evolution of his personal musical style. Despite his German origin, mother tongue, and adopted French culture, Liszt had not ceased to declare himself a Hungarian. It was during those visits, celebrated as the idolized national hero of romantic nationalism at a period of Hungary's struggle for national and cultural independence, that he began to renew his Hungarian roots with more and more sincere feelings.

The early impressions of Hungarian national music that Liszt had not forgotten soon meant more to him then mere exoticism. This type of characteristic national music at its height at the time was by no means folk music, but an idiom of international descent. (Béla Bartók and Zoltán Kodály would discover the ancient Hungarian peasant songs much later in the early twentieth century.) The national music had developed from the *verbunkos*, a recruiting music (from the German *Werbung*) that had flourished since 1780. *Verbunkos* contained elements of Hungarian folk dances as well as Turkish, Near-Eastern, Balkan, and Slavic components—even elements of new Viennese and Italian music seeped into it. This conglomerate and yet characteristic Hungarian national music with its unmistakable stylistic features such as "heel-clicking" cadences, dotted rhythms, and the "Hungarian" or "Gypsy" scale with two augmented seconds, was incredibly popular in Hungary. Hungary adopted it as its primary national symbol of identity. At times it was played on instruments to show resistance to Austrian censorship when national language and costume were forbidden. In the nineteenth century Hungary remained a feudal country without the bourgeoisie and without learned native musicians. The only performers of national music were the Gypsy bands whose characteristic features of interpretation became inseparable from it. It is this reason why it was called "Gypsy-music." Authors of these popular art songs (*magyar nóta*) were, with few exceptions, contemporary dilettante musicians of the Hungarian gentry class who could not write them down. The Gypsy bands could not read music, but learned and played by ear. In the early printed collections, learned musicians belonging to the German minority arranged the melodies for piano.

Both the character and interpretation of that music fascinated Liszt. In his first Hungarian compositions—the first fifteen *Hungarian Rhapsodies* (S 244) and their earlier versions—he wanted to declare his romantic patriotic obligation. Over time, however, Liszt, interested in everything which did not conform, adopted its elements (above all the "Hungarian" or "Gypsy" scale, and the abstractions extracted from it) to his own musical idiom, in a more and more personal, organic, systematic, general, and modern way. These characteristics appear more frequently in his works that have nothing to do with Hungary. They have their special meaning and serve, above all, the expressions of grief, sorrow, and mourning. Yet, not speaking Hungarian and only knowing the circumstances of its music superficially, Liszt had several essential misconceptions concerning this music known as Gypsy music. He thought the melodies were ancient Gypsy folk tunes, fragments of a uniform-but-lost Gypsy epos. In fact, they were only a few decades old and inventions of Hungarian noblemen, often with Hungarian words. What he wanted to do in his *Hungarian Rhapsodies* in his capacity of *rhapsodos,* as he called himself, was to "reconstruct" this "lost Gypsy epos."

These ideas were all nonsense, as we see it now, knowing the real Hungarian and the real Gypsy ("Roma," as they call themselves) folklore. None of these pieces has anything to do with the so-called Gypsy music, except the typical features of Gypsy *Aufführungspraxis.* Liszt, nevertheless, remained convinced of his misconception until the end of his life. In the late 1850s he wanted to formulate his theory in a short preface to his first fifteen *Hungarian Rhapsodies.* The preface Liszt intended grew to a complete volume under the control of Princess Carolyne. In 1859 Liszt published it in Paris under the title *Des Bohémiens et de leur musique en Hongrie* (On Gypsies and on Their Music in Hungary), and, two years later, in Pest, in Hungarian and German translations. In addition to expounding upon Liszt's incorrect theory, the book contained long, tedious, and silly chapters that Princess Carolyne wrote that had nothing to do with the topic, as well as considerable nonsense concerning Hungarian history. Hungarian proper and geographical names were printed with a terrible orthography, making them almost unrecognizable.

The unfortunate book gave rise to a national scandal in Liszt's native country, following a period of the lost war of independence and of suffering under the severest Austrian suppression. His compatriots, the landowner gentry class who lacked musical culture, did not appreciate Liszt's good will. They soon forgot all the fabulous amounts he had given for various institutions in Hungary. Suddenly, he became accused of something similar to high treason. Liszt, the man so much honored in his homeland—had he not even been awarded with a sword of honor, that symbol of gentility—had deprived his nation of its dearest symbol of identity by declaring this so-called "Gypsy music" to be Gypsy indeed and not Hungarian. To make matters worse, he committed his errors in favor of Hungary's most despised national minorities, the Gypsies. The terrible confrontation between Liszt and Hungary that this book produced would have unfortunate consequences in Liszt's later life and even after his death.

WEIMAR, 1848–1861

Liszt summed up his aims in his testament in 1860: "At a certain time (about ten years ago) I envisaged Weimar as a new art period, similar to the one under Carl August, where Wagner and myself should have been leaders just like Johann Wolfgang von Goethe and Friedrich Schiller had been earlier, but unfavorable circumstances destroyed this dream."[15] In 1848 Liszt settled down with Princess Carolyne Sayn-Wittgenstein in Weimar, capital of the German feudal Grand Duchy of Sachsen-Weimar. Liszt served as a conductor, Kapellmeister in extraordinary service, at the court of Grand Duke Carl Friedrich and later of his son Carl Alexander. The princess escaped from Russia with her young daughter Princess Marie Sayn-Wittgenstein, leaving behind the greatest part of her immense fortune. For Liszt, it meant a complete change of life, with restrictions and obligations of several kinds. No longer was he a free, traveling, and glorified artist. Now he had a place to live with a steady job and a commitment to the princess with whom he had to accommodate himself. The princess, when they finally set up house together at the villa Altenburg, ran it as a grand house, constantly receiving guests (including the increasing team of students in Liszt's masterclasses). Liszt no longer had much privacy, even when composing.

He had also his obligations towards the court and the Court Theatre, where he accomplished outstanding and pioneering work as conductor of operatic performances. He revived twenty operas of great value, among them works by Christoph Willibald von Gluck, Mozart, Beethoven, André Grétry, Luigi Cherubini, Schubert, Weber, and Vincenzo Bellini. He also performed twenty-two operas of outstanding contemporaries, including Gioacchino Rossini, Otto Nicolai, Giacomo Meyerbeer, Schumann, Giuseppe Verdi, Peter Cornelius, and, above all Wagner and Berlioz. Liszt led seven world premières, most notably Wagner's *Lohengrin* and Cornelius's *Der Barbier von Bagdad*.

Despite his great expectations, Liszt soon realized that living in Weimar placed severe restrictions on his private life as well as on his capacity as a creative artist. Very much in favor at a court that rigidly clung to old ceremonies and formalities, he did not succeed in making them accept the princess who had been unable to get divorced. Instead of his former admirers that had surrounded him before coming to Weimar, he found himself surrounded by the prejudiced dislikes of the drowsy, envious, petty-bourgeois in this legendary town that still promoted their famous and deceased citizens. Liszt's presence as a foreigner, his French speech, his attitude of a *grandseigneur*, and his unusual attire evoked the growing indignation of the Weimar residents, not to mention his living with a princess who smoked cigars and was married to someone else.

As a conductor, he had to deal with the immense and increasing material difficulties of the small, provincial, declining, and retrograde German principality, which made work almost impossible for him. As a theatre leader, he had to endure—as long as he was able to—all kinds of intrigues. Above all, Liszt the idolized pianist who had stopped playing in public in order to focus on composing suddenly found himself attacked from all sides as a composer. Liszt, the father and master of the new trend of music mocked by the nickname *Zukunftsmusik* or "Music of the Future," had to bear a hostile reception in nearly the whole of Germany. He wrote about his situation in a letter to his great secret love Agnès Street-Klindworth (1825–1906) on 16 November 1860:

If, after settling here in 48, I had wanted to attach myself to the *posthumous* party in music, to be associated with its hypocrisy, and adopt its prejudices etc., nothing would have been easier for me due to my former contact with the chief representatives of this side. . . . It would certainly have had exterior advantages in esteem and approbation; the newspapers who have taken it upon themselves to utter strongly stupidities and insults about me would have excelled their praises to the skies, without my having to do anything for it. . . . But such was not to be my lot; my convictions were too sincere, my faith in the present and the future of art at once too ardent and positive to accommodate myself to the vain formulas of objurgation of our pseudo-critics.[16]

In spite of all these external difficulties and of the internal one, his own restless spirit, his emphasis grew increasingly on composition. In his duties as theatre conductor, he, over time, became a master of handling the orchestra as well. Weimar became the zenith of his activity as a composer—the period where his most popular, monumental works were born or received their decisive version (see Table 1.1).

Table 1.1
Liszt's Major Composition in Weimar

1832–1856	Piano Concerto in E flat major. S 124.
1835–1854	*Années de pèlerinage, première année, Suisse.* S 160.
1837–1858	*Années de pèlerinage, deuxième année, Italie.* S 161.
1837–1851	*Études d'exécution transcendante.* S 139.
1838–1851	*Grandes études de Paganini.* S 141.
1839–1861	Piano Concerto no. 2 in A major. S 125.
1839–1859	*Totentanz.* S 126.
1848–1857	Symphonic poems *Ce qu'on entend sur la montagne* to *Die Ideale.* (S 95–106).
1849	*Funérailles.* S 173/7.
1852–1853	Sonata in B minor. S 178.
1854–1857	*Eine Faust-Symphonie.* S 108.
1855–1856	*Eine Symphonie zu Dantes Divina commedia.* S 109.
1855–1862	*Psalm 13.* S 13.
1855–1858	*Gran Mass.* S 9.
1856–1861	*Two Episodes from Lenau's Faust.* S 110.
	1. *Der nächtliche Zug*
	2. *Der Tanz in der Dorfschenke (Mephisto-Waltz* no. 1)

In addition to many of his major piano works and concerti from this period, he also composed his two large-scale symphonies and the majority of his symphonic poems (S 95–104), a one-movement form he invented. External elements inspired each of his symphonic poems, including Hungarian historical themes (*Héroïde funèbre* and *Hungaria),* themes of antiquity (*Orpheus),* and art

(*Hunnenschlacht*). He based several orchestral compositions on literary works of Johann Gottfried Herder, Hugo, Byron, Goethe, Schiller, and Shakespeare.

The main points of Liszt's style include few themes or short motives suitable to variation and changes of character as well of free use of chromaticism. He also frequently uses "Hungarian" or Gypsy scales and non-diatonic gamuts such as chromatic and whole-tone scales, and individual scale models and constructions.

Although many of Liszt's Weimar orchestral works included theatricalisms and bombastic effects, he influenced a large series of outstanding composers through his various innovations. This list includes César Franck, Camille Saint-Saëns, Claude Debussy, Maurice Ravel, Olivier Messiaen, Wagner, Richard Strauss, Arnold Schoenberg, Bedřich Smetana, Antonín Dvořák, Edvard Grieg, Peter Ilich Tchaikovsky, Modeste Mussorgsky, Nicolai Rimsky-Korsakov, Alexander Borodin, Alexander Skryabin, Sergei Rachmaninoff, Bartók, and Kodály. Nevertheless, Liszt may have never composed as much orchestral music had not Princess Carolyne continued to encourage him in these efforts, even if some of the loud and theatrical sections occurring in his "grand" works were quite likely because of the princess's taste and influence.

Liszt wrote a large portion of his essays in this period as well that contained his ideas concerning problems of art, music, and artists. Nevertheless, they also included the princess's elaborations with her Slavic inclination for loquacity and certain prejudices that in no manner matched the elegant literary French style of the enlightened Parisian, Marie d'Agoult, who had previously assisted him in his essays.

In no other phase of his life did Liszt remain in a single place as in Weimar. He departed only for occasional journeys to take cures, attend music festivals, or visit family or friends. He accompanied the princess and her daughter to Bad Eilsen and later traveled to Aachen to cure his own skin disease. He attended performances of his works in several places in Germany, Prague, Vienna, and Hungary where he was at the world première of his *Gran Mass* in 1856. Upon occasion he visited family or friends. In August 1857 he attended his daughter Cosima and his favorite pupil Hans von Bülow's wedding in Berlin. Between 1853 and 1856 he twice visited with Wagner in Switzerland, who, after the uprising of 1849 in Dresden, succeeded to escape from Germany, thanks to Liszt, and lived there in exile. He traveled to Paris in 1853 to see his mother and children, to Amsterdam in 1854 to attend the foundation of the Music Society of the Netherlands, and to Brussels during the same year to meet his two daughters.

His position in Weimar became increasingly difficult. The delays in Princess Carolyne's divorce proceeding made their position in Weimar socially unendurable. At home, as well as throughout Germany, an anti-Liszt campaign was waged against his works. His authority dwindled to an ever-decreasing extent at the theatre in Weimar because of the new and talented intendant, von Dingelstedt, who, on Liszt's recommendation, had occupied the post in 1857. By 15 December hostility and intrigue became so intense that an open scandal broke out at the première of Cornelius's comic opera *Der Barbier von Bagdad* that Liszt conducted. Liszt promptly resigned. After Princess Marie Sayn-

Wittgenstein had married Prince Konstantin von Hohenlohe-Schillingsfürst (later Lord Steward to the Emperor Francis Joseph) on 15 October 1859, Liszt no longer had reasons to remain in Weimar. After eleven years, it must have been a long and painful process for him to come to this decision. Weimar had turned out to be everything but the "homeland of the Ideal," as Liszt had written to Carl Alexander (Crown Prince at the time) on 6 October 1846 before settling there.[17]

His deception and bitterness in Weimar were crowned by a terrible blow: his twenty-year-old son Daniel, who was talented, amiable, and similar to the young Franz Liszt, fell seriously ill in Cosima's home in Berlin. He died in Liszt's presence. Months later, in May 1860, Princess Carolyne left for Rome in order to petition the pope to dissolve her marriage. Liszt, remaining alone in Weimar, became despondent. As soon as he was able to, he composed the staggering "oraison" *Les morts* on words of Lamennais in memory of his son. In September, he wrote his moving testament.

The year 1860 also saw the publication of protest against the "new music" of Liszt and Wagner that Johannes Brahms, Joseph Joachim, Julius Otto Grimm, and Bernhard Scholz signed. In August 1861, after a Weimar Festival and the foundation of the German General Music Association, Liszt, alone, liquidated his entire household. He left his home and Weimar. His departure meant the end of this exceptional period of ordered life and work some months before his fiftieth birthday. He visited Paris and arrived in Rome on the eve of his birthday to marry the princess the next day. At the last minute, however, the pope prevented the marriage. Alan Walker details the long, dark, and complicated story of this "thwarted marriage" in his *Liszt, Carolyne and the Vatican. The Story of a Thwarted Marriage as it emerges from the original Church documents.*[18]

Leaving Weimar meant an end to an important period of his composing. According to several musicologists, Liszt's compositions during his Weimar period represent the peak of his art. Nevertheless, others and I see his evolution as a composer continuing straight until his death. For me Liszt's output during the last twenty-six years of his life remains the most important, interesting, and moving music he ever wrote. This music with its incomplete and experimental character and without frills or sensationalism became increasingly dark, lonely, personal, and sincere. This music was an outgrowth of his solitary and homeless life, an errant life of an artist growing old who endured many delusions and unfortunate experiences. Liszt could only have composed this music without the princess by his side because this type of music did not correspond to her taste.

ROME, 1861–1869

When Liszt arrived in Rome, capital of the Papal State, the city was passing through its death throes. Though divested of a large part of its territory, Rome was the last island of stubborn resistance to the Risorgimento, the Italian movement of national unification that proclaimed democratic ideas. The troops of Napoleon III, Emperor of France, defended the city. (Liszt, decorated in 1860 with the *Croix d'officier* and in 1861 with that of the *Commandeur* of the *Légion d'Honneur*, was a great admirer of Napoleon III, taking him and his regime for a most democratic and liberal one). In September 1870, with the fall of Louis-Napoléon Bonaparte, Rome "fell." It became the capital of Victor Emmanuel's Kingdom of Italy, and the pope lost his temporal power.

The Roman chapter is the most puzzling period of Liszt's life. When it became clear that he would no longer stay in Weimar, he first wrote to Princess Carolyne, who was already living in Rome, that the Eternal City would not suit him, and they would go somewhere else. (The Princess wrote to Cornelius on 28 July 1865 that she "would rather suffer here [in Rome], than be happy elsewhere."[19]) Liszt arrived for the planned wedding only to find the pope had annulled it at the last minute. This annulment must have been a terrible blow to the princess, but if Liszt felt frustrated or relieved, we do not know. The differences between him and the princess that became more and more pronounced later on suggest that he might have felt relieved. What we do know is that Princess Carolyne would have by all means expected to become his wife. Afterwards, she became increasingly involved in the tenets of religion, sank deeper and deeper into her own exalted, mystical world, and locked herself in her dark rooms. Sometime in 1875 she wrote to Liszt's "cousin" Eduard Liszt in Vienna, complaining bitterly about the "lack of regard for a woman he [Liszt] has accepted *everything* from and should be the husband of."[20] It seems, however, that the topic of their marriage became struck off the agenda for the years to come. Not even the death of Carolyne's husband, Prince Nicholas Sayn-Wittgenstein in March 1864, altered the silence about this issue so far as we know. Liszt and the princess did not live together, although Liszt visited her regularly, despite all of their increasing differences.

Liszt, nevertheless, still did not leave Rome. He established himself in the Eternal City and did not move at all in Rome until 1864. He remained in the city until 1869 and returned frequently, almost every year until his death. Liszt had several reasons to remain in Rome, although he himself did not reveal them. The first was his longstanding attraction towards church music. As early as 1835 in one of his articles, he indignantly lamented the shameful and scandalous situation, the "stupid and pervasive howling" he called it, that prevailed in French churches under the name of church music. His experiences were the same in Italy during 1838 and 1839: the glory of church music in Rome (except in the Sistine Chapel) belonged to the past. Moreover, in Genoa, the unspeakable organ improvisations were based "on bows of the prima donna and the amorous grimaces of the first tenor of last night's opera performance," as Liszt wrote in his essay "Gênes et Florence" in 1839.[21] From his youth, he was interested in Gregorian chant and in the Renaissance masters, Giovanni Pierluigi da Palestrina and Orlando di Lasso. Liszt developed their modality into romantic neo-modality. He composed his first Mass (S 8) for male choir in 1848, the *Gran Mass* between 1855 and 1858, and arrived in Rome with his oratorio *Die Legende von der heiligen Elisabeth* (S 2) in progress. He had not ceased claiming that he believed his chief duty as a composer was to produce new and valuable church music. The brother-in-law of Princess Marie Sayn-Wittgenstein, the later Cardinal Gustav Hohenlohe, living in Rome, held out the promise of seemingly marvelous opportunities for him in the Eternal City and made Liszt believe that he would be able to reform church music according to his own conceptions. No task more appealing could have been offered to him. His dream (and Carolyne's) was for him to become a new Palestrina. It was for this reason that he became an abbé. He received the tonsure on 25 April 1865 and minor orders on 30 July. To join the church had never been a strange idea to Liszt since he had been a sincere Catholic, with a certain attraction towards mysticism. In his early youth, his father and later his mother had prevented him from becoming a priest. Neither was Madame Anna Liszt happy to know that on 23 June 1857 he became *confrater* of the Franciscans in Pest, and she burst into tears when informed about his receiving minor orders. Liszt, nevertheless, soon realized that his reform plans did not interest the church, like those of Gaspare Spontini's large-scale *Rapporto intorno la riforma della musica di chiesa* had in 1839. The church was not inclined to accept new ideas, not even in the field of music. Although he had wanted to become the choirmaster at St. Peter's Basilica, it was impossible for him as a foreigner and still less likely for him as an artist of very subjective religiosity, who as a composer "entered the music of Venusberg into the church." After his many disappointments in the sphere of secular music, he suffered an even worse lack of comprehension and success in the domain of sacred art.

In addition to the irresistible attraction of the marvelous beauty of Rome and its surroundings, Liszt had another more serious reason to settle down there. He hoped with priestly asceticism to overcome his own self, the demon that dwelt within him. Unfortunately, he was not able to. As a result, he became a "piano-playing abbé" (called so by his pupil Carl Tausig in a letter to Cornelius on 24 August 1865) and an "abbé courtesan" (as noted his friend Michelangelo Caetani, Duke of Sermoneta, in a letter to the Grand Duke of Weimar, 21 May 1865).[22] Liszt was seeking tranquility, yearning to create, and yet thirsting for entertainment and success. He continued to perform on the piano with pleasure in the salons of aristocrats, diplomats, and prelates, and also played at numerous benefit concerts in Rome and Tivoli. In the company of distinguished men, beautiful ladies, strong cigars, wine, and cognac, he soon forgot the behavior that was part and parcel of his priestly garb. Even when retiring from the center of Rome, he chose places where visitors could readily reach him. Like Beethoven's "Prayer for inner and outer peace,"[23] Liszt sought peace in various cloisters and apartments during the 1860s. On 20 June 1863 he moved to the cloister "Madonna del Rosario" at the Monte Mario, where Pope Pius IX visited him on 11 July. For a short time when receiving the tonsure on 25 April 1865, Liszt lived in the Vatican apartment of Monsignor Hohenlohe. On 22 November 1866 he moved to the cloister of Santa Francesca Romana at the Forum and traveled in lovely Umbria, staying by the shore of the Adriatic Sea in Grotta Mare with his friend, the Abbé Solfanelli, during July and August 1868. After a short visit between May and June 1865 and then almost every autumn from 1868 until his death, Liszt lived as a guest of Cardinal Hohenlohe at Tivoli in the chilly and uncomfortable Renaissance Villa d'Este, with its marvelous garden of cypresses and fountains.

In Rome, he continued his activity of teaching without pay and held masterclasses in which his many pupils from Italy and as well as from abroad performed. Although his projects concerning a church career and reforms of sacred music proved a fiasco, he resumed his interest in secular, symphonic, and chamber music. Interest in these types of music from "beyond the Alps" had slowly developed in Rome. In some of the concerts Liszt's own works were performed.

From August to October 1864, several journeys took him away from work. He first returned to Germany to take part at Karlsruhe Music Festival. He then visited Munich, Weimar, Berlin, and Paris, and returned to Rome in October. Between 9 August and 12 September 1865, he stayed in Hungary: he attended the première of his *Legend of St. Elisabeth* in Pest, and spent a week in the little town Szekszárd as guest of his best Hungarian friend, Baron Antal Augusz. From the beginning of March until 15 May 1866, he was in Paris for the performance of his *Gran Mass,* including a side trip to the Netherlands. In June 1867 he visited Pest again at the coronation of Francis Joseph I and Empress Elisabeth as King and Queen of Hungary because of the country's compromise with Austria. The ceremony took place in Buda Castle, in the Matthias Church, while Liszt's *Coronation Mass* was performed. In July, he returned to Weimar and Meiningen (Music Festival), directed *St. Elisabeth* at Wartburg castle near Eisenach, and stayed in Munich before returning to Rome. In 1868, his last Roman year, he did not leave Italy, but stayed in the Eternal City except for a short journey to the Villa d'Este.

Several painful incidents occurred making it difficult for Liszt to work at times during the 1860s. On 11 September 1862 he lost his second child: the charming Blandine Ollivier died in Saint-Tropez from complications of childbirth. On 6 February 1866 his mother Anna died in Paris. In addition, his only living child, Cosima, gave him enormous trouble. Liszt knew of Wagner and Cosima's secret love already in 1864 and tried everything possible to save her marriage with von Bülow. In August 1864 he appealed to Cosima's feelings in Karlsruhe and to those of Wagner at Lake Starnberg. In August 1865 he invited Cosima and von Bülow to Pest and Szekszárd for the same purpose of keeping them together. In April 1866 he tried to speak with his daughter in Amsterdam and attempted to convince her again in Munich as late as October 1867. From the Bavarian capital, he secretly paid a short visit to Wagner who was living in Triebschen, Switzerland, after having been exiled by King Louis II because of the scandal around Wagner and the Bülow couple in Munich. Neither Cosima nor Wagner listened to him. Cosima finally left her husband in the summer of 1868 and joined Wagner with her four daughters, two of which were Wagner's children. There followed a terrible, painful break of several years between father and daughter. Wagner and Cosima married in 1870, but it was not until the end of September 1871 that Liszt insisted on reconciliation.[24] The reunion of the three finally took place in September 1872 when Wagner and Cosima visited Liszt in Weimar.

These were the familial sorrows. He also had to endure similar sorrows, in particular, his plans for reforming church music. Never did a failure cause him such tremendous and everlasting grief as the terrible reception of his *Gran Mass* in Paris on 15 March 1866 at St. Eustache Church. Even the amiable reception in Holland in April, where he always had been popular, was a poor consolation to him.

The result of all these external and internal obstacles was that his works did not progress as he would have liked. On 11 November 1867, he wrote to Baron Augusz: "At least 4 or 5 hours a day writing music should be accomplished, without which [...] I am in bad humor and lose any sense of what I am doing in this world."[25] Although neglected for a long time, Liszt's output during his Roman years is not poor at all; on the contrary, it contains compositions in several genres of great value and importance. As a whole, this Roman chapter of his life could be called *L'après-midi d'un Faune,* preceding the last period that the outstanding Hungarian scholar Bence Szabolcsi called "twilight."[26] The Roman years can be appreciated as a huge step forward after Weimar. Liszt composed many of his most beautiful and moving compositions during this period, pushing in several directions trends that would lead to the coming century.

Heroes such as the rebel Prometheus, symbolizing enlightenment, or the ruminating Faust or Hamlet no longer inspired his works. His motto was *caritas* (charity), and *il gran perdono di Dio*—the great remission. His ideals became charitable, and his figures for inspiration became forgiving persons like Saint Elisabeth of the Árpád Dynasty, his patron saint Francis of Paola, Saint Francis of Assisi, or the Redeemer Himself. Literature remained the intermediary, but instead of Byron, Shakespeare, Dante, Schiller, or Nikolaus Lenau, it was the *Fioretti* (the flower garden), the *Cantico del Sol* of Saint Francis of Assisi, and other sacred texts that inspired his music.

He wrote a few independent orchestral pieces. *La notte* (S 699) is a version of the dark and expressive Michelangelo piece entitled *Il penseroso,* from the Italian volume of *Années de pèlerinage,* with a new, explicitly Hungarian middle section. This work and *Le triomphe funèbre du Tasse* (S 517) constitute, with the "oraison" *Les morts* (S 516), the *Trois odes funèbres.*

The diverse piano works were all significant, including the grandiose and staggering funeral piece inspired by J. S. Bach, the variations written on the "Crucifixus" bass theme of the *Mass in B minor: Weinen, Klagen* (S 180) that Liszt composed in memory of Blandine in 1862. Liszt composed another funeral music, a March, in memory of the Habsburg Emperor Maximilian who was executed in Mexico in 1867. This March is an extraordinarily exciting piece and a forerunner of his late style, included in the third volume of *Années de pèlerinage* (S 163). Liszt further enriched the piano's potential for musical color in his *Zwei Konzertetüden* (S 145) and the *Deux Légendes: St. François d'Assise: la prédication aux oiseaux* and *St. François de Paule marchant sur les flots* (S 175).

He composed most of his large-scale sacred works during this period as well. The Mass (S 8) for male choir received its final form in 1869 destined for

Szekszárd. Liszt called it *ma messe Sexardique*. The *Missa Choralis* (S 10), composed in 1865, and the Requiem for male choir (S 12), written in memory of Emperor Maximilian, belong to the best of his oeuvre, while the *Hungarian Coronation Mass* (S 11), completed in 1869, is a more formal, occasional work. The two grandiose oratorios, *Die Legende von der heiligen Elisabeth* (S 2) and *Christus* (S 3), are both long, the first taking three hours and the second even more. Neither of these oratorios is homogenous in style and quality, but each remains of considerable artistic value. Both contain delicately orchestrated and beautiful movements. *Christus*, especially, contains highly dramatic and moving sections. Liszt also composed a number of small sacred choral works often with organ accompaniment. *Mihi autem adhaerere* (S 37), *Pater noster* (S 49), and *Tantum ergo* (S 42) are expressive works, reduced to essentials and composed with the most economic tools, representing Liszt's late, ascetic style. In 1862 he composed the beautiful *Cantico del Sol di Francesco d'Assisi* (S 4) for baritone solo, male choir, and organ that he revised between 1880 and 1881.

His musical language in his Roman period include more extensive and freer use of chromaticism and more frequent use of Gregorian melodies, modality, and his individual neo-modality. Liszt uses Hungarian elements with ever-greater frequency in a more and more idealized, abstract, and individual manner. His piano works move toward impressionism, and his sacred works begin to shed any superfluous elements. All of these changes intensify further in his last period, *La vie trifurquée*.

LA VIE TRIFURQUÉE: WEIMAR-ROME-PEST, 1869–1886

This closing chapter of Liszt's activities lasts seventeen years and constitutes the longest distinct compositional period of his life. When he left Rome in January 1869 at the persuasion of Grand Duke Carl Alexander to continue his work in Weimar, he was fifty-seven. When he died at the end of July 1886, he was nearly seventy-five. The average person and the majority of artists who reach this age are past their creative best. That was not the case with Liszt. Apart from Verdi and Wagner, Liszt was an exception to this rule in the nineteenth century. Arguably, he composed his most mature, intriguing, and expressive works in this last period despite his disappointments and sufferings from melancholy as well as from his physical decline in health. On 4 February 1876 he expressed his own opinion of these works to Olga von Meyendorff, noting his "increasingly poor opinion of my things."[27] However, the end of his career, unlike of those of Verdi and Wagner, was not a brilliant conclusion, full of fresh inspiration like *Otello* and *Falstaff* or a self-apotheosis like *Parsifal*. Liszt's culmination as a composer meant reducing his art to the essential and maintaining a certain unfinished and fragmentary quality that would lead into twentieth-century music.

His style of life as well differed from that of significant composers who reached his age. While many would live in their own homes in perfect comfort, the old Liszt—although complaining about the strains of journeying, and claiming "more than ever, my most ardent wish is to live in seclusion, away from the world, not involved in things—just as you would wish"[28]—the old abbé could not relax in one place. He became a type of Flying Dutchman. Each year of his final period Liszt shuttled between his three "permanent residences," creating his threefold life that he referred to as *ma vie trifurquée*. He usually spent his summers in Weimar where he lived in the Grand Ducal gardener's residence known as the Hofgärtnerei. He often spent his falls in Rome, living in different places including the Vicolo de' Greci, no. 65 Via del Babuino (the princess lived in no. 89 of this street!), in Hotel Alibert, or near Rome in Tivoli at the Villa d'Este. Between November and April Liszt stayed the longest part of each year in the Hungarian capital Pest (called Budapest after November 1873). He lived at 20 Palatine street, 4 Fish Square (which became the first temporary residence of the new Music Academy), in the Hotel Hungaria on the shore of the Danube, and at last in Radial street (today: Andrássy street)—residence of the Music Academy (today called "Old Music Academy") where the Liszt Museum and the Liszt Society are today. These three distant towns—Weimar, Rome, and Budapest—formed the axis of his life where he spent weeks or months nearly every year. There were some exceptions, however. In 1874 he did not go to Weimar because of his resentment against Grand Duke Carl Alexander who omitted sponsoring Wagner's theatre and festival in Bayreuth. In 1872, 1876, 1882, and 1883, he did not return at all to Rome because of his anger with Princess Carolyne. He was upset with the princess's incitement against Cosima and Wagner in the 1870s and her new notorious edition of his "Gypsy Book" in 1881 without his consent.

These were only the "permanent" residences, however. Annually, he visited his cousin Eduard Liszt and his family in Vienna, usually at Easter. From 1873 he often visited the Wagners in Bayreuth, usually in August. In addition, he often was the guest of royal and ducal families in Germany and the Netherlands or attended various music festivals in Germany or Zurich. He returned to Paris in 1878 as one of the judges at the World Exhibition and paid visits to illustrious friends in different parts of Italy, Austria, and Hungary. In 1881, 1882, and 1885 he was honored by festivals in Belgium, organized as *hommages à Liszt*, and during his last spring, he took part at the brilliant celebrations given in his honor in Paris and London. Had his death not prevented him, he would have accepted an invitation to St. Petersburg. "Believe me," wrote von Bülow to his daughter Daniela in December 1881, "movement is a need, a medicine for him [Liszt]. It belongs to his diet."[29]

Liszt did not long for an elegant home of his own. He lived modestly and his way of life was unbelievably ascetic. He absolutely did not care for money. He taught his students without charge and was always ready to help almost everyone who asked. After he had retired as a touring virtuoso, he continued to raise large sums for charitable and cultural purposes, although he himself owned little.

In his "twilight years," Liszt—the traveling black-clad abbé, speaking French and German with sparkling wittiness—could upon occasion be heard as a conductor or a pianist (where he remained unrivalled). With his Mephistophelean smile and sarcastic humor, his wonderful eyes and long white hair, his legendary goodness and tolerance, his brilliant culture and manners of a *grandseigneur*, Liszt remained a captivating, colorful personality with a magic emanation until his end. He still drove the ladies wild and enjoyed the homage of young female pupils who swarmed around him in spite of his growing warts, false or missing teeth,[30] or neglected external appearance (including his worn-out cassock and shabby slippers he had to wear because of his dropsy, which are to be seen now in the Bayreuth Liszt-Museum). He remained a great, radiating, often impetuous, and indefatigable personality, even during the last months filled with great ovations in Western Europe—although upon occasion he fell asleep during a dinner given in his honor.

The extreme contradictions of his character became crystallized. As often as he actually attained the yearned-for creative solitude, he suffered from it as well. He passionately wished for the world and its homage as a man and an artist. The grim struggle against "the old and bitter enemy which is not the little devil of going out into society, but the real demon of extremity in emotion and excitation!"[31] dwelling within him, raged on. He smoked cigars and consumed increasing quantities of alcohol. Carl Lachmund recorded that in 1882 Liszt drank "daily one bottle of cognac and two or three bottles of wine" in addition to drinking absinthe upon occasion.[32] Through his undiminished and sincere faith, nevertheless, Liszt managed to survive his deep depression, weariness of life, and constant dissatisfaction with his own compositions in this last, declining period of health and life.

In his old age Liszt was celebrated in several countries. He had many admirers, but with the passing of time, several fell away from him. He continued to have lady-friends, old and new ones who came forward with arbitrary demands. In addition to the princess, Baroness Olga von Meyendorff née Princess Gortchakova (1838–1926) filled this role. He had some faithful pupils of both sexes—in particular Lina Schmalhausen, August Göllerich, August Stradal, Bernhard Stavenhagen, and István Thomán—who cared for him until the end. Yet he had no close and altruistic friend of his own to whom he could have spoken freely about his intellectual, physical, or psychological problems. Cosima could have been the only suitable person for this task, but she was under the complete influence of Wagner and cared only for her husband and Bayreuth. The aging Liszt was poor, homeless, and lonely after all.

Liszt remained an extraordinary teacher. In Weimar numerous students, several of whom flocked to him solely because of his fame, surrounded him. In Rome his teaching was in a more intimate setting. In Budapest, where he was appointed President of the new Academy of Music in 1875, he taught classes from four to six o'clock four times a week. He consumed a great amount of his time and energy with house concerts held in his apartment in Fish square and later in the concert hall of Radial street. He also was confronted with bureaucratic misunderstandings in Hungary because of its historic and economic situation. Hungary had only recently, after the compromise with Austria in 1867, embarked on a bourgeois and capitalist development. The general attitude, nevertheless, did not keep up with the industrial revolution. Hungary remained stingy, feudal, and provincial in many respects.

His earlier works were played sometimes in Germany, Prague, Vienna, the Netherlands, Belgium, Zurich, and Rome. Performances of his work even spread to America because of the efforts of the conductor Leopold Damrosch. His music was heard little in Paris and London until near his death. In Italy only a narrow circle who had no interest in his secular music esteemed Liszt as a master of sacred music. Because of his presence in Rome, nonetheless, orchestras and chamber ensembles grew in the city, and Liszt often gave advice to the Conservatorio di Santa Cecilia. His church music continued to be neglected in Rome and by the German Cecilians in Regensburg.

Liszt was celebrated at first in Hungary. The country felt honored to have its great master at home for part of the year. King Francis Joseph granted him the rank of a councilor and an annual fee of 4,000 Forints. In 1873 Hungary brilliantly commemorated the fiftieth anniversary of his artistic career, and this tribute gave Liszt great pleasure. On 12 November 1873 he wrote to Cosima: "the success of this feast extraordinary indeed, is complete. No dissonance has troubled the general agreement."[33] He soon found he was laden with "obligations and irritations quite contrary to what I desire" while back in his native land. He continued in his letter to the princess on 7 October 1870: "Now I am to be thrust back into a busy life, and my friends devolve upon me the heavy burden of seeing to the prosperity and glory of all music, sacred and secular, in Hungary!"[34]

Yet, Liszt accepted his burden, and largely because of his self-sacrifices, music institutions and musical life flourished in Hungary.[35] Unfortunately, after a certain time, Hungary grew accustomed to his presence and gradually took him for granted, perhaps, in part, because of its provincial attitude and old resentment concerning his errors in the unfortunate "Gypsy book." (By declaring in his book that Hungarian national music was of Gypsy origin, the Hungarian state refused to initiate him being buried in his native land.)

To make matters worse, the princess, without Liszt's knowledge, republished the book in Leipzig in 1881 with all the old errors intact. In addition, the fiercely anti-Semitic princess rewrote and enlarged the chapter "Les Israélites," adding to the allegations in the earlier version and including the latest slogans of the new race theory. In effect, she formulated one of the first inciting documents on the persecution of the Jews. Not only was this publication an absolutely unfair gesture towards the composer, it could not have happened at a worse historical moment. At the time, of all national minorities of Hungary, it was the Jews, at last achieving their emancipation, who most sincerely desired to become assimilated. Although the Government was liberal, a Parliament Party called "Anti-Semitic" existed promoting anti-Semitic manifestations. Consequently, in 1882, a false "blood trial" started, preceding the Dreyfuss affair in France by some years. A poor kosher butcher of a little village called Tiszaeszlár was accused of killing a young girl to use her blood in the Passover cake. In this tense atmosphere it is easy to imagine what a shocking effect the princess's chapter (under the abbé Liszt's name!) produced. The princess wrote that "the

Jews" were a parasite, unable to assimilate, that "their" very existence was a threat to people in their own countries, and that "this perilously noxious, bloodsucking race, thirsting for power, must be forcibly deported to Palestine."[36] These sentiments conformed perfectly to the slogans of the Anti-Semitic Party in Hungary and of those similar movements in Germany and France. In February 1883, when the Tiszaeszlár trial was still in progress, Liszt felt it necessary—without alluding to the fact that he was not the author of that chapter—to make clear publicly that he was a friend, not an enemy of the Jews. Despite Liszt's noble attitude, the book had terrible consequences for him in the Budapest and in the Viennese press.[37] His compositions were ill-treated with a prejudiced, stupid hatred equal to the princess's notorious chapter.

These events contributed to the indifference and hostility with which many Hungarians viewed Liszt in his final years. Even the performance of his earlier works in Germany and the great ovations he enjoyed so much in Paris and London in the spring of 1886 turned out to be temporary. His late works were declared incomprehensible, and the immortality of his art was questioned. In the decades immediately following his death, when the irresistible charm of his personality could no longer win adherents, Liszt was, for a time, a neglected and scorned composer.

Throughout his life Liszt had been an extraordinarily healthy man in spite of his style of life. Walker documented that his "decline into the infirmities of old age can be traced" from 2 July 1881, when he fell down the stairs of the Hofgärtnerei. "The accident seemed to trigger a number of ailments that until then had been lying dormant within him—including dropsy, asthma, insomnia, a cataract of the left eye, and chronic heart disease. This latter illness would kill him within five years."[38] His symptoms included "swelling of the ankles, loss of appetite, feelings of nausea in the mornings, a serious open wound in the right thigh . . . two fractured ribs with the possibility of bruising of the lungs, [and] pleurisy."[39]

Liszt's final days were spent in Bayreuth and Luxemburg. Cosima, who had refused to meet her father, write to him, or accept his letters after Wagner's death in 1883, had, unexpectedly, personally invited him to come to Bayreuth. At the beginning of July 1886, he attended the wedding of his favorite granddaughter Daniela, renting a private flat in Siegfriedstrasse near Villa Wahnfried. (The street is now called Franz Liszt Strasse, and the flat has been transformed into a Liszt Museum.) Then he visited his friends, the Hungarian painter Mihály Munkácsy and his French wife at their villa in Colpach, Luxemburg. Despite his cold, Liszt returned to the Bayreuth Festival. His cold led to pneumonia, and he died on 31 July 1886. He was buried in Bayreuth in the municipal cemetery.

Significantly, it was in his late music that Liszt managed to accomplish what he wanted as a man and artist: to renounce the world and its glory of personal success. He created some brilliant piano pieces of a completely new, extraordinary kind of enchanting color—*Les jeux d'eaux à la Villa d'Este* (S 163) and *Carillon* from *Weihnachtsbaum* (S 186)—that inspired Debussy to state what an extraordinary old magician Liszt had been. In general, however, Liszt discarded the fancy ornamentation that appealed to the public together with all rhetorical pathos and adornment, external glitter, and everything that did not appertain to the substance of his music and what he wanted to say. This last chapter of his life became the culmination of his creative art, including the process of complete simplification that had begun in the Roman period. In his late music he developed new, never-before-heard innovations and new ways of organizing tones. The asceticism of his music was not for his own sake: its message was more serious, dramatic, expressive, and concise than ever. In his late art with its fundamentally dark tone and portrayals of death, we learn much about a disappointed, lonely, and homeless old man's feelings, sufferings, gloomy presentiments, and feverish visions that he had otherwise carefully concealed. The latest style of Liszt is impregnated through and through with Hungarian rhythms and the elements of the "Hungarian scale," abstracted and individualized to the utmost, even in works, such as his church music, that have nothing to do with his country.[40] In some ways Liszt had expressed these feelings of grief and suffering through his use of these Hungarian elements for a long time.

Liszt's output during his last years includes some large-scale works such as *Die Glocken des Strassburger Münsters* (S 6) on a poem by Longfellow, his most captivating oratorio-like work *Via Crucis* (S 53), the moving *St. Christoph's Legend* (S 47) for baritone solo, women's choir, piano, harmonium, and harp, and a final symphonic poem *Von der Wiege bis zum Grabe* (S 107). He also composed beautiful Lieder such as his setting of Alfred de Musset's *J'ai perdu ma force et ma vie* (S 320), and the staggering, three movements on a quatrain by Hugo: *Le crucifix* (S 342)—two of them chiefly written in 1880, not in 1884.[41] He composed the pieces that constitute the third and final volume of the *Années de pèlerinage* (S 163)—chiefly elegies and dirges which led him originally to call the volume *Feuilles de cyprès et de palmes*.[42] Among his last piano works are the spine-chilling, barbarous Hungarian "dance macabres" such as the late *Hungarian Rhapsodies* nos. 16–19, *Csárdás*, *Csárdás obstiné* (S 225), and *Csárdás macabre* (S 199). He likewise composed the dreary and striking Hungarian funeral marches, including the cycle *Historische Ungarische Bildnisse* (S 205). Among his late, "forgotten," and "hospital pieces" as he referred to them, are the most moving dirges for Wagner: the morbidly beautiful *La lugubre gondola* nos. 1 and 2, (S 200), *R. W. Venezia* (S 201), and *Am Grabe Richard Wagners* (S 202). There are diabolical farces of the *vieillard terrible* Liszt like the late *Mephisto Waltzes*: no. 2 (S 111) and nos. 3, 4, 4/a (*Bagatelle sans tonalité*) (S 216). Liszt also composed the stupefying piano pieces of modern structure and sound like *Nuages gris* (S 199) and *Unstern* (S 208). It was not before the second half of the twentieth century that the real significance and greatness of the late output of Liszt was appreciated. Because in great part to English and Hungarian scholars like Humphrey Searle, Zoltán Gárdonyi, Bence Szabolcsi, Lajos Bárdos, and István Szelényi, these works appear in the repertoire of the greatest pianists today.

NOTES

1. Quoted in *Portrait of Liszt: By Himself and His Contemporaries*, ed. Adrian Williams (Oxford: Clarendon Press, 1990), 373–374.

2. Liszt to Princess Carolyne Sayn-Wittgenstein, 2 June 1876. Quoted in Klára Hamburger, *Liszt,* trans. Gyula Gulyás (Budapest: Corvina, 1987), 196. Virginia Csontos and Paul Merrick translated the letters in German and French quoted in this study.

3. Liszt to Princess Carolyne, 13 August 1856, quoted in *Portrait of Liszt*, 376.

4. Quoted in *Portrait of Liszt*, 374.

5. Quoted in Hamburger, *Liszt*, 78.

6. Quoted in Hamburger, "Musicien Humanitaire," *New Hungarian Quarterly* 27 (Autumn 1986): 85.

7. In November 1873 the three towns Pest, Buda, and Old Buda were united and the name of the Hungarian capital became Budapest.

8. Quoted in Hamburger, *Liszt*, 13–14.

9. Quoted in *Portrait of Liszt*, 29–30.

10. Alan Walker, *Franz Liszt. The Virtuoso Years 1811–1847* (New York: Alfred A. Knopf, 1983), 292–293.

11. *Le Corsaire,* Paris.

12. Robert Schumann to Clara Wieck, 25 March 1840, quoted in Hamburger, *Liszt,* 49.

13. Quoted in *Portrait of Liszt*, 110.

14. Sacheverell Sitwell, *Liszt,* rev. ed. (London: Faber and Faber, 1955), 100.

15. Quoted in Hamburger, *Liszt*, 74.

16. Quoted in Hamburger, *Liszt*, 81. See *Franz Liszt and Agnès Street-Klindworth: A Correspondence 1854–1886*, introduced, ed., and trans. Pauline Pocknell. Franz Liszt Studies Series no. 8, ed. Michael Saffle (Hillsdale, NY: Pendragon, 2000), for more about Liszt's secret relationship to this unusual woman.

17. Franz Liszt, *Selected Letters*, ed. and trans. Adrian Williams (Oxford: Clarendon Press, 1998), 236.

18. Walker, *Liszt, Carolyne and the Vatican. The Story of a Thwarted Marriage as it emerges from the original Church documents*, ed. and trans. Gabriele Erasmi. American Liszt Society Studies Series no. 1 (Stuyvesant, NY: Pendragon, 1991).

19. Quoted in Hamburger, *Liszt*, 120.

20. *Franz Liszt und sein Kreis in Briefen und Dokumenten*, ed. Mária P. Eckhardt and Cornelia Knotik. Wissenschaftliche Arbeiten aus dem Burgenland no. 66 (Eisenstadt: Burgenländisches Landesmuseum, 1983), no. 33. Quoted in Hamburger, *Liszt*, 165.

21. Franz Liszt, "Gênes et Florence," *L'Artiste* (3 November 1839).

22. Both quotations quoted in Hamburger, *Liszt*, 132.

23. Over the score of "Dona nobis pacem" in Beethoven's *Missa Solemnis.*

24. *Franz Liszt Lettres à Cosima et à Daniela,* ed. and annotated Klára Hamburger (Sprimont, Belgium: Mardaga, 1996), 63.

25. Quoted in Hamburger, *Liszt*, 145.

26. Bence Szabolcsi, *The Twilight of Ferenc Liszt*, trans. András Deák (Budapest: Akadémiai Kiadó, 1959).

27. *The Letters of Franz Liszt to Olga von Meyendorff 1871–1886 in the Mildred Bliss Collection at Dumbarton Oaks*, trans. William R. Tyler; introduction and notes Edward N. Waters (Washington, D.C. Dumbarton Oaks, 1979), 229.

28. Liszt to Carolyne, 4 September 1870. Quoted in Hamburger, *Liszt*, 156.

29. Quoted in Hamburger, *Liszt*, 156.

30. For more information see Walker, *Franz Liszt: The Final Years 1861–1886* (New York: Knopf, 1996), 3:511.

31. Liszt to Carolyne, 17 January 1871. Quoted in Hamburger, *Liszt*, 158.

32. Quoted in a supressed passage from the diary of Liszt's pupil, Carl Lachmund in Walker, *Franz Liszt: The Final Years,* 3:412.

33. *Franz Liszt Lettres,* 108.

34. Quoted in Hamburger, *Liszt*, 170.

35. For more information see Dezső Legány, *Liszt and His Country: 1869–1873,* 1 (Budapest: Corvina, 1983) and *1874–1886,* 2 (Budapest: Occidental Press, 1992).

36. Hamburger, "Liszt: Conclusion to a Life," *The Hungarian Quarterly* 38 (Spring 1997), 125–130. A review of Walker, *Franz Liszt: The Final Years.*

37. Walker, *Franz Liszt: The Final Years*, 3:406.

38. Ibid., 403–404.

39. Ibid., 404.

40. For more information, see Hamburger, "Program and Hungarian Idiom in the Sacred Music of Liszt," in *Analecta Lisztiana II: New Light on Liszt and His Music,* ed. Saffle and James Deaville. Franz Liszt Studies Series no. 6 (Stuyvesant, NY: Pendragon, 1997), 239–251.

41. See *Franz Liszt Lettres,* 181.

42. Ibid., 183

2

Liszt's Writings and Correspondence

Charles Suttoni

In thinking about Liszt, one aspect of his activity rarely receives more than passing mention, and that is Liszt the writer, an author whose collected prose filled six volumes,[1] with a new nine-volume edition in progress.[2] His literary works include two book-length monographs plus some fifty other pieces; i.e., reviews, travel articles, program notes, and essays. A notable accomplishment, these writings—much like those of his contemporaries Hector Berlioz, Robert Schumann, and Richard Wagner—can be regarded as an important adjunct to his musical works.

First, however, there is the nagging question of authorship. All the writings date from two distinctly different periods of Liszt's life during which he was involved with two strong, willful women: the first (1835–1841) when he was living and traveling with Marie d'Agoult, and the second (1849–1859) when he was in Weimar with Carolyne Sayn–Wittgenstein. Further, because both women had literary aspirations, documented evidence discloses that each in her own way assisted Liszt in the production of his literary works. But, to what extent? Scholars have been examining and debating that unsettled issue for years,[3] but have at least reached a workable consensus; that is, even if the ladies—Carolyne demonstrably more than Marie—did collaborate in the writing and/or editing of the prose that appeared in print, Liszt himself was basically responsible for the musical matters these works discussed and the ideas they expressed. He did, after all, sign them as their sole author and assumed all public responsibility for them. Thus, they count as his. That point made, it is possible to survey Liszt's prose pieces from the 1830s and the 1850s. They are quite different.

In the 1830s Liszt was an idealistic and outspoken reformer who resented a musician's demeaning role as a paid entertainer in aristocratic houses, who faulted and wished to reform almost every aspect of the French musical establishment, and who extolled Artists as divinely inspired seers working for the betterment of humanity. These ideas prompted his debut as a writer in a long, audacious polemic "On the Situation of Artists and their Status in Society" (1835).[4] In it, he also envisioned a "Religious Music of the Future" that would "sum up both Theater and Church" and fraternally unite "all mankind in rapturous wonder."[5] Liszt's boldness caused a stir, but no real reform.

During these years he also wrote a series of sixteen travel articles or essays for the Paris press, the *Letters of a Bachelor of Music* (1835–1841).[6] Writing candidly, Liszt details his youth, devotion to the piano, concert experiences, rivalry with Sigismond Thalberg, reaction to music in Italy, and his deep feeling for the unity of the arts. The collection, in essence a record of the young Liszt coming to terms with his gifts, is the closest he ever came to writing an autobiography and thus an indispensable source for his future development.

Conditions changed with his move to Weimar in 1848. Liszt assumed the duties of an active Kapellmeister, and the focus of his pen generally shifted from recounting personal experiences to writings,[7] which, while discussing, analyzing, and promoting the works of others, reflected his broader, fundamental, and knowledgeable concern with the history and progress of musical art.

Among his earliest efforts, Liszt wrote a detailed proposal "On the Goethe Foundation in Weimar" (1851),[8] which called for a series of periodic, Olympic-like competitions with writers, painters, sculptors, and musicians all putting forth their best and being amply recognized for it.[9] Even if the plan was too grandly conceived ever to be realized, it did underscore his efforts to help establish Weimar as the *locus classicus* of German cultural history.

About this time Liszt also wrote his biography *Chopin* (1851).[10] Without discounting its value as a tribute, the work, written with Carolyne (herself a Pole) at his side, is a missed opportunity and a disappointment. Instead of providing the unique insights Liszt may have had into his friend, the book is a rather gaseous character portrait, abounding in fanciful flights about genius or the nobility of the Slavic soul. No matter, the dedicated reader can still find the composer of genius hidden beneath the flood of words.

Wagner and his operas, we know, occupied an exalted place in Liszt's estimation, and his first articles about them—*Tannhäuser* (1849) and *Lohengrin* (1851)[11]—are not only the earliest significant appreciations printed anywhere, they also go to considerable lengths to present the innovative nature of Wagner's genius in a sympathetic manner. The vast floods of later Wagneriana may have obscured Liszt's words, but their historical importance for the initial critical reception and public acceptance of Wagner's operas remains unassailable.

For the evolution of opera, however, Liszt wrote an integrated series of essays (1854) on a dozen or so notable operas he had selected for the Weimar repertory.[12] More than mere program notes, "the concrete musical analysis of the works in question is overshadowed by the discussion of the historical position of the opera and its composer, and its relevance to the present."[13] Taken together, Liszt's pieces argue for a far more continuous and cogent line of operatic development than the disjointed Gluck-Rossini-Beethoven-Wagner sequence Wagner himself had put forth in *Oper und Drama* (1851).

Among the other essays on contemporary matters, one that merits special attention is "Berlioz and his Harold Symphony" (1855).[14] Carolyne had initiated it, perhaps to counterbalance all the praise Liszt had lavished on Wagner, but Liszt, moving beyond Berlioz, transformed the lengthy discussion into a rationale for his own symphonic innovations; namely, an aesthetic that not only favored program music, but also fostered the emotional expression and creative importance of the poetic concept underlying the program. It was, in effect, Liszt's way of stating that he represented progress in orchestral music just as much as Wagner did with opera.

This leaves Liszt's last and most controversial book, *The Gypsies and their Music in Hungary* (1859),[15] a work that is significantly marred by a fundamental error and a scandal. The error is that Liszt, fascinated by roving bands of Gypsy musicians in his youth, overstated their importance to the extent that it seemed that Hungarians had no folk music of their own—it was all Gypsy music! (Not so, as Béla Bartók later proved.[16]) The scandal concerns the later 1881 edition of the book. Liszt had entrusted its proofreading to Carolyne, and she, without his knowledge, inserted some blatantly anti-Semitic passages in the chapter dealing with "The Israelites." Gallant to a fault, Liszt assumed responsibility for the publication and thus found himself struggling to disclaim an anti-Semitism he had never felt. Regardless of the edition, then, *The Gypsies* is a dated, problematic work.

There is no simple way to sum up these fifty-plus pieces of wide-ranging prose, except to note that they are all grounded in some way in Liszt's abiding three-fold conception of musical art: an active appreciation of the classics; an ample opportunity to experience the modern; and all possible encouragement for the young and the new. Furthermore, since he never lost his idealism, either in person or in print, one can return to 1840 and the article that many regard as Liszt's most enduring profession of artistic faith. It is the obituary notice of his one-time idol Niccolò Paganini, whom he had come to scorn as an egotist whose "life illuminated no other lives." Continuing, he writes: "May the artist of the future, therefore, joyfully renounce that vain and egotistic role of which Paganini, or so we hope, was the last and illustrious example. May his intentions lay not within but beyond himself. May virtuosity not be an end, but only a means. May he never forget that just as nobility has obligations, so too—and to an even greater extent—genius has obligations!" *Génie oblige!*[17]

Unlike his literary legacy, Liszt's correspondence poses no problems of authorship and style. Liszt wrote his letters plainly enough and much preferred French to German. The problem that Liszt's correspondence does pose, however, is the great, unwieldy mass of it. The basic bibliography of "Liszt Correspondence in Print"[18] cites about 6,500 of his letters, and a recently published Supplement adds several hundred more.[19] Moreover, no collected edition of these letters exists (nor is there any prospect of one in the foreseeable future), meaning that the dedicated reader must deal with the haphazard, sporadic manner in which the letters have been published in the century since Liszt's death. Even if one puts aside the hundreds of articles in which his letters have appeared, a core of over two dozen book-length collections of correspondence remains, most of which are long out-of-print.

In addition to being one of the busiest and most social musical personalities of his day, Liszt was a great communicator. He not only lived his life in public, he was more than willing to share accounts of it with others. In personal terms, his letters provide an almost daily record of his activities as pianist, composer, and conductor, as well as detailing his relationships with his family and a vast circle of friends and acquaintances. In broader terms, moreover, the letters—and those written to him—also describe Liszt's participation in and response to the rich, active life about him, and thus, much like his writings, can be seen as an insider's report on almost every musical development from the 1820s to the 1880s. (He had an uncanny memory for dates, events, and people.)

Given his life, it is not surprising, perhaps, that his published letters are addressed to about one thousand individual correspondents, the list of whom reads like a Who's Who of the mid and late nineteenth century. Still, as with anyone's letter writing, some individuals figure more prominently in it than others; therefore, it might be well to highlight Liszt's correspondence through those closest to him, beginning with his immediate family.

Having lost his father when he was fifteen, Liszt was especially devoted to his mother Anna, a simple, warm-hearted, shrewd woman. She kept house for him in Paris, did any number of commissions while he traveled and, most importantly, provided the home for his children from 1839 to the mid 1850s. Although a selection of his letters to her was published many years ago,[20] a new expanded edition of their mutual correspondence provides a much fuller picture of this deeply personal relationship of Liszt's life.[21]

Blandine, the elder daughter, was in a sense his favorite, and their correspondence can be divided into two parts: her girlhood and her married years as Mme Ollivier.[22] Fatherhood, admittedly, was not one of Liszt's better qualities; he not only let years pass without once visiting his children, he also tended to be a stern parent, constantly admonishing Blandine (and Cosima and Daniel) about their filial piety and obligations. Filled as Blandine's letters may be with their doings and studies, her responses betray the children's rather desperate efforts to live up to the expectations of a famous, demanding, and distant father. The mood changes when Blandine marries and becomes an elegant young matron in Parisian society. She reports on all the political, literary, and musical news, and Liszt responds appreciatively. Who knows what further affectionate relations might have developed had not Blandine died in 1862 when she was only twenty-six years old. Liszt's son Daniel also died early, at age twenty in 1859, and there is no appreciable correspondence with him.

This leaves Cosima, Liszt's only surviving and problematic child. His letters to her and to her daughter Daniela have only recently been published,[23] and the collection raises an important question of the impression created by surviving materials, since letters, as the recipient's private property, can be hidden away or destroyed. That is evidently what has happened here; with one exception,[24] none of Cosima's letters to her father are known, and most of those that he wrote her during her girlhood and her troubled marriage to Hans von Bülow are also missing. A lack of letters, however, cannot be read as a lack of interest because it is apparent from other sources that Liszt never forsook his daughter. Turning instead to what has survived, over eight out of ten of the letters collected here were written after the famous Liszt-Cosima-Wagner reconciliation in 1872. That hard-won capitulation seems to have tapped a stream of fatherly affection for Cosima, giving his newsy communications to her a special feeling of warmth and candor.

Moving beyond the immediately family, Liszt not only had a desire to communicate, he apparently also felt a need for a female confidante, a woman with whom he could correspond and exchange ideas as equals. Those whose friendships he cultivated were all special in some way—intelligent, personable, self-confident, and talented. Although that list is a long one,[25] there are five women with whom he corresponded extensively.

Countess Marie d'Agoult is the first and possibly the most controversial of these. Despite the length and wealth of their correspondence,[26] survival is again a factor because it is all too plain that Mme d'Agoult destroyed virtually all of her early letters to Liszt. Thus, the printed page gives a totally lopsided impression of the circumstances leading to their departure from Paris in May 1835 (i.e., over 100 notes and letters from Liszt with only four in return). Some have used this discrepancy to paint Liszt as the persistent suitor intent upon seducing her from husband and family,[27] but a close examination of other evidence from these years indicates that it was most likely Marie herself who engineered their flight from Paris.[28] Even so, the remainder of their correspondence is an unrivaled source for details of Paris life, the Italian sojourn, and the early years of Liszt's virtuoso tours.

Ironically, one of Liszt's later letters to Marie (10 February 1847) announces that he has just met "a very extraordinary woman—but very extraordinary and eminent."[29] That woman was, of course, Princess Carolyne Sayn-Wittgenstein (though, by preference, she typically dropped the "Sayn" from her title). In one way or another, Carolyne would remain Liszt's companion, emotional anchor, and most enduring correspondent for the next forty years. Their story is well known; her move to Weimar, her futile efforts to secure an annulment, the sequestering of her vast fortune, his move to Rome, their thwarted plans to marry, and her final deterioration into a recluse and religious zealot. Some have called Carolyne meddlesome, and indeed she was because for better or worse she had dedicated her life to Liszt, his well-being, and his stature as a composer-musician.

Forty years can produce considerable correspondence, and it did. The published selection of his letters to her fills four of the eight volumes of his published *Briefe*.[30] As usual, he is the dutiful and diligent correspondent. No occurrence—whether it is the loftiest discussion of human destiny or a small contretemps at a social gathering—fails to find its place in letters to Carolyne. Though, it must be admitted that he is not always totally candid with her.

There has been some criticism that La Mara (Marie Lipsius), who compiled and edited the early, basic collections of Liszt's correspondence, deleted some troublesome or excessively personal passages from the published texts. Later research has shown this to be true—particularly, in this case, some of Liszt's sharp disagreements with Carolyne. This omission, however, is an understandable shortcoming, perhaps, considering that the letters were made public rather soon after Liszt's death. No one, however, can fault La Mara's dedication in collecting them, nor the overall competence with which she presented them.[31]

Carolyne's daughter, Princess Marie, was about the same age as Liszt's Cosima. Marie's life was not a happy one; as heir to her mother's sequestered fortune, she became a pawn in the struggle for it, which ended in her bleak, arranged marriage to an Austrian court official, Prince Konstantin Hohenlohe-Schillingsfürst.

The collection of Liszt's letters to Marie is a mess,[32] an object lesson in what can go wrong when the owner of the collection entrusts it to a young editor who lacks the editorial and historical competence to handle the material properly. Both the English translation, in which the letters are presented, and the supporting apparatus are markedly faulty, and while this is not meant to condemn the volume in total—the substance of the letters is too valuable for that—anyone using it is well advised to use caution. (Lisztians, incidentally, owe a great debt to Princess Marie; Liszt had left all his papers and manuscripts to Carolyne, who, in turn, willed them to Marie, and it was she who gave them to Weimar, establishing the Liszt Archive there.)

Coming to Agnès Street-Klindworth, the story of Liszt's letters to her is a fascinating one. Briefly, Liszt and the beautiful, politically astute Agnès had an intense, passionate, albeit clandestine, affair in the mid 1850s, followed by an equally intense and clandestine correspondence. The affair and the letters might have gone unnoticed had not La Mara located Agnès in 1892, along with a thick packet of neatly preserved, dated, and numbered letters from Liszt. Faced with the possibility of exposing an explicit unknown affair that could prove harmful to Liszt's reputation, the ever prudent La Mara issued a censored, anonymous collection of the letters with the bland title *Letters to a Lady Friend*.[33] Although scholars have known Agnès's identity and the truth behind the letters for a long time, it is only recently that a proper edition of them has appeared.[34] Trysting details aside, the real value of the letters lies in Liszt's candor in discussing the later years at Weimar: his activities, frustrations, compositions, and interest in contemporary politics.

The last of Liszt's special women to merit a collection of her own is Baroness Olga von Meyendorff. Entering his sixties and with Carolyne firmly entrenched in Rome, Liszt probably sensed a need for someone to look after him in Weimar, and Olga was very willing to fill that role. A young widow, beautiful, intelligent, and a gifted pianist, she could also be haughty and downright unpleasant, prompting Liszt on one occasion to complain to Cosima that "her primary nature harmonizes but little with mine, and her second, her tyrannical propensities, is repugnant to me. Still, she has a good and noble heart which wins my affection."[35] Ever tolerant, Liszt accepted Olga as his chamberlaine, traveling companion, and watchdog in Weimar for the last fifteen years of his life. His many letters to her have been published in a good English translation, even though the volume is rather short on the scholarly support a more generous publisher might have provided.[36] Liszt, in any event, is his usual faithful, informative correspondent, especially in his lively discussions with Olga about the political and literary events of the 1870s and 1880s.

Turning to Liszt's male friends and colleagues, pride of place goes to Berlioz. Mutually supportive comrades in Paris, their friendship continued through Liszt's tours and his settling in Weimar, where he arranged three special "Berlioz Weeks" to promote his friend's music. Still, long as it was, the friendship could not survive Berlioz's increasingly acerbic mental state coupled with what he saw as Liszt's preoccupation with the rival Wagner. Although Berlioz did maintain contacts with Carolyne, the anti-Wagnerite who persuaded him to compose *Les Troyens*, the Liszt-Berlioz exchange *per se* trailed off in the late 1850s and, what is worse, has failed to survive intact. We have over 100 letters that Berlioz wrote to Liszt,[37] while virtually all of Liszt's half of the correspondence has been lost—reportedly with the death of Daniel Bernard who was to write a study of the two. Consequently, one can only guess what Liszt wrote to Berlioz, and that is a pity.

Liszt's relations and correspondence with Wagner are studies unto themselves. Eager to memorialize both husband and father, Cosima, working anonymously, edited an incomplete and drastically curtailed edition of their letters in 1888, soon, too soon, after their respective deaths. (The English translation of the correspondence follows Cosima's edition and shares its shortcomings.[38]) Then, with the passing of time, Erich Kloss edited a much superior collection that added letters and supporting material as well as restoring Cosima's deletions.[39] Recently, Hanjo Kesting compiled a new edition; it adds some new, mostly late, letters, but falls rather short in its editorial and scholarly support of the correspondence.[40] Readers thus have a choice, Kloss or Kesting. In either case, the heart of the exchange remains those well-probed years 1849–1861 during which Wagner, a fugitive because of his complicity in the Dresden uprising of 1849, looked to Liszt as his confidant, agent, and promoter in the German states. On balance, there is more of Liszt's concern with Wagner's works than Wagner's interest in Liszt's in the collection.

Liszt also maintained a lengthy correspondence with his pupil and one-time son-in-law Hans von Bülow.[41] It is a collection that is best seen as a record of the extensive professional relations between the two, since virtually every allusion to the emotion fraught Bülow-Cosima-Wagner triangle and its aftermath has been prudently excised. Given Liszt's preeminence in musical life, he also corresponded with just about every composer, performer, and musical journalist of the day. The letters to them, however, must be sought in the Bibliography and Supplement mentioned above.

In broader terms Liszt enjoyed a friendly, respectful relationship with Carl-Alexander of Saxe-Weimar; their exchange limns Liszt's years of service and later residence in Weimar together with his plans and hopes for the city as a cultural center.[42] For his part, Carl-Alexander manifested an amiable interest in Liszt, his works, and well-being, yet remained a little uncomprehending and hesitant, perhaps, about Liszt's artistic agenda.

Liszt carried on an extensive correspondence with Eduard Liszt. Eduard, a half-brother of Liszt's father Adam, was Liszt's uncle, but since Eduard was five years younger than Franz, the two referred to each other as "cousins." "Brothers" might be a better term because their relationship was one of the most enduring and satisfying of Liszt's life. A successful lawyer and jurist, Eduard not only provided a welcome home for his kinsman in Vienna, but also proved a trusted confidant and counselor who also handled many of Liszt's legal and financial affairs. In return, Liszt, lacking a proper heir, transferred his Austrian knighthood—the Order of the Iron Crown—to Eduard and his family in 1866. Although there is no single collection devoted to their correspondence, a good number of the letters to "Liebster Eduard" appear in the *Briefe* and other sources.[43]

Since Liszt's long and frequently complex relations with his native Hungary also played a significant role in his correspondence, there are two notable collections to mention. One reflects Liszt's cherished, lengthy friendship with the Hungarian art patron Baron Antal Augusz, who, as the letters to him testify, worked untiringly to foster Liszt's reputation, compositions, and stature in his homeland.[44] The other shifts its base, so to speak; instead of featuring a single individual, it, like several others in the Liszt canon, is based on the location of the letters. Liszt's *Letters from Hungarian Collections* edited by Margit Prahács is one of the outstanding monuments of Liszt scholarship.[45] Even though it naturally focuses on his manifold activities and contacts in Hungary, its 605 letters are supported by 160 pages of informative and pertinent commentary. Prahács's achievement is a constant joy to work with.

In general, English readers have not been served well in the past. In addition to the translations mentioned—the Wagner-Liszt Correspondence and the letters to Marie Sayn-Wittgenstein and Olga von Meyendorff—only the first two volumes of La Mara's *Briefe* were available.[46] Recently, however, that situation has improved greatly with two collections compiled and translated by the English scholar Adrian Williams. The first is *Portrait of Liszt: By Himself and His Contemporaries*,[47] a collection of over 600 items which, while including a sampling of Liszt's own letters, concentrates mainly on letters and writings about him.[48] Whether in public or in private, Liszt was always news, and a compilation such as this portrays him at his fullest. The other is Liszt's *Selected Letters*,[49] an outstanding volume that contains nearly 950 letters (mostly as substantive excerpts) to over 100 correspondents—with the spotlight mostly on Marie d'Agoult and Carolyne Sayn-Wittgenstein—all backed by the editor's meticulous scholarship. Without discounting the original publications summarized above and which scholars will continue to consult, Williams's selection is a great boon to English readers. It not only taps into Liszt's formidable legacy as a letter writer, but also makes conveniently available a large amount of material from the earlier, out-of-print collections.

Having highlighted the general course of Liszt's correspondence, it is apparent that there are both negative and positive aspects of it to consider. The negative resolves to a matter of convenience. Unlike the letters of Mozart, Beethoven, Chopin, Berlioz, or even Wagner, for example, there is no single, neat set of volumes to which a reader can turn to consult Liszt's letters. Selections help of course, but beyond that the reader is left to seek out the older collections, such as those mentioned above, as well as articles in a vast array of journals and periodicals that can try the resources of even the greatest libraries. This is unfortunate because the difficulty of the search can impede the full understanding of his personal relationships and multifarious activities.

On the positive side, there are the letters themselves (i.e., those already published, allowing that there are more which have yet to be made public). On a personal level, they provide an almost daily account of his activities, contacts, and interest in the events of his time, be they musical, literary, political, or religious. In broader terms, however, Liszt—pianist, composer, conductor, teacher, and ardent champion of musical progress—was the epitome of musical life in the nineteenth century. Thus, the letters also reflect concert practices, music publishing, piano manufacture, the rise of musical journalism and criticism, the importance of music festivals, developments in symphonic composition, the start of national schools, the increasing hegemony of Bayreuth, reforms in church music, not to mention Liszt's unfailing support of young composers or the careers of his many pupils. No other musician, perhaps, has left us a fuller record of his life and times.

NOTES

1. *Gesammelte Schriften,* ed. and trans. (into German) Lina Ramann (Leipzig: Breitkopf & Härtel, 1880–1883; Wiesbaden, 1978) 6 vols.: I *Friedrich Chopin* (trans. La Mara [Marie Lipsius]); II *Essays und Reisebriefe eines Baccalaurens der Tonkunst* (eight early essays from the *Revue et Gazette Musicale* plus twelve "Letters of a Bachelor of Music"); III/1 *Dramaturgische Blätter* (fourteen essays mostly on operatic works); III/2 *Dramaturgische Blätter: Richard Wagner* (essays on *Tannhäuser, Lohengrin, Holländer,* and *Das Rheingold); IV Aus den Annalen des Fortschritts* (six essays on musical personalities of the time); V *Streifzüge* (six miscellaneous essays); VI *Die Zigeuner und ihre Musik in Ungarn* (2d ed. of 1859 work). Also, Serge Gut, "Catalogue complet des oeuvres litteraires," *Franz Liszt* (Paris; Fallois, 1989): 584–587.

2. *Sämtliche Schriften,* ed. Detlef Altenburg (Wiesbaden: Breitkopf & Härtel, 1989–). Three volumes to date: 3 *Die Goethe Stiftung,* ed. Detlef Altenburg and Britta Schilling-Wang (1997); 4 *Lohengrin et Tannhäuser de Richard Wagner,* ed. Rainer Kleinertz (1989); 5 *Dramaturgische Blätter,* ed. Dorothea Redepenning and Britta Schilling (1989).

3. Mária Eckhardt, "New Documents on Liszt as Author," *New Hungarian Quarterly* 95 (Autumn 1984): 181–194.

4. Franz Liszt, *Pages romantiques,* ed. Jean Chantavoine (Paris: F. Alcan, 1912; Paris, 1985), 1–83.

5. Liszt, *Pages romantiques,* 65–67.

6. Franz Liszt, *An Artist's Journey: Lettres d'un bachelier ès musique 1835–1841,* trans. and annotated Charles Suttoni (Chicago: University of Chicago Press, 1989).

7. James Deaville, "A Checklist of Liszt's Writings, 1849–1879," *JALS* 24 (July-December 1988): 86–90.

8. *Sämtliche Schriften* 3. See above n. 2.

9. Liszt evidently liked competitions; he had mentioned them earlier for church music and the Paris salon; Liszt, *Artist's Journey*, 34, 237.

10. Franz Liszt, *Frederic Chopin*, trans. Edward N. Waters (New York: The Free Press, 1963).

11. *Sämtliche Schriften* 4. See above n. 2. Also, Franz Liszt, "Wagner's *Tannhäuser*," *Dwight's Journal of Music* (19 November–17 December 1853).

12. *Sämtliche Schriften* 5. See above n. 2.

13. Mária Eckhardt, "Liszt on Opera," *New Hungarian Quarterly* 116 (Winter 1989): 117. An essay-review of the *Dramaturgische Blätter*.

14. *Source Readings in Music History*, ed. Oliver Strunk (New York: Norton, 1950), 846–873.

15. Franz Liszt, *The Gypsies and their Music in Hungary*, trans. Edwin Evans (London: Reeves, n.d.). 2 vols.

16. "Gypsy Music or Hungarian Music?" in Béla Bartók, *Essays*, selected and ed. Benjamin Suchoff (London: Faber & Faber, 1976), 206–223.

17. Franz Liszt, "Sur Paganini, à propos de sa mort," *Revue et Gazette Musicale de Paris*, 23 August 1840. (trans. C. S.)

18. Charles Suttoni, "Liszt Correspondence in Print: An Expanded, Annotated Bibliography," *JALS* 25 (January–June 1989). It cites some 700 books and articles that present letters written by or to Liszt.

19. Charles Suttoni, "Liszt Correspondence in Print: A Supplementary Bibliography," *JALS* 46 (Fall 1999). It adds about 135 citations to the basic bibliography.

20. *Franz Liszts Briefe an seine Mutter*, trans. (into German) and ed. La Mara [Marie Lipsius] (Leipzig: Breitkopf & Härtel, 1918). 102 letters 1827–1866.

21. *Franz Liszt: Briefwechsel mit seiner Mutter*, ed. Klára Hamburger (Eisenstadt: Amt der Burgenländischen Landesregierung, 2000). 204 letters 1827–1866. Reviewed by Charles Suttoni, *JALS* 49 (Spring 2001).

22. *Correspondance de Liszt et de sa fille Madame Émile Ollivier, 1842–1862*, ed. Daniel Ollivier (Paris: Grasset, 1936). 179 letters.

23. Franz Liszt, *Lettres à Cosima et à Daniela*, ed. Klára Hamburger (Sprimont: Mardaga, 1996). 153 letters 1845–1886. Reviewed by Mária Eckhardt, *Hungarian Quarterly* 146 (Summer 1997): 146–151; Adrian Williams, *Music & Letters* 78/3 (August 1997): 442–444.

24. 31 May 1873. In German trans. in Lina Ramann, *Lisztiana* (Schott: Mainz, 1983), 427–431.

25. La Mara [Marie Lipsius], *Liszt und die Frauen*, 2d ed. (Leipzig: Breitkopf & Härtel, 1919) discusses his relationships with twenty-six outstanding women.

26. *Correspondance de Liszt et de la comtesse d'Agoult*, ed. M. Daniel Ollivier (Paris: Grasset, 1933–1934) 2 vols. ca. 570 letters 1834–1864.

27. Ernest Newman, *The Man Liszt* (New York: Scribner's, 1935) is the most flagrant misuse of this correspondence, and a concerned reader should seek out the severe rebuke of his methods by Carl Engel, *Musical Quarterly* 21 (1935): 230–240.

28. Suttoni, "Liszt and Madame d'Agoult: A Reappraisal," *Liszt and His World*, ed. Michael Saffle (Stuyvesant, NY: Pendragon, 1998), 23–29.

29. *Correspondance de Liszt et de la comtesse d'Agoult*, 2:375.

30. *Franz Liszts Briefe*, ed. La Mara [Marie Lipsius] (Leipzig: Breitkopf & Härtel, 1893–1905) 8 vols. Vols. 4–7 present the letters to Carolyne (1245 letters 1847–1886); vols. 1, 2, and 8 contain letters to various correspondents (1114 items 1823–1886); and vol. 3 those to Agnès Street-Klindworth (see below n. 34).

31. Suttoni, "Liszt Correspondence in Print," 10–13.

32. *The Letters of Franz Liszt to Marie zu Sayn-Wittgenstein*, ed. and trans. Howard E. Hugo (Cambridge: Harvard University Press, 1953). 215 letters 1848–1886. Reviewed by Edward N. Waters, *Notes* 10 (1952–1953): 623–624; Jacques Barzun, *Musical Quarterly* 40 (1954): 110–115; Emile Haraszti, *Revue de Musicologie* 37 (July 1955): 93–101.

33. *Liszt's Briefe*, vol. 3, *Briefe an eine Freundin*. 133 letters 1855–1886.

34. *Franz Liszt and Agnès Street-Klindworth: A Correspondence 1854–1886*, ed. Pauline Pocknell (Stuyvesant, NY: Pendragon, 2000). 160 letters.

35. Liszt, *Lettres à Cosima*: 116. (trans. C. S.)

36. *The Letters of Franz Liszt to Olga von Meyendorff, 1871–1886*, trans. William R. Tyler, introduction and notes by Edward N. Waters (Washington, D.C.: Dumbarton Oaks, 1979). ca. 400 letters. Reviewed by Mária Eckhardt, *Studia musicologica* 22 (1980): 468–474; Sharon Winklhofer, *19th-Century Music* 4 (1980–1981): 266–270.

37. Hector Berlioz, *Correspondance générale*, ed. Pierre Citron et al. (Paris: Flammarion, 1972–1999). 7 vols.

38. *Correspondence of Wagner and Liszt*, trans. Francis Hueffer, ed. W. Ashton Ellis, 2d ed. (New York: Scribner's, 1897; New York, 1973). 2 vols.

39. *Briefwechsel zwischen Wagner und Liszt*, ed. Erich Kloss, 3d ed. (Leipzig: Breitkopf & Härtel, 1910). 330 letters 1841–1882.

40. *Franz Liszt–Richard Wagner Briefwechsel*, ed. Hanjo Kesting (Frankfurt a.M.: Insel, 1988). 351 letters 1841–1882.

41. *Briefwechsel zwischen Franz Liszt und Hans von Bülow*, ed. La Mara [Marie Lipsius] (Leipzig: Breitkopf & Härtel, 1898). 216 letters 1851–1884.

42. *Briefwechsel zwischen Franz Liszt und Carl Alexander, Grossherzog von Sachsen*, ed. La Mara [Marie Lipsius] (Leipzig: Breitkopf & Härtel, 1909). 203 letters 1845–1886.

43. See n. 29 above.

44. *Franz Liszt's Briefe an Baron Anton Augusz, 1846–1878*. ed. Wilhelm von Csapó (Budapest: 1911). 117 letters.

45. Franz Liszt, *Briefe aus ungarischen Sammlungen, 1835–1886*, ed. Margit Prahács (Budapest: Akadémiai Kiadó, 1966). 605 letters.

46. *Letters of Franz Liszt*, ed. La Mara [Marie Lipsius], trans. Constance Bache (New York: Scribner's, 1894; New York, 1969). 659 letters 1828–1886.

47. *Portrait of Liszt: By Himself and His Contemporaries*, ed. Adrian Williams (Oxford: Clarendon Press, 1990).

48. Similarly, *Liszt en son temps*, ed. Pierre-Antoine Huré and Claude Knepper (Paris: Hachette, 1987). Notable for its many extracts about Liszt from the French press.

49. Franz Liszt, *Selected Letters*, ed. and trans. Adrian Williams (Oxford: Clarendon Press, 1998). 946 letters 1811–1886. Reviewed by Patrick Rucker, *JALS* 45 (Spring 1999): 52–59; Ben Arnold, *Notes* (March 2001): 642–644.

3

Liszt in the German-Language Press

James Deaville

One of the least understood and studied topics for Liszt scholarship is the response to him in the daily and musical presses of his day, which produced a massive literature about Liszt.[1] Though still in their infancy at the time, these periodical print media already revealed an eagerness to publish extensively about such a noted personality. Indeed, Liszt was under constant close scrutiny by the press, which—beyond giving his life a modern relevance—may well have influenced how, of the musicians of the era, he seemed to be most involved in reinventing and refashioning himself, as witnessed in his departure from the virtuosic scene in 1847, his taking on of minor orders in the Catholic Church in 1865, and his other excessively public stagings of the private. Thus the role of the press cannot be underestimated as a force in Liszt's life and activities, for it not only potentially influenced him, but it unquestionably had a considerable impact upon presenting him to its readership and his audience. As such, then, study of the Liszt reception in the print media opens new insights into his role in the society and culture of his day, and allows a first overview of developments within the musical press during the nineteenth century.

For this first attempt at a comprehensive study of Liszt in the press, it is important to draw some boundaries because of the volume of available material. Liszt's long-term ties with German-speaking lands, first as traveling virtuoso, then as resident Kapellmeister in Weimar, and finally as occasional visitor to Weimar and other German cities, and the existence of detailed studies devoted to specific periods of the *Liszt-Rezeption* within the German-language print media, like those of Michael Saffle and Dezső Legány, suggest focusing on the press in that area. Chronologically speaking, the first German-language review appeared in 1822, and Liszt's death in 1886 is a reasonable *terminus ad quem* for such a survey, since it demarcates the period during which Liszt could participate in the reception of his own activities and music. And to the extent that Alan Walker recently divided his monumental Liszt biography into three parts,[2] this division makes sense for a study of the reception as well, since the press was keenly aware of (and indeed, exploited) major changes in his life situation.

Finally, a word on the sources consulted for this study. While a variety of documents relevant for a study of *Liszt-Rezeption* exists—articles and reviews in the daily and periodical press, diary and letter passages, books, etc.—the most valuable for assessing his ongoing and developing positions within nineteenth-century society is the reportage in the daily and specialized musical presses. It was the public discourse around Liszt as nurtured by the press(es) that had the greatest effect upon the society of his time. As is the case with any study of reception, these sources are more important for what they tell us about the social and cultural context in which they were written than for their factual value as accurate records of an individual's life[3]—unfortunately, many biographers of Liszt cannot look beyond the inaccuracies of such texts.[4]

The study of music in the print media of the nineteenth century is still in its infancy, so that much of the research regarding contexts for the sources is being undertaken here for the first time. The sixty-five-year span of the survey covers a period of significant change for the German-language daily and musical press, which reflected developments in politics, society, culture and technology. Such a brief study cannot fully consider the writings in the context of the evolving press, even though care must be given to situate the sources historically, and also geographically: the response to Liszt, his performances, and his music in Berlin, for example, differs considerably from that in Vienna or Leipzig for a host of reasons, arising at least in part from the diverse institutions of the press and musical performance.

1811–1847

The first period of Liszt reception (1811–1847) reveals the incipient bourgeois press coming to grips with virtuosity as an artistic phenomenon, which it would come to accept and which would thus draw its attention to Liszt, as virtuoso par excellence. Once Liszt entered the public arena, the German-language press would accompany him for the rest of his life. It took some time, however, for him to obtain more than a passing local interest, for his early appearances could not help but identify him as a child prodigy (*Wunderkind*),[5] with the attached implication of transitoriness. During the course of the virtuoso years, Liszt would establish his reputation with critics and public as international artist of the highest calibre, indeed, as the greatest living performer and the greatest performer of all time, but the reviewers in Vienna can be forgiven if they praised Liszt's concerts from 1822–1823 and then promptly forgot about the prodigy as he disappeared in Paris.[6] That they were quite brief, anonymous reviews in a local music journal (the *Wiener Allgemeine Musikalische Zeitung*) typifies the early years of press coverage of musical events in German-speaking lands. The more important German music periodicals with international coverage through correspondents in foreign cities, in particular the *Allgemeine Musikalische Zeitung* in Leipzig, reported on Liszt's performances in France and England during the 1820s.

Liszt became a commanding figure within the German-language press once he undertook his virtuoso tours within central Europe, to Vienna beginning in 1838, to Pest and Prague (both under Austrian jurisdiction) beginning respectively in 1839 and 1840, and to German cities beginning in 1840.[7] In his exhaustive study of Liszt in Germany, Saffle has already provided trenchant summary observations for the virtuoso Liszt in the German press between 1840 and 1845: "For the most part, this criticism—at least in Germany—was positive, even adulatory. As a pianist Liszt wrung from his reviewers a torrent of praise for his technique, touch, and interpretative abilities; and as a composer, he was less often, but nevertheless quite often, complimented on his talent and accomplishments."[8] The same can be said to hold true for the Liszt reception in Austria and in the important German-language press in cities like Pest and Prague.

Beneath the almost perfunctory adulation, however, the press enlisted Liszt the celebrated performer—perhaps the leading personality of his age—for major cultural and political work. Susan Bernstein has observed that journalism and virtuosity were linked, for "both [were] considered to be fallen or debased facets of music and poetry."[9] Richard Leppert puts both writing about Liszt and Liszt's performance into a broader cultural perspective, addressing the effects of his virtuosity upon his audience (which included journalists and other writers). For Leppert, critics (many of them German) were responding to the "broad range of paradoxical, often contradictory meanings" embodied by the virtuoso: "artist and businessman; inspired superhuman and machine; utterly sincere in character and calculatingly manipulative; authentic and fake; masculine and feminine . . . polarities . . . that characterize modernity itself."[10]

These dual meanings were reflected in the varying responses to Liszt and his virtuosity in the press. Although it is impossible to establish hard and fast rules at that volatile time for the German-language press, newspaper reviews and other non-musical reportage about Liszt, often by non-musicians, tended to be more favorable towards him than the musical press. This duality stands to reason, since daily journalism needed to be in touch with the tastes of its readers, in this case, the masses who adulated Liszt, while it was just that popularity that made the reviewers in the musical press suspicious of him and his performance, even though the critics without exception used extravagant language to describe Liszt's technical and interpretative abilities.[11] The "expert" reviewer of music before 1848—the term "music critic" cannot really be used during this period[12]—was most likely a music theorist-aesthetician, such as Adolf Bernhard Marx or Siegfried Wilhelm Dehn, or a composer-critic like Robert Schumann, and these writers were unlikely to approve music or a phenomenon that had popular roots. The following example shows one of these critics lauding Liszt's artistry while criticizing the superficialities of virtuosity and the blind enthusiasm of his adherents:

Thus the wonderful piano virtuoso Liszt deserved honor and recognition, but no blind veneration, no yoking [of the enthusiast] as beast of burden [pulling] the triumphal wagon of such artistic celebrities! That is the scandal of the century, which today erects a monument to the benefactor of humanity, and tomorrow lowers human dignity, insofar as it strives after the handkerchief of a prima donna, the shoe of a dancer, the lock of hair from the head of a piano player.[13]

Most significantly, Liszt's performance had the effect of destabilizing his gender identity, which invited his opponents in the press to feminize him, and thus dismiss him. His performance of gender unsettled the male critics from the press, who recognized but could not name his sexual ambiguity or—worse yet—ambivalence. For example, he was often portrayed in critical literature as a female hysteric.[14] Once the scholars dig beneath the surface of their representations of Liszt as "lady's man," we begin to see Liszt as sexually ambiguous, or—to cite Leppert again—"publicly [leaping] back and forth across the increasingly higher walls of gender boundaries."[15] This "instability of assigned gender norms" would be both comforting and disconcerting to those who visually "consumed" Liszt as participants in the spectacle of virtuosic performance. The vast array of gestures and demeanor he would use in stage performance, for example, could easily carry the most varied meanings, depending on the diverse subject positions of his audience members. The dangers of the free-floating signifiers released by Liszt's body caused his opponents to try to control him through strategies of opposition, such as feminization.

Of course, the critics did not openly brand Liszt as a woman to express their discomfort over his gender roles. When they did criticize his performance, it was within the broader context of a critique of virtuosity, which indeed must have been an unsettling phenomenon for critics who had dedicated their lives to preserving standards and combatting popularizing tendencies in music. It was above all members of the elite musical press who participated in the discourse against virtuosity during the 1840s, based on the proliferation of charlatan virtuosi who brought in substantial sums and composed trivial music.[16] The dissemination of music as a popular form of entertainment was problematic enough, but then its performance in spectacles that physically enacted sexual identity on stage and fed upon desire within the audience removed the concert experience from the traditions of dignity and control that ruled in other performance venues.[17] Liszt was not spared this criticism, although in his performances the level of artistry was so high that a reviewer like Schumann would have to praise Liszt despite the superficiality of the phenomenon of virtuosity. Of course, non-professional critics in the daily press had a greatly reduced stake in the long-term health of the art, and were likely to be carried away by the same enthusiasm that marked their readers.

The sexing of Liszt was not the only response that his virtuosity brought forth among the audiences of his day. For some spectators, he was a model of bourgeois success.[18] For others, his performance was a distraction from every-day life, a momentary liberation from the oppressive economic and social conditions prior to 1848—in these cases, auditors were swept away into unknown realms of musical appreciation, far from the cares of the day. Here are two examples of reviews from Vienna that illustrate this type of response: "The actual character of his playing reveals itself in an endless power of soul-felt expression, an irresistible force that calls everything its own and draws everything into its realm. . . . Liszt's performance not only leads us onward, but it pulls us along with itself."[19] "Despite his unbelievable, path-breaking technical development, [his achievements] are of such an abstract, ideal character that you forget their creator for the wonderful world of spirit into which he transports us."[20]

The reception of Liszt in the press was augmented by a new form of criticism in the nineteenth century, the caricature. The nineteenth century was an age of seeing, and the spectacle of Liszt gave the new illustrated press ample opportunities to exploit this visual culture to "capture" Liszt. The "illustrated Liszt" in turn promoted the fetishization of his body, which had become a primary component of "Lisztomania."[21] The disappearance of Liszt from public view in 1847, after his withdrawal from public performance, was undoubtedly a factor behind the unfavorable response to that move in the press: robbed of their ability to see, and thus control, Liszt, they lashed out against his entering the realm of the "unseen," of the ineffable in art.[22]

1848–1861

If Liszt learned anything from his years on the stage, it was the value of effective press coverage. Soon after his arrival in Weimar, Liszt took steps (at least initially unpremeditated) that helped turn Weimar into a center for the literary activities of the progressive movement in music. Students who Liszt attracted to Weimar, especially Joachim Raff and Hans von Bülow, began writing for the local papers in Weimar and then, after 1850, in the *Neue Zeitschrift für Musik*, which assured the movement a national profile. Liszt himself added to the literary production of his circle through his books on the Goethe Foundation (1850) and Chopin (1852), and then (beginning in 1854) participated in the German periodical press through a series of articles for the *Neue Zeitschrift*. Although Emile Haraszti overstates the case when he calls Liszt's Weimar a critical "laboratory,"[23] there can be no doubt that the circle around Liszt in Weimar, or more broadly expressed, the Weimar-Leipzig axis of Liszt and Wagner supporters (including the progressive critics at Brendel's Leipzig *Neue Zeitschrift*), worked closely with each other. It is not saying too much that Liszt and his associates developed a press strategy during the early 1850s, so they were able to take advantage of the medium. For example, Liszt's article about Gluck's opera *Orpheus* first appeared in the local *Weimarische Zeitung* of 22 February 1854 within a week after Liszt had conducted it (16 February). A much-extended version of the same article (without local references) appeared two months later in the *Neue Zeitschrift* of 28 April 1854.[24] Between 1880 and 1883 Lina Ramann eventually collected and published (in bowdlerized editions) this and other articles by Liszt, so that the Gluck article appeared in three different contexts during Liszt's lifetime (not counting reprints and translations).

Liszt's associates followed his path through the German press. At first they used the local papers, above all the *Weimarische Zeitung*, which addressed the general public and the Weimar court and attempted to win local adherents for Liszt. (Like Liszt, pupils Raff and von Bülow wrote for the *Weimarische Zeitung*, Bülow also for Weimar's *Deutschland*, and Richard Pohl for the *Weimarer Sonntagsblatt*.) As Raff reports in an unpublished letter from early 1850, these local reports often served to prepare the public for coming musical events: "Among the operas which are to be given here next, I mention *Graf Ory*, the performance of which I have prepared in today's *Weimarische Zeitung* through an article, since it is already going to be staged next week."[25]

The Weimar critics also published in musical and belletristic journals that had a national distribution, above all the *Neue Zeitschrift*, which contributed to the broader basis for the reception of the New-German movement.[26] Bülow well expresses the sentiments of the circle toward Brendel's journal: "I will write for Brendel's paper and no other, 1) because the paper has a respectable, principled, scholarly bearing, [and] 2) because it understands the interests that Wagner and Liszt have in common and there are few people who can write well and intelligently."[27]

Even though they may have exploited the German press in a similar fashion, the critics around Liszt in Weimar each spoke a different language: Peter Cornelius had a moderate, considered tone, while Bülow was notorious for a highly polemical critical style. As the following unpublished letter passage reveals, there were diverse music-critical tactics, even among the polemicists of Liszt's Weimar circle: "This type of battle strategy, where you in disguise sneak up to the side of the opponent and then stick the knife into his ribs, is . . . well suited for Bülow. For my part, I may no longer act like I did years ago. One expects from me that I directly and calmly approach the opponent, face him in full light of day, and knock out his brains with a leaden club."[28]

It is interesting to note that, through the activity of Liszt and his Weimar associates beginning in February of 1854 (the date of Liszt's first "Dramaturgische Blätter"), the *Neue Zeitschrift* took on a "Weimar dialect" in its coverage of the progressive movement in music.[29] Brendel contributed to this unique and substantial Liszt "coverage" through his three articles entitled "Ausflug nach Weimar," which drew special attention to the extraordinary artistic conditions and productions in Weimar.[30] Liszt's articles were particularly attractive to the editor because of Liszt's notoriety. Brendel clearly expressed this in an unpublished letter to Carl Debrois von Bruyck: "The lack of space that I indicated to you is not to be considered the rule. . . . Liszt's articles are responsible, but it is absolutely impossible to do it any other way, and all of the papers in Germany, France, and England would, as one is accustomed to say, lick their fingers if they would have received these articles for publication. I best know what kind of sensation they will make and how much they will be in demand."[31]

Liszt and his associates and pupils also found opposition in the German-language press. Deprived of its ability to consume Liszt visually, and opposing movements of a progressive nature in the conservative atmosphere of the post-revolutionary 1850s, the press was ready and eager to fight the Weimar-Leipzig axis that had established itself as a new direction in art. This opposition was not the daily press that continued to track the activities of Liszt, but rather professional musical journalism, augmented by the new genre of belletristic journals such as the *Grenzboten* and *Westermann's Illustrirte Deutsche Monatshefte*. Heated polemic exchanges, "feather wars," were the watchword of the day in the journals that had become so numerous that competition for readers was fierce.

The German-language press, no longer able to dismiss Liszt as a recreative technician, was forced to regard him as a creative force—as already mentioned, critics would have preferred him to have remained on stage, where he could be seen and thus controlled, rather than dwelling in the domain of the unseen, the ineffable. Indeed, one of the favored strategies of opposition to Liszt and what he represented in Weimar of the 1850s was for the writer to yearn for his virtuoso days.[32] At least that activity gave the public a glimpse of artistic perfection, while works like the program symphonies and symphonic poems were regarded as profaning long-held aesthetic principles.

A variety of publications were available to the conservative opposition, including the *Niederrheinische Musik-Zeitung* in Cologne, the *Signale für die musikalische Welt* in Leipzig, and the aforementioned belletristic journals (which in general supported the status quo). Before the activity of Vienna's Eduard Hanslick beginning in the mid-1850s, however, the conservative forces had no effective spokesman. Furthermore, and perhaps because they were oppositional, they never found one center of operation, nor were their efforts at all co-ordinated. A survey of journal articles from the 1850s would nevertheless give the impression that the New Germans were far outnumbered.

Still, while Liszt was establishing himself in Weimar during the early 1850s, it was Wagner who—by virtue of his recent writings and operas (*Tannhäuser* and *Lohengrin*)—dominated the press. Only when Liszt came before the broader public outside of the confines of Weimar and Thuringia with festival performances of his new sacred music, for example in Gran (1855, *Missa solemnis*) and of his new symphonic compositions in Aachen (1857, *Festklänge*), among many other cities, and with the publication of the symphonic poems beginning in 1856, did he himself take over the position in the vanguard of the New Germans, with important new works before the public (and during a time when Wagner himself produced no new works). In an ironic twist, opponents who had once railed against Liszt's "shallow virtuosity" came to regard it as preferable to his "shallow" compositions of the 1850s. This is apparent in Hanslick's 1857 review of the publication of Liszt's symphonic poems:

When Franz Liszt, the most gifted virtuoso of our time, grew tired of triumphs won with other people's compositions, he set about to surprise the world with large creations of his own. One who is accustomed not only to intellectual activity but also to having his activity crowned with laurels cannot leave the public arena; he can only change it. In Liszt's case it was his intention that the composer should overshadow the virtuoso. Enthusiastic friends and obliging writers heralded this transfiguration as a phenomenon of immeasurable advantage to the development of music. It seems more likely that the musical world has suffered, in the virtuoso's abdication, a loss which the composer's succession can hardly compensate.

He who attentively observed Liszt's artistic individuality during his long career as a virtuoso might pretty well guess the character of his new works. His piano compositions were consistently of such mediocre invention and execution that barely one of them could have claimed lasting existence in musical literature. A profound knowledge of pianistic effect and several interesting ideas are all that can be mentioned with praise. With a virtuoso of genius such attributes may be taken for granted.[33]

While he admits that Liszt was "the most gifted virtuoso of our time," Hanslick cynically yet subtly portrays the achievements of the virtuoso years as shallow, with compositions of mediocre invention and performances intended to gain the laurels of the public. Nevertheless, in comparison with the turn Liszt's life has taken, his prior activities appear acceptable, with Hanslick even recognizing Liszt as a "virtuoso of genius." In his desire to expose Liszt and the symphonic poem as frauds, Hanslick denies Liszt any compositional creativity, including the pre-Weimar piano compositions. Liszt has become the transcendental piano player. The image recurred time and again in the oppositional press of the 1850s,[34] and only weakened as the memory of the virtuoso years faded and as virtuosity itself fell into a type of disrepute.

1861–1886

While Liszt followed different paths after the dissolution of his Weimar, the press itself did not significantly change at that point. Newspapers, music journals, and the belletristic press all continued to report about music and musical events, the medium of publication determined by the nexus of location and significance of event. What did change was Liszt's role within the progressive movement.

The battle fought in the 1850s over the New German School became the major aesthetic dispute for the German-language musical press over the rest of the century, but Liszt played a lesser role in it. As Wagner came to regain the attention of the press during the course of the 1860s and 1870s, with the premieres of *Tristan und Isolde* (1865) and *Die Meistersinger von Nürnberg* (1868) and the preparations and 1876 premiere of *Der Ring des Nibelungen*, as well as the ascendancy of Bayreuth, Liszt figured less. His life and activities still interested the general reader, but—despite such an attempt at promotion through the New German take-over of the Euterpe concert series in Leipzig between 1860 and 1862[35]—his compositions from the 1850s and later did not establish themselves in the concert halls, with two major exceptions: (1) the two oratorios *The Legend of St. Elisabeth* and *Christus* and (2) those works performed at the annual festivals of the *Allgemeiner Deutscher Musikverein*. Also, while Liszt's entry into minor orders in the Catholic Church in 1865 may have interested newspaper readers for a time, this turn to the composition of sacred music did not necessarily excite reader or writer (not at least in comparison with Wagner's music dramas), unless the work was to be performed in their city.

Furthermore, Liszt and his colleagues from Weimar and Leipzig in the 1850s withdrew from activity in the press. With the death of Brendel in 1868, one of the most effective journalistic zealots for Liszt was lost, although Brendel himself had adopted a more conciliatory attitude towards the opposition during the course of the 1860s. The other Weimar critics and writers from the 1850s had dispersed or—like in the cases of Pohl and Cornelius—taken up the cause of Wagner. In the 1870s, the individual forces of Wagnerian propaganda were replaced by a more centralized "operation," based in Bayreuth and featuring such a polemical writer as Hans Freiherr von Wolzogen and focusing on dissemination through the *Bayreuther Blätter* that Wagner had helped to found in 1878.[36] Liszt did not really figure in their writings for a variety of reasons, including his espousal of Catholicism and his personal alienation from Wagner during this period.

One feature of the Liszt reception in his last period was a sanctification of the man and his prior activities. Liszt's withdrawal to Italy, taking on minor orders, and dedication to the composition of sacred music took him away from the aesthetic fray and thus tended to neutralize his position. His absence from the scene in turn allowed critics to focus on and appreciate his career and achievements as a whole, which meant recognizing Liszt's genius as performer and generous spirit, among others. Even though he could not report more favorably about the symphonic poems in 1880 on the occasion of an extraordinary concert of the Gesellschaft der Musikfreunde in Vienna, Hanslick did express the fascination with the great man and his charisma in the following review passage: "We are not in a position to decide whether the Mass and the following tone poems of Liszt delighted or only satisfied, or even somewhat bored, the auditorium. One can never say, when Liszt's compositions are given with the protective magic of his personal presence. The fascinating power of this man is no fable—indeed, many members of the public listen without interest or satisfaction, but their gaze is fixed on Liszt's appearance and—they applaud."[37]

Liszt's piano virtuosity and the phenomenon of Lisztomania associated with it were still fresh in audiences' and critics' memories, thirty years after his departure from the stage. In reporting about a Liszt concert of the Wiener akademischer Wagner-Verein in Vienna in 1879, critic Theodor Helm drew upon the same imagery as a critic from the 1830s or 1840s: "It is certain that the Master was really splendidly disposed this time and, like in his days of youth, knew how to lead the hearts of everyone with magical power into the most inner sanctum of musical art, in which he rules, acts and deeply affects as absolute master."[38]

This same status of Liszt is apparent from an anonymous review from Vienna in the *Allgemeine Zeitung* of 1880: "In the midst of this musical spring, the elevated figure of the Abb[é] Liszt again appeared for the Musikfreunde."[39]

That the reviewer on the one hand praises Liszt's Mass for four-part male chorus and organ and deprecates *Die Ideale* on the other typifies the response to Liszt in the press during the third period of reception. As already mentioned, critics were particularly taken with the oratorios *Christus* and *Die Legende von der heiligen Elisabeth*, although the Psalm settings and Masses also earned him praise from local critics and music journalists. The press of the late nineteenth century loved to play both sides of this quintessentially Romantic and typically Lisztian paradox of sinner and saint, man of the world and man of the cloth.

Because of the increasing celebrity associated with his name, a new type of writing arose within the Liszt reception—the memoirs of Liszt, whether published as a book or in a journal article. Just as pupils flocked to him, both to take something of him and to benefit from his notoriety, so did various writers want to possess him and profit from his name. These "profiteers" ranged from the so-called "Cossack countess" Olga Janina, who published false and injurious memoirs of Liszt,[40] to the musicologist Ramann, who sent Liszt questionnaires to gather accurate information for her account of his life (*Franz Liszt als Künstler und Mensch*). Much of this literature took the form of "My Life with Liszt," whereby a pupil or associate accounted for his/her studies or experiences with Liszt—such reminiscences were popular items for publishers and the press, who wished to cash in on his celebrity themselves.[41]

It should not surprise us that in his last decade or so, Liszt would play an even lesser role in the German press. He had largely forsaken performing or conducting his works, composed music that was not published nor suited for public performance, and generally led a quiet and regulated life. This withdrawal from the public did not sell newspapers, although as an eminent European personality, he still had that potential. In this regard, one could maintain that his death briefly revived Liszt in the print media, to the extent that his passing on 31 July 1886 allowed the German press to reflect upon the accomplishments of his life—tributes in newspapers and music journals were legion, whatever their music-political orientation.

An exploration of Liszt's life necessitates an understanding of the press of his time. As this study of his status in the German press has revealed, many factors came together in the Liszt constructed by the newspapers and journals, including issues of gender and nationality, musical style, and character. As one of the most publicly discussed composers of the nineteenth century, Liszt owed a good portion of his notoriety to the press, to which he and his colleagues significantly contributed. Not only has the *Liszt-Rezeption* yet to receive the scholarly attention it merits, but also the specific activity of Liszt and New-German colleagues in the press on their own behalf requires serious study.

With the widespread critique of virtuosity in Germany of the late nineteenth century, Liszt's name lost some of its lustre after his death, becoming the topic for opposing viewpoints in the press. Curiously, the "posthumous" problem with Liszt was not so much his espousal of program music, which had become an accepted compositional approach, but rather with his character as popularizing charlatan, which was most readily evident in his virtuoso years. He was criticized for having given the public what they wanted, which was a shallow bill of fare, full of superficial and brilliant detail but ultimately devoid of substance. That Liszt's posthumous reputation has powerfully undergone a subsequent shift back to respectability was also the work of writers, such as Peter Raabe, Walker, and Leppert,[42] whose work from a variety of ideological perspectives share the recognition that Liszt is a musical figure who eminently deserves to be brought before the public and understood by it. Although it can never replace artistic achievement, the press can create (or destroy) the basis for the appreciation of a composer, and it did both for Liszt.

NOTES

1. This contribution is based upon studies the present author has undertaken regarding *Liszt-Rezeption*, but several individuals have added valuable insights: Michael Saffle (Virginia Tech), Marischka Olech Hopcroft (UCLA), and Pauline Pocknell (McMaster University). Important first steps on this topic have been made with such studies as Saffle, *Liszt in Germany 1840–1845: A Study in Sources, Documents, and the History of Reception* (Stuyvesant, NY: Pendragon, 1994); Adrian Williams, *Portrait of Liszt by Himself and His Contemporaries* (Oxford: Clarendon Press, 1990); and Dezső Legány, *Franz Liszt: Unbekannte Presse und Briefe aus Wien, 1822–1886* (Budapest: Corvina, 1984). They draw upon the press not only to ascertain opinion of the day towards Liszt and the cultural contexts of his activities, but also to determine specific concert dates and programs.

2. Alan Walker was by no means the first biographer of Liszt to adopt an overall three-period approach to Liszt. Biographer and musicologist Lina Ramann pioneered the tripartite division in her three-volume study *Franz Liszt als Künstler und Mensch* (Leipzig: Breitkopf & Härtel, 1880–1894).

3. One of many examples from Liszt's life was the widely disseminated news of Liszt's death in the fall of 1828. *Le Corsaire* (23 October 1828) may have erred by publishing an obituary, and yet in its error, the paper revealed much about current French attitudes toward virtuosity and stardom.

4. Saffle, *Liszt in Germany,* 65–68, goes to some length to illustrate what he calls "a long-standing prejudice against periodicals as reliable sources of historical information."

5. An important document about the young Liszt is a notice by Martainville in a Parisian paper entitled *Le Drapeau Blanc* (9 March 1824). Walker translates the article into English in his *Franz Liszt, The Virtuoso Years 1811–1847*, rev. ed. (Ithaca: Cornell University Press, 1987), 1:99–100.

6. Liszt's first public appearance took place on 1 December 1822 in the Landständischer Saal of Vienna. It was followed by two further performances in Vienna, on 9 December 1822 and 13 April 1823. These reviews are reprinted in Legány, 17–19.

7. Walker, *Franz Liszt, The Virtuoso Years,* 1:294–295, has a useful table of dates for Liszt's concerts between 1838 and 1847, organized by city.

8. Saffle, *Liszt in Germany,* 203.

9. Susan Bernstein, *Virtuosity of the Nineteenth Century: Performing Music and Language in Heine, Liszt, and Baudelaire* (Stanford: Stanford University Press, 1998), 6. Working from a comparative literature perspective, Bernstein's linguistic analysis in its attempts to establish a mutual relationship between literature and music and its reliance upon the close, comparative reading of texts, unfortunately fails to establish a basis for understanding either the journalistic or the musical milieu of virtuosity, or Liszt himself.

10. Richard Leppert, "Cultural Contradiction, Idolatry, and the Piano Virtuoso: Franz Liszt," in *Piano Roles: Three Hundred Years of Life with the Piano*, ed. James Parakilas (New Haven: Yale University Press, 1999), 281.

11. Here is an example from the Viennese press:

Describe how Liszt played? Oh, your breast always heaved, when the flood of his notes rises, when he bears us along into the romantic realm of the intuitive, unknown upon the wings of his musical passion, beyond all constraints of existence. [Beschreiben wie Liszt spielte? Ach immer schwillt einem der Busen, wenn die Flut seiner Töne steigt; wenn er uns auf den Flügeln seiner tönenden Sehnsucht mit fortträgt in das romantische Reich des Geahnten, Unbekannten, hinweg über alle Befangenheit des Daseyns.] Carlo [Pietro Mechetti], "Franz Liszt," *Wiener Zeitschrift für Kunst* (7 December 1839): 1173–1176.

12. At that time, no writer would have been able to support himself through writing reviews for the press. That changed beginning in the 1850s with the work of Eduard Hanslick, who was able to establish an income and reputation as a full-time critic, which means as a professional music critic.

13. Franz Wiest, "Liszt in Mainz: Kritische Skizze," *Das Rheinland wie es ernst und heiter ist*, 4/89 (6 July 1840), 350–351. Wiest's comment about the pianist's hair is a clear reference to Liszt. ["Darum auch verdiente Ehrung und Anerkennung dem herrlichen Clavier-Virtuosen Liszt, aber keine blinde Vergötterung, kein sich selber als Zugthier einspannen vor den Triumphwagen solcher Kunstcelebritäten! Das ist die Affen-Schande des Jahrhunderts, das heute einem Wohlthäter des Menschengeschlechts Monumente setzt, und morgen die Menschenwürde erniedrigt, indem es um das Schnupftuch einer Primadonna, um den Schuh einer Tänzerin, um die Haarlocke vom Haupte eines Clavierspielers buhlt."]

14. See, for example, a review by Henry Reeve in his *Edinburgh Review* from 1835: "He fainted in the arms of the friend who was turning over [the pages] for him, and we bore him out in a strong fit of hysterics." Cited in John Knox Laughton, *Memoirs of the Life and Correspondence of Henry Reeve* (London: Longmans, Green and Co., 1898), 1:49.

15. Leppert, "Cultural Contradiction, Idolatry, and Piano Virtuoso," 272.

16. Of course, questions of artistic merit for performances and music alike are highly subjective, and one generation's trivial music is the next generation's object of study.

17. Thus it was during this period that the Gewandhaus, among other central European concert institutions, was turning into what has been alternately termed a "church" or a "museum." Deaville explores the situation in the concert halls of Leipzig in his article, "The New-German School and the *Euterpe* Concerts, 1860–1862: A Trojan Horse in Leipzig," in *Festschrift Christoph-Hellmut Mahling zum 65. Geburtstag*, ed. Axel Beer, Kristina Pfarr, and Wolfgang Ruf (Tutzing: Hans Schneider, 1997), 253–270.

18. For a discussion of the meanings attached to Liszt's virtuosity in Vienna, see Deaville, "Liszt's Virtuosity and His Audience: Gender, Class and Power in the Concert Hall of the Early 19th Century," in *Das Andere: Eine Spurensuche in der Musikgeschichte des 19. und 20. Jahrhunderts*, ed. Annette Kreutziger-Herr (Frankfurt: Peter Lang, 1998), 281–300.

19. A. S. [August Schmidt], "Liszt's zweites Concert," *Allgemeine Wiener Musik-Zeitung* (7 March 1846), 114. Schmidt (1808–1891) was the editor of the *Allgemeine Wiener Musik-Zeitung* and as such was probably the most musically trained of the Viennese critics. ["Der eigentliche Charakter seines Spieles offenbart sich in einer unendlichen Kraft seelenhaften Ausdruckes, einer unwiderstehlichen Macht, die alles ihr Eigen nennt und in ihr Bereich zieht . . . Liszt's Spiel zieht uns nicht nur an, es reißt uns mit sich fort."]

20. Ritter v. S. [= Franz von Schober], *Briefe über F. Liszt's Aufenthalt in Ungarn* (Berlin: Schlesinger, 1843), 5–6. ["Seine Leistungen . . . sind bei der unglaublichen, nie dagewesenen mechanischen Entwickelung, so idealer, abstracter Natur, daß man den Schöpfer derselben über die schöne geistige Welt vergißt, in die er uns versetzt."]

21. Thus young women saved his cigar butts in their cleavages. This originates from the book by A. Brennglas, *Franz Liszt in Berlin* (1842), as quoted in Walker, *Franz Liszt, The Virtuoso Years*, 1:372.

22. As argued by such philosophers as Hegel and Schopenhauer, music occupies a special position within the arts because of its non-representational "essence." This idea is an inherently dangerous and subversive position for music, above all when it has no text or descriptive program, for in the realm of free-floating signifiers, it can take on a variety of uncontrolled and unexpected meanings.

23. Emile Haraszti, "Franz Liszt: Author Despite Himself," *Musical Quarterly* 33/4 (October 1947): 507.

24. The fascinating publication history of Liszt's articles from the mid-1850s is presented in the "Überlieferung" section of *Franz Liszt: Sämtliche Schriften*, 5: *Dramaturgische Blätter*, ed. Detlef Altenburg et al. (Wiesbaden: Breitkopf & Härtel, 1989), 160–170.

25. Unpublished letter from Joachim Raff to Kunigunde Heinrich, [Weimar], 14 March [1850]. Raffiana II (uncatalogued), Bayerische Staatsbibliothek, Handschriften-abteilung. ["Von Opern die zunächst hier gegeben werden nenne ich den *Graf Ory*, dessen Aufführung ich heute in der Weimarischen Zeitung durch einen Artikel vorbereitet habe, da es schon nächste Woche in Scene geht."]

26. Despite its significance during the editorship of Franz Brendel, we still lack a study of the *Neue Zeitschrift* during that crucial period, and in particular, of how it may have helped to promote the New German movement.

27. Letter of Hans von Bülow to his mother [Weimar, 1851], published in: *Hans von Bülow. Briefe und Schriften*, 2d ed., Marie von Bülow, *Briefe 1841–1853* (Leipzig: Breitkopf & Härtel, 1899), 1:24. ["Ich werde für die Brendel'sche Zeitung (sonst kein andres Blatt) schreiben: 1) weil das Blatt eine würdige, prinzipvolle, wissenschaftliche Haltung hat, 2) weil es die Interessen, welche Wagner und Liszt gemeinsam haben, versteht und es wenige Leute gibt, die gut und gescheut schreiben können."]

28. Unpublished letter from Joachim Raff to Doris Genast, Weimar, 20 November 1853, 2. Raffiana II (unpublished), Bayerische Staatsbibliothek, Handschriftenabteilung. ["Diese Kriegführung, wo man vermummt an die Seite des Gegners heranschleicht und ihm das Meßer zwischen die Rippen stößt, ist für Bülow auch ganz geeignet. Ich auf meinem Standpunkte darf mich derselben nicht mehr, wie vor Jahren, bedienen. Man erwartet von mir daß ich direct und ruhig dem Gegner entgegengehe, mich ihm am hellen Tage vis-a-vis stelle, und ihm mit einer Bleikeule den Schädel einschlage."]

29. The title page to v. 41, the second half of 1854, identifies the following Weimarians or former Weimarians among the volume's thirty-five contributors: Bülow (in Berlin) and Cornelius, Liszt, Pohl, and Raff (all in Weimar).

30. "Ein Ausflug nach Weimar," *Neue Zeitschrift für Musik* 36/4 (23 January 1852): 37–40; "Ein zweiter Ausflug nach Weimar," *NZfM* 36/11 (12 March 1852): 120–121; "Ein dritter Ausflug nach Weimar," *NZfM* 37/22 (26 November 1852): 225–227; 37/23 (3 December 1852): 237–240; and 37/24 (10 December 1852): 251–254.

31. Unpublished letter from Franz Brendel to Karl Debrois von Bruyck, Leipzig, 11 May 1855. Wiener Stadt-und Landesbibliothek, Handschriftensammlung (I.N. 414431), 3. ["Der bezeichnete Raummangel ist nicht als Regel zu betrachten. . . . Die Liszt'schen Artikel sind schuld, aber es läßt sich schlechterdings nicht anders mache, und—alle Redactionen in Deutschland, Frankreich, England, würden, wie man zu sagen pflegt, die

Finger ablecken, wenn sie diese Artikel zum Druck erhielten. Ich weiß am Besten, welches Aufsehen sie machen und wie viel sie verlangt werden."]

32. See Deaville, "The Making of a Myth: Liszt, the Press, and Virtuosity," in *Analecta Lisztiana II: New Light on Liszt and His Music*, ed. Saffle and Deaville. Franz Liszt Studies Series no. 6 (Stuyvesant, NY: Pendragon, 1997), 181–195.

33. The review originally appeared in the *Neue Freie Presse*; reprinted Eduard Hanslick, "Liszt's Symphonic Poems [1857]," in *Music Criticisms 1846–99*, trans. Henry Pleasants (Baltimore: Penguin Books, 1963), 53–57.

34. One need only browse through the pages of the *Niederrheinische Musik-Zeitung* from the 1850s to ascertain how frequently this tactic was used, intentionally or not.

35. See Deaville, "The New-German School and the *Euterpe* Concerts, 1860–1862: A Trojan Horse in Leipzig."

36. There exists a fairly extensive literature about the Bayreuth circle of critics and writers around Wagner: Winfried Schüler, *Der Bayreuther Kreis* (Münster: Aschendorff, 1971); Mary Ciora, *Parsifal Reception in the Bayreuther Blätter* (New York: P. Lang, 1987); Annette Hein, *"Es ist viel Hitler in Wagner": Rassismus und antisemitische Deutschtumsideologie in den "Bayreuther Blättern"* (Tübingen: M. Niemeyer, 1996).

37. Eduard Hanslick, review in *Neue Freie Presse* (27 March 1880), 2. ["Ob die Messe und die folgenden Tondichtungen Liszt's das Auditorium entzückte oder nur befriedigt, oder gar ein bischen gelangweilt haben, vermögen wir nicht zu entscheiden. Das läßt sich niemals sagen, wenn Liszt'sche Compositionen unter dem schützenden Zauber von Liszt's persönlicher Awesenheit gegeben werden. Die fascinirende Gewalt dieses Mannes ist keine Fabel; gar Viele im Publicum hören theilnahmslos oder unbefriedigt zu, aber Ihr Auge hängt an Liszt's Erscheinung, und—sie applaudiren."]

38. Theodor Helm, "Liszt-Abend des akademischen Wagner-Vereins in Wien," *Pester Lloyd* (7 April 1879), 1. ["Gewiß, daß der Meister diesmal ganz wundervoll disponirt war und, wie in seinen Jünglingsjahren, Aller Herzen mit magischer Gewalt in das innerste Heiligthum des Tonreiches zu führen verstand, in welchem er als unumschränkter Gebieter waltet, rührt und erschüttert."]

39. "Wiener Briefe," *Beilage zur Allgemeinen Zeitung* (13 April 1880), 1. ["Inmitten dieses klingenden Frühlings ist wieder einmal die hohe Gestalt des Abbé Liszt bei den Musikfreunden erschienen."]

40. Olga Janina, *Souvenirs d'une cosaque* (Paris: C. Marpon et E. Flammarion, 1874).

41. A study of these documents would be interesting, perhaps more from the perspective of what they tell us about Liszt's position within his times and in the eyes of his contemporaries than as sources for accurate facts.

42. Peter Raabe, *Franz Liszt: Leben und Schaffen*. 2 vols. (Stuttgart: Cotta, 1931); Walker, *Franz Liszt: The Virtuoso Years*; and Leppert, "Cultural Contradiction, Idolatry, and Piano Virtuoso."

II

The Young Liszt

4

The Early Works

Michael Saffle

Prior to 1847, when he gave up earning his living as a pianist and decided to settle in Weimar, Franz Liszt—or so it has been claimed—composed little music of importance. Certainly, or so it has also been claimed by most of his biographers, he wrote virtually nothing of importance prior to his mid-1830s sojourn in Switzerland and Italy with the Comtesse Marie d'Agoult. One thinks of Eleanor Perényi's caustic observation that the child Liszt's "stunts at the piano—improvisations on *Zitti, Zitti* and the like—bore about the same relation to music that Carême's sugar palaces did to architecture."[1] Even Sacheverell Sitwell, one of the most sympathetic of Liszt's biographers, claimed that the young artist "did not show very much promise" as a composer, and that his early works "cannot be described as at all remarkable, except in their dwelling upon [pianistic] difficulties which only his own consummate technique was capable of solving."[2]

These claims are in large part false. By 1847 Liszt had composed and, in many cases, published more than a hundred piano pieces, songs, chamber works, symphonic works, choral works, and concertos. He had also sketched what eventually became portions of several symphonic poems, and he had composed and scored most of his "first" Piano Concerto in E♭ major as well as a posthumous concerto in the same key.[3] By June 1835, when his "years of pilgrimage" may be said to have begun, he had finished some twenty works, several of them masterpieces. Among the best of these are the three *Apparitions*, the *Fantaisie romantique sur deux mélodies suisses*, and the remarkable one-movement "improvisation" known as the *Harmonies poétiques et religieuses*.

As a composer Liszt was not as precocious as Wolfgang Amadeus Mozart—although what other youthful composer, even Mozart, wrote as much music at as early an age as Franz Schubert did in July 1815? Nor are Liszt's first works of uniformly high quality. Nevertheless, one Monsieur Martainville was not altogether wrong when, in March 1824, he compared the young Liszt's innate talent, exuberance, and musical sensibility to those of his predecessor:

[During the course of a concert in Paris] Liszt gave himself up to his genius in free fantasy. Here words are wanting to express the admiration he excited. After an harmoniously arranged introduction, he took Mozart's beautiful air from *The Marriage of Figaro*, "Non più andrai," as his theme. If, as I have already said, Liszt, by transmigration, is only a continuation of Mozart, it is [Mozart himself] who provided the text [on this occasion]. . . . I cannot help it: since yesterday evening I am a believer in metempsychosis. I am convinced that the soul and spirit of Mozart have passed into the body of young Liszt, and never has an identity revealed itself by plainer signs. The same country, the same wonderful talent in childhood, and in the same art.[4]

To understand how Liszt's early pieces "work," we must realize that many of them sound as if they had been improvised rather than composed. And no wonder. Trained as a brilliant performer who could, upon request (as was the custom of the day), toss off a fantasy with little apparent effort, Liszt seems to have received little or no childhood instruction in counterpoint, fugue, and orchestration. It is scarcely surprising, therefore, that his first substantial published pieces were potpourris or variation sets rather than string quartets and symphonies. Moreover, works like the *Apparitions* and the *Fantaisie romantique* reveal aspects of the keyboard fantasy tradition familiar to music-lovers of the 1820s but almost forgotten today. On the other hand, the presence of sonata and rondo forms in a few of Liszt's youthful pieces cannot be denied. Also noteworthy, particularly to pianists, are the adventurous aspects of his early keyboard writing, including his use of fingered thirds, "coloratura" cadenzas, and rapid repeated-note passages—the last virtual advertisements for Erard's double-escapement-action pianos. As a formalist and even as a fantasist Liszt began as something of a traditionalist; as a keyboard technician, however, and only somewhat later as a harmonist and all-around composer, he rapidly became a revolutionary.

By the early 1830s Liszt had also invented what he later called *partitions du piano*—paraphrases of orchestral works that enabled virtuosos to simulate at the keyboard the power and variety of orchestral sonorities, even those of works like Berlioz's *Symphonie fantastique*. These *partitions* are not mere transcriptions but recreations; the best of them are akin in sophistication to the parody masses of the Renaissance masters—although, in Liszt's case, the "parody" element has to do with remaking orchestral sounds at the piano instead of recomposing collections of notes. In writing about his *partition* of the *Symphonie fantastique*, Liszt explained to Adolphe Pictet: "I took pains conscientiously as if I were to reproduce a holy text to transcribe for piano not only the musical structure but also the individual effects. . . . Though I do not flatter myself to have completely succeeded with this first experiment, nevertheless . . . my intention [has been in these *piano scores*] to follow the orchestra step by step and to leave it only the advantage of mass effect."[5] Of course, in other of his works, especially in his celebrated operatic paraphrases, Liszt sometimes radically altered the notes (as well as the sonorities) of works by composers from Mozart to Richard Wagner. See Chapter 7 for discussion of Liszt's operatic paraphrases and fantasies.

CHILDHOOD (VIENNA), 1822–1823

1822–1823 *Variation über einen Waltzer von Diabelli.* S 147.
1823   Waltz in A major. S 208a.

In 1819, at the age of eight, the child Liszt—his parents called him "Franzi"—began studying piano and composition with Carl Czerny in Vienna; later the boy also took a few lessons in score-reading and sight-singing from Antonio Salieri.[6] Franzi's first completed pieces included a *Tantum ergo* for four-part chorus (S 702), probably composed in 1821 or 1822 and later lost,[7] as well as a variation for piano on Anton Diabelli's famous waltz. This latter work was Liszt's first published composition: it appeared in print on 9 June 1824 in a large volume containing additional variations by forty-nine other composers, including Schubert.

Liszt's variation is not great music, but it is competently written in the style of a Czerny exercise devoted to arpeggiation (compare Examples 4.1 and 4.2).

Example 4.1
Diabelli, Waltz, mm. 1–4

Example 4.2
Liszt, *Variation über einen Waltzer von Diabelli*, mm. 1–4

Moreover, in its showiness as well as its reliance on diminished-seventh chords, this short piece documents Liszt's lifelong enthusiasms for passagework as well as chromatic harmonies—enthusiasms that served him well throughout a long and enormously productive career. Only a few measures long, the tiny Waltz in A major also stems from 1823. Incorporated that year into a ballet-mélange named *Die Amazonen* by its editor Herr von Gallenberg, it survives in several published versions, including an arrangement for guitar.

ADOLESCENCE (PARIS AND LONDON), 1823–1828

1824   *Huit variations* on an original theme. S 148.
1824   *Sept variations brillantes sur un thème de Rossini*. S 149.
1824   *Impromptu brillant sur des thèmes de Rossini et Spontini*. S 150.
1824   *Allegro di bravura*. S 151.
1824   *Rondo di bravura*. S 152.
1825   *Don Sanche, ou Le château d'amour* [opera]. S 1.
1826   *Etude en douze exercices*. S 136.
1827   Scherzo in G minor. S 153.
1828   Two Hungarian recruiting dances (*Zum Andenken*). S 241.

In the fall of 1823 Liszt and his father left Vienna for Paris. Forbidden by Luigi Cherubini to enter the Conservatoire because of his foreign birth—or so the famous story has it—the child Liszt took lessons from Ferdinando Paër and Antonìn Reicha. Precisely what Liszt learned during these lessons we do not know, but by the fall of 1825 he had finished or at least drafted a number of new works. Among them appear to have been several songs (probably for voice and piano); a rondo and fantasia (S 724) as well as a Sonata in F minor and at least two other sonatas—all for solo piano (S 725); a sonata for piano four-hands (S 755); at least one and possibly several concertos or concerto movements for piano and orchestra (S 713); a *New Grand Overture* for orchestra; a trio (S 717) and quintet (S 718)—the instrumentation of both works unknown; and a coda appended to a keyboard exercise by Charles Mayer. With two possible exceptions these works have been lost or misplaced, although in his later years Liszt jotted down from memory a few measures from the F-minor Sonata.[8] The exceptions are the rondo, which may be the same work as the *Rondo di bravura*; and the *New Grand Overture*, which may have been the overture to *Don Sanche*.

Between 1824 and 1825 the young Liszt also completed a set of *Huit variations* on an original theme (published as his op. 1), a set of *Variations brillantes sur un thème de Rossini* (op. 2), an *Impromptu brillant sur des thèmes de Rossini et Spontini* (op. 3), and a *Rondo di bravura* and *Allegro di bravura* (op. 4, nos. 1–2)—all for piano. By October 1825 he had affixed his name as well to a one-act opera entitled *Don Sanche, ou le Chateau d'amour*. Finally, by the end of that year he may have completed, or at least drafted, his *Etude en douze exercices* (published as op. 6 in one edition, as op. 1 in another). All these compositions still exist, although the full score of *Don Sanche* remains unpublished. Collectively—with the possible exception of *Don Sanche*—these pieces demonstrate that, whatever his limitations, the young Liszt had already become a composer of some experience, intelligence, and skill.

Among his earliest published works (they appeared in print together as *Deux Allegri di bravura*), the *Allegro di bravura* and *Rondo di bravura* are often overlooked. The *Allegro* is a monothematic sonata movement of considerable vigor—almost a *moto perpetuo*—consisting of an exposition in E♭ and B♭ major, followed by a development section, then by a recapitulation that presents the single theme several times in the home key. There is little motivic development but plenty of "fantasy" in the striking key changes; consider the introduction, where the tonality shifts at mm. 18–19 abruptly from E♭ minor to D major by way of a "misspelled" augmented-sixth chord (see Example 4.3):

Example 4.3
Liszt, *Allegro di bravura*, mm. 14–19

This introduction is also full of the tremolos, diminished-seventh chords, shifts from major to minor, and other "mysterious" devices that contemporary theorists lumped together under the term *ombra*.[9] In its insistence on only one real melody throughout, its use of mediant chord progressions, and its somewhat digressive character, however, the *Allegro* resembles Schubert more than Beethoven.

The *Rondo di bravura*, on the other hand, is the closest Liszt ever came to writing like Mozart. Cast in sonata-rondo form, it consists of an exposition in E minor and G major (with a strong G-major conclusion), a development full of sequential passages, and an unmistakable recapitulation in E minor/E major. Aside from its use of mediant key relationships, though, the *Rondo* is pretty tame harmonically. More effective in performance are the *Variations brillantes* on a theme of Gioacchino Rossini. Another intriguing, if not entirely successful work, is the potpourri (i.e., fantasy on several tunes instead of just one) known as the *Impromptu brillant* on themes by Rossini and Gaspare Spontini. This is almost certainly the same thing as the "Amusement or, better, Quodlibet on various Themes by Rossini and Spontini" mentioned by Adam Liszt in a letter he addressed to Czerny in July 1824. In spite of dull spots, the *Impromptu* contains several pleasing passages and demonstrates a fine grasp of keyboard technique. It is also a full-fledged sonata movement with a "slow" development or middle section centered in and around the keys of G major, B♭ major, and A♭ major, and a monothematic recapitulation in E major. Most of the *Impromptu* is based on Rossini material; the interpolation at mm. 201ff. of a contrasting theme from Spontini's *Fernand Cortez* anticipates many of Liszt's later and more exciting interpolations, including the *Mal du pays* theme in the *Fantaisie romantique*. Both of these gestures—the development that suggests a slow movement, and the use of interpolated themes—anticipate what William Newman several decades ago dubbed "double-function form."[10] Employed by Liszt with tremendous intelligence and success in several of his finest works, including his Sonata in B minor, double-function form incorporates elements of multi-movement compositions in single-movement pieces.

Of even greater musical interest is the piano piece untitled by Liszt but known today as the Scherzo in G minor. In its arpeggiated thematic material, its considerable reliance on diminished-seventh chords, and its delightfully deceptive modulations—first to F♯ minor (mm. 6–16), then to A major (mm. 20–23) and B♭ major (mm. 59–60), before settling, finally and unmistakably, in the home key of G minor—this lively bagatelle anticipates portions of the *Scherzo und Marsch* Liszt completed and published almost twenty-five years later. Lost for decades, the Scherzo appeared in print for the first time at the end of the nineteenth century, long after its composer's death. By the time it had been jotted down, however, Liszt—then no more than sixteen—had proven himself almost as imaginative as his teacher Czerny (if not quite so accomplished technically) and more inventive than such contemporary keyboard composers as Daniel Steibelt.

The occasionally charming but more often lackluster *Etude en douze exercices* of 1826—actually twelve individual pieces, most of which served as models for the spectacular and celebrated *Etudes d'exécution transcendante* of the early 1850s—are discussed separately in the next chapter.

The most problematic of Liszt's early works is *Don Sanche*. Begun as early as July 1824, this one-act opera seems to have been more or less finished by August 1825, about thirteen months later. Some of its music—possibly much of it—was probably written by Liszt, although he himself later acknowledged Paër's help. Today we may speculate upon how much of the opera was composed by the pupil, how much by the teacher. In one sense it really does not matter: *Don Sanche* is no masterpiece, although a few of its tunes are pleasing. In another sense, however, it does, at least insofar as the question of how Liszt learned to compose for the orchestra is concerned (a question that will be taken up in Chapter 10). Suffice it to say that Liszt may have drafted at least some of the arias and instrumental portions, possibly in piano score, while Paër almost certainly tidied up his drafts, composed the rest of the music, orchestrated the entire opera and, finally, copied out the full score prior to the first performance on 17 September 1825. One fragment of *Don Sanche* is said to survive in Liszt's handwriting, but the score itself—today the property of the Bibliothèque de l'Opéra, Paris—is entirely in Paër's hand.[11]

YOUNG MANHOOD, 1829–1835

1829	*Grande fantaisie . . . sur la Tirolienne de l'opéra La Fiancée d'Auber* (1st version). S 385.
1830–1831?	*Un petit morceau* for violin and piano. S 718c.
1832?	*Die Rose* by Schubert [fantasy/transcription] (1st version). S 556.
1832?	Septet in D minor, op. 74, by Hummel [transcription] (?1st version). S 493.
1832–1834	*Grande fantaisie di bravura sur la clochette de Paganini.* S 420.
1833	*L'idée fixe—Andante amoroso d'après une mélodie de Berlioz* (1st version). S 395.
1833	*Ouverture du Roi Lear* by Berlioz [transcription]. S 474.
1833	*Symphonie fantastique* by Berlioz [transcription]. S 470.
1833–1834	*Harmonies poétiques et religieuses* (1st version). S 154.
1834	*Apparitions.* S 155.
1834	*Grande fantaisie symphonique* on themes from Berlioz's *Lélio.* S 120.
1834	*Grosses Konzertstück über Mendelssohns Lieder ohne Worte* for piano and orchestra. S 257.
1834?	*Fantaisie romantique sur deux mélodies suisses.* S 157.
1834?	*Lyon.* S 156/1.
1835?	Duo [sonata] for violin and piano. S 127.
1835	*Réminiscences de la Juive. Fantaisie brillante sur des motifs de l'opéra de Halévy.* S 409a.

We know far less about Liszt's activities between the death of his father in 1827 and his extended visit to Félicité de Lamennais in 1834 than about any comparable period of his life. What did he do during those years, biographers have asked themselves, besides giving piano lessons and occasional concerts, spending holidays in the country, and falling in love with the aristocratic Caroline de Saint-Cricq? Certainly he composed, perhaps more extensively than we know; among the lost works mentioned in conjunction with these and subsequent years are a "Petit morceau" for cello and piano (1829), a "Sextetto" (c. 1835), an arrangement of the "Clochette" fantasy for piano and orchestra, other concerto movements, and a Sonata in C minor (S 692b) and a Waltz in E major (S 726b) for solo piano. Unfinished compositions from approximately the same period include a draft of what eventually became the E♭ Concerto (S 124), sketches for a "Revolutionary" symphony dating from July 1830 (S 690) and—virtually complete—the *De profundis: Psaume instrumental* (S 691), a kind of tone-poem for piano and orchestra apparently drafted in 1834, only to be completed and recorded in recent years by several pianist-composers.

Among the pieces Liszt wrote and published prior to June 1835, the "Clochette" fantasy, *L'idée fixe*, the *Apparitions* (especially nos. 1–2), the *Fantaisie romantique* on two Swiss tunes, and the *Harmonies poétiques et religieuses*—all for solo piano—take pride of place. These are accomplished, intriguing, even masterful works. Together they display the breadth and depth of Liszt's youthful musical thinking and feeling. By turns glittering and pensive, conventional and experimental, blunt and atmospheric (the last, harmonically, in an almost impressionist sense), they establish their author as one of the most innovative early Romantics. Had he composed nothing else, Liszt would deserve to be mentioned in histories of nineteenth-century European music.

Of the *Apparitions* Searle observes that "the first in particular is a little masterpiece" and that composer and concert pianist Ferruccio Busoni "rightly characterized it as 'romantic, emotional, philosophical, and possessing that breath of Nature which in art is achieved so rarely and with such difficulty.' "[12] It is difficult to write about so capricious yet coherent a quasi-improvisation except in terms of its elements—themselves a striking blend of *ombra*, ornamented operatic Italianate melody, experimental notational gestures, and harmonic audacity. Consider, for example, just one of its passages (see Example 4.4). Without seeming ever to settle anywhere, yet without modulating in an obvious fashion, Liszt manages in this passage to wander with aplomb from F♯ major through G♭ major, its enharmonic equivalent, then to E♭ major and B♭ major (the latter the enharmonic major mediant of F♯), and finally to G major (the Neapolitan major of F♯). The second *Apparition*, a somewhat more light-hearted, although equally quirky piece, is followed by the delightful third, a "Fantasy on a Waltz of Franz Schubert." As Alan Walker observes, no one who hears the *Apparitions*, especially the first, "can confound the authentic voice of Liszt" with that of his contemporaries.[13]

If the *Apparitions* represent one aspect of Liszt's early output, the transcriptions represent another. True, the first version of Schubert's *Die Rose* is anything but faithful to its model, filled as it is with decorations Liszt himself saw fit largely to remove a few years later when he prepared a second version for publication in 1835. On the other hand, the transcriptions of Berlioz's *Symphonie fantastique* and *Ouverture du Roi Lear* are as painstakingly accurate as they are spectacularly and successfully pianistic. So is that of Hummel's celebrated Septet, a *partition* Liszt must have begun and may even have completed as early as 1832,[14] and one he undoubtedly performed on several occasions during his German concert tours of the 1840s.[15] *L'idée fixe*, on the other hand, is not a transcription but a kind of meditation on Berlioz's famous *Fantastique* theme, a charming and often-overlooked work in a style altogether Liszt's own.

The *Fantaisie romantique* is a far more complex composition, a dreamy, somewhat discursive, but largely successful symphonic poem for piano. Like *Apparition* no. 1 it is thoroughly imbued with pianistic allusions to ornamented *bel canto* melody: the principal theme returns again and again, occasionally punctuated with quasi-improvisational cadenzas. The *Fantaisie* also contains potpourri elements in the form of familiar, interpolated melodies. There are suggestions of programmism: the names of and performance directions for its two interpolated themes—the *Ranz des Vaches* and *Mal du pays*—as well as the music of its transitions conjure up images of mysterious and beautiful mountain vistas and even of "profound" religious sentiments; note, for instance, the designation "religioso" at m. 178. Too, we find suggestions in the *Fantaisie* of double-function form, with the *Mal du pays* as slow movement, the *Vivace* as scherzo. At the same time the work as a whole, excluding the introductory passages, functions as a single-movement sonata form. Finally, at its end,

Example 4.4
Liszt, *Apparition* no. 1, mm. 26–39

beginning in m. 512, fragments of the *Ranz* and its principal transformation are presented over an extended pedal-point of arpeggiated chords that bring the *Fantaisie romantique* to an idyllic conclusion.[16]

Concerning the remarkable individual piano piece entitled *Harmonies poétiques et religieuses,* I must again agree with Searle: this "free improvisation, mostly without time or key signature, and far bolder than any previous attempts in the same direction,"[17] is indeed superior to the revised version published years later as part of a multi-movement suite also named *Harmonies poétiques.* In fact, in its original incarnation the *Harmonies* stands, perhaps, as Liszt's first masterpiece. Why he suppressed it in the thematic catalogs of his works he prepared decades later for Breitkopf & Härtel we do not know. Perhaps the work had for him a special significance; in a letter he addressed to Marie d'Agoult in October 1833, he asked for a copy of his "little *harmonie lamartinienne* without key or bars" and observed in passing that it reminded him "vividly of an hour of suffering and delight."[18] Among the many intriguing and innovative devices and gestures of the original *Harmonies poétiques* are the use of numerals to "count out" beats in measures otherwise unsupplied with time signatures, and its emotionally charged performance directions—including, in this work and the *Apparitions,* such words and phrases as *tristamente* (sadly), *quasi niente* (as if it were nothing), *distinctamente* (distinctly), and *molto pronunziato la melodia* (forcibly emphasizing or "speaking" the tune). Up to the time of its composition, the *Harmonies* boasted perhaps the most harmonically inconclusive conclusion in music history. Still another noteworthy aspect of this piece is its use of thematic transformation—a device, it is often claimed (erroneously), that Liszt "patented" in his symphonies and symphonic poems. Virtually every measure of *Harmonies* is derived from a consecutive three-note ascending and descending figure, first heard several times in the opening measures of the left hand (see Example 4.5):

Example 4.5
Liszt, *Harmonies poétiques et religieuses* (1834), mm. 1–2

Presented subsequently in an *agitato* passage (mm. 27–30; see Example 4.6) and in half-notes against a repeated-note figure consisting of alternating quintuplets and sextuplets, versions of the motif also appear in several transitional passages, and—finally—as the "principal subject" of the piece (designated *Andante religioso*; see Example 4.7):

Example 4.6
Liszt, *Harmonies poétiques et religieuses*, mm. 29–32

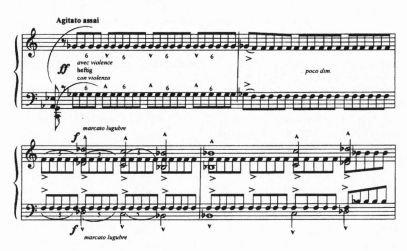

Example 4.7
Liszt, *Harmonies poétiques et religieuses*, mm. 60–63

This last example reflects Liszt's admiration for Beethoven's late works—an influence acknowledged explicitly in such works as the Fantasy for piano and orchestra on themes from *The Ruins of Athens,* and implicitly in portions of such later works as the symphonic poem *Ce qu'on entend sur la montagne* and the *Missa solemnis* composed for the consecration of Esztergom Cathedral. Nor was this all Liszt produced in his childhood and youth. *Lyon,* a brief and bold musical statement of political concerns, is as forthright as the *Apparitions* and *Harmonies* are indirect; it even incorporates stirring references to the *Marseillaise.* And Liszt may even have began one of his greatest tributes to Beethoven—his transcriptions of all nine symphonies for solo piano—prior to June 1835; we know he worked on the first of them between July of that year and October 1836.[19]

NOTES

1. Eleanor Perényi, *Liszt: The Artist as Romantic Hero* (Boston and Toronto: Little, Brown, 1974), 16. Other experts pay more attention to the early works. See, for example, Humphrey Searle, *The Music of Liszt*, 2d rev. ed. (New York: Dover, 1966), 1–19.

2. Sacheverell Sitwell, *Liszt* (London: Cassell, 1955), 17. Sitwell claims to be writing only about the music Liszt wrote prior to the July Revolution of 1830, but he goes on to ignore most of Liszt's works from 1828–1835.

3. See Jay Rosenblatt, "New Wine in Old Wineskins: Franz Liszt's Concerto in E-flat major, Op. Posth." *The Pendragon Review* 1/1 (Spring 2001): 7–31.

4. Cited in Alan Walker, *Franz Liszt: The Virtuoso Years, 1811–1847*, rev. ed. (Ithaca, NY: Cornell University Press, 1987), 1:99–100.

5. See Liszt's letter to Pictet of September 1837. Quoted in NLE, ii/16: xi (italics added).

6. See also Johann Harich, "Franz Liszt—Vorfahren und Kinderjahre," *Öster-reichische Musikzeitschrift* 26 (1971): 503–514.

7. For additional information about many of Liszt's lost works, as well as about a few works recently rediscovered, see Friedrich Schnapp, "Verschollene Kompositionen von Franz Liszt," in *Von deutscher Tonkunst: Festschrift zu Peter Raabes 70. Geburtstag*, ed. Alfred Morgenroth (Leipzig: C. F. Peters, 1942), 119–152. Fascinating observations also appear in "The Greatness of Franz Liszt: Leslie Howard Talks to Martin Anderson," *Fanfare* 23/2 (November-December 1999): 62–81.

8. A facsimile of these measures appears as an illustration in Schnapp, "Verschollene Kompositionen von Franz Liszt."

9. Or "mood of mystery." Similar "mysterious" devices may be found in the "Wolf's Glen" scene from Weber's *Der Freischütz* and the introduction to the first movement of Beethoven's Sonata in C minor ("Pathétique"), op. 13.

10. For an explanation of double-function form, see William S. Newman, *The Sonata Since Beethoven*, 3d ed. (New York: W. W. Norton, 1983), 373–377.

11. I would like to thank Dudley Newton for providing information about the *Don Sanche* score and facsimiles for study. Indirect evidence exists that Liszt did in fact have a hand in *Don Sanche*. See Paul Merrick, "Original or Doubtful? Liszt's Use of Key in Support of his Authorship of 'Don Sanche,' " *Studia musicologica* 34/3–4 (1992): 427–434.

12. Searle, *The Music of Liszt*, 13.

13. Walker, *Franz Liszt: The Virtuoso Years*, 1:157.

14. Auguste Boissier, the mother of Valerie Boissier (who took piano lessons from Liszt in the early 1830s), claims her daughter's teacher had transcribed the Hummel Septet by 13 March 1832. See NLE ii/ 8: xiii.

15. Several hundred of Liszt's concert programs are presented in Michael Saffle, *Liszt in Germany, 1840–1845: A Study in Sources, Documents, and the History of Reception* (Stuyvesant, NY: Pendragon, 1994). Additional information about Liszt's early performances is available in Geraldine Keeling, "Liszt's Appearances in Parisian Concerts, 1824–1844," *LSJ* 11 (1986): 22–34; and 12 (1987): 8–22.

16. For a more fulsome discussion of the *Fantasie romantique* and ways in which it embodies principles of the fantasy tradition, see Saffle, "Liszt and the Traditions of the Keyboard Fantasy," in *Liszt the Progressive*, ed. Hans Kagebeck and Johan Lagerfelt (Lewiston, MA: Edwin Mellen, 2001), 159–184.

17. Searle, *The Music of Liszt*, 11.

18. Cited in Franz Liszt, *Selected Letters*, ed. and trans. Adrian Williams (Oxford: Clarendon, 1998), 20. If Liszt is referring in this letter to the single-movement piano

piece *Harmonies poétiques et religieuses*, we may assume that work had at least been drafted by 1833.

19. See Lina Ramann, *Franz Liszt als Künstler und Mensch* (Leipzig: Breitkopf & Härtel, 1880), 1:452; and NLE ii/18: xii.

Dating Liszt's early works is difficult. I have tried to do so precisely, but precision is not always possible. A variety of scholarly studies contain useful clues. In his documentary biography of Schubert, for instance, Otto Erich Deutsch provides the information that Liszt was "eleven years old" [*Knabe von 11 Jahren*] when his Diabelli variation was written; this means it almost certainly dates from 1823. See Deutsch, *Schubert: die Dokumente seines Lebens* (Kassel: Bärenreiter 1964), 241–242. On the other hand, standard reference works frequently get dates wrong. The *Fantaisie romantique*, for instance, is often dated "1835" or "1836," but a manuscript recently acquired by the French National Library preserves part of it and is dated 1834 in Liszt's hand. See Saffle, "Liszt Manuscripts in the Bibliothèque Nationale, Paris: A Preliminary Catalog." *Analecta Lisztiana I: Proceedings of the "Liszt and His World" Conference Held at Virginia Polytechnic Institute and State University, 20–23 May 1993* (Stuyvesant, NY: Pendragon, 1998), 135.

Interestingly enough, many of the errors in the literature reinforce notions of Liszt beginning to compose later in life. Yet other early works, rumored to exist, simply do not. In his new translation of Liszt's letters, Williams mentions in an aside that the first version of *La romanesca* (S 247) dates not from the early 1840s but from 1832; he even gives its place of publication (*Selected Letters*, 6). Unfortunately, the information is false: the "Romanesca" published as a supplement to the *Gazette Musicale de Paris* in April 1833 is an arrangement of the tune for violin and piano by the fiddler Beriot and has nothing to do with Liszt's later and much more imaginative fantasy. I would like to thank Cecile Reynaud for providing a photocopy of the edition in question.

III

Keyboard Music

5

Piano Music: 1835–1861

Ben Arnold

The catalog of Liszt's works in the second edition of the *New Grove Dictionary of Music and Musicians* lists 338 separate numbers for his solo piano compositions, including original works, paraphrases, and transcriptions. Within these numbered sets are nearly 400 individual works and versions, bringing his total output for solo piano to well over 700 pieces. Approximately 300 of these are original works; the rest are transcriptions or paraphrases, including nearly sixty compositions based on the composer's works in other genres. Liszt's enormous output is not surprising considering his faith in the capacity of the piano "to assimilate, to concentrate all musical life within itself and, on the other hand, its own existence, its own growth and individual development. It is simultaneously, as an ancient Greek might say, a *microcosm* and a *microthea* [a miniature world and a miniature god]."[1] While the quality of this output is uneven, Liszt surely accomplished the goal he set out as early as 1837: "My first course, my dearest ambition, would be to leave pianists who come after me some useful lessons, an outline of some advancements that I made—a work, in short, that worthily represents my studies and diligent efforts as a young pianist."[2] Claude Debussy once wrote, "Liszt's genius is often disordered and feverish, but that is better than rigid perfection, even in white gloves."[3] Liszt's visceral and imaginative keyboard writing rarely approaches "white-glove perfection," yet it remains vibrant, challenging, and, at times, provocative even today.

Liszt's most intensive years of touring and performing as a solo pianist were between 1835 and 1847. During his "years of pilgrimage" (1835–1839) and his three world tours (1840–1847), he composed his first cycles of programmatic pieces, his most virtuosic etudes, and his compositions based on folk music, particularly from Hungary and Switzerland. Before the age of thirty Liszt had already completed his *Album du Voyageur* (1835–1838) and the seemingly insurmountable versions of his *Vingt-quatre grandes études* (1837) and *Etudes d'exécution transcendante d'après Paganini* (1838–1839). The majority of his unrevised compositions from these touring years consisted of showpieces for his own performances, including galops, waltzes, dances, and numerous paraphrases and transcriptions.

Liszt moved to Weimar in February 1848 and remained in his full-time position there until August 1861. By the time he left Weimar, he had composed his most famous piano works, establishing a legacy as one of the eminent composers in the nineteenth century. Over the course of these fourteen years in Weimar, he revised almost all of his major compositions conceived during his virtuoso years. Believing that some of this music was too extravagant, bold, and individualistic, he curtailed many of the technical difficulties and reigned in his over-enthusiastic gestures. He completely rewrote the Magyar pieces as the *Hungarian Rhapsodies*, further revised his *Harmonies poétiques et religieuses*, turned parts of the *Album du voyageur* into his first book of the *Années de pèlerinage*, and reworked his collection of virtuosic etudes, taming them considerably in 1851. Furthermore, he composed his most important large-scale works for piano, his most significant orchestral and piano and orchestra compositions, and carried out his greatest experimentation with large-scale forms, combining "double-function" forms with multi-movement sections all within a large sonata form. In all these pieces from his youth to his maturity of Weimar, Liszt displays an overwhelming devotion to musical expression.

Liszt's piano music between 1835 and 1861 is as diverse and contradictory as he was himself. His music often verges on the autobiographical, stemming from his travels, readings, and personal experiences. A man who toured nearly all of Western Europe by his mid-thirties, he was influenced wherever he went, writing "nationalistic" pieces on a dizzying array of melodies representing countries from Spain to Russia, or England to Hungary. He was influenced by folk traditions in these countries as much as he was by more formal operatic productions, particularly those of the *bel canto* Italian composers with their long *cantabile* melodies. A bevy of individual composers, musicians, and writers inspired him—from Ludwig van Beethoven, Carl Maria von Weber, Hector Berlioz, Niccolò Paganini, and Frédéric Chopin to Dante Alighieri, William Shakespeare, Johann Wolfgang von Goethe, Lord Byron, and Victor Hugo.[4] And through it all, Liszt's religious beliefs and struggles remained with him, finding outlets in his music at every stage of his life even though he could, at the drop of a hat, represent the diabolic, the sinister, and the malevolent with equal competency.

Liszt's technical arsenal displays an overpowering assortment of open octaves, chromatic scales, double thirds, four-octave arpeggios, tremolos, trills, instrumental recitatives, and three-hand effects. His harmonic palette is broad enough to embrace and experiment with the tritone, the augmented triad, and unresolved seventh and ninth chords. His subjects range from the religious to the devilish, the spiritual to the tragic, the political to the ecstatic. He can entice with the most seductive melody or dishearten with the darkest death march. He can paint a picture of a lake or a storm or set out on a spiritual quest for meaning. His piano can emulate the full orchestra or a single violin. He can thrill with the most acrobatic pianistic combinations ever contrived in his time or calm the savage beast with the most poetic and expressive utterances obtainable on the piano. He experiments with notation, both rhythmic and melodic, using various signs for rhythmic flexibility and numerous staves for clarity of display. Richard Hudson credited some of Liszt's experiments in rhythm, suggesting that he "is a key figure in the history of tempo rubato, for it was his diverse and changing concept of the device which influenced later performers and composers."[5] Liszt composes in many types of forms from traditional binary, ternary, and sonata to unusual and new fusions of forms based on his idea of thematic transformation. He writes in nearly all of the romantic genres, including those adopted by Chopin whose influence is readily apparent: etudes, waltzes, ballades, berceuses, nocturnes, polonaises, even a mazurka as well as sonatas, legends, variations, and Schumanesque cycles. While the majority of his piano music is programmatic, Liszt is still at home in writing formally consistent abstract music in the style of a waltz, mazurka, or sonata. His overriding method of development is through the variation technique he employs ingeniously in so many of his large-scale works. As arguably the greatest improviser of his age, Liszt possessed the ability to find fresh and imaginative transformations of thematic material—a feat that remains impressive more than a century later.

MULTI-PIECE SETS

Album d'un voyageur

Liszt lived in Switzerland from June 1835 to October 1836. Although he had visited the country on two previous occasions, it was this lengthy stay that most greatly influenced him as he encountered the Swiss landscape and its rich folk-music tradition. He expressed these experiences in his first multi-piece set, *Album d'un voyageur* (S 156) which he assembled between 1837 and 1838, although a few of the pieces were written earlier. He originally planned for the *Album* to include piano compositions inspired by his travels. The first part was to be a potpourri of artistic works that evolved from his trip, while the second was to be more characteristic of folk-like pieces representing national styles and music of the areas he traveled. The *Album* contained nineteen separate pieces published in three books: *Impressions et poésies, Fleurs mélodiques des Alpes,* and *Paraphrases.* As a whole the *Album* represents a composite musical portrait of Liszt's interest at the time with its diverse body of original works, improvisations on themes of others, and pieces based on folk material.

With the exception of *Lyon* and *Psaume,* the first and last pieces found in the first part, Liszt revised the others for inclusion in the first book of *Années de pèlerinage,* which will be examined below with their revisions. The editors of the NLE commented that "Liszt regarded this revision as being synonymous with the invalidation, or withdrawal, of the earlier series. And so that there would be no possibility of performing or spreading the work, Liszt bought back the publication rights and the plates of the *Album d'un voyageur* from the work's publisher, Haslinger, in 1850. Nor did he permit the cycle to be included in the catalogue of his works."[6] These works, consequently, have rarely been performed in their first versions, and *Lyon* and *Psaume* have not entered the active repertoire.

Lyon (1833–1834), the opening work of the cycle and the earliest of these compositions to be composed, represents Liszt at his most defiant and belligerent. Prefaced with a quotation from Abbé Félicité Lamennais, *Vivre en travaillant ou mourir en combattant* (to live working or die fighting), this opening work (*Allegro eroico*) is also among his most bombastic and in stark opposition to the prayerful *Psaume* that concludes the *Impressions et poésies*. Highly sectionalized by two main motives that begin in C major, *Lyon* contains loads of dotted rhythms, open octaves, repeated chords, and tremolos almost always at the *fortissimo* level. This piece also illustrates Liszt's early attempts of more specific notations using open double lines to indicate pauses shorter than a fermata, closed double lines for acceleration, and single lines for deceleration. *Psaume* (subtitled *de l'église à Genève*) is prefaced with a quotation from Psalm 42: "As the hart panteth after the water brooks, so panteth my soul after thee, O God." The least worthy work in this first part of the *Album*, Liszt treats the opening diatonic theme in chordal style, reduces its texture upon its initial restatement, and expands it to more open arpeggiated chords on the third statement. A brief coda contains the theme in diminution and stretto followed by florid arpeggios. With only five chromatic chords in the entire work, it is one of Liszt's dullest and least imaginative works found in his early music. It is possible, nonetheless, that this extreme diatonicism represents the piety and purity of his religious thought at the time.

The second part of the *Album, Fleurs mélodiques des Alpes*, most likely dates from the first five months of 1838. This part contains nine untitled pieces based on folk tunes or themes of Ferdinand Huber (8b and 9b), ranging from less than two minutes in length to slightly more than seven. Liszt heavily revised two pieces in the *Années*: 7b (*Lento* in E minor/G) as *Le may du pays* and 7c (*Allegro pastorale* in G) as *Pastorale*. 7c, for example, is over twice as long as its revision *Pastorale* and contains about seventy measures of a contrasting B section in C and A♭ major that Liszt omits in his revision.

The forms of these pieces are sectionalized and often ternary, requiring limited virtuosity. They exhibit a pastoral and graceful nature, although Liszt counters at times with contrasting dance or march sections as in 8a, 8c, and 9a. 9a (*Allegretto* in A♭), for example, juxtaposes martial, dance-like, and sentimental salon music in a playful manner. Indeed 9a and 9c seem to be forerunners of his *Hungarian Rhapsodies* at times with their collective jagged syncopations, alternating registers, ostinatos, pedal points, changing meters, and modal writing. 8b (*Andante molto espressivo* in G minor), based on themes of Huber, also has a section reminiscent of the *cymbalon* effect in some of the *Hungarian Rhapsodies*. It is the longest and most difficult of the set and most prominently features etude-like writing with tremolos and double notes similar to the first Paganini Etude. Overall, its evocative mood and expressive melody make it among the most attractive in the second part. The other pastoral theme of Huber that Liszt uses appears in 9b (*Allegretto*), which includes bell effects that Liszt notates on three staves (mm. 27–39). 8c (*Allegro moderato*) is also interesting because of its use of the Lydian mode over pedal points in much of its first ninety-seven measures. It contains sharply contrasting sections, including a polonaise at the *Allegro decision* (mm. 109–132).

The third part of the *Album* includes lengthy *Paraphrases* Liszt wrote on themes of Huber and von Knop; it was composed in 1835 and 1836, and published in 1836 as *Trois airs suisses*. During his late period Liszt revised each of these airs slightly, shortening the first two significantly, and published them in 1877 as *Trois morceaux suisses*. The first, *Improvisata sur le ranz de vaches de F. Huber*, is an improvised pastiche of showpiece techniques. No doubt the writing is incredibly effective for its purpose, but the overall integrity of the music does not raise this above the barnstorming pieces that mark some of his early music. Liszt bases most of his variations on the opening diatonic horn call that he uses with echo-effect in the opening statement.

The second, *Un soir dans les montagnes* (An Evening in the Mountain), works better because of its programmatic associations. It opens with a lovely, pastoral theme that captures the peaceful qualities of night. A tremendous storm (*Allegro agitato*) full of chromatic moanings, brilliant octaves, double thirds, and raging trills and tremolos abruptly interrupts this repose. The melodic material is not as defined as the *Orage* of the *Suisse année*, creating a better and more evocative depiction of the storm. The stillness of the night returns with the opening material to close the work.

The last paraphrase, *Rondeau sur le ranz de chèvres de F. Huber*, is considerably shorter than the other two and not as tedious as the first paraphrase in the set. It is consistently more cheerful, brimming with clever virtuosic effects at a breakneck tempo. The pace slows only for thirty measures at the *Un poco ritenuto il tempo* before launching again into the brilliant fireworks of the opening sections. The piece contains many alternate passages, including difficult right-hand glissandos in double-thirds.

Années de pèlerinage, Books I and II

Liszt assembled his first two books of the *Années de pèlerinage* during his Weimar period, although the majority of first versions of the works originated during the 1830s and 1840s. Near the end of his life he published the third book of this collection under the same title. The entire *Années de pèlerinage*, therefore, consists of three volumes and twenty-six individual pieces, counting the supplement to the Italian years that Liszt added in 1859.

Scholars have discussed the individual cycles for years, but Andrew Fowler recently suggested that the collection of pieces functions as a megacycle:

Années de Pèlerinage, as with Wagner's *Ring* cycle, is a monumental work reflecting aspects of the Romantic aesthetic that its composer helped define. The work serves as a musical expression of the life experience of its composer and contains within a single opus the documentation of his well-known sympathy with specific Romantic ideals such as the search for new means of expression as well as the integration of music with the visual and literary arts.[7]

However these works function, whether as individual pieces (which is how they are most often performed), unified cycles (as commonly analyzed), or as a megacycle, many of the individual numbers represent Liszt's ability to evoke nature, art, or ideas into music and illustrate the range of his compositional interests.

Between 1848 and 1854 Liszt assembled the first set of pieces: *Années de pèlerinage, première année, Suisse* (S 160). Humphrey Searle praised Liszt for his innovative depiction of landscapes in music in this cycle: "In it [the *Suisse année*] we see romantic landscape painting at its best. . . . Liszt, by the freshness of his vision, did succeed in contributing an entirely new element to the music of his time, and one which he left as a legacy to subsequent generations of composers."[8] Based largely upon the *Album d'un voyageur*, Liszt selected and revised seven of these works, complemented by two additional works: *Eglogue* (1836) and *Orage* (1854). In 1852 Liszt remarked in a letter to Carl Czerny that his *Album d'un voyageur* "will reappear very considerably corrected, increased, and transformed."[9]

Most of the pieces in the first *Année* are related to Switzerland via folksong, place, or textual prefaces. Four employ Swiss folk songs of some type: *La chapelle de Guillaume Tell* uses a Swiss Alpine horn melody; *Pastorale* an Appenzell *Kuhreigen*; *Eglogue* the *Ranz de chèvre* (a Swiss shepherd's song); and *Le may du pays* an Appenzeller *Ranz des vaches*. Only *Pastorale* and *Les cloches de Genève* do not include mottoes or prefaces, and *Les cloches* appeared with a quotation from Byron only in the *Album* version. These prefaces range from the opening one-line Swiss motto found in *La chapelle de Guillaume Tell* and short fragments from Byron or Schiller in nos. 2, 4, 5, and 7, to extensive writings of Sénancour for *Vallée d'Obermann* and *Le mal du pays*. Without hearing a note of music, the textual references and titles provide specific settings by which to listen to this programmatic music:

La chapelle de Guillaume Tell	"One for All—All for One" (Swiss motto)
Au lac de Wallenstadt	". . . thy contrasted lake, With the wild world I dwelt in, is a thing Which warns me, with its stillness, to forsake Earth's troubled waters for a purer spring." (Byron's *Childe Harold*)
Au bord d'une source	"In the rustling coolness begins the play of young nature."[10] (Schiller's *Der Flüchtling*)
Orage	"But what of ye, O tempests! is the goal? Are ye like those within the human breast? Or do ye find, at length, like eagles, some high nest?" (Byron's *Childe Harold*)

Vallée d'Obermann	"What do I want? what am I? what may I demand of nature? . . . I feel, I exist only to exhaust myself in untamable desires, to drink deep of the allurement of a fantastic world, only to be finally vanquished by its sensuous illusion." (Selections from Sénancour's *Obermann*)
	"But as it is, I live and die unheard, With a most voiceless thought, sheathing it as a sword." (Selection from Byron's *Childe Harold*)
Eglogue	"The morn is up again, the dewy morn With breath all incense, and with cheek all bloom, Laughing the cloud away with playful scorn And living as if earth contain'd no tomb." (Byron's *Childe Harold*)
Le mal du pays	"Nature has put the most forcible expression of romantic character in sounds, and it is especially by the sense of hearing that you can render perceptible by a few impressions and in a striking manner both extraordinary places and things." (Selection from Sénancour's *Obermann*)
Les cloches de Genève	["I live not in myself, but I become Portion of that around me."] (Byron's *Childe Harold*: 1st version; omitted in *Années*)

The nine works creating the program could be characterized as follows: After a triumphant, "political" opening (1), the music proceeds to calm nature writing (2–4) and storm and unrest (5–6), before returning to a more pastoral atmosphere (7–8) and ending with the symbolic tolling bells of Geneva (9). *La chapelle de Guillaume Tell* progresses from the opening slow chords in a chorale-like setting of an Alpine horn melody through *pianissimo* left-hand tremolos and double-dotted motive to close in a grand and noble manner, shifting through the keys of A♭ and E♭ to a resolution in C major.

Liszt begins his Swiss nature writing with *Au lac de Wallenstadt*, one of his earliest and best water pieces. Almost the entire work consists of a triplet sixteenth-note pattern alternating with four sixteenths, creating the uneven waves or ripples in calm water (broken for the first time at m. 86). Marie d'Agoult wrote that it was at Lake Wallenstadt that "Franz composed for me a melancholy piece, imitative of the sighing of the waves and the rhythm of the oars, that I have never been able to hear without weeping."[11] *Pastorale,* although designated *Vivace,* remains soft throughout in its lilting 12/8 and 6/8 rhythms, and *Au bord d'une source* continues this mood with its delightful, brilliant, and energetic style, especially its cadenza-like interludes, transitions, and *fortissimo* climax from mm. 46 to 50. The uninspired *Le mal du pays*, too, retains a folk simplicity and charm, and suggests a sense of the vast stretches in nature with its wide, open spacing in mm. 105–109; so does *Eglogue* which concludes in A♭ major with a surprising

N–V$_9$–I cadence after a long break. *Les cloches de Genève*, dedicated to Liszt's daughter Blandine on her birth, 18 December 1835, also continues this pastoral nature, although the serenity provided by the bells summons up religious or at least ethereal connotations.

In contrast to his peaceful nature writing, Liszt uses the ferocious storm of *Orage* to destroy the serene impression of sunny Swiss days. *Orage* begins *fortissimo* and rages throughout with its tumultuous octave passages, double thirds, tremolos, chromatic scales, and four-octave arpeggios, even in its somewhat contrasting second section that appears in F♯ major, a tritone away from the first theme. Part of its structural purpose, nonetheless, is to prepare the way for *Vallée d'Obermann*,[12] the most extraordinary work of the cycle.

Vallée d'Obermann represents Liszt at his programmatic best and illustrates some of his finest examples of thematic transformation. Fowler wrote, "*Vallée d'Obermann* is one of the earliest single-movement large scale piano works intended to express a specific literary conceit musically. The composer/pianist becomes Obermann, and through the piano, which acts as conduit, the hero experiences the overwhelming, unpenetrable forces of Nature. This is a seminal work, symphonic in scope, and a precursor to Liszt's symphonic poems."[13] The second version opens with a descending scalar passage that forms the primary material for the entire composition, and the frequent stops and starts suggest its searching quality (see Example 5.1).

Example 5.1
Examples of Liszt's thematic transformation in *Vallée d'Obermann*, mm. 1–4

Liszt, *Vallée d'Obermann*, mm. 20–25

Liszt, *Vallée d'Obermann,* **mm. 75–78**

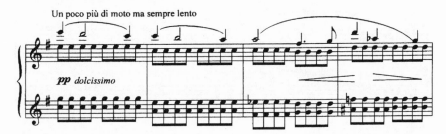

Liszt, *Vallée d'Obermann,* **mm. 170–171**

Liszt, *Vallée d'Obermann,* **mm. 180–181**

Liszt, *Vallée d'Obermann,* **mm. 188–189**

Liszt, *Vallée d'Obermann,* **mm. 214–216**

The transformations of the first 118 measures are of the contemplative type, but at the *Recitativo* beginning at m. 119 the restless and energized quest begins with its turbulent tremolos and impressive octaves. A contrasting transformation begins at m. 170 in E major and conveys the peaceful assurance that something meaningful has been found. Liszt inverts the opening melody at m. 180 to create a sublime and glorious moment leading directly into a blissful state starting at m. 188. Largely because of this section, Searle asserted that *Vallée d'Obermann* is a "real paean of joy."[14] While moments of ecstasy are present, this joy is cut tragically short by a dramatic pause and an abrupt descending restatement of the opening theme. This epiphany proves to be an illusion, since the final descending statement harmonized with two augmented chords creates a heartbreaking close to this incredible pursuit. Liszt as Obermann almost finds life's answer and the happiness he seeks, only to realize that it is a mirage. Liszt captures this search in an unparalleled musical manner, creating one of his most successful philosophical and evocative works. In the end, this work of trials, tribulations, hope, and jubilation, ends in tragedy, or in Byron's words in the preface, "But as it is, I live and die unheard, / With a most voiceless thought, sheathing it as a sword."

Liszt's conversion of the *Album* to the *Suisse année* included alterations ranging from slight adjustments to extensive rewritings. Originally *Au lac du Wallenstadt* and *Au bord d'une source* were joined, but the pieces were separated in the *Suisse année,* although they still share the same key. The composer made minor changes to *Au lac du Wallenstadt,* but the original conception of *Au bord d'une source* was more difficult and etude-like compared to its light and delicate revision.[15] The *Pastorale,* on the other hand, was based on the first twenty-two measures of 7c (*Allegro pastorale*) of the *Fleurs mélodiques des Alpes.* 7c is over twice as long as its revision and contains about seventy measures of a contrasting second section that Liszt omits in his revision. The original also concludes with the opening A theme instead of the B theme used to close the revised version. Likewise, the first eighteen measures of *Le may du pays* are based, with slight variation, on the first seventeen measures of 7b (*Lento*), but the *Allegro vivace* section that follows in 7b differs entirely from the contrasting section in the revision.

More dramatic reconstructions are seen in the opening and concluding works of the cycle. The two versions of *La chapelle de Guillaume Tell* differ in almost every instance, making these pieces individual works based on the same theme; they share only the melody that begins in m. 4 of the revision. The first version is more pretentious and experimental with its predilection for the tritone and the forcefully virtuosic with its pounding octaves, chords, and tremolos. The strong introduction and coda of the first version broaden the scope of William Tell's chapel from the more single-minded portrayal of the revision. Likewise, the revised *Les cloches de Genève*, the final work of the *Suisse année*, is a highly abbreviated revision of the earlier piece (188 vs. 269 mm.). Moreover, the entire original version, a largely unknown pictorial gem, is developed from a single piece of opening thematic material; the contrasting B theme found in the revision is not present in the original. The first forty-five measures of both versions are nearly the same, but the chiming of the bells plays a more obvious role in the original at mm. 19–27. The remainder of the original version fully elaborates the lovely opening material and patiently depicts the bells and Geneva in their various guises. The return of the main theme at the *Andantino* section at m. 203 displays an exquisite nocturne-like filigree over a left-hand melodic line. The lyrical and calm coda further develops the main theme in clever harmonic guises, ending the working perfectly with harmonizations of the opening bells. Nearly twelve minutes long in performance, Liszt may have found this work too long for its material, and thus an unfitting end to the first book of the *Années de pèlerinage*.

The most fascinating of his revisions for the *Suisse année* involved transforming the core elements from the earlier version of *Vallée d'Obermann* into a tighter and more logical construction. The original version provides most of the material that appears in the revision, but Liszt changes the order, texture, or melodic content in nearly every measure, including important adjustments to the ending.

Overall modifications of these types illustrate Liszt's methods of achieving balance and proportion when assembling a cycle. Had he not revisited these works, the cycle would have been longer and less manageable as a whole. Indeed, this cycle seems to be more than a collection of Swiss pieces as Karen Wilson and Dolores Pesce have pointed out.[16] Pesce wrote, "If *Les cloches* can be interpreted to symbolize a higher faith, then Liszt's [Suisse] *Année* . . . represents more than a travelog of Swiss sights and sounds. Its order and typology of pieces suggest a spiritual journey as well."[17] Unlike the *Album,* which is a hodgepodge of pieces, the first book of the *Années de pèlerinage* seems to be structured both musically and thematically as a cycle.

Liszt published the second volume of the *Années* with Schott in 1858, but had composed the seven pieces that constitute the *Années de pèlerinage, deuxième année, Italie* (S 161) between 1838 and 1849. Whereas the Swiss book deals primarily with nature, the Italian book touches on art works—sculpture, painting, and literature—of masters such as Dante, Michelangelo, Raphael, Petrarch, and Salvator Rosa.

The inspiration behind Liszt's *Sposalizio* (1838–1839) was Raphael's *Lo Sposalizio della Vergine* (Marriage of the Virgin) in the La Brera Museum in Milan. Joan Backus discussed the "marriage" of art and music in this piece:

Liszt's musical procedures can allow a subtle interplay between the musical form and an external idea, a reciprocal relationship in which each contributes to the creation of a significant and expressive musical form. *Sposalizio* offers a particularly illuminating example of the way this concept of musical perspective functions in Liszt's music. Not only does it demonstrate several aspects of Liszt's conception of evolving form, but it also projects a remarkable sense of musical perspective that is parallel to the visual perspective of Raphael's canvas.[18]

The opening four measures present two diatonic motives that permeate the entire work. The only other thematic material appears in m. 38 in G major and serve as the second-theme area. Liszt cleverly combines this new theme with the first motive at m. 78 for a dignified statement of both themes in E major. Backus asserted that, "Just as the two visual planes of Raphael's canvas are united through converging perspective lines, the two aural planes of Liszt's composition are here brought together in a capitulatory synthesis."[19] Liszt's primary use of only two keys, E and G, for the entire piece—restrictions not that common with him—further strengthen these two perspectives.

Liszt based his *Il penseroso* (1838–1839) on a statue of Michelangelo in the San Lorenzo Church in Florence. It is a severe, *Lento* march in C♯ minor with almost constant dotted rhythms presented primarily in the mid-to-lower register of the keyboard. The opening eight-measure phrase is repeated a minor third higher in its next two statements, outlining the diminished triad E–G–B♭. A walking bass intensifies its somberness, until a unique moment of lightness appears in the remarkable sequential passage at mm. 33–39, the last so anticipatory of Wagner's chromatic writing. Liszt also occasionally uses the augmented triad, minor ninth, and tritone in this highly personal work. Decades later he reused material from this gloomy march for *La notte* (S 699), the second of his *Trois odes funèbres* (S 112).

Liszt composed his *Canzonetta del Salvator Rosa* sometime before 1849, unknowingly basing it on a text of Giovanni Battista Bononcini. Liszt published Bononcini's text over the notes of the score throughout its four pages. The *Canzonetta*, the least significant of the works in the cycle, almost seems to be out of place with its dance-like, frivolous nature: it consists of little more than strophic variations moving from A major to F♯ minor and returning to A with a small coda attached to the end. The monothematic work becomes overly monotonous in its prevailing diatonicism. Liszt, perhaps, is illustrating the text which deals with a person moving about but always remaining the same.

The three *Sonetti del Petrarca* appeared as songs between 1838 and 1839. Liszt published the piano transcriptions of them in 1846 (S 158) and later revised them around 1850 for publication in the *Années*, reversing the order of the first two sonnets. The three transcriptions are among the most played in the cycle, and Derek Watson claimed they "rank among the finest lyric works of Liszt."[20]

Sonetto 47 appears in D♭ major for both piano transcriptions, but in A♭ major for the song version. All three bear different tempo instructions at the beginning as well as varying introductions. (See Chapter 15 for discussion of the three song versions of the sonnets.) The revised piano version published in the second book of the *Années* is much simpler, and the texture is significantly reduced from the first version for piano. After a tentative introduction in the revised version, a beautiful, single-line melody appears over an undulating accompaniment in D♭. When the theme returns in this modified strophic form, it appears a tritone away in the key of G major. Unusual, too, is the way the third stanza begins in E major before segueing gently into tonic major for the completion of the stanza.

The revised version of *Sonetto 104* follows closely the original piano transcription with some simplification of accompanying material. The greatest change reduces the elaborate introduction from twenty-one measures to six. Both versions are the most virtuosic of the three transcriptions and the most agitated and passionate. In a modified strophic form as well, the last version of the sonnet starts impetuously, presenting the main theme simply. The second statement is more varied, but the technical fireworks inundate the third strophe with its cadenzas, double and alternating thirds, and repeated octave passages. The work closes quietly, nevertheless, and provides a calm transition into the third sonnet.

Liszt makes more substantial changes in the piano versions of the *Sonetto 123*. In the revision he omits the elaborate cadenza of m. 8, dramatically lightens the accompaniment throughout, adds more syncopation, and extends the climatic section from mm. 49 to 60. The revised work itself is among Liszt's most beautiful and serene works, containing moments of exalted beauty, particularly with the elegant tranquility of the *Più lento* section (m. 41) and its close.

The first version of the *Après une lecture du Dante, fantasia quasi sonata* (*Dante* Sonata) dates from 1839,[21] although it did not reach its final form until 1849. While it deals with Dante's *Commedia*, the title itself stems from a Hugo poem.[22] The *Dante* Sonata has received considerable criticism over the years, even among Liszt supporters such as Searle.[23] From the number of recordings in the past decade, however, pianists have appeared eager to perform this work which must count among Liszt's best large-scale compositions.

This sonata/fantasy expresses Hugo's take on the diabolical nature of Dante's *Inferno* in battle with the spiritual side of his *Paradiso*. While it conforms to sonata format, as many writers have suggested, it also incorporates fantasy elements that make the sonata designation questionable (see Table 5.1). One of Liszt's earliest works to rely heavily upon the tritone, the "sonata" also depends upon the perfect fourth and fifth that triumphantly appear in m. 211. The opening 102 measures suggest the inferno by means of a dissonant focus on the tritone (motive x), minor seconds (motive y), sinister scales (motive z—mm. 25–28), and a chromatic *lamentoso* first theme (see Example 5.2). It is only after the establishment of F♯ major and the appearance of the second theme at m. 103 that the passionate, religious side of the equation begins to be balanced. Liszt often associates *fff* writing and F♯ major as religious ideas as seen in many of his later works.[24] The development begins immediately with a wrestling match between the opening diabolical themes and the noble and sublime themes in F♯ major.

This confrontation continues until the recapitulation occurs at the upper register tremolos at m. 290 that mark the return of tonic D major. Thomas Mastroianni speculates this return "seems to provide a glimpse of Paradise."[25] When the tritone motive makes its last appearance in the left hand (mm. 318–323), Liszt almost seems to ignore or override it as he passes on to a joyous paradisiacal conclusion. When motive x appears triumphantly at m. 366, it is once again the descending perfect fifth (motive x') that had battled with the tritone motive, firmly resting in the victorious key of D major over a long tremolo pedal.

Table 5.1
Liszt, *Dante* Sonata

Section	Measures	Key	Theme/Motive	Tempo
EXPOSITION 1–114				
Introduction	1		mot. x, y, z	*Andante maestoso*
1st Theme	35	D minor	th. 1	*Presto agitato assai*
Transition	73		mot. x, z	
2nd Theme	103	F♯	th. 2	
DEVELOPMENT 115–289				
	115		mot. x, y	*Tempo I (Andante)*
	124	V/F♯	th. 1	*Andante (quasi improvvisato)*
	136	F♯	th. 2	*Andante*
	157	F♯	th. 1	*più tosto ritenuto . . .*
	167	F♯	th. 1	
	181		mot. x, y	*Allegro moderato*
	199		th. 1, mot. z	
	211	A♭ (seq.)	mot. x'	*Più mosso*
	233		mot. x', z	
	250	B major	th. 2, mot. z	
Retransition	273	V/D minor	th. 1	*Tempo rubato...*
	283		mot. x'	
RECAPITULATION 290–373				
2nd Theme	290	D	th. 2	*Andante*
	306	D	th. 2	*Allegro*
	318		mot. x	
CODA 326–373				
	326	D	th. 1	*Allegro vivace*
	339	D	th. 1	*Presto*
	366	D	mot. x'	*Andante (Tempo I)*

Example 5.2
Liszt, *Dante* Sonata, Themes and Motives
Motive x, mm. 1–2

Motive y, mm. 3–4

Motive z, mm. 25–28

Theme 1, mm. 35–37

Theme 2, mm. 103–107

   In 1861 Schott published an appendix to the Italian volume entitled *Venezia e Napoli* (S 162). Around 1840 Liszt had written a set of four pieces under this collective title (S 159)—*Lento, Allegro, Andante placido,* and *Tarantelles napolitaines*—but the set was not published in his lifetime. When he revised *Venezia e Napoli* in 1859, he reduced the plan to three pieces to be played without break. Liszt based each work on a different pre-existing theme: (1) *Gondoliera* on *La biondina in Gondoletta, Canzone del Cavaliere Peruchini*; (2) *Canzone* on *Nessùn maggior dolore, Canzone del Gondoliere (nel 'Otello') di Rossini*; and (3) *Tarantella* on Neapolitan songs by Guillaume Louis Cottrau.
   The first of the three revised compositions starts with a calm sixteen-measure introduction before the main theme, taken from the third piece of the original *Venezia e Napoli,* begins. Liszt intersperses a delicate cadenza between repetitions of this theme that later becomes intertwined within the third variation decorated by light, cascading arpeggios. He simplifies the trill pattern that in the original was with the inner fingers of the right hand while the thumb and little finger played continuous parallel tenths—a passage requiring an immense hand. The *Canzone* contains sixty-fourth-note trills and tremolos throughout over which appears its jagged theme. The *Tarantella,* based on the fourth of the original pieces in the set, presents *Presto* triplet figures in the bass with its main theme appearing at m. 13. Liszt varies this theme with fast repeated notes and introduces the bravura second theme at m. 74. He plays with these ideas throughout the fast sections until a calming *Canzone napoletana* middle section provides appropriate contrast to the brilliant tarantella. Florid cadenzas, chromatic passages, and elaborate arpeggios lead this section back to the fast opening material. The music crescendos and accelerates to *prestissimo* for its remarkable conclusion.
   The first two pieces of the unpublished version were not used in any way for the revision. The first piece, *Lento,* is based upon a gondolier's song that Liszt later used in his symphonic poem *Tasso* (see Chapter 10, "Orchestral Music" for

additional information). He treats the theme to a series of imposing variations that are nearly orchestral in scope with fast scales, tremolos, and alternating open octaves. The second piece is rather bland and obviously the least important of the set. The first part repeatedly states a dotted rhythm while the *Allegretto* section is pleasant but characterless.

Harmonies poétiques et religieuses

Liszt composed a single piece entitled *Harmonies poétiques et religieuses* in 1834 based on Alphonse de Lamartine's collection of poems of the same name (discussed in Chapter 4). Lamartine strongly influenced Liszt, leading him to plan a larger set of pieces based on his poetry over the next two decades and culminating in the well-known 1853 version of the cycle also entitled *Harmonies poétiques et religieuses*. Our understanding of the evolution and history of the pieces that comprise this cycle, however, changed when Albert Brussee published an edition of the 1847 cycle that formed the basis of the better known 1853 version.[26] Brussee's work centered on the N9 sketchbook at the Goethe- und Schiller-Archiv in Weimar; he proposed that Liszt intended this cycle as a set and that the composer had completed part of it. Brussee's evidence led him to propose a twelve-piece cycle in the 1847 version that greatly differs from the final 1853 cycle shown in Table 5.2 (bracketed names not supplied by Liszt):

Table 5.2
Liszt, *Harmonies poétiques et religieuses*

1847 Cycle	1853 Cycle
[*Invocation*]	*Invocation*
Hymne de la nuit	*Ave Maria* (new)
Hymne du matin	*Bénédiction de Dieu dans la solitude*
Litanies de Marie	*Pensée des morts*
[*Miserere d'après Palestrina*]	*Pater noster*
Pater noster, d'après la psalmodie de l'eglise	*Hymne de l'enfant à son réveil*
Hymne de l'enfant à son réveil	*Funérailles* (new)
[*Pensée des morts*]	*Miserere d'après Palestrina*
La lampe du temple	*Andante lagrimoso*
[*Encore un hymne*]	*Cantique d'amour* (new)
Bénédiction de Dieu dans la solitude (?)	
[*Postlude*][27]	

Liszt composed or arranged much of the 1847 cycle while staying at the estate of Princess Carolyne von Sayn-Wittgenstein. He had previously written four of the works that he incorporated into the cycle. Of these, he had only published the 1834 version of the *Harmonies poétiques et religieuses* which provided the basis of both versions of the *Pensée des morts* in the 1847 and 1853 cycles. The other three works remained unpublished until the Brussee edition in 1997: *Litanies de Marie*; *Hymn de l'enfant à son réveil*; and *Prélude*. Brussee included the eleventh piece, *Bénédiction de Dieu dans la solitude,* in the 1847 cycle because of eighteen pages missing at this point in the N9 sketchbook that he speculated had once contained this masterpiece of Liszt's. The 1847 cycle remains more closely connected with Lamartine and exhibits a more cohesive spiritual nature than the revised 1853 cycle. Liszt based nos. 1–3 and 7–9 of the 1847 cycle on poems of Lamartine; the remaining numbers have religious connections, with the exception of the last two (not counting the *Bénédiction* which also embodies a Lamartine connection). Of the twelve pieces that comprise the 1847 cycle, Liszt retains aspects of nine in his heavily revised and reconsidered 1853 version. He reorders much of the cycle, drops three pieces completely (nos. 2–4), and adds three or four new works (depending whether the *Bénédiction* is included in the earlier version or not): *Ave Maria, Funérailles,* and *Cantique d'amour.*

Of the three works Liszt did not revise for the 1853 cycle (*Hymne de la nuit, Hymne du matin,* and *Litanies de Marie*), the *Hymne de la nuit* is the most forward-looking. Lasting nearly seven minutes, it opens with a couple of themes exhibiting a Mendelssohnian gentility that provide almost all of the material for the work's transformations. Although the *Hymne* builds to a *ff* climax at m. 52, it is quite delicate and refined overall in its nocturne-like character. Liszt's unusual use of the extreme upper register of the keyboard (mm. 76–83) is a surprising venture in so early a work. *Litanies de Marie,* the longest piece in the cycle composed before 1 November 1847, is also a substantial work that contains some lovely and little-known music. The second version consists of a series of transformations of four different themes that remain primarily in major keys. One of Liszt's brooding, searching moments opens the introductory section (mm. 1–44), followed by a prayerful second idea (mm. 45–56) and a beatific, *cantabile* A♭-major theme (mm. 57–100). The fourth main theme arrives in m. 114 and continues this tranquility and atmosphere of elevated, religious thought. With the return of the transposed and varied opening section (m. 129), no new thematic material is presented; instead, the remaining half of the piece consists of episodic transformation of the four themes. While a static quality pervades much of the writing, it remains effective in its portrayal of a meditative and unpretentious serenity. Unfortunately, the third piece, *Hymne du matin,* based on the Lamartine poem of the same title, is not as successful and suffers from its episodic nature and an uninspired and plodding march section (mm. 47–86). Brussee maintained Liszt completed this piece on 27 October 1847 and that it follows the outline of the poem with its depiction of mysterious night, the arrival of the sun, and day-time energy.[28]

Far and away the best-known pieces of the 1853 cycle are *Funérailles* and *Bénédiction de Dieu dans la solitude.* Liszt composed *Funérailles* anew in October 1849 in memory of Hungarian leaders killed during the Hungarian War of Independence in 1848 and 1849.[29] One of his most performed works, famous for its depiction of mourning bells in the beginning and its daring octave passages in the C section, this classic evokes an intense emotional quality with its dramatic opening and principal theme in addition to its hair-raising, octave C section. The lamenting second theme poses a perfect foil to the intensity of the other sections. Its form is much simpler with an introduction and three sections that reappear in order, the octaves returning only as a brief coda at the end. This composition deserves its place among the magisterial works of Liszt.

A poem from Lamartine that revels in the renewed sense of peace and joyous contentment after a time of uncertain restlessness prefaces the masterpiece of the set, *Bénédiction de Dieu dans la solitude*. The longest piece in the cycle and among the most elegant compositions Liszt ever penned, "the *Bénédiction*," Searle wrote, "is indeed almost unique among Liszt's works in that it expresses that feeling of mystical contemplation which Beethoven attained in his last period, but which is rarely found elsewhere in music. . . . The touching simplicity of the final passage shows that Liszt, like Beethoven, could express the most sublime thoughts in completely unadorned language when the mood was upon him."[30]

Kentner claimed the work is cast in ABA form, "being very clear-cut,"[31] but Dolores Pesce asserted that "the composite form [of both *Bénédiction* and *Funérailles*] is ABCA'B'C' where B' and C' signal abbreviated returns and A' signals a more expansive texture."[32] She clarified her position, stating that "the subsequent appearance of C' and B' functions more as a coda that lends harmonic confirmation than as a recall of earlier sections."[33] Clearly a disagreement exists about the work's form and a variety of elements that disguise it. Neither analyst considered mm. 43–85 a contrasting section, one in which neither the opening melody nor the F♯-major key is present (see Table 5.3 below).

Table 5.3
Liszt, Bénédiction de Dieu dans la solitude

Measure	Section	Theme	Key	Comments
1	A	1	F♯	*Moderato*
21		1'	F♯	restatement and varied—at m. 26
43	B	2	—	
51		2'	—	
67		2"	—	
86	A'	1"	F♯	return of F♯ and opening theme
104		1"'	F♯	varied restatement with rolled chords
148		1^{iv}	F♯	*Tempo 1*—closing idea of first section
178	C	3	D	*Andante*
186		3'	D	restated an octave higher
222	D	4	B♭	*Più sostenuto...* from postlude, 1847 cycle
234		4	D♭	restatement
252	A"	1^{v}	F♯	*Tempo 1*
271		1^{vi}	F♯	
308		1^{vii}	F♯	closing idea (similar to 148–178)
330	Coda	4', 2"	F♯, —	*ritenuto ad libitum*
349		3"	F♯	

Liszt retains an ostinato pattern similar to the A theme, but that in itself is not enough to keep this only within the A section. Furthermore, this thematic idea never returns in the same way upon the return of the A section. If this is seen as a B section and the two middle sections (mm. 178–252) as the C section (or a development section), the work could be viewed, perhaps, as a rondo or a sonata-rondo with coda (ABACDA' coda) since the A theme returns each time in F♯ in its transformations at mm. 86 and 252. Another oddity of the work is that mm. 148 and 308 function formally as closing sections would in a sonata form, making it appear that Liszt's form becomes part of the enigma of the piece itself.

Example 5.3
Liszt, *Bénédiction de Dieu dans la solitude*, Themes

Theme 1, mm. 1–9

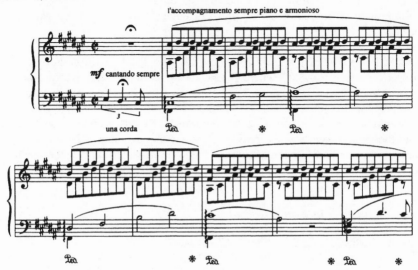

Theme 2, mm. 40–49

Theme 3, mm. 178–186

Theme 4, mm. 222–226

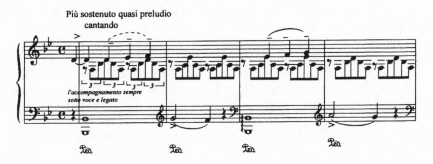

The marvel of the *Bénédiction* is the way it leads logically from the sublime to the passionate. When the first theme returns to F♯ (m. 86) and begins to build through sequential passages to the first climatic moment of the work (mm. 132–148, each chord is perfectly positioned and proportioned. The first climax is fitting and not over-powering, yet Liszt is able to enhance it again upon its parallel return (mm. 287–308). The coda that begins at m. 330 is almost a stream-of-consciousness reflection upon the preceding music. The penultimate cadence on D major is a stroke of genius.

Liszt composed two additional new pieces for inclusion in the 1853 cycle. The first is his calm and noble transcription of an *Ave Maria* he had originally composed for chorus and organ; the second is his *Cantique d'amour,* evidently composed for Princess Carolyne to whom he dedicated the entire 1853 cycle. The *Ave Maria* uses repeated octaves in the treble, antiphonal recitatives and chordal statements, and a beautiful, diatonic B♭-major melody over which Liszt places the text *Ave Maria, gratia plena* that he restates in B minor (m. 65) and E♭ major (m. 82) before returning to the tonic (m. 103). The composition ends with a fragmented coda, becoming one of Liszt's earliest piano works to conclude *perdendo* with a single, unaccompanied line. *Cantique d'amour* closes the cycle in its initial key of E major. This rather sentimental and at times pretentious love song is a single-minded pursuit of an enchanting theme. What begins softly as a single-line, cello melody in the middle register of the keyboard accompanied by harp-like arpeggios increases in complexity, texture, and dynamics to lead to an exuberant and ardent transformation beginning at m. 108. The cycle concludes with a tremendous crescendo, closing on eight, E-major chords.

The remaining pieces have often led critics such as Searle[34] and Kentner[35] to write disparagingly about this cycle. Of these criticized pieces *Pensée des morts* is the most important. Its revision process illustrates how Liszt transformed this revolutionary early *Harmonies poétiques* into these later versions. He based the untitled eighth piece of the 1847 cycle on his 1834 work and various sketches from his sketchbook N9, including the central section on Psalm 130, writing the words *De profundis clamavi ad te, Domine* in the score (mm. 43–70). He transfers the first thirty-nine measures and mm. 63–119 of his original *Harmonies* unchanged into this intense version, interpolating additional music between these two sections and concluding with different material not found in the original *Harmonies*. After a serious introduction, Liszt presents the *De profundis* chant, alternating low and high statements accompanied by tremolos and extended, cascading arpeggios. The character shifts at m. 59 when the tremolo and arpeggio activity ceases and the chant resounds, without decoration, in full chords. These chordal statements fade away and, after a "very long silence," Liszt returns to the original *Harmonies* music beginning in G major (*Andante religioso*). The revised work closes with a final chordal statement of the *De profundis,* rounding it out with further unification. This version considerably expands the original *Harmonies* but omits twenty-three measures contained in its middle section. It succeeds, however, with its overriding severity and profundity, and exhibits one of Liszt's darkest mental states from this period of his life.

Although Liszt's final version of *Pensée des morts* appears similar to the earlier versions, he makes a number of changes that dramatically effect the piece. First, he provides meter signs (5/4, 7/4, and 4/4) where he had previously indicated no meter at all. Second, he makes the opening less stark by omitting the bass counterpoint of the previous versions and leaves the recitative measures unaccompanied from the beginning. This revision succeeds following the sublime *Bénédiction*, although it takes away some of the drama of the earlier version. Third, Liszt extends the section after the initial cadenza, making it more triumphant than the earlier version. Fourth, he jumps straight to the chordal presentation of the *De profundis* (m. 58) but scores the passage an octave lower and omits the earlier tremolo and arpeggiated sections. Fifth, he returns at m. 61 to the opening idea before the G-major *Andante religioso* that he omits in the revised version. Sixth, instead of the *Andante religioso*, Liszt adds an *Adagio*, also in G major that, with its harp-like accompaniment, is more radiant but less fitting with the first parts of the work. The return of the chant in the previous version was more effective than this placid conclusion.

Of the remaining five pieces in the cycle, the *Invocation* is the most satisfying musically. In 1847 Liszt based an untitled introduction that formed the foundation of the later *Invocation* almost entirely on a descending bass line, an ascending melody over triplet, repeated chords, and tremolos. The piece, in which Liszt copied out the entire poem in the manuscript, provides a strong, uplifting invocation to a life of solitude and religious reflection, ending *fff* in E major.[36] Liszt's revision is over three times as long as his original version—203 measures compared to the original 61. It opens with similar repeated chords and a single-note melody above the chords, but the melody, lowered an octave, creates a more intense opening as it rises higher and higher in its melodic extensions. A new, jagged motive appears over the repeated chords somewhat reminiscent of his earlier *Vallée d'Obermann* (m. 25), and introduces a grandiose motive followed by descending open octaves (m. 52). These ideas reappear in various triumphal guises until the work closes *fff* in E major. All in all, Liszt adds a rough vigorousness to the serenity of the first version and in the process, creates a more epic beginning to the 1853 cycle. In his discussion of Liszt's religious keyboard music, David Gifford wrote that *Invocation* "is the perfect model for the musical characteristics present in many of the religious piano works. All of the three themes are based on the cross motive in some way . . . the tonality is E major . . . and the final page has repeated plagal cadences."[37]

One of the surprises in examining these rewritings is the work known as *Prière d'un enfant à son réveil*—a title Liszt provided in his correspondence when he mentioned he had composed it in 1840. Extraordinarily peaceful and loving, this three-minute prayer displays a more romanticized and fuller harmonic accompaniment than the composer employs in his later two versions of the melody known as *Hymne de l'enfant à son réveil*. In revising the prayer as *Hymne de l'enfant à son réveil*, he doubles its length by adding a fifty-five measure, contrasting *Andantino* section at the end and varying the opening theme in new and creative ways. Liszt reduces the texture by slightly accompanying the melody in its initial statement, but elaborates more in restatements beginning in mm. 39, 43, and 94. At m. 110 he adds a new *Andantino* section with a treble, repeated-chord figuration that closes the work. The revision may fit better as a component in this larger cycle, but Liszt did not necessarily improve the content of the original *Prière*. In his 1853 version of the *Hymne de l'enfant à son réveil* he makes only minor modifications, briefly extending the coda and altering the density of the chords throughout much of it.

In a similar reflective vein is the untitled *Andante lagrimoso* that stems from the earlier *La lampe du temple*. Liszt changes the poems it was originally based on, curtails the piece significantly, and raises the tonality from G minor to G♯ minor. Although the music of the first forty-one measures is similar in both versions, the composer changes the accompaniment figures from sixteenth notes to triplet eighths. He also removes the climatic material from the earlier work to create a more somber piece throughout and, unlike the previous version, restates the opening motive at the end. While there is nothing to offend in the composition, its length and lack of variety prevent it from playing a significant role in the cycle.

Liszt's two most severe works in the *Harmonies*—*Miserere d'après Palestrina* and *Pater noster, d'après la psalmodie de l'eglise*—are also the weakest. He creates his slow and ponderous *Miserere d'après Palestrina* by combining ideas from two works from the 1847 cycle, tacking on the elaborate arpeggiated figures from the earlier *Encore un hymne* to the untitled fifth piece in the cycle. A chant-like recitation of a repeated melodic idea opens the first twelve measures of the *Miserere* (a setting from Psalm 51), followed by twelve measures of right-hand tremolos prior to rapid arpeggios eighteen measures later. This combination of styles works better than one might think in creating a reflection on what Liszt thought, incorrectly it turned out, was a theme by Palestrina. Similarly, Liszt based his somewhat austere setting of the Lord's Prayer, *Pater noster, d'après la psalmodie de l'eglise*, on his earlier work for male chorus. Words in Latin appear above each note in an almost exclusively syllabic style; the setting seems to change keys for every phrase, concluding decisively with a C-major "Amen." Liszt's revision of *Pater noster* mainly concerns modifications in the texture and accompaniment.

The 1853 cycle *Harmonies poétiques et religieuses* contains more notable works than the earlier cycle, but thematically it is more loosely organized, making it less successful in performance as a single composition. The popularity of the *Bénédiction* and *Funérailles* also make performances as a cycle seemingly erratic because of the obscurity and quality of several of the other pieces.

Etudes

Counting both original and revised works, Liszt composed fifty-eight etudes, ranging from some of his earliest pieces, *Etudes en douze exercises* (S 136) in 1826, to his last two programmatic etudes of the early 1860s, *Waldesrauschen* and *Gnomenreigen* (S 145). Twenty-five of these represent Liszt's final thoughts and are the most performed of his etudes; the other thirty-three are earlier versions that he later revised. The twelve Etudes of 1826 are rarely performed as are the notoriously difficult sets from the late 1830s: the *Vingt-quatre grandes études* (S 137), of which only twelve were written, and the *Etudes d'exécution transcendante d'après Paganini* (S 140). Liszt revised and simplified both of these sets in 1851, renaming them *Etudes d'exécution transcendante* (S 139) and *Grandes études de Paganini* (S 141). In his later years from 1868 to around 1880, he compiled a twelve-volume exercise book entitled *Technische Studien* (S 146); these studies, however, are not self-contained, independent pieces, only exercises in the truest sense of the word.[38]

Transcendental Etudes. Liszt's greatest set of etudes, the twelve 1851 *Etudes d'exécution transcendante* (Transcendental Etudes), have the most complicated history of his keyboard studies. Beginning in 1826 with the original set of twelve, he later revised and expanded them in 1837 and again in 1851. Examining these studies, almost all of them reworked over a twenty-five-year period, illustrates Liszt's compositional style from each period of his life—or, as Ferruccio Busoni described, "in seed, in growth and finally in self-clarification."[39]

Although Liszt called them "etudes" throughout their permutations, only the 1826 set is truly etude-like, focusing as it does on particular technical problems. The original twelve pieces that he wrote as a young teenager in 1826 show the influence of his teacher Czerny with their simple repeated patterns often centered on a particular technical demand. Liszt arranged them, starting in C major, by relative major and minor keys, proceeding through the flat side of the circle of fifths. The forms are often clear, employing traditional ABA (e.g., nos. 1 and 11), ABAB (no. 4), or ABA'CA' (no. 9) often followed by a brief coda.

The 1826 version provides the basis for all but one of the 1837 *Vingt-quatre grandes études* (see Table 5.4). Liszt retains the key structures of the 1826 set for his 1837 version, except for transposing his 1826 seventh Etude from E♭ major to D♭ major, making it the eleventh of the second version. In 1837 he adds a new composition in E♭ major to retain his key organization. None of the works in the first two sets have programmatic titles but contain generic tempo indications. The fourth of the 1837 set was reworked and published independently with the title *Mazeppa* in 1840, eleven years before Liszt undertook revisions of the other etudes in 1851.

Table 5.4
Liszt's op. 6 Etudes and Revisions in 1837 and 1851

Op. 6, 1826	1837	1851
No. 1 in C *Allegro con fuoco*	*Presto*	*Preludio: Presto*
No. 2 in a *Allegro non molto*	*Molto vivace*	*Molto vivace: a capriccio*
No. 3 in F *Allegro sempre legato*	*Poco adagio*	*Paysage: Poco adagio*
No. 4 in d *Allegretto*	*Allegro patetico*	*Mazeppa: Allegro*
No. 5 in B♭ *Moderato*	*Egualmente*	*Feux follets: Allegretto*
No. 6 in g *Molto agitato*	*Largo patetico*	*Vision: Lento*
No. 7 in E♭ *Allegretto con molto espressione*	No. 11 in D♭ *Lento assai*	*Harmonies du soir: Andantino*
- - - - -	No. 7 in E♭ *Allegro deciso*	*Eroica: Allegro*
No. 8 in c *Allegro con spirito*	*Presto strepitoso*	*Wilde Jagd: Presto furioso*
No. 9 in A♭ *Allegro grazioso*	*Andantino*	*Ricordanza: Andantino*
No. 10 in f *Moderato*	*Presto molto agitato*	*Allegro agitato molto*
No. 11 in D♭ *Allegro grazioso*	(not included)	(not included)
No. 12 in b♭ *Allegro non troppo*	*Andantino*	*Chasse-neige: Andante con moto*

In his 1837 revisions Liszt transforms each of his original etudes into a massively difficult piece that often sheds its original structure and focus. He, in effect, creates new compositions that only superficially resemble the models upon which they are based. The 1837 revisions usually do not limit keyboard technique as do traditional etudes. Liszt incorporates more melodic interest into the revised etudes and makes incredible virtuosic demands, consisting of interlocking patterns, tremolos, wide stretches and leaps, and presto scales, arpeggios, repeated chords, and octaves. He substantially lengthens the individual etudes to nearly three times their original length on the average—only the first Etude is shorter than its 1826 counterpart—and radically alters most of them, frequently changing tempos and meters. Etudes nos. 3, 6, 9, 11, and 12 retain a slow to moderate tempo, but the remaining seven are quite fast. In the third Etude, for example, Liszt slows the tempo from *Allegro sempre legato* in the 1826 version to *Poco adagio* at the beginning of the 1837 version and changes the meter from 4/4 to 6/8. In the 1826 version each hand performs the same material, usually a tenth apart, in continuous eighth notes; some melodic notes are held and emphasized. Liszt begins the revised version with a beautiful melody in octaves that he restates and varies throughout the Etude. The original Etude provides the accompaniment and harmonic structure, but the revised melodic content is so distinct that it seems like an entirely different work. The 1837 version concludes, moreover, with an additional *Presto agitato assai* that completely changes the character of the piece. The 1837 revisions, along with the 1838–1839 Paganini studies, represents the virtuoso Liszt at his most revolutionary and daring; they are studies meant for few others than himself because of their daunting technical requirements.

The 1851 version of the *Transcendental Etudes* simplifies the demands of the previous version to some degree, although it retains more than enough virtuosity for professional pianists. Liszt provides titles for all but two, nos. 2 and 10. The composer's maturity shows in these revisions through his textural reductions, increased notational clarity, and refined artistic judgment. (Only the seventh Etude of the 1837 set is often considered better than its later counterpart.) While Liszt only makes minimal changes to the first and ninth Etudes in his last revisions, the other ten receive significant alterations, ranging from expanded introductions and endings to cutting substantial sections. In the 1851 version of no. 11 *Harmonies du soir,* for example, Liszt extends the poetic introduction by two measures and removes the bell references, replacing the open octaves with slow alternating octaves. He also removes the *Quasi presto* and *Allegro vivace* sections and completely revises the middle *molto espressivo il canto* section by lightening the texture dramatically. He also reduces the vast number of wide stretches in the revision, makes significant harmonic changes, and rewrites much of the accompanimental material. Examples 5.4 and 5.5 illustrate how difficult a passage from the 1837 version of Etude no. 2 is and how Liszt simplified it in 1851 without losing the intended effect.

Example 5.4
Liszt, *Transcendental Etude* no. 2 (1837), mm. 6–10

Example 5.5
Liszt, *Transcendental Etude* **no. 2 (1851), mm. 6–10**

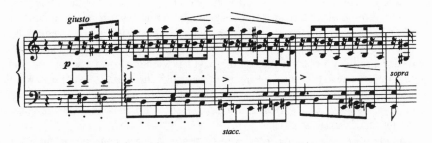

To illustrate the development of these etudes from their conception to their final form, I examine four of the most brilliant and respected of the Etudes (nos. 4, 5, 8, and 10) below. The final version has little to do with the first ideas Liszt presented as a fifteen-year-old composer.

The 1826 version of the fourth Etude in D minor, *Allegretto,* incorporates cross-hands passages with *piano* legato thirds in each hand. It is among the simplest of the early etudes built from an ABAB form with coda. In the 1837 version Liszt nearly doubles the length of the work, transforming it into a pianistic symphonic poem in a triumphal manner. Technically the study still concentrates on thirds but this time between wide chordal leaps. The fast thirds in both hands in the variation beginning in m. 25 are incredibly difficult to perform, and he simplifies them in his final revision. The 1837 version contains a contrasting *leggiero* middle section still employing thirds but often with repeated octaves and thirds. After a flurry of *fortissimo* open octaves, the *Allegro animato* returns with the opening material that remains brilliant with additional, fascinating variations to the end.

When Liszt published another version of this piece in 1840 under the title *Mazeppa,* he altered both the beginning and ending, starting with an eleven-chord *forte* introduction and closing with a seven-measure, triumphant D-major ending. Other than some thinning of texture and simplification, *Mazeppa* is highly similar to the 1837 version.

In his 1851 version Liszt further expands the introduction, adding slashing, *fortissimo* rolled chords and sweeping scale passages in each hand to set up the musical representation of the journey on horseback. Although he simplifies the opening statement by removing some left-hand octaves, he notates the first twenty-one measures of his new version on three staves for clarity in reading. He concludes with another expansion of the coda, setting up a recitative that allows Mazeppa to rise from his fallen horse and be crowned king triumphantly in D major.

The 1826 version of the fifth Etude in B♭ major (*Moderato*) concentrates on repeated, dotted eighth-note/sixteenth-note rhythms played legato throughout much of the work. *Fortissimo* ascending scale passages, sometimes accompanied by descending quarter-note chords, occasionally interrupt this rhythmic pattern. The Etude possesses little musical interest outside of its opening theme on which

Liszt so brilliantly based his revision in 1837. Indeed Liszt makes an impressive leap from the *Moderato* of the earlier version to the *Egualmente* version, with its constantly evolving thirty-second-note passages in single-note scales and arpeggios, tremolos, and maddening leaps. Liszt wrote few pieces so indebted to subtle filigree and to capricious yet gracious double notes all at a remarkable tempo. Along with the tenth Etude of the 1851 set, it counts among his greatest keyboard studies. In his last version he makes few changes to its sound; he thins the texture in a place or two, but his most valuable alteration is to the end which is more delicate and better suited to the idea of the title he gives it: *Feux follets*, usually translated as "will-o'-the-wisp." Leo Weiner made an orchestral transcription of this work in 1934.[40]

The eighth of the original Etudes in C minor, *Allegro con spirito*, curiously resembles Chopin's C-minor "Revolutionary" Etude with its predominant, running left-hand sixteenth notes. Liszt's sixty-four-measure first attempt, however, is only a ghost of the nearly quadrupled versions that follow. He does not add the mythological title *Wilde Jagd* (Wild Hunt) until the 1851 version, but the 1837 version is one of the wildest pieces, hunt or not, that Liszt wrote. Russell Sherman asked even of the later version, "Does it demand this many forces to capture a puny fox? What are they hunting here, dinosaurs or the Abominable Snowman?"[41] The meter changes to 6/8 from its original 4/4, and the tempo increases to *Presto strepitoso*. The work starts with a thirty-second-note unison flourish in the bass that Liszt simplifies to alternating sixteenth notes in the 1851 revision. He greatly expands his original idea and takes his theme through many transformations both lyrical and disjointed. The calm and gentle E♭-major section provides a contrasting respite from the frenzied hunt. The opening material returns more forceful than before, changing, like *Mazeppa*, to tonic major with an extended peroration of the opening thematic material, including broken octaves in both hands, treacherous right-hand octave leaps, and a relentless drive to the *fff* close. The 1837 version, which ends too abruptly, is given an additional brief descending scale in the 1851 version to bring the massive work to a more suitable close. Liszt also truncates the section before turning to C major in the revision which tightens the work formally and makes it superior to the previous version.

The tenth Etude, *Moderato* in F minor, consists of continuous sixteenth-note triplets in both hands a sixth apart—most often in stepwise motion but upon occasion arpeggios as well. Liszt includes some short leaps in mm. 15–16, but the Etude remains in the same style throughout. In the 1837 edition he increases the tempo to *Presto molto agitato* and replaces the parallel sixths with alternating left- and right-hand triads. While the early study maintains its *Moderato* tempo, Liszt adds a *Presto feroce* section and closes with a *Prestissimo agitato ed appassionata assai* coda. He also adds an octave melody beginning at m. 22 (taken from the melodic material added at m. 3) that provides welcome contrast to the opening figuration. Furthermore, he greatly magnifies the technical difficulties using extreme leaps, awkward accompaniment ideas within the melody hand, rolling two-octave, left-hand arpeggios, and brilliant open octaves. He dramatically simplifies this Etude in his 1851 revision, omitting two lengthy sections (including the *Presto feroce*), thinning the texture, and removing the nearly impossible technical feats of the 1837 version. Liszt greatly improves this untitled work to make it among the most frequently performed and respected *Transcendental Etude*.

Paganini Etudes. Although Liszt heard Paganini play in 1831, he did not publish his *Etudes d'exécution transcendante d'après Paganini*—which he had begun as early as 1832—until 1838–1840. Liszt based five of the pieces on Paganini's solo violin Caprices and the other, *La campanella*, on the third movement of Paganini's Violin Concerto in B minor. Although these etudes are often listed as Liszt's original works, they are piano transcriptions of Paganini's violin music rather than Liszt's original compositions. In 1851 Liszt revised, simplified, and edited them as *Grande études de Paganini*; both versions are identical from a structural standpoint. Liszt dedicated both sets to Clara Schumann.

Both versions of the first Etude in G minor are framed with brilliant opening and closing cascading arpeggios and scales. The study proper consists of a single-note melody played over constant tremolos notated for the left hand alone in the first seventeen measures of the first version, but for only eight in the revision. Liszt refines the second version by redistributing material to different hands and simplifies awkward writing in mm. 41–43 and 51–54. This imposing Etude, in either version, makes a grand opening when the studies are performed as a set.

The second Etude in E♭ major is in ABA form. In his revised version Liszt makes no major changes in the dramatic octave study that constitutes the B section but often thins out the texture of the A section, replacing thirds with single notes, full chords with intervals or open octaves, and shortening extended thirty-second-note flourishes. Its delicate and capricious nature makes it one of the most successful of the set, even though it is overshadowed in popularity by the next Etude.

By far, the most performed of these studies is the revised version of *La campanella* with its engaging wide leaps, repeated notes, chromatic scales, and open octaves all within a brisk tempo (*Allegretto*). The two versions differ from each other in tempo (*Allegro moderato* versus *Allegretto*), key (A♭ minor versus G♯ minor), and musical material. Liszt employs another theme of Paganini in the first version that he omits in the second. Liszt greatly improves the second version by tighter unity in structure and by including the high treble sixteenth-note skips starting at m. 4. In the earlier version Liszt employs grace-note figures which give it a more spasmodic feeling. He also incorporated the *campanella* theme in two other gargantuan and elaborate paraphrases: *Grande fantaisie di bravura sur la clochette de Paganini* (S 420) composed between 1832 and 1834 and *Variations de bravoure pour piano sur des thèmes de Paganini* dating from 1845.

The fourth Etude in E major appears in three highly distinct versions, the first two published in 1839. Versions one and two (*Andante quasi Allegretto*) contain considerable parallel writing and are much denser in texture than the revised 1851 Etude. The first version uses many parallel sixths or octaves for the first twelve measures and is far superior to the second version (see Example 5.6).

Example 5.6
Liszt, *Etudes d'exécution transcendante d'après Paganini* no. 4, version 1 (1839), mm. 1–2

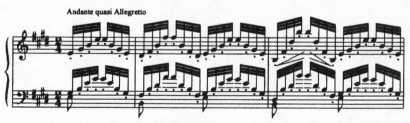

Version two opens with thick, thirty-second-note chords for which Liszt writes *leggieramente*—something almost impossible on the modern piano (see Example 5.7). This version contains difficult double-third accompanimental passages, *fff* alternating chords, and wide stretches. The second version ends *Maestoso* with a *marcatissimo* coda that sounds highly ineffective compared to his skillful revision in 1851.

Example 5.7
Liszt, *Etudes d'exécution transcendante d'après Paganini* no. 4, version 2 (1839), mm. 1–2

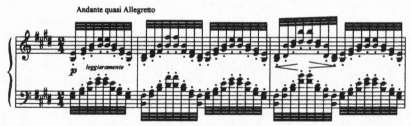

The last version is unique in Liszt's piano music with its notation consisting of only one stave, literally imitating the violin with its restriction to the treble clef and violin range (see Example 5.8). He changes the tempo to *Vivo* and cleverly uses crossing hands to reduce this work to a delicate and almost elf-like nature.

Example 5.8
Liszt, *Grande études de Paganini* no. 4 (1851), mm. 1–2

In the same key as the previous Etude, Liszt's *La chasse*, begins in the first version with treble thirds and sixths in both hands in imitation of the flute. The answer to this theme is a similar pattern imitating the horn in a contrasting register. This version adds sixteenth-note figurations (mm. 25–28) and repeated octaves (at the *Più animato*) that Liszt omits in the revision, and contains difficult parallel octaves and chords that he replaces with glissandos in the later version. He also writes fifty-two measures of optional passages in the first version, which, if chosen, almost creates another study.[42] The 1851 version is the least virtuosic of the *Paganini Etudes* and, like the preceding E-major Etude, lighter and more elegant than the other etudes in the set.

Liszt based his sixth and concluding Etude in A major on Paganini's grand finale to his *24 Caprices*. Liszt faithfully follows the eleven variations that Paganini wrote on his theme, adapting for the keyboard the material Paganini wrote so idiomatically for the violin. Liszt's two versions of this Etude have significant changes in almost each variation, and even the theme itself is simplified in the revised version with single notes replacing open octaves. Liszt simplifies some of the incredibly difficult passages of the first versions, namely the nearly unrealizable parallel tenths in the alternate passage in variation 6, the treacherous rolled chords in variation 8, and some intricate leaps in the last variation. He completely rewrites variation 2, omitting the counter melody begun in the fifth measure of the original version and removes the four-against-three rhythmic pattern of the first version in the fourth variation. The final version, nevertheless, retains much of the original virtuosity and includes brilliant writing for the piano with examples of extended trills, alternating chords, open octaves, parallel thirds, and four-octave arpeggios.

Miscellaneous Etudes. Liszt composed a few isolated etudes outside of his large sets. His brief *Morceau de salon, étude de perfectionnement* (S 142) dates from 1840, and he revised it as *Ab irato: Grande etude de perfectionnement* (S 143) in 1852. Both pieces begin *Presto impetuoso* and maintain that energy, except for a brief sixteen-measure contrasting section designated *Più moderato* in *Ab irato*. A melodic line over rolling multi-octave, thirty-second-note arpeggios characterizes both. A similar contrasting section appears in the earlier *Morceau de salon*, but Liszt did not indicate any relief from the fast tempo. Except for the slow section in *Ab irato*, both works are based upon a stepwise, six-note figure varied throughout. Liszt also adds a final statement of the motive in the penultimate measures of *Ab irato* that is not present in the earlier version.

Liszt's *Trois études de concert* (S 144), composed between 1845 and 1849, were published in Paris as *Trois caprices poétiques* with the individual titles by which they are now best known, *Il lamento*, *La leggierzza*, and *Un sospiro*—titles Liszt more than likely did not supply. The first Etude in A♭ (*Il lamento*) is among Liszt's longest works in the etude genre. It opens with a four-note melodic motive he extends and develops throughout the work followed directly by a chromatic Chopinesque cadenza. This *A capriccio* section reappears in the coda framing the lyrical inner workings. Like Chopin's op. 10, no. 3 study, the *Allegro cantabile* section requires a single melodic note in the top part of the right hand while the lower notes of the same hand provide accompanimental figures. This pattern appears over an arpeggiated, nocturne-like left hand as Liszt alters it chromatically in various registers of the keyboard. Although the Etude begins and ends in A♭ major, it passes with ease through many, often unrelated, keys including A, G, B, D♯, F♯, and B♭.

Starting *in medias res* with its many fast, delicate, and *pianissimo* chromatic sixteenth notes, the second concert Etude in F minor (*La leggierzza*) maintains an almost phantasmal quality throughout. Liszt uses chromatic thirds and sixths, illusive irregular rhythmic subdivisions (particularly septets), fluid meter changes (e.g., 4/4, 7/4, 4/4, 9/4, and 4/4 between mm. 43 and 53), avoidance of the first beat, and understated cadenzas to evoke the atmosphere of lightness and illusion found in its title.

The third and most famous Etude of the set in D♭ (*Un sospiro*) is known for its beautiful melody gracefully plucked out by alternating hands over *legatissimo* cascading arpeggios that create an adroit, Thalbergian three-hand effect. Liszt's melody consists of single notes, thirds, or broken octaves, and appears at times in each register (lower, middle, and upper) of the keyboard. At the end of m. 52 Liszt himself often improvised a cadenza, and the NLE provides three brief optional cadenzas that Liszt wrote for several friends and students: Professor Henrik Gobbi, Auguste Rennebaum, and Lina Schmalhausen. The edition also provides a haunting and enigmatic conclusion with ascending half-note major chords passing in contrary motion over a descending whole-tone scale.[43]

Magyar Dallok and *Hungarian Rhapsodies*

Liszt wrote twenty-two pieces that fall under the category of *Magyar dallok—Ungarische Nationalmelodien* (S 242) between 1839 and 1840. Most likely stimulated by his visits to Hungary in 1839 and 1840, he composed the first eleven in four volumes between 1839 and 1840 and nos. 12–17 between 1846 and 1847 published as *Magyar Rhapsodiák/Ungarische Rhapsodien* (S 242). Liszt failed to publish nos. 18 to 21 but published no. 22 "Pester Karneval" in 1848. Of these twenty-two works, all but five—nos. 1–3 and 8–9—became better known in their revisions and recompilations as *Hungarian Rhapsodies*.

The first three *Magyar dallok* are short pieces in slow tempos (*Lento, Andantino,* or *Sehr langsam*); none is highly distinctive. The first in C minor is unmetered and presented in a question and answer format. The second in C major has syncopation and Hungarian gestures in three short sections but does not hold the rhythmic energy so often found in the later rhapsodies. The third in D♭ major—the most developed of these with its thirty-two measures and three distinct sections—also fails to warrant further development in the rhapsodies.

The other two *Magyar dallok* that Liszt did not revise, nos. 8 and 9, are more distinguished than the first three. He based no. 8 in F minor on a single idea, a slow funeral march of considerable merit. Liszt's imaginative and artful changes in the accompaniment create interest throughout, even though the unremitting gloom is broken only by the surprising shift to four F-major chords that conclude the march. The ninth *Magyar dallok* in A minor, at 249 measures and approximately ten minutes, is a significant work on its own, worthy of inclusion in the later *Hungarian Rhapsodies*. It opens *Lento* with an elaborate *cymbalon* effect of tremolos, trills, and rapid scales in sixths and thirds requiring ample virtuosity. At m. 44 the tempo shifts to *Quasi presto*, and the sprightly *friska* begins with several short repeated sections. This amusement is again broken (m. 123) with a sudden change to the opening tempo and a shift to D minor. The *Quasi presto* returns in A minor (m. 150) and proceeds without interruption to its joyous conclusion in A major.

Liszt also simplified some of the earlier *Magyar* pieces in their conversions to *Hungarian Rhapsodies*, in particular, nos. 13–17. *Magyar Rhapsodiák* no. 15 in D minor was the basis for the seventh *Hungarian Rhapsody*; however, he truncated this version in the revision and in many ways weakened a work that has more interest than its reincarnation. He omits two substantial sections, including mm. 93–101 and a beautiful B-major slow section (mm. 179–255).

Liszt assembled the majority of his nineteen *Hungarian Rhapsodies* between 1851 and 1853 when he published the first fifteen. The last four are late works stemming from his last years and discussed in Chapter 6. With the exceptions of the first (based on a discarded *Consolation*) and the second (newly written), the other *Hungarian Rhapsodies* (nos. 3–15) include revisions and re-combinations of *Magyar dallok* and *Magyar Rhapsodiák* pieces. Most of the Rhapsodies (nos. 3–4, 7–11, and 13) are based on only one previous piece, and four (nos. 5, 12, 14, and 15) combine two pieces.

Of all the Rhapsodies no. 6 is the most heterogeneous in its conception. It consists of a *Magyar Rhapsodiák* (no. 20) and three different pieces from the *Magyar dallok* (nos. 4, 5, and 11) that Liszt also used in his three *Ungarische Nationalmelodien* (S 243). The entire *Magyar dallok* no. 5 opens the Rhapsody embellished by an extension and cadenza used in his first *Ungarische Nationalmelodien*. *Magyar dallok* no. 4 (*Ungarische Nationalmelodien* no. 2) follows immediately as the *Presto* section in C♯ major. The *Andante* from *Magyar Rhapsodiák* no. 20 is not nearly as extended or ornamented as the original version that includes a number of *cymbalon* effects. The B♭-major *Allegro* with its repeated notes and octaves comes directly from the *Allegretto* of the eleventh *Magyar dallok* (and third *Ungarische Nationalmelodien*), but Liszt extends the work with octaves in contrary motion to intensify its dramatic conclusion. Each section appears in a different key as well, starting in D♭ major, modulating to C♯ major and B♭ minor, before ending in B♭ major.

The moods of the fifteen rhapsodies are generally upbeat and entertaining, although two in particular show a more serious side. Liszt's least rhapsodic Rhapsody no. 5 "Héroïde-élégiaque," (*Lento, con duolo*), is a funeral march with the fewest conspicuous contrasts between sections. The tenebrous bent of the opening brightens to a limited degree in the B section, but the overall atmosphere relies more on themes of resignation and introspection than the other rhapsodies. His fourteenth Rhapsody, later arranged as his *Hungarian Fantasy* for piano and orchestra, also begins as a funeral march, *Lento quasi Marcia funèbre*, set in a low register of the keyboard in F minor. Unlike the fifth Rhapsody, however, it moves to F major twenty-five measures after it opens and becomes heroic (*Allegro eroico*) before closing *Vivace assai* with an impressive coda. In absolute contrast is the good-natured fun found in the famous second Rhapsody and the consistently joyous eighth and ninth Rhapsodies in E♭ major. The lighthearted tenth Rhapsody is the most etude-like of the rhapsodies, full of scales in contrary motion, octaves and tenths, and even glissandos in the *Vivace* section; on the other hand, Liszt's fourth Rhapsody, *Quasi Adagio-altieramente,* seems so whimsical it borders on the banal. Each theme progressively becomes more humorous and fanciful in this insouciant trifle with brilliant cadenzas and closing *Presto* open octaves.

These rhapsodies provide a combination of virtuosic tasks and improvisatory delicacies, usually ending with intimidating pyrotechnical features. Except for the third and fifth, all have bravura *fortissimo* endings. Often included are scintillating trills, cadenzas, rapid thirds, repeated notes, open and interlocking octaves, and wide leaps. Liszt changes registers abruptly on a regular basis. For example, Rhapsody no. 3 in B♭ major begins in the lowest register of the keyboard with a stern, *pesante* melody. The B section, contrarily, utilizes only the upper register with its light and impish, quasi-cadenza writing. All are primarily in duple meters and sectionalized to some degree, often with startling contrasts of tempo and style. Only the fifth Rhapsody retains its original tempo indication throughout (although the editors of the NLE have supplied some possible changes). Liszt applies the term *a capriccio* to nearly half of the first fifteen rhapsodies, and the term specifically "denotes metrical irregularity."[44]

These compositions are indeed mercurial and capricious with contrasting episodes that can require up to a dozen significant and often abrupt tempo changes within a single rhapsody. Most are built around the *verbunkos* idea of a slow beginning (*lassu* or *lassan*) with a faster conclusion (*friss* or *friska*), but the sixth and ninth have slow sections after fast passages before returning to their brisk conclusions. The forms range from ABA' (no. 3) and ABAB (no. 5) to more elaborate ABABACABDECA of the twelfth—with each return a variant of the original section. His *Hungarian Rhapsody* no. 11 contains four distinct sections, each in a different key with a progressively faster tempo, moving from *Lento a capriccio* to *Prestissimo.* Ten of the fifteen begin in minor keys, but the majority end in major keys. Hungarian elements include coloristic grace-notes, Hungarian scales, and *cymbalon* effects. The opening *lassan* sections in Rhapsodies nos. 7 and 11 display the most elaborate *cymbalon* effects. The eleventh, in particular, has a striking, shimmering effect with its delicate tremolos and sixty-fourth-note configurations.

Liszt's second Rhapsody, along with his seventh, displays the clearest use of the *lassan* followed by the *friska.* The most famous and frequently performed of the rhapsodies, the second entered the popular culture through more than a dozen films and cartoons, including *Rhapsody Rabbit* with Bugs Bunny (1946), *The Cat Concerto* (1947), *Who Framed Roger Rabbit* (1988), and *Shine* (1996). Liszt composed this work anew, without incorporating any of his previous compositions. Its opening C♯-minor *Lento a capriccio* and *Andante mesto* provide some of Liszt's best themes in these rhapsodies. Although maintaining a slow tempo and capricious character, he still interposes brilliant, delicate cadenza passages on three occasions in its ABCA'B'A" formal structure. The *friska* begins *Vivace* with the theme first heard in the *lassan* (m. 35) that leads into fast, repeated notes and alternating broken-octave patterns. The *Tempo giusto-vivace* introduces a variety of new themes and plenty of fireworks, with its dotted rhythms, wide leaps, open and interlocking octaves, and flashy scales. The energy lessens only twelve measures before the optional cadenza, and the closing *Prestissimo* restores the frenetic pace of the *friska* with a bravura close in F♯ major.

Rhapsody no. 12, based on five different themes, is the most unified of the set. The opening idea returns several times in the beginning, in a transformed version at m. 88, in the middle of the work (*Tempo 1*—m. 104), and at the *Adagio* at the end. Liszt achieves greater unity through repetition of themes, although the same alternating structure of the genre is employed overall. The third theme presented first in m. 35, for example, also returns at the close for the *fff* summation. The highly episodic work contains eleven tempo changes and numerous abrupt emotional shifts.

Liszt's fifteenth *Hungarian Rhapsody* is one of seven different piano versions and transcriptions of the *Rákóczy March* published in the NLE, including the thirteenth *Magyar Rhapsodiák,* two transcriptions of the orchestral versions, and two simplifications of previous versions. The Rákóczy melody "was the very embodiment of the strivings for national independence and freedom in Hungary."[45] The thirteenth *Magyar Rhapsodiák—Rhapsodies hongroises* is the most fascinating of these works, much more difficult than the simplified Rhapsody that is better known. In its previous incarnation Liszt uses glissandos in thirds, rapid repeated notes, wide leaps, and strenuous trills while playing the melodic passage in the same hand. He based his fifteenth *Hungarian Rhapsody* on *Magyar Rhapsodiák* nos. 10 and 13. It is in a large-scale minuet and trio form, with the opening idea in ABA and the trio section in CDCDC. After an extensive cadenza, the opening ABA returns with a coda based on the A theme in tonic major. Furthermore, pianists such as Vladimir Horowitz have been so enchanted with the fifteenth Rhapsody as to make their own versions of it. Horowitz rewrites the cadenza completely and ornaments a great deal of the work.

Much has been written about the *Hungarian Rhapsodies*, and performers have been including them on their concerts throughout the twentieth century. The pieces have had a troubled history, nevertheless, and require special performance abilities to succeed. Alfred Brendel wrote, "It is above all the Rhapsodies that come to life through the improvisatory spirit and fire of the interpreter; they are wax in his hand like few other pieces in existence."[46] Ernest Hutcheson summed up their status in the middle of the twentieth century:

To qualify as a critic of piano music it is fashionable to adopt a sneering attitude toward Liszt's Hungarian Rhapsodies. This may be because the critic must needs maintain a superiority to public taste, and public taste in its ignorance adores the rhapsodies, applauding them frenetically whenever they are performed. The young recitalist, ever in search of that elusive phantom the 'effective end piece,' finds it incarnated in these dazzling works. For nearly a century the world's best artists have not disdained to play them.[47]

Consolations

Liszt composed six works that he published in 1850 as the *Consolations* (S 172)—a title that he derived from one of two possible authors. The editors of the NLE claimed that the title "was in all probability taken by Liszt from the volume of poetry with the same title of the French literary historian and poet Joseph Delorme, pseudonym of Charles Sainte-Beuve (1804–1869),"[48] an idea that Alan Walker also endorsed.[49] Maria Eckhardt and Ernst-Günter Heinemann indicated that Lamartine's poem *Une larme, ou Consolation* was more likely to be the source.[50] Walker described the background for these works: "Their reflective, self-communing character reveals a new and much more thoughtful Liszt: this is music tinged with a secret sorrow. It first stirred to life under Liszt's fingers in the Altenburg, when the tragedy of his liaison with Carolyne had begun to penetrate his soul."[51]

The earliest *Consolation* (no. 5) dates from 1844, while nos. 1, 2, 4, and 6 come from 1848. The third and most popular of the set, *Lento placido*, replaced an earlier work that became part of Liszt's *Hungarian Rhapsody* no. 1. The first two and last two *Consolations* in E major contrast with the middle two works in Db major, an augmented second lower.[52] (Both keys are often associated with love or religious themes in Liszt's music.) The first four pieces are in duple meter and the last two in triple. Most of these compositions are tightly constructed upon limited melodic material with which Liszt develops through variation and transformation. All of them are meditative to some degree, particularly the first five that are slower and do not contain any loud passages at all. The third is the longest and most similar in style to Chopin's Nocturnes, although the fifth, *Andantino,* also owes a great deal to Chopin with its use of thirds and harmonic progressions (particularly mm. 12–18). Liszt based no. 4, *Quasi adagio,* on a theme by the Grand Duchess Maria Pavlovna that begins in chorale style and no. 5 on an earlier pieced entitled *Madrigal.*[53] Because a star appeared above the printed score of the fourth *Consolation*, it has on occasion been subtitled *Stern Consolation*. Compared to the others, no. 5 appears the most stately, almost religious or philosophical in nature. The sixth *Consolation* owns the fastest tempo of the group, *Allegretto sempre cantabile,* and also possesses the most intense crescendo and extroverted music of the cycle, making it imperative that performers remember the meditative and reposed spirit of the genre. These often-played works had an early famous admirer. Frederich Nietzsche recorded, "On this day, I played Liszt's 'Consolation' quite a bit, and I feel how the tones have infiltrated their way into me and resound in me in spiritualized form."[54]

LARGE-SCALE WORKS

Ballades

Liszt wrote two Ballades between 1845 and 1853, most likely influenced by Chopin's four works with this title.[55] Liszt began his Ballade no. 1 in Db major

(S 170) in 1845 but did not complete it until 1849 when he dedicated it to Eugène von Sayn-Wittgenstein, a Russian sculptor related to Princess Carolyne's husband. The subtitle *Le chant du croisé* that once was associated with the work appears to be the work of a French publisher and not a title that Liszt added.[56] Rena Mueller pointed out that Liszt's working title for the original material went through several name changes before arriving at Ballade, first being known as *Galop Bohémien* and *Dernier illusion.*[57]

The Ballade, in clear ternary form with a brief introduction and coda, begins with a *Preludio* of eleven measures that, with its two-phrase structure of legato and contrasting staccato passages, sets out the conceptual material for the entire work. The beautiful A section in D♭ major (*Andantino, con sentimento*) consists solely of the legato theme that Liszt thematically transforms five more times. The most fanciful transformation places the theme in the left hand with expressive filigree of treble trills, thirty-second-note patterns, and a *leggierissimo* cadenza over it. The contrasting B section in A major (*Tempo di marcia, animato*), however, relies exclusively on staccato notes and includes an expanded version of the same introductory staccato material. Each of the two parts in this section repeats. He significantly transforms the first, a somewhat trivial march, from its initial statement. The second part begins each phrase with an ascending *rapido* scale that Liszt complicates even more from a technical standpoint by adding a similar, simultaneous descending pattern in the left hand. The piece returns to D♭ major for the A section and further transformation of legato material. At its close the B material returns briefly, using both themes to present a quick, uplifting coda. The first Ballade remains an outstanding, tightly organized work that makes a fine companion piece to the larger and more dramatic second Ballade.

Two other works have a connection with the first Ballade. Liszt based his Piano Piece no. 2 in A♭ (S 189a) on the same theme that he used for the main theme in his Ballade no. 1. Since he began his first Ballade in 1845, the material probably comes from that date although it is unknown whether Liszt extracted this excerpt into a separate piece or incorporated it into the Ballade. The brief work of only twenty-four measures with its repeated A section, nonetheless, is highly reminiscent of Chopin with its melodic thirds and calm, rocking accompaniment. Liszt bases the B section on material from the first section with an addition of only one measure in the theme to alter it slightly. He also drafted a Piano Piece in D♭ (S 189b) that is a brief forty-second work almost identical to a portion of the Ballade (mm. 12–29).

The Ballade no. 2 in B minor (S 171) was Liszt's next important large-scale piano work after the Sonata in B minor, and the two works were written "virtually at the same time."[58] James Parakilas claimed that Liszt's second Ballade is such a new conception of the genre that he questioned "how much it really belongs to the ballade genre at all."[59]

Like the Sonata, the second Ballade is in sonata form, although it departs from some of the usual practices.[60] The first-theme group of the exposition begins in B minor (mm. 1–35) and is restated exactly down a step to B♭ minor (mm. 35–69). Liszt's predilection for restatement in different keys troubled some critics, but this is a common and effective device available to nineteenth-century composers breaking away from the classical traditions. This part of the exposition states three distinct themes: (1) a single bass line over daring and restless chromatic scales; (2) at the *Lento assai* (m. 20) a theme based upon the same four-note ascending scale as the first theme that began in m. 3, although its character is restful and distinctive with its open spacing; (3) the charming theme that immediately follows the second and which returns for a more significant statement in the second-theme area.

After statements of the first-theme area, Liszt begins a somewhat martial and developmental transition *Allegro deciso* (m. 70) that uses the first two themes. Pesce and Gunther Wagner argued that the development section begins at this point, but this material is new to begin with and makes the exposition so short as to not be self-standing. I prefer to call this a transition section, after which Liszt moves to the second-theme area in D major (mm. 135–161)—the expected relative major relationship. Liszt states the fourth theme, a lyrical single-line melody with a distinctive turn figure followed by a gentle transformation of theme 3. Granted, this is a short second-theme area; because of its new theme and tonal stability, however, it seems to function well in this capacity.[61] The development opens with the chromatic scales and theme 1 of the exposition, modulating through various keys and breaking out into cascading interlocking octaves. Theme 2 serves as a retransition to the recapitulation that begins with theme 4 restated in tonic B major (m. 225). The second-theme area begins the recapitulation, followed by theme 3 in B major as well. A *cantabile* statement of theme 1 appears in a noble and surprising transformation. As a closing idea, theme 4, which began the recapitulation, returns and leads to the heroic and *grandioso* transformation of theme 1 in the coda. The rapid scales Liszt supplied as an option are much more effective than the bombastic chords he indicated for those same measures (mm. 292–299). Liszt also reconsidered the finale and settled for the more elegant, graceful, and softer close using theme 3. He contemplated two other endings: the first contained twenty-nine measures beginning and ending with loud interlocking octaves, and the second, a more developed closing, with a loud *Presto* section followed by bombastic chords and similar interlocking octaves.[62]

The second Ballade remains one of Liszt's most successful large-scale works and a major contribution to the Ballade genre. Parakilas's assessment of the B-minor Ballade on the history of the Ballade is worth noting:

This Ballade can be seen to have had an influence on the genre, and especially on a number of large-scale and serious piano *ballades* composed in its wake by students and disciples of Liszt. For the composers of these *ballades* . . . Liszt's Second Ballade seems to have opened up the genre to musical forms other than Chopin's and narrative types other than that of the ballad. While Liszt's work is in its way profoundly indebted to Chopin, its importance in the history of the *ballade* lies precisely in its distance from Chopin: it freed the genre from any particular tie to ballads, making the title *'ballade'* available for narrative piano pieces on many different models and, by the end of the nineteenth century, making *'ballade'* the preeminent name for programmatic piano pieces, as 'symphonic poem' was for programmatic orchestral works.[63]

Polonaises

Liszt published two Polonaises (S 223) in 1852 obviously modeled on the famous dances of Chopin. The first is rarely heard, but the second continues to be played and recorded. Liszt's first foray into this genre was to create an unusual, large work with some of the trimmings of the Chopinesque polonaise. Emotionally, however, his 1850 *Polonaise mélancolique* no. 1 in C minor is darker, less emphatic, and at times nearly amorphous compared to those of Chopin. What other Polonaise, for example, returns the main theme in 4/4 and as a *Quasi Cadenza improvisata* in the middle of the work? Liszt also creates an odd, almost surreal effect with his elaborate parallel sixths and thirds in this 4/4 polonaise (mm. 184–210). Furthermore, unlike Chopin, Liszt never repeats anything exactly for any length of time, varying each idea upon its reappearance. While the work is in C minor, its contrasting section beginning at m. 70 and returning at m. 215 appears in E♭ and C to lighten the overall somberness of the polonaise. All of this is not to say that there are not heroic, virtuosic moments. The *Allegro energico* section (mm. 147–181) meets the requirements of a distinguished polonaise, but immediately following it is the cadenza-like return of the A section. Just when the ending seems to be grandiose, Liszt undercuts it fifteen measures from the end with a brooding figure *mp* in the bass. The last eight bars of *fortissimo* seem strained and hollow after such a surprising interjection.

Liszt's 1851 Polonaise No. 2 in E major, *Allegro pomposo con brio,* begins with a four-measure, introductory fanfare that also provides transitions between themes in the work. The piece, not as tightly constructed as Chopin's models, displays a clear ABACA'B'A form with coda. The extended C section in A minor contains some developmental elements that give the overall form sonata-rondo inclinations. The transformation of the heroic and chordal *fortissimo* A theme into the soft, delicate filigree idea after the extended cadenza (m. 140), however, is quite remarkable and atypical of Chopin's style. Liszt's Polonaise seems to be more of a Polonaise-fantasie with its elaborate cadenzas and unusual transformation of themes.

Grosses Konzertsolo

Liszt composed his *Grosses Konzertsolo* (S 176) between 1849 and 1850 and dedicated it to his friend Adolf Henselt (1814–1889), the noted pianist and composer. Henselt evidently was unable to learn the work because of its difficulties, and Carl Tausig (1841–1871), in turn, became the first ever to play it.[64] Liszt also arranged it as his *Concerto pathétique* for two-pianos (S 258) and for piano and orchestra (S 365).

Liszt's Sonata in B minor has so overshadowed the *Grosses Konzertsolo* that it is intriguing to speculate how it would have been received without the Sonata in the picture. Surely, the *Grosses Konzertsolo* would then be considered one of Liszt's most important keyboard compositions. While pianists have recorded the

Sonata over two hundred times and perform it on a regular basis, the *Grosses Konzertsolo* seldom appears on either the concert stage or on recordings.

The similarities between the two works are conspicuous. Both use the same terminology for comparable events in the works: *Allegro energico, Andante sostenuto, Grandioso,* and *Stretta.* The second theme of the Sonata also appears regularly in the *Grosses Konzertsolo* and is used similarly, beginning in m. 46. The *Grandioso* themes are both heroic and short-lived with similar denouements. Both *Andante sostenuto* sections are lyrical, but more importantly, almost motionless in their beginnings. The original ending of the Sonata before Liszt revised it was also in the same mold as that of the *Grosses Konzertsolo.* Needless to say, both large-scale works require extraordinary virtuosity and display intriguing formal plans, working both as sonata form and as a multi-movement structure.

Unlike the Sonata in B minor, however, the *Grosses Konzertsolo* has twenty measures of optional passages and does not include the slow and soft beginning or ending that give the Sonata such profundity. The *Grosses Konzertsolo* only changes key signatures seven times, compared to sixteen in the Sonata. The slow movement arrives much sooner in the *Grosses Konzertsolo* (m. 145) compared to m. 330 in the Sonata, consequently providing the Sonata with a more epic plan. For all its virtuosity, Liszt wrote the Sonata entirely on two staves, whereas he has sixteen measures on four staves in the *Konzertsolo.* In his manuscript of the *Konzertsolo,* he evidently considered notation that made the section even have six staves. "As a matter of fact it cannot be established whether Liszt omitted the ossia for musical reason, or simply because he wanted to avoid having a 6-stave score."[65]

The form of the *Grosses Konzertsolo* is as intriguing as that of the Sonata and can be seen as a double-function form, having three distinct movements within a mirrored, arch-like sonata form (see Table 5.5). The work's twenty-nine-measure introduction, based upon motives w and x, is somewhat tonally unstable and unsettled because of its rhapsodic and developmental nature (see Example 5.9).

Example 5.9
Liszt, *Grosses Konzertsolo,* Themes and Motives
Motive w, mm. 1–3

Motive x, mm. 6–7

Motive y, mm. 46–49

Motive z, mm. 60–63

Theme 1, mm. 30–35

Theme 1a, mm. 102–108

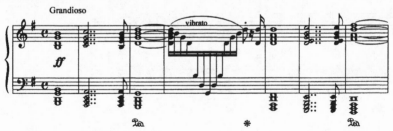

Theme 2, mm. 145–152

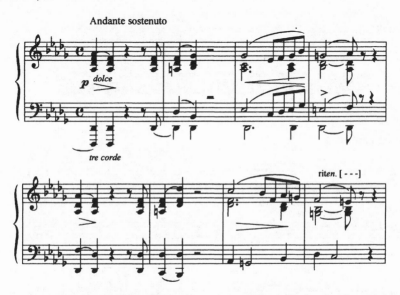

Other analysts see the first twenty-nine measures as the first-theme area, but this analysis creates an extraordinarily short first-theme area without a true transition or modulation to the second-theme area. Considering the first theme at m. 30 establishes the key of E minor for the first time, and this theme returns in various guises at key moments throughout the work. Furthermore, considering the modulation to G major and the *grandioso* statement of the second theme (m. 102) makes perfect sense from a key relationship, even if the second theme is based upon the first. I have labeled the second theme 1a to show its similarity to theme 1, but it is not exactly the same theme, and Liszt distinguishes between the two themes upon their returns as well, both their pitches and characteristics. After the contrasting development section or second movement (mm. 145–234), these two themes are mirrored exactly in the recapitulation or third movement (mm. 235–350) with theme 1a' returning in G major, rather than E minor. The original first theme returns in tonic E minor as the second theme at m. 328. The development section, which Liszt added later, also has a five-part structure that alternates its new theme 2 with the earlier motive y to create an inner five-part, arch-like structure. The coda begins, as did the development section, with a statement of theme 2 mutating to tonic major for the first time in the work. Formally, the *Grosses Konzertsolo* closes with an apotheosis based on the *grandioso* idea of theme 1a.

Table 5.5
Liszt, *Grosses Konzertsolo*

Measures	Motives	Key	Dynamics	Movements/Tempo indications
Introduction				**1st Movement**
1	mot. w, x	unstable	*f*	*Allegro energico*
Exposition [30–144]				
1st Theme Area				
30	Th. 1	E minor	*p*	*patetico, accentuato, assai il canto*
Transition				
46	mot. y		*f*	*molto rinforz. ed appassionato*
60	mot. z			*agitato*
74	mot. w, x		*f*	*molto energico e marcato*
2nd Theme Area				
102	Th. 1a	G major	*ff*	*Grandioso*
129	Th. 1a'		*pp*	*marcato ed espressivo assai il canto*
Development [145–234]				**2nd Movement**
145	Th. 2	D♭ major	*p*	*Andante sostenuto*
161	mot. y		*(p)*	*dolcissimo*
170	Th. 2	D♭ major	*(p)*	
189	mot. y		*p*	
200	Th. 2	D♭ major	*ff*	*a tempo con maestà*
Retransition				
217	mot. y		*(f)*	*Allegro agitato assai*
Recapitulation [235–350]				**3rd Movement**
1st Theme Area				
235	Th. 1a'	G major	*f*	*a tempo, più moderato*
Transition				
252	mot. z			*Più mosso – agitato*
266	mot. w, x			*molto energico e marcato*
320	mot. y			*pesante*
2nd Theme Area				
328	Th. 1'	E minor	*p*	*Andante, quasi marcia funebre*
Coda [351–418]				
351	Th. 2	E major	*p*	*sempre cantabile*
371	Th. 1a, mot. y	E major	*ff*	*Tempo giusto, moderato*
388	Th. 1a	E major	*ff*	*Allegro con bravura*

Scherzo und Marsch

Liszt composed his neglected *Scherzo und Marsch* (S 177) in 1851 and first entitled it *Wilde Jagd—Scherzo*. The Scherzo presents the ironic and sardonic quality of Liszt's diablerie better than many of his other works. As a whole it is extremely virtuosic with its fast tempos and repeated notes, scales patterns (particularly in the left hand), open octaves, and alternating chords. The mocking Scherzo begins *Allegro vivace, spiritoso* with a simultaneous 2/4 and 6/8 meter marking that constitutes the first half of the total work, followed by the March that enters *Allegro moderato, marziale* in B♭ major (m. 388). The Scherzo returns (m. 478), and the March reappears as well in the coda, prompting Kentner to write, "It is as if religion were doing battle with the Devil. In the end there is victory for religion, but not as unqualified as is usual in Liszt"[66] (see Example 5.10).

Example 5.10
Liszt, *Scherzo und Marsch*
Motive a

Motive b

Motive c

Motive d

Theme 1

Theme 2

Theme 3

Liszt continues his experiments with formal procedures in this work. Table 5.6 indicates that the work could be seen as large-scale rondo form (ABA'CA" coda). Others see it as an expanded sonata form with two developments and two recapitulations. A simpler way of viewing it would be as an expansion of the minuet and trio form with the A section up to the March and the March serving as the trio section equivalent. The return of the Scherzo (m. 478) would then be the da capo of this structure. However it is analyzed, it is apparent that during his early years in Weimar the major piano works that Liszt wrote were breaking new ground with their formal experimentation.

Table 5.6
Liszt, *Scherzo und Marsch*

Measures	Key	Themes	Sonata Form	Rondo Form
1	D minor	mot. a, b, c	Introduction	A
10	E♭ major	restatement of mot. a, b, c		
19	D minor	Th. 1	Theme 1 Area	
43		Trans. motive d (with mot. a)		
51		Th. 1'		
76		Transition mot. d, (mot. a)		
87	A minor	Th. 2 (based on mot. a)	Theme 2 Area	
104		Th. 2A		
116		Closing 1 Octaves (mot. c')		
128		Closing 2 (mot. c)		
154		based on intro. motives	Dev. 1	B
172		developing Th. 1		
200		Fugue – based on mot. c'		
276		Retransition		
292	D minor	Th. 1' (omits 14 mm.)	Recap. Theme 1 Area	A'
302		Trans. mot. d		
314	D minor	Th. 2	Theme 2 Area	
330		Th. 2A		
342		Closing 1 Octaves (mot. c')		
341		Closing 2 (mot. c)		
388	B♭ major	(A) Th. 3	Dev. 2 – March	C
420		mot. a		
423		(B) Contrast away from tonic		
450	B♭ major	(A) Th. 3 restatement		
478	D minor	Introduction	Recap. Theme 1 Area	A"
496	D minor	Th. 1		
521		Trans. mot. d (with mot. a)		
528		Th. 1"		
553		Trans. mot. d, (mot. a)		
567	D minor	March/Scherzo mot. c"	Coda	Coda
575	D major			

Sonata in B minor

Liszt's Sonata in B minor (S 178) stands without doubt as his greatest single compositional accomplishment. Of all his works the Sonata captures the imagination of performers, listeners, and scholars to an enormous degree. Scholars have written considerably about the Sonata, and performers have commercially recorded it more than any of his other monumental works. Liszt completed the Sonata on 2 February 1853 and dedicated it to Robert Schumann who had dedicated his magnificent Fantasy in C to Liszt in 1839.

Its history, nevertheless, has been problematic. It was greatly misunderstood by many, even though friends like Wagner, Hans von Bülow, and Arthur Friedheim greatly esteemed the Sonata. Johannes Brahms supposedly fell asleep while Liszt performed it for him, Clara Schumann detested it even though Liszt dedicated it to her husband, and professional critics were baffled by it. In April 1880, more than twenty-five years after it was written, Charles Bannelier proclaimed, "Liszt's Sonata . . . is more a fantasy, a framework for a symphonic poem, than a sonata. New things require new names; why keep the classic designation for a work whose liberty of form is driven to excess? No doubt there is an underlying programme; we were not given it, but we are not too sorry, because we would probably not have appreciated to a significantly greater extent the chaotic beauties which comprise a good half of this very long musical narrative."[67] Wagner, on the other hand, added on 5 April 1855:

[Karl] Klindworth has just played me your great Sonata! We spent the day alone together: he dined with me, and afterwards I made him play for me. My dearest Franz you, too, were here in the room with me—. The Sonata is beautiful beyond belief; great, lovable, deep and noble,—as sublime as you yourself. I was most profoundly moved by it, and all my troubles here in London have suddenly been forgotten. . . . It was wonderful! . . . many, many thanks for such infinite enjoyment![68]

Liszt presents his Sonata without any program or extra-musical thought whatsoever. Its dramatic and evocative nature has led numerous writers, nonetheless, to insist on creating their own programs for the work. Speculations range from the Faust legend, which was the first and most persistent, to Liszt's autobiography in music[69] or from the Fall of Man[70] to its representation of the divine and diabolical as seen in Milton's *Paradise Lost*.[71] Antal Boronkay in his edition of the Sonata in the NLE wrote:

Some of his [Liszt's] contemporaries (Wagner, Köhler) saw it as an artistic portrait of the composer himself. Ever since the work has often been called the 'Faust Sonata', mainly because of thematic similarities with the characters of the Faust symphony. On this basis the fugato of the Sonate [sic] suggests Mephisto, the cantando theme of the *Andante sostenuto* can be paralleled to the Gretchen movement, and the *Allegro energico* theme brings to mind the energetic figure of Faust.[72]

The list of performers and scholars who also think of the Sonata in Faustian terms include Claudio Arrau,[73] Alfred Brendel,[74] Serge Gut,[75] and Bertrand Ott[76] among others. Kenneth Hamilton confessed, "I feel compelled to admit, in blatant contradiction to everything I have written about the Sonata and programmaticism, that when playing this page [with the return of the *Grandioso* theme in tonic major] I cannot avoid thinking of the final defeat of Mephistopheles and the redemption of Faust."[77] Recently, David Wilde offered a Jungian interpretation,[78] and Charles Rosen threw his fanciful reading into the arena: "A literal and naïve interpretation is inescapable. The source of Liszt's Sonata is not only Beethoven and Schubert but Byron (above all the Byron of *Manfred* and *Childe Harold*), the popular Gothic novel, and the sentimental religious poetry of Lamartine. Even the saccharine religious art of the style known as Sainte-Sulpice plays a role in some of the most remarkable pages of the Sonata."[79]

The Sonata can readily be divided into three movements because the breaks at mm. 331 and 460 are too extreme in mood, character, and key to think otherwise, or into four movements as William Newman and Walker suggested, with the fourth movement coinciding with the recapitulation at m. 533. It first and foremost makes sense to think of it as three or four movements to be played without pause. Beethoven often combined movements in his sonatas and symphonies without break, and it seems likely that Liszt followed in this tradition without great difficulties. Nevertheless, the marvel of this thirty-minute long Sonata is that it also can be viewed in light of a larger sonata form. The one-movement scheme is so grand and the themes so intertwined, nonetheless, that it is troublesome for scholars to agree on how it functions as one movement.

Table 5.7 indicates the wide-ranging ideas writers have on the Sonata's form.[80] None of the authors listed completely agree on major sections. Collectively, they proposed at least three different scenarios for the first theme, development, recapitulation, and coda. The only area of complete agreement concerned the second-theme area (m. 105). Rey Longyear strongly argued for the fugue as recapitulation, but others viewed it either before or after this event. Longyear maintained that those who consider the fugato to function as a development section, forget "the numerous examples of the past where thematic and tonal recapitulations do not coincide. . . . [Alan] Walker calls the transition [m. 32] the 'first subject proper;' it is really a point of tonal departure in the exposition and the juncture with the home tonic in the recapitulation. Liszt was fully cognizant of the relationship of the closing theme to the 'hammer-blows' of the motive in the first theme."[81] Hamilton, on the other hand, declared, "Fugal development sections themselves are not unusual, Beethoven's op. 101 and 106 sonatas contain famous examples, but to begin one after an already extensive development, including an Andante movement, was unprecedented."[82] Similar difficulties arise in determining the beginning of the coda. Longyear and Sharon Winklhofer suggested the coda began at m. 650, but Searle, Watson, and Hamilton proposed the *Presto* (m. 673); Newman and Walker started the coda at the *Prestissimo* (m. 682). However critics see the work, Béla Bartók highly praised its structure: "But from the formal point of view it is absolutely perfect (a rare thing with Liszt) and a revolutionary innovation."[83]

Table 5.7[84]
Liszt, Sonata in B minor
One-Movement Sonata Form Comparison by Selected Authors

Measures	Section	Newman 1969	Longyear 1969, rev. 1973, 1988	Winklhofer 1978	Searle 1980	Walker 1989	Watson 1989	Hamilton 1996
1	*Lento assai*		Intro.		Expo. Intro.	Intro.	Intro.	Intro.
8	*Allegro energico*	Expo. 1st.	Expo. 1st.	Expo. 1st	1st	Expo. 1st	Expo. 1st	Expo. 1st
32		Trans.	Trans.	(tonal pres.) Trans.				Trans.
45								2nd
105	*Grandioso*	2nd	2nd	2nd	2nd	2nd		
153			Closing	Cadential Area	3rd			
171								
179			Dev.					
205	*Allegro energico*			Dev. 1 Trans.	Dev.		Dev.	Dev.
277								
331	*Andante sostenuto*	Dev.		Dev. 2		Dev.		
453				Recap.				
460	*Allegro energico*		Recap.					
531				(tonal pres.)	Recap.		Recap.	
533		Recap.	Trans.			Recap.		Recap. Sec. Dev.
555	*Più mosso*							2nd
600		2nd	2nd					
650	*Stretta quasi presto*		Coda	Coda 1				
673	*Presto*				Coda	Coda	Coda	
682	*Prestissimo*	Coda						Coda
711	*Andante sostenuto*			Coda 2				
729	*Allegro moderato*							
750	*Lento assai*							

Table 5.8
Liszt, Sonata in B minor

Measures	Key	Section	Themes	Tempo markings
1	G minor	Introduction	1	*Lento assai*
8	---		2, 3	*Allegro energico*
32	B minor	Expo: 1st-Theme Area	2, 3, 1	
105	D major	2nd-Theme Area	4, 2	*Grandioso*
123	---		2, 3	*dolce con grazia*
153	D major		3	*cantando espressivo*
179	---	Closing Area	2, 3	
205	---	Development	2, 1	*(Allegro energico)*
255	---		3	
277	---		2, 1	
297	---		4	
301	C♯ minor—		3	*Recitativo*
302	---		4	
306	F minor—		3	*Recitativo*
310	---		3, 2	
331	F♯ major		5	*Andante sostenuto*
349	A major		3, 2	
363	F♯ major		4	
376	G minor		4, 2	
397	F♯ major		5	
433	F♯ major		3	
453	F♯ major		1	
460	B♭ minor- E♭ major (fugue)		2, 3	*Allegro energico*
533	B minor	Recap: 1st-Theme Area	2, 3	
555	E♭ major, E minor		1	*Più mosso*
569	---		2, 1	
582	V/B (F pedal)		2, 3	
600	B major	2nd-Theme Area	4	
616	B major		3	*cantando espr. senza slentare*
642	---	Closing Area	2	
650	---		3	*Stretta (quasi presto)*
673	B minor-B major	Coda	1	*Presto*
682	B major		2	*Prestissimo*
700	B major		4	
711	B major		5	*Andante sostenuto*
729	B major		3, 2	*Allegro moderato*
750	B major		1	*Lento assai*

The opening, ponderous descent of the Sonata takes its point of departure from the despair found in his *Vallée d'Obermann,* setting the stage for an epic undertaking (see Example 5.11). This type of unadorned opening is a trademark of Liszt. Carl Dahlhaus explained that this "practice of starting primarily from abstract elements, from elementary structures of pitch and rhythm, rather than from themes and motives in which rhythm and pitch content 'coalesce,' is one of Liszt's ideas that made music history, if not in the nineteenth century, at least in our own."[85]

Example 5.11
Liszt, Sonata in B Minor, Theme 1, mm. 1–3

Liszt repeats this simple idea, altering three notes of the scale by half steps and consequently creating two augmented seconds so prevalent in Hungarian music. He transforms this theme numerous times throughout the work as well as the next two themes that follow it. At m. 8 the heroic, angular second theme appears in noble octaves, followed immediately by the sinister third theme rattling in the lower register of the keyboard (see Examples 5.12 and 5.13).

Example 5.12
Liszt, Sonata in B Minor, Theme 2, mm. 8–11

Example 5.13
Liszt, Sonata in B Minor, Theme 3, mm. 13–15

No substantial new themes appear until the fourth *grandioso* theme resounds with its arrival of D major (see Example 5.14).

Example 5.14
Liszt, Sonata in B Minor, Theme 4, mm. 105–110

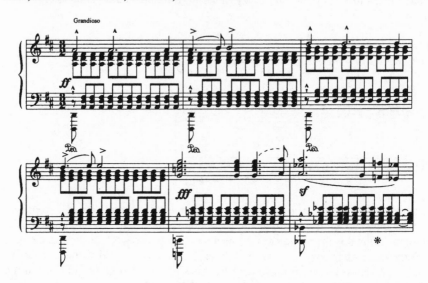

These four themes unify the Sonata more tightly than any other of this length and in the remaining 80 percent of the Sonata to follow, the composer adds only one additional theme, the exquisite *Andante sostenuto* theme in F♯ major (see Example 5.15).

Example 5.15
Liszt, Sonata in B Minor, Theme 5, mm. 329–338

Weaving in and out among these five themes, Liszt creates a mosaic of enigmatic beauty through thematic combinations, diminution, augmentation, fragmentation, register exchanges, rhythmic variation, and contrapuntal ingenuity. Only 22 measures out of 760 repeat exactly; all the rest is transformed, sometimes so elusively that it is nearly beyond recognition even after several hearings. Liszt develops the themes almost at once, combining the second and third themes for the beginning of the exposition and the arrival of B minor at m. 32. He turns the *Allegro energico* theme into a virtual octave etude with imitation between right and left hands (mm. 55–81) before sequencing the first theme and moving it from the deep bass to the treble and back. He continues to develop the second-theme area after the *grandioso* D-major theme, transforming the character of both the second (*dolce con grazia*) and third (*cantando espressivo*) themes by subduing their determined and invigorating initial statements through changes of texture, augmentation, and dynamics.

Long before the development section starts at the *Allegro energico* (m. 205), Liszt, like Beethoven, has been actively employing developmental strategies. Nevertheless, the development—one of the longest in the nineteenth century—lasts 327 measures or approximately 43 percent of the Sonata, compared to only 204 measures for the exposition and 227 for the recapitulation and coda. Liszt develops each of the four themes through a series of brilliant octaves, chromatic scales, thrilling leaps, and dazzling arpeggios. Most curious is the stripped-down version of theme four (m. 297) presented in a manner of almost barbaric primitivism. Its fragmented version modulates after an *appassionato* recitative, but its transformation has intrigued Szász to suggest it represents the crucifixion of Christ.[86]

The major reason for the expansion of the development section is the addition of the fifth theme in F♯ major (m. 331). In the Faustian explanation, this theme represents Gretchen or in Merrick's interpretation it represents Christ.[87] While the *Andante sostenuto* serves as a second movement as well as part of the development section, it continues to develop the other themes, modulating several times in the process. After the glorious return of the fifth theme *fff* (m. 395), Liszt establishes a magical repose in the midst of this bustling excitement (mm. 415–459). The opening theme returning *ppp* (m. 453) heralds an engaging fugue based on the second and third themes—or what some scholars see as the third movement, others the recapitulation, and others a continuation of the development. Winklhofer argued that the recapitulation begins at m. 453 with the return of the opening theme, even though it is stated a minor second lower. The fugue itself (which Bartók wrote was "flashing with the very sparks of hell"[88]) is in B♭ minor, also a minor second lower than the expected tonic. Even though something momentous is occurring with the beginning of the fugue, the "wrong" or "false" key and the spectral nature of the three-voice fugue are too unsettling to establish a strong feeling of recapitulation. It is only after this final developmental wizardry that Liszt presents the home key and material precisely as we heard it before (m. 533). Not only have we arrived at B minor, the ensuing twenty-two measures are the only ones that repeat literally in the entire work. From this point, the recapitulation follows the general outline of the exposition quite closely, before the coda begins with the *Presto* octaves (m. 673). These precipitous octaves based upon the first two themes of the Sonata move from *Presto* to *Prestissimo* and lead to the compelling restatement in triplets of the *grandioso* theme in tonic major. Finally, Liszt delivers the earthshaking apotheosis at m. 710 that a work of this length demands. The long silence marked by several rests and a fermata is necessary to deal emotionally with the nostalgic reminiscences that float through the remainder of the coda. Even though we have already heard the material many times before, this reaffirmation provides the supreme enchantment of the Sonata with the most sublime forty-nine measures Liszt penned. He recalls the fifth theme immediately after the rest, and then the first three themes return in the opposite order that they first appeared. The *Lento assai* descending scale repeats exactly this time, except for its deletion of the octaves, and each time ends, unlike its initial appearance, with an augmented second. A series of five treble chords look upward for the conclusion of the work in B major. When the last note fades away (a full eighth note, not a staccato note as some performers play), the reverent silence indicated by the fermata over the rest is essential to the performance of the work. Certainly by reconsidering this coda, Liszt reached some degree of acceptance and peace with the tumultuous despair and angst that began the work. The Sonata would not have earned the respect it has today had Liszt not changed the ending. His original thought, as noble as it was, would have been a *grandioso* overkill that could never have competed with this beatific ending.[89]

Rhapsodie espagnole

In 1858 Liszt composed his famous *Rhapsodie espagnole: Folies d'Espagne et Jota aragonesa* (S 254)—the last work influenced by his travels in Spain. It is his greatest evocation of Spanish music long before the French impressionists turned their attention to that exotic country. Based on two Spanish themes, the Rhapsody begins *Lento a fortissimo* with heavy chords, dotted rhythms, roaring tremolos, and brilliant arpeggio flourishes that develop into an elaborate cadenza, nearly a minute long in performance. So concerto-like in its opening, it is easily understood why Busoni made a transcription of it for piano and orchestra. After this sparkling cadenza, the *Andante moderato* presents the first Spanish theme, *Folies d'Espagne* (m. 12), that consists of an eight-bar, unaccompanied tune with its grace-notes and thirty-second-note pungent thrusts stated in the bass. The variations begin immediately with a jagged, staccato version that leads to a descending, legato theme (m. 44). The variations take on a march-like pattern (even though remaining in triple meter), followed by an alternating chromatic passage that serves as a transitional interlude. The brilliant variation with chordal leaps follows and is reinforced with open octaves in each hand, speeding to the *Allegro animato* with its martial rhythm and ascending treble scales. These scales cleverly lead into the second theme, *Jota aragonesa* (m. 136)—a sparkling, delicate tune in D major played *pianissimo* in the upper register of the keyboard. The *Jota aragonesa* continues with its sensuous graceful thirds and light appoggiaturas before a couple of brilliant variations leads to a lyrical section, *Un poco meno Allegro* (m. 312). The texture thins dramatically and a stillness falls over the piece for a brief respite. A splendid new theme in thirds emerges in F major (m. 337), and treble trills and delicate filigree over the new theme lead to a playful variation of the beginning *Jota* theme that runs away into a lengthy, bravura transition. A strong retransition (m. 416) and brilliant octaves lead eventually to a variation of the new theme, *Sempre presto e ff* (m. 540). Liszt is only warming up at this point. He proceeds to have a scherzando-like variation in thirds, followed by treacherous leaps that returns to the *Non troppo allegro* opening theme (m. 635). The work concludes with a final statement of the new theme closing in D major.

MISCELLANEOUS WORKS

Berceuse

Liszt drafted the first version of his *Berceuse* (S 174) in 1854 for a collection to honor the marriage of the Austrian empress Elisabeth. In 1854 he wrote to Louis Köhler that "perhaps the continuous pedal D♭ will amuse you. The thing ought properly to be played in an American rocking-chair with a Nargileh for accompaniment, in *tempo comodissimo con sentimento*, so that the player may, willy-nilly, give himself up to a dreamy condition, rocked by the regular movement of the *chair-rhythm*."[90] Except for the last ten measures, it appears throughout on three staves. While both versions share a similar state of contemplation, the first is reserved and bare compared to the later virtuoso version. As a meditative work, this version surpasses the revision for its peacefulness and passive quality; nothing appears forced or contrived. Even though the pieces are obviously related, they should also be considered distinct and separate works because of the extent of the elaboration in the second.

Liszt published the second version of his *Berceuse* in 1865. In a letter to Eduard Liszt on 22 May 1863, he described returning to the idea of the *Berceuse*: "Weariness or something of the sort carried my thoughts back to my "*Berceuse*." Various other *Berceuses* rose up in my dreams. Do you care to join my dreams? It shall not cost you any trouble; without touching the keyboard yourself, you will only need to rock yourself in the sentiments that hover over them."[91] More than any other work that Liszt ever wrote, this second version is a daydream—vague, static, delicately mercurial with more *pianissimo* treble elaboration per measure than any of his other works. The slow and lengthy introduction seems to go nowhere—in fact, it almost never seems to begin. When the first theme starts in D♭ major (m. 30), the momentum halts several times with fermatas. As ephemeral as the work is, it also requires amazing technique and control to play the thirty-second-note passages in thirds and sixths, and at the same time let the music float in its quasi-improvisatory way. For the first *ppp* cadenza supposedly "Liszt played . . . [it] and the following *pp* runs 'like a soundless shadow' with the inner part of the fingertips, with a completely relaxed hand."[92] With its *Andante* tempo and more than a hundred measures, this work seems nebulous and shadow-like. Except for *mf* (m. 82) and *crescendo* (m. 84) markings, the entire piece nearly whispers with its fourteen *pp* and seven *ppp* indications in addition to terms such as *perdendo* and *dolcissimo*. While Liszt certainly pays tribute to Chopin with a piece similar to his, Liszt, as he often does, takes the idea to the extreme and creates an extraordinary piece for its time.

Dances

Liszt composed some major dance pieces during the Weimar years, including waltzes and mazurkas, as well as the larger polonaises already examined. The latest research indicates that Liszt originally composed *Der Tanz in der Dorfschenke* (*Mephisto Waltz* no. 1, S 514) for piano and that it is not a transcription of the second part of his *Zwei Episoden aus Lenaus Faust: Der Tanz in der Dorfschenke* for orchestra.[93] The *Mephisto Waltz* no. 1 dates sometime between 1856 and 1861 and remains one of his best-known works. Liszt printed excerpts from Lenau's *Faust* to specify the details of the work's program, but the waltz succeeds on its own with imaginative virtuosic writing for the piano. Its programmatic nature, though, is explicit following the text with Mephistopheles and Faust attending the wedding festivities. Mephistopheles takes the fiddle and plays wildly (prompting Liszt's introduction), and Faust dances his brunette out of doors to seduce her (the sensuous middle section) at which Mephistopheles laughs mockingly (m. 452). Even the nightingale of the poem makes an appearance at m. 835 (*Ritenuto il tempo*) before the lovers drown in the sea of ecstasy.

The Waltz begins with its famous "tuning" fifths repeated and climaxing with its main theme at m. 111 in A major. This theme repeats at m. 205 and serves as a closing theme at m. 295. The sensuous, seductive middle section begins in Db major at m. 339 with its suggestive tritones. New material representing Mephistopheles' laughter breaks up this scene at the *Presto* (m. 452). The main theme returns at the *Più mosso* at m. 644 (but not in the tonic key) and again at m. 692. A demonic coda begins at m. 737 with *Presto* octaves and treacherous right-hand-octave leaps before breaking into a flashy cadenza. After the nightingale appears, a quick and brutal crescendo builds to a flurry of interlocking octaves to close the dance.

The NLE published two insertions that lengthen the Waltz by over 150 measures for the first time in 1982.[94] These measures prolong the transition or closing idea before the Db-major section enters at m. 339. The most extensive addition is another transformation of the Db theme where Liszt continues the mood established at the beginning of the section. He also has a considerable number of alternative passages for the performer to choose from as well. In 1904 Busoni made his own piano transcription based on Liszt's orchestral work.

The next most significant Waltz from this period is Liszt's *Valse impromptu* (S 213), based on an earlier *Petite Valse favorite* (S 212). A wonderful, elegant waltz in Ab major, the *Valse impromptu* begins *Vivace scherzando* with a thirteen-measure introduction and *leggierissimo* treble cadenza. The main theme contains a lively triplet figure on the downbeat of each measure whereas the contrasting and statelier second theme consists of slower note values. Each section repeats, creating a tight ABAB form with coda, which alternates both themes in a clever and enticing way. Though not particularly virtuosic, the *Valse* contains some challenging right-hand leaps and rapid cadenza-like passages. Liszt performed this waltz in his concerts in St. Petersburg in 1842.

Liszt's other waltzes from this time were published as a set. His *Trois caprices-valses* (S 214), composed between 1850 and 1852, are each reworkings from earlier pieces. The first Caprice, *Valse de bravoure* taken from his 1836 *Grande valse di bravura* (S 209), is of the splendid, virtuoso mien with its rapid and brilliant trills, octaves, and double-note patterns (thirds and sixths in particular). Unlike the second Caprice that was a radical revision of the earlier Waltz it was based upon, this bravura Caprice simplifies the earlier, extraordinarily challenging Waltz with its wide leaps and double thirds. This Waltz contains elements that lend themselves to sonata form ideas, although the development section consists only of themes from the second-theme area. The recapitulation is truncated, and the fourth theme first stated at m. 105 becomes a transformed theme that begins the development and coda.

The second Caprice (S 214/2) reworks the earlier *Valse mélancolique* (S 210) from 1839. Liszt retains the two main themes but greatly alters the entire constitution of the earlier work. The tempo markings change from *Allegretto* to *Andantino espressivo,* and a series of soft arpeggios that establish the pensive tone of the so-called Waltz replace the rather flamboyant introduction. At m. 40 (*Quasi andante*) the first semblance of a waltz begins. This portion is exactly the same as the earlier version, but the section ends differently with a transition of introductory arpeggios that leads to the second waltz idea. Liszt delays the downbeat from the first waltz, giving it a more syncopated lilt, and adds more elaborate ornamentation from the earlier version. He abbreviates and subdues the climatic *Più mosso* section from the first version and a fanciful, *pianissimo* cadenza leads to the melancholy return of the opening waltz theme. The Caprice closes with the arpeggios of the introduction and a poignant cadence to tonic.

Liszt's third Caprice (S 214/3) comes from his 1842 *Valse a capriccio sur deux motifs de Lucia et Parisina* (S 401), which incorporates two themes from Donizetti's operas. The lengthy Waltz opens with a fast *Allegro vivace* introduction that leads to the Lucia motive starting at the *Meno allegro.* The first half is devoted to this theme. A couple of delicate, *leggierissimo* cadenzas hover amidst Donizetti's sensuous theme. At the *Allegro appassionato* the second theme appears in robust and cheerful octaves. A variation of the Lucia theme interrupts this outburst before returning to the second theme (*Vivace*) to close. The Waltz is well conceived and among his most thrilling pieces in waltz form.

Liszt's *Mazurka brillante* (S 221) dates from 1850 and begins with a diatonic, eight-measure flourish with its characteristic dotted rhythms and third-beat accents. The opening E-major A section has a pleasing eight-measure melody first stated in sixths and then restated *forte* in octaves with an inner third. The B section begins at m. 24 with a variation of the opening theme, starting with its quintuplet left-hand figure in G♯ major. The A theme returns varied after a brief *Cadenza ad libitum* in the ossia. Liszt changes the mood at the F-major *Più moto* section with its ascending thirds. Its contrasting D section with parallel sixths

(*Vivamente con grazia*) gives the piece a particular élan. At the *a tempo* an exact restatement of the first ABA section occurs before leading to a virtuosic variation of the C and D themes at the *Più moto* that closes the dance.

Between 1838 and 1841 Liszt composed three works with "galop" in their titles. The first is probably his clever *Grand galop chromatique* (S 219), dating from around 1838. One of his war-horses during his touring days,[95] it lasts only four minutes, but its energy never wavers, nor does the *Presto* tempo ever falter. The joyous, *fortissimo animato* is a fitting coda to a grand exercise in non-serious, fun-loving, pianistic acrobatics. Liszt also published a simplified version shortly after in 1840 or 1841. The second slight *Galop de bal* (S 220) lasts less than a minute and does not require the virtuosity of the first at all. Liszt composed his last original *Galop* in A minor (S 218) in 1846. For a galop it is an extremely long work, nearly twice as long as the *Grand galop chromatique* or eight times as long as his *Galop de bal*. Clearly Liszt has enough time to illustrate his keyboard pyrotechnics and that he does with wide leaps, bravura octaves, trills, and three-hand effects. The quirky and slightly winding introduction, nonetheless, appropriately sets the stage for the strange galop theme that, Mephisto-like, descends chromatically into a parody of itself. Liszt relishes its return throughout the work. The last third of the piece mutates to A major where it ends with an array of octaves.

During this period of time Liszt also composed numerous little waltzes and "feuilles d'album" which he dedicated to friends. He composed his *Feuilles d'album* in A♭ (S 165) in 1844 and dedicated it to Gustave Dubousquet. In three parts opening *Allegro vivace* with a loud nine-bar introduction, the first theme contains some syncopation with its entry on the second beat and is highly diatonic. The repeated second section consists of a melody in staccato octaves for the most part. The following third section is softer and more legato. Liszt varies the first two themes upon their return to create an ABCA'B' form with a brief introduction and coda. His 1841 *Albumblatt in walzerform* (S 166)—not published until 1908—is less than a minute long with its melody entirely in open octaves ending on a *ff* A-major chord. Liszt also composed a brief *Ländler* in A♭ (S 211) in 1843. A delightful waltz, with regular repeated four-bar phrases in an ABA form, it lasts less than a minute and makes an elegant encore with its delicate, non-virtuosic manner.

Marches

Liszt produced five independent marches for piano between 1848 and 1861, often arranging them for piano four-hand and/or orchestra as well. The most successful of these ceremonial works are the *Festmarsch zur Säkularfeier von Goethes Geburtstag* (S 227) written in 1849 (revised in 1859) and the *Zweite Festmarsch nach Motiven von E Hz S-C-G* (S 522) on motives of Ernst II, Duke of Sachsen-Coburg-Gotha composed between 1858 and 1859. Following a twenty-six-measure introduction, the 1859 version of the *Festmarsch zur Säkularfeier von Goethes Geburtstag* begins a distinguished march theme that is somewhat reminiscent of Wagner's early style. The more heroic parts of the section come only towards its close before breaking out, surprisingly for a march, into a cadenza. The middle section *dolce grazioso* is not in a march meter at all, but in 3/2 and the style, still reminiscent of Wagner, is noble and at times sublime. It rises to a short outburst near the end of the section and returns to the opening march theme. Liszt tacks on an extensive coda that, unfortunately, adds little to the work with its *fortissimo* interlocking octaves, tremolos, and dotted chords ending triumphantly in E♭ major. The *Zweite Festmarsch* begins *Allegro pomposo e deciso* in the lowest register of the keyboard and builds to a heroic entry for the D-major march. With this clever entrance, the march proceeds strongly with slight reference to earlier Chopin polonaises. The pleasant and almost cheerful theme of the trio section begins in B♭ major, and Liszt subjects it to elaborate and clever ornamentation on its restatement, creating his most imaginative trio section in his marches and, with this virtuosity, elevating the work beyond the typical formulaic marches. The A section returns, more eminently than before with Liszt pulling out further technical tricks of the trade.

Of Liszt's remaining marches from this period, his C-major *Huldigungsmarsch* (S 228), composed in 1853 for the inauguration of Prince Carl Alexander, also succeeds as a festive, celebratory march. Liszt revised the straightforward ABA march in 1857 and later incorporated the quieter middle section in B major into his *Weimars Volkslied*. The most unusual feature is its extensive passage of dotted rhythms from mm. 32 to 46. On the other hand, his *Vom Fels zum Meer!: Deutscher Siegesmarsch* (S 229) in E♭ major, composed between 1853 and 1856, is a delightful work that does not particularly sound like his other music. It is joyful throughout and contains humorous moments, particularly in the trio section with its light, staccato accompaniment, echo effects (mm. 54–67), and disguised return of the trio theme at m. 92. A long coda concludes the light-hearted, almost tongue-in-cheek march. The earliest and least significant march is his *Marche héroïque* (S 510) that dates from around 1848 but remained unpublished in his lifetime. The first section of the work derives from his choral work *Arbeiterchor*, but Liszt created a new middle section for his march. The G-major *Più moderato* theme is warm and graceful—almost too beautiful for the trio of a march! The flippant nature in much of the work flaws this non-heroic march, leading to moments of unintentional humor.

TRANSCRIPTIONS

From 1835 to 1861 Liszt transcribed numerous works of his own and major works of others. In addition to his opera transcriptions and paraphrases discussed in Chapter 7, Liszt also arranged many vocal and instrumental pieces for piano solo. While the paraphrases illustrate his own imaginative individuality, he also took great pains to make literal transcriptions of works that he admired. He explained to Adolphe Pictet in September 1837:

I applied myself as scrupulously [in transcribing Berlioz's *Symphonie fantastique* for piano solo] as if I were translating a sacred text to transferring, not only the symphony's musical framework, but also its detailed effects and the multiplicity of its instrumental and rhythmic combinations to the piano. . . . I called my work a *partition de piano* [piano score] in order to make clear my intention of following the orchestra step by step and of giving it no special treatment beyond the mass and variety of its sound.[96]

In the 1830s Liszt arranged Berlioz's *Symphonie fantastique* (S 470), *Marche des pélerins de la Sinfonie Harold en Italie* (S 473), *Ouverture du Roi Lear* (S 474), and *Ouverture des Francs-Juges* (S 471), and in 1860 returned with his *Danse des Sylphes de La damnation de Faust* (S 475). He made the first arrangements of three of Beethoven's symphonies (nos. 5–7) (S 464) and the *Marche funèbre* movement from the third (S 464/3) in 1837, *Capriccio alla turca sur des motifs de Beethoven (Ruines d'Athènes)* (S 388) in 1846, and the *Fantasie über Beethovens Ruinen von Athen* (S 389) in 1852. These transcriptions effectively transform the piano into an orchestra of one capable of unheard-of-before pianistic effects. In his 1865 publication of the complete Beethoven symphonies, Liszt confessed, "My aim has been attained if I stand on a level with the intelligent engraver, the conscientious translator, who comprehend the spirit of a work and thus contribute to the knowledge of the great masters and to the formation of the sense for the beautiful."[97]

Liszt took on smaller works as well. He arranged a couple of the most famous chamber pieces from the age, Beethoven's Septet, op. 20 (S 465) in 1840 and Hummel's Septet (S 493) in 1848. His 1850–1851 transcription of Ferdinand David's twenty-four short pieces for violin and piano known as *Bunte Reihe* (S 484) are utterly enchanting. Arranged in major and minor keys, these pieces move from C major by half steps to B minor like Bach's Preludes and Fugues. Each piece has an individual title (e.g., Scherzo, *Erinnerung*, and Mazurka) and is clear in structure and musical elaboration. Some of Liszt's most literal transcriptions can be seen in Bach's *Sechs Präludien und Fugen für die Orgel* (S 462) that he made between 1842 and 1850.

His transcriptions of choral music include Mendelssohn's *Wasserfahrt und Der Jäger Abschied* (S 548) and Weber's *Leyer und Schwert* (S 452) in 1848. He also composed the *Deux transcriptions d'après Rossini* (S 553) of which the first *Air du Stabat mater* is based on an aria and the second, *La charité*, a sacred chorus. He also made piano arrangements of three of his own pieces for male chorus and published them as *Geharnischte Lieder* (S 511) in 1861. The first (*Vor der Schlacht*) and last (*Es Rufet Gott uns mahnend*) are similar in character and, though titled individually, were originally different settings of the same war-like poem. In E major *Vor der Schlacht* begins with heroic flourishes, followed by a martial repeated figure. *Es Rufet Gott uns mahnend* begins in C major (*Marziale*), shifts to A major at m. 13 for its main theme, and modulates immediately back to C. For six measures (mm. 46–51) it shifts to D♭ major before quickly returning to C for the close, remaining basically loud throughout. The piece that separates these two, *Nicht Gezagt,* opens in a dark, brooding way. At the *Un poco più mosso* the rolling arpeggio figures lead to a passionate outcry with *fortissimo* repeated chords. Immediately, however, the opening motive returns, and the piece ends quietly in A♭ major.

Liszt transcribed over 140 songs of other composers and twenty-one of his own for piano solo. He had transcribed all but eighteen of these songs before 1861, including all his transcriptions of Beethoven, Chopin (S 480), Dessauer (S 485), Franz (S 488 and 489), Mendelssohn (S 547), Mercadante (S 411), Rossini (S 424), and Schubert. His transcriptions of fifty-two Schubert songs are the most of any one composer, but Liszt also arranged eighteen songs by Beethoven, including the six songs that constitute *An die ferne Geliebte* (S 469). His earliest Schubert transcription, *Die Rose* (S 556), dates from 1833 and his last, the second version of *Die Forelle* (S 564) and his *Müllerlieder* (S 565), were composed in 1846. Most important, perhaps, are his selections from *Schwanengesang* (S 560) and *Winterreise* (S 561), both arranged between 1838 and 1839. During his German tours between 1840 and 1845, Liszt performed Schubert's *Erlkönig* sixty-five times (more than any of his operatic paraphrases).[98] While most of his Schumann transcriptions appeared after 1861, Liszt composed *Zwei Lieder* (S 567) in 1861 and his famous *Liebeslied (Widmung)* (S 566) sometime between 1846 and the 1860s.

In addition to his *Liebesträume* arrangements (S 541) and *Petrarch Sonnets* that are well known as piano pieces in their own right, Liszt arranged fifteen of his other songs, including two versions of his *Die Loreley* (S 532)—the second of which he composed in 1861. He published two others, *Il m'aimait tant!* (S 533) and *Ich liebe dich* (S 542a), independently. In 1843 and 1847 he arranged the remaining twelve in two volumes entitled *Buch der Lieder* (S 531 and 535–540), although the second was never published in his lifetime. The six arrangements in the 1843 *Buch der Lieder* follow the songs closely, but Liszt occasionally adds a flourish here or there, changes registers, or doubles vocal lines. All of these arrangements are of the first version of songs that he later revised. The last of the six, *Angiolin dal biondo crin*, strays further from its original with intriguing variations to the modified strophic song. In some ways the imaginative piano writing improves the song overall. The most successful transcription is the second, *Am Rhein*, with its continual river accompaniment. The only song Liszt transcribed for piano in its revised form was *Die Loreley*. This second version corresponds closely to the song except for a brief cadenza at mm. 21–22 and a much more elaborate one followed by a different ending at mm. 122–135. Unlike the first version, he places a running text in the score itself instead of just printing the text at the beginning of the piece as he did in the *Buch der Lieder*. The second *Buch der Lieder* contains six of Liszt's French settings of Hugo. Liszt later revised the first four of these songs and consequently the transcriptions are different from the songs as we know them today. These transcriptions, nevertheless, are engaging and *Oh! quand je dors* and *Comment, disaient-ils*, in particular, should be better known. The last transcription, *Gastibelza*, is the most brilliant pianistically-speaking of the set and a little-known contribution to Liszt's virtuosic repertory.

Liszt's music up to and through his Weimar period displays outstanding and traditional romantic values. Not long after leaving Weimar Liszt radically changed his compositional style. In the following years Liszt would, for the most part, embrace the austere instead of the popular, the divine instead of the worldly, and the despondent instead of the hopeful. As in late Beethoven Liszt's last years produced treasures of the most pensive and individualistic kind far out of sync with his contemporaries and his era.

NOTES

1. Franz Liszt, *An Artist's Journey: Lettres d'un bachelier ès musique 1835–1841*, trans. and annotated Charles Suttoni (Chicago: The University of Chicago Press, 1989), 47.

2. Ibid., 48.

3. Claude Debussy, *Monsieur Croche the Dilettante Hater*, trans. B. N. Langdon Davies (New York: Viking, 1928), reprinted in *Three Classics in the Aesthetic of Music* (New York: Dover, 1962), 40.

4. Liszt was an avid reader throughout his life and well-versed in the literature of his day. See Arnold, "Franz Liszt: the Reader, the Intellectual, the Musician," in *Analecta Lisztiana I: Liszt and His World*, ed. Michael Saffle. Franz Liszt Studies Series no. 5. (Stuyvesant, NY: Pendragon, 1998), 37–60.

5. Richard Hudson, *Stolen Time: The History of Tempo Rubato* (Oxford and New York: Clarendon Press, 1994), 254.

6. NLE i/6: x.

7. Andrew Fowler, "Franz Liszt's *Années de Pèlerinage* as Megacycle," *JALS* 40 (July-December 1996): 127.

8. Humphrey Searle, *The Music of Liszt*, 2d rev. ed. (New York: Dover, 1966), 29.

9. *Letters of Franz Liszt*, ed. La Mara [Marie Lipsius], trans. Constance Bache (New York: Greenwood Press, 1969), 1:130.

10. In säuselnder Kühle / Beginnen die Spiele / Der jungen Natur.

11. Quoted in Adrian Williams, *Portrait of Liszt: By Himself and His Contemporaries* (Oxford: Clarendon Press, 1990), 68.

12. Later in life Liszt returned to *Vallée d'Obermann*, adapting it on three occasions for violin, cello, and piano, indicating his continued interest in this early work. See Chapter 9.

13. Fowler, "Motive and Program in Liszt's *Vallée d'Obermann*," *JALS* 29 (January-June 1991): 11.

14. Searle, *The Music of Liszt*, 27.

15. The NLE prints an eight-measure addition for the ending of the piece that Liszt evidently wrote for Giovanni Sgambati in 1863.

16. See Karen Wilson, "A Historical Study and Stylistic Analysis of Franz Liszt's *Années de pèlerinage*" (Ph.D. diss., University of North Carolina, 1977), and Dolores Pesce, "Expressive Resonance in Liszt's Piano Music," in *Nineteenth-Century Piano Music*, ed. R. Larry Todd (New York: Schirmer, 1990), 355–411.

17. Pesce, "Expressive Resonance in Liszt's Piano Music," 360–361.

18. Joan Backus, "Liszt's *Sposalizio*: A Study in Musical Perspective," *19th-Century Music* 12/2 (Fall 1998): 175.

19. Ibid., 181.

20. Derek Watson, *Liszt* (New York: Schirmer, 1989), 246.

21. The traditional date has been 1837. For the compositional history of the *Dante Sonata*, see Sharon Winklhofer, "Liszt, Marie d'Agoult, and the Dante Sonata," *19th-Century Music* 1/1 (July 1977): 15–32.

22. See William S. Newman, *The Sonata Since Beethoven* (Chapel Hill: University of North Carolina Press, 1969), 362–363 for a literal translation of the poem.

23. See Searle, *The Music of Liszt*, 32.

24. See Alan Walker, *Franz Liszt: The Weimar Years 1848–1861* (New York; Knopf, 1989), 2:154, n. 49. Walker wrote that "it cannot be an accident that so much of his 'divine' or 'beatific' music unfolds in the key of F-sharp major."

25. Thomas Mastroianni, "The Italian Aspect of Franz Liszt," *JALS* 16 (December 1984): 14.

26. See Franz Liszt, *Harmonies Poétiques et Religieuses* (1847 Version), ed. Albert Brussee. 2 vols. (Huizen, Holland: B.V. Muziekuitgeverij XYZ, 1997). Brussee also published these findings in the *JALS* 44 (Fall 1998): 1–23. Leslie Howard recorded the 1847 cycle in 1996. See Liszt, *Litanies de Marie* ("Music intended for a first cycle of *Harmonies poétiques et religieuses*"). The Complete Music for Solo Piano 47 (Hyperion, CDA67187 [1997]).

27. Liszt, *Harmonies Poétiques et Religieuses*, ed. Brussee, 1:ix.

28. Ibid., 1:39.

29. For Liszt's reaction to war and revolution in his time, see Arnold, "Liszt and the Music of Revolution and War," in *Analecta Lisztiana II: New Light on Liszt and His Music*, ed. Saffle. Franz Liszt Studies Series no. 6 (Stuyvesant, NY: Pendragon, 1997), 225–238.

30. Searle, *The Music of Liszt*, 55.

31. Louis Kentner, "Solo Piano Music (1827–1861)," in *Franz Liszt: The Man and his Music*, ed. Alan Walker (New York: Taplinger, 1970), 129.

32. Pesce, "Expressive Resonance in Liszt's Piano Music," 366.

33. Ibid., 366.

34. See Searle, *The Music of Liszt*, 55.

35. See Kentner, "Solo Piano Music," 131.

36. Rena Charnin Mueller, "Liszt's 'Tasso' Sketchbook: Studies in Sources and Revisions" (Ph.D. diss., New York University, 1986), 267.

37. David E. Gifford, "Religious Elements Implicit and Explicit in the Solo Piano Works of Franz Liszt" (D.M.A. diss., University of Missouri-Kansas City, 1984), 46.

38. Howard recorded one of these: *Sprünge mit der Tremolo-Begleitung*, no. 62 on Liszt, *The Complete Paganini Études*. The Complete Works for Solo Piano 48 (Hyperion CDA67193 [1998]).

39. Liszt, *Complete Etudes for Solo Piano*, ed. Ferruccio Busoni, Series I: Including the Transcendental Etudes (Leipzig; Breitkopf & Härtel, 1910–1911; Reprint. New York: Dover, 1988), v.

40. Liszt, *Feux follets*, arranged for orchestra by Leo Weiner (Budapest: Rózsavlögyi, 1934; Miami: Edwin F. Kalmus, n.d.)

41. Liszt, *Transcendental Etudes* (Albany Records TROY028-2 [1989]).

42. Howard records this version with all the optional passages: Liszt, *The Complete Paganini Études*.

43. See NLE i/2: 35 and 38.

44. NLE i/3: xi.

45. NLE i/18: xvi.

46. Alfred Brendel, *Musical Thoughts and Afterthoughts* (Princeton: Princeton University Press, 1976), 84.

47. Ernest Hutcheson, *The Literature of the Piano: A Guide for Amateur and Student* (New York: Alfred A. Knopf, 1948), 255.

48. NLE i/9: xiv.

49. Walker, *Franz Liszt: The Weimar Years*, 2:145.

50. Franz Liszt, *Consolations*, ed. Maria Eckhardt and Ernst-Günter Heinemann (Munich: G. Henle, 1992), vi.

51. Walker, *Franz Liszt: The Weimar Years*, 2:145.

52. Enharmonically this is C♯ major that would be a minor third down and a common key relationship in the romantic period.

53. See Everett Helm, "A Newly Discovered Liszt Manuscript," *Studia musicologica* 5 (1963): 101–106, for details about the two compositions.

54. From Nietzsche, *Werke* 3:113, quoted in Susan Bernstein, *Virtuosity of the Nineteenth Century, Performing Music and Language in Heine, Liszt, and Baudelaire* (Stanford: Stanford University Press, 1998), 110.

55. See Günther Wagner, *Die Klavierballade um die Mitte des 19. Jahrhunderts* (Munich and Salzburg: Katzbichler, 1976). Wagner discusses specific borrowings from Chopin in his first work of the genre that Chopin established with such élan.

56. See "Preface," in Liszt, *Balladen*, ed. Mueller and Heinemann (Munich: G. Henle, 1996), v.

57. Mueller, "Liszt's 'Tasso' Sketchbook," 213–217.

58. Liszt, *Balladen*, Mueller and Heinemann, v.

59. James Parakilas, *Ballads Without Words: Chopin and the Tradition of the Instrumental Ballade* (Portland, OR: Amadeus, 1992), 101.

60. For differing analyses of the work, see Parakilas, Pesce, Wagner, and Márta Grabócz, *Morphologie des oeuvres pour piano de Liszt: Influence du programme sur l'évolution des formes instrumentales* (Budapest: MTA Zenetudományi Intézet, 1986), 186–189.

61. Parakilas argued that the second theme does not start at m. 135. "In view of the unusual structure of the work, it is misleading to call this new melody the 'second theme,' as Kentner and Grabócz call it. It is rather a new part of the thematic progression already established. So far it serves to introduce and, in Grabócz's word, 'underline' the character of the co-theme; later it takes on more life of its own," 104.

62. Both endings are included in Liszt, *Balladen*, Mueller and Heinemann.

63. Parakilas, *Ballads Without Words*, 113–114.

64. NLE i/5: x.

65. NLE i/5: 22.

66. Kentner, "Solo Piano Music," 100.

67. *La Revue et Gazette musicale de Paris* (25 April 1880), 133, quoted in Katharine Ellis, *Music Criticism in Nineteenth-Century France: La Revue et Gazette musicale de Paris, 1834–80* (Cambridge: Cambridge University Press, 1995), 154.

68. *Selected Letters of Richard Wagner*, ed. and trans. Stewart Spencer and Barry Millington (London and Melbourne: J. M. Dent & Sons, 1987), 337.

69. See Peter Raabe, *Franz Liszt: Leben und Schaffen* (Stuttgart: J. G. Cotta, 1931; Reprint. Tutzing: Hans Schneider, 1968), 2:60.

70. See Paul Merrick. *Revolution and Religion in the Music of Liszt* (Cambridge: Cambridge University Press, 1987), 293–295.

71. See Tibor Szász, "Liszt's Symbols for the Divine and Diabolical: Their Revelation of a Program in the B Minor Sonata," *JALS* 15 (1984): 39–95.

72. NLE i/5: xi.

73. See Claudio Arrau, "Conversation with Claudio Arrau on Liszt," *Piano Quarterly* 23 (Spring 1975): 10.

74. See Alfred Brendel, *Music Sounded Out: Essays, Lectures, Interviews, Afterthoughts* (New York: Farrar Straus Giroux, 1990), 173–180.

75. See Serge Gut, *Franz Liszt* (Paris: Editions de Fallois/L'Age d'homme, 1989), 326–327.

76. See Bertrand Ott, "An Interpretation of Liszt's Sonata in B Minor," *JALS* 10 (December 1981): 30–38 and 11 (June 1982): 40–41.

77. See Kenneth Hamilton, *Liszt: Sonata in B Minor*. Cambridge Music Handbooks (Cambridge: Cambridge University Press, 1996), 46.

78. See David Wilde, "Liszt's Sonata: Some Jungian Reflections," in *Analecta Lisztiana II: New Light on Liszt and His Music*, 197–224.

79. See Charles Rosen, *The Romantic Generation* (Cambridge: Harvard University Press, 1995), 491.

80. Information for this table and much of the discussion of the Sonata in B minor comes from the following: Hamilton, *Liszt: Sonata in B Minor*, 32–48; Rey M. Longyear, *Nineteenth-Century Romanticism in Music*, 3d ed. (Englewood Cliffs, NJ: Prentice Hall, 1988), 152; William S. Newman, *Sonata Since Beethoven*, 3d ed. (New York and London: W. W. Norton, 1983), 373–378; Humphrey Searle, "Franz Liszt," in *The New Grove: Early Romantic Masters: Chopin, Schumann, Liszt*, rev. Sharon Winklhofer 1 (London: Papermac, 1985), 274–277; Walker, *The Weimar Years*, 2:151–157; Watson, *Liszt*, 240–241; and Sharon Winklhofer, *Liszt's Sonata in B Minor: A Study of Autograph Sources and Documents* (Ann Arbor, MI: UMI Research Press, 1980), 127–168.

81. For other views, see a similar table in Serge Gut, "A 'Reply' to Alan Walker," *JALS* 30 (July-December 1991): 52.

82. Rey M. Longyear, review of *Franz Liszt*. Vol. 2. *The Weimar Years, 1848–1861* by Walker, *JALS* 26 (1989): 70–71.

83. Hamilton, *Liszt: Sonata in B minor*, 45.

84. Béla Bartók, "Liszt's Music and Today's Public," in *Béla Bartók Essays*, selected and ed. Benjamin Suchoff. No. 8 in the New York Bartók Archive Studies in Musicology (New York: St. Martin's Press, 1976), 452.

85. Carl Dahlhaus, *Nineteenth-Century Music*, trans. J. Bradford Robinson (Berkeley and Los Angeles: University of California Press, 1989), 241. His comments pertain specifically to Liszt's *Bergsymphonie* but are also applicable to the Sonata.

86. See Szász, "Liszt's Symbols for the Divine and Diabolical," 39. "This study began on the day when I realized that the crucifixion music of Liszt's *Via crucis* is almost identical with a section of his Sonata in B Minor. I refer to the only place in the Sonata where dissonant chords alternate with recitatives."

87. Merrick, *Revolution and Religion in the Music of Liszt*, 293.

88. Bartók, "Liszt's Music and Today's Public," 452.

89. See MW, ii/8, vi for the original ending to the Sonata that Liszt discarded.

90. *The Letters of Franz Liszt*, 1:190. A "Nargileh" is, according to the *Oxford English Dictionary*, "An Oriental tobacco-pipe in which the smoke passes through water before reaching the mouth."

91. Quoted in *Letters of Franz Liszt*, 2: 47.

92. NLE i/11: 80.

93. See LW, 14: 808.

94. See NLE, i/15: 124, 127–128.

95. Saffle documented seventy performances of Liszt's *Grand galop chromatique* between 1840 and 1845 in Germany and wrote that it "is possibly the most popular piece in his 1840s German repertory." *Liszt in Germany, 1840–1845: A Study in Sources, Documents, and the History of Reception*. Franz Liszt Studies Series no. 2 (Stuyvesant, NY: Pendragon, 1994), 72 and 187.

96. Liszt, *An Artist's Journey*, 46.

97. MW. "Preface," trans. C. E. R. Mueller. F.B.: 2 [n.p.]

98. Saffle, *Liszt in Germany*, 187.

6

Piano Music: 1861–1886

Ben Arnold

After Liszt left Weimar and his position as Kapellmeister in August 1861, he eventually settled in Rome, arriving there on 20 October. He immediately turned to compositional subjects of a more religious nature for much of the next decade, and, in 1865, he received four degrees of the priesthood. He devoted himself, in particular, to choral music for the church and, therefore, reduced his compositions for piano during this time. Not only did his music become more religious, but his style became increasingly austere as each year passed, exhibiting thinner textures, more potent dissonances, and freer forms.

By the time he started his tripartite life in Rome, Budapest, and Weimar in 1869, he already realized how far-reaching his compositions were and how out of step they were with the public; consequently, he did little to promote his own music. In a letter to Camille Saint-Saëns on 19 July 1869 Liszt noted, "Thus I have judiciously made up my mind not to trouble myself about my compositions any further than the writing of them, without in the least thinking of spreading them. Supposing that they have any value it will always be found out soon enough either during my life or afterwards."[1] He reinforced this idea in a letter to Princess Carolyne on 9 February 1874, "As a musician my only ambition has been and will be to throw my javelin into the undefined spaces of the future. . . . Provided that this javelin be of good temper and not fall again to earth, the rest does not matter to me at all!"[2] During these years he actively discouraged people from performing his music. He lamented to Professor Julius Stern on 4 February 1875, "Owing to critical circumstances . . . I have, as a rule, to dissuade people everywhere from giving performances of my scores."[3]

He continued to compose, though, as if he had no choice in the matter. In a letter to Otto Lessmann, 8 September 1881, Liszt explained, "There is so much admirable music written that one is ashamed to write any more. With me it only happens in cases of urgency and from inner necessity."[4] A few months later he wrote to Saint-Saëns, "Yet I go on writing—not without fatigue—from inner necessity and old habit. We are not forbidden to aspire toward higher things: it is the attainment of our end which remains the note of interrogation."[5] A couple of years later he expressed his disillusionment to the Princess on 29 September 1883: "Despite the inevitable interruptions, I continue to write page after page of music, and only cross out and erase. The majority of things I could write do not seem to me to be worth the effort!"[6] Even with his fame and enormous record of published compositions, publishers rejected some of his works. Several pieces remained unpublished in his lifetime, and a few were not published until a century after his death.

Indeed, his piano works from the last twenty-five years of his life did anticipate much of what happened during the late nineteenth and early twentieth centuries. Works such as *St. François de Paule marchant sur les flots*, *Les jeux d'eaux à la Villa d'Este*, *Angelus!*, and *Abendglocken* illustrate Liszt's anticipation of the full-blown impressionists, just as *Unstern! Sinistre, disastro, Nuages gris, Trauervorspiel*, and *Bagatelle ohne Tonart* were forerunners of the expressionists.[7] During his last years Liszt entered into a world far different from his youthful emphasis on speed and virtuosity for an adoring concert audience. Instead, he wrote little piano music for the public, increasingly turning to the instrument to convey his sincere religious beliefs or some of his disheartening, distressing, and innermost fears and thoughts. His short, troubled works are often saturated with strains of longing, resignation, depression, and death, indicating a time of gloom, confusion, and even bitterness in his life. These themes manifest themselves in elegies and laments, seeming to infiltrate the very basis of his increasingly severe style. His music often evokes mystical dream-like states or breaks into macabre, almost surreal dances. Occasionally pieces seem to stop rather than end; others are inconclusive fragments pointing the way to early Webern. Collectively they rely on non-functional harmony, parallelism, tritones, whole-tone scales, augmented seconds, augmented triads, recitatives, tremolos, elusive cadences, and other striking dissonances. The augmented triad particularly fascinated Liszt in his late years, and his use of it is important in the history of harmony. R. Larry Todd emphasized this point: "Arguably, Liszt was the first composer to establish the augmented triad as a truly independent sonority, to consider its implications for modern dissonance treatment, and to ponder its meaning for the future course of tonality. Liszt's accomplishments in these areas were considerable and support in no small way his position, in Busoni's phrase, as the 'master of freedom.' "[8] Readily apparent, as well, in most pieces are their lack of virtuosity and their tight, introspective, and retrained qualities. Often the texture is reduced to single lines and becomes almost recitative-like in appearance.[9] Paul Henry Lang summarized Liszt's accomplishments, "Franz Liszt occupies a unique position in the history of modern music; most of our accomplishments in the field of harmony, orchestration, and construction originated in his inquisitive and inspired mind."[10]

At the same time Liszt's faith and optimism brought forth several religious compositions, many of which used major tonalities with limited chromaticism. For all his preoccupation with death and religion, the aging Liszt could still surprise with a vigorous rhapsody, a wild *czárdás*, or an operatic paraphrase promptly displaying the trademarks of his virtuosic skill.

Liszt's music had outgrown the romanticism of the first half of the nineteenth century. The idea that music had to be beautiful was slipping away in the same era that God would be pronounced dead. Liszt, pioneer that he was, moved music away from tonality and toward the acceptance of more and more dissonance. Bence Szabolcsi explained:

Indeed, this music is rarely *beautiful* if this term is to mean the accustomed sensuous beauty of romantic music. It has become haggard and sharp-featured, harsh and mordant, sometimes even caustic, yet, more swirling and nightmarish, more demonic and threatening than any music before. It often strikes us as the flare-up of a single idea: it is perhaps more like an idea than music, rather a scream or râle than melody, and it is perhaps due to just these traits that this music appears as vaticination.[11]

After analyzing several of Liszt's late pieces James M. Baker maintained, "Thus, a full twenty years in advance of the composers generally recognized as the pioneers of atonality, Liszt had already explored this new musical world."[12]

ANNÉES DE PÈLERINAGE, TROISIÈME ANNÉE

The cycle that best demonstrates Liszt's twofold preoccupation with faith and death in his late years is his bold and experimental *Années de pèlerinage, troisième année* (S 163) which appeared in print in 1883 (although the seven individual works date between 1866 and 1877; see Table 6.1).

Table 6.1
Années de pèlerinage, troisième année

1. *Angelus! Prière aux anges gardiens* (1866–1877)[13]
2. *Aux cyprès de la Villa d'Este* (3/4) (1877)
3. *Aux cyprès de la Villa d'Este* (4/4) (1877)
4. *Les jeux d'eaux à la Villa d'Este* (1877)
5. *Sunt lacrymae rerum* (1872)
6. *Marche funèbre* (1867)
7. *Sursum corda* (c. 1877)

Liszt completed the first four and the last piece of the cycle in 1877. The first, fourth, and seventh pieces are religious and the second, third, fifth, and sixth are laments. The cycle begins and ends in E major, and five of the pieces conclude on complete major triads in G (no. 2), F♯ (nos. 4 and 6), A (no. 5), and E (no. 7). The first and third pieces end on more original, single-note, recitative-like patterns. Although several works contain highly chromatic and dissonant passages evident in Liszt's late style, stretches of complete diatonicism are also prominent, for example, in *Aux cyprès de la Villa d'Este* (4/4), *Les jeux d'eaux à la Villa d'Este,* and concluding portions of the last two works of the cycle. Many use single-line melodies (often restated in open octaves), ostinatos, and frequent sequential passages (mm. 49–53, 56–60 in *Aux cyprès*, 4/4). All but the first contain dramatic use of tremolos.

The three religiously-oriented pieces play key positional roles since they form the beginning, middle, and end of the cycle. In effect, they encapsulate the four threnodies. The opening work, *Angelus! Prière aux anges gardiens*, and the closing, *Sursum corda* (Lift up your hearts),[14] share the key of E major, *Andante* tempo, ostinato patterns, and occasional use of triadic and diatonic themes. Their moods, however, are quite dissimilar. *Angelus!* is soft and prayerful in 6/8 (*Andante pietoso*) with shimmering, impressionistic, treble ostinatos and graceful themes while *Sursum corda* (*Andante maestoso, non troppo lento*) uses repeated, pedal eighth notes throughout, a whole-tone scale in mm. 66–70, and is largely loud and pompous, requiring four staves between mm. 71–77 for the *fff* restatement of the opening theme that remains *fff* to the end. Although *Angelus!* has a similar, but brief E-major outburst at m. 157, it returns to its elegance immediately and ends enigmatically with a single, unaccompanied line on tonic E.

Les jeux d'eaux à la Villa d'Este has more musically in common with *Angelus!* with its focus on the upper register of the keyboard and the peaceful nature of the flowing water. It is the most accessible and performed work from this cycle with its impressionistic water music that so influenced the French impressionists, particularly Debussy and Ravel. It is replete with double-note tremolos and thirty-second notes, refined left-hand trills, and major-ninth chords. Above the D-major section in m. 144 where Liszt first breaks into three staves, he writes in Latin: "sed aqua, quam ego dabo ei, fiet in eo fons aquae salientis in vitam aeternam" (but the water that I shall give him shall be in him a well of water springing up into everlasting life) from the *Gospel of St. John* 4:14. Because of the extreme use of sequential development, the key relationships throughout are fluid and the music is quite diatonic for late Liszt. *Les jeux d'eaux à la Villa d'Este*, with the serenity of his earlier *Bénédiction* and its exquisite keyboard writing, is elevated to the top tier of his compositions from the last decade.

The four laments are darker and more ponderous works that focus attention on the lower register of the keyboard compared to the religious pieces in the cycle. The first two threnodies (as Liszt preferred to call them[15]) share the same title (*Aux cyprès de la Villa d'Este*) and are distinguished by different time signatures (3/4 and 4/4). Inspired by his stays at the Italian palace at Villa d'Este over the years, Liszt worked on them concurrently in September 1877. He described one of them, probably the first in 3/4, as "a fairly gloomy and disconsolate elegy; illumined toward the end by a beam of patient resignation."[16]

Aux cyprès de la Villa d'Este (3/4), contains blocks of contrasting textures unified by a four-note melodic cell and major-to-minor mutations. The two-note, diminished-fourth bass ostinato in octaves introduces the work followed by a statement of the four-note melodic cell that opens with an augmented sonority in m. 4. Liszt emphasized the augmented chord several times in the work, particularly at mm. 25–26 and 29–30. The ostinato pattern also establishes the frequent mutations from major to minor that permeate the work, beginning in mm. 12–13 (see Examples 6.1 and 6.2).

Example 6.1
Liszt, *Aux cyprès de la Villa d'Este* (3/4), mm. 1–8

Example 6.2
Liszt, *Aux cyprès de la Villa d'Este* (3/4), mm. 9–18

The texture abruptly changes to a lilting G-minor arpeggiated accompaniment (similar to another lament, *La lugubre gondola*) with an expanded version of the opening cell and a leap of a minor sixth displacing the half-step motion at the end of the original motive. A new stepwise motive appears *fortissimo* at m. 47 and returns at m. 131. The arpeggiated ostinatos that accompany renewed statements of the four-note motive beginning in m. 63 break into more difficult and bravura cascading arpeggios that climax at m. 107 into descending chords and *fff* tremolos. The work features the major-minor interchange from mm. 175 to the end, finally concluding on a tonic G-major triad.

Aux cyprès de la Villa d'Este (4/4), contains elements of an ABA' form disguised by a dramatic introduction and an extended, almost nebulous coda (see Table 6.2). It begins with a Tristanesque five-note cell suggesting E minor and characterized by a drop of a perfect fifth followed by a rising chromatic passage (see motive x in Example 6.3).

Example 6.3
Liszt, *Aux cyprès de la Villa d'Este* (4/4), mm. 1–3 (motive x)

Table 6.2
Aux cyprès de la Villa d'Este (4/4)

Measures	Section	Theme/Motive	Key	Comments
1–30	Introduction	x		fragmented, long pauses
30–38	A	A	Db major	
39–46		A	C minor	
47–53		A	Bb major	
53–60		A	Bb minor	
61–67	Transition	x		
68–75	B	B	F♯ major	diatonic, harp–like
76–95		C		
96–105		x'	F♯ minor	
106–115		B	A major	
116–135		C		
136–145		x'	A minor	
146–153		B	C major	
154–161		C		
162–169	A'	A'	Db major	theme in bass
170–177		A'	C minor	
178–184		A	Bb major	exactly like 47–53
184–191		A	Bb minor	exactly like 53–60
192–207	Coda	x"		
208–225		B and x		combines B and x
226–240		B	E major/ C♯ minor	
241–244		x		unaccompanied

A *pesante* variation introduced by two falling tritones and ascending minor seconds immediately follows the second statement of motive x. The A theme begins in Db at m. 30 and is restated three times in C minor, Bb major, and Bb minor, alternating major and minor modes. The opening x motive serves as an interlude to the B section with its contrasting arpeggios, diatonicism, and upper register focus which makes it more similar to the religious pieces. The B section contains three statements of themes B and C that modulate from F♯ major, through A major, to C major, a tritone away from the initial statement of the themes. Between each of these modulations, a variant of motive x separates the appearance of these new themes. The music abruptly moves up a half step, returning with the opening A theme back in D♭ major, although this time the theme is stated in octaves in the bass (m. 162). The A theme repeats through the same keys as before, and motive x—now with the fall of the tritone instead of a fifth (mm. 192–193)—begins the mysterious coda based on motive x and the B themes. The work concludes hauntingly with an unaccompanied statement of motive x in its major mutation. Dolores Pesce observed that, "the coda does not serve, as it traditionally has, to confirm a tonic already established, but instead becomes itself the area of resolution."[17]

The last two laments stem from political events and feature dotted rhythms and march-like components. Liszt's *Sunt lacrymae rerum*, subtitled *En mode hongrois* and originally entitled *Thrénodie hongroise*, refers to the failed Hungarian uprising of 1848–1849 instead of the Fall of Troy to which Virgil's line "Sunt lacrymae rerum" refers. Liszt dedicated his *Marche funèbre* (1867) to the memory of Maximilian I, the assassinated emperor of Mexico, and includes a preface, "In magnis et voluisse sat est" from Propertius. Although both begin dissonantly in despair, both end with a triumphal air.

Dedicated to Hans von Bülow, *Sunt lacrymae rerum* contains numerous Hungarian elements. The NLE editors elaborated:

The so called kalindra (Phrygian, with two augmented seconds) scale, forming the opening and the closing scale of the work, was considered by Liszt to be just as Hungarian as the so called gypsy scale, named 'ungarisch' by Lina Ramann, which likewise contains two augmented seconds and also occurs in this piece. Apart from the scales it is also possible to list among the principal characteristics of the Hungarian style the *verbunkos*-style march rhythm and the piece's anticipations full of pathos.[18]

In addition Liszt uses recitative-like, single-line melodies, a descending three-note pattern forming a tritone between the first and third notes, augmented triads, triple dotted rhythms, and alternating extreme high and low registers.

Marche funèbre opens *Andante maestoso, funebre* with one of Liszt's darkest gestures in the lowest register of the keyboard. The march in dotted rhythms at m. 10 prevails throughout the first half of the work. Starting at m. 50, however, the music leaves the bass clef for the first time, and the texture thins to a single melodic line with sparse accompaniment. The term *Recitativo* appears at m. 68—the only use of the term in the cycle—and includes brief segments of a whole-tone scale. The recitative leads to an unusual tremolo (mm. 88–103) that rises and falls, stopping on a *fortissimo* F♯-major chord. The mood surprisingly changes once again with a triumphant variant of the march theme in F♯ major. It concludes with twenty-four measures of completely diatonic F♯ major, cadencing on a second-inversion tonic triad.

Since the third book of the *Années* features such despairing music and an often dissonant language, it has never been as popular as the earlier two. Only

Les jeux d'eaux à la Villa d'Este is performed regularly from this set, and it is by far the mildest of the group. The cycle as a whole, nevertheless, contains some of Liszt's strongest late compositions and is certainly as personal, if not more so, than the earlier cycles. In her fascinating article on this cycle, Pesce argued also for a strong Hungarian connection to the cycle:

On the most obvious level *Année 3* suggests a spiritual journey that carries us through Liszt's reflections on death (four threnodies) and the consolation he found in Christianity (three religious pieces). But that reflection on death has another component, his sense of personal loss and yearning for his homeland. . . . To judge by the exuberant tone of the final piece, *Sursum corda*, Liszt's spiritual journey eventually anchors itself in consolation and hope in God. But the triumphant treatment of the *Szózat* fragment in the penultimate *Marche funèbre* suggests that this consolation is fueled by faith in his native Hungary.[19]

RELIGIOUS PIECES

While writing numerous religious choral compositions during his Rome years, Liszt also contributed a few solo piano works on religious themes that often feature triplet rhythmic figurations, *fff* climaxes, and large quantities of major keys and chords—particularly leaning toward E major and the upper register of the keyboard. Some contain chant-like passages, and several are of a serene and spiritual type. Liszt often seems to equate a jubilant, assured force with his personal view of religious expression. When he harnesses this exultant compulsion, the works are usually more sophisticated and successful.

The most important of his spiritual compositions from the Rome years, his *Deux Legends: St. François d'Assise: la prédication aux oiseaux* and *St. François de Paule marchant sur les flots* (S 175), are also his most often performed works on Biblical themes. Composed in 1863 and first performed in Pest in 1865, Liszt also made orchestral transcriptions of them in 1863 and published the piano solo version in 1866, dedicating them to Cosima. In the piano score he included a brief preface of his own and a lengthy quotation for each piece telling the story behind the compositions.

The first Legend, *St. Francis of Assisi: The Sermon to the Birds*, is taken from the sixteenth chapter of the *Fioretti di San Francesco*. Liszt wrote, "That which might be called the 'spiritual motive' of the following composition, is drawn from one of the most touching episodes of the life of St. Francis of Assisi, which is told with the inimitable grace of simplicity."[20] Liszt apologized for both the limitations of the piano as an instrument and of himself as a composer in trying to bring this story alive in music. While traveling with some companions, St. Francis noticed a large number of birds in the trees he was passing. He asked his companions to wait and went to preach to the birds. The birds were so transfixed that "not one moved during the whole sermon; nor would they fly away until the Saint had given them his blessing. . . . While the holy Father thus spoke to them, the little birds opened their beaks and stretched out their neck, and, spreading their wings, all reverently bowed their heads to the earth, and by their acts and their songs, showed that the sermon filled them with great joy."[21] After St. Francis finished the sermon, "the birds rose into the air" dividing into four groups each flying in different directions, "singing their wonderful songs" to the four corners of the world.[22]

Inspired by this story, Liszt creates one of his most elegant piano tone poems. The first seventy measures, written exclusively in treble clef, are full of extraordinarily evocative bird songs. (It would not be until the music of Ollivier Messiaen that such bird-like sounds emanated again from the piano.) Liszt's technical presentation of the birds includes thirty-second-note scales and arpeggios, grace-notes, and sparkling trills, all at the *piano* level. Liszt musically represents St. Francis at m. 51 with a single-note *recitativo* statement. The birds respond, and this exchange between man and birds continues several times before the sermon proper begins with the serious change of tone at m. 71 (*Solenne*). At m. 85 St. Francis and the birds are heard together, beginning the *dolcissimo* statement of soft repeated chords high in the upper register of the keyboard that turn into quivering tremolo patterns (m. 104) and build to the only loud section of the piece. The *recitativo* (m. 131) has a amiable, *Parsifal*-like religiosity. The conclusion presents a dialogue between St. Francis and the birds with distinct recitative passages separated by delicate bird motives.

The second Legend, *St. Francis of Paola Walking on the Waters,* depicts a more dramatic and stormy setting based upon Giuseppe Miscimarra's *The Life of St. Francis of Paola.* The story relates the miracle of St. Francis of Paola walking across the water after the boatmen refused to take him across. The boatman had responded, "If he is a Saint . . . let him walk on the waters, and work miracles."[23] St. Francis spread his cloak on the water and, with his companions, sailed upon this self-made vessel "to the amazement of those of Arena, who watched from the shore, as it rapidly hastened through the waters, crying out after him in terror and tears, and beating their hands as did also the sailors on the barque, and their unfriendly master, who implored pardon of him for the refusal of his request, and begged him to come into his ship."[24] Liszt hung a painting of this story in his Blue Room at the Altenburg.[25]

Liszt's second Legend begins *Andante maestoso* in common time with a unison statement in the bass. He restates the theme immediately up a third and harmonizes the theme in tonic E major with chords above bass tremolos that begin the representation of waves. Sixteenth-note triplet patterns first interrupt the tremolos and soon become thirty-second-note, cascading, left-hand waves. Over these patterns are sequential statements in slow-moving note values. The rapid figurations appear for five measures unaccompanied to prepare for the return of the opening theme over the impressionistic painting of the waves (m. 41). At m. 64 Liszt transforms the melody into the bass, and the music soon breaks into violent, jagged ascending passages. One of Liszt's longest and most effective crescendos emerges from m. 85, starting *piano* in the bass and building to the glorious *fortissimo* setting of the E-major theme (m. 103). Everything stops for the expressive recitative section marked *Lento* (m. 139). The opening unison theme returns softly deep in the bass, and the right-hand chords steadily rise to build to the *fff* conclusion with treble double-note arpeggios over majestic left-hand octaves.

The remaining Rome pieces on spiritual themes are less pictorial and ambitious. Liszt's 1862 *Ave Maria für die grosse Klavierschule von Lebert und Stark (Die Glocken von Rom)* (S 182) in E major is among the most competent and imaginative of these works. It begins with a five-note introduction and returns at the end of the piece fully harmonized. The first section contains a constant sixteenth-note accompaniment to establish a calm and flowing atmosphere. At m. 41 low notes at the extreme range of the piano sound like distant bells according to Liszt's markings. With the upper register chords also sounding in alternation, an impressionistic section begins on three staves (mm. 46–52). Liszt transforms the main theme in the *Più adagio* section and *poco a poco animando il tempo (ma poco)*. From mm. 86 to 105 the focus seems to be the tolling bells that build to a *fff trionfante* climax on three staves at the extreme ends of the piano (as well as seeming to anticipate Wagner's use of bells in *Parsifal*). These patterns decrescendo to *pianissimo* before the *più lento* close of the work in E major.

Liszt made a rather odd pairing of his *Alleluja* and a transcription of Arcadelt's *Ave Maria* (S 183). The *Alleluja*, which uses themes from Liszt's *Cantico del Sol di San Francesco d'Assisi*, is among his least successful piano music. The euphoric and ecstatic epiphany that he attempts turns into rather purgatorial bombast with its incessant *fortissimo* triads—likely the most substantial number of such major chords in his music. The *Ave Maria* (S 183/2) is as pure and angelic as the *Alleluja* is noisome.

Two of Liszt's virtuoso religious works composed in 1864, *Urbi et orbi, bénédiction papale* (S 184) and *Vexilla regis prodeunt* (S 185), were not published until in 1978 in the NLE. Both contain text above borrowed chants or hymns, but both suffer from the same euphoria as the *Alleluja*. *Urbi et orbi, bénédiction papale* at least has a contrasting chant phrase (on occasion similar to the *Dies Irae* theme) that Liszt states in single lines and in quieter and more reflective ways (e.g., the rippling right-hand triplets over the chordal theme in m. 42). His *Vexilla regis prodeunt* based on Venantius Fortunatus's Medieval Latin hymn, on the other hand, relies far too much on its *Maestoso, marziale* fanfares, triplet sixteenth-note arpeggios (i.e., mm. 32–32), left-hand roaming octaves, and heavy blocked chords in the right hand hammering out the hymn tune. The brief respite at the *Più lento* (m. 81), where Liszt quotes the hymn in single notes in the left hand and above it in canonic imitation thirds and chords, cannot save the work that accelerates once again with open, triplet-eighth octaves, climaxing with a *fff* "Amen" in E major.

In the 1860s Liszt also completed a number of piano transcriptions from his own religious works, including his *Drei Stücke aus der heiligen Elisabeth* (S 2, 1857–1862), *Zwei Orchestersätze aus dem Oratorium Christus* (S 3, 1862–1866), *Slavimo slavno Slaveni!* (S 503, c. 1863), *Salve Polonia* (S 518, c. 1863), and the 1867 *Benedictus* and *Offertorium* from the *Hungarian Coronation Mass* (S 501). The latter pieces are distinguished by their Hungarian elements, particularly in the *Offertorium*. The exquisite *Benedictus* opens quietly and serenely; it builds to an elevated religious peroration with *fortissimo* repeated chords before closing with its opening serenity. In 1864 Liszt also arranged his *Weihnachtslied II: Christus ist geboren* (S 502), a brief twenty-measure, F-major piece first written for chorus, and *L'hymne du Pape* (S 530), a rather loud and diatonic E-major work that he transcribed from an 1843 organ piece and included as part of *Christus*.

Liszt's output of original religious piano music diminished somewhat after starting *La vie trifurquée* in 1869, but he continued to write small religious pieces and transcribe several of his religious works of other genres. His forty-eight-measure *Sancta Dorothea* (S 187), which dates from 1877, is another of his contemplative pieces from his old age. Saint Dorothea's festival "is celebrated by the Church on February sixth, the same day Liszt's mother died in 1866, giving this work a particular autobiographical poignancy."[26] Except for the last ten measures, it flows evenly with continuous triplet eighth notes with the melody arising from the main beats of these triplets. At m. 39 the triplet pattern ceases and the rhythmic energy slows to stolid, hymn-like quarter and half notes, ending on a treble E-major triad. Oddly enough, Richard Strauss saved the manuscript of this piece for posterity.[27]

One of Liszt's last overtly religious pieces originally conceived for piano was his *In festo transfigurationis Domini nostri Jesu Christi* (S 188), dating from 6 August 1880. Its opening four-note motive in the bass serves as a ground bass for the next two phrases over which appears a broken C-major chord. The music modulates up a step to a broken Db-major chord for the next eight measures. After three blocked chords mm. 5–20 are restated a major third higher. At the end of this section both hands move to the treble clef as the music ascends to depict Christ's Transfiguration. The last seventeen measures contain only harp-like rolled chords in the upper register of the piano closing with a *pianissimo* $V_{6/4}$ to I_6 cadence on F♯ major.

Between 1878 and 1879 Liszt transcribed *Via Crucis* (S 504a) and two books of chorales, *Zwölf alte deutsche geistliche Weisen* (S 50), for piano. While the chorales are simple and intended for personal use (although displaying occasional striking harmonizations), *Via Crucis* is an apt piece of forbidding religious music even as arranged for solo piano (see Chapters 8 and 13 for versions for chorus and for organ). Fluctuating between simple chorales and ostinato patterns of Station II to the continuously chromatic nature of Stations IV, VIII, X, and XIII, and the stark minor and augmented chords of Station XI, Liszt wields together a hybrid form that is unique in nineteenth-century pianism with its patient, almost at times vacuous, blend of austerity and religiosity. Around 1880 Liszt transcribed his *San Francesco (Preludio per il Cantico del sol di S. Francesco)* (S 499a) and in 1881 his *Cantico di San Francesco* (S 499). Between 1880 and 1884 he transcribed for piano the *Deux Polonaises de l'oratorio Stanislaus* (S 519) and his *In domum Domini ibimus (Zum Haus des Herren ziehen wir)* (S 671) for piano or organ in 1884.

In addition to making transcriptions of many of his own religious works, Liszt turned to some earlier religious works to make free paraphrases of other composers. His 1862 paraphrase of *A la Chapelle Sixtine after Allegri and*

Mozart is an odd combination Liszt assembled to show "the misery and anguish of man['s] moan[ings] in the *Miserere*; God's infinite mercy and his hearing of prayer answer and sing in the *Ave verum Corpus*. This touches upon the most sublime of mysteries which reveals [to] us that Love triumphs over Evil and Death."[28] It opens with a chaconne on Allegri's *Miserere* that builds into a forceful outburst of *molto energico* chords and four-octave arpeggios moving *pp* to *ff* and back measure by measure. Mozart's beautiful motet follows in B major but is interrupted by another burst of the *Miserere* before repeating again in F♯ major. Liszt also made a literal transcription of the *Ave verum Corpus* for organ solo near the end of his life. Sometime around 1862 he made moving transcriptions of the *Confutatis* and *Lacrymosa* from Mozart's Requiem (S 550). More than a decade later, between 1877 and 1882 Liszt fashioned a part-transcription, part-paraphrase of the *Agnus Dei* from Verdi's Requiem (S 437). This piece never rises above a *piano* dynamic, but its lyrical intensity builds through its thickening texture (and harmonic surprises) before a fragmented coda winds the work down to a solemn close.

LAMENTS

With the death of two of his children Daniel and Blandine in 1859 and 1862, Liszt turned increasingly toward elegiac compositions in memory of loved ones or toward works on the topic of death. During the last twenty-five years of his life he contributed a significant number of individual laments and dirges.

In 1862 Liszt completed his imposing *Variations on the theme of Bach: Weinen, Klagen, Sorgen, Zagen* (S 180) "inspired by the death of his eldest daughter Blandine."[29] Liszt dedicated this troubled, plaintive set of variations to the great pianist Anton Rubinstein. The original key signature remains throughout the work—atypical of Liszt in his large works with their numerous key changes—until the last forty measures with its mutation to tonic major. After the epic *fortissimo* thematic presentation in the lower register of the keyboard, the variations begin simply in the middle-to-upper range of the keyboard, quietly and sorrowfully. Liszt develops the theme through various alternating-hand and repeated-note patterns, octaves, and rapid arpeggios. One of his longest instrumental recitatives within a large-scale composition appears at the *Lento: Recitativo* that leads directly into the *Quasi Andante, un poco mosso* (m. 230) where the texture remains thin and the atmosphere pensive. At the *Quasi Allegro moderato* a bass pedal begins over which the theme appears, building to its horrific *fff* climax at m. 312. An unaccompanied treble line leads to F major and the chorale of assurance and acceptance, *Was Gott tut, das its wohl getan* (Everything that God has done is well done), that also ends Bach's cantata. The arrival of the major mode and the diatonic chorale after ten minutes of such acute chromaticism and dissonance generates a magical moment in Liszt. The sun has broken forth and the ascending *fortissimo* theme in F of more than two octaves symbolizes the triumph over tragedy and grief. Alfred Brendel wrote that "the entry of the chorale is a miracle of tenderness."[30]

Liszt composed an earlier prelude on this theme, *Weinen, Klagen, Sorgen, Zagen: Präludium nach Joh. Seb. Bach* (S 179) in 1859 and published it in 1863. While the variations begin and end *fortissimo*, the smaller prelude starts and finishes softly in F minor and provides a more intimate setting, although it too is a series of variations. Not only is this prelude a tribute to Bach but also a glorious reflection on a poignant theme. This prelude incidentally "was the last piece Horowitz ever played."[31]

Dating from 1859 to 1869 Liszt composed his cycle *Trois odes funèbres* for orchestra and made various arrangements of it. The first piece of the cycle, *Les morts* (S 516), exists in versions for piano solo, orchestra with male chorus, piano duet, and organ solo. The second, *La notte* (S 699) which was based on material from his *Il penseroso*, appears in versions for solo piano, piano duet, and violin and piano. He revised the final version of the piano piece in 1866. The third ode, *Le triomphe funèbre du Tasse* (S 517), shares material with his symphonic poem *Tasso* and was arranged for solo piano and piano duet. These odes are highly personal works as Liszt explained to his mother on 8 May 1863:

Some months after Daniel's death I reread the verses called *Les Morts* that Lamennais published in a volume of his miscellany. Each of them hangs on, or rather ascends to, this simple and sublime exclamation: "Blessed are the dead who die in the Lord." This is the resounding of God's mercy in the human soul and the revelation of the mystery of life and death through the infinite beatitude of His love. In reading Lamennais's verses I translated them involuntarily into music. I wrote down these chords, as feeble and helpless as they may be.[32]

Liszt prefaced *La notte* with a quotation from Michelangelo[33] and included the comment that "Being unable to see or feel is a blessing." The origins of the third ode appear less personal since Liszt deals with Tasso's funeral, but Searle noted that "this work clearly symbolises the idea that Liszt's true fame, like Tasso's, would not come about until after his death."[34] Furthermore, "Liszt felt so strongly about the works that he asked in a note on the score that *Les morts* and *La notte* should be played at his own funeral; but his wish was not fulfilled, and both works remained unperformed until 1912."[35]

Les morts begins *Lento assai* with a descending single-note line in the bass followed by brief, ascending chromatic octaves and half-diminished-seventh chords over a tremolo. Several long fermatas in mm. 8, 11, 14, and 21 fragment the entire introduction along with other extended rests and recitative passages. The main theme that provides hope and reassurance throughout the dark, solemn counterpart of the work appears at mm. 21–26—a theme based on a series of rising chords stated *dolcissimo* in A♭ major. Over this passage Liszt places the text *Heureux les Morts, qui meurent dans le Seigneur!* (Blessed are they who die in the Lord!). The following music contains grave chordal passages, diminished chords, and foreboding bass octaves. Sixteen measures of tremolo passages lead to the peroration of the A-major *Maestoso assai* theme presented *fff* on three staves. After this extended passage of passionate chords and octaves, the *Recitativo* idea returns (m. 136), followed by the final statement of the rising chordal theme in E major with its harp-like rolled chords undergirded by pedal octaves in the bass. Paul Merrick wrote, "Liszt's music captures the extraordinary atmosphere of the poem exactly. . . . *Les morts* is not just a piece of music, but a psychological document, a key to the understanding of Liszt as man and musician."[36] *Les morts* demonstrates Liszt's faith with its ethereal placidity at the end.

La notte, a somber, emphatic C♯-minor funeral march, begins *Lento funebre* with repeated E-minor and then augmented triads in the low register of the keyboard before reaching tonic at m. 5. The ominous opening is only relieved by a transitional passage to the B section that consists of a descending series of suspension chains. Echoes of the funeral march reappear before a single line emerges from the bass to reach the *dolcissimo* of the B section (m. 54) where Liszt placed the quotation from Virgil's *Aeneid*, "remembering sweet Argos as he dies."[37] This lengthy and contrasting B section is arguably autobiographical, graced by its tender Hungarian cadences and augmented-second scale steps.[38] Since Liszt wrote these odes after deaths in his family and wanted to have this particular piece played at his funeral, it seems possible that the loving way he enhances and repeats the signature cadence he uses so much in his *Hungarian Rhapsodies* might symbolize himself. This lament is one of Liszt's most personal, heart-felt, and autobiographical outpourings. The funeral-march A section returns at m. 137 with left-hand tremolo passages and penetrating augmented sonorities. After its initial statement a spectral, surreal passage strangely interrupts the descending *pianissimo* from G♭, F, E, E♭, to D major (mm. 150–154). The moment is brief because tremolos emerge and two measures later *fortissimo* octaves sound. At m. 162 the march returns in full force, slowed as before with the chain of suspensions. Fragments of the death march faintly echo over the next fifteen measures to close the engaging and *lagrimoso* work. Its seriousness and profundity set this march apart from Liszt's other pieces and even those of Beethoven and Chopin who wrote some of the most intense funeral pieces for piano in the nineteenth century.

Le triomphe funèbre du Tasse continues the quality of the previous two pieces of the cycle. Its plaintive, descending opening is soon followed by a noble theme accompanied by tremolo patterns that leads to a lush cantabile section. *Le triomphe* is more dignified and peaceful than the first two laments, although it contains triumphant elements that provide a fitting tribute to one of Liszt's most heartfelt and little-performed cycles.

Liszt's two small works entitled *Elegie* date from 1874 and 1877. His *Elegie I (Schlummerlied im Grabe)* (S 196) in memory of Marie von Moukhanoff opens with a twenty-measure introduction representative of the austere recitative-like style of his late period. The main theme presented at the *a tempo* marking, however, is in A♭ major and more characteristic of his earlier Weimar period with its romantic leanings. The first two notes establish the descending, minor-second motive heard throughout much of the work. Liszt inverts the theme to an ascending second (m. 37) and varies the opening theme with a triplet accompaniment beginning in m. 51. This transformation leads to the passionate climaxes of the work at mm. 68–74 and 85–91. Atypical of Liszt he repeats sixteen measures exactly.

Dedicated to Lina Ramann, *Elegie II* (S 197), like many of Liszt's late works, looks forward at the same time it retains romantic and almost nostalgic characteristics of the past. The ultra romanticism of the *dolcissimo amoroso* section stands in stark contrast to the sparse texture of the opening *Quasi Andante* with a single-note line ascending over two-and-a-half octaves and only one chord supporting the eight-measure phrase.

Wagner served as the subject for four of Liszt's late elegiac pieces. The first of these, *La lugubre gondola* (S 200/1), dates most likely from December 1882. Liszt provided more information about *La lugubre gondola* than perhaps any of his other late piano works. He wrote to Princess Carolyne on 14 January 1883: "Would you be so kind to thank Sgambati for his intention of making my *Lugubre gondola* known. I doubt that it will achieve success in concerts—considering its sad and somber character, hardly mitigated by some daydreaming."[39] A few weeks later on 9 February 1883 he complained: "Here [in Budapest] I can hardly get down to my *real* work. It was easier for me in Venice. There, I wrote various things, among them a *third* elegy, dedicated to Lina Ramann. Don't be frightened by the title, 'die Trauer Gondel' ('la gondola lugubre'). As you know, I bear in my heart a deep sorrow; now and then it has to break out in music."[40] A couple of years later Liszt shared the origin for his work in a letter to Ferdinand Táborszky on 8 June 1885: "As though it were a presentiment, I wrote this *élégie* in Venice six weeks before Wagner's death." He added, "Now I should like it to be brought out by Fritzsch (Leipzig), Wagner's publisher, as soon as I receive it from you in Weimar."[41]

The work (in 6/8) is in a tripartite form, with the second section a major-second transposition of the first. The first two sections are based upon the undulating barcarole accompaniment that give the feeling of Venetian canals. The poignant, single-line melody and the cross-relations (that occur, for example, in mm. 6, 13, and 17) establish the bitterness that underlies much of the lament. Each of the sections closes with a descending, single-line pattern. Liszt based the third section upon the first two, but the constant tremolo accompaniment and the lower register destroy the lilting rhythmic ostinato of the earlier sections. The music fades to nothingness with the last three measures containing only *ppp* tremolos in the lowest register of the piano.

Liszt composed the second *La lugubre gondola* in 1885 (S 200/2), and it also exists in a version for violin (or cello) and piano (see Chapter 9 for a discussion of this arrangement). This version in 4/4 is related to, but extremely different from, the earlier version, opening with a thirty-four-measure introduction consisting largely of broken diminished chords and recitative-like passages. The ostinato figure from the first version appears in a modified form in m. 35 and in the same 4/4 meter of the introduction rather than the 6/8 of the first version. While the mood resembles that of the first, the melody is distinct until m. 43 where the melodic ideas appear similar. Like the previous version this section repeats, but down a minor second rather than a major second. The undulating left-hand figure continues in the next section that consists chiefly of chords of long values, resolving a minor second down every two measures and forming major-to-minor harmonies. Liszt marks this section *Un poco meno lento* and further labels it *dolcissimo, dolente*. At m. 109 the music breaks out into a more romantic texture with blocked chords in the left hand and open octaves in the right with a transformation of the lyrical material beginning in m. 35. This outburst builds to a tremendous climax that leads to a restatement and transposition of the diminished chords in the introduction. After the recitative statement, a series of blocked minor chords descend and return to where they started. After a variant of these chords, a single line emerges that forms the last seventeen measures of the piece, which ends with whole notes moving from a G to a G♯. Pesce described the way the outer parts frame the inner sections of this work: "These outer parts suggest disjointed, improvisatory utterances; at the very end, the sense of aimlessness is reinforced by a bare, stripped down fragment of a whole-tone scale. As seen in *La lugubre gondola* no. 1, we sense here the true welding of form and idea to which Liszt aspired."[42]

Although Liszt informed Malwine Tardieu on 6 March 1883, "To great grief silence is best suited. I will be silent on Wagner, the prototype of an initiatory genius,"[43] he composed two elegies soon after Wagner's death. Göllerich claimed Liszt composed the first of these, *R. W. Venezia* (S 201), in March 1883. Unlike *Am Grabe Richard Wagners* that Liszt wrote a few months later, this work lashes out in its despondency. Its opening broken augmented chord starts at the lowest C♯s on the keyboard. This seven-note pattern in one guise or the other sounds eleven consecutive times with chromatic chords resonating over the disheartening ostinato the pattern creates. This section ends with a striking series of ascending augmented triads that crescendo nearly stepwise and lead into the heroic remembrance of Wagner. Beginning with triplet-eighth fanfares in B♭ major, Liszt states this heroic figure eleven times in a series of modulating sonorities. The music crashes on an F-augmented chord in the upper register of the keyboard that dwindles down in unison notes in each hand resting on low C♯s an octave above the beginning notes of the piece.

Liszt's final tribute to Wagner, *Am Grabe Richard Wagners* (S 202), relinquishes the anger and despair of *R. W. Venezia*. In this work Liszt reflected upon his friend by citing Wagner's own music. The editors in the NLE noted, "The first four bars are virtually identical with *Excelsior*, the theme of the introduction to the two movement oratorio work *Die Glocken des Straßburger Münsters* written in 1874, and they are also related strongly to the mood of the Lord's Supper motif in Wagner's *Parsifal*. And the closing section (bar 46 onwards) quotes the *Parsifal* bell-motive."[44]

The work opens with a single-line, augmented triad in the lower register just as the earlier *R. W. Venezia* did.[45] Liszt continues the ascent of the phrase, however, without redirecting the augmented triad as he did in his earlier tribute to Wagner. By the ninth measure and the *pianissimo* B-major sonority that appears there, Liszt has already come to terms with Wagner's death. While the augmented chord appears in key places later in the piece, it is always in the upper register, soft and delicate. The lament concludes with the *Parsifal* bell-motive starting in the treble and descending softly to stop on a single C♯ in the middle of the keyboard. Cannata pictorially suggested that "with all the ceremony and ritual now over, with his contemplation of Wagner's death at an end,

Liszt now invokes guardians of the temporal world, and entrusts the protection of his friend's grave to the perpetual care of the Grail Knights—as if, upon walking away, he could turn and see them standing watch."[46] This work exists in two versions other than the piano solo: for organ (or harmonium) and for string quartet, with harp *ad. lib.*

Liszt's 1885 elegy, *Trauervorspiel und Trauermarsch* (S 206), is among his most forward-looking piano works. The twenty-two-measure *Trauervorspiel* (*Andante lugubre*) consists of a descending artificial scale that repeats exactly six times with rhythmic right-hand chords in the bass clef. This material builds steadily to a *fortissimo* climax on an augmented chord. Allen Forte commented, "*Trauer-Vorspiel*, in common with many other of the very last compositions, does not exhibit tonality, as a vestigial feature or otherwise; its musical structure is entirely dependent upon pitch-class sets and their interrelations, as expressed over the temporal span of the work."[47] Without a break the *Trauermarsch* (*Andante maestoso funebre*) begins with a harsh introduction in the bass with the single notes F, F♯, G, B♭, and C♯. The last four notes, taken from Mihály Mosonyi's piano piece *Gyászhangok Széchényi István halálára* (Lamentations on the Death of István Széchényi),[48] form a striking bell-motive that appears throughout the march. Liszt specifically indicated that these notes "are to be played throughout with a broad '*staccato*.' "[49] Similar to the *Trauervorspiel*, the *Trauermarsch* begins *mp* and continues its intensification until it climaxes in a *fortissimo* culmination (m. 93). The energy drops quickly to longer note values, upper register, and *mp espressivo* (m. 97) until the opening motive returns to build quickly to a *fff* conclusion with a final statement of the omnipresent motive.

Historische ungarische Bildnisse

Liszt's series of dirge-like *Historical Hungarian Portraits* (S 205) was his last major project for piano, largely assembled and composed in 1885, although not published until 1956. Szabolcsi described these portraits as "just one powerful funeral song."[50] Three of them—those for Mosonyi, Vörösmarty, and Petőfi—appeared earlier as separate compositions but were adapted and revised for this series. Liszt's portrait of Petőfi has the most complicated history of the set since it originated from Liszt's 1874 melodrama *The Dead Poet's Love*. Liszt had earlier adapted a portion from the melodrama in 1877 and entitled it *Dem Andenken Petőfis*. Liszt's portrait of Mosonyi is the longest of the set and one he had composed as *Mosonyis Grabgeleit* around 1870. The tribute to Teleky is almost note-for-note the same as the *Trauermarsch* except for omitting several of the quieter measures from the work and replacing the *Andante maestoso funebre* heading of the *Trauermarsch* with a single word *Lugubre*. Liszt composed the remaining works in 1885 specifically for the series. Except for numbers six and seven that he had previously written, none of the compositions is longer than three minutes. Controversy has surrounded the order of pieces, but Table 6.3 provides an updated order:[51]

Table 6.3
Order of *Historische ungarische Bildnisse*

Stephan Széchényi (1791–1860), founder of the Hungarian Academy of Sciences
Franz Deák (1803–1876), a politician
Ladislaus Teleky (1811–1861), a writer sentenced to death
Josef Eötvös (1813–1871), Minister for Religion and Education in Hungary
Michael Vörösmarty (1800–1855), a prominent poet
Alexander Petőfi (1823–1849), a revolutionary poet active in the 1848 uprising
Michael Mosonyi (1815–1870), composer whom Liszt admired

Liszt was concerned about the unification of the cycle and added a number of features while revising and editing the work to ensure continuity within it. He added or changed intervals and scale patterns, and wrote new introductions and conclusions. In her analysis of Liszt's additions to copies in the Library of Congress, Linda W. Claus indicated Liszt's concern, "This structural unification is shown by the consistent insertion of descending-fifth and chromatic-scale motives at important areas of formal articulation. . . . These new preludes and postludes, with their anticipation or echoing of important motivic material, also demonstrate Liszt's concern for creating a high degree of unity within individual movements."[52]

From the unyielding *Feroce* introduction of Széchényi with its *fortissimo* open octaves to the solemn and peaceful close on a D-major chord in first inversion in the Mosonyi elegy, Liszt travels through the most intense darkness of any of his cycles. The first five of the works are stark marches, often including loud staccato open octaves and falling perfect fifths. The Teleky portrait is full of musical venom and the harshest of the group, but Liszt tempers the following march in Eötvös with an amiable *Più moderato* B section (mm. 44–83).

Of the seven works of the series, the masterful portrait of Petőfi serves as a foil to the earlier five pieces with its mournful charm. After a slow, single-line recitative, a doleful and angular melody with its grace-notes and dotted rhythms begins. The sublime middle section, *grazioso e dolce,* with its soothing ostinato pattern and syncopated melody, modulates upward for another restatement. The climax consists of a *grandioso* return of the opening melody replete with *fortissimo* tremolos under descending open octaves. After what appears to be closing chords in the upper register of the keyboard, Liszt adds a single-note restatement of the main theme closing with a quiet four-note descending motive. The closing portrait of Mosonyi opens *Langsam* with funeral bells in the bass (somewhat in the style of *Funérailles*) and contains a graceful section with thirteen measures of 5/4 meter, one of most extended passages of irregular meter in Liszt's late works. All in all, it is not that surprising that it took seventy years after his death for this cycle to appear in print.

RHAPSODIES, DANCES, AND MARCHES

Rhapsodies

In the last five years of his life, Liszt returned to the notion of the *Hungarian Rhapsodies* and contributed four more pieces to the genre (S 244). These later contributions have little in common with the vitality and vigorousness of the first fifteen. Each exhibits Liszt's late style with its sparseness and austerity. Each is in a minor key and contains more dissonance than the earlier rhapsodies. By far the longest of these is no. 19 at over ten minutes in length. The two shortest he ever wrote are nos. 17 and 18, each lasting only slightly longer than three minutes.

Rhapsody no. 16, *Allegro* in A minor (1882) combines a percussive, syncopated, and almost Bartókian style with a pensive *lassan* (m. 27) of extended trills, tremolo patterns, and harp-like filigree. It has a sardonic quality throughout and never gets off the ground the way the finales of the earlier rhapsodies do.

The seventeenth Rhapsody, *Lento* in D minor (1883), opens with a gruff, bass ostinato and single-line, recitative-like pattern that leads to a soft, tranquil, repeated pattern in the treble. This theme appears in treble open octaves before starting the louder and faster section that ends harshly on B♭ octaves. Interesting is Liszt's use of chords made of fourths that Searle suggested derived "from the 'Hungarian' intervals of F–G♯ and B♭–C♯."[53] Jim Samson wrote that the "most remarkable [of the last four rhapsodies] is the seventeenth, a curiously brief, elliptical piece which welds together the seemingly incompatible worlds of Hungarian scales and 'modern' symmetrical harmonies based on augmented triads and superimposed 4ths."[54]

Rhapsody no. 18, *Lento* in F♯ minor (1885), also follows the *lassu/friss* format of the previous two. The first forty measures (*Lento*) are soft and distinguished with two-note slurs and trill patterns. The *Presto Friss* uses staccato notes predominantly both in chords and open octaves. It is slightly humorous and ends unexpectedly.

The last Rhapsody, *Lento* in D minor (1885) after the *Czárdás nobles* of Ábrányi, is one of Liszt's most sophisticated rhapsodies with considerable rhythmic variety and contrapuntal inner voices in the extended *lassan*. It features melodic augmented seconds several times in the opening section and incorporates numerous types of trills and double-note passages. Oddly enough a passage (mm. 46–49) and its repeat (mm. 67–70) sounds strikingly like Sergei Rachmaninoff's music. The *Vivace Friss* beginning at m. 130 revives Liszt's clever and energetic writing displayed in some of the earlier rhapsodies amidst the more dissonant elements that are still present in his late style. Although the majority of the second section remains in D minor, it moves to D major at m. 400 and ends strongly in D major with some augmented seconds thrown in for good measure. Some of the passagework is extremely awkward and difficult, but this imaginative Rhapsody represents a major achievement by the seventy-four-year-old Liszt.

Liszt also composed what is, in effect, a miniature *Hungarian Rhapsody*. His two-minute, *Puszta-Wehmut (Die Werbung)* (S 246, 1871) contains two parts (*lassu/friss*) with the slow idea returning as a small coda to conclude the work. It is an arrangement of a song by Ludmilla Gizycka, née Zámoyská on a text by Lenau (see Chapter 9 for a discussion of its arrangement for violin and piano).

Dances

Liszt was drawn to many types of dances throughout his career, but late in his life he focused primarily on the waltz and *czárdás*. These works are not typical dances though. Liszt certainly stretches the definition of the waltz even to the point of writing one in a duple meter. He also incorporates more dissonance, unexpected harmonies, and tonal ambiguities in some of these compositions.

Liszt composed his *Quatre valses oubliées* (S 215) in his seventies, the first on 23 July 1881 and the other three (nos. 2–4) in 1883. Bote & G. Bock in Berlin published the first three in 1884, but the last was not published in Liszt's lifetime. With the word *oubliées* in their titles, it is not surprising to find that these are not typical waltzes; at times, they almost appear not to be waltzes at all. Each is in 3/4 time, but the last three in particular rarely sound like waltzes. When they do, he immediately obliterates that sense of dance with rests or atypical rhythmic figurations.

The first *Valse oubliée* is the most conventional, at least until m. 140 when it turns inward and reflective. It opens with paired staccato seventh chords lightly cascading down the piano. The waltz itself, beginning in m. 17, contains a swaying waltz rhythm with beats two and three slurred in the left hand. The theme outlines a major-ninth chord in mm. 17 and 18 and does not clearly establish a key. Each eight-measure phrase repeats throughout the section, and Liszt restates much of the material up a second. The waltz breaks forth in an *appassionato fortissimo* section (m. 89), but the composer specifically instructs the performer to "play it in an elegiac mood, not too waltz-like"[55]—an unusual instruction in the middle of a waltz! The introductory chords return and the waltz seemingly starts over (m. 107). The key signature changes from six sharps to two flats, and the major ninth outlined in the first statement of this theme is now turned into a minor ninth. After the restatement of the phrase the piece suddenly disintegrates into an eighth-note-trill pattern and into full-blown trills by m. 155. The passionate theme of m. 89 reappears (m. 160), but this time softly with a gentle broken-chord accompaniment. It, too, begins to meander after its second statement, wandering in fragments up the keyboard. The accompaniment figure comes to rest on a single note B and the last seventeen measures are unaccompanied fragments of the waltz in single notes—only a reminiscence of the past. The waltz literally just fades away *dolcissimo*.

The second Waltz is the least waltz-like, the fastest, and the most forward-thinking of the group. Becoming a waltz of irony rather than of entertainment, it illustrates Liszt's disillusionment with the idea of the waltz and the age that it once represented. Marked *Allegro vivace*, it begins with quite an un-waltz-like pattern. The jagged rhythm with each of the three beats not emphasized is certainly atypical—seemingly more of an etude with its repetitive motivic patterns. After breaking out into double and treble trills (m. 65), a waltz-like theme emerges in sixths. Liszt uses the curious term *garbato*, which means "courteous" or "kind," but still fails to provide the left-hand accompaniment to signify a waltz. That occurs at m. 111 with a theme consisting totally of sixths—perhaps the most ironic waltz theme written in the nineteenth century with its mordant appoggiaturas and syncopated melody. The tempo slows, altering the mood at the *un poco meno mosso (ma poco)* before it leads into transitional materials that turn into double trills. Much of this material repeats, before playfully leading to a strange twist in the waltz. At m. 304 Liszt slows the tempo again and creates repeated quarter notes that cadence on dissonance chords and are likewise repeated. He interpolates this stern pattern with the *scherzando* figures that began the waltz. After a brief rest (m. 376) the trill idea resumes in the treble portion of the piano. After more than twenty measures of trills with no waltz-like patterns to be seen, this odd waltz concludes on five A♭-major rolled chords at the extreme upper range of the keyboard.

Liszt cleverly bases his third "forgotten" Waltz on a three-note, ascending stepwise motive simply stated at the beginning. The nature of the waltz changes significantly in m. 76 with a figuration made of repeated seconds and thirds, more in 6/8 than in 3/4. These repeated patterns appear over a single-note pedal point and are highly impressionistic. After more than forty measures of this idea, the three-note motive returns—this time in repeated open octaves. Like many of Liszt's late works, this waltz ends with single notes; interestingly enough, the three-note, ascending motive seemingly will outline D♭ major until, with a nasty surprise, Liszt flattens the third note to F♭ rather than F♮. He provides an alternative ending that adds little to the piece, other than concluding it on an F♭-major chord.

The final Waltz in the series is hardly a waltz for the most part. It consists of similar three-note figures found in the previous Waltz and becomes waltz-like only with the new theme in m. 105, *Quasi presto, ma pomposo*. This theme repeats at m. 168 but in a much lighter texture and with softer dynamic markings—in other words without the *pomposo* feeling. The piece dissolves into single-note lines and concludes on a series of arpeggiated treble chords chiefly over an E pedal. It is surely a bizarre Waltz.

Continuing the idea of his first *Mephisto Waltz*, Liszt turned again to the idea of Mephisto in dance form during the last decade of his life, composing five additional pieces on this theme. He composed the earliest of these, the *Zweiter Mephisto-Walzer* (S 515), between 1878 and 1881 and dedicated it to Saint-Saëns. Liszt simultaneously penned the four-hand version and later transcribed a version for orchestra (S 111). The Waltz begins with a five-note theme that outlines a tritone and then sets about accentuating that dissonance with melodic repetitions of notes B and F. The idea restates, moving to the perfect fifth, but the *diabolus in musica* is already established The startling and tonally unstable introduction leads to a similar main theme in E♭ major. This opening exposition contains five basic themes that return within the section before Liszt casts the dreamy middle part (*Quasi l'istesso tempo, Un poco moderato*) as he did in his first *Mephisto Waltz*. After the slow section the music winds its way back to the opening material in tonic E♭ major and proceeds accordingly until the last fifteen measures of the work. Instead of concluding on E♭ as expected, it abruptly, with no forecasting at all, leaps from E♭ to repeated notes on B♮s. The opening tritones reappear, and the work concludes hammering out octave Bs, making the ending more unnerving than the beginning.

Dating from 1883 Liszt's *Dritter Mephisto-Walzer* (S 216) carries a key signature of D♯ minor. Although it ends on D♯s, it, nevertheless, contains numerous augmented and diminished triads and seventh chords to disguise the tonal structure of the dance, not to mention the nine key signature changes. Even though entitled a waltz, it is either 4/4 or 12/8 throughout. Liszt bases the extended work on five motives presented within the first forty measures and transforms them imaginatively throughout. The first motive consists of single notes outlining an incomplete D♯-major-ninth chord that repeats four times without resolution (mm. 1–5). He immediately restates this motive with parallel triadic accompaniment. The second motive (m. 11) consists chiefly of first inversion minor triads repeated in triplets and descending by steps with minimal melodic interest. The third motive (m. 19) is made up of a neighbor motive in 12/8 time, and the fourth (m. 26), primarily a rhythmic idea and most reminiscent of the first *Mephisto Waltz*, is a harmonic version of the opening with the grace-note E♯ providing the completed ninth chord. Most playfully diabolical is the fifth motive, starting in m. 35 with its beat-three trills. From these raw materials Liszt weaves together a fascinating web of thematic and virtuosic transformations. Only mm. 196–212 are not obviously derived from these motives, and these measures contain elements of the third motivic idea. Although the work as a whole is demanding with its fast open octaves, interlocking chords, rapid sixteenth-note arpeggios, and *vivamente* repeated notes and chords, it is not of the fiendish difficulty of the first *Mephisto Waltz*.

Liszt composed his fourth *Mephisto Waltz* in March 1885 in ternary form. The outer parts contain loud and brilliant octave writing with the first part exhibiting his classic restatement of the main theme a second higher. He notates much of these sections on three staves for clarity of performance. The *Espressivo* section beginning at m. 73 reduces the texture to a soft, single line in the right hand somewhat reminiscent of the first *Mephisto Waltz*. The A section returns in varied form in m. 105, extending the introductory material until m. 137 when the main theme returns full force. For the coda the tempo accelerates with continued *fortissimo* octaves.

Liszt dedicated his 1882–1883 *Mephisto Polka* (S 217) to his student Lina Schmalhausen. The polka demonstrates one side of Liszt's diabolical humor with its clever use of appoggiaturas and brilliant right-hand filigree passages. The dance begins with a sixteen-measure introduction that forecasts the first theme and establishes two of the most important motivic ideas that run throughout the piece. First is the sextuplet neighboring figure that immediately echoes in m. 3. Second is the use of a grace-note idea that appears in m. 2. One of these two figures is within nearly every measure of the work except between mm. 81–96 and 169–188. The polka is essentially a series of variations upon the rather trite theme that begins in m. 17. Much of the writing moves to the upper register of the keyboard beginning at m. 89, and from this point until the end, over 100 measures are notated completely within the treble clef. Throughout the variations Liszt develops the material in an improvisatory manner. Ending on F♮ after cadencing on the F♯-major-minor-seventh chord is a comic stroke of genius. The polka contains numerous alternative measures that make the work much more difficult, although it is challenging even without taking the optional passages. The *Mephisto Polka* represents Liszt at his most whimsical and delightful in his old age—an amazingly clever little morsel for a seventy-two-year-old.

Liszt composed his last Mephisto piece, *Bagatelle ohne Tonart* (216a), originally as his fourth *Mephisto Waltz*; he, nevertheless, gave another work that title and this one is better known as *Bagatelle Without Tonality*. It has elements comparable to the earlier waltzes, particularly the section moving out of the trill on C♯ between mm. 149 and 176 that so resembles the first *Mephisto Waltz*. In an ABA' form with coda, the *Bagatelle* uses a sextuplet in m. 13 in a similar way in which he used in the *Mephisto Polka* two years before. The B section consists only of alternating chords in the right and left hands followed by a quick cadenza passage. The A section returns at once in m. 87, omitting the first four bars. Liszt states the main idea a minor third higher (m. 95) with the blocked chords in the right hand and the sextuplet in the left. After the six-measure trill on C♯, the Waltz closes with brilliant right-hand figurations that stop in mid stream. After a moment's rest, Liszt has a final flourish of ascending, staccato, and diminished chords that stops on two rolled G♯, fully-diminished-seventh chords. The work is not atonal in the sense of twentieth-century atonality, but Liszt enjoyed experimenting with the idea of expanding tonality to the point where it becomes vague and tenuous. Bernard Lemoine wrote, "The concept of tension followed by relaxation (i.e., the resolution of dissonance to consonance) [in the *Bagatelle ohne Tonart*] has been scrupulously avoided and Liszt has, by the very denial of this tonal axiom, taken a giant step towards the twentieth-century styles of Schoenberg, Berg, Webern, and their followers."[56] Liszt, nevertheless, writes many basic major and minor triads throughout the *Bagatelle* and employs enough repetition of chords and notes to provide tonal indications at several points in the work. The opening flourish accentuating the tritone gives the impression of a strikingly unusual piece for its time.

Liszt penned three works with *czárdás* in the title, which demonstrate his capacity for writing virtuosic works during his old age—particularly the *Csárdás macabre*. A *czárdás*—a Hungarian dance that usually contains a slow, free introduction (*lassan* or *lassu*) followed by a rapid, wilder type of dance (*friss* or *friska*)—is similar in style to a *Hungarian Rhapsody*.

Liszt composed the first of these, the *Csárdás macabre* (S 224), during 1881 and 1882. Its innovative nature includes use of repeated open fifths and the percussive effects associated with Bartókian and Stravinskyesque primitivism. Liszt himself wrote on his copy of the score: *Darf man solch ein Ding schreiben oder anhören?* (May one write or listen to such a thing?)[57] The introduction based in the lower register of the keyboard sets out the major rhythmic and melodic motive of the work. This particular rhythm repeats ten times through the first forty measures of the work. A clever single-note transition theme appears between mm. 41 and 48 and returns at comparable moments within the work. The first part of the main section begins with bare open perfect fifths in both hands that last for thirty measures (see Example 6.4).

Example 6.4
Liszt, *Csárdás macabre,* **mm. 1–9**

Measure 88 begins a dance fragment based to some degree on the single-line theme from the introduction (see Example 6.5).

Example 6.5
Liszt, *Csárdás macabre,* **mm.88–91**

A new theme appears (m. 133) that Liszt varies later in the work (see Example 6.6).

Example 6.6
Liszt, *Csárdás macabre,* **mm.133–136**

At m. 162 Liszt quotes a well-known folk-song *Ég a kunhhó, ropog a nád*[58] (see Example 6.7) and plays with this idea until the single-note introduction theme leads into a treble staccato theme (m. 229) based on Example 6.6.

Example 6.7
Liszt, *Csárdás macabre*, mm. 159–166

A fragmented version of Example 6.4 links a new and more virtuosic variation on the folk song that closes out the first half of the work. These themes repeat in exact order, presenting the folk song down a minor third from the original statement. The dance concludes with a rather extensive coda based principally on the a and b motives and confirms that Liszt had not lost his flair for extroverted and virtuosic works.

In 1884 Liszt published two *Czárdás* (S 225), the first simply titled *Czárdás* and the second *Czárdás obstiné*. *Czárdás* is the shortest and least virtuosic of the three in this genre, and *Czárdás obstiné (Presto)* is the most carefree and insistent. Both dances incorporate single-note patterns in the right hand and repeated blocked chords in the left. *Czárdás* is distinguished by its thin, recitative-like texture in its closing section. A four-note, descending motive first stated in mm. 7–8 permeates the *Czárdás obstiné,* which contains more virtuoso elements, with scintillating open octaves in the right hand and fast sixteenth-note passages beginning in m. 149.

No discussion of the dances would be complete without briefly mentioning Liszt's fascinating piano transcription and elaboration of Saint-Saëns's *Danse Macabre* (S 555), made within a short time after the orchestral premiere in 1875. The dance is so Lisztian in spirit and conception that Liszt must have felt he was arranging one of his own works. He obviously enjoyed experimenting with some of his favorite themes: unresolved harmonic tritones, alternating hands, brief fugal writing, thematic combination and transformation, and bravura octaves, tremolos, and trills all upon a sprightly diabolical subject. Searle went so far to suggest that Liszt made "a great improvement on the original work!"[59]

Marches

Liszt continued to write occasional marches up to 1884. He wrote versions of his *Ungarischer Marsch zur Kronungsfeier in Ofen-Pest am 8. Jun 1867* (S 523) for piano four-hand and orchestra as well in 1870. He followed with his *Ungarischer Geschwindmarsch* (S 233) in 1870–1871 while he was in Hungary.

This three-minute quick-march, *Schnell und ungestüm,* is fast throughout and in ABA form. It displays Hungarian characteristics with its frequent augmented-scale patterns and grace-notes; it ends like a rhapsody with its *fortissimo* dotted rhythms in the *Più allegro* coda.

In December 1883 Liszt composed a *Bülow-Marsch* (S 230) in honor of his former son-in-law Hans van Bülow. In his preface Liszt praised Bülow: "In the world of art, Hans von Bülow, for the past thirty years, has signified, exemplified, and further all that is noble, genuine, lofty and enlightened in creative work."[60] Liszt also arranged the March for duet, and his pupil Karl Goepfart arranged it for orchestra. For an honorary march it has a lugubrious opening and a tender, almost lethargic, middle section *Un poco meno allegro, ma poco.* The March moves from the most diatonic *fortissimo* C-major chordal writing to extraordinary descending chromatic chords and octaves that become somewhat tedious. Before returning to the louder, dramatic portions of the March, Liszt substitutes in the treble realm a playful, unmarch-like staccato octave section. The music modulates to Ab major after a restatement of the descending chromatic passages for the return to the noble nature of the March. The martial mood continues as it returns to nearly forty measures of diatonic C major at the *fortissimo* level.

The last of Liszt's late marches is the *Siegesmarsch—Marche triomphale* (S 233a) in Eb major, most likely written in 1884. Formally it is a clear ABCA'BC'A" with the A idea and its staccato triadic arpeggios serving as introduction, interlude, and coda between the two major sections B and C. The B section (mm. 10–37) is the most elaborate with its *fortissimo* chords and scintillating sixteenth-note flourish nearly every other measure. The C section provides a quiet contrast, originally (*espressivo cantando*), but in its return becomes *forte* to lead to the grand climatic end.

MISCELLANEOUS CYCLES

Etudes

Liszt composed his *Zwei Konzertetüden* (S 145) sometime between 1861 and 1863. Although they are known today as *Waldesrauschen* (Forest Murmurs) and *Gnomenreigen* (Dance of the Gnomes), these titles are not present on the autograph manuscripts.[61] Liszt dedicated his last two etudes to one of his pupils, Dionys Pruckner, and contributed them to the Siegmund Lebert and Ludwig Stark piano method. *Waldesrauschen* contains almost continuous sixteenth-note sextuplet arpeggios often constructed over non-functional seventh and ninth chords. Over or under this figuration, as the case may be, Liszt requires a legato melodic line, either in single notes or octaves. Although the etude is one of Liszt's most monothematic works (repeatedly varying the opening left-hand melody), it is also highly chromatic and changes key signatures ten times in its ninety-seven measures. It builds to its first climax at the return of Db major at m. 61 and then displays an ecstatic outburst in its treacherous *stringendo molto e sempre fortissimo ed appassionato* section at m. 71. The opening arpeggios and original theme reappear quietly to end the work *perdendosi ppp*. After Queen Elisabeth heard Liszt's *Waldesrauschen*, she wrote a poem about it.[62]

Gnomenreigen is one of Liszt's cleverest and most facetious works, sparkling in its *Presto scherzando* tempo. While primarily in compound duple or compound triple meter, the imaginative, interlocking writing between the hands creates the buoyant effects of the piece. In distinct sections (ABAB'CA'B" Coda), its A theme recurs each time in F♯ minor, with its contrasting B section appearing in A, B♭, and F♯ major. The brief developmental C section in G minor (mm. 77–102) provides the only contrast from the two main themes.

Five Hungarian Folksongs

Liszt's ties to his homeland seemed to grow greater in his later years as he turned to Hungarian subjects for many of his works. In 1873 he based his Five Hungarian Folk Songs (S 245) on actual songs, and all but the first include the text at the beginning of the piece. The pieces alternate slow and fast tempos, beginning with slow. Each of the fast songs lasts under a minute, and the longest slow song, number five, less than two minutes. These pieces then are Hungarian miniatures in the style of *verbunkos* in 2/4 meter with dotted rhythms, often short/long rather than the typical long/short. Several contain the rapid treble flourishes at cadences and alternate major and minor modes, but none of them requires much virtuosity.

Weihnachtsbaum

Weihnachtsbaum (S 186), a collection of twelve short pieces, combines an odd assortment of arrangements as well as nationalistic music of Hungary and Poland. The first four are for piano or "Armonium," but the remainder seemed conceived solely for piano. Some pieces are simple and others require significant virtuosity, although the cycle appears more appropriate for the soirée or home than for the concert hall. Liszt dedicated it to his granddaughter Daniela von Bülow. On New Year's Day 1874, he wrote to Princess Carolyne about the pieces he called *Christbaum* at the time: "They will not in the least be 'scientific' works or pompous, but simple echoes of my youthful emotions—these stay indelible through all the ordeals of the years!"[63] Liszt would turn to these "echoes" for several more years before settling on their final publication in 1882.

The first four pieces of the cycle are transcriptions of traditional Christmas songs, and Liszt wrote words over portions of music in the first two. He based the *Psallite—Altes Weihnachtslied* on a Christmas choral by Michael Praetorius (1571–1621), *O heilige Nacht!* on a traditional carol, *Die Hirten an der Krippe* on the famous tune *In dulci jubilo*, and *Adeste fideles* (better known as *O Come All Ye Faithful*) on the seventeenth-century Latin hymn. Each of these arrangements is simple and straightforward. *Adeste fideles* contains a few surprising harmonizations and additions, and *O heilige Nacht!* alternates harmonized versions with unaccompanied melodies. In *Die Hirten an der Krippe*, one of the jewels in the cycle, Liszt utilizes a clever and appealing ostinato in the left hand that provides a new twist to *In dulci jubilo*, until m. 72 when it becomes the melody itself for a brief moment

The fifth and sixth pieces change the cycle from its simple song arrangements. Both the *Scherzoso: Man zündet die Kerzen des Baumes an* (Lighting the Tree) and *Carillon* require considerable virtuosity in their fast tempos. The double thirds and open octaves of the *Scherzoso* and the *quasi trillo* alternating harmonic thirds and fourths in the right hand of the *Carillon* make these pieces as challenging as etudes at times. Both primarily use the treble register of the piano, setting a sprightly and merry mood.

The playful antics of the previous pieces cease with the *Schlummerlied* (Slumber Song), set initially in F♯ major (although it ends vaguely without cadencing on tonic). For a sleep-inducing piece, it displays considerable activity with the constant humming and sixteenth-note, trill-like patterns. Its character is easeful for the most part, but the music incorporates ample counterpoint, striking modulations, and hand crossings into the mix to provide some intensity, almost to the point of restlessness towards the end. The eighth selection, *Altes provençalisches Weihnachtslied*, provides the wake-up music after the *Schlummerlied*. The playful B-minor song, noted for its three-measure phrases in the opening section of the ABA form, resembles the *Scherzoso* with its use of thirds.

The ninth piece, *Abendglocken* (Evening Bells), is impressionistic with its tranquil and suspended ostinato patterns. Most effective is the *Andante quieto* section (mm. 99–125) with its three levels of low open octaves, middle-register octave ostinato, and upper register bells on octave Bs. The tenth piece *Ehemals!* (*Jadis*), is somewhat peculiar with its sparse, brooding introduction, interlude, and conclusion on single notes and rising seconds in long-note values. Liszt admirably varies the single melody that constitutes the body of the music and closes the work with a surprising cadence on a diminished-seventh chord (mm. 119–120).

The last two nationalistic pieces, *Ungarisch* and *Polnisch*, seem out of character with the rest of the cycle because of their bravura and extroverted manner. Searle suggested Liszt included them because they are representative portraits of the "Hungarian" Liszt and the "Polish" Princess.[64] *Ungarisch* is the most boorish of the group with its pompous march replete with dotted rhythms, repetitive motives, and triplet eighth fanfares. At less than two minutes long, Liszt does not tend to subtleties as he does in the concluding piece. The last and longest piece of the cycle, *Polnisch*, opens tenderly with its *Andante* forecasting of the main theme in B♭ minor. The second theme with its frolicsome, jagged rhythms and staccato notes lead into a type of *Mazurka di bravura* with *fortissimo* full chordal writing and brilliant octaves. The bombastic coda concludes in a manner far removed from the opening transcription that began this strange, miscellaneous cycle.

Fünf kleine Klavierstücke

Between 1865 and 1879 Liszt wrote *Fünf kleine Klavierstücke* (S 192) for Baroness Meyendorff, although Leslie Howard indicated there is no evidence they were meant as a cycle.[65] The first four pieces were published in 1928 and the last only in the 1960s.

In 1865 Liszt based the first of these five short piano pieces on an earlier song, *Gestorben war ich,* set to the text of Ludwig Uhland. Liszt had also arranged the song for piano and published it as his second *Liebestraum.* In *Klavierstück* no. 1 Liszt adds a new introduction and a contrasting addition to the B section, but much of the melodic material remains the same and in the same key. The introduction is a series of broken diminished chords each followed by a fermata. The piece has a simple, song-like melody restated in octaves. The B section moves the melodic line to the bass, providing a crescendo to the climatic five-note descending phrase that Liszt repeats three more times. The opening theme returns to round out the charming piece in a clear ABA form. Nicholas Cook suggested that this piece

is not fully intelligible as a composition in its own right. But it gives the impression of being something more than a nostalgic reminiscence of its predecessors. Its opening measures, for instance, are not merely a reminiscence of the opening measures of *Liebestraum* No. 2 but also a criticism of them: fifty notes in the 1865 version do the work that took sixty-six in the *Liebestraum.* . . . *Kleine Klavierstück* No. 1 can be regarded as a critical reinterpretation of *Liebestraum* No. 2.[66]

The second piece in A♭ major (1865) has a song-like melody accompanied by syncopated chords. As in the preceding piece, Liszt restates the melodic line in octaves and intensifies the accompaniment. The contrasting section *un poco animato* with the melodic pattern alternating in the bass and the treble is a thematic transformation of the opening ideas. The music builds to a surprising *fff* climax for such a short piece and ends with another variation of the first theme.

The third and fourth piano pieces are only twenty-five and twenty-one measures respectively and both in F♯ major. They are so short that they seem to be fragments rather than worked-out compositions. The third *Sehr langsam* (1873) repeats a four-measure descending phrase six times in various guises, all *pianissimo* and *dolcissimo.* The fourth *Andantino* (1876) is another quiet and gentle song based upon a brief two-measure theme. Although it has more contrast beginning in m. 8 with a faster and louder section, it quickly returns to a simple re-harmonization of the opening theme to close on a F♯-major arpeggiated chord.

Dating from 1879 *Sospiri!* (Sighs), the last piece of the cycle, is monothematic in its approach. The introduction forecasts the main melody presented at m. 11 *dolce amoroso,* and Liszt subtlety and imaginatively transforms the temperate theme until the surprising arrival of the *sf* half-diminished chord in m. 80. The piece ends jarringly with this half-diminished-seventh chord moving directly to a *pianissimo* fully-diminished-seventh chord. *Sospiri* is the highlight of the set.

OTHER MISCELLANEOUS WORKS

Much of Liszt's late music defies easy classification. Several of his late miniatures represent his darker side, and a few of these pieces exhibit his most futuristic music. In 1881 he composed two pieces *Unstern! Sinistre, disastro* (S 208) and *Trübe Wolken (Nuages gris)* (S 199) that have become much discussed in the Liszt literature today because of their adventuresome characteristics.

The title *Unstern! Sinistre, disastro* indicates misfortune—an evil or unlucky star—and Liszt portrays this sentiment graphically in the first eighty-two measures. In no other work does his fascination with the tritone and augmented sonorities appear so startling and modern (see Example 6.8).

Example 6.8
Liszt, *Unstern! Sinistre, disastro*, mm. 67–84

Forte wrote, "This opening passage, in its austerity and its economy of means with respect to the musical processes it represents, is strongly reminiscent of the music of Anton Webern."[67] The opening phrase contains a melodic tritone and concludes on a harmonic tritone, all performed *mf* and *pesante*. The music has difficulty starting with its frequent silences in mm. 6, 11, 16, and 21. The inexorable side of evil, though, begins with double-dotted rhythms in m. 21. From this point the motion of the piece continues unchallenged until m. 84. The first augmented triad appears at m. 25, and its most unusual use is exhibited in a series of triads beginning in m. 58 that ascend stepwise for two octaves. These triads crescendo, building to an overwhelmingly dissonant climax with an added tritone (m. 71)—certainly one of the most discordant passages in nineteenth-century music (again, see Example 6.8). At m. 84, however, the religious side of his nature appears, as if Liszt appeared uncomfortable with too much anguish. The music changes abruptly with its sustained, chordal passages that he suggests to be played in the style of an organ. This hymn-like texture that begins with two major chords, however, is also tainted with dissonance. By m. 101 the inauspicious mood of the first section reasserts itself, and a sinister unison chromatic passage interrupts the chordal texture. The hymn-like chords resume but without purpose, plodding along until exhausted. The work disintegrates into a series of whole tones in the bass of the keyboard ending on a single note. *Unstern* ranks as Liszt's most daring venture into Cimmerian hopelessness and paints in absolute terms the apathy that troubled him so desperately during his last years.

Alan Walker proposed that *Nuages gris,* composed on 24 August 1881, is autobiographical: "This was a bleak month for Liszt. Seven weeks earlier he had fallen down the stairs of the Hofgärtnerei and had sustained severe injuries. He had expected to make a swift recovery, but the healing process was slow, and it was compounded by his other difficulties, which now included dropsy and failing eyesight."[68] *Nuages gris* is one of Liszt's most haunting works and, according to Forte, "represents a high point in the experimental idiom with respect to expressive compositional procedure."[69] The opening motive includes a tritone and repeats four consecutive times, with faint left-hand tremolos accompanying the last two of these statements. After a series of augmented chords punctuating over the bleak tremolos, Liszt restates the opening theme (m. 25) and adds a counter melody above it. In m. 33 a variation begins on the augmented triads (mm. 9–20). In place of the two layers of blocked chords over tremolos, Liszt creates three levels with a series of undulating left-hand passages that alternate between half steps B♭ and A—the exact chords from the earlier section but now broken—and, above all, an open-octave, ascending chromatic line in the treble. After a measure of silence, the piece ends with two treble rolled chords of unresolved dissonance. Throughout the work the dynamic level never rises above *piano.* Mauricio Kagel incorporated Liszt's *Nuages gris* into his own *Unguis Incarnatus est* (1972),[70] and Stanley Kubrick relied on *Nuages gris* for a shocking scene at the morgue in his last film, *Eyes Wide Shut.* Leonard Ratner commented:

The restless, unresolved dissonances of 'Nuages gris' the isolated figures, the sense of alienation—these have a clear affinity with the somewhat later expressionism of the Viennese composers Mahler and Schoenberg. . . . [*Nuages gris*] is a musical bellwether that indicated what was happening and what would happen in European music: sound, with the assistance of symmetry, would take over; harmony would be absorbed into color and lose its cadential function.[71]

Two years later in 1883 Liszt composed another striking piece based on a poem by one of his students, Antonia Raab: *Schlaflos! Frage und Antwort, Nocturne* (S 203). Liszt includes several optional passages, including a substantial cut of eighteen measures and an alternate ending. Out of seventy-five possible measures, twenty-five are different (not counting the cut of eighteen measures), making in effect two different versions—each containing two parts. The first, *Schnell und leidenshaftlich*, asks the question, while the second, *Andante quieto*, provides an answer. The first section, beginning in E minor, consists of tumultuous and continuous left-hand, eighth-note arpeggios in the bass that create the sleepless anxiety of the question. The right-hand melody is usually in single notes or octaves and becomes quite chromatic until the section abruptly ends; after a silence a recitative bridge marked *Ritenuto* segues into the second section stated in E major. While the first section was wild and stormy, the second is chorale-like and calm, soft, and controlled. In the first ending the work concludes with a single-note line in its last nine measures. The alternate ending concludes peacefully with a complete E-major triad.

The year before he died Liszt composed *En rêve—nocturne* (S 207) in Rome. It remains *piano* throughout and contains the frequent Lisztian ostinato in the left hand with a single-note line above it in the right. In its variation that follows, the single-note line is enriched with an inner voice to establish further the vague harmonies of the first section. From mm. 13 to 20 an unaccompanied treble line separates the two sections of the piece. In m. 35 treble trills begins that ascend stepwise to the closing treble chords, finally closing on a B-major triad.

Several of these small miniatures are quite charming as well and not at all so austere and dissonant as the music just discussed. These represent a nostalgic Liszt who could still write beautiful and tonal music with ease. Dating from sometime after 1860, Liszt's *Klavierstück in F-sharp* (S 193) was found after his death, and scholars are uncertain of its date of composition. It retains a warm, romantic, and even Chopinesque feeling that would place it before his extreme late period. It is much like a nocturne with its rolling, arpeggiated left hand and its somber and elegant mood set by the lithesome melody in thirds. Although marked *Appassionato* at the beginning, Liszt also writes *dolcissimo* which gives a better feeling for the work. This miniature deserves greater prominence among Liszt's small character pieces.

Liszt's Piano Piece in A♭ (S 189), composed in May 1866, was thought to be lost for some time. The Liszt Society with the assistance of William Wright and K. W. Souter, however, located a previously published copy and reissued the small piece in 1988.[72] Even though it begins in A♭ major with a single-line melody and gentle triplet accompaniment, Liszt immediately transposes the beginning theme up a step to A major. He restates the opening theme with octaves in A♭ (m. 23) and slightly alters the accompaniment figure. As before he transposes this variation to A major, winding his way back to A♭ through a series of modulating chords. It is a charming, nocturne-like piece limited to its initial thematic material.

Dedicated to Baroness Meyendorff, Liszt composed the *Impromptu* (*Nocturne*) in F♯ major (S 191) in 1872. An earlier version of the work exists entitled *Nocturne*. With its repeated-chord opening theme and question-and-answer response alternating between treble and bass themes, it is an attractive and passionate work displaying Liszt's romanticism even at this late date.

In 1877 Liszt composed two of his most tranquil late pieces: *Recueillement* (S 204) and *Resignazione* (S 187a). *Recueillement,* written "at the invitation of F. Florimo for the erection of a monument to Bellini in Naples,"[73] never rises above a *forte* dynamic marking. It opens *Un poco lento* with arpeggios for the first section consisting of major and minor chords for the most part, with augmented sonorities in mm. 3–5. The second section, a brief chorale, leads to a strong cadence on C♯ major to begin the third section. Liszt experiments with alternating upper register patterns with low chords (mm. 59–68) as he varies the five-note melody that began in m. 44. A coda based on the B section begins in m. 77, and the piece ends softly on repeated C♯-major chords. *Resignazione*— one of his calmest and shortest pieces—requires no virtuosity at all. In only twenty-nine measures it consists primarily of a four-part choral-like texture, ending with a five-measure, single-note line in the middle register of the keyboard. Even in its simplicity Liszt holds the listener's attention through his striking harmonic progressions and chromaticism.

Dating from around 1879, Liszt's only Toccata (S 197a) is more of an etude than any of his later works. Its *Prestissimo* tempo and youthful vigor (somewhat reminiscent in spirit to *Gnomenreigen*) as well as its harmonic simplicity make it quite different from Liszt's late, more introspective works. The first twenty-three measures are entirely played on white keys as is most of the piece, until it modulates to E♭ major in m. 43. The first eighteen measures consists of continuous sixteenth notes alternating in groups of four between the hands. In m. 19 an ostinato pattern of thirds and fifths begins in the left hand, and in m. 35 the right hand begins a series of arpeggios that last until the opening idea returns. The mood of the piece changes when the music focuses on the low register of the keyboard and lightens only as the work concludes with its treble rolled chord on A minor.

Liszt also wrote a couple of trifles that remain interesting today. In 1868 upon the request of Marquise de Blocqueville (a daughter of a general under Napoleon), Liszt composed a musical portrait of her, basing his thirty-two measures on two other similar portraits she had requested from Henri Herz (1835) and Francis Planté (1868). The little piece, *La marquise de Blocqueville, un portrait en musique* (S 190), has three distinct sections moving from G to F♯ minor and finally to F♯ major. The idea of the musical portrait gained prominence in the twentieth century with Virgil Thomson who "painted" over two hundred "musical" portraits of individuals he knew.[74]

Liszt's most amusing piece is his *Carrousel de Mme Pelet-Narbonne* (S 214a), dating between 1875 and 1881. In only forty-three measures, it foreshadows Bartók's *Bagatelles* and shorter pieces for *Mikrokosmos*. The first section, *Allegro intrepido* in A minor, uses percussive and repeated open fifths in the bass, and the second (*un poco moderato*) and third—both in A major—are more delicate and playful. The textures are sparse throughout. Although the work could hardly be considered virtuosic, the clever writing makes the piece difficult to perform effectively. Anecdotally, this work was first improvised as a character description. Joseph Banowetz elaborated on its compositional history:

During the 1870's the Meyendorff family was renting a house from Madame Pelet-Narbonne in Weimar. The good lady, apparently of rather portly proportions, had been seen by Liszt riding on a carrousel at the carnival which was in town. The sight of the corpulent and ungainly woman struck Liszt as extremely funny, and to describe her he improvised this little piece for the Baroness. Delighted at this, she made him immediately write it out.[75]

Liszt's *Wiegenlied (Chant du berceau)* (S 198) starts out as one of his charming, light works but moves into a different realm. The piece, in two parts with the second a variation of the first, never rises much above the *piano* dynamic level. *Wiegenlied* begins with a four-measure rhythmic ostinato that provides the left-hand accompaniment for the majority of the work. Over this ostinato Liszt writes a slow but lilting melody usually in thirds or sixths. As the work progresses however, it becomes more harmonically complex as the tritone inserts itself into the ostinato pattern. The work in C major in its beginning dissolves into leanings a tritone away in F# minor, before closing on a single-line, three-note descending pattern. The same material is found in the first movement of Liszt's *Von der Wiege bis zum Grabe* and *Die Wiege* for four violins.[76]

The *Romance Oubliée* (S 527) is Liszt's response to a publisher who wanted to reprint his earlier *Romance*. In 1880 he wrote it not only for piano, but also for viola and piano, violin and piano, and cello and piano. He gives the indication of *Andante malinconico* and with its opening single-line, five-note motive establishes an aura of languor and sadness in its 9/8 rhythm. The piece begins to intensify at m. 18 and builds with repeated chords to a *forte* section that is immediately curtailed by a single-line, quasi-cadenza section. The rest of the piece is elegiac with its half-note motives, often in augmentation of the opening motive, and the rolling eighth- and sixteenth-note arpeggios. The work succeeds in its thoughtful depiction of nostalgia and regret.

OTHER TRANSCRIPTIONS

Other than his transcriptions dealing with religion or lamentation, Liszt continued to transcribe his own works and those of others on a host of multifarious themes. Most important of his own works for piano include his solo version of *Totentanz* (S 525) that was published in 1865 and deserves to be heard much more than it is. Overshadowed by the piano and orchestra version, the solo version is highly effective, differing only slightly from the better-known version. As well, his 1877 transcription of "Gretchen" from his *Faust Symphony* (S 513) remains warmly beautiful even without the resources of the orchestra.

Shortly after he had revised the original organ *Präludium und Fuge über der Namen BACH* in 1870, Liszt transcribed his *Fantasie und Fuge über das Thema B-A-C-H* (S 529) for piano solo. He had also made a piano transcription of the first version dating from around 1855 or 1856 that was not published until 1983 in the NLE known as *Präludium und Fugue über das Motiv B-A-C-H*. The Fantasy immediately spells out Bach's name in German notation (B♭, A, C, B♮) in the lower register of the piano with a ferocious *fortissimo* opening. Partly because of the chromatic nature of the motive, this work is one of Liszt's most adventuresome large-scale compositions. He uses this B-A-C-H theme in all types of manners, in augmentation, diminution, melodically, and accompanimental in a variety of harmonic textures. It permeates the musical fabric of the entire work in a surprisingly dissonant manner. The beginning rhapsodic prelude remains extremely loud and rough except for a couple of brief, softer transitional passages. The fugue itself, though, begins *pianissimo* and *misterioso* in an *Andante* tempo. Not long after the four voices enter Liszt changes the tempo to *Allegro con brio* (m. 142) and the *fortissimo* and almost violent mood of the opening returns for much of the work. Brazen, interlocking octaves fly by with loud tremolos, quick arpeggios, and majestic, thick chords. Right to its conclusion, Liszt continually develops the B-A-C-H motive, making this music as unrelenting as it is monumental.

Late in his life Liszt became quite involved with the music of Russian composers. He transcribed or paraphrased a large number of Russian compositions from the 1870s until his death, including the *Polonaise* from Tchaikovsky's *Eugene Onegin* (S 429), two songs of Anton Rubinstein (S 554), and two excellent tarantellas based on music of Alexander Dargomïzhsky in 1879 (S 483) and César Cui in 1885 (S 482). Liszt even wrote fifteen measures in 1880 entitled *Prelude to Borodin's 'Chopsticks' Polka* (S 207a) solely to prove that he had been enchanted with an edition that Alexander Borodin had assembled of paraphrases on the "chopsticks" theme. These fifteen measures are insignificant from a musical point of view. They illustrate, nonetheless, Liszt's humor and his generosity in aiding other composers.[77] A year before he died Liszt based a short piece on a couple of Russian folksongs: *Abschied–Russiches Volkslied* (S 251). It is a tonal work in the Aeolian mode and is entirely diatonic except for four measures where the lowered second scale degree give it a Phrygian flavor. The brief work *(Andante)* requires no virtuosity, and much of the writing is in four-part harmony.

Gerald Abraham called some of these last pieces "strangely beautiful things which if they are romantic in any sense of the word are but ashes of romanticism. . . . they mark the birth of modernism as much as the old age of romanticism."[78] From the serious religious music Liszt wrote during his Rome years, to the fragmented experimentation of his last years, his music from these twenty-five years seems as genuine, if not more so, than the music before this time. Whether tonal or approaching atonality, or portraying a fat lady on a carrousel, whipping off a *Mephisto Waltz* or a *Hungarian Rhapsody*, extemporizing on a famous operatic scene, or expressing his unbearable grief for those he most loved, Liszt never ceased to express himself through his music right to the end of his dying days. This voluminous outpouring of music for solo piano with its unflagging innovations in keyboard performance, formal structure, and harmonic language paved the way, in one manner or the other, for an astounding number of composers in the following generation.

NOTES

1. *Letters of Franz Liszt*, ed. La Mara [Marie Lipsius], trans. Constance Bache (New York: Greenwood Press, 1969), 2:184.

2. *Franz Liszt's Briefe*, ed. La Mara [Marie Lipsius], 8 vols. (Leipzig: Breitkopf & Härtel, 1893–1905), 7:57–58. ["Ma seule ambition de musicien était et serait de lancer mon javelot dans les espaces indéfinis de l'avenir. . . . Pourvu que ce javelot soit de bonne trempe et ne retombe pas à terre—le reste ne m'importe nullement!"]

3. *Letters of Franz Liszt*, 2:272.

4. Ibid., 2:382.

5. Ibid., 2:391.

6. *Franz Liszt's Briefe*, 7:388. ["Malgré force interruptions, je continue de noircir du papier de musique, et ne fais que biffer et raturer. La plupart des choses que je saurais écrire, ne me paraissent pas en valoir la peine!"]

7. For an additional list of Liszt's impressionistic pieces, see Gerald Abraham, *A Hundred Years of Music* (London: Duckworth, 1938), 277.

8. R. Larry Todd, "The 'Unwelcome Guest' Regaled: Franz Liszt and the Augmented Triad," *19th-Century Music* 12/2 (Fall 1988): 93.

9. See Arnold, "Recitative in Liszt's Solo Piano Music," *JALS* 24 (July-December 1988): 3–22.

10. Paul Henry Lang, *Music in Western Civilization* (New York: W. W. Norton, 1941), 872.

11. Bence Szabolcsi, *The Twilight of Liszt*, trans. András Deák (Budapest: Akadémiai Kiadó, 1959), 40.

12. James M. Baker, "The Limits of Tonality in the Late Music of Franz Liszt," *Journal of Music Theory* 34/2 (Fall 1990): 170.

13. David Cannata argued this earlier date for *Angelus!* instead of the customary 1877 in his "Perception & Apperception in Liszt's Late Piano Music," *Journal of Musicology* 15/2 (Spring 1997): 191–206. *Angelus!* is the only work in the cycle that Liszt arranged for string quartet (S 378), organ (S 378/1), and harmonium or piano—although he only changes the texture in eight measures (mm. 157–164) to indicate the harmonium version.

14. *Sursum corda* takes its title from "part of a short dialogue between the celebrant and the congregation that focuses on the Preface [of the mass] that follows." See Cannata, "Perception & Apperception in Liszt's Late Piano Music," 193.

15. From Villa d'Este on 27 September 1877 Liszt wrote of the cypress pieces: "I shall call them *Thrénodies*, as the word *élégie* strikes me as too tender, and almost worldly." *The Letters of Franz Liszt to Olga von Meyendorff in the Mildred Bliss Collection at Dumbarton Oaks*, trans. William R. Tyler, introduction and notes by Edward N. Waters (Dumbarton Oaks: Trustees for Harvard University, 1979), 293.

16. *The Letters of Franz Liszt to Olga von Meyendorff*, 292.

17. Dolores Pesce, "Expressive Resonance in Liszt's Piano Music," in *Nineteenth-Century Piano Music*, ed. R. Larry Todd (New York: Schirmer, 1990), 372.

18. NLE i/8: x–xi.

19. Pesce, "Liszt's *Années de Pèlerinage*, Book 3: A 'Hungarian' Cycle?" *19th-Century Music* 13/3 (Spring 1990): 228.

20. Franz Liszt, *Sonata in B Minor and Other Works for Piano*. From the Franz Liszt-Stiftung edition, ed. José Vianna da Motta (New York: Dover, 1990), 167.

21. Ibid., 167.

22. Ibid.

23. Ibid., 182.

24. Ibid.

25. Alan Walker, *Franz Liszt: The Weimar Years 1848–1861* (New York; Knopf, 1989), 2:75.

26. Joseph Banowetz, ed. *Franz Liszt: An Introduction to the Composer and His Music* (Park Ridge, IL: General Words & Music, 1973), 4.

27. MW, 14: 815.

28. Cited in NLE ii/12: xii. *Briefwechsel zwischen Franz Liszt und Carl Alexander, Groherßoz von Sachsen*, ed. La Mara [Marie Lipsius] (Leipzig: Breitkopf & Härtel, 1909), 115.

29. Searle, *Music of Liszt*, 101. See Chapter 8 for a discussion of the organ arrangement of *Weinen, Klagen, Sorgen, Zagen*.

30. Alfred Brendel, *Musical Thoughts and Afterthoughts* (Princeton: Princeton University Press, 1976), 83.

31. Murray Perahia, "Reflection & Comments," *Horowitz: The Last Recording* (New York: CBS Records and Sony Classical, SK 45818 [1990]), 5.

32. *Franz Liszt: L'artiste—Le Clerc. Documents inédits*, ed. Jacques Vier (Paris: Les Éditions du Cèdre, 1951), 121. ["Quelques mois après la mort de Daniel, j'ai relu les strophes appelées les 'Morts', que Lamennais a publiées dans le volume de ses mélanges. Chacune d'elles retombe ou plutôt remonte à cette simple et sublime exclamation: 'Heureux les morts qui meurent dans le Seigneur.' C'est le retentissement de la miséricorde de Dieu dans l'âme humaine et la révélation du mystère de la vie et de la mort par l'infinie béatitude de son amour.

En lisant les strophes de Lamennais, je les traduisais involontairement en musique. J'ai noté ces accords, quelque faibles et impuissants qu'ils soient."]

33. The entire preface reads,
"Grato m'è il sonno, e più l'esser di sasso.
Mentre che il danno e la vergogna dura,
Non veder, non sentir m'è gran ventura
Però non mi destar, deh'—parla basso!"

34. Searle, *The Music of Liszt,* 103.

35. Ibid.

36. Paul Merrick, *Revolution and Religion in the Music of Liszt* (Cambridge: Cambridge University Press, 1987), 264.

37. "dulces moriens reminiscitur Argos" in *Virgil's Works: The Aeneid, Eclogues, and Georgics*, trans. J. W. Mackail (New York: The Modern Library, 1950), X, 782.

38. See Theodore Edel, "Liszt's La Notte: Piano Music as Self-Portrait," *JALS* 42 (1997): 43–59.

39. *Franz Liszt's Briefe*, 7:370–371. ["Veuillez avoir la bonté de remercier Sgambati de son intention de faire connaître ma *lugubre Gondola*. Je doute qu'elle obtienne du succès aux concerts—vu son caractère triste et sombre, à peine mitigé par quelques ombres de rêverie."]

40. Franz Liszt, *Selected Letters,* ed. and trans. Adrian Williams (Oxford: Clarendon Press, 1998), 897.

41. *Letters of Franz Liszt*, 2:473. Liszt refers to the solo piano work as the transcription of the piano and violin (or cello) work.

42. Pesce, "Expressive Resonance in Liszt's Piano Music," 402.

43. *Letters of Franz Liszt*, 2:432.

44. NLE i/12: xiv.

45. For further relationships between these two pieces, see Cannata, "Perception & Apperception in Liszt's Late Piano Music," 178–207.

46. Ibid., 207.

47. Allen Forte, "Liszt's Experimental Idiom and Music of the Early Twentieth Century," *19th-Century Music* 10/3 (Spring 1987): 221.

48. NLE, i/12: xv.

49. Ibid., 91.

50. Szabolcsi, *The Twilight of Liszt*, 39.

51. See LW, 820.

52. Linda W. Claus, "An Aspect of Liszt's Late Style: The Composer's Revisions for *Historische, Ungarische Portraits*," *JALS* 3 (1978): 5–6.

53. Searle, *The New Grove Early Romantic Masters*, 1:317.

54. Jim Samson, "East Central Europe: the Struggle for National Identity," in *Music and Society: The Late Romantic Era From the mid-19th century to World War I*, ed. Samson (Englewood Cliffs, NJ: Prentice Hall, 1991), 226–227.

55. NLE, i/14: 43.

56. Bernard C. Lemoine, "Tonal Organization in Selected Late Piano Works of Franz Liszt," in *Liszt Studien 2. Referate des 2. Europäischen Liszt-Symposions Eisenstadt 1978*, ed. Serge Gut (Munich and Salzburg: Emil Katzbichler, 1981), 130.

57. NLE i/12: xi.

58. NLE i/14: xi–xii.

59. Searle, *The Music of Liszt*, 115.

60. MW, ii/10: 205.

61. For discussion of compositional dates and title information, see "Preface" to Franz Liszt, *Zwei Konzertetüden*, ed. Maria Eckhardt and Wiltrud Haug-Freienstein (Munich: G. Henle, 1994), vi.

62. See Franz Liszt, *Selected Letters*, 906.

63. *Franz Liszt's Briefe*, 7:49. ["Ce ne seront nullement des oeuvre de science, ou d'apparat, mais de simples échos de mes émotions de jeunesse—celles-ci restent indélébiles à travers toutes les épreuves des années!"]

64. See Searle, *The Music of Liszt*, 110. Searle speculated that "the two latter are portraits of Liszt himself and the Princess respectively—*Jadis* recalls their first meeting."

65. See Franz Liszt, *The Late Pieces*. The Complete Music for Solo Piano 11 (Hyperion CDA66445 [1991]), 5.

66. Nicholas Cook, "Rehearings: Liszt's Second Thoughts: *Liebestraum* No. 2 and Its Relatives," *19th-Century Music* 12/2 (Fall 1988): 170–171.

67. Forte, "Liszt's Experimental Idiom," 222.

68. Walker, *Franz Liszt: The Final Years 1861–1886* (New York: Alfred A. Knopf, 1996), 3:441.

69. Forte, "Liszt's Experimental Idiom," 227.

70. See François Decarsin, "Liszt's *Nuages Gris* and Kagel's *Unguis Incarnatus est*: A Model and Its Issue," trans. Jonathan Dunsby, *Music Analysis* 4/3 (1985): 259–263.

71. Leonard Ratner, *Romantic Music: Sound and Syntax* (New York: Schirmer, 1992), 267.

72. Franz Liszt, *Piano Piece No. 1 in A Flat*. Liszt Society Publications (Aylesbury: Bardic Edition, 1988), n.p.

73. LW, 14: 815.

74. See Anthony Tommasini, "The Portraits for Piano by Virgil Thomson" (D.M.A. diss., Boston University, 1982).

75. Banowetz, *Franz Liszt,* 1.

76. NLE, i/12: xiii.

77. See Guy S. Wuellner, "Franz Liszt's Prelude on 'Chopsticks,' " *JALS* 4 (December 1978): 40. After Liszt had written Borodin thanking him for the volume, Liszt's letter was published in Russia and immediately pronounced a forgery by Borodin's enemies. Consequently, Liszt wrote these measures to place before Borodin's own polka and appeared in the second edition of the pieces in Liszt's own manuscript to prove that he had contributed to this small volume. Wuellner concluded that Liszt's fifteen measures "add up to much more than a few moments of music: they are a touching testimony of a great artist willing to stand with his fellow composers against adversity— armed only with his genius and a simple childish tune."

78. Abraham, *A Hundred Years of Music*, 70.

7

Opera Paraphrases

Charles Suttoni

The opera paraphrase is something of a problematic form. Reviled by some as an aberration,[1] it nonetheless dominated the concert stage for much of the nineteenth century in an age when pianists of the day performed the music of their own time. That was only as it should be. Opera ruled the lyric stage. It was living theater that provided an ever-fresh supply of popular melodies, and it was the public's familiarity with these melodies that drew them to both the opera house and the concert hall.

Pianists were quick to capitalize on opera's popularity, and that appeal, coupled with the instrument's improvements in mechanical action and sonority, led to ever more ingenious elaborations of operatic material. Virtually every concert program from about 1830 to 1860 included opera fantasies, with each pianist usually writing his or her own, and it was these pieces, not the piano works of Ludwig van Beethoven, Franz Schubert, or even Frédéric Chopin and Robert Schumann, that provided the standard concert fare of the period.[2] Liszt's rival Sigismond Thalberg, great pianist that he was, built his reputation almost entirely with such works, but it remained for Liszt to cultivate the form to its fullest.[3]

Opera paraphrases were an integral part of Liszt's musical personality, a point Ferruccio Busoni stressed when he wrote that "anyone who has listened to or played the finale of *Lucrezia*, the middle section in B-major in *Norma* or the slow movement in *Sonnambula* without being moved has not yet arrived at Liszt."[4] In broader terms, Johannes Brahms remarked in the 1880s that "whoever really wants to know what Liszt has done for the piano should study his old operatic fantasies. They represent the classicism of piano technique."[5] Both points are well taken. Liszt not only incorporated his command of the piano's action and sonorities into these works, he eventually became uncommonly sensitive to the dramatic nature of the operatic material he chose to elaborate. A simple potpourri of "favorite" tunes was not for him. Furthermore, since our present-day reliance on a presanctified repertory of century-old operas was totally alien to Liszt's time, the operas he paraphrased were almost all contemporary works by living composers. Typically he wrote these pieces within a few years, if not within months, of an opera's premiere.

Liszt composed fantasies and paraphrases of one type or another throughout his entire career. Because the works of any given period naturally reflect his interests and activities at the time, it is advantageous to survey these pieces period by period.

THE YOUNG YEARS, 1824–1829[6]

1824   *Impromptu brillant sur des thèmes de Rossini et Spontini.* S 150.
1829   *Grande fantaisie sur la tyrolienne de l'opéra La fiancée.* (Auber) (revised in the late 1830s and again around 1842). S 385.

Allowing that Liszt's first brush with operatic material came when he was only twelve years old in a modest, Czernyesque impromptu on themes from four popular operas of the early 1820s, his first real involvement came with the Auber *Tyrolienne* five years later. Although called a *Grande fantaisie*, it is actually a traditional introduction, theme, and variations. The theme is a folksy tune from Act II, while the variations—as artful and extended as they may be—make the most of the rapid and elaborate passagework that characterized the virtuosity of the 1820s and marked the now neglected works not only of Carl Czerny, but of Friedrich Kalkbrenner, Henri Herz, and Johann Hummel as well. Since young Liszt had cut his pianistic teeth, as it were, on this voluble, brilliant pianism, it would be some time before he would wean himself from the bravado of playing clutches of notes as quickly as possible.

PILGRIMAGE YEARS, 1835–1837

1835   *Réminiscences de La juive.* (Halévy) S 409a.
1835–1836   *Divertissement sur la cavatine 'I tuoi frequenti palpiti.'* (*Niobe*, Pacini) S 419.
1835–1836   *Réminiscences de Lucia di Lammermoor.* [Sextet] (Donizetti) S 397.
1835–1836   *Marche et cavatine de Lucia di Lammermoor.* (Donizetti) S 398.
1836   *Grande fantaisie sur des thèmes de l'opéra Les Huguenots.* (Meyerbeer) S 412.
1836   *Réminiscences des Puritains.* (Bellini) S 390.
1837   *Hexaméron. Grandes variations de bravoure sur la marche des Puritains.* (with Thalberg, Pixis, Herz, Czerny, and Chopin) S 392.

Even if Liszt in his mid-twenties began to develop his distinctly resonant sound with this group of works, he continued to revel in brilliant passagework for its own sake. Both factors are evident in the Pacini piece, a protracted *improvviso*, with lyric touches, on an eccentric, staccatoish little cavatina. A showpiece for his prowess, Liszt played it frequently at his early concerts, including his famous encounter with Thalberg in 1837.

Traveling and away from Paris in the late 1830s, Liszt evidently sought to keep his name alive by writing fantasies of the big, hit operas of the day. He usually cast these pieces in a broad tripartite form—that is, a dramatic opening section, an extended lyric interlude, followed by a bang-up finale that typically included references to earlier themes. Generally speaking, these early fantasies are overly long and overly ambitious, and while many of their details are sensitively rendered, they are flawed to the extent that Liszt sometimes allows an overweening virtuosity to subvert the character of the melodies he includes. In *La juive*, it is the delicately exotic Bolero that suffers. With *Lucia*, the two parts of which Liszt had conceived as a single extended work, even the sympathetic Andre Schaeffner remarked: "To Edgardo's cavatina ["Tu che a Dio"] Liszt abruptly attaches the finale of the second act and there . . . indulges himself in his eccentricities of extreme virtuosity."[7] Small wonder, then, that the publisher Hofmeister split *Lucia* in two, thereby freeing its self-contained opening section—an adroitly crafted paraphrase of the Sextet "Chi mi frena" with its own brief introduction and codetta—to take on a popular concert life of its own,[8] while the far longer *Marche et Cavatine*, with its inappropriate finale, fell into neglect.

I puritani underwent similar radical surgery. Originally written as an extended tripartite work based on related incidents from Act I—Arturo's arrival, his declaration of love for Elvira, and her joy at becoming a bride—the piece may embody a cogent dramatic point of view, but again it is Liszt's tendency to overstate and accelerate his material that detracts from the fantasy's total effect. (Liszt had such supreme command of the keyboard that it seems churlish at times to chide him for unleashing his fingers to the utmost, as he does in pieces like *I puritani*.) Eventually, it was not the publisher, but Liszt himself who detached Elvira's scintillating Polonaise "Son vergin vezzosa" from the Fantasy and performed it as an independent concert piece.

I puritani also provided the theme—the spirited duet and march "Suoni la tromba" from Act II—for that virtuoso novelty, the *Hexaméron*.[9] A composite work to which six pianists each contributed a variation, it furnishes an instructive mixture of differing piano styles of the 1830s. In addition to his variation, Liszt also provided the introduction, transitions, and finale. He is the only one of the six known to have performed the work in concert.

In 1836 Liszt turned to Meyerbeer's *Les Huguenots*. Thalberg had written a potpourri-like fantasy that featured three unrelated highlights from this blockbuster: the Bathers' Chorus in Act II, the chorale "Ein' feste Burg," and the Rataplan in Act III. Liszt countered with a totally different conception of the opera. Gerhard Winkler, in a detailed comparison between the two approaches, notes: "Liszt's composition is a Fantasy on the Grand Duo, the great love duet at the close of Act IV"[10] between the Catholic Valentine and her Huguenot lover Raoul. With the duet as the centerpiece, Liszt frames it with corollary themes relating to the massacre of the Protestants, the lovers' deaths, and a forceful peroration of "Ein' feste Burg." The work, as a result, focuses on and conveys what Liszt regarded as the dramatic core of the opera, an approach he would refine and master in his coming Fantasies.

VIRTUOSO YEARS, 1839–1847

1839   *Fantaisie sur des motifs favoris de l'opéra La sonnambula.* (Bellini) S 393.
1840   *Réminiscences de Lucrezia Borgia.* (Donizetti) rev. 1848. S 400.
      1. Trio du seconde acte.
      2. Chanson *à boire (Orgie)-Duo-Finale.*
1840   *I puritani. Introduction et polonaise.* S 391 (from S 390).
1841   *Réminiscences de Robert le diable. Valse infernale.* (Meyerbeer) S 413.
1841   *Réminiscences de Norma.* (Bellini) S 394.
1841   *Réminiscences de Don Juan.* (Mozart) S 418.
1842   *Fantasy on two themes from Le nozze di Figaro.* (Mozart) S 697. (Completed by Busoni.)
1844   *Marche funèbre de Dom Sébastien.* (Donizetti) S 402.
1846   *Tarantelle di bravura d'après la tarantelle de La muette de Portici.* (Auber) S 386.

With the start of his decade-long virtuoso tours late in 1839, Liszt was in need of opera fantasies that he could perform at his concerts, producing in the process some of the most notable examples of the genre. The Donizetti pieces of the time, however, still tend to be needlessly elaborate and overblown, even though the second *Lucrezia* Fantasy, the first composed, does include the Finale that so impressed Busoni.

Bellini fares much better. Liszt's *Sonnambula* is a grandly contrived concert piece that is most notable for a daunting passage that combines a reunion of themes—"Ah! non giunge" and "Ah! perche non posso odiarti"—with a trill:

Example 7.1
Bellini/Liszt, *Sonnambula,* **mm. 262–269**

But, if Liszt's Fantasy—appealing as sections of it may be—seems overly episodic and lacks a cogent dramatic impact, it is the opera's inconsequential tale of Amina, the sleepwalker who innocently wanders into a nobleman's bed chamber, that is essentially at fault.

Norma is a different story. Liszt had evidently become so annoyed at the press's incessant linking of his name with Thalberg's that he determined to out-do Thalberg in his rival's own style. Liszt even went so far as to describe his *Norma* sardonically as "a fantasy all charged and supercharged with arpeggios, with octaves and with those drab commonplaces that are supposed to be brilliant and extraordinary."[11] Even so, he succeeded most impressively with *Norma*. By judiciously selecting seven themes that highlight Norma's tragic conflict between her responsibilities as a Druid priestess and her emotions as a woman and mother, he not only focused on the dramatic core of the opera, he also fashioned a piece that proceeds just as inexorably to its climactic close. As for the B-major section, "Qual cor tradisti," that Busoni cited, it is by all counts one of the most ingenious and sublime pages ever written for the piano, maintaining as it does, three distinct voices while filling the keyboard with sound.

Example 7.2
Bellini/Liszt, *Norma*, mm. 190–194

If Liszt's paraphrase of *Norma* has any fault, it is the stretto combination of themes (mm. 345–354) that interrupts the drive to a climax in the finale. (It is, incidentally, the same pairing that Thalberg had included in his own fantasy on *Norma* six years earlier.) Some bolder pianists have taken to omitting the stretto, and the piece is much the better for it.

With Meyerbeer's highly successful *Robert le diable*, Liszt also centers his Fantasy on a single character. Not Robert, Duke of Normandy, of the title, but his demonic father Bertram, who, having sold his soul to the Devil, must deliver Robert in his place to avoid damnation. The *Valse infernale*—Bertram's big scena "De ma gloire éclipsée" backed by a chorus of black demons in Act III—is a high point of the opera, one that Liszt, following his usual practice, "enriches" by adding two other themes: the ballet, "Séduction de jeu," and the Knights' entry in Act II.[12] The appeal of Liszt's *Robert*, a huge sensation in its day, is the gleeful abandon with which he treats Meyerbeer's high-camp demonism and the great skill with which he combines the various themes.

Liszt's *Don Juan*[13] is a third work to reduce the essence of an opera to the dramatic portrayal of its protagonist. Broadly structured in Liszt's preferred tripartite form, the Fantasy is an impressively conceived piece whose succeeding sections seem to make the most of the piano's sonic possibilities. The work opens with an ominously scored montage of themes relating to the Commendatore's vengeance on the Don and its writing is as "orchestral" as Liszt ever gets in his transcriptions. The Don's attempt to seduce Zerlina—the duet "Là ci darem la mano"—forms the substantial lyric center. Here, too, Liszt remains close to his source in that he presents the scene as a true duet,[14] which contrasts the Don's suave baritone blandishments with Zerlina's increasingly flustered treble responses, a distinction he maintains throughout the ensuing, well-developed variations. The Don's animated "Fin ch'han dal vino," then forms the basis for the lengthy finale. Admittedly, some critics seem to have taken exception to letting this gleeful, amoral aria have the final say, or substantially so,[15] but Liszt, in purely musical terms, was still committed to the brilliant finale and this sturdy theme is the only one in the opera that, taken in context, has both the propulsion and verve required for his purposes. The grandest of the Liszt paraphrases,[16] the work almost magically manages to make sweeping demands on both piano and pianist while remaining virtually free of virtuosity for its own sake.

The same cannot be said of *Figaro*, a work known only in the Busoni-completed version.[17] The themes are "Non più andrai" and "Voi, che sapete." As a lyric respite, Cherubino's winsome *canzona* is treated resonantly (in tenths) and discreetly enough, but the great bulk of the piece, as we have it, is given over to a boisterous, bombastic, bravura paraphrase of "Non più andrai." The incongruity of tune and treatment is fascinating, so let the virtuosi flail away!

Lastly, there is Liszt's trenchant, expert version of the Auber Tarantella, a work "in which all the virtuoso possibilities are gathered together in a perfectly lucid framework."[18] After this he would compose no more opera paraphrases for his own use.

WEIMAR AND ROME, 1848–1868

1848	*Salve Maria de Jerusalem.* (*I Lombardi,* Verdi) S 431.
ca. 1849	*Ernani. Paraphrase de Concert.* (Verdi) rev. 1859. S 432.
1849	*'O, du mein holder Abendstern' Rezitativ und Romanze aus der Oper Tannhäuser.* (Wagner) S 444.
1849	*Halloh! Jagdchor und Steyrer aus der Oper Tony.* (Ernst II, Duke of Saxe-Coburg-Gotha) S 404.
1849–1850	*Illustrations du Prophète.* (Meyerbeer) S 414.
	1. *Prière, Hymne triomphale, Marche du sacre.*
	2. *Les Patineurs, Scherzo.*
	3. *Choeur pastoral, Appel aux armes.*
ca. 1850	*Valse de concert sur deux motifs de Lucia et Parisina.* (Donizetti) S 214/3. Earlier version S 401, 1842.
1852	*Zwei Stücke aus Tannhäuser und Lohengrin.* (Wagner) S 445.
	1. *Einzug der Gäste auf der Wartburg.*
	2. *Elsas Brautzug zum Münster.*
1852	*Bénédiction et serment, deux motifs de Benvenuto Cellini.* (Berlioz) S 396.
1853	*Andante Finale et Marche de l'opéra König Alfred.* (Raff) S 421.
1854	*Aus Lohengrin.* (Wagner) S 446.
	1. *Festspiel und Brautlied.*
	2. *Elsas Traum.*
	3. *Lohengrins Verweis an Elsa.*
1859	*Miserere du Trovatore.* (Verdi) S 433.
1859	*Rigoletto. Paraphrase de concert.* (Verdi) S 434.
1859	*Phantasiestück über Motive aus Rienzi.* (Wagner) S 439.
1860	*Spinnerlied aus Der fliegende Holländer.* (Wagner) S 440.
1861	*Valse de l'opéra Faust.* (Gounod) S 407.
1861–1862	*Pilgerchor aus der Oper Tannhäuser.* (Wagner) S 443.
1865	*Illustrations de l'Africaine.* (Meyerbeer) S 415.
	1. *Prière des matelots.*
	2. *Marche indienne.*
ca. 1865	*Les sabéennes, berceuse de l'opéra La reine de Saba.* (Gounod) S 408.
1867	*Isoldens Liebestod: Schluss-Szene aus Tristan und Isolde.* (Wagner) rev. 1875. S 447.
1867	*Fantaisie sur l'opéra hongrois Szép Ilonka.* (Mosonyi) S 417.
ca. 1868	*Les Adieux. Rêverie sur un motif de l'opéra Roméo et Juliette.* (Gounod) S 409.
1868	*Don Carlos. Coro di festa e Marcia funebre.* (Verdi) S 435.

When Liszt retired from the concert stage in 1847 his involvement with the opera paraphrase changed significantly. No longer composing for his own use, he began writing for others; that is, to help promote their operas, to provide them with concert material, or simply to fulfill publishers' commissions, the Liszt name being a strong selling point. The scope of his paraphrases also changed. Rather than trying to distill an entire opera into a single fantasy, he turned his attention to a given scene or episode, supporting his conception of it, if needs be, with related thematic material. Furthermore, his creative emphasis shifted so that the dramatico-melodic content of a scene generally assumed more importance than the pianistic elaboration of it. If virtuosity *per se* was to be held in check, however, Liszt continued to employ a number of compositional techniques—introductions, development sections, reharmonizations, and added codas—to convey his personal approach to the material cited and to fashion it into an independent piano piece. These creative considerations can be taken as background for the two dozen paraphrases of these years, a miscellaneous lot indeed.

Of the Meyerbeer groups, for instance, *Le Prophète* is an homage to a respected old friend, while *L'Africaine* is a publisher's commission. Their designation "Illustrations" harks back to Liszt's transcriptions of the Beethoven Symphonies, which he had termed "the work of an intelligent engraver."[19] Thus, one can well imagine the most engaging of these pieces, the fleet-fingered Scherzo, *Les Patineurs*, as a musical engraving of the famous ice-skating scene in *Le Prophète*. The paraphrases of scenes from *Tony, König Alfred,* and *Szép Ilonka* (Pretty Helen) can also be taken as homages to the colleagues who wrote the operas. Yet, despite some effective writing, they remain as unfamiliar as the operas on which they are based. The Berlioz piece—two complementary themes fashioned into a single, solemnly paced crescendo—is a pointed reminder that Liszt was staging *Benvenuto Cellini* in Weimar when he wrote it.

As for Gounod, the pieces drawn from *The Queen of Sheba* and *Romeo and Juliette* are notable for their reserve and sensitivity, but remain as unfamiliar as their operatic sources. The Waltz from *Faust*, on the other hand, is a concert favorite and deservedly so. Cast in broad ABA form, the work begins with a robust paraphrase of the Waltz in Act II. The ensuing lyric section opens with Faust's approach to Marguerite in the Waltz scene, but takes on significance by leaping to the climax of the love duet "O nuit d'amour," ecstatically set in trills. And then, with this brilliantly spare bit of writing, the Waltz theme returns in ever more ingenious and forceful guises to complete this satisfyingly balanced composition.

Example 7.3
Gounod/Liszt, *Faust,* **mm. 362–376**

The Verdi paraphrases of this period—beginning with the resonant rendition of the lovely prayer "Salve Maria" in *I Lombardi*—are all pieces that focus on a single well-known scene. They include the Quartet from *Rigoletto* (a pianist's favorite), the Miserere from *Il Trovatore,* and the peroration to Charlemagne "O Sommo Carlo" from the third act of *Ernani* (a much reduced excerpt from an earlier unpublished Fantasy on the opera). Liszt composed these three last works specifically for Hans von Bülow to play in his concerts. Some years later when *Don Carlos* first premiered (1867) publisher Ricordi commissioned Liszt to write a piece on it, and the composer complied with a modestly demanding, dark-toned reading of the Grand Finale, Act III, Sc. 2.

Coming to the long series of Wagner Paraphrases,[20] it is important to recall that the Wagner-Liszt compositions were an integral part of the ongoing, complex relations between the two and thus entailed a greater personal involvement than was generally true of the other paraphrases. There is no doubt, however, why Liszt wrote them: "Appearing at the beginning of the fifties," he stated, "such transcriptions only served as modest propaganda on the inadequate piano for the sublime genius of Wagner."[21] Wagner, for his part however, after waxing enthusiastic about Liszt's transcription of the Overture to *Tannhäuser* (S 442), seemingly adopted an indifferent air about them, none too pleased, perhaps, to have another name associated with his music, or even altering it, as Liszt was increasingly wont to do.

Except for the pedestrian, lackluster Fantasy on three themes from *Rienzi* (another concert work for Bülow), Liszt's earlier Wagner pieces tend to be near-transcriptions of the originals, with special attention paid to Wagner's orchestral coloring. Yet, from the start, Liszt, as he did in all his paraphrases, personalized, i.e., revised, the works by making alterations and by shaping them into independent piano pieces. Thus, he subtly rewrites the accompaniment to the recitative of *Abendstern*, or he recapitulates the Festival (Prelude to Act III) in *Lohengrin* after the Bridal Song, or he deletes a portion of Wagner's *Elsas Traum*. Perhaps the most subtle yet far-reaching change occurs with *Isolde's Liebestod*. Although its four introductory bars are usually passed over without special comment, they are, in fact, essential to Liszt's concept; namely, a quotation from the second act love duet at the words "sehnend verlangter Liebestod" (ardently longed for love-death). Thus, the great finale that Wagner had originally designated as Isolde's "Transfiguration," became in Liszt's hands her "Liebestod," and so it has remained ever since.

LAST YEARS, 1871–1882

1871	*'Am stillen Herd' Lied aus Die Meistersinger von Nürnberg.* (Wagner) S 448.
1872	*Ballade aus Der fliegende Holländer.* (Wagner) S 441.
1875	*Walhall aus Der Ring des Nibelungen.* (Wagner) S 449.
ca. 1879	*Aida. Danza sacra e duetto final.* (Verdi) S 436.
1879	*Sarabande und Chaconne aus dem Singspiel Almira.* (Handel) S 181.
1879	*Polonaise from Eugene Onegin.* (Tchaikovsky) S 429.

1882   *Feierlicher Marsch zum heiligen Graal aus Parsifal.* (Wagner) S 450.
1882   *Réminiscences de Boccanegra.* (Verdi) S 438.

The last group of paraphrases alternates, as needed, between Liszt's earlier concert-based style and the spare, harmonically daring mood of his other late piano works. Among them, the Polonaise from *Onegin* is a reminder of former days—a resounding, harmonically enhanced rendition of Tchaikovsky's spirited dance. The publisher Jürgenson commissioned it and paid handsomely for Liszt's efforts. Also, the *Almira* piece is not really a paraphrase, but a set of ingenious variations on Handel's Sarabande, with the Chaconne introduced toward the end as contrast. Liszt composed it as a concert piece for his English pupil Walter Bache.

Of greater importance are the late Wagner pieces which, as noted, became increasingly personal conceptions independent of their opera sources. "Am stillen Herd," for instance, may start out as a replica of Walther's scene with the Meistersingers in Act I, but, somewhat like the song, becomes so elaborate that it develops into a striking, purely Lisztian *improvviso* on the melody. With the Ballad from *The Flying Dutchman,* Liszt alters the flow and structure of Wagner's work so radically by rewriting sections and interpolating themes (e.g., the Dutchman's motif) that one commentator wrote: "This transcription is, as it were, an imaginary staging of *The Flying Dutchman* fashioned after Liszt's compositional technique on the basis of Wagner's motifs."[22] Much the same reshaping occurs with the brief *Walhall* paraphrase in which Liszt condenses and molds the *Ring's* Walhall and sword motifs to his own ends. So too with the Solemn March to the Holy Grail, a rather morbid assemblage of four thematic motifs: the bells, knights' march, holy fool, and the grail itself. Yet, if *Parsifal* is "the supreme song of divine love . . . the miracle work of the century" that Liszt said it was,[23] this piece with its dogged, fifty-eight-bar ostinato and blatant climaxes is at best an enigmatic representation of it. It could be, as Winkler has proposed in a closely argued study, that Liszt had turned against the composer so that "Liszt's reworking is" in reality "a proceeding against the 'theatrical showman' Wagner in Wagner's own name."[24] In other words perhaps, not a paraphrase, but a caricature of the contrived religiosity of the scene. That may be, but the reader can only judge for himself. As it stands, the *Parsifal* paraphrase is Liszt's final, intensely personal yet cryptic evocation of Wagner.

Liszt continued to paraphrase works of Verdi as well. The *Aida* paraphrase is an appealing, sensitively scored work that seems to delight in sending Verdi's themes off in all manner of exotic melodic and harmonic directions. With *Boccanegra*, Liszt's long series of opera-based compositions comes to a close. Why *Boccanegra*? Ricordi may have commissioned it, following, as it does, the opera's 1881 revision. Or, perhaps, it was simply that the aged Liszt sensed an affinity with Doge Simon—both men had been acclaimed heroes in their own day and way, and each had had serious problems with his daughter. What better identification, then, than Liszt would shape his piece around the opera's closing scene in which the dying Boccanegra blesses his daughter's marriage. Whatever its inspiration, it is a modest, somber, and subdued piece with no hint of the former virtuoso in its writing.

Some four dozen pieces composed over sixty years, these works are both a mirror and an integral part of Liszt's activity and output. Much like the symphonic and Lieder transcriptions, the paraphrases attest to his total belief in the piano's ability to assimilate and reproduce the complete range of musical art, but unlike them, the paraphrases are freer in their choice of thematic material and in their manner of presenting it. Such freedom also raises the question of appropriateness, since all paraphrases ultimately relate back to the dramaturgy of the operas themselves. In these terms, a number of the earlier fantasies were indeed overly ambitious and too much the vehicle for virtuoso prowess. In the 1840s, however, when Liszt decided to focus his thematic selections on the dramatic essence of an opera as he saw it and to tailor his pianism to enhance its effect, he produced three of the greatest works in the concert fantasy genre; the *Réminiscences of Norma, Robert le diable,* and *Don Juan.*

Liszt scaled the later works more modestly, but they are no less idiosyncratic evocations of specific scenes or episodes, supported at times with related themes. Although all of them have their individual merits, those based on *Rigoletto, Faust, Tristan und Isolde,* and *Onegin* have, more or less, established themselves in the pianists' repertory. The post-virtuoso paraphrases also include the Wagner pieces, which, in purely musical terms, manifest Liszt's increasingly personal and independent interpretation of their Wagnerian sources. Finally, at the close, with *Aida* and *Boccanegra,* the virtuoso is long gone, and the aged Liszt confines himself to his ever-personal interpretation of the music alone.

NOTES

1. Liszt's own biographer Peter Raabe wrote in 1931 that "Die Opernfantasie war als Kunstform nie wirklich lebendig und ist jetzt sicher tot." [The Opera Fantasy was never truly viable as an art-form and is now surely dead.] *Franz Liszt: Leben und Schaffen* (Stuttgart: J. G. Cotta, 1931; Tutzing: Hans Schneider, 1968), 2:32.

2. Charles Suttoni, "Piano and Opera: A Study of the Piano Fantasies Written on Opera Themes in the Romantic Era" (Ph.D. diss., New York University, 1973) gives a history of the form and its many composers.

3. Liszt's efforts are discussed by: Andre Schaeffner, "Liszt transcripteur d'Opéras italiens," *La Revue musicale* 9 (1928): 89–100; Dieter Presser, "Die Opernbearbeitung des 19. Jahrhunderts," *Archiv für Musikwissenschaft* 12 (1955): 228–238; David Wilde, "Transcriptions for Piano," *Franz Liszt: The Man and His Music,* ed. Alan Walker (New York: Taplinger, 1970), 168–200; Suttoni, "Piano and Opera," 244–323; Sieghart Döhring, "Réminiscences: Liszts Konzeption der Klavierparaphrase," *Festschrift Heinz Becker,* ed. J. Schläder and R. Quandt (Laaber: Laaber Verlag, 1982), 131–151; Kenneth Hamilton, "The Operatic Fantasises and Transcriptions of Franz Liszt: A Critical Study," (Ph.D. diss., Oxford University (Balliol College), 1989); András Batta, "Die Gattung Paraphrase im Schaffen von Franz Liszt—Die musikalische Hassliebe Liszts," in *Der junge Liszt: Referate des 4. Europäischen Liszt-Symposions Wien 1991. Liszt Studien 4,* ed. Gottfried Scholz (Munich and Salzburg: Emil Katzbichler, 1993), 135–142. For Liszt's Wagner paraphrases, see below n. 20.

4. Ferruccio Busoni, *The Essence of Music and other Papers*, trans. Rosamond Ley (London: Rockliff, 1957), 150. The papers were first published 1907–1922.

5. Quoted in Arthur Friedheim, *Life and Liszt: The Recollections of a Concert Pianist*, ed. Theodore L. Bullock (New York: Taplinger, 1961), 138.

6. In this, as in later lists, the date is that of the original composition. The lists for the most part omit later revisions, alternate versions for duet and two pianos, unpublished works, and strict transcriptions (e.g., the Overture to Rossini's *William Tell*, Wagner's *Tannhäuser*, etc.).

7. Schaeffner, "Liszt transcripteur," 96. ["A l'air de Raimond [Edgardo] . . . brusquement Liszt enchaîne le finale du deuxième acte et là . . . se livre à ses excentricités de haut virtuose."]

8. Franz Liszt, *Piano Transcriptions from French and Italian Opera*. Selected with an Introduction by Suttoni (New York: Dover, 1982) includes *Lucia* and a dozen of the later Liszt paraphrases.

9. Humphrey Searle, *The Music of Liszt*, 2d ed. (New York; Dover, 1966), 33–34 gives the origins of the piece.

10. Gerhard J. Winkler, "'Ein'feste Burg ist unser Gott.' Meyerbeers Hugenotten in den Paraphrasen Thalbergs und Liszts," in *Der junge Liszt. Referate des 4. Europäischen Liszt-Symposions Wien 1991. Liszt Studien 4*, ed. Gottfried Scholz (Munich and Salzburg: Emil Katzbichler, 1993), 109. ["Liszts Komposition ist eine Fantasie über das Grand Duo, das grosse Liebesduett am Schluss des vierten Aktes."]

11. Liszt's letter of dedication to Marie Pleyel, January 1844, which the publisher Schott engraved and included in the first edition of the piece. It was also reprinted in a number of journals of the time. See Suttoni, "Liszt's Letters: Réminiscences of Norma," *JALS* 8 (1980): 77–79. ["Une fantaisie toute chargés et surchargés d'arpèges, d'octaves et de ces ternes lieux communs, prétendus brillians et extraordinaires."]

12. Döhring, "Réminiscences," 140. The article presents a detailed analysis of the piece, as well as of *Norma* and *Don Juan*.. ["Dass noch zwei weitere Themen aus der Oper verarbeitet sind, entspräche durchaus der Lisztschen Praxis, die Übertragung einer Einzelnummer gegebenenfalls mit zusätzlichem Material anzureichern."]

13. By titling his work *Don Juan* instead of the expected *Don Giovanni*, it is clear that Liszt was thinking of the much expanded and highly melodramatic version of Mozart's work that was being given at the Paris Opéra as *Don Juan* and which had opened in 1834. See Suttoni "Piano and Opera," 283–284.

14. Here, as in many of his other opera-inspired works, Liszt was uncommonly sensitive to the original vocal registers of the melodies he included.

15. Busoni, for instance, after praising Liszt's "unerring perception of what is important in [the opera]," goes on to object that "the *Don Juan* Fantasy treats sacred themes [sic] in altogether too worldly a fashion." Busoni, *Essence of Music*, 92.

16. The conceptual aesthetic of the work is discussed at length by Albrecht Riethmüller, "Franz Liszts 'Réminiscences de Don Juan,' " in *Analysen: Festschrift für Hans Heinrich Eggebrecht*, ed. W. Breig, et. al. *Beihefte zum Archiv für Musikwissenschaft* 23 (Stuttgart: Steiner, 1984), 276–291.

17. Liszt had originally written a much longer Fantasy that included the Menuet from *Don Giovanni*, which Busoni deleted. Hamilton, "Liszt Fantasises—Busoni Excises: The Liszt-Busoni 'Figaro Fantasy,' " *JALS* 30 (1991): 21–27.

18. Presser, "Opernbearbeitung," 236. ["In der Tarantella aus Aubers 'Muette de Portici' werden alle virtuosen Möglichkeiten in einer vollendet übersichtlichen Anlage zusammengefasst."]

19. "Préface aux symphonies de Beethoven," *Franz Liszt: L'artiste—L'clerc*. ed. J. Vier (Paris: Les Éditions du Cèdre, 1950), 150. ["Je serai satisfait si j'ai accompli la tâche du graveur intelligent."]

20. See Franz Liszt, *Complete Piano Transcriptions from Wagner's Operas*, Introduction by Suttoni (New York: Dover, 1981). Also, see Ursula Hirschmann, "Die Wagner Bearbeitung Franz Liszts," in *Richard Wagner und die Musikhochschule München. Schriften der Hochschule für Musik München* 4, (Regensburg: Bosse, 1983), 103–121; Helmut Loos, "Liszts Klavierübertragungen von Werken Richard Wagners; Versuch einer Deutung," in *Franz Liszt und Richard Wagner. Musikalische und geistesgeschichtliche Grundlagen der neudeutschen Schule. Referate des 3. Europäischen Liszt-Symposions. Eisenstadt 1983. Liszt Studien 3*, ed. Serge Gut (Munich and Salzburg: Katzbichler, 1986), 103–118; Dorothea Redepenning, "'Zu eig'nem Wort und eig'ner Weis' . . . Liszts Wagner-Transkriptionen," *Die Musikforschung* 39 (1986): 305–317; David Huckvale, "Massive Reductions: Wagnerian Piano and Vocal Scores," *Wagner* (London) 13 (1992): 60–82.

21. Letter to Breitkopf & Härtel, 23 November 1876. *Letters of Franz Liszt*, 2:307.

22. Redepenning, "Liszts Wagner-Transkriptionen," 312. ["Diese Übertragung ist gleichsam eine imaginäre Inszenierung des *Fliegenden Holländers*, gestaltet nach Liszts Kompositionstechnik auf der Basis von Wagners Motiven."]

23. Letter to Carolyne Sayn-Wittgenstein, 2 August 1882. Franz Liszt, *Selected Letters*, ed. and trans. Adrian Williams (Oxford: Clarendon, 1998), 883.

24. Winkler, "Liszt contra Wagner. Wagnerkritik in den späten Klavierstücken Franz Liszts," in *Liszt Studien 3*, ed. Serge Gut (Munich and Salzburg: Emil Katzbichler, 1986), 199. ["Liszts Bearbeitung ist ein Prozess gegen den 'Schauspieler' Wagner—das Wort im Sinne Nietzsches—im Namen Wagners."]

8

Organ Music

Marilyn Kielniarz

Liszt's interest in the organ dates from at least 1836, when Adolphe Pictet detailed Liszt improvising on the large Mooser organ in Freiburg's St. Nicholas Church. Liszt taught himself to play the *pedal-flugel* or *pedalier* during the next decade and presented his first and only recital as an organist in 1843 at Moscow's Evangelical Church of SS. Peter and Paul. He offered the program as a benefit for the church's orphan asylum, and included two Beethoven transcriptions and a Handel fugue. Liszt's only other known public performance as an organist occurred under Karl Gille, for whom he appeared as the accompanist in Mendelssohn's *Hear My Prayer*.

Despite few appearances as an organist, Liszt held an interest in the instrument through many musical activities and by way of close friendships. The composer, for example, was appointed to the examining jury for the musical instrument division at the 1878 Paris Exposition. As a result, he played many times upon the large organ Cavaillé-Coll built in the Trocadero. Charles Marie Widor witnessed Liszt at this organ, and remarked: "His hands seemed to spread like fans over the manuals."[1]

Beginning in the Weimar years, prominent organists were among Liszt's close circle of friends. Alexander Winterberger (1834–1914) and Alexander Wilhelm Gottschalg (1827–1908) were students of Johann Gottfried Topfer (1791–1870), Weimar's Municipal Organist and Seminary Professor, and closely linked with the composer. Liszt selected Winterberger as the organist to premiere *Ad nos* for the 1855 dedication of the Merseburg Cathedral organ. Together, they spent much time preparing the work for performance. Winterberger took a recital tour of Holland the following year, during which he received outstanding reviews for performances of *Ad nos* and *B-A-C-H*. Liszt became acquainted with Gottschalg following the latter's appointment to the

Weimar court as organist. Their close relationship may be evidenced, among other things, by Liszt's dedicating three organ works to Gottschalg: *Evocation,* the transcription of Arcadelt's *Ave Maria,* and *Weinen, Klagen, Sorgen, Zagen.* Gottschalg figures heavily within the entire category of Liszt's organ transcriptions and was responsible for much work related to the actual production of these compositions. Liszt and Gottschalg also frequented various churches, listening to the organs as well as engaging in coaching sessions.

LISZT'S ORGAN COMPOSITIONS[2]

The commonly held attitude concerning Liszt's organ works includes two primary points: compositions for the instrument are few in number and may best be described as examples of thematic transformation garbed in bravura display. To be sure, three works, his *Fantasy and Fugue on Ad nos* (S 259), *Prelude and Fugue on B-A-C-H* (S 260), and *Weinen, Klagen, Sorgen, Zagen* (S 673), are well-known organ compositions and feature dramatic, virtuoso passagework. Liszt, nevertheless, composed a great deal of other literature intended for, or playable upon, the instrument, including over forty transcriptions, arrangements, paraphrases, and short pieces. *Ad nos, B-A-C-H,* and *Weinen, Klagen, Sorgen, Zagen* share some similarities as regards basic compositional approach. These pieces, however, do not share the common mark of thematic transformation. Similarly, not every Liszt organ work features thematic transformation as a compositional tool, nor does it necessarily display virtuosic passagework. The composer conceived repertoire for the instrument throughout his life, and the organ works parallel compositional developments found within his oeuvre. Liszt's organ works form three distinct categories: the large-scale, monumental pieces; transcriptions of works he wrote for other musical media; and pieces from his final compositional period. For many, the three large, dramatic pieces that took shape during his years in Weimar characterize Liszt's writing for organ.

The Monumental Works

Liszt considered his first composition for organ, the *Fantasy and Fugue on Ad nos, ad salutarem undam* "as one of my least bad productions."[3] First begun in 1842 and completed in 1850, Breitkopf & Härtel published it in 1852 for organ/pedal piano, as well as for piano four hands. Liszt composed it during this same period in which he worked on piano transcriptions of six large Bach organ works (BWV 543–548: Preludes and Fugues in A minor, C major 4/4, C major 9/8, C minor, E minor, and B minor, S 462). As with numerous other pieces by Liszt, the work also appears in alternate form as a piano duet from 1852.

Liszt designed *Ad nos* as a single, thirty-minute movement based on a chorale theme from Meyerbeer's opera, *Le Prophète,* sung by three Anabaptists preaching to an onlooking crowd.

Example 8.1
Meyerbeer, *Le Prophète*, chorale theme

Much of the composition's style reflects the years Liszt spent as a virtuoso pianist and demonstrates his use of thematic transformation as a compositional device. Contrary to its title, *Ad nos* contains three main sections: a fantasy, an *Adagio*, and a concluding fugue. These sections often feature rhapsodic, dramatic treatments of the theme, in addition to exploring unusual and striking harmonies. The composition is filled with bravura, pianistic passagework—an approach far different than that of other large organ pieces from the same period. Another uncommon feature is that its fugal section does not adhere to traditional structure and takes the common Lisztian approach of abandoning strict formal convention at the conclusion of the exposition. In general, Liszt most often utilizes the theme sequentially, preferring to make use of small, primarily four-note statements. This technique allows for much sectional repetition, which is seldom absent at any point within the work. Liszt increases the juxtaposition of thematic fragments as the composition progresses.

Ad nos begins with a lengthy introduction, leading to rhapsodic treatment of the chorale theme (mm. 1–7). The work's first primary section, a fantasy, extends over 200 measures; characterized by arpeggios, pedal trills, recitatives, and virtuosic cadenza passages for both manuals and pedal, it conveys a brilliant, often pianistic approach to organ composition. Dotted rhythms help create a general sense of tension and are omitted only when rapid passagework demands straightforward rhythmic delineation of thematic fragments. Beginning with the introduction, the entire fantasy concentrates most heavily on development of the chorale-theme head. A secondary compositional motive, a fanfare-like figure based on the first eight notes of the theme tail, is introduced in m. 141 (see Example 8.2).

Example 8.2
Liszt, *Ad nos*, mm. 141–144

The fantasy concludes with a series of pauses and recitatives whereby the composer reduces the excitement and tension created through earlier technical "gymnastics." Begun in C minor, the fantasy concludes with a transitory passage leading to F♯ major, a tritone away. Of particular interest to organists, Liszt does not offer many specifics in the fantasy about registration aside from dynamic indications and the rare stop reference (mm. 141 and 150: *Tromba*). He also provides little assistance to the performer in the way of directives pertaining to manual assignments and changes.

The second major section, a lyric *Adagio*, begins at m. 243 by way of a single tenor voice stating the complete chorale theme (mm. 243–250). The *Adagio* contains harp-like arpeggios and melodic dialogue. The development of the theme tail assumes primary importance within this section. In contrast to the pianistic fantasy, the *Adagio* conveys a compositional approach far more orchestral in nature. Among the numerous settings of the theme, Liszt reflects his fascination with the works of J. S. Bach in m. 357 by stylistically recalling the arpeggiated fifteenth variation of the Baroque master's Passacaglia and Fugue in C minor (see Example 8.3).

Example 8.3
Liszt, *Ad nos*, mm. 357–360

As in the preceding fantasy, Liszt does not provide the organist registrational specifics within this section, except for the indication of dynamic levels. Given such freedom, the lyric, orchestral *Adagio* presents the organist a wide array of opportunities through which to explore the instrument's solo colors. Uncommon to organ repertoire, Liszt presents the performer with an option for a "shortened version," the elimination of mm. 335–397. A passage of extended modulatory arpeggios interrupts thematic statements toward the end of the *Adagio* (mm. 425–433). The double bar at the end of m. 433 signals a renewal of thematic statements: partial single-line iterations coupled with chordal answers. This transitory passage gradually finds its way to A♭ major, and concludes with a single pedal note and the rare registrational directive to change the stops, *die Register wechseln* (m. 444–446).

A brilliant, *forte* cadenza connects the *Adagio* to the fugue (*Allegro deciso*). The passage begins with a series of diminished chords answered by rising trills and incorporates a return of pianistic writing with rapid broken octaves chromatically descending the full compass of the instrument (mm. 470–475). The cadenza is also important from a basic structural standpoint: it contains the composition's harmonic center in m. 493, a prominent dominant-seventh chord on G (mm. 490–492).

The composition's final primary section, a fugue, provides clear recapitulation with the return of dotted rhythms, original tonal center, and reappearance of the fanfare motive. The fugue subject states the entire chorale theme and appears, respectively, in the bass, tenor, alto, and soprano voices.

Example 8.4
Liszt, *Ad Nos,* **mm. 492–499**

Liszt abandons formal fugal design at the conclusion of the exposition and fills the fugue with highly technical passages and a number of directives associated with articulation. Numerous trills, arpeggios, broken octave figurations, and a passage with rapidly changing harmonies over a pedal point contribute to increasing musical tension. Dynamic markings support the general mood and never fall below a *forte* within this final portion of the composition. Unlike the fantasy and *Adagio,* the fugue contains several sections that do not utilize pedal. Nonetheless, a few highly technical passages for pedal may still be found, and the final cadenza features material for solo pedal. A double bar at the beginning of m. 738 heralds a final, grand thematic statement in C major. Marked *Adagio,* Liszt sets the theme within the context of a concluding chorale (mm. 738–741). He follows the slowly moving theme with sequentially descending material based on the fanfare motive. Four half-note chords, expanding in contrary motion away from the center of the keyboard, lead to the final seven measures which feature a C-pedal point. Following the registrational approach of the earlier sections, there is an absence of notations except for dynamic markings. The *fortissimo* dynamic level associated with the concluding chorale indicates use of the organ's full tonal resources, bringing the lengthy work to a massive close.

Without question, *Ad nos* holds a unique place within the genre of organ literature. Few works are presented on such a grand scale or place such challenging demands on both performer and instrument. To underscore the work's complexity, three different compositional styles are featured: organistic, pianistic, and orchestral. This work offers a seemingly limitless scope of material, appearing to reflect the great and varied musical potentials Liszt felt during his early Weimar years.

Another large-scale composition Liszt began during the Weimar years is the *Prelude and Fugue on B-A-C-H* (1855–1870). Liszt had planned its premiere for the 1855 dedication of the Merseburg Cathedral organ; he failed to complete the work in time for the event, however, and *Ad nos* was performed in its place. The composition displays many similar characteristics to the dedicatory work, including transformation of a theme throughout, virtuoso passagework, pianistic writing, cadenzas, and a fugal section with its concluding chorale. *B-A-C-H* places more technical demands upon manual work than that for pedal. Unlike *Ad nos,* except for a cadenza-like passage of trills (mm. 243–249), the pedal is used for little more than thematic and harmonic underpinning. Liszt also makes considerable use of the theme's inherent chromaticism as a structural element, and *B-A-C-H* attests to the composer's growing interest in the expansion of tonality, doing so with tonal shifts occurring so frequently that it is often quite difficult to determine key centers. Liszt revised *B-A-C-H* in 1870 (published by Schuberth) and also published a version for piano solo the next year. It is the second version that is most familiar and discussed below.

Perhaps the most noticeable characteristic of the composition is Liszt's use of chromaticism seen in the "B-A-C-H" motive begun on B♭: it eventually appears in all twelve transposition levels during the prelude's eighty measures (see Example 8.5).

Example 8.5
Liszt, *B-A-C-H*, mm. 1–2

At times, the work seems to be little more than a study in diminished harmonies, with many passages formed by sequences quickly moving through various tonal centers (mm. 55–58). The prelude's cadenza-like passagework finds its climax in m. 68, where dramatic chords and traditional harmonies mark a *fortissimo* thematic statement at the original tonal level. Similar to *Ad nos,* Liszt does not provide the organist with an abundance of registrational directives save for dynamic markings and indications of crescendo and decrescendo.

A short bridge featuring a chromatic, descending single line connects the prelude with the fugue (mm. 75–80). This brief passage also serves to reduce the organ's tonal resources suddenly and quickly, as Liszt directed in m. 81 of the fugue (*pp, misterioso*). Liszt presents the "B-A-C-H" motive at the beginning of the fugue subject, followed by two descending groups of four eighth notes. He states the motive at the ninth transposition level, starting on Gb. The full subject expanded from the "B-A-C-H" motive underscores Liszt's development of chromaticism by utilizing eleven of the twelve chromatic pitches (the twelfth pitch is added with the first note of the countersubject). The countersubject, characterized by a descending chromatic line, further clouds the identification of tonal center (see Example 8.6).

Example 8.6
Liszt, *B-A-C-H*, mm. 81–87

As in *Ad nos,* Liszt abandons strict conformation to traditional fugal structure at the conclusion of the exposition. The fugue gradually builds in dynamic level following the exposition, with the composer eventually indicating full organ (*volles werk*) at m. 130. Passagework characterized by rapidly descending minor scales and punctuating thematic statements identifies a new *Allegro* section within the composition.

Within the active passagework and trills, harmonies from G to C♯ are explored. Liszt presents the option of an *ossia* to the organist, replacing mm. 130–166 with a slightly less technically-demanding presentation of the same musical material (i.e., eighth-note arpeggios replacing rapidly descending scales and the elimination of accompanimental trills). A clear change in musical approach appears in m. 169 when Liszt recalls the beginning of the fugue with a single pedal line stating the subject. Liszt, however, now sets the subject *forte,* and accompanies it with ascending passagework derived from both the countersubject and subject tail. Twelve measures of ascending scales combined with chordal statements of the subject lead to the work's final, bravura passages.

Among other compositional features, the "B-A-C-H" motive alternates in retrograde (D♯-E-C♯-D) with the original motive in the pedals. See retrograde motive bracketed in Example 8.7.

Example 8.7
Liszt, *B-A-C-H*, mm. 200–204

A long series of diminished arpeggios eventually leads to solo pedal trills and a bridge connecting to the composition's concluding section, *Maestoso/ Grave*.

Reminiscent of *Ad nos,* lengthy *fortissimo* chords using traditional harmonies occupy the final measures of the composition. Recalling an earlier passage found near the conclusion of the prelude, Liszt climactically sets the four-note "B-A-C-H" motive within a basic B♭-tonal center (mm. 257–259). Completing the work's catalog of dramatic writing techniques, the juxtaposition of extreme dynamic levels appears in the final ten measures, comparing the organ's softest sounds with its loudest and most forceful. Additionally, the final five measures of the composition do not utilize the "B-A-C-H" motive at all, but present an extended B♭ plagal cadence over a pedal point (mm. 283–292).

A comparison of the 1870 *B-A-C-H* version to the original 1855 composition reveals a slight decrease in length—the original containing 302 total measures to the revised version's 292. The revision, nonetheless, includes approximately twenty changes from the original, totaling 113 measures. While the changes contain little new or different material, the 1870 version reflects Liszt's increased knowledge of the organ, presents more dramatic tension, and shows streamlined compositional technique. He eliminates many doublings between left hand and pedal in the later version, as well as numerous instances of awkward pedal writing. Increased texture in many chordal passages produces a fuller organ sound than found in the original. The revision also shows Liszt more fully exploring chromaticism and expanding concepts of tonality. The composer preferred the revision, finding the original inferior by comparison.

Example 8.8
Liszt, *B-A-C-H*, version 1, m. 71

Example 8.9
Liszt, *B-A-C-H*, version 2, m. 68

Weinen, Klagen, Sorgen, Zagen is another familiar Liszt organ work, even though it first appeared as a work for piano (a praeludium from 1859). The composition did not take its present shape as an extended series of variations until 1862, following the death of Liszt's elder daughter, Blandine. Liszt transcribed it for organ in 1863, and Korner published it in 1865. Liszt based the work on two themes of Bach, the basso continuo theme from the first chorus of Cantata no. 12: *Weinen, Klagen, Sorgen, Zagen* and the "Crucifixus" of the *B Minor Mass*. (The vocal writing of the "Crucifixus" is nearly identical to that found in the first chorus of Cantata no. 12, written a half step lower.) Similar in style to the *Prelude and Fugue on B-A-C-H, Weinen, Klagen, Sorgen, Zagen* demonstrates innovations in approach to traditional harmony.

The thirty variations begin in the manner of a typical passacaglia, showing progressive rhythmic and chromatic metamorphoses, and utilize continual variation technique instead of thematic transformation. As in *B-A-C-H* and *Ad nos* Liszt closes the composition with a chorale, in this case the final movement from Cantata no. 12, "Was Gott tut, das ist wohl getan."

Weinen, Klagen, Sorgen, Zagen begins with a sixteen-measure introduction based on the cantata's basso continuo theme (see Example 8.10).

Example 8.10
Liszt, *Weinen, Klagen, Sorgen, Zagen*, mm. 1–4

A double bar midway through m. 16 indicates the initial statement of the basso continuo theme. The complete statement, an eight-measure period featuring mirrored construction, contains two iterations of the passacaglia-like bass line. Little of the actual motivic material found within the next sixteen measures is Liszt's own; rather, it is a paraphrase and reduction of the opening nine measures from the first chorus of Bach's Cantata (see Example 8.11).

Example 8.11
Liszt, *Weinen, Klagen, Sorgen, Zagen*, mm. 16–24

A melodic "sighing motive" directly recalls the *Crucifixus* (and vocal writing from the first chorus of Cantata no. 12), and identifies syncopation as the composer's primary tool for rhythmic development. Variation 2, characterized by increasing rhythmic complexity, specifically utilizes melodic pitches on weak beats juxtaposed with a constant quarter-note statement of the bass line (mm. 24–25). Close paraphrasing of Bach continues until the end of m. 27, at which point a freely composed, descending chromatic line appears in the uppermost voice. The continual stream of eighth-note motives initiated in m. 30 foreshadows variation 3. Succeeding variations increase the complexity of texture, rhythm, range, and harmonic content. Liszt briefly suspends the eight-measure thematic period with variation 5 (mm. 48–51).

Paraphrases of motivic material from the first chorus of Bach's Cantata continue through the sixth variation. This particular variation corresponds to mm. 25 through 32 of Cantata no. 12 (see Example 8.12), where Bach provides a change of text ("Angst und Not sind der Christen Tranenbrot") and texture (polyphony replaced by homophony). Liszt's paraphrase of the Bach work reflects a similar stylistic change (see Example 8.13).

Example 8.12
Bach, Cantata no. 12, mm. 25–29

Example 8.13
Liszt, *Weinen, Klagen, Sorgen, Zagen*, mm. 52–56

Variation 7, beginning in m. 64, presents material Liszt freely composed and brings to a climax the rhythmic tension created through previous variations. The composer offers an *ossia*, presenting the option for both reduced texture and range (mm. 68–72). This first large section of *Weinen, Klagen, Sorgen, Zagen* concludes with closely related variations 8 through 10, characterized by a lessening of dramatic tension and lowering of tessitura. Variation 10 makes use of a dotted rhythmic figure, which quickly evolves into a two-note ostinato and serves as transition into the next major compositional section (mm. 80–82).

Variations 11 through 19 form the work's second primary division and show a gradual unleashing of the organ's full tonal resources surrounded by virtuosic technical display. Written entirely for manuals, the composition's pace quickens by way of continually accelerating triplets, set as accompaniment to the more slowly moving theme (mm. 92–93). Variation 14 hides the theme within a flurry of rapid passagework, marking the first time during *Weinen, Klagen, Sorgen, Zagen* that the theme is not clearly heard.

Example 8.14
Liszt, *Weinen, Klagen, Sorgen, Zagen*, mm. 114–115

Succeeding variations develop an ostinato of triplets, during which Liszt couples a decrescendo with a ritardando, gradually bringing the rapid passagework to a quiet close (mm. 151–154).

The third section of *Weinen, Klagen, Sorgen, Zagen* is quite lengthy, (mm. 155–320) and explores an entire spectrum of musical drama through diverse variations. A double bar and meter change precede variation 20 at m. 155. Both halves of this variation present stark octaves at a *forte* dynamic level, showing considerable contrast to the hushed conclusion of variation 19 (mm. 155–157). Succeeding variations employ a rising tessitura and various virtuosic displays, including quick scale patterns and rapidly ascending and descending arpeggios over diminished harmonies. Variation 25 initiates rhythmic and thematic ambiguity.

These variations no longer demonstrate clear bi-partite construction. Heightened chromaticism and thematic extensions of the tail become commonplace, continuing to the composition's concluding chorale. Increased complexity is not limited to pitch: alternating measures of 4/4 and 5/4 appear in the first half of variation 26. A registrational directive also appears, indicating the drawing of full tonal resources (*volles werk*) (mm. 187–191).

Variation 27 provides sharp contrast with its sudden reduction in range and dynamic level. Transitory in nature, this variation descends chromatically through two octaves and gradually brings rhythmic activity to a halt. The fourteen measures of variation 28 present a *pianissimo* recitative and conclude with a chromatically descending three-note figure, forming the motivic foundation for variation 29.

Variation 29 gradually accelerates to a meter change at m. 248, and once again shows Liszt providing tonal strain. The two halves of variation 30, utilizing a single musical line, are used as a brief transition between the unique thematic presentations of earlier variations and sequential repetition—the compositional device defining succeeding variations. Measures 300–320 dramatically close the third portion of *Weinen, Klagen, Sorgen, Zagen* through increased acceleration and expansion of range. Diminished harmonies, lack of cadential figures, a *volles werk* directive, and the eventual simultaneous utilization of all ten fingers and both feet characterize this climactic passagework (see Example 8.15).

Example 8.15
Liszt, *Weinen, Klagen, Sorgen, Zagen*, mm. 312–313

A harmonically meandering, single-line recitative ushers in the concluding chorale. Liszt sets the hymn's phrases over traditional harmonies in F major and alternates between *piano* and *forte*. The chorale concludes with an extension of ascending stepwise passagework and, underscoring the hopeful sentiment expressed in the original chorale text, the work moves to a triumphant conclusion.

The score of *Weinen, Klagen, Sorgen, Zagen* contains more specific registrational notations and manual assignments than found in either *Ad nos* or *B-A-C-H*. Gottschalg's name appears on the dedication, and it is likely that the organist contributed specific performance directives for the composition. Arguably, of the three monumental works, *Weinen, Klagen, Sorgen, Zagen* represents Liszt at his most mature level of compositional development, particularly in his writing for the organ. The work is technically and musically challenging, yet does not serve as a mere showpiece for technical display. Virtuosic writing combined with musical sensitivity conveys the full range of emotions Liszt experienced during this time of his life. The work also presents balance between pianistically-based writing and that which is more organ-like in approach. *Weinen, Klagen, Sorgen, Zagen* may have originated as a praeludium for piano, but, in its final form, is without question a work written for and well suited to the organ.

Organ Transcriptions

Various original works of the composer, dating primarily from the Weimar years, provided a source for later organ transcriptions. Scholars face one fundamental problem regarding these transcriptions: to whom should actual credit for the compositions be given? In many cases Gottschalg was critical to the production of these compositions. Most individuals, nevertheless, continue ascribing ultimate credit to Liszt, based on the sheer number of changes, additions, and other detailed annotations he made in various manuscripts and source materials.

Foremost among transcriptions of Liszt's orchestral works for organ is Gottschalg's transcription of Liszt's symphonic poem, *Orpheus*.[4] Gottschalg carefully transcribed it around 1860, and Liszt made detailed alterations to the draft. Schuberth later published the corrected work in Gottschalg's *Repertory*—a major source for a number of Liszt's organ compositions. Robert Schaab made another manuscript of the transcription that features suggestions for registration and contains many of Liszt's notations. A second large work for organ that Schuberth published, *Introduction, Fugue and Magnificat from the "Dante" Symphony*, bears similarity to *Orpheus* in the transcription process: Gottschalg's "revision" is combined with Liszt's numerous notations, additions, and changes in the production of a work for organ. *Andante religioso* (1861), while based on a theme from Liszt's first symphonic poem, is not a direct transcription of the larger work. This work may be found in Gottschalg's *Repertory*.

Many choral works also provide material appropriate to organ performance, including the *Introduction from St. Elisabeth* (with transcription assistance from Karl Muller-Hartung), and several pieces carrying the title *Ave Maria*. Gottschalg originally transcribed the 1853 *Ave Maria*, and Liszt added extensive corrections and annotations. Both compositions offer suggestions for registration, with directives for *Ave Maria* specifically based on the Ladegast organ in the Merseburg Cathedral. Liszt based another *Ave Maria* (S 659) on a composition he thought by Arcadelt. Gottschalg's name appears in the dedication to the score, which contains numerous registrational suggestions and directives for manual changes. A third *Ave Maria* (1869) appears in versions for solo voice and organ/harmonium and for four-part chorus and organ. *Evocation à la Chapelle Sixtine* (S 658) is a "fantasy" based on Mozart's *Ave Verum Corpus* and Allegri's *Miserere*. The first edition of this composition for organ, harmonium or *Pedalflügel* (Korner, 1865) carries a dedication to Gottschalg and offers remarks on registration and manual assignments. Liszt conceived *Slavimo slavno slaveni!* (S 668) as a hymn for male chorus and organ, and it received its first performance at the Church of St. Hieronymus in Rome during 1863 as part of a millennial commemoration of Saints Cyril and Methodius. Liszt extracted the *Offertorium* (S 667) from the larger *Hungarian Coronation Mass*, which he composed for solo voices, choir, orchestra, and organ to celebrate the coronation of Francis Joseph I and Elisabeth in June 1867. The *Offertorium* was missing from the *Mass* when first performed and appeared later in Gottschalg's *Repertory*. Even though the full title of *Tu es Petrus* (S 664, 1867) documents its source as the oratorio *Christus*, a form of the composition appeared earlier as the organ work, *Der Papst Hymnus* (ca. 1863, S 261; published for harmonium/organ in 1865). Liszt eventually arranged the piece for chorus, with this form of the composition inserted into *Christus*. Liszt composed his *Weimars Volkslied* (S 672) to words by Peter Cornelius around 1862. He also composed earlier versions for male chorus and orchestra, male chorus and organ, and male chorus and piano (1857).

Liszt further made organ transcriptions of works he originally conceived for piano. *Les morts*, written in memory of Liszt's son, Daniel (1860), is drawn from *Trois odes funèbres* no. 1, and appears in some performing editions by the title, *Trauerode* (S 268/2). *Zur Trauung* (1883) is an arrangement of *Sposalizio*. Three of six *Consolations* (1850) were later reworked for organ: *Adagio* (*Consolation* IV in Db major), *Consolation* V in E major, and *Trostung* (*Consolation* VI in E major). *Trostung* offers the most independence from an original version, being a rather free adaptation of the piano composition. The *Consolations* are not immune from the common question of "true" transcription authorship. Sándor Margittay noted in his performing edition of Liszt organ works: "Several organ and harmonium transcriptions of each of these pieces have been made by unidentified arrangers."[5] Gottschalg claimed "in the Preface of the 'Historisches Album' that he had made 'diverse arrangements' of the works included," among which may be found the *Consolations*.[6] In any case, scholars credit Liszt for these transcriptions based on his numerous corrections and annotations found in various source materials.

Finally, Liszt transcribed numerous works by other composers. Included in this category are transcriptions of three compositions by J. S. Bach (Introduction and Fugue from the cantata, *Ich hatte viel Bekummernis*, BWV 21; *Adagio* from the Fourth Sonata for Violin and Harpsichord, BWV 1017; and the opening chorus from the cantata, *Aus tiefer Not schrei ich zu dir*, BWV 38). Liszt also transcribed two preludes of Chopin (piano preludes, op. 28, nos. 4 and 9) and a motet of Orlando di Lasso (*Regina coeli laetare*). Additionally, there are transcriptions of compositions by Otto Nicolai (*Ecclesiastical Festival Overture on the Chorale "Ein feste Burg ist unser Gott,"* op. 31); Giuseppe Verdi (*Requiem: Agnus Dei*); and Richard Wagner (*Tannhäuser: Pilgrims' Chorus*). The earliest of these transcriptions dates from 1852 (Nicolai's *Ein feste Burg*) and the latest from 1886, the year in which Liszt died (Mozart's *Ave Verum*). Liszt produced most of the transcriptions in the 1860s, and many bear close association with Gottschalg. In general, works within this category do not offer writing idiomatic to the organ; yet, all but one of the works includes writing for pedal (the exception being Verdi's *Agnus Dei*). Registrational directives and

manual notations appear in only two transcriptions; directives in an additional
transcription are limited solely to manual notations.

Compositions of the Late Period

Liszt produced a number of short, austere works for keyboard during his
final years. In recent decades, these pieces have assumed great importance for
scholars within the overall study of nineteenth-century compositional innovation
and experimentation. Piano works figure most prominently within this category;
however, there are several organ works and organ versions of compositions: *Ave
maris stella* (S 669, second version 1868); *Excelsior* (S 666, ca. 1874); *Salve
Regina* (S 669) and *Resignazione* (S 263) from 1877; *Gebet* (S 265, 1879); *San
Francesco* (S 665, 1880); *Ungarns Gott* (1881); *O sacrum convivium* (ca. 1881);
Am Grabe Richard Wagner (S 267) and *Nun danket alle Gott* from 1883; and *In
domum Domini ibimus* and *Introitus* (1884). Additionally, several multi-
movement works date from the late period, including *Via Crucis* (S 674a,
1878–1879), *Rosario* (S 670) and *Missa pro Organo* (S 264) from 1879, and
Requiem (S 266, 1883). Finally, it is appropriate to list compositions designated
for harmonium (clavier): *Ave maris stella* (first version, 1868); the four
movement *Weihnachtsbaum* (1876); *Ave Maria II* (1869); *Angelus! Prière aux
anges gardiens* (1877); and *Ave Maria* (fourth work by this title, 1881).

Bence Szabolcsi suggested that these late works show the creation of a new
type of expression for Liszt: a sequence or portrayal of dramatic scenes.[7] These
organ compositions often portray one particular event and may incorporate
significant dramatic contrast. The term "abstract" best describes this music
which places little reliance on bravura display. Liszt engages in new
experiments regarding the concept of harmony and frequently utilizes devices
such as augmented chords, dissonant intervals as structural components,
pentatonic passages, modal scales, and the avoidance or blurring of cadences.
He also employs melodies that are often speech-like or declamatory in nature.

Some scholars have suggested the concept of timbre became less important
to Liszt during his final years. Many of the short, non-orchestral works indicate
performance on "keyboard." This point may be carried further: the works
specifically designated for organ may occasionally offer general suggestions for
registration, but several, such as the multi-movement *Via Crucis,* give little or
no indications for organ color. During this same period, Liszt also produced a
number of compositions that could be performed as instrumental solos or
chamber works, suggesting decreased importance of specific instrumental color.
Humphrey Searle suggests this habit was probably one of convenience for Liszt
more than for any other reason.[8]

The late compositions show Liszt working in genres far different than those
of the 1840s and 1850s. Funeral pieces and works based on death poetry figure
prominently among pieces from his final years. As he aged Liszt turned
increasingly toward the production of sacred music. It is known that he aimed to
create a new type of church music, more expressive than that of his

contemporaries, featuring "fresh" harmonies surrounding traditional liturgical frameworks. He met considerable resistance from the Church, however, as well as from publishers. Pustet, a prominent religious publishing firm, rejected three of his works, *Via Crucis, Septem Sacramenta,* and *St. Francis' Hymn to the Sun.*

Via Crucis. The fifteen movements of *Via Crucis* provide excellent source material on which to base a discussion of typical compositional innovations and features from Liszt's final years. Comments produced from this study may be successfully applied to other late works. *Via Crucis* exists in three different arrangements, a phenomenon common to pieces from Liszt's final years: vocal soloists, chorus, and organ/piano accompaniment; organ/harmonium solo; and piano solo.

Via Crucis depicts Christ's passion through a prelude (based on the Latin hymn, "Vexilla Regis") and the fourteen stations of the cross. It offers a typical late-Lisztian approach to form: the structure of each movement results from continual development of the smallest available motivic unit. Ongoing repetition of the basic unit often occurs with slight alterations. The Gregorian intonation appears throughout *Via Crucis,* traditionally carries the text ("O Crux") and serves as a unifying motive throughout the multi-movement composition.[9]

Example 8.16
Liszt, *Via Crucis*, basic motive known as the "cross motif"

Via Crucis also provides another approach common to other late works: many passages are comprised of little more than single notes or octaves. Such transparency stands in marked contrast to the textural complexity of Liszt's earlier organ works (Station XII, m. 1). *Via Crucis* offers a rich study in new approaches to harmony. Among the various movements are passages based on unresolved chromaticism as in mm. 1–6 of Station IV and mm. 1–5 in Station VIII. Modal passages are common as well, most of which result from the use of Gregorian chant as an underlying thematic source (Vexilla: mm. 11–14).

Liszt's late works, often characterized as foreshadowing atonality and music of the twentieth century, reflect his interest in redefining harmony and experimenting with a replacement for tonality, *ordre omnitonique.* He composed a *Prelude Omnitonique,* but the manuscript disappeared in 1904 after being placed on exhibition in London. Liszt worked toward a free and equal use of all twelve chromatic pitches, and utilized several elements to meet this end. A number of innovations related to this concept are presented in the movements of *Via Crucis.* For instance, a whole-tone scale is used with prominence in Station X beginning with m. 19. A basic feature of the whole-tone scale, the augmented fourth, appears with consistency throughout *Via Crucis,* as well as other works from Liszt's late years. Liszt uses the augmented fourth as a motive (Station VI, mm. 1–4), as the interval of sequence (Station V, mm. 3 and 13), and as the final notes of a movement (Station V, mm. 51–52). Other traditionally dissonant intervals, such as the second and seventh, find frequent use in the late works, and often appear in the movements of *Via Crucis* as seen in Station X, mm. 1–3. Another technique appropriate to the *omnitonique* concept is that of pedal point unrelated to the harmonies appearing against it (Station V, mm. 50). Additionally, Liszt begins and ends nearly every movement of *Via Crucis* on different and/or harmonically unrelated pitches.

Liszt's late works do not limit innovations to pitch and/or harmonic content. Although rhythm may seem secondary in importance to new harmonic approaches, Liszt supports an overall sense of musical ambiguity through various ways he utilizes rhythm and tempo. In *Via Crucis* he designates six movements *Lento* and nine *Andante*, and, coupled with various rhythmic devices, often creates the sense of lost pulse through syncopation (Station IV, mm. 1–2), shifting accents (Station I, mm. 16–22), and sections of silence (Station X, mm. 9–11).

Brief consideration of three other works provides additional insight into Liszt's compositional language from the late period. Liszt scored *Am Grabe Richard Wagners* (1883) for three possible timbres: piano, string quartet with harp *ad libitum,* and organ or harmonium. This extremely intimate work demonstrates many characteristics common to other late works: brevity (fifty-five measures long), transparency of texture, frequent use of pedal point, ambiguity of rhythm, slowly evolving harmonies, and key signatures often unrelated to the musical material with which they are surrounded. Liszt produced this work on Wagner's seventieth birthday, marking the three-month anniversary of his friend's death. Included with the composition is the following inscription: "Wagner once reminded me of the similarity between his *Parsifal* motive and my *Excelsior* which was written earlier (*Einleitung zu den Glocken von Strassburg).* Let this mention remain here in as much as he accomplished the greatness and sublimity of the present art."[10] The work is contemplative and reflective, aptly belying the composition's title, and filled with numerous dynamic markings in place of specific registrational suggestions. Liszt composed *Introitus* the following year (1884), although it was not published until 1890. He builds this brief work (only seventy-nine measures) upon various series of modulating chords within a sequential framework. Quarter-note passages in octaves punctuate the chorale-like writing, and slowly moving harmonies over pedal point comprise the final third of the composition. Unlike *Am Grabe,* a full range of dynamic markings appear, including one registrational indication for full organ (*volles werk*). Liszt composed *Resignazione* in 1877, while staying at the Villa d'Este. This brief work contains only four phrases within twenty-nine measures, yet demonstrates compositional language found throughout the late works: ambiguous tonality, frequent use of melodic sequence, chorale-like writing juxtaposed with monophonic passages, and lack of rhythmic complexity. The work projects ultimate simplicity of approach, including an absence of dynamic and registrational marks.

Numerous twentieth-century composers later explored Liszt's ideas of vague tonality, the expression of a single idea or mood, rhythmic ambiguity, and conciseness of compositional approach. The keyboard works from his final years demonstrate a new, daring approach to music and present considerable contrast to Liszt's earlier compositional language.

Liszt's organ works reflect great complexity and diversity of approach, revealing the composer's interest in producing works for a keyboard instrument capable of creating colors and dramatic effects far different from that for the piano. His initial lack of practical knowledge about the organ was more than overcome by close personal and musical relationships. Equally important were various opportunities with organist friends that may be best described as "experiential learning sessions." Recent publications of scholarly, "collected" performing editions have been successful in making the composer's organ works better known to performers and researchers alike. Continued familiarity with examples from the entire genre of Liszt organ works will assist in revealing a composer of far greater complexity and depth than apparent through knowledge limited solely to *Ad nos, B-A-C-H,* and *Weinen, Klagen, Sorgen, Zagen.* Liszt's compositions for organ assume an important place within the repertoire for the instrument and occupy a notable place among his entire compositional output.

NOTES

1. Quoted in Milton Sutter, "Liszt and His Role in the Development of 19th Century Organ Music," *Music/American Guild of Organists* (January 1975): 36.
2. Performing editions of the music contain much information about Liszt's organ works. Among the various editions presently available, both the Margittay and Haselböck editions offer historical and descriptive material devoted to each composition. Of particular interest is Haselböck's anticipated tenth volume, promising critical notes about the organ works, "organs of Liszt," and the Weimar "circle of organists." See Sándor Margittay, ed., *Franz Liszt: Összes orgonzmuve. Sämtliche Orgelwerke* (Budapest: Editio Musica Budapest, 1970) and Martin Haselböck, ed., *The Complete Works for Organ,* 10 vols. (Vienna: Universal Edition A.G, 1985–).
3. Harvey Grace, "Liszt and the Organ," *Musical Times* (August 1917): 358.
4. Schuberth published an organ version of *Orpheus,* and Breitkopf & Härtel published an additional version for two pianos.
5. Margittay, *Franz Liszt,* 2:29.
6. See Haselböck, "Preface," *Franz Liszt: The Complete Works for Organ,* vol. 4.
7. Bence Szabolcsi, "Liszt and Bartók," *New Hungarian Quarterly* (January 1961): 3–4.
8. Humphrey Searle, *The Music of Liszt,* 2d rev. ed. (New York: Dover, 1966), 112.
9. See Chapters 10 and 13 for other Liszt works using the "cross motif."
10. Margittay, *Franz Liszt,* 4:1.

IV

Instrumental Music

9

Chamber Music

William Wright

Liszt's works in the field of chamber music are minor in comparison with those of other masters ranging from Franz Joseph Haydn and Wolfgang Amadeus Mozart to Dmitry Shostakovich. Liszt's chamber music, nevertheless, enriches the repertoire and warrants careful study. More than forty works are known to exist, although several are unpublished and remain in libraries and private collections (see Table 9.1 for a listing of Liszt's chamber compositions and arrangements). For ease of discussion, each composition has been categorized in one of the following groups:

   a. Liszt's own chamber works
   b. Liszt's chamber arrangements of other composers' works
   c. Others arranging Liszt's works with his annotations

In the majority of cases these works are duos Liszt composed mainly for piano and one other instrument. The first group includes the *Grand duo concertant sur La romance de M. Lafont "Le marin"* (S 128) for violin and piano—a composition he originally conceived in collaboration with the celebrated French violinist Charles-Philippe Lafont (1781–1839). Works by other composers that Liszt approved but in which he made no corrections or additions have been excluded. In this category, for example, is Camille Saint-Saëns's piano trio of Liszt's symphonic poem *Orpheus*. Today, scholars can give a fuller, more accurate, and up-to-date assessment of this genre through increased information on Liszt's original chamber works and transcriptions following recent intensive searches for his musical manuscripts, letters, concert programs, playbills, and reviews.

Liszt's involvement with chamber music began in childhood and continued throughout the rest of his life, even during the years between 1838 and 1848 when he was traveling great distances and giving innumerable solo performances throughout Europe and Asia Minor. Adam Liszt, his father, was an amateur cellist, guitarist, violinist, and pianist. Alan Walker noted that "Adam held frequent chamber-music evenings in his house at which he and his friends from neighbouring communities took part. . . . The young Liszt was surrounded by music from his early years."[1] Throughout much of his life, he took part in duos, trios, and larger concertante works that he and others wrote.

Liszt's chamber works composed between 1823 and 1835 include three works now lost (a trio[2] and quintet[3] from 1825 and an early sextet[4]) and the *Grand duo concertant*.[5] Two extant arrangements for violin and piano, *Zwei Walzer* (S 716b)[6] and two untraced violin and guitar transcriptions were published around the middle of 1825. It was the custom during the period for Stephen Heller, Henri Herz, Friedrich Kalkbrenner, Ignaz Moscheles, George Osborne, Theodore Labarre, Charles de Beriot, and others to write duo concertanti in collaboration with partnered instrumentalists. Liszt followed suit with violinist Nicholas Mori and flautist Antonio Minasi in London in 1827,[7] probably with others in Paris during the years 1828 to 1834,[8] and certainly with Lafont in Geneva in 1835. The three early London duos were probably similar in form to the 1835 Lafont/Liszt *Grand duo concertant* that consists of an introduction, theme, variations, and finale.

Table 9.1
Liszt Chamber Compositions and Transcriptions
(excluding untraced works, a few extant fragments, and works in private collections)

Violin and Piano

ca. 1823	Zwei Walzer. S 126b.
ca. 1835	Duo [sur des themes polonais]. S 127.
ca. 1835, rev. 1849	*Grand Duo concertant sur La romance de M.[Charles-Philippe] Lafont "Le [départ du jeune] marin." S 128.*
ca. 1853	*Rhapsodie hongroise no. 12* (Joachim arranged violin part). S 379a.
1864	*Die drei Zigeuner. S 383.* (paraphrase)
ca. 1865	*La notte. S 377a.*
ca. 1869	*Benedictus und Offertorium aus der Ungarischen Krönungsmesse.* S 381.
	Epithalam zu E[duard] Reményis Vermählungsfeier. S 129.
1874	*[Première] Élégie. S 130.*
1877	*Zweite Elegie. S 131.*
1880	*Romance oubliée. S 132.*
ca. 1883	*Die Zelle in Nonnenwerth. S 382.*
ca. 1885	*La lugubre gondola. S 134.*

Violin and Organ/Harmonium

ca. 1868	*Benedictus und Offertorium aus der Ungarischen Krönungsmesse.* S 678.

Viola and Piano

1836	Berlioz's *Harold in Italy. S 472.*
1880	*Romance oubliée. S 132.*

Cello and Piano

1852	28 m. fragment, Wagner's "O du mein holder Abendstern." S 380.
ca. 1871	10.5 m. fragment *Enchaînement*. S 382a.
1874	[*Première*] *Élégie*. S 130.
1875	Duo in G major [Unpublished].
1877	*Zweite Elegie*. S 131.
1880	*Romance oubliée*. S 132.
ca. 1883	*Die Zelle in Nonnenwerth*. S 382.
ca. 1885	*La lugubre gondola*. S 134.

Cello and Organ

1870s	*Consolation* nos. 1 and 4, de Swert/Liszt: *Enchaînement de F. Liszt*.

Trombone and Piano

1862	*Cantico di San Francesco* [Unpublished].

Trombone and Organ

ca. 1862	*Cujus Animam*: Rossini/Liszt. S 679.
1862	*Cantico di San Francesco* [Unpublished].
1862–1863	*Hosannah*. S 677.

Piano Trio

1848	*Rhapsodie hongroise* no. 9 "Pester Karneval." S 379.
1870s	*Tristia, Vallée d'Obermann*: Lassen/Liszt. S 723a,b,c.

String Quartet

1880 and 1882	*Angelus!* Prière aux anges gardiens. S 378.

String Quartet [and Harp, ad. lib.]

1883	*Am Grabe Richard Wagners*. S 135.

String Quintet

1882?	*Angelus!* Prière aux anges gardiens. S 378.

Cello, Piano, Harp, and Harmonium/[organ, ad. lib.]

1874	[*Première*] *Élégie*. S 130.

Violin, Piano, Harp, and Harmonium/[organ, ad. lib.]

1870s	"Gretchen" from Liszt's *Faust Symphony* that Leopold Alexander Zellner arranged
	Die drei Zigeuner later arranged by Jenö Hubay published in 1931 as the Liszt/Hubay *Hungarian Rhapsody* for violin and orchestra.
	Zámoyská's *Puszta Wehmut*. S 379b.
	Die Wiege. S 133. (for four violins)

Voice, violin, and piano

Walther von der Vogelweide

LISZT'S OWN CHAMBER WORKS

Liszt composed his first large-scale chamber work, *Grand duo concertant* for violin and piano (S 128), based on Lafont's romance *Le marin* around 1835.[9] He revised it in Weimar around 1849, and Schott and Richault published the revision in 1852. August Göllerich suggested Schott published the first version in 1836.[10] On 1 June 1835 Liszt left Paris for Geneva, and on the first day of October he and Lafont took part in a charity concert in the Swiss town. Prince Emilio Belgiojoso arranged the concert at which Liszt and his new partner performed the *Grand duo concertant* in aid of refugees who had fought for the Unification of Italy. The Lafont *Romance* was probably more widely known at that time by its full title, *Le départ du jeune marin*. According to a letter Liszt wrote to Joachim Raff on 20 November 1849,[11] what they performed was a collaborative arrangement of the song. The 29 September 1835 issue of *Le fédéral* cited the piece in a reprint of the concert program, adding further confirmation by adopting the accepted formula of words for a joint work: "Duo concertant exécuté par MM. Liszt et Lafont."[12] On 6 October 1835 the composition was later mentioned in *Le fédéral* in a review of the performances.[13]

On 9 November 1839 while in Trieste, Liszt provided more proof of their collaboration in his letter to Marie d'Agoult. "Send me very soon via the Embassy, the piece I composed with Lafont."[14] The violinist Albert Sebestyén added: "It is interesting that Lafont also composed a duo on the same theme ('Le marin'). Numerous measures are identical in both compositions, and a further number only show very small deviations. In 1835 both works existed in manuscript only. Lafont's composition was published in 1838."[15] Sebestyén, however, erred when he implied that the 1835 Liszt/Lafont manuscript was identical to Liszt's 1852 published version of the work. The revised Schott publication consists of an introduction, theme, four variations, and a finale that Bärenreiter republished in 1971 with Liszt's *Epithalam* (S 129).

Liszt's revised *Grand duo concertant,* a brilliant concert piece in A major, has a dramatic opening with sudden mood, tempo, and dynamic changes. During a tranquil *Andantino* the violin introduces the thematic material above a restrained accompaniment, and the violin dominates in variation 1 with florid and ornamental passagework. Variation 2 begins and closes with the melody played pizzicato amid rapid swirling keyboard sixteenth notes interspersed with sudden shifts from bravura or delicate interplay. A six-measure linking passage leads into the key of D major at variation 3, an *Allegretto Pastorale*, with featured ascending and descending arpeggios, recitative, and cadenza. Variation 4, a tarantella, is a tour de force, and the chromatic double thirds and sixths at the end of this section precede the martial finale.

Liszt's next important chamber work was his Duo in C♯ minor (S 127) for violin and piano, based on Frédéric Chopin's C♯-minor Mazurka, op. 6, no. 2. Liszt wrote to his mother on 26 July 1835 while in Geneva and mentioned *un Duo pour piano et violin sur une Mazourk de Chopin.*[16] Liszt probably composed it around 1835. The sonata for violin and piano in three movements (1830?) that Göllerich[17] mentioned in 1908 and Peter Raabe[18] in 1931 may relate to an earlier version.[19] It certainly cannot refer accurately to the manuscript at present in Weimar in Liszt's youthful hand: a four-movement work, which, contrary to Sharon Winklhofer's suggestion, is probably not in the typically classical style of Liszt's early lost chamber works.[20] Walker gave the completion date of the composition as "1848 or later."[21]

In 1942 Dr. Friedrich Schnapp examined the Weimar manuscript that was evidently written in collaboration with a violin expert[22] and identified material from Chopin's Mazurka, op. 6, no. 2 in the Liszt autograph. The American pianist Eugene List and violinist Tibor Serly studied the work in the late 1950s. Serly used the autograph as a basis for his own arrangement of the piece, making some melodic and harmonic alterations and omitting several measures of Liszt's original composition. In 1964 the Southern Music Publishing Company published the Liszt/Serly composition as Liszt's Duo (Sonata), as it is now erroneously described.[23] Albert Sebestyén studied both the manuscript and Serly's own arrangement of the work in the early 1970s and found that Serly had altered Liszt's chamber work much more than he had claimed in this introduction to the 1964 publication. Sebestyén made an analysis of each of the four "movements" of the autograph and printed score and included his observations in his article, "Liszts Originalkompositionen für Violine und Klavier."[24] He noted that at m. 90 of the first movement [Serly edition] two measures that are in the autograph are missing from the printed score, and that the last three measures of the second movement have been contracted into two measures with different harmonies. He noticed also at m. 354 of the third movement two measures of motivic material are missing that are in the autograph and immediately before the cadenza of the fourth movement that Serly had appended a triple time measure to two measures of duple time.

Liszt's Duo in C♯ minor—*Moderato, Tema con variazioni, Allegretto,* and *Allegro con brio*—is characterized not only by some highly effective Chopinesque writing but also by thematic transformation. Two themes from Chopin's Mazurka are heard in a variety of guises throughout the piece, and Liszt introduces an additional Polish melody in the *Allegro con brio* section. The tempo changes and arpeggio figurations salient in the final coda of Serly's published score are absent from Liszt's autograph. The Liszt Society intends to publish an Urtext edition of the Liszt Duo in C♯ minor in the near future.

While in Weimar during June 1875 Liszt collaborated in the composition of a Duo in G major for cello and piano. It has five sections: *Allegretto, Andante, Allegro con fuoco, Lento,* and *Vivace,* all written in a markedly Hungarian style. The autograph of this unpublished composition is in the Bibliothèque Musicale Gustav Mahler in Paris. Liszt almost certainly corrected and completed a violin and piano arrangement of the work concurrently with the cello and piano version. The Viennese antiquarian Heinrich Hinterberger sold the violin and piano version, another eight-page manuscript dated June 1875 and signed by Liszt, to an unknown buyer in 1935.[25] Hinterberger described the work as containing "numerous corrections and remarks by Liszt . . . the last page written entirely by Liszt,"[26] which also relates to the June 1875 Liszt cello and piano manuscript in the Gustav Mahler library. It is clear from a study of the Paris autograph that some other person arranged the cello and piano version, that Liszt made many corrections, added a four-measure introduction at the beginning of the piece before the *Allegro con fuoco* and *Vivace* sections, and appended a seventeen-measure ending. The wife of Frederick Goldbeck donated the eight-page cello and piano manuscript to the Paris library around 1991 or 1992 shortly after her husband's death.

Liszt, often with the aid of other performers, arranged nearly a dozen of his own piano, vocal, or choral works as chamber music. These works most frequently included violin and piano, but he also arranged works for trombone and organ, string quartet or quintet, and piano trio.

Liszt probably collaborated on arrangements of two of his *Hungarian Rhapsodies,* no. 9 "Pester Karneval" (S 379) for piano trio and no. 12 for violin and piano.[27] Little is known about the origins of the "Pester Karneval" arrangement, but the second edition of the *New Grove Dictionary of Music and Musicians* gave the date of composition as 1848. After Liszt's death, however, Fritz Volbach, editor at Schott, examined the Weimar manuscript, and Schott published Volbach's edition of the arrangement in 1892. The Liszt Society reprinted the work in 1996.[28] Considerably more is known about the twelfth *Hungarian Rhapsody* cited by August Göllerich.[29] In the autumn of 1850 Joseph Joachim accepted Liszt's invitation to become leader of the Weimar Orchestra. It was a brief stay, lasting from late 1850 until January 1853. While there, Joachim dedicated his recently completed Violin Concerto in G major, op. 3 to Liszt who in turn dedicated to Joachim his *Hungarian Rhapsody* no. 12 in C♯ minor for piano. Liszt later revised the work, adding a partially sketched out violin part that Joachim completed. Neither Raabe, Searle, nor Winklhofer catalogued this collaborative composition, which the Liszt Society subsequently identified as S 379a.

Some twenty years were to elapse before this violin and piano arrangement appeared in print for the first time when Schuberth published it in 1871 with a reprint of the piano version at Liszt's request. Writing to Alexander Gottschalg on 11 November 1870 Liszt commented: "The already available dedication would not be suitable for these pieces, and especially unsuitable for Joachim's [violin] part."[30] Joachim became increasingly disaffected with Liszt and his music during this period. Following the young violinist's appointment in Hanover in 1853 as concertmaster to the royal court and subsequent meeting with Johannes Brahms and violinist Eduard Reményi (1830–1898) later that year, the breakup of the Liszt/Joachim partnership became inevitable. Joachim transferred his allegiance to Brahms, and, partly as a result, Liszt and Reményi forged an enduring link between them. Liszt composed or arranged at least five violin and piano compositions for Reményi between 1864 and 1872 (*Die drei Zigeuner, Benedictus, Offertorium, La notte,* and *Epithalam*) and probably two or more arrangements for violin and organ.[31]

Liszt completed the first of these arrangements for Reményi *Die drei Zigeuner* (S 383) on 9 May 1864 in the Madonna del Rosario, Rome. Liszt's 1864 violin and piano version—written four years after his publication of the voice and piano setting—is a more extended work. Liszt features the Gypsy scale prominently in this chamber arrangement, and although the autograph of the piece is apparently lost, the quasi-improvisatory nature of the music may reveal its genesis. The first public performance was given at the Karlsruhe Music Festival in August that year. At some later date the manuscript came into the possession of fellow Hungarian, violinist Jenö Hubay, who had Kahnt publish it in 1896. Later, Hubay made an arrangement for violin and orchestra that Universal published in 1931 as the Liszt/Hubay *Hungarian Rhapsody* for violin and orchestra.[32]

The precise date Liszt arranged *La notte* (S 377a) for violin and piano is unknown. On 9 August 1865 Reményi received the piece from Liszt and the two musicians gave its first public performance on 5 September 1865 in the home of Baron Antal Augusz in Szekszárd. Sebestyén wrote, "On 10 August 1865 the *Zenészeti Lapok* reported: 'Franz Liszt spent the afternoon yesterday with Ede Reményi. . . . On this occasion he surprised Reményi with his newest composition: Funeral March [*Trauermarsch*] which they played together.' "[33] The diary of Baron Augusz's daughter Anna proves that this was *La notte*. She recorded, "In the evening [5 September] Monsieur l'Abbé played his very beautiful composition, 'La notte' together with M. Reményi."[34] Robert Charles Lee first published the arrangement in 1963 in *Five Late Works of Liszt*, and Boccaccini and Spada later published it in Rome in 1983. Both the autograph and a copyist's copy are in the Library of Congress. This chamber work—one of Liszt's mourning pieces—is an arrangement of the orchestral version of *La notte* (S 112/2), which is itself based on the musical material of *Il penseroso* (S 161/2) for piano solo. Liszt also based his violin and piano transcription on Buonarroti Michelangelo's poem *La notte* which depicts an Italian sepulchral scene. Liszt adds a quotation from Virgil's *Aeneid* at the beginning of the F♯-minor passage, "dulces moriens reminiscitur Argos" (canto X, line 782).

Two other pieces that Liszt arranged for Reményi were the *Benedictus* and *Offertorium* for violin and piano (S 381). The precise dates of these compositions and their first performances are unknown. On 14 July 1869 Liszt wrote to Baron Augusz from Rome:

I have finished the revision of the 'Coronation Mass' and made a four handed arrangement of the 'Offertorium' and 'Benedictus' for your daughters [Anna and Helene]. . . . Herbeck will send you the four hand arrangement—also 2 pages: the same 'Benedictus' and 'Offertorium,' arranged for piano and violin. Could you please give them [i.e., the violin and piano arrangement] to Reményi. I want him to use them in his concerts.[35]

Schuberth (Leipzig) issued the violin and piano arrangements separately in 1871.

Liszt may have made arrangements of *Benedictus* and *Offertorium* (S 678) for violin and organ or harmonium in collaboration with Gottschalg around 1868. Dezső Legány noted, "On 25 October 1868 Reményi travelled to Szekszárd where he performed 'Benedictus' and 'Offertorium' from Liszt's 'Missa Coronationalis' to organ accompaniment."[36] Liszt sent revised proofs of the arrangements to Schuberth at the beginning of September 1871, and the pieces appeared in print shortly afterwards. They were also included in *Gottschalg's Repertorium für die Orgel* about this time.[37] The instrumental specification at the beginning of the Benedictus copy in the Goethe- und Schiller-Archiv, Weimar, reads: *Violine / Orgel [Gottschalg] [oder Harmonium] [Liszt]*. In 1987 Martin Haselböck published these pieces in volume eight of *Franz Liszt Sämtliche Orgelwerke*.

Liszt composed *Epithalam* (S 129) for violin and piano in celebration of Reményi's marriage to Gizella Fay on 10 February 1872. The first performance took place at a musical evening given by Count Imre Széchényi on the preceding day. The piece appeared in print in the periodical *Apollo 1* later that year, and Táborszky and Parsch published the arrangement in Pest soon after. *Epithalam* relates closely to the piano version of the work until the music reaches its climax at m. 60, a *fortissimo* chordal flourish ushering in sixteen measures of vigorous duo interplay. The melody then rises lark-like above rapidly shifting tonalities, and the work ends with a brief violin cadenza, a slowly ascending recitative and two *pianissimo* tonic chords.

Liszt arranged two of his works for trombone and organ or piano. The first, *Cantico di San Francesco,* is unpublished and was unknown until the Japanese musicologist Wataru Fukuda brought Liszt's arrangement to the attention of scholars at the 1996 Budapest Liszt Conference. In his paper published two years later in the *Liszt Society Journal,*[38] he mentioned that neither William Bates[39] nor Martin Haselböck[40] made reference to the version. Nor did Raabe or Searle include it in their catalogues, although Mária Eckhardt cited the manuscript of this work in her 1993 catalogue of music belonging to the Liszt estate. Fukuda conceded that the unknown transcription may have been an earlier version of *Hosannah* for organ and optional trombone (S 677) and that Gottschalg may also have shared this view. He dated the arrangement "just prior to March 11, 1862."[41] The introductions of both works "have almost the same melody and harmony and both include the same 'head motif.' "[42] Fukuda suggested Liszt composed and copied his second work for trombone and organ *Hosannah* (S 667) between 15 April 1862 and 29 September 1863. Liszt in collaboration with Gottschalg made this arrangement specifically for the Weimar Court trombonist, Eduard Grosse. Liszt made many emendations to Gottschalg's written trombone part, and Kühn published the arrangement in the Weimar 1870 *Töpfer Jubelalbum.*

Winklhofer cited the *A magyarok Istene* autograph (S 381a) in the Budapest National Széchényi Library as a brass woodwind chamber work.[43] The unpublished manuscript, however, is more likely the wind-band accompaniment to *A magyarok Istene* for men's chorus and wind band that Eckhardt described.[44]

Liszt made at least three arrangements of *Angelus!* (S 378) from his third book of *Années de pèlerinage.*[45] Between 22 and 23 September 1880 while in Sienna, Italy, Liszt made his first string quartet arrangement of the piece. A performance of this version or a later version was given in Weimar in April 1882.[46] A photocopy of the September 1880 Liszt manuscript was brought to the attention of scholars in 1980.[47]

Liszt composed a string-quartet arrangement of *Angelus!* for Ettore Pinelli of the Santa Cecilia Academy in Rome while there in January 1882.[48] A third quartet version that Schott published in 1883 reappeared in an 1887 reprint that included a version for quintet or string orchestra edited by Walter Bache. Bache suggested that Liszt had added the double bass part in the autumn of 1882, and the quintet version was first performed in Prague in 1883. Both editions are held in the British Library. Amadeus Verlag of Winterthur, Switzerland reissued the 1883 Liszt string quartet arrangement in 1985. The Liszt Society republished the version for quartet, quintet, or string orchestra in the *Liszt Society Journal* in 1989.[49] Liszt had a special liking for *Angelus.* In 1883 he commented on the work in Carl Lachmund's presence. Lachmund noted, "This is a favourite with me," Liszt said, "—though I do not generally like my own music—notwithstanding it is not a very perfect piece. But you know, a parent loves the defective child the most."[50]

In 1880 Liszt's publisher sent him a copy of his *Romance in E* for piano (S 169) with a request for its reprint. Instead, Liszt transformed the piece into a new four-minute composition, *Romance oubliée* (S 132) for viola and piano. Liszt had heard Hermann Ritter playing the new five-string viola alta during Wagner's initial performance of *Der Ring des Nibelungen* in Bayreuth between 13 and 17 August 1876. Liszt was impressed with the new instrument and later composed the *Romance oubliée* for viola and piano.[51] He also arranged versions for violin or cello and piano as well as for piano solo. The Hanover publisher Arnold Simon published all of these in 1881. Liszt's *Romance oubliée* for viola and piano was published a year after the only other known Liszt work for the two instruments, his *Harold in Italy* transcription.[52] The little *Romance* opens with a few measures of unaccompanied viola, followed by an expressive recitative immediately after m. 38. The work ends with a passage strikingly similar to the *Canto Religioso* "arpeggiato" measures in the second movement of Berlioz's *Harold Symphony*.

Around 1882 Liszt arranged the first movement of his symphonic poem *From the Cradle to the Grave* for four violins and entitled it *Die Wiege* (S 133). He scored a lengthy passage in the slow movement of his *Faust Symphony* for the same combination of instruments in 1857. The manuscript was for some time in the possession of Nadine Shahovskaya née Helbig (1847–c.1923) and remains unpublished. At present it is in a private collection in Rome. Liszt dedicated his Violin Prelude (S 721) to the daughter of Nadine Helbig, probably while in Rome in January 1886.[53] This piece, possibly a birthday gift, remains untraced.

In July 1874 during a stay at the Villa d'Este, Liszt composed his [*Première*] *Élégie* (S 130)[54] in two versions for cello, piano, harp, and harmonium and for piano alone. He dedicated the piece to the memory of Madame Moukhanoff. When Kahnt published it the following year, a further chamber arrangement for cello and piano had been added. A violin and piano version with the violin part arranged by Nándor Plotényi was printed in 1876. Liszt's first *Élégie* received its première performance during Madame Moukhanoff's memorial concert at Weimar's Tempelherrhaus on 17 June 1875.

In October 1877 at the Villa d'Este Liszt composed his *Zweite Elegie* (S 131) in two versions: the first for piano alone and the second for violin or violoncello with piano accompaniment that Kahnt published in 1878.[55] Liszt dedicated the second *Elegie* to Lina Ramann, who, not long before, had written a long and laudatory article on the first *Élégie* published in two successive issues of the *Neue Zeitschrift für Musik* in March 1877. In a letter to her, following the publication, Liszt wrote, "I will compose a volume of Elegies for you—according to your directions—*religioso* at the close."[56]

Am Grabe Richard Wagners (S 135) exists in two chamber music versions: for string quartet and for string quartet and harp. Liszt made the arrangements on 22 May 1883 in Weimar, and the Liszt Society published them in 1956.

Amadeus Verlag reissued the string quartet arrangement with the republished *Angelus* quartet transcription of Liszt in a 1985 edition. Liszt prefaced the piece with the following note: "Wagner once reminded me of the likeness between his *Parsifal* theme and my previous written 'Excelsior'! May the remembrance remain here. He has fulfilled the great and sublime in the art of the present day."[57] Walker suggested that "the model for this theme as Wagner acknowledged, was *Excelsior*! (the prelude to Liszt's cantata *The Bells of Strasbourg*). Wagner had heard a performance of that work in Liszt's company when the two composers were together in Budapest for a joint Liszt-Wagner concert in March 1875."[58] There is a clear allusion to the *Parsifal* bell-motive in the final ten measures of this short piece. Lachmund, an American pupil of Liszt, recorded a possible variant of S 135 "an arrangement by Liszt of the *Parsifal* bell-music for cello, with piano part" performed in his master's presence by the Weimar cellist, Leopold Grützmacher and pianist Alfred Reisenauer on 15 June 1875.[59]

Liszt originally composed *La lugubre gondola* (S 134) for piano solo in December 1882 while he was visiting Wagner in Venice (see Chapter 6 for further discussion of the piano version). At that stage Liszt had dedicated it to Ramann. This first version of the piece was published in 1916 when it was included in Georg Kinsky's catalogue of the Heyer collection of instruments and manuscripts published by Breitkopf & Härtel. In his 22 February 1883 letter to Ramann, Liszt indicated that he wished Kahnt to publish it in the summer of that year.[60] Liszt, however, either mislaid or decided to withdraw the manuscript. When he wrote to the Hungarian publisher Ferdinand Táborszky on 8 June 1885, he referred to two versions of *La lugubre gondola*, one for piano and violin or violoncello, and the other, a transcription for piano solo (the second piano version of the piece). Liszt stated his intention to have both pieces published by E. W. Fritzsch, who was Wagner's publisher.[61] By this time Liszt had withdrawn the dedication to Ramann, and Fritzsch published the second piano version at the end of 1885.

Kinsky gave a full account of the history of *La lugubre gondola* in his catalog of the Heyer collection. He believed that despite similarities in thematic material and construction, the two versions (the original one in 6/8 time and the later extended version in common time composed two years after Wagner's death) can justifiably be regarded as two different pieces based on the same fundamental theme. Kinsky observed that the opening five notes of the cello part of this darkly brooding late piece present a clear allusion to Wagner's *Tristan und Isolde*.[62] The version for violin or cello and piano, based on the Weimar manuscript and not on the less extended string arrangement Liszt had intended Fritzsch to publish, appeared posthumously in a 1994 István Szelényi Editio Musica Budapest publication. Tibor Von Bisztriczky and Albert Sebestyén gave the first performance of the Szelényi version for violin and piano in Sopron (Odenburg) on 27 November 1974.

LISZT'S CHAMBER ARRANGEMENTS OF OTHER COMPOSERS' WORKS

In 1836 Liszt transcribed Berlioz's four-movement symphony *Harold in Italy* for viola and piano (S 472), two years after his published keyboard arrangement of Berlioz's *Symphonie fantastique*. Like the latter, the arrangement exhibits Liszt's consummate ability in recreating orchestral sound pianistically and his considerable skill in knowing when to omit, add to, or alter Berlioz's material in order to produce appropriate keyboard or chamber solutions. An examination of three selected passages from the orchestral score of *Harold in Italy* and Liszt's transcription serves to highlight when Liszt occasionally deemed it prudent to veer from the original.

Evidence that Liszt may initially have found mm. 73–90 in the first movement less straightforward to transcribe is found in a draft fragment of the measures in the National Széchényi Library in Budapest.[63] The autograph reveals an early Liszt intention to retain in the transcription the double thirds and fourths featured in the ascending sixteenth-note triplets of the orchestral upper strings. It is clear from a study of Liszt's published score that he later abandoned the idea and opted for fifths, sixths, and single notes. This decision involved Liszt in the insertion of some additional material. For example, although the first and second violas play the fifth notes of A♯ and C♯ at mm. 73 and 77 in the Berlioz score, Liszt substituted F♯ in the piano part at this point. He also opted to incorporate several single notes during m. 79 and to include a G♯ and C♯ during the second to last and last beats of the same measure: accidentals that are nowhere in evidence at the equivalent point in Berlioz's symphony. The absence of C♯ at the beginning of m. 88 of Liszt's transcription and clearly in evidence in the orchestral flute part at the same point in the Berlioz score was not as a result of Liszt's decision to leave it out, but rather because the publisher Brandus failed to put it in. Unfortunately, this aberration has crept unobserved into some recent performances of the work.

During the second movement of the symphony the woodwind and strings play as if in solemn antiphon above an onward pizzicato, and gradually recreate the pilgrims' song and their almost furtive tread. Seven measures before the celebrated *Canto Religioso* section characterized by the solo viola's relentless eighth-note arpeggios, Liszt inserts several transcribed notes for the instrument that do not feature in the solo viola part at the same point in the orchestral score. In Liszt's transcription of the work the solo viola part continues from mm. 162–168 while in Berlioz's score the viola part suddenly stops at m. 162. Why is this? Liszt clearly decided at m. 162 of his piano transcription that he could not leave the violist or the listener with an unfinished melody. At the same point in the orchestral score the melody is transferred from solo viola to solo bassoon. During the *Allegro Assai,* the opening thirty-one measures of the third movement of the orchestral score, the solo viola remains silent while the second oboes and clarinets imitate the drone of the Abruzzian bagpipes. Liszt by contrast employs the solo viola throughout the passage to produce a similar effect.

Liszt was not only a close friend of Berlioz for many years, but also of the violist Chrétien Urhan. Liszt made the arrangement in 1836 not only to promote the music of Berlioz but probably with a view to performing the composition with Urhan. (Urhan had been solo violist at the first performance of Berlioz's *Harold in Italy* at the Paris Conservatoire on 23 November 1834 and on many later occasions.) Liszt subsequently mislaid the manuscript, and it was only found in 1877.[64] Two versions of the work were published two years later by Leuckart of Leipzig (first edition) and Brandus of Paris (second edition). The autograph of the first version is preserved in the Staatsbibliothek zu Berlin, and the library of the Paris Conservatoire holds the second edition engraver's copy.[65] Gerard Billaudot issued a 1990 edition of the *Harold in Italy* transcription based on Liszt's arrangement, revised and annotated by François René Duchable and Gerard Causse.

Extant Liszt chamber arrangements of other composers' works include Gioacchino Rossini's *Cujus animam* for organ and trombone (S 679) and Countess Ludmilla Gizycka née Zámoyská's *Puszta-Wehmut* for violin and piano (S 379b).[66] The first is a transcription from Rossini's *Stabat Mater* that Liszt originally wrote for piano in 1847 and arranged for organ and trombone around 1862. Although the Rossini/Liszt trombone and organ arrangement is modeled on the 1847 piano version, the keyboard writing in the later Liszt piece is technically less demanding. In the earlier arrangement the piano plays the short *quasi improvisato* passage immediately before the coda at m. 117 that the trombone plays in the latter. Schott published this arrangement in 1874, and the piece has been included with *Hosannah* (S 667) in the eighth volume of *Franz Liszt Sämtliche Orgelwerke* edited by Haselböck.

The second work is an arrangement Liszt made of an untraced composition by Zámoyská that may have been written in 1871 around the same time of the piano version. The first edition of *The New Grove Dictionary of Music and Musicians* cited *Puszta-Wehmut* as being in the private collection of H. Cardello, New York. This little csárdás, *Puszta-Wehmut*, or "Longing for the Plains" was inspired by the poem, *Puszta-Wehmut*, written by Nikolaus Lenau (1802–1850). The Liszt D-minor piano version of the piece that Táborszky published in 1885 opens with a low double E before rising slowly. The notes of this introduction are written in the bass clef in smaller type and may signify the existence of a Liszt cello part. It is possible that the chamber version previously owned by the late Cardello may be a cello and piano arrangement. Nineteenth-century cello writing can easily be confused with violin music of the period. It was common practice at that time for cello parts to be written an octave higher than pitch. Liszt's Duo for cello and piano in the Paris Biblothètheque Musicale Gustav Mahler is, or was until the spring of 1999, wrongly cataloged as a Liszt piece for violin and piano.

On 10 June 1852 Liszt composed a fragment for the celebrated cellist Bernhard Cossmann in Weimar of Wagner's Romance, "O du mein holder Abendstern" (S 380) from *Tannhäuser* for cello and piano. *Die Musik* published the autograph in May 1902. Cossmann had been principal cellist during a

Weimar performance of Wagner's *Tannhäuser* on 31 May 1852 and was featured prominently in Wolfram's song in Act III, scene ii. Liszt probably provided Cossmann with the manuscript, a twenty-eight measure ending to the *Romance*, to enable them to perform a cello and piano transcription of the song. On 8 October 1993 the Scottish cellist Myra Chahin and William Wright gave the first modern performance of the reconstructed *Romance* at the International Liszt Congress in Washington, D. C.[67]

OTHERS ARRANGING LISZT'S WORKS WITH HIS ANNOTATIONS

Around 1868 Belgian cellist, Jules de Swert (1843–1891) arranged Liszt's six *Consolations*[68] for cello and piano while engaged as a teacher at Weimar's Hochschule and as solo cellist at the Royal Chapel. Breitkopf & Härtel published the transcription in or shortly before 1870. The same year another Belgian cellist, Ernst de Munck (1840–1915), succeeded de Swert as first cellist in the court orchestra and came into contact with Liszt. De Munck and Liszt performed the *Consolations* during a series of matinées at the Grand Duke of Weimar's Palace in July 1871, although it is possible they only played *Consolations* I and IV.[69] Liszt likely wrote the ten-and-a-half-measure passage linking the two about this time, which is known today as the *Enchaînement de F. Liszt* (S 382a).

During the latter part of his career, de Munck became professor of cello at the Royal Academy of Music in London. After his death a copy of de Swert's arrangement of *Consolation* no. 1 with Liszt's added linking passage was lodged in the Academy library. Breitkopf & Härtel republished de Swert's arrangement of the set of the six pieces in the spring of 1990. The Liszt Society's publication in 1992 of the six Liszt/de Swert *Consolations* included the first appearance of Liszt's *Enchaînement*.[70] Cellist Mark Bailey of the Edinburgh Quartet and Wright gave its first modern performance on 21 July 1991.

Around 1880 the Danish composer Edward Lassen (1830–1894) made a transcription of Liszt's *Vallée d'Obermann* for piano trio in Weimar. Liszt added a new introduction, made some corrections, and later created two further versions by altering the copyist's manuscript and sketching an alternative ending.[71] The three arrangements (S 723a,b,c),[72] identified and reconstructed by Wolfgang Marggraf in 1986, appeared in print for the first time in a Liszt Society publication, *Ferenc Liszt: The Complete Works of Liszt for Pianoforte, Violin and Violoncello* (1996). The first modern performance of the third version was given in Budapest in 1986, and a modern première of the first two versions were given by violinist Deborah Fox, cellist William Howard, and pianist Leslie Howard at the Australia House, London, on 25 November 1993.

Liszt also made corrections and added material in his own hand to an unpublished arrangement of "Gretchen" from his *Faust Symphony* that Leopold Alexander Zellner arranged for violin, harp, harmonium, and piano. Göllerich cited an orchestral arrangement of this Weimar manuscript, held in the Liszt

Academy in Budapest, and Liszt's first *Élégie* arranged for cello, piano, harp, and harmonium as works for small orchestra.

In the summer of 1841, Liszt and his family visited Nonnenwerth, an island in the Rhine, and Liszt wrote the song *Die Zelle in Nonnenwerth* (S 382) that he published in 1843. Ludwig L. Frank possibly arranged a version for violin or cello and piano. On the title page of the version for piano solo (third edition) that Tonger of Cologne published in 1877 is the following: "Instrumentation by Ludwig L. Frank."[73] The second edition of the *New Grove Dictionary of Music and Musicians*, however, cited a violin or cello and piano version by Liszt and printed by Tonger in 1883. Raabe and Winklhofer suggested that Liszt did not make any chamber arrangements of the song. In 1992 the Liszt Society published a cello and piano version of the work[74] and will soon publish a violin and piano version based on the Weimar Liszt manuscript with pasteovers in another hand and accompanying string parts copied by Wilhelm Weber, dated 21 August 1883. The first performance was given in Budapest on 16 March 1885.

With few exceptions Liszt's original chamber works and the chamber arrangements he made of some of his own pieces and those of others are rarely heard. The recent Liszt Society's publication of *The Complete Music for Violoncello and Pianoforte* (1992) and *The Complete Music for Pianoforte, Violin and Violoncello* (1996) have made more of the arrangements accessible for performers. Recent attempts by several artists to make the transcriptions better known to the musically discerning merit applause.

NOTES

1. Alan Walker, *Franz Liszt: The Virtuoso Years 1811–1847* (New York: Alfred A. Knopf, 1983), 1:58.

2. The complete cello part of the D♭ major 1825 trio for piano, violin, and cello (S 717), consisting of ten manuscript pages Bittermann of no. 69 Rue de Clery, Paris copied for Liszt, was sold in Paris on 6 November 1997 at a Laurin, Guilloux, and Buffetaud sale. Liszt added numerous autograph annotations regarding interpretation to the copied cello part. The manuscript of the piano part was sold at Stargardt in July 1998. He composed the work in three movements: *Allegro Moderato, Andante non troppo*, and *Rondo*. A Liszt A-major string trio fragment held in the Goethe- und Schiller-Archiv in Weimar is unrelated to this work. Michael Saffle suggested that Liszt may have continued to experiment with several other ensemble compositions before his years in Weimar. Saffle posed the possibility of the "Miserere" fragment [F- PN, Ms 163v] being an arrangement for piano and instrument(s). See Saffle, "Liszt's Music Manuscripts in Paris," *Analecta Lisztiana 1* (Stuyvesant, NY: Pendragon, 1998), 123. Also, see *Marie Poème* S 701a.

3. See La Mara [Marie Lipsius], ed. *Klassisches und Romantisches aus der Tonwelt* (Leipzig, 1892), 260. Liszt was almost certainly one of a small number of Parisians devoted to the performance of chamber music at this time. Members of the Baillot Quartet and others gave performances in the homes of prominent musicians, and Liszt's 1825 trio (S 717) and quintet (S 718) were probably written for such a gathering. Liszt continued to attend and participate in chamber concerts as a young pianist and composer, and remained one of Baillot's enthusiastic admirers.

4. On 26 July 1835 Liszt sent a letter to his mother in Paris asking her to send several of his manuscripts, including the "sextet copied by the Pole [S 718d]." See *Franz Liszt: Briefwechsel mit seiner Mutter*, ed. and trans. Klára Hamburger (Eisenstadt: Amt der Burgenländischen Landesregierung, 2000), 65.

5. More and more often in the 1820s two famous virtuosos—one a pianist and the other a violinist—would appear in joint concerts and create their own repertoire. The genre became known as "Duo brilliant" usually under joint authorship. How the actual compositional work was done remains a mystery, but the technical aspects were defined, each virtuoso taking charge of his own instrument. See Boris Schwarz, *French Instrumental Music Between the Revolutions 1789–1830* (New York: Da Capo, 1987), 272.

6. Liszt's *Zwei Walzer* for violin and piano were almost unknown until they were identified as S 208a in "Liszt's Violin Music: The Liszt Society's Information Sheet no. 1" in *The Liszt Society Newsletter* no. 71, (September 1999). The British Liszt Society intends to republish the pieces with other presently unavailable Liszt violin and piano works: [*Première*] *Élégie* (S 130), *Zweite Elegie* (S 131), *Romance oubliée* (S 132), *La lugubre gondola* (S 134), *La notte* (S 377a), *Rhapsodie Hongroise* XII (S 379a), *Benedictus* and *Offertorium* (S 381), *Die drei Zigeuner* (S 383), and the 1883 unpublished violin and piano version of *Die Zelle in Nonnenwerth*. The pieces will be included in a forthcoming Liszt Society Publication: *Ferenc Liszt, The Complete Music for Violin and Pianoforte*. Liszt's *Zwei Walzer* in A major for violin and piano were included as nos. 4 and 5 in "Sieben Walzer für Violine und Pianoforte von M. Pamer, H. Payer und F. List [sic]," published by Mathias Artaria of Vienna. The pieces were advertised in the *Wiener Zeitung* on 26 August 1825. The whereabouts of Liszt's two violin and guitar waltz arrangements published concurrently, also in A major, remain unknown. See Alexander Weinmann, *Beiträge zur Geschichtes des Alt-Wiener Musikverlages*, Reihe 2, Folge 14. *Verzeichnis der Musikalien des Verlages Maisch-Sprenger-Artaria* (Vienna: Universal Editions, 1970), 46.

7. While in London in 1827, Liszt had been introduced to the leading English violinist Nicholas Mori. On 2 June they performed to critical acclaim their violin and piano duo on Rossini's *Semiramide* (S 718a) at the Royal Society of Musicians' Grand Festival (see the *Morning Post*, 4 June 1827). The boy flautist, Antonio Minasi, also played with Liszt during this sojourn. On 5 June 1827 during Liszt's third sojourn, they performed together *The Fall of Paris ms, a Military Air* with variations for flute and piano (S 718b) at the Drury Lane Theatre (see the Drury Lane Theatre Playbill, 5 June 1827). On 26 May 1827 the *Times* in its supplementary issue first noticed this duo, another collaborative composition of Liszt's. The Liszt/Mori violin and piano duo and the Liszt/Minasi flute and piano duo received their first mention in the Liszt literature in 1991. See Wright, "Liszt's London Appearances in 1827," *LSJ* 16 (1991): 9. The present whereabouts of the two 1827 London manuscripts are unknown. The title of a third 1827 London duo, *Fantasie on the French Air, 'Le petit Tambour,'* that Liszt and Mori composed for a performance at the Drury Lane Theatre on 8 June 1827 came to the attention of the author in October 2000 (see the Drury Lane Theatre Playbill, 8 June 1827).

8. While in Paris between 1827 and 1834, Liszt likely composed duos with violinists Karl Ebner, Theodore Hauman, Antonio James Oury, and others. After his father's death in 1827, Liszt returned to the French capital and soon renewed his friendship with fellow Hungarian Ebner. They had performed together in Munich in 1823. "The Duo for piano and violin executed by MM Litz [sic] and Ebner" on 23 February 1828 at the Salons Dietz may well have been a work written by them both. See Geraldine Keeling, "Liszt's Appearances in Parisian Concerts: 1824–1844," *LSJ* 11 (1986): 25. Performances Liszt and former Belgian law student Hauman gave in Paris on

10 April 1828 and 15 April 1833 probably featured the *Grand duo concertant* as did the concert with Liszt and Oury on 15 December 1829. See Keeling: 27, 29, and 33.

Hauman composed his *Grandes variations sur la Tyrolienne de La fiancée d'Auber*, op. 7 for violin and piano or orchestra probably around the time Liszt composed his own 1829 arrangement of the same *Tyrolienne*. See "François Joseph Fétis," *Biographie universelle des musiciens* (Paris, 1835–1844), 4:244–245.

9. Friedrich Schnapp gave the date of composition as around 1837. See Schnapp, "Verschollene Kompositionen Franz Liszts," in *Von Deutscher Tonkunst: Festschrift zu Peter Raabes 70. Geburtstag*, ed. Alfred Morgenroth (Leipzig: C. F. Peters, 1942), 128. Schnapp cited an 1841 lost chamber arrangement of Liszt on page 131 of the same publication: "Grand Fantasie on God Save the Queen and Rule Britannia for Piano Quartet" (S 718e). Michael Short wrote, "This work is mentioned in Lina Ramann, *Franz Liszt als Künstler und Mensch*, 2:311. Apparently Ramann derived her information from the first issue of Julius Schuberth's Hamburg publication, *Blätter für Musik und Literatur*. The work was advertised as follows: 'In addition, we have acquired the rights and will publish during course of the year, Liszt, Dr. Fr., Paraphrase, Gr. Fantasie über "God Save the Queen" und "Rule Britannia" for piano and orchestra.' (Full score, orchestral parts, for piano duet and as a Piano Quartet)." See Michael Short, "The Doubtful, Missing, and Unobtainable Works of Ferenc Liszt (1811–1886)," *LSJ* 24 (1999): 40.

10. August Göllerich, *Franz Liszt* (Berlin: Marquardt, 1908), 280.

11. Helene Raff, "Franz Liszt und Joachim Raff im Spiegel ihrer Briefe," *Die Musik* 1 (2 November 1901): 291.

12. Cited in Albert Sebestyén, "Franz Liszts Originalkompositionen für Violine und Klavier," in *Liszt-Studien 1. Kongress-Bericht Eisenstadt 1975*, ed. Wolfgang Suppan (Graz: Akademische Druck- u. Verlagsanstalt, 1977), 173.

13. Robert Bory, *Une retraite romantique en Suisse. Liszt et la Comtesse d'Agoult* (A Lausanne, SPES edition, 1930), 55.

14. *Correspondance de Liszt et de la Comtesse d'Agoult*, ed. Daniel Ollivier (Paris: Grasset, 1933–1934), 1:284.

15. Sebestyén, "Franz Liszts Originalkompositionen für Violine und Klavier," 173.

16. *Franz Liszt: Briefwechsel mit seiner Mutter*, 66.

17. Göllerich, *Franz Liszt*, 280.

18. Peter Raabe, *Franz Liszt: Leben und Schaffen* (Stuttgart: J. G. Cotta, 1931), 2:313.

19. Further evidence of Liszt's early chamber works is revealed in a letter written around 1830 or 1831 to Monsieur Curie: "I hope to have the pleasure of seeing you at David's [probably Félicien David, the Saint-Simonist] on Monday. I will be bringing a little piece for piano and violin (*un petit morceau* [S 718c]). You won't need to practise it, since with your talent it will be plain sailing." (*Franz Liszts Briefe* 8:4). The whereabouts of this work is unknown.

20. Humphrey Searle, "Franz Liszt," in *The New Grove: Early Romantic Masters 1: Chopin, Schumann, Liszt*, rev. Sharon Winklhofer (London: Papermac, 1985), 301. Searle more accurately stated that Duo (S 127) was written "in a rather more classical style than most of Liszt's other works from this period." Liszt's early lost chamber compositions were probably written often in air and variation form.

21. See Alan Walker, "Liszt's Duo Sonata," *Musical Times* 116 (1975): 620–621 and Walker, *Franz Liszt: The Weimar Years 1848–1861* (New York: Alfred A. Knopf, 1989), 2:47.

22. Rena Charnin Mueller, "Liszt's Catalogues and Inventories of His Works," *Studia musicologica* 34 (1992): 232.

23. Liszt never referred to this work as a sonata, nor divided it into separate movements. Serly was first to describe this composition as a "four-movement work." See Serly's article in the *New York Times* (14 February 1960) and his introductory note in the Southern Music publication of the work.

24. Sebestyén, "Franz Liszts Originalkompositionen für Violine und Klavier," 164–173.

25. See ibid., 173.

26. Quoted in Ervin Major, Card Catalogue Eleven (Budapest: Institute of Musicology of the Hungarian Academy of Sciences, 1935), item 76.

27. Albert Sebestyén suggested that Liszt may have made a violin and piano arrangement of his fifth *Hungarian Rhapsody,* "Héroïde-élégiaque." Liszt and Nándor Plotényi performed it on a Liszt Sunday matinée in Pest on 8 January 1871. Sebestyén wrote, "The performance was reported in *Zenészeti Lapok* (15 January 1871) under the wrong title *Héroïde Funèbre.*" See Sebestyén, "Franz Liszts Originalkompositionen für Violine und Klavier," 176.

28. See Leslie Howard, ed., *Ferenc Liszt: The Complete Music for Pianoforte, Violin and Violoncello.* Liszt Society Publications 11 (Edinburgh: The Hardie Press, 1996).

29. Göllerich, *Franz Liszt,* 280.

30. Alexander Wilhelm Gottschalg, *Franz Liszt in Weimar und sein letzten Lebensjahre,* ed. Carl Alfred René. Letter no. 21 (Berlin, 1910). Cited in Hans Rudolf Jung, *Franz Liszt in seinen Briefen* (Athenäum: German Democratic Republic. 1987), 216 and 477.

31. Liszt had intended to write a violin concerto for Reményi around 1860. The Hungarian National Library in Budapest has a page of manuscript in Liszt's hand relating to this work. Albert Sebestyén suggested Liszt may have made violin and piano arrangements of two movements from *Christus:* "Hirtenspiel an der Krippe" and "Die heiligen drei Könige" [Marsch]. "Liszt and Reményi performed 'Hirtenspiel' at the home of Baron Antal Augusz in Pest on 3 May 1869, and both pieces in Pest on 27 November 1870 and 5 March 1871 at Liszt's Sunday Matinées. There are relevant press reports in *Zenészeti Lapok* (9 May 1869) and *Pesti Napló* (28 November 1870). Although Ede Sebestyén mentioned these performances in his book *Franz Liszt's Concerts in Budapest* [1944], no information on sources is given. I owe all my information about the sources to Dezső Legány." See Sebestyén, "Franz Liszts Originalkompositionen für Violine und Klavier," 176.

32. Jenö Hubay's violin and piano arrangement of Liszt's *First Valse Oubliée* and *Valse Impromptu* are also currently available in publications by Edition Musica Budapest.

33. Sebestyén, "Franz Liszts Originalkompositionen für Violine und Klavier," 174.

34. Albert Hadnagy and Margit Prahács, *Liszt szekszárdi kapcsolantairól: Tanulmányok Tolna megye történetéböl* vol. 2 (Szckszárd, 1960). Cited in Sebestyén, "Franz Liszts Originalkompositionen für Violine und Klavier," 178.

35. *Franz Liszt's Briefe an Baron Anton Augusz, 1846–1878,* ed. Wilhelm von Csapó. (Budapest, 1911), 153.

36. Dezső Legány, "Reményi and Liszt," *LSJ* 22 (1997): 23.

37. Schuberth issued Gottschalg's most important publication, *Repertorium für die Orgel* in three volumes.

38. Fukuda, "An Unknown Version of Liszt's *Cantico di San Francesco,*" *LSJ* 23 (1998): 17–26.

39. William Bates, "The Haselböck Edition of Liszt's Organ Works," *JALS* 28 (1990): 42–68.

40. Martin Haselböck, ed. *Franz Liszt: The Complete Works for Organ.* 10 vols. Vienna: Universal, 1985–.

41. Fukuda, "An Unknown Version of *Cantico di San Francesco*," 25.

42. Ibid., 25.

43. Searle, "Franz Liszt," in *The New Grove Early Romantic Masters*, 356.

44. See Mária Eckhardt, *Liszt's Music Manuscripts in the National Széchényi Library* (Budapest: Akadémiai Kiadó, 1986), 141 and 238.

45. Göllerich cited *Die Vier Jahreszeiten*, an unfinished Liszt string quartet in his 1908 "Franz Liszt" catalog of works. According to information Ferruccio Busoni gave to Göllerich, Liszt had drafted a sketch of the first movement and part of the second around 1880. Göllerich also mentioned an *Allegro Moderato* in E major for violin and piano as a Liszt work. Raabe stated that Aloys Obrist, curator of the Hofgärtnerei (1902–1920), informed Göllerich of the piece. Göllerich also attributed the arrangement of *Au bord d'une source* for three violins to Liszt, although Edmund Singer made this Schott publication. Ernst Rentsch actually made the arrangement of *Lebe Wohl* (*Gesammelte Lieder* no. 44) for violin and piano that Göllerich attributed to Liszt and that Kahnt published.

Göllerich cited a cello and piano transcription of the same song as another Kahnt publication and Liszt's work. No mention of the piece appears in any of the Kahnt catalogues. The Kahnt publication of *Mignon* (*Gesammelte Lieder* no. 1) for cello and piano that Göllerich attributed to Liszt, was made by either Friedrich Grützmacher, son of Leopold, or Friedrich Grützmacher, pupil of Karl Drechsler. Liszt likely had sight of the manuscripts of several of the above and of the chamber compositions by Robert Pflughaupt and others. Liszt would certainly have had occasions to make corrections or add material.

46. *Franz Liszt's Briefe*, ed. La Mara [Marie Lipsius]. 8 vols. (Leipzig: Breitkopf & Härtel, 1893–1905), 8:341.

47. See photocopy of the arrangement in Eősze László: *119 Római Liszt Dokumentum* (Budapest: Zeneműkiadó, 1980), 102–106.

48. The author is grateful to Kenneth Souter for this information.

49. See "Music Section," *LSJ* 14 (1989): 37–46.

50. Alan Walker, ed., *Living with Liszt from the Diary of Carl Lachmund: An American Pupil of Liszt 1882–1884*. Franz Liszt Studies Series no. 4 (Stuyvesant, NY: Pendragon, 1995), 232.

51. Chrétien Urhan had performed on a violin alto, a five-stringed violin with the lowest note C below middle C, at his Paris concerts during the 1830s.

52. A few years after the publication of Liszt's *Romance oubliée* chamber versions, two of his contemporaries, Konrad Adam Stehling (1824–1902) and Friedrich Hermann (1828–1907) made viola and piano arrangements of Liszt works. Augener of London published Stehling's transcription of *Consolation* no. 5 in 1886/87 and Hermann's arrangement of the six *Consolations* in 1903.

53. See "Franz Liszt in Rom. Aufzeichnungen von Nadine Helbig," *Deutsche Revue* (January 1907): 74.

54. See *Franz Liszts Briefe*, 2:258.

55. See ibid., 7:203.

56. Lina Ramann, *Lisztiana: Erinnerungen an Franz Liszt in Tagebuchblättern, Briefen und Dokumenten aus den Jahren 1873–1886/1887*, ed. Arthur Seidl and Friedrich Schnapp (Mainz and New York: B. Schott's Sons, 1983), 113.

57. See manuscript of the piano version of Liszt's *Am Grabe Richard Wagners* held in the Cary Deposit, Pierpont Morgan Library, New York.

58. See Walker, *Franz Liszt: The Final Years*, 3:432.

59. See Walker, *Living With Liszt*, 185.

60. *Franz Liszt Briefe*, 2:348–349.

61. Ibid., 2:380–381.

62. Musikhistorisches Museum von Wilhelm Heyer in Coln: Katalog von Georg Kinsky, vol. 4, *Musical Autographs* (Coln: J. P. Bachem, 1916), 729.

63. Eckhardt, *Liszt's Music Manuscripts in the National Széchényi Library*, 166–169.

64. See *Franz Liszts Briefe* 2:257.

65. Manuscript no. [F – PN, MS 171]. See Saffle, "Liszt's Music Manuscripts in Paris," 126.

66. See Liszt's letter to Ludmilla Zámoyská dated 28 July 1871 in Zoltán Hrabussay, *Liszt's Unknown MSS in Slovakia* (Bratislava: Hudobnovedné stúdie, IV, 1990), 189.

67. A facsimile of this reconstructed song transcription appeared in Wright, "The Transcriptions for Cello and Piano of Works by Liszt," *JALS* 35 (1994): 46–48.

68. Liszt's concatenation of *Consolations* nos. 1 and 4 may also be considered as a Liszt cello and organ piece. A Liszt cello and organ arrangement appears to have been included in a Beethoven Centenary Concert in Weimar on 28 May 1870 and later at Merseburg Cathedral on 7 June of that year, performed by the German cellist Karl Fitzenhagen (1848–1890) with organ accompaniment. Legány suggested that *Consolations* nos. 1 and 4 were probably played (see his *Liszt Ferenc and His Country, 1869–1873*, 51). This would explain the inclusion of handwritten three-manual German organ registration at the top left-hand corner of the first transcribed *Consolation*. See photocopy of de Swert's first transcribed *Consolation* in Wright, "The Transcriptions for Cello and Piano of Works by Liszt," 30.

Ernst de Munck spent around seven years as court cellist in Weimar and was engaged to perform another sanctioned Liszt pairing: Liszt/de Swert *Consolations* nos. 1 and 3 to organ accompaniment at the "Altenburg Musikfest" on 28 May 1876. See the *Neue Zeitschrift für Musik* (1876): 227–228. On 29 April 1877 in the same town, de Munck and resident organist Bernard Sulze performed one of the Liszt/de Swert *Consolations* transcribed for cello and organ. See Legány: *Liszt and His Country: 1874–1886*, 53 and 73. Liszt's *Consolation* no. 4 for organ had been in print since 1867.

Liszt took part in a cello, piano, and organ performance of Chopin's *Marche funèbre*, op. 35 at a concert in Jena Cathedral on 2 July 1877. See Alfred Habets, *Liszt and Borodin*, ed. Rosa Newmarch (London: Digby, Long, and Co., 1895), 108 and 126. The manuscript of Chopin's Funeral March that Gottschalg arranged for organ with Liszt's corrections is held in the Liszt Academy, Budapest. This manuscript and the untraced cello part may have been used for the 2 July 1877 performance. See Short, "The Doubtful, Missing, and Unobtainable Works of Ferenc Liszt," 47.

69. The September 1871 issue of the *Musical Standard* reported the series, 224.

70. See Howard, ed., *Ferenc Liszt: The Complete Music for Violoncello and Pianoforte*. The Liszt Society Publications 10 (Edinburgh: The Hardie Press, 1992). The volume also includes *Élégie* (S 130) with optional parts for harp and harmonium or organ, *Zweite Elegie* (S 131), *Romance oubliée* (S 132), *La lugubre gondola* (S 134), *Die Zelle in Nonnenwerth* (S 382), and Leslie Howard's conjectural reconstruction of "O du mein holder Abendstern" (S 380).

71. See Wolfgang Marggraf, "Eine Klaviertrio-Bearbeitung des 'Vallée d'Obermann' aus Liszts Spätzeit," *Studia musicologica* 28 (1986): 301–302.

72. Liszt entitled the final version *Tristia, La vallée d'Obermann*. This third version is a somber representation of Sénancour's *Obermann* and Ovid's elegy *Tristia*.

73. The author is grateful to Rena Charnin Mueller for this information.

74. Imre Sulyok and Imre Mező cited only a Liszt violin and piano transcription of *Nonnenwerth*. See NLE, i/17: xv.

10

Orchestral Works

Michael Saffle

For decades historians have told us that Liszt turned to orchestral music only in 1848, after he had retired from his "years of transcendental execution" and settled in Weimar, where he served for more than a decade as Kapellmeister to the grand-ducal court. This is not quite true. We do not know when Liszt wrote out his first orchestral score, but it cannot have been later than the mid-1830s. As a child he was supposed to have composed several "grand overtures," and it is just possible that he scored these himself; unfortunately, the pieces have disappeared. (He was also supposed to have composed—which, one might think, would also mean "have orchestrated"—his youthful opera *Don Sanche*, but the evidence suggests his teacher Ferdinando Paër actually wrote out the full score. See Chapter 4 for a brief discussion of this issue.)

We know Liszt toyed in 1830 with plans for a "Revolutionary" symphony (S 690); in the second volume of his *Franz Liszt*, Peter Raabe reproduced in facsimile sketches for that work, jotted down during the July Revolution.[1] Contemporary accounts tell us that, by the end of the 1830s, Liszt had performed in public piano-orchestral versions of several of his keyboard fantasies. Did he score them himself? Perhaps. We know he prepared an orchestral accompaniment for his *Lélio* fantasy (S 120); the manuscript survives in the Goethe- und Schiller-Archiv, Weimar. By 1839 Liszt had also drafted two quite different piano concertos: one an early version of the Concerto in E♭ major he revised for publication in 1849, and the other the so-called "Concerto Op. Posth." that Jay Rosenblatt reassembled from fragments of early works and published for the first time a few years ago. Finally, in August 1845 Liszt composed, rehearsed, and conducted at the Beethoven Festival in Bonn a cantata in honor of the composer, one he himself had orchestrated (S 67). These last few works may not be masterpieces, but all of them are unquestionably orchestral.

On the other hand, Liszt devoted only a decade or so largely to orchestral composition; most of his important symphonic works date from or at least were begun between 1849 and 1859. From these years, too, date drafts or finished versions of his finest pieces for piano and orchestra, substantial portions of his oratorios *Christus* and *Die Legende von der heiligen Elisabeth*, and all of his finest work for chorus and orchestra: the *Missa solemnis* composed for the consecration of the Cathedral at Esztergom in Hungary (and known today by the German name of that city as the *Gran Mass*). True, he also produced some orchestral music after he left Weimar in 1861; it was during the mid-1860s, for example, that he finished *Christus* and wrote another fine mass for the coronation in 1867 of Francis Joseph I as King of Hungary. Afterwards, however, Liszt mostly ignored the orchestra, and aside from a final symphonic poem he produced little for large ensembles during the last decade of his life.[2]

As an orchestral composer Liszt was both conservative and innovative. Occasionally he daydreamed about writing parts for wind machines and projecting pictures to "illustrate" his symphonic poems, but most of the time he composed for a conventional mid-nineteenth-century orchestra: woodwinds in pairs, three or four horns, two trumpets, two or three trombones and tuba, timpani, and strings. To this ensemble he often added parts for piccolo, English horn, bass clarinet, one or more additional trumpets (including trumpets in E and F), harp, and "battery" (triangle, cymbals, snare drum, bass drum, and gongs); occasionally he also called for a third flute, a third bassoon, a second harp, chimes, and organ. See Example 10.1, which reproduces the first page of *Ce qu'on entend sur la montagne*, the first of the published symphonic poems and one scored for a large "Lisztian" orchestra.

Only a few of Liszt's scores call for "gimmicks" his contemporaries might have considered radical: the muffled bass-drum roll at the opening of *Ce qu'on entend*, for instance (again, see Example 10.1), or the part for narrator in *Les morts* (see Example 10.17)—if, that is, Liszt intended the French words he wrote into the latter score to be read out loud. We should remember, however, that both Berlioz and Schumann also called for narrators in some of their orchestral scores, and that, by 1830, Berlioz had also called for sponge-headed drumsticks and many other special percussion effects in his *Symphonie fantastique*. In many ways Liszt's orchestration of the 1850s looks back to Berlioz's even as, in certain respects, it anticipates Wagner's.

Instead of novelty or complexity, Liszt specialized as an orchestrator in transparency. Only when necessary did he double parts, and then most often to give his string parts more emphasis. Almost never did he produce muddy-sounding or poorly-balanced passages, as Schumann and even Brahms sometimes did; certain murky effects in *Tasso* are an exception, introduced for programmatic purposes (see Example 10.3). Instead, Liszt's more heavily scored passages are forthright rather than merely exaggerated; his sectional scoring, especially for winds, is noteworthy for its clarity and logic, and his use of solo instruments is both infrequent and highly effective. Liszt also wrote well for percussion; consider the delightful and mostly understated military passages in *Hungaria*. On occasion he may have employed cymbals and other noise-

Example 10.1
Liszt, *Ce qu'on entend sur la montagne*, mm. 1–4

makers a bit too enthusiastically—his excessive use of the triangle in his first Piano Concerto long ago inspired wits to dub that work the "Triangle Concerto"—but as the years passed his orchestration, in general, grew more subdued. By the 1880s his scoring had become downright sparse, and in *Von der Wiege bis zum Grabe*, his last symphonic poem, there is almost nothing sonorous or "effective" at all.[3]

Liszt's orchestral compositions and transcriptions fall into four principal categories: the thirteen symphonic poems, the two symphonies, a group of original but less-familiar and generally smaller-scale pieces, and ensemble arrangements of works originally composed for other forces. Except for the arrangements, almost all of these works are discussed below in roughly chronological order. Insofar as the Weimar years are concerned, they are also discussed under such subheadings as "Symphonic Poems," "Symphonies," and "Miscellaneous Works."

WEIMAR, 1848–1861[4]

1830–1856	*Héroïde funèbre*. S 102.
1830–1857	*Hungaria*. S 103.
1838–1854	*Mazeppa*. S 100.
1840–1854	*Tasso: Lamento e trionfo*. S 96.
c. 1845–1854	*Les préludes*. S 97.
1840s–1859	*Eine Symphonie zu Dantes Divina commedia*. S 109.
1840s–1861	*Eine Faust-Symphonie*. S 108.
1845?–1854	*Ce qu'on entend sur la montagne*. S 95.
1849–1857	*Festmarsch zur Goethejubiläumsfeier*. S 115.
1850–1855	*Prometheus*. S 99.
1853–1854	*Festklänge*. S 101.
1854	*Orpheus*. S 98.
1857–1858	*Die Ideale*. S 106.
1857–1860	*Künstlerfestzug zur Schillerfeier 1859*. S 114.
1857–1861	*Hunnenschlacht*. S 105.
1858–1861	*Hamlet*. S 104.
1860	*Festmarsch nach Motiven von E. H. zu S.–C.–G.* S 116.
1860	*Les morts (Trois odes funèbres* no. 1). S 112/1.
c. 1861	*Zwei Episoden aus Lenaus Faust*, S 110.

After settling in Weimar Liszt devoted himself for several years not merely to composing orchestral music, but to rehearsing, conducting, and performing it as well. He did not approach these tasks empty-handed: instead, he brought with him some practical experience as a conductor as well as sketches and drafts for portions of what later became six of his symphonic poems: *Hungaria, Héroïde funèbre, Tasso, Ce qu'on entend sur la montagne, Les préludes*, and *Mazeppa*.

The inspiration for *Hungaria* and *Héroïde funèbre* dates back to the "Revolutionary" symphony sketches of 1830, although prior to the late 1840s Liszt seems to have done little more than think about finishing that legendary work. Drafts for several parts of *Tasso* date from August 1847, when they were written down in three- or four-stave format in the so-called "Tasso sketchbook" belonging today to the Goethe- und Schiller-Archiv, Weimar (shelf-number N5). Another part of that work—in this case a melody Liszt heard a Venetian gondolier sing—was borrowed from part of the *Album d'un voyageur* (S 156), engraved for publication in 1840 but finally printed and sold for the first time more than a decade later. Sketches for *Ce qu'on entend* date from the mid-1840s and were recorded in another Weimar sketchbook (shelf-number N1). Portions of what became *Les préludes*—the unfinished *Les quatre Élémens* (S 80), settings of poems by Joseph Autran for chorus and piano, as well as an instrumental introduction to them—date from the mid-1840s. Early versions of *Mazeppa*— one incorporated into the *24 Grandes Etudes* of c. 1838 (S 137), another in the form of an independent piano piece published as early as 1840 (S 138)—were later reworked and republished, first as part of the *Etudes d'exécution transcendante* (S 139), then as part of a symphonic poem; additional sketches for one or both of these revisions as well as for *Ce qu'on entend* may also be found in the "Tasso sketchbook."[5] Finally, Liszt brought to Weimar at least the ideas of, and possibly musical sketches for, both his *Faust* and *Dante* symphonies.

In 1848 Liszt seems immediately and by himself to have begun scoring some of these pieces. A complete orchestral draft in his own hand of *Héroïde funèbre*, completed in the fall of 1849, survives today in the collections of the Paris Conservatoire (Bibliothèque Nationale). For the most part, however, he hired skilled collaborators to prepare fair draft copies of the first few symphonic poems. The idea was to save time and trouble: for each work Liszt jotted the music down on two, three, or four staves, complete with orchestral suggestions; next, his assistant worked these sketches up into full-fledged scores; finally, Liszt corrected these drafts and returned them for recopying. At first he employed the industrious August Conradi; later Liszt turned to Joachim Raff, a more imaginative musician and an equally industrious one. Unhappily for Liszt's reputation, however, Raff claimed in correspondence—later published—that he had taught Liszt to orchestrate![6] There is no real evidence for this claim, but Liszt probably did adopt one or more of his assistant's orchestral suggestions.

After the early 1850s Liszt either worked alone or, occasionally, corrected and edited orchestral arrangements of his own compositions prepared by others; examples of such arrangements include the orchestral transcriptions of Liszt's *Hungarian Rhapsodies* nos. 2, 5–6, 9, 12, and 14 (S 359) that Ferdinand Doppler prepared, and that the composer himself touched up and "authorized" prior to publication. Liszt's competence as a mature orchestrator does not prove, however, that as the years passed he always knew his own mind. Liszt was forever a reviser, even a fussbudget; often, it seems, he considered published pieces works-in-progress and dozens of his printed scores are filled with additional "corrections" and alternate passages. It is for this reason that no Liszt work can be considered "finished" at the very least until its publication; a fair copy of *La triomphe funèbre du Tasse* owned by the Library of Congress, with corrections in the composer's hand, proves that Liszt added the published percussion parts just before the work received its premiere performance in 1877—and that for a work ostensibly completed in 1866!

The Symphonic Poems

Liszt was not the first to compose single-movement orchestral compositions of a markedly programmatic or extra-musical expressive character. Many operatic overtures, such as Gioacchino Rossini's overture to *Guillaume Tell*, consist largely of narrative "moments" strung together to "summarize" larger wholes; other pieces, such as Felix Mendelssohn's *Fingal's Cave*, reflect their creators' travels and personal experiences. On the other hand, Liszt invented the term "symphonic poem" and, in his own thirteen *sinfonische Dichtungen*, he established a tradition that was taken up and expanded upon by a host of other composers, including Paul Dukas, Antonín Dvořák, Edvard Grieg, Edward MacDowell, Jean Sibelius, Bedřich Smetana, Pyotr Ilich Tchaikovsky, and Richard Strauss. Liszt's principal contribution to the evolution of the genre, however, was in demonstrating how orchestral music could represent the extramusical through a combination of absolute and programmatic elements. Of great importance among the more traditional elements he employed is the sonata idea also employed by Franz Joseph Haydn, Wolfgang Amadeus Mozart, Ludwig van Beethoven, Franz Schubert, and a host of other late eighteenth- and early nineteenth-century masters. Also important is double-function form, which combines elements of single-movement sonata form with suggestions of multi-movement organization.[7] Of great importance among his more programmatic and innovative musical gestures are: a pioneering use of topics and thematic transformation; explicit allusions to literature and art in the form of titles, textual quotations, and the like; and, occasionally, references to pre-existing tunes and other musical "signs" that convey extra-musical significance.

Musical programmism is a challenging subject and one that still raises the hackles of many performances and scholars. At times—to contradict Humphrey Searle's assertion that his subject was "not interested in the minute pictorialism into which the symphonic poem later degenerated," and that, for him, "the story, if any . . . was merely the symbol of an idea"[8]—Liszt did in fact represent in sound particular characters and events. Examples include the distant trumpets that announce Mazeppa's rescue, "Ophelia's theme" in *Hamlet* (Liszt himself wrote that the theme was "about" her), the "clock at Elsinore" depicted— according to some scholars[9]—in the same work, and the nightingale's song in *Der nächtliche Zug* (see Example 10.16).

More important, Liszt told the same kind of story—what Searle may have meant by "an idea"—over and over again. This tale, one of suffering followed by triumph, incorporates what Keith Johns calls "paired dualities . . . archetypes like death and rebirth, or struggle and victory . . . expressed musically through explicit and implicit programmatic elements: topics, musical motives and their transformations, harmonic relationships, and so on."[10] Liszt made certain that most of his symphonic stories ended happily; he even added an "Apotheosis" to *Die Ideale*, a work otherwise associated with rather pessimistic sentiments. In other words, Liszt's programmatic pieces do tell stories, although they tell them in various ways and, in so doing, draw upon various traditions, expressive schemes, and specialized techniques, including sonata form and thematic transformation. Alan Walker's suggestion that Liszt's titles and programs are little or nothing more than "prefaces" or "letters to the general public" disclosing only "the source of [the composer's] inspiration" rather than anything about the compositions themselves seems unlikely, especially in light of Johns's painstaking semiotic analyses and the narrative response of so many listeners to almost all of these works.[11]

Topics (or *topoi*) are musical "places" or "points" of style: collections of melodic, harmonic, rhythmic, textural, instrumental, and accompanimental gestures associated with particular classes or groups of people, physical locations, states of mind, and social activities. Alternately, theorist Kofi Agawu has defined them as "subjects of musical discourse" and as "signs."[12] Among the topics employed by Classical composers were the *galant* style, associated with cheerfulness and aristocratic elegance; hunting music, associated with excitement and the bucolic; the *empfindsamer Stil* (or "sensitive style"), associated with an almost neurasthenic melancholy and delicacy of expression; pastoral music, associated with peasants and Arcadian shepherds; and the "learned" style, associated with thoughtfulness and intellectual power as well as with certain religious feelings and situations—the last particularly because complex counterpoint was often associated with and found in organ and church music.

Liszt himself used topics as narrative devices, establishing "story lines" by stringing appropriate topical statements together. Sometimes, too, he used transformations of one or more melodies, treated in various topical ways, as bases for musical stories or situations; *Les préludes*, for instance, presents transformations of a single theme in terms of triumphal, military, amorous, and pastoral stylistic circumstances. To make his narrative purpose plain, and to help listeners follow his particular story line, Liszt also provides literary programs (i.e., summaries in words) for many of his orchestral works.

Some of Liszt's symphonic poems are more immediately semiotic ("programmatic") than structural ("absolute" or "abstract"). Many people, for instance, can hear a wild horseback ride "in" *Mazeppa* and a battle between Christians and pagans "in" *Hunnenschlacht*; imaginative individuals (Liszt provided no explicit literary program) can even hear in *Hungaria* a series of struggles by the Magyars to throw off their Austrian oppressors. Other symphonic poems, however, seem to be more about structure than semiotics or stories; *Festklänge*, for instance, is certainly celebratory, but it is also quite obviously and largely "about" sonata form and the resolution of harmonic tensions.

Often, it seems, performers and scholars want everything their own way: either programmism or absolute music, with no in-between position possible. This distinction is false to Liszt's own sentiments, set down in a letter to Louis Köhler. Concerning his symphonic compositions in particular, Liszt wrote:

For, however others may judge of the things, they are for me the necessary developments of my inner experiences, which have brought me to the conviction that *invention* and *feeling* are not so entirely *evil* in Art. Certainly . . . *forms* (which are too often changed by quite respectable people into *formulas*) 'First Subject, Middle Subject, After Subject, etc., may very much grow into a habit, because they must be so thoroughly natural, primitive, and very easily intelligible.' Without making the slightest objection to this opinion, I only beg for permission to be allowed to decide upon the forms by the contents.[13]

In other words, each work should be judged on its own merits. In any one composition Liszt may have included particular narrative details (which Searle disliked) *and* told an archetypal tale (which Johns believes he did) *and* employed traditional structural, harmonic, and topical gestures as well as innovative musical processes such as thematic transformation.

Each of Liszt's first twelve (or "Weimar") symphonic poems is discussed below according to order of publication in the definitive edition of the 1860s. Nine of the symphonic poems were issued more or less together by Breitkopf & Härtel (Leipzig) in 1856–1857; the remaining three appeared in print for the first time somewhat later: *Die Ideale* (no. 12 in the later, definitive edition) in 1858, *Hunnenschlacht* (no. 11) and *Hamlet* (no. 10)—the last composed—in 1861. Because *Von der Wiege bis zum Grabe* was written much later and published only in 1883, it is discussed in another section of this chapter.

The symphonic poems could, of course, be considered from other perspectives. One of these involves their original purposes: about half of them—*Tasso, Les préludes, Orpheus, Prometheus,* and *Hamlet*—either began life as overtures to other literary or musical works or could have served such functions. Another perspective involves religious content: *Ce qu'on entend, Les préludes, Hunnenschlacht,* and *Von der Wiege* are all frankly Christian works; *Orpheus* and *Prometheus,* on the other hand, are ostensibly "pagan" but in places sound "Christian" to modern ears; *Mazeppa* seems to be pagan through and through. Some of the poems have national biases (*Hungaria*) or literary associations (*Tasso, Prometheus, Hamlet,* and *Die Ideale*) or embody vaguely secular rather than explicitly sacred concerns (*Festklänge* and *Héroïde funèbre*). Musicologist Paul Merrick has argued that the "bewildering external variety" of Liszt's output in no sense contradicts his personal search for redemption.[14] This may be true, but it does not always seem true. Liszt was not invariably successful as a composer, nor was he a man with a single, simpleminded set of personal and professional concerns.

Ce qu'on entend sur la montagne (Symphonic Poem no. 1). The earliest sketches for *Ce qu'on entend sur la montagne* (literally, "What is Heard on the Mountain"), the first in published order of the symphonic poems, date from the mid-1840s; in 1847 Liszt is supposed to have played themes later used in that work to the Princess Carolyne zu Sayn-Wittgenstein. An early version of the piece, orchestrated by Raff, was performed in Weimar in 1850; later Liszt reworked the entire composition several times—on at least one occasion with Raff's assistance—and had it performed again in Weimar on 7 January 1857.

Like *Die Ideale,* the last of the first twelve poems (in published order), *Ce qu'on entend* is what musicologist Rey Longyear has called a work of "philosophical" programmism: one that depicts ideas rather than individuals or events.[15] Based on a poem of the same name taken from Victor Hugo's *Feuilles d'automne,* Liszt's "Mountain Symphony" appeared in print for the first time accompanied by a short synopsis: "The poet hears two voices: one immense, splendid, and full of order, raising to the Lord its joyous hymn of praise—the other hollow, full of pain, swollen by weeping, blasphemies, and curses. One speaks of nature, the other of humanity! Both voices struggle nearer to each other, cross over, and melt into one another, till finally they die away in a state of holiness."[16] Hugo's poem, itself much longer and even more rhapsodic in character, was also printed at the beginning of the original Breitkopf & Härtel edition and reprinted in the unfinished *Gesamtausgabe* (or "complete edition") issued by the same firm between 1907 and 1936. These editions also contain programs or at least comments or poetic quotations that Liszt or one of his amanuenses wrote for all of the remaining symphonic poems except *Festklänge*, *Hungaria*, and *Von der Wiege bis zum Grabe*.

Ce qu'on entend is an enormous work, truly symphonic in length, but its overall musical structure is that of a sonatina—i.e., a sonata incorporating either a brief development section or none at all. The first or expository portion of the work fills mm. 1–520 and the second or recapitulatory its remainder (mm. 521–989). Harmonically the work opens in Eb major, modulates to and then away from G major in its central passages, and finally returns to Eb. Interestingly and appropriately, Liszt incorporates developmental passages in both halves of the work; furthermore, his sophisticated use of secondary harmonic relationships not only adds variety and color to the work but helps tell its story effectively.

We cannot pause to examine every aspect of this remarkable composition, but one deserves mention: Liszt's innovative use of topics. In *Ce qu'on entend*, in fact, he invents several of his own. The work's opening measures, for example, present what Johns identifies as a new kind of pastoral music—one suggestive not of shepherds and sunny Greece, but rather of "undulating or 'oceanic' string figures"—with, later on, "a horn call symbolic of the 'bugles of war' " and possibly intended to suggest man at his most bestial or "natural" (see Example 10.1).[17] Another topic, one that Liszt borrowed from Beethoven's "Choral" Fantasy and Ninth Symphony but very much made his own, is the hymn, associated in *Ce qu'on entend* and other works with transcendence. The final presentation of the chorale tune Johns dubs "Contemplation and Peace"—marked *Andante religioso* at m. 479 and scored first for three trombones and tuba, then for oboes, clarinets, and bassoons—epitomizes both this topic and the general purity of Liszt's writing for wind instruments.[18] Still another topic is the cantilena, suggestive of love, beauty, and romance. Frédéric Chopin too used cantilenas in instrumental compositions, but without programmatic associations; originally they hearken back to the Italian operatic melodies of Gaetano Donizetti and Vincenzo Bellini. A beautiful if somewhat unusual example of a Lisztian cantilena, presented by solo violin, harp, and woodwinds, appears for the first time in *Ce qu'on entend* beginning at m. 246 (see Example 10.2).

In *Ce qu'on entend* Liszt tells an unusual musical tale of struggle and vindication that is symmetrical—for just as the poet must climb the mountain, where he encounters the sublime, so must he make the return journey. Thus we have struggle and climax in the first half of the composition, with struggle, climax, and resolution in the second. This work is the most seemingly spontaneous of Liszt's orchestral compositions—a "spontaneity" purchased at considerable cost, as the Weimar sketchbooks and manuscripts reveal; it also calls for one of the largest ensembles he employed and it is especially richly scored. What a pity that Liszt, in his later years—and even before he left Weimar—turned his back on such an approach to symphonic composition and on such resources![19]

Example 10.2
Liszt, *Ce qu'on entend sur la montagne*, mm. 246–253

Tasso: Lamento e trionfo (Symphonic Poem no. 2). Although we know Liszt was familiar as early as 1840 with at least one of the motifs he later used in this work, and although the "Tasso sketchbook" contains drafts dating from 1847 for much of what eventually became the completed symphonic poem, *Tasso* itself is characteristic of the composer's early Weimar years. In its first version it was performed in August 1849 at celebrations honoring the centenary of Goethe's birth; ostensibly, then, it may be thought of as associated with Goethe's play *Torquato Tasso*. On the other hand, Liszt's music and its program are more concerned with suffering and apotheosis than "about" particular historical or literary events. Raff may have helped orchestrate the first version of this work, but Liszt revised it himself comprehensively at least twice, the second time in 1854.

For the most part *Tasso* is the product both of inspired design and careful attention to detail. Its four principal sections present "scenes" associated with the Italian Renaissance poet's character and career. Or, as Liszt wrote in the preface to the original edition:

Tasso loved and suffered at Ferrara; he was revenged at Rome; his glory still lives in the popular songs of Venice. These three periods are inseparable from his immortal memory. To render these in music, I felt I must first call up the spirit of the hero as it now appears to us, haunting the lagoons of Venice; next we must see his proud and sad figure, as it glides among the fetes of Ferrara—the birthplace of his masterpieces; finally, we must follow him to Rome, the Eternal City, which, in holding forth to him his crown, glorified him as a martyr and poet.

In fact, *Tasso* is divided into four topical sections: these depict or suggest suffering (mm. 1–61), pride (mm. 62–164), courtly life (mm. 165–382), and triumph (mm. 383–584). All four sections employ transformations of the same thematic material. In this scheme, too, there are suggestions of single-movement sonata form as well as that of a multi-movement symphony; the prideful funeral-march music suggests a second or slow movement, while the courtly music (*Allegretto mosso con gracia*) is an actual minuet—Liszt's only use of this eighteenth-century topic.

Unusual orchestral touches occur especially in the funeral march, where Liszt pits horns and bassoons against a harp arpeggio to suggest the murkiness of Venetian lagoons (see Example 10.3). Immediately afterward we hear Tasso's spirit rise from these depths and glide across the waters as the first violins take over the melody presented initially in mm. 62–74 by the bass clarinet. The clarity of its form, the forthrightness of its programmism, and the good humor of its concluding stretto (mm. 558)—the last full of trumpet fanfares and percussion sounds, a passage Searle criticizes as "Liszt at his most bombastic"[20]—make *Tasso* perhaps its composer's most accessible symphonic poem and the one most reminiscent of Rossini's and Weber's operatic overtures.

Example 10.3
Liszt, *Tasso*, mm. 74–79

Les préludes (Symphonic Poem no. 3). None of Liszt's symphonic poems is better-known, more deeply loved, and more often burlesqued than this composition. Inspired, initially, by Autran's series of poems on the subject of the four classical elements (earth, air, fire, and water) and drafted by Liszt in part as a prelude to his settings of those poems for chorus and piano, the work we know today as *Les préludes* somehow was transformed during the early 1850s into an altogether different work: one scored entirely for orchestra and devoted to the subject of our preparation for the life to come.[21] Ostensibly modeled in its instrumental form on a poem by Lamartine, *Les préludes* was published with a program drafted by Liszt's colleague, the pianist and conductor Hans von Bülow:

What else is our life, but a series of preludes to that unknown Hymn, the first and solemn note of which is intoned by Death?—Love is the glowing dawn of all existence; but what is the fate where the first delights of happiness are not interrupted by some storm, the mortal blast of which dissipates its fine illusions, the fatal lightning of which consumes its altar; and where in the cruelly wounded soul which, on issuing from one of those tempests, does not endeavor to rest his recollection in the calm serenity of life in the fields? Nevertheless, man hardly gives himself up for long to the enjoyment of the beneficent stillness which at first he has shared in Nature's bosom, and when "the trumpet sounds the alarm," he hastens, to the dangerous post, whatever the war may be, which calls him to its ranks, in order at least to recover in the combat full consciousness of himself and entire possession of his energy.

Searle has called this statement "purely artificial . . . put in [i.e., published] to describe the music and to bear a vague relation to Lamartine's poem" when, in reality, the work "is not the philosophical meditation commonly believed, but a description of Mediterranean atmosphere."[22] The chief objection to Searle's hypothesis is that Liszt's music matches Bülow's program fairly closely. After an introduction we hear a powerful opening statement of the principal theme followed by passages depicting love, storms, the countryside, and war; finally a recapitulation of the powerful opening seems to suggest "the first and solemn note . . . intoned by Death" reflected in our own lives.

Les préludes is organized around a single theme presented in a series of transformations associated with several topics. One of these is the cantilena, here representing romantic love. The remaining topics are Classical in origin: they include *Sturm und Drang* music, representing the tempestuous in both nature and culture; more or less conventional pastoral music, representing the out-of-doors; military music, representing war; and an "Apotheosis" (representing impending death and the life to come). Because Liszt used trumpets and percussion in many of his apotheoses, however, his celebrations may strike us today as a bit militant. In fact, they are mostly intended to be heard in spiritual terms; thus the conclusion of *Les préludes* anticipates a Christian heaven rather than some sort of pagan Valhalla. This last point is worth making if only because certain Nazi propaganda films employed this work as background music ostensibly illustrative of that movement's spurious greatness. Ironically, too, Liszt cited it as an example of both his success as an orchestral conductor and his lack of success as a composer of any kind with the general public. Writing to the Baron Antal Augusz on 30 December 1856, he confessed sarcastically:

According to the newspaper report I appeared in St. Gallen as a *pianist* [the previous fall]. You can again see how bent people are on performing me a good service . . . I enclose from the St. Gallen newspaper the published program of the concert, for which I conducted the first part and Wagner the second ([Beethoven's] *Sinfonia eroica*). The excellent performance given my two symphonic poems—*Orpheus* and *Les préludes*—must surely have been disagreeable to some "well-wishers" (*Wöhlers*) whose kind has spread everywhere; therefore they had nothing more pressing than to indulge in my *imaginary* piano playing. . . . One of their leaders said recently, entirely naïvely: "If we do not stir ourselves up and resist quite energetically, the public might easily find Liszt's compositions to their taste. Forward, therefore, Handel, Bach, Haydn, Mozart, Beethoven, Mendelssohn, and all the classic composers, and so leisurely slay the living with the dead."[23]

True, Liszt's symphonic poems did not achieve the success they might have enjoyed with contemporary audiences, although by no means were they systematically suppressed. Today, thanks to explanations in music-appreciation textbooks concerning thematic transformation, *Les préludes* is the only one of the symphonic poems known by name to several generations of American college students.

Orpheus (Symphonic Poem no. 4). Performed for the first time in conjunction with a production of Christoph Willibald von Gluck's *Orfeo ed Eurydice* conducted by Liszt in 1854, *Orpheus* is the first symphonic poem (in order of publication) to have been composed and revised entirely after its composer settled in Weimar. The shortest of the poems, *Orpheus* was a personal favorite of Wagner's, and with good reason: it is a consummate example of Liszt's ability to compose marvelous music of an altogether acceptable "abstract" kind *and* to employ variation techniques and unusual harmonic progressions in order to tell a "story" both passionately and—within the limitations of his medium and methods—quite precisely. *Orpheus* is also supposed to have been inspired as much by an Etruscan vase in the Louvre as by Gluck's opera, making it—together with *Hunnenschlacht* and *Von der Wiege bis zum Grabe*—an example of visual rather than verbal programmism.

In his foreword, however—like Coleridge in his preface to *Kubla Kahn*—Liszt pretends that *Orpheus* is somehow incomplete:

If I had been going to work out my idea in full, I should like to have portrayed the tranquil civilizing character of the songs, their powerful empire, their grandly voluptuous tones, their undulation sweet as the breezes of Elysium, their gradual uplifting like clouds of incense, their clear and heavenly spirit enveloping the world and the entire universe as in an atmosphere, as in a transparent vesture of ineffable and mysterious harmony.

Example 10.4
Liszt, *Orpheus*, mm. 197–213

But Liszt did work out his idea "in full"—although *Orpheus* is unusual among his symphonic poems, as Johns points out, in that it is concerned with "no archetypal program, only a series of fluctuating images."[24] Among many beautiful passages its conclusion especially is accepted as one of the supreme moments of nineteenth-century orchestral music. In these few measures a marvelously delicate final statement of the principal theme by the English horn, accompanied by two harps (one accentuating the theme with harmonics) and the upper strings, gives way at m. 202 to a statement by muted strings and winds of chromatic harmonies that calls Wagner's "magic fire" to mind and that concludes as subtly as does Isolde's "Love-Death" in *Tristan* (see Example 10.4). The two harps, of course, symbolize Orpheus—who, according to legend, played the lyre so beautifully that he was able to charm beasts and even the Lord of the Underworld with his transcendent music-making.[25]

Prometheus (Symphonic Poem no. 5). In a lengthy and discursive "program" for this symphonic poem, itself composed for the unveiling in 1850 of the Herder monument in Weimar, Liszt or one of his colleagues mentions Herder's drama *Prometheus Unbound*, Liszt's own choral settings of some of its texts and his overture to them, and, finally, the myth of Prometheus the Bringer of Fire—a myth that "has always in the liveliest manner appealed to the imagination by its hidden symbolical accordance with our strongest instincts, our bitterest sorrows, and our happiest forebodings." The kernel of the program, however, lies in its last lines; in spite of their apparent vagueness, they describe precisely the topical and expressive character of the music: "Suffering and Apotheosis! Thus compressed, the fundamental idea of this too-true fable demanded a sultry, stormy, and tempestuous mode of expression. A desolating grief, triumphing at least by energy and perseverance, constitutes the musical character of the piece now offered to notice."

Cast in sonata form, complete with introduction (mm. 1–26), exposition (mm. 27–160), development (mm. 161–236), and recapitulation (mm. 237–390), *Prometheus* suggests many extra-musical things.[26] It makes those suggestions not only through reference to the original Greek legend (in its title), but also through its association with Herder's drama (by way of its program), and even—thematically, harmonically, and structurally within the content of Liszt's music—through its incorporation of passages from his Herder choruses, the *Chöre zu Herders Entfesseltem Prometheus* (S 69). Consider too its striking use of topics. One of these is the fugue, exemplary of the "learned style" in eighteenth-century music but used by nineteenth-century composers in a variety of procedural and programmatic circumstances. Johns hears in the fugal passages of *Prometheus* a reminiscence of the "Chorus of the Muses" (i.e., music that acclaims Prometheus as hero) and consequently identifies this specialized "musical symbol" as a "celebration of Humanity."[27] Merrick, on the other hand, considers Liszt's fugues (including that found in the Sonata in B minor) illustrative of a "process of purification" that invokes Merrick's own archetypal religious analysis of Lisztian narrative in terms of lament, prayer, struggle, and salvation.[28]

Liszt probably intended most or even all of these things to be heard in *Prometheus*, although he almost certainly would have preferred Merrick's sacred interpretation to Johns's secular one. On the other hand, Liszt hated musical complication for its own sake and condemned the use of fugue in many contemporary sacred compositions.[29] Moreover, he must have wanted his listeners to enjoy his clean, powerful, persuasive orchestral writing. Examples of such writing include the final statement of what Johns calls the "promise of redemption" theme in the strings and winds. Here, as in earlier and similar but less forceful statements of this theme, the music shifts effortlessly between tonic and mediant chords (A major and C♯ major in mm. 368–369), "brightening" the overall sound and mood; Liszt also uses the piccolo to double the violins and make things even brighter. Note that the remaining parts for winds and strings involve almost no doubling at all; instead, every instrument or group of instruments plays an independent musical role. The effect is one of marvelous clarity in the midst of a full-fledged orchestral tutti (see Example 10.5).

Example 10.5
Liszt, *Prometheus*, mm. 364–370

Mazeppa (Symphonic Poem no. 6). Unlike *Ce qu'on entend, Les préludes, Orpheus,* and *Die Ideale*—all of which employ expressive or ideological programs that may strike modern listeners as ambiguous or vague—*Mazeppa* tells a clear-cut and familiar story: that of the legendary Cossack chieftain condemned to death by his own countrymen. Tied to his horse, Mazeppa is turned loose on the steppes of Asia to suffer, yet is somehow rescued, triumphantly restored to life, and given a crown by his new and adoring subjects. The final stanza of Hugo's poem, printed in its entirety as a preface to the published score, reads:

> He cries out with terror, in agony gasping,
> Yet ever the neck of his hippogriff clasping,
>   They heavenward spring;
> Each leap that he takes with fresh woe is attended;
> He totters — falls lifeless — the struggle is ended —
>   We hail him then king!

Suffering and Apotheosis indeed! In this case, however, it is difficult to discern a spiritual element among the details of the story.

Except for the harps in *Orpheus* and a few other works, and for a few incidental percussion instruments, the orchestra required for *Mazeppa* is the largest—and among the loudest—Liszt ever employed, calling as it does for piccolo, English horn, bass clarinet (in D), and three bassoons as well as a battery and a full-fledged ensemble of woodwinds, brasses, and strings. *Mazeppa* is vigorous, even violent music; it opens with a shriek (depicting, I imagine, the crack of a whip), it is full of pounding hoofbeats, toward the end it moans and groans quite convincingly, and it concludes with a series of wind-band effects reminiscent of the final measures of Berlioz's *Roman Carnival* Overture and the "Orgy of the Brigands" from his *Harold en Italie*. Structurally *Mazeppa* recalls the several versions of Liszt's etude in that it consists mostly of a series of variations on a single theme; it differs from its keyboard predecessors, however, in being outfitted with a massive introduction, a very much expanded "slow movement" (Mazeppa faces death), and a colossal final celebration on a theme borrowed from Liszt's *Arbeiterchor* of 1848 (S 82).[30] Variety is provided by the lovely B♭-major variation beginning at m. 122 and, of course, by the *Andante* death-passage mentioned above (mm. 404–436).

"*Mazeppa*," Searle informs us, "is unfortunately not one of Liszt's finest creations," although he qualifies this opinion by adding that some of its music "is exciting enough in a rather obvious kind of way."[31] True. Liszt was a marvelous creator of effects, but his best works—and this symphonic poem is not one of them—consist of *more* than effects.

Festklänge (Symphonic Poem no. 7). Ostensibly composed to celebrate his marriage to the Princess Sayn-Wittgenstein—a wedding that never took place[32]—*Festklänge* (Festival Sounds) is among Liszt's most intelligently constructed and effective orchestral works. With the exception of *Hungaria*, it is the only symphonic poem that lacks an explicit literary program or other definite form of extra-musical inspiration; *Hamlet* refers through its title and at least one of Liszt's performance directions to Shakespeare's characters and play, while *Von der Wiege* we know to have been modeled on what Searle calls "a very bad painting" by the composer's countryman Mihály Zichy.[33]

Festklänge is also unusual in its close adherence to the conventions of early nineteenth-century single-movement sonata form—consisting, except for a brief "slow-movement" excursus near its beginning (mm. 47–62), of a straightforward but sophisticated exposition (mm. 63–230), development (mm. 231–362), and recapitulation (mm. 363); several of these sections also incorporate references to the opening introductory passage. The coda resolves with great effectiveness and skill the harmonic question posed for the first time in mm. 11–23, when C-major flourishes are presented over a B♭ pedal point: is the piece in C major or F major? (Beethoven raised a similar but much more succinctly stated version of the same question in the opening measures of his First Symphony.) In fact the piece is in C major, although we are finally convinced of that only as the work hastens to its end.[34]

Although *Festklänge* has no known program, it contains two unusual and possibly programmatic passages: mm. 208–215 and 488–495 incorporate polonaise music that may be intended to suggest the Princess's Polish origins (see Example 10.6 for the first of these passages). Another interesting feature of this work are the numerous alternate connecting passages Liszt provided for abbreviated performances or for use by less experienced instrumentalists. In the Eulenberg miniature score these fill thirty-six pages (the work itself fills only eighty-eight); in performance they radically alter the sense and form of the music. In other words, *Festklänge* is an orchestral example of that tinkering spirit that inspired Liszt to add *ossias*, cadenzas, transitional passages, and fingerings to so many of his published piano pieces. These are not the only cuts that Liszt suggests for his symphonic poems; one of those provided for *Prometheus* may even have programmatic significance.[35] It is difficult to see, however, what might be gained by replacing large parts of the less explicitly programmatic *Festklänge* with almost equally lengthy sections of alternate passagework.

Héroïde funèbre (Symphonic Poem no. 8). Ostensibly derived from the so-called "Revolutionary" symphony of Liszt's youth—he inserted a reference to that effect in the lengthy foreword he drafted for the original Breitkopf & Härtel edition—*Héroïde funèbre* is a fine example of double-function form. The opening funeral march constitutes both exposition and "first movement"; it also introduces both a "slow movement" as its "trio" section and a scherzo-like "third-movement" passage that serves both developmental and initial recapitulatory functions; finally, the march itself reappears and concludes the recapitulation.[36]

Example 10.6
Liszt, *Festklänge*, mm. 204–208

Among the earliest symphonic poems Liszt orchestrated throughout, *Héroïde* makes effective use of such military instruments as piccolo, massed brasses, and a battery that includes tam-tam and chimes. The *Più lento* section, on the other hand, includes a lovely cantilena, reminiscent harmonically of the composer's famous *Liebestraum* no. 3 (S 541/3). Also among *Héroïde*'s beauties is a characteristic mediant modulation, from D♭ major to B♭ major and back in m. 161, just before the tune—presented for the first time by the horns beginning in m. 153—returns in octaves in the upper strings (see Example 10.7, especially mm. 183–185 where the theme returns). Liszt's lengthy program rhapsodizes somewhat incoherently about catastrophes, ruins, and disasters as well as an almost carnivalesque parade in honor of the fallen dead, but the overall musical impact of the composition itself is one of majesty and beauty. Among its more breathtaking passages is a powerful unison statement of the principal theme— heard only once, toward the beginning of the work—by F trumpets and trombones (see Example 10.8, beginning in m. 108).

Example 10.7
Liszt, *Héroïde funèbre*, mm. 178–185

Example 10.8
Liszt, *Héroïde funèbre*, mm. 107–112

Little-known today, *Héroïde funèbre* is a work that deserves to be performed more frequently. If anything, Searle underestimated its importance when he called it "a fine example of Liszt's mature style."[37]

Hungaria (Symphonic Poem no. 9). Searle also called *Hungaria* a "Hungarian Rhapsody on an extended scale."[38] Again he underestimated the importance of a remarkable composition. Lengthy and richly scored, this symphonic poem without program is nevertheless a work of concision as well as power and orchestrational skill. Like *Héroïde funèbre, Hungaria* opens with a rising stepwise motif, associated in this and other of Liszt's works with struggle or combat; again like *Héroïde*, it suggests several movements rolled into one, although its allusions to double-function form are neither tidy nor easily explained. Somewhat more immediately comprehensible is its single-movement sonata scheme, consisting of an exposition that incorporates an introduction and "first theme"—or set of themes—derived from Liszt's *Heroischer Marsch im ungarischen Styl* of 1840 (S 231), as well as a "second theme" in B major (*Allegro eroico*). These passages are followed by a substantial developmental passage, *Agitato molto,* and by a funeral march that suggests a slow movement. Finally, a breathtaking recapitulation that begins in D major and includes a celebratory restatement in D major of the second theme—complete with massed winds and percussion—concludes with a coda launched by a stretto that recalls some of the harmonic surprises of the development.

Example 10.9
Liszt, *Hungaria*, mm. 360–364

Among the many colorful touches in *Hungaria* are passages employing the so-called "Hungarian minor" scale (e.g., D / E / F / G / A / B♭ / C♯ / D), two brief and touching solo-violin cadenzas (mm. 136–142 and 146–152) that punctuate the work's opening passages, powerful unison statements by all three F trumpets, and spectacular development sequences in which the first and second themes are combined in counterpoint with an arpeggiated motif presented for the first time more fulsomely in the "slow movement"—all this offset by drum rolls, tremolo violin passagework, piccolo flourishes, and accented interjections by the battery. See Example 10.9, which illustrates one moment of this splendid and tightly controlled pseudo-confusion. In this passage the first theme is presented by the horns in mm. 362–364, the second theme by three F trumpets (the parts written on two staves) in m. 360, and the "slow movement" theme anticipated by figures in the bassoons, trombones, tuba, and lower strings.

Hamlet (Symphonic Poem no. 10). Less luxurious in its instrumental effects than *Hungaria*, less tightly organized than *Festklänge* and *Prometheus*, Liszt's tenth published symphonic poem and the last written (ostensibly to complete the set) has inspired several explorations of its purported programmatic intent.[39] Except for a single comment in the score, however, Liszt left us no explicit information about the work's extra-musical associations, and that comment—to the effect that the theme introduced in mm. 160 "refers to Ophelia" (*auf Ophelia hindeutend*)—would seem to suggest that *Hamlet* is a dual character portrait of the melancholy prince and his doomed lover. Reinforcing this interpretation is the fact that the "Ophelia theme" is a transformation of another principal theme (Hamlet's?) introduced in mm. 33–36.

Completed only in 1858, *Hamlet* is in some sense a response on Liszt's part to a performance of Shakespeare's play he attended two years earlier. Cast in the title role was Bogumil Dawison, a famous actor of the day. To Agnès Street-Klindworth Liszt later confessed that Dawison "did not create an uncertain dreamer crushed by the weight of his mission, as has been generally envisioned ever since Goethe produced his theory (in *Wilhelm Meister*); instead he presented an intelligent, enterprising prince, full of significant political concepts, who is waiting for the appropriate moment to wreck his vengeance and achieve his ambition of being crowned in his uncle's stead."[40] Certain parts of *Hamlet* are indeed "enterprising," but others are not. Structurally, passages featuring the "Ophelia theme" suggest a slow movement near the middle of the work; they themselves are punctuated by development-like *Sturm und Drang* material intended, perhaps, to hint at Hamlet's tormented inner life. More interesting to historians of musical style is the passage, beginning at rehearsal letter "D," that may have provided the inspiration for a similar passage near the end of *Fêtes*, the second of Debussy's *Nocturnes* for orchestra.

Of Liszt's thirteen symphonic poems, *Hamlet* is the only one that ends "unhappily," concluding as it does with a funeral march and thus contradicting both Johns's and Merrick's archetypal tales of ultimate salvation or triumph. Perhaps this is because of its literary model, although *Die Ideale*—unlike Schiller's poem—ends "happily"; so too, in spite of the historical setbacks suffered by his native land in 1848–1849, does *Hungaria*. Overall I cannot agree with Searle that "of all Liszt's symphonic poems this is the one which most merits revival and frequent performances." On the other hand, Searle is correct when he notes that "even in Liszt's lifetime it was not properly appreciated," and that its first performance "did not take place till 1876 in Sondershausen."[41]

Hunnenschlacht (Symphonic Poem no. 11). None of the symphonic poems, not even *Mazeppa*, is more boisterous than *Hunnenschlacht*; none, not even *Hamlet*, is more initially confusing, at least in terms of conventional musical form.[42] On the other hand, there is no real need for detailed structural analysis where the "Battle of the Huns" is concerned. In this work we encounter "real" program music: here is a frank portrayal in sound of pitched battle and, more specifically, of barbarians being beaten back and Christians winning the day. (The barbarians get much of the liveliest music, though. They often do.) The historical event on which the work is based took place in A.D. 451 between the Huns, under Attila, and the Romans, ruled at that time by Theodoric. This event, and the composer's imagination, provided material for portions of the two rather different programs—one in German, the other in French—Liszt prepared for early published editions of the work.

Inspired by Wilhelm von Kaulbach's painting of the same name, Liszt's symphonic poem is presented musically as a series of contrasts, especially that of pagan (i.e., "exotic") vs. Christian (i.e., "diatonic") musical elements. Or, as Liszt put it in his French program, between the forces of "fury" (the Huns) and "serenity" (the Christians). Of great importance both programmatically and structurally is the sudden appearance of the *Crux fidelis* theme, representing the Christians, amid the hubbub of battle. See Example 10.10: at mm. 261–265 the Christian theme, scored for organ or for wind choir and piano, and captioned *dolce religioso*, is followed without interruption by an arpeggiated theme that, according to Johns, represents the Roman forces. In this instance the hymn tune symbolizes not so much generalized transcendence as the literal presence of "a sacred song rising in the sky."[43] The concluding Apotheosis is, as one might expect, more than a bit martial in character.

Die Ideale (Symphonic Poem no. 12). Among the longest and, to those unfamiliar with its workings, the most discursive of the symphonic poems, *Die Ideale* is "explained" by the appearance in the full score of lengthy excerpts from Friedrich Schiller's poem of the same name. Although it is organized loosely in sonata form, this complex composition is perhaps best listened to semiotically—i.e., in terms of its topical references to the emotional sense of Schiller's observations on the idealism of youth that ultimately gives way to disillusionment. Liszt tacked his apotheosis onto Schiller's somewhat pessimistic verse. Johns has identified many of the thematic statements that crop up throughout the work—describing, for instance, the descending stepwise theme that first appears in mm. 4–9 as "loss of youthful inspiration," the transformation of this theme that appears for the first time at mm. 262–265 as "inspiration and the power of creation," and so forth.

Example 10.10
Liszt, *Hunnenschlacht*, mm. 261–269

Liszt was scarcely indifferent to the structural aspects of his score; Searle, for one, believes that, as composition progressed, "musical construction became more important" than programmism,[44] and Johns observes that programmatic elements of the score also do purely musical duty. Thus the "friendship" motif (mm. 515–519), for example, can be understood as functioning "both structurally as the theme of the Trio portion of the funeral march, and semiotically as a call to action."[45] The work's overall double-function scheme is reflected in the titles Liszt chose for its four sections. "Aspirations" (*Aufschwung*, mm. 26–449), the first of these, is preceded by a brief introduction and incorporates aspects of exposition and opening movement; "Disillusionment" (*Enttäuschung*, mm. 450–564), the second, combines aspects of development and slow movement; "Pursuit" or "Toil" (*Beschäftigung*, mm. 565–676), the third, combines aspects of recapitulation and scherzo; and the Apotheosis (mm. 677–869), the fourth, aspects of recapitulation and coda.[46]

The Symphonies

Liszt completed only two multi-movement symphonies. Both works are essentially the product of the composer's early and middle Weimar years; both were widely criticized as well as praised by his contemporaries; and both (unlike *Die Ideale*, *Héroïde funèbre*, and *Hamlet*) may be considered staples of the concert repertory—although the *Dante*, calling as it does for baritone solo and male chorus as well as a substantial orchestra, is expensive to produce and has not been often heard in European and American concert halls since World War II. It should be pointed out that both symphonies are, in certain respects, not so much musically inferior to the best of the symphonic poems as of lesser historical interest; in other words, they are less stylistically innovative and seem to have been less influential on other composers. Furthermore, although both symphonies contain great beauties, they have not proven themselves as appealing as *Tasso* and *Mazeppa*, nor as accessible as *Les préludes*.

The Faust Symphony. Liszt claimed on several occasions that three books were of central importance to him throughout most of his life: *The Imitation of Christ* by Thomas à Kempis, Dante's *Commedia*, and Goethe's *Faust*. The last, introduced to him by Berlioz in 1830, provided the inspiration for his most ambitious orchestral composition, a "character study" in three movements of the wayward and intellectual Faust, the beautiful and naïve Gretchen, and the cunning and ultimately impotent Mephistopheles. In a sense these studies— collectively entitled *Eine Sinfonie zu Goethe's Faust in drei Charakterbildern*— rank as Liszt's only full-fledged multi-movement symphony; the *Sinfonia zu Dante's Divina Commedia* was truncated and altered during composition, while the so-called *Bergsymphonie* (or "Mountain Symphony," another name for *Ce qu'on entend sur la montagne*) is cast in a single movement.

Liszt began thinking about a "Faust symphony" between 1840 and 1845, and fragments intended for such a work survive in the so-called "Sardanapale" sketchbook owned by the Goethe- und Schiller-Archiv (shelf-number N4).[47] Apparently he was stirred to take up this project again on account of performances of Schumann's scenes from *Faust*, which Liszt himself conducted in August 1849, by a performance Berlioz mounted in Weimar in 1852 of his own *Damnation du Faust*, and especially by a visit novelist George Eliot and her husband paid to Weimar in August 1854 to pursue researches into Goethe's life and career.

In any event, Liszt completed a preliminary draft of the entire work in October 1854; this fascinating document is preserved in the collections of the Hungarian National Library, Budapest, and deserves to be published today in a critical edition.[48] Dissatisfied, however, Liszt asked Raff to make a fair copy of a somewhat different version. Unfortunately, Raff's copy has disappeared and we cannot today judge its significance; all we know is that by September 1855 Liszt himself had prepared yet another draft and rehearsed it twice with the Weimar orchestra. Revisions continued until 1857, when the symphony was given its first complete performance. A second performance, incorporating further revisions, took place in August 1861 as part of that year's *Tonkünstlerversammlung* meeting.

Several useful analyses of the symphony have appeared in print, and I shall not attempt to summarize them here.[49] Suffice it to say that "Faust," the work's first movement, is a study not only of this fascinating and not altogether admirable literary figure, but of the possibilities of conventional sonata form. The entire instrumental edifice is based primarily on a remarkable theme consisting of four arpeggiated augmented triads (see Example 10.12, mm. 54–57, clarinets and cellos). Technically—but only technically—it constitutes perhaps the first "twelve-tone" row in music history, although Liszt treats it expressively rather than serially. Other themes may be also be discerned in "Faust," and some have been given names appropriate either to their dramatic implications (e.g., "Passion," "Pride," and "Love") or to Liszt's performance directions (e.g., *Affettuoso, Expressivo,* and *Appassionato*).[50]

It is possible, therefore, to work out a detailed program for the movement as a whole, and even for the symphony, although Liszt did not provide one. Merrick has done so, at least to the extent of pointing out religious elements in its organizational details.[51] Suffice it to say that Faust as a character is presented partly in terms of his philosophical temperament (i.e., in terms of shifting harmonies, uneasy rhythms, and other "complexities"), and partly as a "good man," a striver after truth. Gretchen, on the other hand, is depicted in her preternaturally sweet and pretty second movement solely as "girl"; the more disturbing aspects of her personality and activities in Goethe's drama—that she succumbs to seduction, is overcome with remorse, commits a heinous crime, and goes mad—are avoided altogether. In the "Gretchen" theme (see Example 10.11: the theme itself begins in m. 15) we catch a glimpse not so much of the composer as chauvinist—in many ways Liszt was ahead of his time in terms of his admiration for and encouragement of accomplishments by women—as of an overriding nineteenth-century concern: the placing of "good women" on public pedestals. Similar musical depictions of Goethe's heroine—all of which stop at, or at most glance into, the drama's disturbing Part I conclusion—may be found in Gounod's opera and, with certain modifications, in Berlioz's dramatic symphony. Furthermore, Liszt anticipates Gretchen's theme in "Faust," implying (intentionally or not) a feminine aspect or side to his protagonist's psychological makeup.

Example 10.11
Liszt, *Faust* symphony, second movement ("Gretchen"), mm. 13–24

The most intriguing and inventive programmatic aspect of the symphony is the depiction, in its third movement, of Faust's dangerous and deceitful companion. This is accomplished not so much through music of the Devil's own, as through caricatures of Faust's music. As Christian dogma would have it, Satan cannot create; he can only ridicule and pervert. Parody gives the "Mephistopheles" movement a special piquancy; besides, Liszt was a marvel when it came to diabolical music. In one of many superb passages (see Example 10.12) Faust's theme appears in mm. 8–11, beginning on the note G in the clarinets and cellos and "decorated" with chromatic figures in the violas and bassoons. The overall effect, after a lot of preliminary screaming and shouting, is at once comic and hollow: after all, we say to ourselves (as Liszt wished us to), we have heard that tune before; can't Satan do better than that? Gretchen's theme, however, cannot be perverted (at least in Liszt's take on the story) and appears in "Mephistopheles" only in its original form, linking the two movements and thereby providing structural continuity in what is a lengthy, difficult, and emotionally demanding masterpiece. A concluding Apotheosis in the form of a choral ode on the final lines of *Faust*, Part II (the only allusion to that part of Goethe's drama), affirms the importance of the Eternal Feminine and suggests that the Devil can never triumph over God.

Example 10.12
Liszt, *Faust* symphony, third movement ("Mephistopheles"), mm. 47–58.

The Dante symphony. Precisely when Liszt decided to compose what became his *Sinfonia zu Dante's Divina Commedia* we do not know. Certainly he was thinking of such a work as early as the 1840s; he even considered employing a wind machine to suggest the storms of Hell![52] One motif, that of the *diabolus in musica*—the diminished fifth (B–F) or augmented fourth (F–B)—appears frequently in both his *Après une lecture de Dante: Fantasia quasi sonata*

(S 161/7) and in the first movement of the published symphony; perhaps, then, Liszt thought about an orchestral tribute to Dante as early as 1838, when he began work on the "sonata." In 1855 he told Wagner about his plans, writing on 2 June of that year:

So you are reading Dante. He's good company for you, and I for my part want to provide you with a kind of commentary on that reading. I have long been carrying a Dante Symphony around in my head—this year I intend to get it down on paper. There are to be 3 movements, Hell, Purgatory, and Paradise—the first two for orchestra alone, the last with chorus. When I visit you in the autumn I shall probably be able to bring it with me; and if you don't dislike it you can let me inscribe your name on it.[53]

Later—the story is a familiar one in the literature—Wagner talked Liszt out of writing a third movement, arguing that no human composition could depict adequately the glories of Paradise.[54] Unfortunately, little work had been done on the work prior to Wagner's advice; most of the score was drafted during the early months of 1856 and Liszt thus was able more easily to give up his heavenly plans. Searle considers Liszt's decision to jettison the project third movement "a pity"—adding that, although "Liszt was certainly more at home in the infernal than the celestial regions . . . the task should not have been beyond his powers. As it is, the listener is left in the transitional state of Dante at the end of the Purgatorio movement, where he gazes up at the heights of Heaven and hears its music from afar."[55] A tempestuous premiere performance took place in 1857, with the composer as conductor; much of the criticism was foolish, but Liszt learned something from the experience and revised the score prior to its publication in 1859.

Extrapolated, Searle's remarks about depictions of Heaven and Hell in Liszt's music raise important issues about the completed symphony. Why did Liszt, who knew Dante's poem well, depict so little of it in his music? The *Inferno* must have suggested more to him than musical fire and brimstone, punctuated by a cameo of Paolo and Francesca engulfed in their shared sin of passion—a story, true, that had great personal significance for Liszt and his secret lover, the mysterious Agnès Street-Klindworth.[56] And what of the *Purgatorio*? That *cantica* contains some of Dante's greatest verse; in Liszt's symphony, however, it is reduced to a musical sunrise followed by a lengthy and gradually brightening fugal "transition." The concluding apotheosis, a setting of several lines from the Magnificat appended to the end of the two-movement work, captures neither the splendid procession at the top of Dante's mountain nor the full-fledged glories of his *Paradiso*.

The first movement, "Hell," may strike many listeners as chaotic. Of course Dante's Hell *is* chaotic; it is home to the City of Dis, filled with the shrieking and moaning of the damned. Fortunately, Liszt provides the conductor with a little commentary: above a declamatory figure in the trombones and tubas in mm. 1–4, he presents in the score several lines from Canto III, beginning with the words *Per me si va nella citta dolente* (Through me the road to the City of Desolation). After two additional statements of the same motif and more of

Dante's text, a second motif announces what might be called the ideological theme of the first movement, presented by the trumpets and horns beginning in m. 12; above this tune appear the words *Lascia te ogni speranza, voi ch'entrada* (Abandon every hope, you that enter here). See Example 10.13, which reproduces part of the latter passage.

Example 10.13
Liszt, *Dante* symphony, first movement ("Hell"), mm. 8–14

The rest of the lengthy introduction is, in effect, an enormous clustered upbeat before the tonic key of D minor is affirmed in m. 64, at the beginning of the exposition. The rest of the movement follows both the rough outlines of single-movement sonata form (a developmental passage begins at m. 280 and something like a recapitulation at m. 465) and a multi-movement composition (the development can also be heard in part as a "slow movement"—the Paolo and Francesca cameo—and in part as a "scherzo"—beginning at m. 395; the recapitulation also serves as "final movement"). This double-function pattern is fleshed out by additional programmatic musical allusions to the wails and groans of the damned.

To suggest Paolo and Francesca Liszt uses the harp nicely to portray not merely the shivers of desire that coursed though the lovers' veins during their earthly lives, but also the winds of lust that blow them about in Hell (see Example 10.14, m. 295, and note that Liszt provides an alternate piano part in case a harp is not available). The lovers themselves are suggested first by clarinets and bassoons in mm. 287–295, then by other instruments; again, see Example 10.14. Later a cantilena, above which Liszt quotes Francesca's lament that the saddest thing in death is to remember the pleasures of one's past life, appears and is repeated in a somewhat slower section (*Andante amoroso*) beginning at m. 354. Appropriately, the harp has the final word—one of Liszt's successes at this and other moments in his orchestral compositions is that his instruments seem veritably to *speak*—and whisks the lovers away in a cadenza constructed entirely from diminished-seventh chords (mm. 393–394). The mutterings that follow, as we have seen, suggest a scherzo movement and return us more explicitly to the agonies of the damned.

Liszt's depiction of the Abyss is charming (no oxymoron intended) and his programmatic touches ingenious: consider his effective use of the bass clarinet's lowest notes as well as his alternation of 7/4 and 4/4 meters to suggest both suppleness and confusion on the parts of Paolo and Francesca. Nevertheless, the emotional thrust of this beautiful interlude misses Dante's moral point: Francesca was neither repentant nor reasonable, and she is to blame for her own damnation. On the other hand, should Liszt have tried to capture her arrogant self-justification in music? Or should he have stuck to *Sturm und Drang* for the entire movement? The former alternative might have been beyond his powers, while the latter would have been aesthetically unsatisfactory.

The second movement opens by suggesting in sound the dawn that greets Dante and Virgil at the beginning of the *Purgatorio*. Today this depiction, twice repeated (mm. 1–32 and 33–67), may also suggest to many listeners the "prelude" to *Das Rheingold*, which Liszt may not have known in 1856 and certainly did not slavishly imitate. In any event, where Wagner's monolithic and harmonically static prelude evokes primordial grandeur, Liszt's introduction is harmonically supple and orchestrally translucent. After this, however, the movement loses a sense of overall coherence, although the splendid fugue that starts at m. 129 is remarkable. Johns, as we have seen, associates fugal passages in Liszt's symphonic poems with "suffering humanity." Certainly there is suffering in Purgatory, but there is also hope. Thus, from a wayward and seemingly directionless chromatic exposition, Liszt's fugue grows gradually more "penitential." Is it coincidental that, prior to m. 149, the orchestration is almost identical to Bach's and the music's mood similar to that of the first Kyrie from the B-minor Mass? (see Example 10.15). Only gradually does it become brighter, less intricate, and more celebratory.

Example 10.14
Liszt, *Dante* symphony, first movement, mm. 287–295

Example 10.15
Liszt, *Dante* symphony, second movement ("Purgatory"), mm. 151–159

The fragments of a Magnificat that follow provide a fitting conclusion, but not altogether a coherent one. Scored for a chorus of women's voices, this extended coda incorporates rising arpeggiated figures that link it with the dawn music in a subtle but suitable manner. Another figure, Liszt's "musical fingerprint" (F#–G#–B at m. 314)[57]—Merrick calls these notes the "Cross motif"—would seem to tie this affirmative passage to dozens of others in his output, including the triumphal climax of the Sonata in B minor. Still, it is not altogether clear that we have arrived in Paradise. There are many fine things in

"Purgatory," including some splendid writing for woodwinds, but as a whole it seems to me inadequate to its literary model.[58]

Miscellaneous Works

Liszt's fascination with the Faust legend extended beyond Goethe's drama. In his *Zwei Episoden nach Lenau's Faust* Liszt composed two pieces of music, entitled respectively *Der nächtliche Zug* (The Night Procession) and *Der Tanz in der Dorfschenke* (Dance at the Village Inn). Together, this pair of tone-poems comprise a massive "Introduction and Scherzo" for large orchestra. Unfortunately, the "Dance" is almost always performed by itself—and then, more often, in its version for solo piano, better-known as the celebrated *Mephisto-Waltz* no. 1.

Der nächtliche Zug is a masterpiece, albeit a rather odd one, of musical picture-painting. In this work Liszt portrays with remarkable vividness Lenau's description of a spring night in a forest: we hear—as well as "see" and "feel"— the clouds sliding overhead, the warm wind caressing our shoulders, and the nightingale's song throbbing through the trees (see Example 10.16). Then a magical procession appears: priests in white robes, carrying torches, chant the *Pange lingua* in celebration of St. John's Eve (24 June)—when, according to European folk traditions, spirits walk abroad in the darkness. Lenau writes that Faust is overcome by these impressions and, burying his face in his horse's mane, weeps bitter tears. Liszt captures these emotions with wonderful skill; he also includes quotations from Lenau's poem at several places in his published score.

In musical terms, the piece is largely a fantasy on the *Pange lingua* melody. Among other motifs, this tune incorporates Liszt's "musical fingerprint," here transposed on its first appearance to C♯–D♯–F♯. Especially important to the work as a whole is the two-note rising figure we encountered in several of the symphonic poems. Presented chromatically, it appears in the declamatory passage depicting Faust's anguished melancholy toward the end of the composition; presented diatonically, it plays an important role in the forest murmurs that greet him near its beginning. The motif even appears in the nightingale's meticulously depicted song, especially the piccolo part in m. 43 (again, see Example 10.16). Searle is right in calling this work "one of Liszt's finest" and in proclaiming its neglect "unintelligible."[59]

Der Tanz in der Dorfschenke tells a simpler tale of revelry and escape. In topic and form a more or less conventional waltz, it includes a marvelously devilish tune and lots of instrumental flourishes. Toward the end of the movement a sensuous interlude or trio, marked *Poco a poco più moderato*, inter-rupts the Devil's manic fiddling (itself marked *selvaggiamente*, or "savage"); we hear Faust whirl out of the Inn with a dark-haired girl in his arms; next the nightingale makes a brief reappearance; this is followed by a harp cadenza— itself reminiscent, structurally and programmatically, of the similar cadenza in the first movement of the *Dante* symphony; and the movement finishes in a flourish of trumpets, triangle, and cymbals. Liszt's orchestration in *Der Tanz in der Dorfschenke* is a marvel of understated clarity; here, as elsewhere, he erects a skeletal tradition upon which later Romantic masters like Richard Strauss heaped mounds of sonic flesh in such symphonic poems as *Ein Heldenleben* and *Till Eulenspiegel's Merry Pranks*.

Example 10.16
Liszt, *Der nächtliche Zug*, mm. **41–47**

The occasional orchestral marches Liszt mostly composed as part of his responsibilities to the Weimar court have never become concert favorites; in them is comparatively little of the ingenuity expended upon the symphonies and symphonic poems. As Searle suggests, several of these works were cobbled together from bits and pieces of other compositions; thus the *Künstlerfestzug* of 1859 makes use of themes from the cantata *An die Künstler* (S 70) composed originally in 1853 and performed successfully four years later.[60]

Les morts (Deaths), on the other hand, is anything but occasional. It seems almost to consist of three quite different but fortuitously conjoined musical fragments: an orchestral meditation on death; a ritornello for men's chorus and orchestra, in Latin, on the words "Blessed are they that die in the Lord" (a text also set by Brahms, in German, as part of his *Deutsches Requiem*); and—perhaps—a melodrama or recitation based on words by the Abbé Félicité de Lamennais, Liszt's youthful spiritual mentor. The meditation consists of alternating topical passages suggesting thoughtfulness, calm beauty, and triumph—the last incorporating not only such military instruments as cymbals and snare drum, but Liszt's "Cross motif" or "musical fingerprint." To all this the chorus adds its refrain over and over again. The same refrain appears in French in Lamennais's text, which Liszt copied in its entirety between staves of the score and which he may have intended to be read aloud during performances. See Example 10.17, in which the choral ritornello appears in mm. 77–81.

Example 10.17
Liszt, *Les morts***, mm. 73–81**

As we have seen elsewhere, Liszt often entered quotations into his scores; one of the most interesting appears above mm. 55–65 in *La notte* (Night), the second of the Funeral Odes. In Virgil's *Aeneid* (Book X, line 782) these words—"Dying, he remembered sweet Argos" (*Dulces moriens reminiscitur Argos*)—have to do with perishing far from home. Perhaps Liszt, who completed "Night" while living in Rome—see below—thought of himself as also dying someday far from home. One thing more: Liszt asked that both *La notte* and *Les morts* be performed at his funeral, but this request was overlooked or ignored. In fact, neither work was performed publicly until 1912, and neither was published prior to their joint appearance in 1916 in the Breitkopf & Härtel *Gesamtausgabe*.

ROME AND ELSEWHERE: THE FINAL YEARS, 1861–1886

1863–1884 *Salve Polonia* (interlude from the unfinished oratorio *St. Stanislaus*). S 113.
1863–1864 *La notte* (*Trois odes funèbres* no. 2). S 112/2.
1866–1877 *La triomphe funèbre du Tasse* (*Trois odes funèbres* no. 3). S 112/3.
1880–1881 *Second Mephisto Waltz*. S 111.
1881–1883 *Von der Wiege bis zum Grabe*. S 107.

Of Liszt's later works for orchestra, by far the most important are *La notte* and *Von der Wiege bis zum Grabe* (From the Cradle to the Grave). *La triomphe funèbre du Tasse* (The Funeral Celebration of Tasso) is a postlude on musical materials from the symphonic poem of the early 1850s; it comprises the third of the Funeral Odes. Searle considered this work autobiographical; according to him, "Liszt felt that he, like Tasso, would only be really appreciated after his death."[61] Everything else Liszt scored for orchestra during the two decades prior to his death is either substantially less important than these two pieces or represents an arrangement of a work originally conceived for non-orchestral forces.

Von der Wiege bis zum Grabe, Liszt's last symphonic poem, was ostensibly inspired by a painting and deals with subjects—especially struggle, death, and rebirth—that preoccupied the composer throughout his life. Divided into three sections, *Von der Wiege* opens with a lullaby (*Die Wiege*)—an unusual topic for Liszt, but one he employed in a few other works—scored only for violins and violas, two flutes, and harp. In spite of the limitations of both his subject matter and performing forces, Liszt manages to avoid the overtly sentimental; his music may not appeal to every taste, but it is in no sense kitschy. A second section, *Der Kampf um's Dasein* (The Struggle for Existence), scored for full orchestra, can be considered the work's development section; only at m. 250 does the full-fledged presentation of a theme never previously heard in that form suggest recapitulation. A final section, *Zum Grabe: die Wiege des zukünftigen Lebens* (To the Grave: The Cradle of the Life to Come)—scored without parts for piccolo or trombones—seems sweet and "drifting." Reminiscence and repetition are important features of the symphonic poem as a whole; consider the introductory passage in the "Struggle" section (mm. 129–173), which is repeated a whole step higher beginning at m. 174.

Example 10.18
Liszt, *Von der Wiege bis zum Grabe*, mm. 380–405

In the *Grabe* section—see Example 10.18—Liszt begins by recalling motivic and rhythmic material from the "Struggle" section, especially the syncopated figure and parallel thirds that appear in the clarinets (mm. 380ff.) and in the violins and flutes (mm. 385ff.), and that appeared originally in m. 194. This is followed by a passage in descending parallel thirds (mm. 398–404) reminiscent of *Die Wiege*, mm. 88–94. Liszt liked to tie up his musical parcels neatly, especially later in life. Carefully constructed but emotionally understated and somewhat indistinct expressively, *Von der Wiege* is nevertheless an interesting piece, although one that has never found much favor with concert audiences.[62]

Most of Liszt's minor orchestral works, including the several marches identified earlier in this chapter, are of comparatively little interest. One exception is *Salve Polonia*, if only because Liszt intended it to form part of his unfinished oratorio *Die Legende dem heiligen Stanislaus* (S 688). For a description of *Die Legende von der heiligen Elisabeth*, an oratorio Liszt did complete, and for a little additional information about another number intended for *Stanislaus*, see Chapter 13.

NOTES

1. See the inserts in Peter Raabe, *Franz Liszt*, rev. Felix Raabe (Tutzing: Hans Schneider, 1968), vol. 2 ("Liszts Schaffen"). Other sketches for the symphony are preserved today in the "Revolutionary Symphony sketchbook" belonging to the Goethe- und Schiller-Archiv, Weimar (shelf-number N6).

2. Adequate and up-to-date book-length studies of Liszt's symphonic music as a whole are non-existent. The broadest-based works in print are Max Chop, *Franz Liszts symphonische Werke, geschichtlich und musikalisch analysiert*, 2 vols. (Leipzig: Reclam, 1924–1925); and Alfred Heuss, *Erläuterungen zu Franz Liszts Sinfonien und sinfonischen Dichtungen* (Leipzig: Breitkopf & Härtel, 1912). Keith T. Johns's *The Symphonic Poems of Franz Liszt* (Stuyvesant, NY: Pendragon, 1998) is based on that author's 1986 dissertation; unfortunately, it covers only the works in question. Georgii Vilgelmovich Krauklis's *Simfoncheskie poemy F. Lista* (Moscow: "Muzyka," 1974) is not only in Russian, but hard to find; so is Marina Voronova's less extensive "Simfoniceskaja poema Lista v ee svjazjah s literaturjoz Romanticeskoj poemoj," in *Pamjati N. S. Nikolaevoj* [In Memory of N. S. Nikolaeva: Festschrift] (Moscow: Moscow Conservatory, 1996), 36–41. An important pamphlet, Franz Brendel's *Franz Liszt als Symphoniker* (Leipzig: C. Merseburg, 1859), is now a collector's item. Also useful, although it contains no musical examples, is Carl Dahlhaus's "Liszts Idee des Symphonischen," in *Liszt-Studien 2*, ed. Serge Gut (Munich and Salzburg: Emil Katzbichler, 1981), 36–42. Other valuable articles on various Liszt symphonic works, including the *Faust* symphony, may be found in *Liszt und die Weimarer Klassik*, ed. Detlef Altenburg (Laaber: Laaber-Verlag, 1997). For additional studies of individual symphonic works and problems associated with them, see Saffle, *Franz Liszt: A Guide to Research* (New York: Garland, 1991), 289–302.

3. A useful introduction to Liszt's orchestration appears in Alan Walker, *Franz Liszt: The Weimar Years, 1848–1861* (New York: Alfred A. Knopf, 1989), 2:300–337.

4. The dates given below for each composition represent the full span of years, from the earliest sketches known or hypothesized to publication or the first performance of the published version (whichever came first). In several cases precise dates are difficult to determine. A useful synopsis of much of this information—experts still disagree over the dates and orderings of these compositions—may be found in Walker, *Franz Liszt: The Weimar Years*, 2:301–303.

5. For additional information about this sketchbook and some of the orchestral sketches in it, see Rena Charnin Mueller, "Liszt's 'Tasso' Sketchbook: Studies in Sources and Revisions" (Ph.D. diss., New York University, 1986).

6. Raabe attempted to refute this claim in his doctoral dissertation on Liszt's early orchestral works; see *Die Entstehungsgeschichte der ersten Orchesterwerke Franz Liszts* (Leipzig: Breitkopf & Härtel, 1916). Unfortunately, it has persisted well into the twentieth century. The claim itself was made public in Helen Raff, "Franz Liszt und Joachim Raff im Spiegel ihrer Briefe," *Die Musik* 1 (1901–1902).

7. I must take exception with Johns on this point: there is much more of the sonata tradition in the symphonic poems than he and other commentators have uncovered.

8. Humphrey Searle, *The Music of Liszt*, 2d. rev. ed. (New York: Dover, 1966), 77.

9. See Johns, *The Symphonic Poems of Franz Liszt*, 77.

10. Ibid., 10–11.

11. See Walker, *Franz Liszt: The Weimar Years*, 2:305. Walker goes on to quote from what he considers merely to be the preface to *Orpheus*, then asks, "Will it help us to pictorialize the music that follows?" (306). Perhaps or perhaps not; each individual constructs his or her own interpretation. *Orpheus*, however, is the exception that proves the rule regarding Liszt's psychological story-telling in orchestral sound. For a detailed discussion of programmism and Liszt's symphonic poems, see Vera Micznik, "The Absolute Limitations of Programme Music: The Case of Liszt's 'Die Ideale,' " *Music & Letters* 82 (1999): 207–240.

12. Kofi Agawu, *Playing With Signs: A Semiotic Interpretation of Classic Music* (Princeton, NJ: Princeton University Press, 1991), 19 and 49.

13. Quoted in Paul Merrick, *Revolution and Religion in the Music of Liszt* (Cambridge: Cambridge University Press, 1987), 283.

14. Ibid., 308–309.

15. See Rey M. Longyear, "Structural Issues in Liszt's Philosophical Symphonic Poems," in *Analecta Lisztiana I: Proceedings of the "Liszt and His World" Conference Held at Virginia Polytechnic Institute and State University, 20–23 May 1993,* ed. Saffle (Stuyvesant, NY: Pendragon, 1998), 247–270.

16. Quoted in Johns, *The Symphonic Poems of Franz Liszt*, 79. Subsequent quotations from Liszt's programs (with some of them he was "assisted" not only by Bülow, but by the Princess Sayn-Wittgenstein and others of his coterie) are taken from Searle's revisions of the Eulenberg pocket scores or have been translated by the present author from those editions.

17. Johns, *The Symphonic Poems of Franz Liszt*, 25.

18. Ibid., 80.

19. Published analyses of *Ce qu'on entend* include Dahlhaus, "Liszts Berg-symphonie und die Idee der Symphonischen Dichtung," in *Jahrbuch des Staatlichen Instituts für Musikforschung Preussischer Kulturbesitz 1975* (Berlin 1976), 96–130; and Manfred Kelkel, "Wege zur 'Berg-Symphonie' Liszts," in *Liszt-Studien 3*, ed. Serge Gut (Munich and Salzburg: Emil Katzbichler, 1986), 71–89.

20. Searle, *The Music of Liszt*, 71.

21. A valuable study of this metamorphosis and one that supports the relevance of a Lamartine-like program for Liszt's symphonic poem, is Alexander Main, "Liszt after Lamartine: 'Les préludes,' " *Music & Letters* 60 (1979): 133–148.

22. Searle, "The Orchestral Works," in *Franz Liszt: The Man & His Music*, ed. Walker (London: Macmillan, 1971), 289.

23. *Franz Liszt's Briefe an Baron Anton Augusz, 1846–1878,* ed. Wilhelm von Csapó (Budapest: Franklin, 1911), 81–82. [Aus der Zeitungsnachricht zu Folge welcher ich mich in *St. Gallen* als *Pianist* produziert haben sollte, kannst Du wieder ersehen wie

sehr man befleissigt ist, mir in der Presse gute Dienste zu leisten und der Wahrheit gemäss über meine Wirksamkeit zu berichten. . . . Anbei sende ich Dir das in der St. Galler Zeitung veröffentlichte Programm des Conzerts, wovon ich den I-ten Theil und Wagner den II-ten (Symphonia eroica) dirigierten. Die vortreffliche Aufführung, welche meine 2 symphonischen Dichtungen—'Orpheus' und 'Präludes'—fanden, mussten sicherlich einige *Wöhlers* (deren Geschlecht überall verbreitet ist) unangenehm berührt haben; desswegen hatten sie nichts eiligeres, als sich über mein *imaginäres* Clavierspiel zu ergehen. . . . Einer ihrer Chefs sagte neulich ganz naïv 'wenn wir uns nich sehr energisch umthun und wehren, so kann das Publikum leicht Geschmack finden an der Liszt'schen Composition. Also vorwärts *Händl* [sic], *Bach, Haydn, Mozart, Beethowen* [sic], *Mendelsohn* [sic], und alle Classiker, und so recht gemächlich die Lebenden mit den Todten todt geschlagen.]

24. Johns, *The Symphonic Poems of Franz Liszt*, 60. See also note 11 above.

25. Additional information about this work appears in Sigfrid Schibli, "Franz Liszt: 'Orpheus,' " *Neue Zeitschrift fur Musik* 147/7–8 (July-August 1986): 54–56.

26. A useful study of the literary and cultural background of this symphonic poem is Paul Bertagnolli, "From Overture to Symphonic Poem, From Melodrama to Choral Cantata: Studies of the Sources for Franz Liszt's *Prometheus* and his *Chöre zu Herder's 'Entfesseltem Prometheus'* " (Ph.D. diss., Washington University, 1998). A summary and refinement of this study is scheduled to be published soon in the proceedings of the international Liszt conference held at the Villa Serbelloni, Bellagio, Italy, during December 1998.

27. Johns, *The Symphonic Poems of Franz Liszt*, 45.

28. See "Liszt's Programmatic use of Fugue" in Merrick, *Revolution and Religion in the Music of Liszt*, 267–282.

29. See Merrick, *Revolution and Religion in the Music of Liszt*, 268, which quotes Liszt on the subject of fugues in undistinguished nineteenth-century religious compositions.

30. Several studies of the etudes, including *Mazeppa*, have appeared in print; the most useful especially for the relationship between those pieces and the symphonic poem, remains August Stradal, "Liszts Mazeppa-Werke," *Neue Zeitschrift für Musik* 78 (1911): 577–583 and 597–601. See Chapter 5 in the present volume.

31. Searle, *The Music of Liszt*, 73.

32. The complex history of Liszt's marriage plans is clarified by Walker and Gabriele Erasmi in *Liszt, Carolyne, and the Vatican: The Story of a Thwarted Marriage* (Stuyvesant, NY: Pendragon, 1991).

33. Searle, *The Music of Liszt*, 116.

34. See also Saffle, "Liszt's Uses of Sonata Form: The Case of 'Festklänge,' " in *Liszt 2000: Selected Lectures Given at the International Liszt Conference in Budapest, May 18–20, 1999*, ed. Klára Hamburger (Budapest: Liszt Ferenc Társaság, 2000), 201–216.

35. See Merrick, *Revolution and Religion in the Music of Liszt*, 275, which suggests that the optional cut "which would leave out the recapitulation of the stormy *Allegro molto appassionato*, thus passing directly to the 'triumph' music" reinforces the notion that in this work, as in others, "the fugue represents the transitional between the prayer and its fulfillment."

36. For an analysis of this work's structure and style largely in terms of funeral pieces by Beethoven, Chopin, and other nineteenth-century figures, see Linda Popovic, "Liszt's Harmonic Polymorphism: Tonal and Non-tonal Aspects in 'Héroïde funèbre' " *Music Analysis* 15/1 (March 1996): 41–55; and Friedrich Riedel, "À propos de l'Héroïde

funèbre: Quelques caractéristiques stylistiques de musiques de Liszt, de ses prédécesseurs et de ses contemporains," *La Revue musicale* 405–407 (1987): 29–35.

37. Searle, *The Music of Liszt*, 74.

38. Ibid., 74

39. See, for instance, Edward Murphy, "A Detailed Program for Liszt's 'Hamlet,' " *JALS* 29 (1990): 47–60.

40. Quoted in Johns, *The Symphonic Poems of Franz Liszt*, 74.

41. Searle, *The Music of Liszt*, 75.

42. For a study of this subject, see Manfred Kaiser, "Anmerkungen zur Kompositionstechnik Franz Liszts: Am Beispiel der 'Hunnenschlacht,' " in *Liszt-Studien 1. Kongress-Bericht Eisenstadt 1975*, ed. Wolfgang Suppan (Graz: Akademische Druck- u. Verlagsanstalt, 1977), 125–129; see also Wolfram Steinbeck, "Musik nach Bildern: Zu Franz Liszt's *Hunnenschlacht*," in *Töne, Farben, Formen: Über Musik und die bildenden Künste: Festschrift Elmar Budde zum 60. Geburtstag* (Laaber: Laaber-Verlag, 1995), 17–38. With regard especially to Liszt's use of "exotic" musical materials, including those employed in *Hunnenschlacht*, see James Deaville, "Liszts Orientalismus: Die Gestaltung des Andersseins in der Musik," in *Liszt und die Nationalitäten*, ed. Gerhard J. Winkler (Eisenstadt: Burgenländisches Landesmuseum, 1996), 163–195.

43. Johns, *The Symphonic Poems of Franz Liszt*, 56.

44. Searle, *The Music of Liszt*, 76.

45. Johns, *The Symphonic Poems of Franz Liszt*, 70.

46. Additional insights into the structure of this composition may be found in Macklenburg, "Liszt und seine Ideale," *Bayreuther Blätter* (1926): 153–169.

47. See László Somfai, "Die Gestaltwandlungen der 'Faust-Symphonie' von Liszt," reprinted in *Franz Liszt: Beiträge von ungarischen Authoren*, ed. Hamburger (Budapest: Corvina Kiadó, 1978), 292. According to Mueller ("Liszt's 'Tasso' Sketchbook," 166), this manuscript source dates from 1846–1860.

48. Additional information about this draft may be found in Mária Eckhardt, *Liszt Manuscripts in the National Széchényi Museum* (Stuyvesant, NY: Pendragon, 1986), 86–87.

49. See, for instance, Dahlhaus, "Liszts 'Faust-Symphonie' und die Krise der symphonischen Form," in *Über Symphonien. Beiträge zu einer musikalischen Gattung: Festschrift Walter Wiora zum 70. Geburtstag* (Tutzing: Hans Schneider, 1979), 129–139; Constantin Floros, "Die Faust-Symphonie von Franz Liszt. Eine semantische Analyse," in *Franz Liszt*, ed. Heinz-Klaus Metzger and Reiner Riehn (Musik-Konzepte 12, 1980), 42–87; Vernon Harrison, "Liszt's Faust Symphony: A Psychological Interpretation," *LSJ* 4 (1979): 2–5; and Klaus Wolfgang Niemöller, "Zur nicht-tonalen Thema-Struktur von Liszts 'Faust-Symphonie,' " *Die Musikforschung* 22 (1969): 69–72. Basic analyses of sonata form in "Faust," the symphony's first movement, appear in several standard textbooks on the symphony as a genre and on nineteenth-century European music. A respectable synopsis of this symphony as a whole may be found in Walker, *Franz Liszt: The Weimar Years*, 2:329–334; and of both the *Faust* and *Dante* symphonies in Searle, "The Orchestral Works," 304–315.

50. Friedrich Pohl is responsible for some of these names. See Walker, *Franz Liszt: The Weimar Years*, 2:330.

51. See Merrick, *Revolution and Religion in the Music of Liszt*, 301–302.

52. See Eckhardt "Liszt à Marseille," *Studia musicologica* 24 (1982): 192.

53. Quoted from Franz Liszt, *Selected Letters*, 375.

54. See Searle, "The Orchestral Works," 310.

55. Ibid., 310–311.

56. An exciting new study of Liszt's relationship with this woman, consisting primarily of a carefully annotated translation of their surviving letters, is *Franz Liszt and Agnès Street-Klindworth: A Correspondence, 1854–1886*, ed. and trans. Pauline Pocknell (Hillsdale, NY: Pendragon, 2000).

57. This figure (printed as Example 8.16) is also found in the *Crux fidelis* theme from *Hunnenschlacht* and a host of Liszt's other works. Merrick discussed it at some length in *Revolution and Religion in the Music of Liszt*. Merrick calls it the "Cross motif"; so did Liszt himself. Robert Collet uses the term "musical fingerprint" to identify it; see Collet, "Choral and Organ Music" in *Franz Liszt: The Man and His Music*, 323.

58. Comparatively few useful analyses of the *Dante* symphony have appeared in print. Among the best of them is Jean-Pierre Barricelli, "Liszt's Journey through Dante's Hereafter," *Bucknell Review* 26 (1982): 149–166. Barricelli's article was reprinted in *JALS* 14 (1983): 3–15.

59. Searle, "The Orchestral Works," 314.

60. See Searle, *The Music of Liszt*, 95–96.

61. Searle, "The Orchestral Works," 317.

62. See Jürgen Schläder, "Der schöne Traum vom Ideal. Die künstlerische Konzeption in Franz Liszts letzter Symphonischen Dichtung," *Hamburger Jahrbuch für Musikwissenschaft* 6 (1983): 47–62, for a reproduction of Zichy's painting as well as analytical diagrams and additional information about this symphonic poem.

11

Piano and Orchestra Works

Jay Rosenblatt

Franz Liszt composed seventeen works for piano and orchestra, a sizable repertory in a genre naturally attractive to a nineteenth-century virtuoso. Curiously, he rarely performed these works during his career and, of the seventeen, published only seven (see Table 11.1). Why did the greatest pianist of the century have such an ambiguous relationship with the most virtuoso of genres? The answer is that Liszt's aspirations for his concertos went beyond mere display. From the earliest surviving examples, we see him moving away from the older model exemplified by Mozart and early Beethoven and still practiced by contemporaries such as Johann Nepomuk Hummel and Frédéric Chopin. Liszt not only worked towards a greater integration of soloist with orchestra, but he used the concerto to forge the fundamental principles of his compositional style. These concertos presented new demands, musically as well as technically, and Liszt hesitated to put the results before the public. Given that so few of them were published, it can come as a surprise that Liszt's work in the concerto genre extended from 1825 to 1885, a period exceeded only by the years he devoted to his works for solo piano. A complete survey reveals the significance the concerto had in his development.

FIRST MATURITY

Aside from three concertos the teenage Liszt wrote in the 1820s (and which are lost),[1] the earliest surviving works for piano and orchestra were completed in close succession in 1834–1835. These include the first version of Concerto no. 1 in Eb major, the *Grande fantaisie symphonique* on themes from Berlioz's *Lélio, De profundis,* and the work known as *Malédiction.* Musical factors also unify these works. With the exception of Concerto no. 1, they are all in one continuous movement, revealing Liszt's desire to organize large-scale structure in ways that go beyond the conventional three-movement form.[2] He also uses various internal means, some obvious such as the restatement towards the conclusion of a theme from earlier in the work (Concerto no. 1 and the *Grande fantaisie symphonique*), and some more subtle such as his first tentative employment of thematic transformation (*De profundis* and *Malédiction*). In addition, the *Grande fantaisie* and *De profundis* make use of a unifying rhythmic motive found throughout each work. All of these devices may be considered incipient stages of the techniques found in the great works of the Weimar years, including the symphonic poems and the Sonata in B minor. Finally, the piano part is integrated into the musical argument from the first measures, leaving behind the classical tradition of an orchestral exposition and following the standard set by Carl Maria von Weber in his Konzertstück in F minor, op. 79 (1821), and Felix Mendelssohn in his Concerto no. 1 in G minor, op. 25 (1831) and *Capriccio brillante*, op. 22 (1832).[3]

Table 11.1
Liszt's Works for Piano and Orchestra[4]

Composed	Published	Composition
1825		(Piano Concerto)—Lost. S 713.
1825		(Piano Concerto) — Lost. S 713.
1827		(Concerto in A minor)—Lost. S 716.
1834		*Malédiction*. S 121.
1834		*Grande fantaisie symphonique*. S 120.
1835		*De profundis, psaume instrumental*. S 691.
1839		*Hexaméron*. S 390.
1839		Concerto in E♭ Major, op. posth.
1849	1851	Carl Maria von Weber's Polonaise brillante, op. 72. S 367.
1849–1852	1865	*Fantasie über Motive aus Beethovens "Ruinen von Athen."* S 122.
1832–1856	1857	Concerto no. 1 in E♭ Major. S 124.
1839–1861	1863	Concerto no. 2 in A Major. S 125.
1849–1863	1864	Fantasie über ungarische Volksmelodien. S 123.
1849–1864		*Totentanz*. S 126.
1850		*Grand solo de Concert*. S 365.
1852	1858	Franz Schubert's *Wanderer Fantasy*, op. 15. S 366.
1885		Concerto in the Hungarian Style. S 714.

Grande fantaisie symphonique

The first work to be completed appears to have been the *Grande fantaisie symphonique*.[5] In an "étude biographique" that appeared in the *Gazette musicale de Paris* of 14 June 1835, the writer noted: "We must make particular mention of his *Fantaisie symphonique sur le chant du Pêcheur et le choeur des Brigands* of Berlioz, the latest and most important work of Liszt. He composed it last autumn, during his stay at La Chênaie with the Abbé Lamennais."[6]

Liszt may have also referred to this work in a letter to the Countess Marie d'Agoult: "I will benefit here by finishing a new enormous Fantasy, of which I wrote two-thirds at La Chênaie; the remainder is done in my head."[7] These references date the origins to September 1834, when Liszt visited the home of the Abbé Félicité de Lamennais, and, as the first performance was announced for Berlioz's concert of 23 November, Liszt must have been successful in completing the work over the next month.[8] According to the reviews, it was not performed at this time, but whether because it was not completely copied, required revision, or proved too difficult for the orchestra in rehearsal is unclear, and the only known fact is that Liszt did not appear on the program at all.[9] Perhaps Berlioz was referring to this cancellation when he wrote: "This work, before reaching the public, had to conquer the prejudice and difficulties which never fail to attack all lofty unconventional output."[10] The premiere finally took place at Liszt's own concert of 9 April 1835.[11]

As noted, the *Grande fantaisie* is based on a work by Berlioz. It is not surprising that Liszt turned to Berlioz for inspiration, since they were close friends at this time, and Liszt was eager to promote Berlioz's music. Thus in 1833, Liszt prepared a piano transcription of the *Symphonie fantastique,* which he published the following year at his own expense, then he turned his attention to a paraphrase for piano and orchestra on its sequel. Berlioz's inspiration is also apparent in the title, "fantaisie symphonique" being a simple reversal of "symphonie fantastique." The source work, *Le retour à la vie* (later titled *Lélio*), consists of six short pieces written over the period 1830–1831 and collected by Berlioz into a work that was intended to continue the story begun in the *Symphonie fantastique.* From these six movements, Liszt chose two of the most tuneful that also contrast well with each other: *Le pêcheur* and the *Chanson de brigands.* First is the opening number of Berlioz's score, a setting of a ballad by Goethe, *Der Fischer*, that tells the story of a water nymph who loves a fisherman to his death. The four verses were translated into French and set in A minor to a modified strophic form for voice and piano.[12] The *Chanson de brigands*, third of the six movements, is a swaggering dramatic scene for bass, male chorus, and orchestra. It is in F major and essentially strophic.

The *Grande fantaisie symphonique* stands as the first of Liszt's extended one-movement forms, although in this case the internal division is simply a slow section (based on *Le pêcheur*) followed by a fast section (based on the *Chanson de brigands*).[13] His brief description in the letter to d'Agoult quoted above summarizes the work's distinctive features: the *Grande fantaisie* was an "énormité" by contemporary standards—nearly twenty-five minutes—thus it is quite long for a single-movement work, and "fantasy" implies a certain freedom in form. Each section begins with a straightforward statement in the original keys of the source material, which is subjected to increasingly elaborate variation in the manner of Liszt's operatic paraphrases. Liszt also uses two of the techniques noted above to bind the work together. From the second number in Berlioz's score, the *Choeur d'ombres,* he borrowed a rhythmic motive, which appears several times throughout the score (see Example 11.1).[14] In addition, he takes twenty-one measures from the section devoted to *Le pêcheur* and restates them towards the end of the piece, immediately before the coda.

Example 11.1
Liszt, *Grande fantaisie symphonique*, mm. 74–75

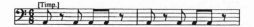

Discussion of the *Grande fantaisie* is a good place to take up the question of Liszt and orchestration. The quality of the orchestral writing led Peter Raabe to suspect that "it is unlikely the instrumentation stems from Liszt," a statement echoed by Humphrey Searle.[15] Contrariwise is the comment by Robert Collet: "The orchestral writing is curiously helpless and overloaded, without even a faint foretaste of the mastery that Liszt eventually achieved."[16] We are left to wonder: is the orchestration so good that it could not be by Liszt or so bad that it must be? For the first part of the question, a portion of Liszt's autograph of the orchestral score recently surfaced at auction, thereby settling the matter. As for its quality, the orchestration is competent and performable, as has been demonstrated in several recent recordings, and Liszt's contemporaries had nothing but praise for this aspect of the work: "The instrumentation of this vast composition is fresh, picturesque, incisive, but of an intricacy that renders the task of the orchestra quite difficult. It is passionate, extravagant, unexpectedly powerful, like the performing ability of the author."[17] Evidence of Liszt's ability can also be seen in the autograph score for *De profundis,* composed a few months later. Here we find no signs of inexperience, such as errors in transposition or clefs. Furthermore, passages such as the contrapuntal figure beginning at m. 130 (see Example 11.2) are so completely idiomatic for the strings and so resistant to piano transcription that they give lie to the idea that Liszt "played the orchestra on the piano and the piano on the orchestra."[18] Liszt's ability in this area was never questioned during his life, and such challenges were issued only much later.[19]

De profundis

Although La Chênaie served as the workplace for the *Grande fantaisie symphonique,* it was the inspiration for *De profundis.* Liszt wrote of it to Lamennais on 14 January 1835: "Before [my visit in July], I will have the honor of sending you a small work, to which I had the audacity to attach a great name—yours. It is a *De Profundis*—for orchestra. The plainchant that you love so much is contained within the faux bourdon [sic]. Perhaps this will please you a little; at any rate I have done it in memory of several hours passed (I would like to say *lived*) at La Chênaie."[20] Liszt entitled the work, *De profundis* (*Psaume instrumental*), and dedicated it to "M[onsieu]r l'abbé de Lammenais." As for the "fauxbourdon," this refers to the harmonized setting of the psalm tone used in plainchant for chanting psalms, in this case Psalm 129 (130), that generates much of the musical material for the work. The manuscript of *De profundis* is also significant as it is the earliest complete autograph of an orchestral work by Liszt, fully scored and numbering over 900 measures. Yet despite this effort on Liszt's part, it remained unfinished: the music breaks off at the end of a page, although recent attempts to complete *De profundis* suggest that only a coda is lacking.[21]

Example 11.2
Liszt, *De profundis*, mm. 130–137, strings only

De profundis is in one continuous movement that lasts, even without its conclusion, well over thirty minutes. It is carefully organized into exposition, extensive development, "scherzo-like" interlude, and recapitulation. The use of these terms is very appropriate, as the structure works both as a large sonata form and a multi-sectional work, an approach which strikingly foreshadows the "double-function" form found in the Sonata in B minor.[22] Liszt's sonata form begins in a traditional manner, with a group of themes in D minor followed by a transition to a theme in F major. This orchestral phrase anticipates the "De profundis fauxbourdon," which immediately follows in the piano in F♯ minor (see Example 11.3) and is repeated by the orchestra, almost as a priest leading a congregation in worship. One is reminded of Lamennais's concept of the artist as "the prophet of the future," as well as Liszt's own essay from 1834, where he states: "But today, at a time when the altar creaks and totters, today when the pulpit and religious rites have become matters of doubt and derision, it is essential that art leave the temple, that it stretch itself and seek to accomplish its major developments in the outside world."[23] Central to the work is an extensive piano cadenza, which includes a transformation of the "De profundis" theme in A♭ major (see Example 11.4), again followed by a statement in the orchestra. In addition to its placement at the exact midpoint, this long passage establishes a tonal pole to the opening in D minor that is a tritone removed. Finally, the recapitulation begins along expected lines, but at the point where the original "De profundis fauxbourdon" was heard, the music segues into a concluding section that takes the A♭ version of the theme and transforms it into a march in D major (see Example 11.5). This concluding section is, in a sense, a natural continuation of the recapitulation, because the transformed theme is one that has not yet been stated in the key of D. When we consider *De profundis* alongside the *Grande fantaisie symphonique,* we see Liszt experimenting with various techniques to bind together a large single movement form. In the *Grande fantaisie,* Liszt's strategy is to restate music heard earlier in the work, but he makes no attempt to integrate the repeated material. With *De profundis,* we see Liszt trying to work out a solution along more organic lines and, in the process, anticipating his later innovations.

Example 11.3
Liszt, *De profundis,* mm. 188–193

Example 11.4
Liszt, *De profundis,* mm. 405–408

Example 11.5
Liszt, *De profundis,* mm. 822–825, piano only

Malédiction

The last work by Liszt from this period that may be considered a concerto is *Malédiction* for piano and strings, published posthumously in 1914.[24] Several misunderstandings have accrued to the work as a result of this edition. The editor took the liberty of indicating the string parts in the plural, thus suggesting that Liszt intended a work for piano and string orchestra. An examination of the copyist's manuscript, the only surviving score aside from sketches, reveals string indications in the singular, and this fact, along with the recognition that such sextets were a well-known genre of chamber music in the 1830s, suggests that Liszt intended a piece of chamber music, not a concerto. The editor erred further in taking Liszt's scrawled pencil indication above the first system of music as a title. It has long been recognized that the word *malédiction* (curse) is only a programmatic label for the opening theme, and other labels are found throughout the work: *orgueil* (pride) at m. 17, *pleurs—angoisse—songes* (tears, anguish, dreams) at m. 68, and *raillerie* (jesting) at m. 118.[25] Far more elusive has been the date of composition. Speculation has ranged over a span of fifty-eight years, with most commentators concentrating on the years between 1827 and 1848. An important clue was first detected by Sharon Winklhofer, when she observed the paper's watermark, "KOOL 1833."[26] This is, of course, only a *terminus post quem,* and other manuscript evidence suggests 1834–1835, the same period as the *Grande fantaisie symphonique* and *De profundis.*[27]

Aside from the questions of genre and title, the penciled words throughout the score reveal another preoccupation of Liszt, that of program music, and there are several other clues that offer insight into this aspect of *Malédiction*. Liszt recycled parts of the piece in later programmatic works: the opening measures are found in *Orage* (*Années de pèlerinage, première année, Suisse*), and the theme at m. 17 is used in the *Faust Symphony*, where it is the only musical material in the third movement ("Mephistopheles") that has no counterpart in the first ("Faust").[28] In addition, Liszt originally included a transcription of Schubert's song, *Du bist die Ruh*, placing it before the coda (*Molto animato, quasi Presto*). This information is not enough to formulate a coherent program, although it suggests that Liszt had a detailed one in mind. As for the musical aspects, the work lasts about fifteen minutes and is in one continuous movement with some aspects of sonata form. For example, there is a clear sense of recapitulation at m. 243, however the theme labeled *raillerie*, heard in G major to close the first part of the piece, never returns to round out the structure. Thematic transformation is also found, especially in the coda.

While the evidence is by no means conclusive, it is useful to speculate that these works were composed within months of each other with a specific goal in mind. Liszt was becoming increasingly active as a performer, and he may have been developing a repertory for himself that could display his talents as a superb pianist and innovative composer. The concert of 9 April 1835 was the first to feature a work for piano and orchestra, the prime vehicle for any virtuoso, and the manuscript score of Concerto no. 1, identical in layout to the manuscript of the *Grande fantaisie,* suggests that this work was slated next for presentation. Furthermore, the extensive *étude biographique,* which appeared as the lead article in the *Gazette musicale* of 14 June 1835, demonstrates that Liszt had enlisted the press, and all the evidence together reveals a well-orchestrated blitz to bring Liszt's name before the public. In addition, all biographical indications, including the letter quoted above to the Abbé Lamennais, indicate that Liszt had no intention of leaving Paris at this time. An unforeseen turn of events made it impossible to benefit from these well-laid plans, however: by May, Marie d'Agoult realized she was pregnant, and by June, Liszt had joined her in Basel. Any plans for making an impression as a composer and pianist were temporarily put aside.

The final curious aspect of these works for piano and orchestra is that Liszt abandoned all but one of them. Once settled in Geneva, he requested several of his manuscripts, including the Concerto no. 1, the *Grande fantaisie symphonique, De profundis,* and perhaps *Malédiction.*[29] One can assume that he hoped to perform or, at least, revise these compositions, but only the *Grande fantaisie* was played (once more, on 18 December 1836), and *De profundis* was never finished. In addition, themes from *Malédiction* were incorporated into other works, and the "De profundis fauxbourdon" and its transformation were used in *Pensée des morts,* the fourth item in *Harmonies poétiques et religieuses* (1853). Such actions offer a sure sign that the original compositions had been relegated to the scrap heap and would not see publication during his life. Within a few years, Liszt turned his attention to a new series of works for piano and orchestra, and the only work from this period that he would salvage is the one that later came to be known as his Concerto no. 1.

THE THREE CONCERTOS OF 1839

It was not until September 1839 that Liszt returned to the concerto genre. His third and final child with Marie d'Agoult had been born in Rome the previous June. After the usual handing off of the baby to a wet nurse, the couple retired to San Rossore for about six weeks in late August and September, where they rented a house on the "Gombo" estate.[30] San Rossore was a last time together in seclusion, as Liszt and d'Agoult had decided to separate for the winter so that Liszt could concertize.[31] Liszt also used this time to prepare a repertory for piano and orchestra that he could play on such a tour: his orchestral score for Concerto no. 2 has an inscription at the end, "Gombo, 13 Sept [18]39," and other manuscript evidence suggests that while at the estate he worked on a revised version of Concerto no. 1, composed a new Concerto in E♭ major, and devised orchestrations for his *Réminiscences des Puritains* and *Hexaméron.*[32] Such a flurry of activity is reminiscent of the concertos prepared in 1834–1835, and, not surprisingly, the concertos from 1839 also share musical features.

At first glance, the orchestration appears to be a step backward from the earlier works. The orchestra often doubles the piano, resulting in a lack of transparency in the texture. But Liszt may have had a good reason for such doubling. If it is true that he wrote these works to play on tour with orchestras of unknown size and proficiency, then he was only being pragmatic by keeping the parts simple. The orchestral parts to Concerto no. 1 are more adventurous than the others, but this is likely because it was a revision of a work written under different circumstances (some passages were taken over with little change). In addition, the instrumentation of all these works is quite modest, with the exception of the Concerto in E♭ major and *Hexaméron,* which call for a *trompette à clefs* (keyed trumpet), an instrument that by 1839 was not used much outside of Italy.

Concertos nos. 1 and 2 and the Concerto in E♭ major are further unified by the compositional devices with which he had begun to experiment in the works from 1834–1835: the novel use of one-movement forms and the use of thematic transformation toward structural ends. All three works are in one continuous movement, and they all recapitulate their various themes towards the end in transformed guise and in the key of the work. The state of the first and second concertos in 1839 can be summarized briefly. Concerto no. 1 is recognizably the work we know today with much (but not all) of the thematic material. Differences can be found in the working out of the themes in the opening movement and the *Quasi adagio* (here simply *Adagio*), and in the recapitulation of the themes in the closing section. The situation is similar in Concerto no. 2, where one of the most beautiful transformations is lacking (see Examples 11.15 and 11.16 below). But of all these works, it is the Concerto in E♭ major which shows the greatest evidence of Liszt's "double-function" form.

Concerto in E♭ major, op. posth.

A unique aspect of the Concerto in E♭ major, and one which it shares with the *Transcendental Etudes,* is the use of earlier compositions to craft a new work, in this case, publications from the 1820s. In a letter of March 1836, Liszt requested the following: "Please take the trouble to search in my trunk or at the bottom of the armoire for four pieces of music by Franz Liszt that were published 13 or 14 years ago by the Demoiselles Érard. Here are the titles: *Variations* sur un thème original dédiées à Sébastian Érard, *Variations* dédiées à Mme. Panckoucke, Deux Allegri di Bravura (2 pieces) dédiées au Comte Amadé."[33] The theme from the Érard variations (*Huit variations,* op. 1) and motives from the two works dedicated to Amadé (*Allegro di bravura* and *Rondo di bravura,* op. 4) were ultimately incorporated into the Concerto. In the same letter Liszt requested his Études, op. 6. He reworked these pieces as the *Vingt-quatre grandes études* (predecessors to the *Transcendental Etudes*), publishing them in 1839, and the new set may be regarded as a summation of the musical and technical advances of the decade.[34] The reworking of compositions from Liszt's youth may be said to mark a new beginning for the twenty-seven-year-old composer. Similar to his impact in the solo repertory, Liszt may have wanted to make a contribution to the concerto genre.

In the Concerto in E♭ major, the "double-function" form is particularly evident. Here we have a slow introduction followed by four distinct sections (*Allegro—Andante—Allegro—Allegro vivace*) that also work as a sonata form (exposition—[slow movement]—development—recapitulation), with the slow movement also functioning as a secondary key area. The thematic cross relations between sections also underline the form: the slow introduction anticipates all of the thematic material, the development concentrates exclusively on the themes of the exposition, and the recapitulation states all the themes, including that of the slow movement, transformed and in E♭ major. Further, Liszt's use of his source material reinforces this scheme. The opening measures of the *Allegro di bravura* serve as an ostinato in the introduction (see Example 11.6) as well as the opening theme of the exposition (see Example 11.7).[35] For the slow movement, Liszt used the theme of his *Huit Variations,* stating it intact (see Example 11.8) and subjecting it to development within the section. The recapitulation marks Liszt's most extravagant use of transformation, with a considerable change of emotional mood for each theme (compare Example 11.9 with 11.7 and Example 11.10 with 11.8). Finally, Liszt reserves one theme for restatement in E♭ major in the closing measures. It is a variant of Example 11.7, first heard at the end of the exposition (see Example 11.11) and also used in the development, but never in E♭. By saving it for the end and stating it in a triumphant transformation, Liszt has increased the sense of closure while at the same time bringing the piece to a brilliant conclusion. He would again use this device in the revisions of Concertos nos. 1 and 2 in 1849 as well as other works from his Weimar years.

Example 11.6
Liszt, Concerto in E♭ Major, op. posth., mm. 1–4

Example 11.7
Liszt, Concerto in E♭ Major, op. posth., mm. 42–45, piano only

Example 11.8
Liszt, Concerto in E♭ Major, op. posth., mm. 134–137

Example 11.9
Liszt, Concerto in E♭ Major, op. posth., mm. 266–269

Example 11.10
Liszt, Concerto in E♭ Major, op. posth., mm. 346–353, piano only

Example 11.11
Liszt, Concerto in E♭ Major, op. posth., mm. 122–125, strings only

Despite five new concerted works in his portfolio, the only one that he played during his *Glanzperiode* was his arrangement of *Hexaméron,* which was performed for the first time in Leipzig on 31 March 1840.[36] Why did Liszt not perform these works during the height of his popularity, when it would have been easy for him to do so? A survey of his concert programs reveals that, when a work for piano and orchestra was needed, he invariably turned to Carl Maria von Weber's Konzertstück, op. 79, or, less often, *Hexaméron.* The reason may lie in the reception of the one work of his maturity previously performed, the *Grande fantaisie symphonique.*[37] Although all of the reviews remarked on his dazzling pianistic ability, even the positive review by Berlioz noted that the work contained *quelques longeurs* and *abus de modulations enharmoniques.*[38] Others were more blunt: "We remark . . . that we do not like very much the *Grande fantaisie symphonique* of Berlioz, notwithstanding the fine talent of Liszt."[39] An unsigned review in the *Revue musicale* offered the following advice: "If he perseveres while improving, if he preserves his individuality while rejecting his thought that spoils it, that shocks the sensitive ear, then there will be for him a career as a composer as there is a marvelous one as performer."[40] Most damning of all was an observation from the Parisian correspondent for a German periodical:

The composition by Liszt, in which at present, as in all works of this kind, the thread of ideas—when they are available—immediately gets lost, contains, aside from much that is brilliant, considerable confusion, even disorder, in which neither a thought nor a goal is to be found. In such fantastic painted surroundings [Gemälderamen], one no doubt believes . . . without orderly thoughts, without order and coherence, it was tossed out by a child with a lively imagination, raw and disordered to the wide world.[41]

Given such comments, it seems as if Liszt's ego did not allow him to jeopardize his success with experimental works such as his three concertos.

THE WEIMAR YEARS

Liszt was settled in Weimar by February 1848, and Princess Carolyne von Sayn-Wittgenstein soon joined him. Much of his attention was devoted to preparing his piano works for publication as well as fulfilling his obligations as Kapellmeister. By 30 May 1849, however, he was writing to a friend, hinting that he had some new work for August Conradi, his regular copyist at this time: "What has become of Conradi? Thank him for the copy of the Bach fugues (of which I equally thank you, always with pleasure) and tell him that if he has nothing better to do, I would ask him to give me the pleasure of coming to Weimar as soon as he sees fit, to make a fair copy of the two scores of my Concertos (now completely finished) and others."[42] Hans von Bülow also knew of these works, as he wrote to his mother on 21 June 1849: "As Liszt has communicated to me, so is the rumor truly confirmed, that he has begun larger works, that several piano concertos with orchestral accompaniment lie ready in his desk."[43] Conradi must have begun his task by mid-summer, for Liszt was able to write to Joachim Raff on 1 August: "The scores of my two concertos . . . are now completely copied."[44] But Bülow's "several" suggests more than the two works indicated in Liszt's letter, and, by October, Conradi had prepared copies of no less than six works for piano and orchestra: Concertos nos. 1 and 2, *Totentanz*, and transcriptions of Weber's Polonaise brillante, op. 72, his own *Capriccio alla Turca sur des motifs de Beethoven*, and a Hungarian Rhapsody.[45] These copies were bound in three luxurious volumes with the coat of arms designed for Liszt by the Princess Wittgenstein embossed in gold tooling on the cover. Each volume bears the inscription on the flyleaf in the hand of Liszt or the Princess, *terminée le 21 Octobre 1849*, the day before Liszt's 38th birthday. Obviously, the works were not finished on that day, and the presentation was probably the Princess's idea for a birthday gift. Nevertheless, their collection together speaks of a concentrated effort as well as the continued importance of the genre for Liszt.[46]

Within a few months of Conradi's work, Liszt instructed Raff, now his resident copyist, to write out yet another full score of Concerto no. 1. Raff's tenure began on or shortly before 1 December 1849.[47] His very first task must have been to prepare the new copy of Concerto no. 1, and this beautifully copied score titled "Première Concerto Symphonique pour Piano et Orchestre" is duly annotated at the end of the last measure at the bottom of the page: *Copié par Joachim Raff. Eilsen 8. Dec: 49.* Within two months, Liszt had also revised Concerto no. 2, and by February 1850 Raff was able to report the completion of this copy.[48] It is unclear why Liszt would need new scores of Concertos nos. 1 and 2 so soon after Conradi's copies, and one can only speculate that he thought he might soon publish them. Instead, Liszt turned his attention to a variety of other piano and orchestra projects. He transcribed Franz Schubert's *Wanderer Fantasy* (Fantasy in C major, op. 15) as well as his own *Grand solo de concert*,[49] and he also readied for publication his transcription of Weber's Polonaise brillante. A letter of 11 April 1851 to the Princess Wittgenstein noted a performance of the Polonaise by one of his students,[50] the first performance of any piano and orchestra work since his *Glanzperiode*. Transcriptions and students came together again, when, two years later, Bülow's first concert tour prompted Liszt to rummage through his desk drawer to provide him with suitable concerto vehicles. The result was the revision of the *Capriccio alla Turca* and *Hungarian Rhapsody*, and a letter of Bülow's reveals that new copies of these scores were complete by 27 January 1853.[51] Bülow left around May, and a letter from Liszt of 12 May reveals that his thoughts regarding concerto revisions did not end with his pupil's departure: "Concerning music, I have completed my Sonata [in B minor] and a second ballade—and at this moment I have finished the revision for the definitive fair copy of my two concertos and *Totentanz*."[52]

Nevertheless, two years passed before Liszt returned to these works, and the occasion was the first performance of any of the original concertos. He had now gone through three fair copies of Concertos nos. 1 and 2 and two for *Totentanz*, and he must have been apprehensive about offering such a work to the musical world. He therefore chose the circumstances that would unquestionably show it in its best light. In February 1855, Liszt scheduled the second "Berlioz Week" in Weimar, where the composer was in residence to supervise performances of his own works, and it was during this week on 17 February that Concerto no. 1 was premiered with the finest pianist of the day as soloist (Liszt) and the finest conductor on the podium (Berlioz). Liszt also allowed Bülow to perform the work in September,[53] and by March of the following year, Bülow was charged with correcting the copies in existence and creating new copies.[54] All this activity was preparatory to publication,[55] and Concerto no. 1 appeared early in 1857 with a dedication to his fellow pianist, Henry Litolff.[56] The *Wanderer Fantasy* transcription was also prepared for publication around this time, and it appeared later that same year.

Liszt soon turned his attention to Concerto no. 2. The work had its premiere on 1 January 1857 with his pupil, Hans von Bronsart, as soloist, and Liszt himself on the podium. It was to Bronsart that Liszt dedicated the work: "For my part, allow me also a dedication: my second Concerto shall belong to you and your name is already placed on the title page."[57] Liszt was well aware of the novelty of Concerto no. 2 and wrote Bronsart with advice on rehearsing the work: "The Concerto was sent to you yesterday evening—and in the case that you play it I ask you to rehearse it carefully and, *before the rehearsal,* to play it with the score to the conductor in order to impress the correct tempos of the movements that I wish."[58] In the following months, Bronsart performed the work on tour along with the transcriptions of Weber's Polonaise brillante and Schubert's *Wanderer Fantasy*.[59] The following year Liszt also allowed his student Carl Tausig to play Concerto no. 2 in public.[60] It was not until 1861, however, that he finally prepared the manuscript for the engraver. Liszt wrote the Princess on 10 January concerning the work: "At the moment that your letter arrived, I was in the act of reviewing my second Concerto, of which, incidentally, I have made various improvements, which have taken me four or five days."[61] The publication appeared two years later.

Concerto no. 1 in E♭ major

This Concerto had the longest gestation period of any of the works for piano and orchestra. Liszt may have completed the first version by the end of 1832, as he observed in a letter: "I have prepared and for a long while worked out several instrumental compositions, among them . . . a *Concerto* after a plan that I think will be new, and whose accompaniment remains to be written."[62] Based on a copyist's manuscript of the work from around 1835, this is a plausible (if somewhat vague) description. Here we find a work in three movements, all laid out on a grand scale. Several aspects suggest that Liszt used Beethoven's *Emperor Concerto* as a model: the key scheme is E♭ major for the outer movements and B major for the slow movement, the second and third movements are connected with a bridge passage, and the last movement is in triple time (here 3/4, not 6/8). Thematic material is mostly recognizable from the final published version: the opening was probably very similar (it cannot be said for certain, as several pages were torn from the manuscript), the slow movement begins with the same theme as the *Quasi adagio,* and the last movement uses the theme from the "triangle" Scherzo (although the idea of the triangle itself had not yet occurred to Liszt).[63] Perhaps the most interesting feature is found in the third movement, where the principal theme from the slow movement returns just before the Coda. The Scherzo is simply halted with a fermata, and there is no attempt to rhythmically integrate the interpolation. Although a somewhat crude effect, this restatement may be the "new plan" to which Liszt referred in his letter.

The revision of 1839 gave the work its one-movement form, and the version of 1849 is very recognizable as the work we know today (including the well-known use of the triangle), with subsequent revisions being more of refinement, especially in the area of orchestration. Among the aspects that Liszt brought into focus is, of course, the "double function" form, again a single-movement work that can also be heard as a four-movement structure: *Allegro—Quasi adagio—Scherzo—Allegro marziale.* Liszt has further added continuity with an extensive transition section before the final movement that recalls the opening of the Concerto, and the opening measures themselves yield a rhythmic motive which recurs throughout the work. Perhaps most impressive of the techniques employed is that of thematic transformation, used in the *Allegro marziale* to recapitulate all of the themes heard earlier. Liszt himself was aware of what he had achieved, and his description of it, in a letter of 26 March 1857, can serve well to illustrate the distinctive features:

The fourth movement of the Concerto (from *Allegro marziale*)

corresponds with the second movement *Adagio*

and is only a concise Recapitulation with refreshed, enlivened rhythms of earlier materials and contains no new motive, which will be quite evident to you from a perusal of the score. This manner of binding together and rounding off an entire piece by its conclusion is rather my own; it completely maintains and justifies itself from the standpoint of musical form.

The trombones and basses

take the second part of the motive from the *Adagio* (B major)

the next following piano figure

is none other than the bringing back of the motive, which was given in the *Adagio* by the flute and clarinet,

so also the closing passage a variant and intensification in major of the motive of the Scherzo

until finally the first motive

on the pedal of the dominant Bf accompanied by trill figuration

appears and the whole is concluded.[64]

In addition, Liszt reserved one theme for restatement at the conclusion of the work, and, as in the Concerto, op. posth., this theme too is based on the opening motive (see Example 11.12).

Example 11.12
Liszt, Concerto no. 1 in E♭ Major, mm. 61–63

Concerto no. 2 in A major

Liszt's two published concertos represent a remarkable contrast in character, with the E♭ major being "dionysian," while the A major is more "apollonian." The differences go much deeper, however: whereas Concerto no. 1 has four main sections, Concerto no. 2 is more episodic, more fantasia-like, changing mood with greater frequency. The binding factors are again thematic use, including the development and transformation of the opening (see Example 11.13). This theme returns many times throughout the Concerto, most remarkably in its transformation as a march, recalling a similar use in *De profundis* (see Example 11.14). There is also a more subtle use of thematic transformation, as can be seen by comparing the theme first heard in B♭ minor with its return in E major some fifty measures later (see Examples 11.15 and 11.16). It is this theme that is reserved for restatement in A major in the final measures of the work.

Example 11.13
Liszt, Concerto no. 2 in A major, mm. 1–7

Example 11.14
Liszt, Concerto no. 2 in A major, mm. 408–411

Example 11.15
Liszt, Concerto no. 2 in A major, mm. 140–144

Example 11.16
Liszt, Concerto no. 2 in A major, mm. 200–202

THE ROME YEARS

Following his move to Rome in October 1861, Liszt continued to revise for publication works that lay in his portfolio from the Weimar years. Bülow may have initiated a correspondence regarding *Capriccio alla Turca sur des motifs de Beethoven* and the *Hungarian Rhapsody* (his letter is lost), and Liszt wrote to him on the subject in Autumn 1863, asking him to write the orchestral reduction for a second piano in both works.[65] The *Hungarian Rhapsody* appeared the following year in two-piano score as well as full score; the reduction was indeed by Bülow and the work was dedicated to him. This edition also contains the first use of the title, *Fantasie über ungarische Volksmelodieen* [sic]. It was Liszt himself who prepared the Beethoven transcription for publication, writing not only a two-piano score but a version for solo piano, all appearing in 1865. He also decided on a new title, to make a clear distinction between the older para-phrase and these new publications, and the work appeared as *Fantasie über Motiven aus Beethovens Ruinen von Athen.*[66]

Bülow was also involved with the publication of Liszt's final work for piano and orchestra. He urged Liszt to issue *Totentanz,* and in a letter of 12 November 1864, Liszt responded to Bülow's request:

With regard to *Totentanz,* I am unable to make up my mind whether to have it appear before you have heard it played. Permit me, then, very dear friend, a postponement that will not last longer than six months, I hope. You will tell me then explicitly if you believe that I can risk publishing such a monstrosity, and in the meantime please thank Siegel for his courageous intentions.[67]

He apparently began thinking about the work within a few days, for on 26 November he wrote Bülow that he had written the publisher to arrange not only for publication in full score, but also a version for piano solo.[68] The work appeared the following year with a dedication to Bülow, who was also the soloist at the premiere on 15 April 1865.

Totentanz

With *Totentanz*, we return to the program realm that so much of Liszt's music occupies, but while there is no doubt of a "dance of death," the debate over the inspiration of the work goes back to Liszt's lifetime. Richard Pohl wrote the program note for the premiere, and he dwelt at length on a series of woodcuts by Hans Holbein, *Der Todtentanz*, even to the point of assigning specific images to some of the variations.[69] This information must have come from Liszt himself, as Pohl had been a member of the composer's intimate circle since the 1850s, and it is further confirmed by an oblique reference in a letter to Bülow: "The idea of giving the first exhibition of *Totentanz* in Basel is extremely well advised. If it is a fiasco, we will blame it on Holbein, who has corrupted the taste of the public."[70] But in a conversation with Lina Ramann that took place in 1886, Liszt contradicted this idea. She recounted the occasion shortly afterwards:

Siloti rehearsed *Totentanz*—which he was to play today in the second concert. Again I sat near Liszt. His remarks made the work clearer to me. The program (by R. Pohl) named Holbein as the point of departure.

"Where did you come upon Holbein? In Chur?," I asked.

"Not at all!—Pisa—," he answered laconically—"I don't know how Pohl came by his idea. In Italy I saw many such pictures. One in Pisa captivated me—*Dies irae* always lay near me."

"Freiburger Cathedral 1836," I interrupted.

"There I improvised on that theme on the organ."—"Do you see these little cupids?"—he suddenly continued—(Siloti played with wonderful grace the first variation), "you will find them in Pisa in the work of Orcagna."[71]

When Ramann came to write about the work in her biography of Liszt, she made the connection explicit:

One has mistakenly named Hans Holbein the younger's "Todtentanz" as the work which had inspired the master to a musical response and searched from this the meaning of his variations. To me alone personally did he give the communication that it was not Holbein's work but rather the well known mural found in the hall of the Campo Santo in Pisa: "The Triumph of Death" by the Florentine Andrea Orcagna—the father of all "Totentänze"—the stimulus of our master for his paraphrase.[72]

Ramann's assurance aside, the question of inspiration is a difficult one, and over the long gestation period of *Totentanz*, both art works may have had an influence. But this is all to beg the question of programmatic implication: Liszt as a devout Roman Catholic used the "Dies irae" with full knowledge of its spiritual significance, and when we take into account the inclusion of the "De profundis fauxbourdon" in the versions of 1849 and 1853, there appears to be a deeper level of meaning which remains hidden. Note also that the work was prepared for publication in the months before Liszt took the four minor orders of priesthood.

    Totentanz stands apart from many of his works, being a theme and variations. While variation is at the heart of Liszt's compositional process ("thematic transformation" is, of course, a form of variation), he wrote very few works in this form, mainly in the earlier part of his career. But while Liszt follows the form, he also allows his variations to evolve into development and further interpolates two lengthy cadenzas at important structural points. The theme is indicated in the subtitle to the work: "Paraphrase über Dies irae," the first part of the Sequence from the Requiem Mass. Liszt used a variant that differs from the more familiar version found in the *Liber Usualis,* and a manuscript copy titled "Prose des Morts" found among his papers may have been in front of him as he composed the work (see Example 11.17).[73] Thus the first part of *Totentanz* is based on the "Première Strophe," with an introduction, theme, and five variations, with the fourth and fifth variations quite expanded, and the fifth leading into an extensive cadenza that prepares the next group. For the next variations, Liszt used the "Deuxième Strophe," and though only "variation six" is so indicated in the score, it is clearly followed by six additional variations. Again, the final variation is expanded and leads into a cadenza that brings back the "Première Strophe," which is developed into an exciting conclusion.[74] Pohl may have summed up the work best, when he wrote: "It is no cheerful, entertaining genre painting that is here unrolled, rather a serious, affecting character piece, whose poetic content goes far beyond the boundaries of 'concert variations.' "[75]

    Liszt's interest in the concerto genre continued until the end of his life. At some point in 1885, a favorite student of his, Sophie Menter, requested a work for piano and orchestra. Liszt wrote to her on 3 August 1885: "The Sophie Menter Concerto is begun and will be completely written in Itter."[76] He was, of course, quite old by this time, and A. W. Gottschalg noted in his diary for 18 September: "Liszt has begun a new piano concerto for Sophie Menter. It will be completed with difficulty."[77] It is presumed that he completed the concerto during a visit to Itter in mid-October.[78] The work was listed as "Concerto in the Hungarian Style" in a catalog by August Göllerich,[79] and while there is no trace of a composition under this name, it has also been identified with the work for piano and orchestra published under Menter's name as *Hungarian Gypsy Songs.*[80] An anecdotal account states that Menter presented some form of Liszt's score (perhaps a two-piano version) to her friend, Tchaikovsky, with a request to orchestrate it, keeping Liszt's identity a secret as Tchaikovsky did not think highly of Liszt as a composer.[81] Tchaikovsky did, in fact, orchestrate *Hungarian Gypsy Songs,* perhaps in September 1892 when he visited Itter, but without Liszt's manuscript, it is not possible to document this work as Liszt's "Sophie Menter Concerto." It is also not clear why Menter would publish a work by

Liszt under her own name. Nevertheless, the case has been argued on stylistic grounds, and Maurice Hinson has stated, "any pianist who has played much Liszt will have no difficulty in assigning the work to Liszt."[82]

Example 11.17
Liszt, *Prose des Morts*

Prose des Morts

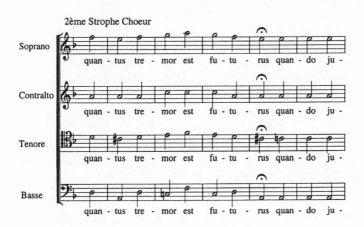

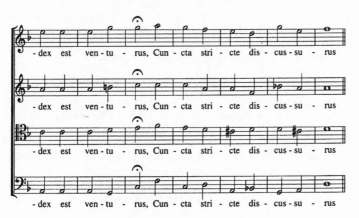

Two months later, Liszt received a transcription of his two-piano *Concerto pathétique*, written by another student, Eduard Reuss. Liszt not only endorsed the transcription, but also made various emendations, both to the orchestration and to the piece itself, adding measures to the beginning and the end.[83] That same month he wrote Breitkopf & Härtel, paving the way for publication,[84] and he was concerned about various details just a month prior to his death.[85]

Liszt turned to the concerto genre at several important junctures in his creative life. Following a fallow period that began shortly after the death of his father,[86] he wrote his first mature works for piano and orchestra, including his first extended work using a "double function" form, *De profundis*. Then on the eve of his *Glanzperiode*, he wrote three works that continued to pursue this idea, including a revision of Concerto no. 1, the first version of Concerto no. 2, and a third concerto, also in E♭ major. Finally, before launching the series of symphonic poems and preceding such works as the *Faust* and *Dante* symphonies and the Sonata in B minor,[87] Liszt prepared six piano and orchestra compositions, refining further his ideas of the "double function" form in new versions of Concertos nos. 1 and 2. Even *Totentanz* may play into this scenario, its final version coming in the months before Liszt took the four minor orders of priesthood. As a genre, the concerto stands midway between the worlds of the soloist and that of the orchestra, and Liszt, himself safely ensconced in one and ready to move into the other, perceived this genre as the best medium to try out his most advanced musical thoughts.

NOTES

1. The evidence for two of these works is found in a letter of 14 August 1825 from Adam Liszt (Liszt's father) to Carl Czerny; see La Mara [Marie Lipsius], *Klassisches und Romantisches aus der Tonwelt* (Leipzig: Breitkopf & Härtel, 1892), 260. Ignaz Moscheles mentions in a diary entry from June 1827 a Concerto in A minor that he heard Liszt play in London, but it is unclear whether this work is one of the concertos from 1825 or a third concerto; see Ignaz Moscheles, *Recent Music and Musicians: As Described in the Diaries and Correspondence,* edited by his wife and adapted from the original German by A. D. Coleridge (New York: Henry Holt & Co., 1875), 94. These documents are further discussed in Jay Rosenblatt, "The Concerto as Crucible: Franz Liszt's Early Works for Piano and Orchestra" (Ph.D. diss., University of Chicago, 1995), 168–172.

2. The early version of Concerto no. 1 will be discussed below in the context of the final version.

3. While there is no documented contact between Liszt and Mendelssohn at this time, Mendelssohn was in Paris in 1832, and both of these works were published by 1833. As for Weber, Liszt's admiration for this composer is well known, and his Konzertstück was in Liszt's repertory as early as his performance of it on 24 November 1833.

4. Table 11.1 is based on worklists of Humphrey Searle and Sharon Winklhofer, "Franz Liszt," in *The New Grove Early Romantic Masters I: Chopin, Schumann, Liszt* (New York: Norton, 1985), and Peter Raabe, "Verzeichniß aller Werke Liszts" in *Franz Liszt,* rev. ed. (Tutzing: Hans Schneider, 1968). The dates under "Composed" differ from these sources and are the result of the present author's research. Note that this table does

not include transcriptions for which no manuscripts survive; for a listing of these works, see Friedrich Schnapp, "Verschollene Kompositionen Franz Liszts," in *Von Deutscher Tonkunst: Festschrift zu Peter Raabes 70. Geburtstag,* ed. Alfred Morgenroth (Leipzig: C. F. Peters, 1942), 119–153.

5. This is the title as inscribed by Liszt on the flyleaf of the only surviving score, although the work is frequently referred to today as the "Lélio Fantasy," after the work by Berlioz on which it is based.

6. Joseph d'Ortigue, "Etudes biographiques: Frantz Listz [sic]," *Gazette musicale de Paris* 2 (14 June 1835): 204.

7. *Correspondance de Liszt et de la Comtesse d'Agoult,* ed. Daniel Ollivier, 2 vols. (Paris: Éditions Bernard Grasset, 1933–1934), 1:124.

8. See *Gazette musicale de Paris* 1 (16 November 1834): 371.

9. See, for example, the concert reviews in *Gazette musicale de Paris* 1 (7 December 1834): 394, and *L'artiste* 8 (1834): 217. In *L'artiste*, the reviewer specifically remarked that the work, though announced, was not performed.

10. "Concerts de M. Listz [sic]: (*Hôtel-de-Ville, salle Saint-Jean*)," *Journal des débats* (25 April 1835): [1].

11. Several secondary sources list the premiere as 24 November 1834, an error that can be traced back to Emile Haraszti in his "Le problème Liszt," *Acta Musicologica* 9 (1937): 127. See also Humphrey Searle in the *Grove Dictionary of Music and Musicians* (1980); Peter Raabe, *Franz Liszt,* 2 vols., second enlarged ed. (Tutzing: Hans Schneider, 1968), 2:20 (Zusätze); introduction to Franz Liszt, *Grande Fantaisie symphonique über Themen aus Hector Berlioz' "Lélio" (Lelio-Fantaisie) für Klavier und Orchester,* ed. Reiner Zimmermann (Leipzig: Breitkopf & Härtel, 1981).

12. This description is based on the work as published in 1833. When Berlioz revised it, he deleted one strophe, altered the others, and added a reference to the *idée fixe* from the *Symphonie fantastique.*

13. Liszt appears to have used the term "symphonique" to indicate a work in one continuous movement. When he requested his manuscript of *De profundis,* he described it as "un autre concerto symphonique," and he used the title "concerto symphonique" in the manuscripts of Concerto nos. 1 and 2 from 1849.

14. This device was first observed by Ralph Locke in his review of the edition by Zimmermann; see *Notes: The Quarterly Journal of the Music Library Association* 41 (1984): 384.

15. See Raabe, *Franz Liszt,* 2:311, and Searle, *The Music of Liszt,* 2d rev. ed. (New York: Dover, 1966), 10. Searle's one piece of evidence is based on a misunderstanding of Liszt's use of the French word "bon"; see Rosenblatt, "The Concerto as Crucible," 156–157.

16. Robert Collet, "Works for Piano and Orchestra," in *Franz Liszt: The Man and His Music,* ed. Alan Walker (London: Barrie & Jenkins, 1970), 251.

17. *Gazette musicale de Paris* 2 (12 April 1835): 131 (review of the first performance).

18. This comment was made by Joachim Raff, Liszt's amanuensis from 1849 to 1856, in a letter of December 1849; see Helene Raff, "Franz Liszt und Joachim Raff im Spiegel ihrer Briefe," *Die Musik* 1 (1901–1902): 390.

19. The issue of Liszt and orchestration is discussed at length in Rosenblatt, "The Concerto as Crucible," 127–160 ("Who Orchestrated Liszt's Works?").

20. *Franz Liszt's Briefe,* ed. La Mara [Marie Lipsius], 8 vols. (Leipzig: Breitkopf & Härtel, 1893–1904), 1:12.

21. This question is discussed in Rosenblatt, "The Concerto as Crucible," 448–450. There are presently three editions of the work: Joseph Ács (Eschweiler: Edition Joseph

Ács, 1989), Michael Maxwell (unpublished), and Rosenblatt (unpublished). The unpublished scores have been recorded, Maxwell's by pianist Philip Thomson with the Hungarian State Orchestra conducted by Kerry Stratton (Hungaroton, HCD 31525, 1991), and Rosenblatt's by pianist Steven Mayer with the London Symphony Orchestra conducted by Tamás Vásáry (ASV, CD DCA 778, 1991) and Leslie Howard with the Budapest Symphony Orchestra conducted by Karl Anton Rickenbacher (Hyperion 67403/4, 1998).

22. The term "double function" was first used by William S. Newman in his discussion of the Sonata in *The Sonata Since Beethoven* (Chapel Hill: University of North Carolina Press, 1969), 371–378.

23. Franz Liszt, *An Artist's Journey: Lettres d'un bachelier ès musique, 1835–1841*, ed. and trans. Charles Suttoni (Chicago: University of Chicago Press, 1989), 236–237. A discussion of Lameness' thought can be found in the Introduction, xix–xxi.

24. *Malédiction* first appeared as part of MW, i/13.

25. See for example Raabe, *Franz Liszt*, 2:54–55.

26. See Winklhofer, Review of "Liszt, Franz [Ferenc]" in *The New Grove Dictionary of Music and Musicians, 19th-Century Music* 5 (Spring 1982): 260.

27. On the complex question of the work's date, see Rosenblatt, "The Concerto as Crucible," 294–313.

28. Searle observes: "Mephistopheles takes possession, as it were, of Faust, whose leading themes now appear distorted and cruelly misshapen." "The Orchestral Works" in *Franz Liszt: The Man and his Music,* 308.

29. Letter of 28 July 1835, first published in a mutilated German translation in *Franz Liszts Briefe an seine Mutter*, ed. La Mara [Marie Lipsius] (Leipzig: Breitkopf & Härtel, 1918), 19–22. A complete transcription in French with annotations can be found in Rosenblatt, "The Concerto as Crucible," 426–433. There has been some debate over the precise identification of the items in Liszt's letter; compare Friedrich Schnapp, "Verschollene Kompositionen von Franz Liszt," in *Von Deutscher Tonkunst: Festschrift zu Peter Raabes 70. Geburtstag,* ed. Alfred Morgenroth (Leipzig: C. F. Peters, 1942), 124–127; Rena Mueller, "Liszt's Catalogues and Inventories of His Works," *Studia Musicologica* 34 (1992): 231–232; Rosenblatt, "The Concerto as Crucible," 214–219.

30. See Dario Simoni, *Un soggiorno di Francesco Liszt a San Rossore* (Pisa: Nistri-Lischi, [1936]), 12; also Walker, *Franz Liszt: The Virtuoso Years, 1811–1847,* rev. ed. (Ithaca: Cornell University Press, 1987), 1:269.

31. See Jacques Vier, *Franz Liszt: L'artiste—Le clerc* (Paris: Les Éditions du Cèdre, 1951), 55 (letter of 28 August 1839, to Lambert Massart). The impetus for these tours is often explained as part of Liszt's very public response to the desire of the Beethoven Committee in Bonn to erect a statue, but this was only a convenient explanation for a decision he had made months earlier.

32. These arrangements will be discussed in Chapter 12. Aspects of the manuscripts, including paper types and handwriting, are discussed in Rosenblatt, "The Concerto as Crucible," 112–114. The Concerto in E♭ major was first published in 1989 by Editio Musica Budapest.

33. Unpublished letter, Bayreuth, Richard Wagner Museum (II C b–103); see also *Briefe an seine Mutter,* 29.

34. Despite the title, only twelve études were published. They become the *Études d'exécution transcendante* only in Liszt's final revision, published in 1851.

35. This process of derivation is explored in Rosenblatt, "Old Wine into New Wineskins: Franz Liszt's Concerto in E-flat major, Op. Posth.," *Pendragon Review* 1 (2000). Note that it is as a result of basing his Concerto on a theme from the *Allegro di*

bravura, a work that begins in E♭ minor, that Liszt came to write two Concertos in E♭ major in the 1830s.

36. See the review in the *Allgemeine musikalische Zeitung* (1 April 1840): column 299.

37. All of the known reviews are summarized, including extensive quotations, in Rosenblatt, "The Concerto as Crucible," 275–288. I am grateful to Geraldine Keeling for supplying copies of the more obscure periodicals, based on her research of Liszt's concerts.

38. "Concerts de M. Listz [sic]," *Journal des débats* (25 April 1835): 2. The article is signed "H***," Berlioz's usual designation until 20 June 1837, at which point he signed his own name.

39. Raymond de Saint-Félix, "Concerts Listz [sic] et Berlioz," *L'artiste* 12 (1836): 295.

40. "Concert de M. Liszt: au bénéfice d'une famille pauvre," *Revue musicale* 9 (12 April 1835): 116.

41. "Paris im Januar 1837," *Caecilla* 19 (1837): 128.

42. *Franz Liszt: Briefe aus ungarischen Sammlungen 1835–1886,* ed. Margit Prahács (Kassel: Bärenreiter, 1966), 66 (to Franz Croll).

43. Hans von Bülow, *Briefe und Schriften,* ed. Marie von Bülow, 2d ed. (Leipzig: Breitkopf & Härtel, 1899–1907), 1:180. See also Liszt's letter of 12 July 1849 to Lambert Massart, where he also mentions *Totentanz*; see Vier, *Franz Liszt: L'artiste—Le clerc,* 94.

44. "Franz Liszt und Joachim Raff im Spiegel ihrer Briefe," 287.

45. The last two works were published under the titles: *Fantasie über Motiven aus Beethovens Ruinen von Athen* and *Fantasie über ungarische Volksmelodien.* The source for the *Hungarian Rhapsody* was no. 21 in his first series of these works, later revised as no. 14 in the second series. See "Orchestral Transcriptions" for further discussion.

46. See also Mueller's discussion of this manuscript complex, "Liszt's 'Tasso' Sketchbook: Studies in Sources and Revisions" (Ph.D. diss., New York University, 1986), 159–163.

47. See "Franz Liszt und Joachim Raff im Spiegel ihrer Briefe," 291.

48. See ibid., 397.

49. Also known as the *Grosses Concert-Solo,* this was a work originally written in 1849 for a piano competition at the Paris Conservatoire. Liszt's arrangement remains unpublished.

50. See *Franz Liszt's Briefe,* 4:87.

51. See Bülow, *Briefe und Schriften,* 1:501.

52. *Briefwechsel zwischen Franz Liszt und Hans von Bülow,* ed. La Mara [Marie Lipsius] (Leipzig: Breitkopf & Härtel, 1898), 21.

53. *Franz Liszt's Briefe,* 3:46–47 (22 September 1855).

54. *Briefwechsel Liszt-Bülow,* 172–173 (14 March 1856).

55. See *Franz Liszt's Briefe,* 4:336 (15 September 1856).

56. *Franz Liszt's Briefe,* 8:129. La Mara dated this letter between 12 January and 15 March, but a more precise date can be ascertained by referring to *Briefwechsel Liszt-Bülow,* 193 (30 January [1857]). Note that the work appeared simultaneously in two editions, full score and two-piano, the orchestral part arranged for a second piano by Liszt himself. The two-piano score was apparently a novel idea for its time; see *Briefwechsel Liszt-Bülow,* 322–323 (12 November 1864).

57. Unpublished letter in the Goethe- und Schiller-Archiv (MS 58/5), 14 January 1857. Bronsart had dedicated to Liszt a trio for piano, violin, and cello.

58. Unpublished letter in the Goethe- und Schiller-Archiv (MS 58/8), 23 March 1857.

59. Unpublished letters in the Goethe- und Schiller-Archiv (MS 58/8, 16, 17), 23 March, 11 September, 5 October 1857.

60. *Franz Liszt's Briefe*, 4:409 (11 March 1858).

61. *Franz Liszt's Briefe*, 5:122.

62. Robert Bory, "Diverses lettres inédites de Liszt," *Schweizerisches Jahrbuch für Musikwissenschaft* 3 (1928): 10 (12 December 1832, to his student, Valérie Boissier).

63. Note, however, that Liszt had given the triangle a prominent role in the *Grande fantaisie symphonique*.

64. *Franz Liszt's Briefe*, 1:273–274; also Lina Ramann, *Franz Liszt als Künstler und Mensch*, 3 vols. (Berlin: Breitkopf & Härtel, 1880–1894), 3:337–338 (to his uncle, Eduard Liszt); corrected after comparison with the original in the Pierpont Morgan Library, New York (Koch 1057).

65. See *Briefwechsel Liszt-Bülow*, 318, also quoted in "Orchestral Transcriptions."

66. See *Briefwechsel Liszt-Bülow*, 323.

67. Ibid. The Leipzig publisher C. F. W. Siegel published both *Totentanz* and *Fantasie über Motiven aus Beethovens Ruinen von Athen*.

68. Ibid., 324–325.

69. See Richard Pohl, "Liszts symphonische Dichtungen: Ihre Entstehung, Wirkung und Gegnerschaft," in *Franz Liszt: Studien und Erinnerungen, Gesammelte Schriften über Musik und Musiker* 2 (Leipzig: Bernhard Schlicke [Bathasar Elischer], 1883), 401–402; also the review by J. von Arnold, "Concertmusik: Franz Liszt, 'Todtentanz,' " *Neue Zeitschrift für Musik* 61 (6 October 1865): 353–355.

70. *Briefwechsel Liszt-Bülow*, 327 (9 December 1864). Actually, Bülow gave the first performance in The Hague.

71. Lina Ramann, *Lisztiana: Erinnerungen an Franz Liszt in Tagebuchblättern, Briefen und Dokumenten aus den Jahren 1873–1886/87*, ed. Arthur Seidl, rev. Friedrich Schnapp (Mainz and New York: B. Schott's Söhne, 1983), 331. Alexander Siloti was a noted Russian pianist who at this time was participating in Liszt's masterclasses.

72. Ramann, *Franz Liszt als Künstler und Mensch*, 3:343. The fresco has since been attributed to Francesco Traini.

73. This manuscript is in the Goethe- und Schiller-Archiv (Z18, no. 9) and contains six strophes, of which only the first two are reproduced here. Mueller has identified the hand as that of the Princess Wittgenstein; see "Liszt's 'Tasso' Sketchbook," 363.

74. An earlier version of *Totentanz* was published by Ferruccio Busoni (Leipzig: Breitkopf & Härtel, 1919). Here the "De profundis fauxbourdon" is given its own (brief) set of variations, inserted before the coda, and in the coda Liszt contrapuntally combines the "De profundis" and "Dies irae" melodies. In this context, it should be noted that Busoni misinterpreted the manuscript evidence, and though the title page states that it is the 1849 version, it is, in fact, the version from 1853.

75. Pohl, "Liszts symphonische Dichtungen," 402.

76. Margit Prahács, "Liszts letztes Klavierkonzert," *Studia Musicologica* 4 (1963): 195; also *Briefe aus ungarischen Sammlungen 1835–1886*, 447. See also Ramann, *Franz Liszt als Künstler und Mensch*, 3:342, n. 5. Itter was Menter's country seat in Tyrol.

77. A. W. Gottschalg, *Franz Liszt in Weimar und seine letzten Lebensjahre*, ed. Carl Alfred René (Berlin: Arthur Glaue, 1910), 155.

78. See Prahács, "Liszts letztes Klavierkonzert," 198; also *Briefe aus ungarischen Sammlungen 1835–1886*, 285 (letter of 25 September 1885, to Menter).

79. See August Göllerich, *Franz Liszt* (Berlin: Marquardt & Co., 1908), 281. See also Raabe, *Franz Liszt,* 363, where Göllerich is quoted as explicitly making the identification.

80. See Maurice Hinson, "The Long Lost Liszt Concerto," *JALS* 13 (June 1983): 53–58.

81. See ibid., 57–58.

82. Ibid., 54.

83. See *Franz Liszt's Briefe*, 2:383 (4 November 1885), also quoted in "Orchestral Transcriptions."

84. See ibid., 384–385 (November 1885).

85. See ibid., 396 (22 June 1886, to Reuss). Liszt's involvement in this edition has been debated, as he received no credit on the title page. These letters make clear, however, that the changes from the two-piano version belong to him.

86. A frank letter to Moscheles summarized the situation: "I know that these four or five years, which have slipped away between my childhood career and the beginning of my maturity (from 1829 to 1833 or 34), have been unfortunate in many respects." *Franz Liszt in seinen Briefen*, ed. Hans Rudolf Jung (Berlin: Henschelverlag, 1987), 64 (28 December 1837, in German translation). The complete letter can be found in the original French in Rosenblatt, "The Concerto as Crucible," 438–441.

87. This statement must be qualified, as two of the symphonic poems existed in earlier versions that Liszt considered concert overtures. For *Tasso, lamento e trionfo* (Symphonic Poem no. 2), see Mueller, "Liszt's 'Tasso' Sketchbook," 278–303. On the complicated history of *Les préludes* (Symphonic Poem no. 3), see Andrew Bonner, "Liszt's *Les Préludes* and *Les Quatre Élémens*: A Reinvestigation," *19th-Century Music* 10 (Fall 1986): 96–101.

12

Orchestral Transcriptions

Jay Rosenblatt

Liszt's orchestral transcriptions serve much the same purpose as his transcriptions in other mediums. Following his piano solo arrangements of songs and instrumental music, the earliest of his orchestral transcriptions were written for piano and orchestra as vehicles for himself or his students. Later transcriptions take works originally meant for the drawing room, such as songs and piano pieces, and bring them into the concert hall. Again the intention is similar to that of his piano transcriptions. Such arrangements helped promote composers whose works might not otherwise be heard in such surroundings (certainly true of Schubert in 1860) and also took advantage of the rise of the symphony orchestra and the concert season as we understand it today. That this change took place during Liszt's lifetime underscores the sharp divide between the virtuoso arrangements (all written before 1851) and the song and orchestral transcriptions (beginning in 1857). As a result, the orchestral transcriptions differ from genres such as Liszt's piano music, where his entire development can be viewed. These transcriptions can best be examined as a complement to his compositions in other areas, particularly the concerto and the great orchestral works of the Weimar years (see Tables 12.1–2).[1]

GLANZPERIODE

In the weeks leading up to his first concert tour, Liszt and the Countess Marie d'Agoult rented a house on the "Gombo" estate in San Rossore,[2] where he prepared a repertory of pieces for piano and orchestra that he could play in concert.[3] Thus in addition to three concertos, Liszt wrote his first orchestral transcriptions, arrangements for piano and orchestra of his *Réminiscences des Puritains* and *Hexaméron*.[4] Both of these works were originally for piano solo

Table 12.1
Franz Liszt, Orchestral transcriptions of his own works

Arranged	Published	Composition
Piano and Orchestra		
1839		*Hexaméron* (from S 392).
1849	1864	*Fantasie über ungarische Volksmelodien* (from S 242/21). S 123.
1849	1865	*Fantasie über Motive aus Beethoven's Ruinen von Athen* (from S 388). S 122.
1850		*Grand solo de concert* (from S 176). S 365.
Voice and Orchestra		
1860	1863	*Mignon* (from S 275/3). S 370.
1860	1863	*Die Loreley* (from S 273/2). S 369.
1860	1872	*Die drei Zigeuner* (from S 320). S374.
1850s?	1872	*Drei Lieder aus Schiller's Wilhelm Tell:* 1. *Der Fischerknabe;* 2. *Der Hirt;* 3. *Der Alpenjäger* (from S. 292). S 372.
1858,	1877	*Jeanne d'Arc au bûcher* (from S 293/1) rev.1874. S 373.
1886	1886	*Die Vätergruft* (from S 281). S 371.
Orchestra		
1857–60	1875	*Ungarische Rhapsodien:* no. 1 in F; no. 2 in D; no. 3 in D; no. 4 in D minor; no. 5 in E; No 6, "Pester Karneval" (from S 244/14, 2, 6, 12, 5, 9). S 359.
By 1859	1860	*Festmarsch nach Motiven von E. H. z.* S (from S 522). S 116.
1863	1984	*Deux Légendes* (from S 175). S 354.
c. 1862–63		*A la Chapelle Sixtine* (from S 461). S 360.
c. 1862–63		*Der Papsthymnus* (from S 261). S 361.
1864		*Vexilla regis prodeunt* (from S 185). S 355.
1865	1871	*Rákóczy Marsch* (from S 242, 244). S 117.
1875	1877	"Benedictus," *Hungarian Coronation Mass* (from S 11). S 363.

Table 12.2
Franz Liszt, Transcriptions of other composers'sworks

Piano and Orchestra		
1849	c. 1851–53	Weber: *Polonaise brillante,* op. 72. S 367.
By 1852	c. 1857–58	Schubert: *Grosse Fantasie in C Major,* op. 15. S 366.
Voice and Orchestra		
1860	1863	Vier Lieder von Franz Schubert: 1. *Die junge Nonne;* 2. *Gretchen am Spinnrade;* 3. *Lied der Mignon;* 4. *Erlkönig;* 5, *Der Doppelgänger;* 6. *Abschied.* Published only nos. 1–4. S 375.
1871	1872	Schubert: *Die Allmacht.* S 376.
1883		Korbay: 1. *Le matin* (Bizet); 2. *Gebet* (Geibel). S 368.
1884		Zichy: *Der Zaubersee* (ms. destroyed). S 377.
Orchestra		
1859–60	1870	Schubert: *Märsche:* 1; 2. *Trauer-Marsch;* 3. S. 363.
1865	1868	Bülow: *Mazurka-Fantasie,* op. 13. S. 353.
1873	1873	Béni Egressy and Franz Erkel: *Szózat und Hymnus.* S 353.
1877	1905	Cornelius: 2nd overture to *Der Barbier von Bagdad* (orchestrated from sketches). S 352.
1881		Julius Zarembski: *Danses galiciennes.* S 364.

and fall into the category of operatic paraphrase. They also take themes from the same opera by Vincenzo Bellini, *I puritani,* itself written for Paris and heard for the first time on 24 January 1835. The opera was very successful, and, with Liszt still resident in Paris, it would be surprising if he did not see it performed. *Réminiscences des Puritains* was published in 1837 during the relatively quiet period of his sojourn in Switzerland. It follows the typical format of such paraphrases, treating several selections from the opera and ending with a brilliant setting of the polonaise from the end of Act I. *Hexaméron* came to life under considerably more colorful circumstances. The Princess Cristina Belgiojoso requested variations on "Suoni la tromba" from six of the leading piano virtuosos resident in Paris, with the idea of having each of them play them as part of a charity soirée in her salon. Whatever other pieces were performed on 31 March 1837, this work was not among them, and a letter from the Princess to Liszt of 4 June makes it clear that the composers were slow in producing their contributions.[5] Once Liszt had the variations in hand, he added an Introduction, Finale, and connecting passages to make a substantial work. Unfortunately, there are no surviving score or parts for the piano and orchestra version of *Réminiscences des Puritains,*[6] but an incomplete score of *Hexaméron* exists in the Gesellschaft der Musikfreunde in Vienna. It is presumably this arrangement that was played several times by Liszt, the first performance taking place in Vienna on 31 March 1840.[7]

Hexaméron

The title pages of the earliest editions of the piano solo version include "Hexaméron" at the top, followed by "Morceau de Concert" and "Grandes Variations de Bravoure," with each phrase describing a different facet of the work.[8] "Hexaméron" is the biblical six days of creation, here referring to the six pianists who contributed to the work, the "concert piece" considers the substance, twenty minutes in duration and requiring great virtuosity, and the "variations," the general structure, although Liszt's contributions bring it closer to an operatic paraphrase. The lengthy introduction and statement of the theme are by Liszt and take up 98 measures of a total of 450, which indicates the size of his contribution (see Table 12.3). Sigismond Thalberg is given first place, and his variation is quite brilliant, while at the same time following the theme closely. Liszt gives himself second position, and he has created a great contrast, not only in a slower tempo, but also in the freedom with which he treats the theme, both harmonically and melodically. Next is the variation of Johann Peter Pixis, again bravura, and before preceding to a variation of similar brilliance by Henri Herz, Liszt inserts a brief *ritornello.* Carl Czerny comes next, but as his variation is about to conclude, Liszt cuts short his former teacher and inserts a connecting passage that modulates to E Major (the rest of the work is in A♭ major), followed by the *Largo* variation of Frédéric Chopin. With all participants having had their say, Liszt adds a transition back to A♭ major and a lengthy "Finale," largely of original material, although he quotes briefly from the variations of Thalberg and Herz and extensively from the variation of Pixis at the *Allegro animato* (m. 392).

Table 12. 3
Organization of *Hexaméron*

(measures):	1–66	67–98	99–122	123–158	159–185
Piano solo version:	Introduction	Theme	Var. I (Thalberg)	Var. II (Liszt)	Var. III (Pixis)
Orchestral score:	Introduction	Theme	Var. I (Thalberg)	Var. II (Liszt)	(omitted)

(measures):	186–195	196–219	220–250	251–289	290–306
Piano solo version:	*Ritornello*	Var. IV (Herz)	Var. V (Czerny)	*Fuocoso molto energico*	Var. VI (Chopin)
Orchestral score:	(omitted)	Var. III (Herz)	(omitted)	(omitted)	(omitted)

(measures):	307–316	317–363	364–391	392–450
Piano solo version:	[transition]	Finale: *Molto vivace quasi prestissimo*	*Tutti*	*Allegro animato*
Orchestral score:	(omitted)	(omitted)	(omitted)	Finale: (159–177 inserted before 392)

Liszt must have decided early in the work's genesis that *Hexaméron* would also be a work for piano and orchestra: there is a *ritornello* in mm. 186–195, presumably to be played by the orchestra and engraved in smaller notes, a *tutti* in mm. 364–391, with an instruction to omit the passage if played without orchestra, and an additional two staves in mm. 406–414 that contain a separate piano part to be played "avec accompagnement d'Orchestre."[9] Nevertheless, he may not have prepared his arrangement by the time of publication: few instrumental indications are found in the published version, and the only surviving orchestral score severely abridges the work, omitting the *ritornello* and *tutti* passages as well as a few of the variations. This observation leads to the question of whether the arrangement is Liszt's. A copyist wrote the score, and perhaps for this reason Peter Raabe was of the opinion that it was "probably not by Liszt."[10] Raabe's prejudice against the idea that Liszt could capably orchestrate in the 1830s is apparent in other entries in his catalog of works, but it is not based on any evidence.[11] On the contrary, when we compare the orchestration to the three concertos of 1839, for which there are autograph scores, we find many similarities in approach and note that the instrumentation is identical to the Concerto in E♭ major, op. posth., including the use of a *trompette à clefs.* At the time, the keyed trumpet was increasingly being replaced by the valve trumpet, except in Italy, and it was an exceptional choice for any composer. In short, there is little reason to reject Liszt as orchestrator, and the use of this particular trumpet ties the work to the other concerto.

As noted, the version of *Hexaméron* in the orchestral manuscript is abridged. Following the variation by Liszt, the score jumps to the one by Herz, and from there to the *Allegro animato,* expanded to a complete statement of the Pixis variation, which in this context is now heard for the first time (see Table 12.3). Apparently the copyist had trouble following one aspect of Liszt's thought. After underlaying the original piano version on the lowest staves of the score (except for Thalberg's variation, which was intended to be unaccompanied), the copyist began to write Pixis's variation beneath the orchestration for Herz's. He wrote fourteen measures before realizing that it did not work with the orchestral parts and left the piano lines blank for the remainder of the piece. It is a simple matter to envision the copyist's dilemma: Liszt must have written out his orchestration in score without the piano part and instructed the copyist to take it from the published edition, but he may not have indicated clearly the cuts to the original version.

Why reduce the work? *Hexaméron* in its uncut form lasts more than twenty minutes, which would have been quite long in the context of Liszt's concerts. Liszt seems to have realized this when he performed the work, since the more detailed reviews indicate that he made cuts in the solo version. For example, when Liszt played the work in Vienna on 8 and 14 May 1838, the reviewer noted that the Czerny variation was not heard at the earlier concert.[12] A review of a concert on 31 October 1840 in Hamburg noted the omission of the variations by Pixis, Czerny, and Chopin,[13] precisely the portions missing in the orchestral score. These omitted variations also match a two-piano version that Liszt is known to have played during these years.[14] The piano and orchestra version of *Hexaméron* may have been intended to be a "Konzertstück," a sub-genre of the concerto, usually lasting twelve to fifteen minutes. Such pieces were in one continuous movement, often a slow introduction followed by an *Allegro* in sonata form, although, as Weber's Konzertstück suggests, there was much variety as well. It was especially popular in the 1830s, with examples by Chopin, Mendelssohn, and (later) Schumann, and Liszt's three concertos of 1839 also fall into this category. Thus, whatever Liszt's intention when he composed *Hexaméron,* he considerably shortened the work in his arrangement for piano and orchestra.

EARLY WEIMAR YEARS

Liszt took up the duties of full-time Kapellmeister in Weimar in 1848, and by October 1849 he had prepared six works for piano and orchestra, copied and bound into three volumes.[15] Thus one volume contained new versions of his Concertos nos. 1 and 2, another the earliest version of *Totentanz,* and the third, transcriptions of works originally for piano solo, titled in his own hand: "Capriccio Turc de Beethoven, Polonaise de Weber, Rhapsodie Hongroise."[16]

These transcriptions all had some connection with his *Glanzperiode*: the *Hungarian Rhapsody* was the twenty-first and last of a series prepared during the 1840s; *Capriccio alla turca sur des motifs de Beethoven* was his paraphrase on movements from the incidental music to a play, *Die Ruinen von Athen*, published in 1847; and Weber's Polonaise brillante, op. 72, was a natural successor to his many performances of the same composer's Konzertstück. Liszt continued this series of transcriptions with piano and orchestra versions of his *Grand solo de concert* in 1850 and Schubert's *Wanderer Fantasy* (Fantasy in C major, op. 15) in 1851.[17] Note that Liszt himself was careful to distinguish these works from his "original compositions" and in the thematic catalog published in 1877 characterized them as "Orchestrirungen (mit Pianoforte principale)."[18]

With Liszt's concert career ended, the main purpose for these transcriptions was as vehicles for his growing cortège of students, and performances began to take place in 1851. The Polonaise was performed for the first time on 13 April with Salomon Jadassohn and the Weimar orchestra conducted by Liszt,[19] and the *Wanderer Fantasy* soon followed on 14 December in Vienna, with Count Hardegg (himself a student of Czerny's) and the orchestra of the Gesellschaft der Musikfreunde conducted by Joseph Hellmesberger.[20] Liszt thought highly of his Weber transcription and wrote of it to his friend Theodor Kullack on 15 June 1852:

It is especially with a view to enlarging the concert repertory that I have undertaken my bit of work and for the progress that I have made in [the art of] orchestration. . . . You will see that I have done my best to serve the few pianists (the number is exceedingly restricted, I know), who would be eager to play at their concerts pieces that make a distinguished impression. Perhaps you would do me the honor and the favor to attempt this Polonaise one time in public, and in that case the success of it would be brilliantly assured.[21]

Liszt encouraged Kullack to bring it to the attention of the Berlin publisher A. M. Schlesinger, and he included a list of precise engraving instructions. Schlesinger published the work soon thereafter, making it Liszt's first composition with orchestra to be widely available. It was dedicated to the pianist, Adolf Henselt.

It was Hans von Bülow who provided the impetus for revisions to the *Capriccio alla turca* and the *Hungarian Rhapsody*. Bülow had been Liszt's student since 1851, and within two years he was preparing for his first concert tour. For the task, Liszt returned to his bound volume of transcriptions, and he had new versions ready by January 1853.[22] Bülow left around May, and the first performance of both works took place in Budapest on 1 June with Ferenc Erkel conducting. "It was an unparalleled triumph, according to what everyone says," he wrote to his mother the day after the concert.[23] He also wrote Liszt of the success, who responded on 8 June: "I am delighted that the Hungarian Rhapsody with orchestra did not fail to make its effect. I have the proofs of it (for piano solo) on my desk, and I have just inscribed your name for the dedication . . . . You will gratify and give me pleasure by popularizing these works . . . in

Hungary."[24] Once the tour was completed, however, the transcriptions were allowed to languish. Liszt turned his attention to his original works for piano and orchestra, giving the first performance in 1855 of the Concerto no. 1 (as soloist) and in 1857 of the Concerto no. 2 (as conductor), and arranging for publication of both shortly thereafter. In 1857, he also published his transcription of Schubert's *Wanderer Fantasy*.

Not until his years in Rome did Liszt return to his piano and orchestra transcriptions, and again it was Bülow who played an important role in preparing these works. Liszt wrote him in Autumn 1863:

Cosima will have informed you of my proposition concerning the publication of the two pieces: "Rhapsodie hongroise" and "Caprice turc," with accompaniment of a second piano only, without the orchestral score, but embellished with several indications of the instruments. If indeed you would like to take upon yourself the writing of the accompaniment for the second piano, I would be very much obliged to you.[25]

The *Hungarian Rhapsody* appeared the following year in two-piano score as well as full score; the reduction was indeed by Bülow and the work was dedicated to him. Here we find the title, *Fantasie über ungarische Volksmelodieen* [sic], but it is unclear whether it stems from Liszt. In a thematic catalogue from 1855, the work is listed as *Ungarische Rhapsodie* no. 14, after the revised version in the second cycle of *Hungarian Rhapsodies* for piano solo. There is also a copy of the first edition from Bülow's estate that has the title "FANTASIE" crossed out every time it appears and *Ungarische Rhapsodie* written in crayon, probably by Bülow himself.[26] Perhaps the title was the idea of the publisher.

Liszt also made certain that Bülow was involved with the Beethoven transcription, as a letter of 5 April 1864 to the publisher Haslinger shows:

With regard to the publisher of the *Capriccio alla turca* (on motives from the Ruins of Athens) with orchestral accompaniment I have nothing more to decide. H. von Bülow possesses the manuscript, which I prepared about twelve years ago for his concert use, and [gave] to him, along with other scribbling, as a gift of *music without value*. . . . I request that you come to an understanding over it with Bülow, since the manuscript is his property, and I reserve for myself merely the review of the last proofs.[27]

Nevertheless, Liszt himself wrote the two-piano score as well as a version for piano solo, and they appeared along with the full score in 1865. At this time, the work also gained a new title. In a letter to Bülow dated 12 November 1864, Liszt wrote of his idea to change the name to "Fantasie" to put some distance from the earlier solo work, and he asked Bülow's opinion.[28] Thus it was published as *Fantasie über Motiven aus Beethovens Ruinen von Athen*, with a dedication to the Russian pianist, Nicolas Rubinstein.

Of the work of his Weimar years, the one transcription that Liszt never revised for performance or publication was that of his *Grand solo de concert*. Perhaps the reason is that Joachim Raff, Liszt's amanuensis from 1849 to 1856, had also prepared an orchestration. No score survives of this arrangement, but

Raff noted in a letter of February 1850: "I have orchestrated his Solo and copied it twice."[29] Some of Raff's claims in his letters have been subject to question, however.[30] In this case, his comment seems straightforward enough, but it is odd that he should have undertaken the task around the time of Liszt's own arrangement, and one wonders if he is referring to revisions of Liszt's orchestration. But although the arrangement was forgotten, the piece was not. Published as a piano solo in 1851, Liszt arranged it for two pianos, completing it by 1856, and titling it *Concerto pathétique*. The work became a true concerto in the 1880s, when his student, Eduard Reuss, arranged it for piano and orchestra. Reuss sent Liszt the score, and Liszt responded in a letter of 4 November 1885:

Thanks and praise for your *excellent* orchestral arrangement of the "Concerto pathétique." It seems to me effective, well proportioned, carried out with fine and correct understanding. I had only little things to change: but a few supplements to the original were suitable, in order to give the piano virtuoso his proper place. Thus, in various spots, approximately 50–60 measures in all, that I have appended to your manuscript. Also the beginning should begin 10 measures earlier, and the ending should end 22 measures later.[31]

That same month he wrote Breitkopf & Härtel, paving the way for publication,[32] and he was concerned about various details just a month prior to his death.[33] In a typical gesture, he did not ask for, nor did he receive, credit on the title page for his emendations. As for his own arrangement, the manuscript remains unpublished, although Humphrey Searle prepared a score in 1949 for performance on the BBC, and Leslie Howard has recorded his own edition as part of his survey of Liszt's piano music.[34]

Fantasie über ungarische Volksmelodien

Liszt's attempts to capture the music of Hungary in transcription are centered in his two cycles of *Hungarian Rhapsodies*. The beginnings of the first cycle date from 1840, four volumes containing eleven works for piano solo that he published under the bilingual title *Magyar Dallok—Ungarische Nationale Melodien*. These were followed by a number of other piano works on Hungarian themes, with the cycle resuming only in 1846 with another six works, now under the title *Magyar Rhapsodiák—Rhapsodies hongroises*. Liszt intended to continue the cycle, and there are manuscript copies in the Goethe- und Schiller-Archiv in Weimar with *Ungarischen Rhapsodien*, nos. 18–21, dating from the following year. These last works were never published, perhaps because Liszt had already begun to plan a new cycle of *Hungarian Rhapsodies*: the work later titled *Hungarian Rhapsody* no. 2 was completed by 27 March 1847, and the first two rhapsodies of the second cycle were published by 1851. These two works were newly composed, but for the continuation of the second cycle in 1853 (nos. 3–15), Liszt returned to the publications from the 1840s and reworked the various themes into new compositions. The second cycle represents the *Hungarian Rhapsodies* as we know them today.[35] Despite the abuse these works have taken over the years, Liszt himself had great affection for his *Hungarian Rhapsodies* and revised them for publication in various mediums over the course of several decades.

The *Hungarian Rhapsodies* are similar to Liszt's operatic paraphrases in that he freely adapts several themes to create a new work. Typically, he uses the *verbunkos*, an older dance form that begins in a slower tempo (*lassan*) and ends considerably faster (*friss*).[36] For the *Fantasie über ungarische Volksmelodien* (usually referred to as *Hungarian Fantasy*), Liszt used as a basis no. 21 from the first cycle. There are five themes in this work. Although the work begins in E minor, the same first theme proclaims itself by m. 25 in E major, where it is marked *Allegro eroico* (see Example 12.1). The middle section includes a theme marked *Poco allegro tempo capriccioso* (see Example 12.2), followed by an *Allegretto à la Zingarese* which alternates with another melody (see Examples 12.3 and 12.4). Finally, the concluding section is based on a melody labeled *Koltói Csárdás* in the score (see Example 12.5). The key scheme is worth noting as well: it begins in E minor, moving soon to E major; the *tempo capriccioso* begins in C♯ major, returning to E major; the *Allegretto* is in A minor, and the theme with which it alternates is in F major; the final *csárdás* is also in F major. The lack of a "closed" key structure ultimately was a concern to Liszt, although he would not correct it until the piano solo revision in the second cycle, where the work became *Hungarian Rhapsody* no. 14.

Example 12.1
Liszt, *Hungarian Rhapsody* no. 21 (first cycle), *Allegro eroico*

Example 12.2
Liszt, *Hungarian Rhapsody* no. 21 (first cycle), *Poco allegro tempo capriccioso*

Example 12.3
Liszt, *Hungarian Rhapsody* no. 21 (first cycle), *Allegretto à la Zingarese*

Example 12.4
Liszt, *Hungarian Rhapsody* no. 21 (first cycle), *Allegro vivace*

Example 12.5
Liszt, *Hungarian Rhapsody* no. 21 (first cycle), *Vivace assai*

To prepare his transcription for piano and orchestra, Liszt wrote out an orchestral score (without a piano part), indicated a few emendations in the manuscript copy of the piano version,[37] and instructed August Conradi, his regular copyist at this time, to prepare a new score which combined all the parts. This version is faithful to the original version for piano solo with two important distinctions: Liszt appears to have omitted the *tempo capriccioso* section,[38] and he inserted two reprises of the *Allegro eroico* theme, first prior to the *csárdás*, where it is heard in D♭ major, and then before the coda, where it is heard in E major and F major. The return of this theme is an attempt to unify the work on two levels. First, the cyclic nature of repeating a theme in a later section adds thematic unity. For the second, the return of the *Allegro eroico* before the coda is heard in each of the two keys that are the pillars of the work, which is an attempt to provide tonal unity.

Liszt returned to his arrangement, presumably at Bülow's request, and revised the score, completing it by January 1853. It was at this time that he inserted a new episode, which he derived from the opening of *Hungarian Rhapsody* no. 10 from the first cycle (see Example 12.6). He provides a foretaste of the theme in a brief piano cadenza, inserted at the beginning of the piece (m. 17). From there, it takes the place of the *tempo capriccioso* (which is omitted entirely), beginning with a longer cadenza marked *Molto adagio, quasi fantasia* (m. 104). He also uses the new theme in a short passage following the first restatement of the *Allegro eroico* theme (m. 236), and he uses its opening motive as counterpoint in the *Allegretto à la Zingarese* section (beginning at m. 188) and in the closing *csárdás* (m. 348), thus creating a thematic unity that runs the entire course of the piece.

Example 12.6
Liszt, *Hungarian Rhapsody* no. 10 (first cycle), *Adagio sostenuto a capriccio*

With these changes in mind, it is interesting to compare the revision of the *Hungarian Fantasy* with the revision of the piano solo version, especially as Liszt was preparing nos. 3–15 of his second cycle of *Hungarian Rhapsodies* at about the same time. He indicated in a letter of 16 April 1852 that he planned to publish a "rather thick volume" of these works the following winter,[39] and we know from his letter to Bülow (quoted above) that he was correcting proofs in June 1853. Thus work may have overlapped on the new version of the *Hungarian Fantasy* and *Hungarian Rhapsody* no. 14. Liszt appears to have based the Rhapsody on the version from the first cycle, while at the same time borrowing a few ideas from the piano and orchestra version. The result is a mixed line of descent, as shown in Figure 12.1. Thus in *Hungarian Rhapsody* no. 14, he retained the *tempo capriccioso* section from the earlier solo version but included the restatements of the *Allegro eroico* theme from the Fantasy. In addition, he transposed the entire opening section up a half step, to F minor and F major, thus providing the tonal unity lacking in the earlier versions. Why did he not bring the two works into agreement with each other? Certainly the new theme added to the *Hungarian Fantasy* maintains the mood of the work, which would have been disrupted by the lightheartedness of the omitted *tempo capriccioso*. Or perhaps the new theme lent itself better to a piano cadenza, something not necessary in a solo version. Whatever the explanation, the different versions of this *Hungarian Rhapsody* underline Liszt's flexible attitude toward his own compositions.

Figure 12.1
Stemma for *Hungarian Fantasy*

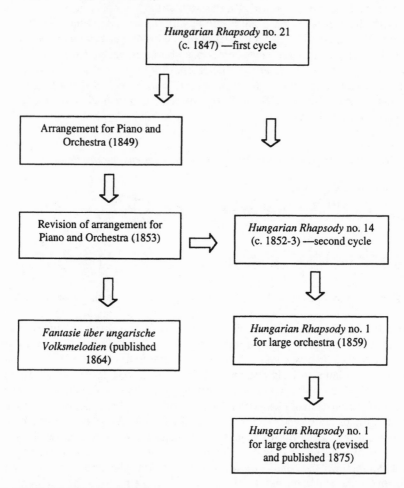

LATER WEIMAR YEARS

With many of his major works through the press, including the symphonies, symphonic poems, and piano cycles, Liszt turned his attention to orchestral transcription. Such activity had not been of interest to him before this point, outside of the piano and orchestra transcriptions and some earlier abortive attempts. One is tempted to assign the inspiration to the receipt of Franz Doppler's transcriptions of six *Hungarian Rhapsodies*. The first of these is dated February 1857 (no. 2 in C♯ minor, transposed to D minor), and others are dated from 1859 and 1860. Clearly the idea of transferring a work written for the piano to the orchestra began to appeal to him, and around this time Liszt orchestrated a *Festmarsch nach Motiven von E. H. z. S.,* first performed at a concert conducted by Bülow in December 1859.[40] Therefore, when Johann Herbeck, conductor of the Vienna Philharmonic concerts and supporter of Liszt's music, requested transcriptions of Schubert's marches, Liszt was happy to oblige. According to his letter of 28 December 1859, Liszt planned to send Herbeck the scores of the first two marches the next day: "It is to be hoped that Herbeck will be pleased with the orchestration of the Schubert marches. This small task is, in my opinion, quite well done, and I will resume [my work on] them, as they offer much that is attractive to me. Soon will follow the four other marches, which will make a full half dozen."[41] Within a month he had prepared another two, a *Trauermarsch* in E♭ major and a *Hungarian March* in C minor, "which can be played one after the other."[42]

Once stimulated, Liszt produced an outpouring of additional transcriptions the following December: "Besides, my orchestration of the *Reitermarsch* of Schubert having been a success—I have decided to orchestrate a half dozen *Lieder* of Schubert, as well as three of my own: *Mignon, Loreley* and the *drei Zigeuner.*"[43] The next day he wrote to the publisher C. F. Kahnt,[44] where he listed the songs of Schubert that he had transcribed: "*Erlkönig, Gretchen, junge Nonne, Doppelgänger, Mignon,* and *Abschied.*"[45] Kahnt was only interested in the transcriptions of his own songs, and the works were in press by the following August.[46] As for the Schubert songs, four were published in 1863. Of the remaining two, the manuscript of *Der Doppelgänger* remains unpublished in the Goethe- und Schiller-Archiv in Weimar, while that of *Abschied* is listed as *nicht auffindbar* in Raabe's worklist.[47] It is perhaps a great irony that Hector Berlioz wrote an arrangement of *Erlkönig,* his only transcription of a Schubert song, in the same year.

Liszt also may have been inspired by the singing of Emilie Genast, daughter of the Weimar actor Eduard Genast and a singer at the Weimar Hofoper. In Bülow's concert in Berlin of 14 January 1859, she performed *Die Loreley* under circumstances which can only be considered hostile.[48] As a result of the backlash from this incident, Liszt himself came to Berlin to participate in a concert of 27 February, where Genast performed songs of Schubert and Liszt's *Mignon.*[49] She also performed his songs at a private gathering on 2 March, including *Die Loreley.*[50] Later that year in Leipzig, she again sang Liszt's songs. "It will be difficult for any of those present ever to forget that performance: Liszt at the piano, and in front of him, interpreting the *Loreley,* Emilie Genast, one of the finest *Lieder* singers of the time!"[51] In gratitude, Liszt dedicated *Die drei Zigeuner* to Genast, writing on the manuscript: "Fräulein Emmy Genast. Ihr ganz devoter Zigeuner F. Liszt."[52] Remembering that all three of his transcribed songs were associated with Genast and that she also sang songs of Schubert (the texts of three of the published transcriptions are suitable only for a woman), it is perhaps not surprising that upon publication, the Schubert songs were dedicated to her (the transcriptions of his own songs were published without dedication). The title page reads "An Frau Emilie Merian-Genast," and, considering that 1863 was also the year she was married, the dedication may have been a wedding gift.

Ungarische Rhapsodien für grosses Orchester

It is unfortunate that many descriptions of these arrangements use the phrase "orchestrated with the assistance of Franz Doppler," as if to imply that Liszt could not have written the transcriptions without him. With such works as the symphonic poems, symphonies, and concertos behind him, this is obviously not the case. Franz Doppler (1821–1883) is best remembered today for his flute compositions, and his active career was mostly as a flutist. Although born in Poland, he established himself in Hungary, beginning as principal flutist at the German Theater in 1838 and moving to the Hungarian National Theater in 1841. He also made a reputation as a composer, with five operas produced between 1847 and 1857. By 1858 he was in Vienna at the Court Opera, again as flutist and later as conductor. Doppler first met Liszt in Weimar while on tour in 1854. Their contact during the following years is unknown, as are the circumstances behind the first transcription in 1857. Liszt had no reason to request such orchestral arrangements, and it is likely that Doppler prepared them on his own initiative, beginning with the most popular, no. 2 in C♯ minor. He made a straightforward transcription of the piano solo version and sent it to Liszt, perhaps for his approval, perhaps to request assistance in having it published. We can assume that Liszt encouraged his efforts, for by 1860 Doppler had produced five additional arrangements.[53] Ultimately these works became a collaborative effort, the published score proclaiming "bearbeitet vom Componisten und F. Doppler." Note also that these transcriptions have their own numbering, somewhat independent of the piano solo versions (see Table 12.4).[54]

Liszt could never keep his hands off his own works. Once he received Doppler's colorful but otherwise faithful transcriptions, he began to see the possibility for changes not only to the orchestration but also to the music itself. The manuscript scores in the Library of Congress are full of such alterations, including many pasted-over passages. Thus, wherever the orchestral version differs substantially from the piano solo version, the alteration can be traced back to Liszt himself. Some of these changes amount to the extension of a phrase (see Examples 12.7 and 12.8), and in the case of the *tempo capriccioso* section in no. 1, Liszt added a few measures from the earlier piano solo version (no. 21 of the first cycle, discussed above). More substantial revisions can be found in the codas to several of the transcriptions, which were rewritten. Also interesting is a comparison with the piano four-hand versions that Liszt published at the same time as the orchestral scores. Although these follow the orchestral versions closely in many respects, in some cases the piano writing returns to that of the piano solo version, in others it becomes a new texture, and in no. 1, we find a new coda, different from all previous versions. In short, the four-hand versions are in some ways yet another reworking of the same material.

Table 12.4
Numbering of *Hungarian Rhapsodies*

Orchestral Transcription (1857–1860)	Piano Solo Version (second cycle, 1851–1853)	Dedication
no. 1 in F Minor	no. 14 in F Minor	Hans von Bülow
no. 2 in D Minor and G Major	no. 2 in C♯ Minor	Count László Teleky
no. 3 in D Major	no. 6 in D♭ Major	Count Anton Apponyi
no. 4 in D Major	no. 12 in C♯ Major	Joseph Joachim
no. 5 in E Major	no. 5 in E Major	Countess Sidonie Reviczky
no. 6 "Pester Karneval"	no. 9 "Pester Karneval"	H. W. Ernst

Example 12.7
Liszt, *Hungarian Rhapsody* no. 3 (orchestral version), mm. 11–14 (in Liszt's own arrangement for piano four hands)

Example 12.8
Liszt, *Hungarian Rhapsody* no. 6 (second cycle), mm. 11–13

Die Loreley

As with all of his transcriptions, when he returned to *Die drei Zigeuner,*
Mignons Lied, and *Die Loreley,* he could not resist the temptation to adjust
certain passages. Liszt transferred some of the virtuosic piano figuration of *Die*
drei Zigeuner to the instrument most identified with the Gypsy, the violin,
rewriting the passages to create brief cadenzas. In the case of *Mignon,* it became
quite a different work, with recognizably the same melody, as can be seen by
comparing the two versions in Raabe's edition.[55] *Die Loreley* shows subtle but
no less significant adjustments by Liszt to his original conception. The earliest
version of the song dates back to 1841, although it was first published in a piano
transcription as part of his *Buch der Lieder* in 1843. A revised version was
published in 1856, and Liszt's orchestral transcription is based on this edition.
Finally, he prepared a new piano transcription, which was published in 1862.
Comparing the three later versions, it is interesting to observe the passages that
Liszt revised. For example, the transition following "gewaltge Melodie," a mere
two measures in 1856, is extended to eight in the orchestral transcription. This
passage apparently gave Liszt much trouble: he treats it differently in the piano
transcription, and Raabe includes these measures as they appear in a later French
edition, where they are again quite different.[56] Also noteworthy are the
concluding measures, where each version is almost a variation of the other (see
Examples 12.9, 12.10, and 12.11). The orchestral version displays the delicate
instrumental effects that Liszt could command by this time: the violas suggest
the gentle waves, accompanied by the violins, *ponticello,* the winds used
sparingly but effectively, and the colorful use of *pizzicato.* In composing this
ending, Liszt appears to have been guided by the orchestral effect he knew he
could achieve and not an abstract musical concept.

Example 12.9
Liszt, *Die Loreley* (piano and voice), conclusion

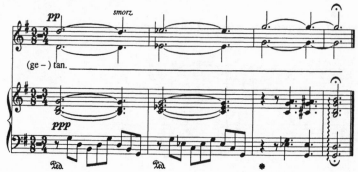

Example 12.10
Liszt, *Die Loreley* (orchestral transcription), conclusion

Example 12.11
Liszt, *Die Loreley* (piano transcription), conclusion

LAST YEARS AND FINAL TRANSCRIPTIONS

In the years that followed the flurry of arrangements in 1859 and 1860, Liszt returned only sporadically to the orchestral transcription. During his time in Rome, he prepared orchestral versions of his *Légendes,* dated 23–29 October 1863 and written at about the same time as the works for piano solo (*San Francesco d'Assisi* and *San Francesco di Paola*).[57] He also wrote transcriptions of two other works with spiritual associations, *A la Chapelle Sixtine*, originally for piano, and *Der Papsthymnus,* originally for organ.[58] Nor did he forget Schubert, and he was able to combine a favorite composer with another religiously-themed work, taking Schubert's song, *Die Allmacht* (D 852), and arranging it for tenor, men's chorus, and orchestra in 1871.[59] Although published in Schubert's lifetime as op. 72, no. 2, it is hardly one of his best-known songs, and one wonders if Herbeck again played a role in the transcription. It is known from a worklist of 1865 that Herbeck possessed Schubert's unfinished manuscript on the same text of a version for chorus.[60] Perhaps Liszt was intrigued by this idea and, rather than complete an unfinished draft, carried the idea of a choral work into an orchestral transcription of Schubert's original song. It was also around this time that Liszt finally issued his transcriptions of the Schubert marches (1870) and the *Hungarian Rhapsodies* (1875).[61]

Liszt also made the occasional transcription to promote the music of those close to him. For Hans von Bülow, Liszt orchestrated the piano piece, *Mazurka-Fantasie,* op. 13, which he completed in November 1865. As he wrote to Bülow: "The orchestration of your *Mazurka-Fantasie* has already given me great pleasure, which is increased again by the pleasure you will receive from it. I must therefore thank you doubly."[62] He also transcribed the *Danses galiciennes* of his student Juliusz Zarembski in 1881.[63] In contrast, Liszt quickly came to regret another task of transcription. As he wrote to the Princess Wittgenstein on 26 April 1883: "The principal obstacle [to not writing sooner] was an absurd willingness to have promised one of my godsons, Francis Korbay, born in Pest, well established in New York, to orchestrate two of his songs, which he intends to sing soon in London. This task didn't appear to me to require more than four or five mornings—mistake! It took more than twice that time to make the thing presentable."[64] From another letter, we learn that he needed to rework the song itself, for a total of more than twenty-five hours labor.[65]

Liszt's final transcription was of one of his own songs, *Die Vätergruft*. He had written it as early as 1844, and in a letter of 7 February 1859, he expressed a desire to orchestrate it.[66] When he finally returned to the song in the last year of his life, it seemed to take on additional meaning. August Stradal was with Liszt at this time: "The last piece on which he worked was the orchestration of the accompaniment to his setting of Uhland's ballad *Die Vätergruft*. Knowing him to be engaged on such a work had a most melancholy effect upon me: the feeling came to me that he himself would now be 'descending to the coffins of his forefathers.' "[67] With an eerie foreboding of Liszt's death, the text concludes: "In a cold spot stood / a coffin yet unfilled / this he took as his bed of rest / for a pillow he took his shield. / He clasped his hands / about his sword and slept / the sound of the spirits fell silent / and all around was still."[68] The new arrangement was performed for the first time during Liszt's visit to England on 9 April 1886. Thus a medium which had served him only intermittently over the years was found suitable to convey his final musical thoughts.

NOTES

1. Tables 12.1 and 12.2 are based on information from the thematic catalog of Liszt's works published by the composer, *Thematisches Verzeichniss der Werke, Bearbeitungen und Transciptionen von F. Liszt,* neue vervollständigte Ausgabe (Leipzig: Breitkopf & Härtel, [1877]; reprint, London: H. Baron, 1965), 7–11, 13, and supplemented by the worklists of Humphrey Searle and Sharon Winklhofer, "Franz Liszt," in *The New Grove Early Romantic Masters I: Chopin, Schumann, Liszt* (New York: Norton, 1985), and Peter Raabe, "Verzeichniß aller Werke Liszts" in *Franz Liszt,* rev. ed. (Tutzing: Hans Schneider, 1968), as well as my research outlined in this chapter.

2. See Dario Simoni, *Un soggiorno di Francesco Liszt a San Rossore* (Pisa: Nistri-Lischi, [1936]), 12; also Alan Walker, *Franz Liszt: The Virtuoso Years, 1811–1847,* rev. ed. (Ithaca: Cornell University Press, 1987), 1:269.

3. See the discussion in Chapter 11, "Piano and Orchestra Works."

4. For completeness, we must mention the *Divertissement sur la Cavatine de Pacini "I tuoi frequenti palpiti"* and *Rondeau fantastique sur un thème espagnol "El contrabandista,"* both published in 1837. Each title page has the following statement: "Ce morceau a été écrit d'abord pour Piano et Orchestre." There is, however, no sign that these arrangements ever existed. See also Friedrich Schnapp, "Verschollene Kom-

positionen von Franz Liszt," in *Von Deutscher Tonkunst: Festschrift zu Peter Raabes 70. Geburtstag,* ed. Alfred Morgenroth (Leipzig: C. F. Peters, 1942), 128 (items 22 and 23).

5. See Walker, *Franz Liszt: The Virtuoso Years, 1811–1847,* 1:242.

6. The only evidence for this version is three references in letters to the Countess d'Agoult; see *Correspondance de Liszt et de la Comtesse d'Agoult,* ed. Daniel Ollivier 2 vols. (Paris: Éditions Bernard Grasset, 1933–1934), 1:284 (9 November 1839), 325 (6 December 1839), 346 (29 December 1839).

7. See *Franz Liszt's Briefe,* ed. La Mara [Marie Lipsius], 8 vols. (Leipzig: Breitkopf & Härtel, 1893–1904), 1:33 (27 March 1840, to Robert Schumann); also the review in the *Allgemeine musikalische Zeitung* (1 April 1840), column 299.

8. As was typical of the time, the work was published simultaneously in four countries in 1839; see NLE, ii/3: xi, 157. The title page of the Haslinger edition is reproduced in Ernst Burger, *Franz Liszt: Eine Lebenschronik in Bildern und Dokumenten* (Munich: Paul List Verlag, 1986), 91 (item 161); also in English translation, *A Chronicle of His Life in Pictures,* trans. Stewart Spencer (Princeton: Princeton University Press, 1989).

9. The passage marked "tutti" (mm. 364–391) and the additional staves in mm. 404–414 are lacking in the NLE. No explanation is given for these omissions in the Critical Notes.

10. Raabe, *Franz Liszt,* 2 vols., second enlarged ed. (Tutzing: Hans Schneider, 1968), 2:271.

11. This issue is discussed in detail in Jay Rosenblatt, "The Concerto as Crucible: Franz Liszt's Early Works for Piano and Orchestra" (Ph.D. diss., University of Chicago, 1995), 127–160 ("Who Orchestrated Liszt's Works?").

12. Dezső Legány, *Franz Liszt: Unbekannte Presse und Briefe aus Wien 1822–1886* (Vienna: Böhlaus Verlag, 1984), 44.

13. I am grateful to Geraldine Keeling for providing me with this information on the basis of her extensive research into Liszt's concert programs.

14. The score is in the Goethe- und Schiller-Archiv, unpublished. Note that this version differs from the two-piano score published in 1870, at which time Liszt made further cuts while adding a *Largo maestoso* section in Db major.

15. See the discussion of this manuscript complex in Rena Charnin Mueller, "Liszt's 'Tasso' Sketchbook: Studies in Sources and Revisions" (Ph.D. diss., New York University, 1986), 159–163.

16. The volume is presently in the Library of Congress. A letter states that it was purchased from one of Liszt's students, Frederic W. Riesberg: "After the composer's death [Riesberg] went to his house to express his sympathies and Liszt's house keeper [sic] suggested that he select something that had belonged to the composer, as a token of memory." (Letter of Walter Schatzki, 11 June 1954, sent with the score.)

17. The date for both of these works is uncertain. The *Grand solo,* also known as the *Grosses Concert-Solo,* was originally written in 1849 for a piano competition at the Paris Conservatoire and published in 1851. The orchestral arrangement is of the first version, lacking the *Andante sostenuto* section, which was added around December 1850, thus the arrangement probably dates to earlier that year. As for the Schubert transcription, the earliest reference is found in a letter to the Princess Wittgenstein; see *Franz Liszt's Briefe,* 4:107 ([4–5 May 1851]).

18. See *Thematisches Verzeichniss der Werke, Bearbeitungen und Transcriptionen von F. Liszt,* 13. The *Grand solo* arrangement is not listed in the catalog, as its contents are limited to published works (see discussion of the *Grand solo* below).

19. See *Franz Liszt's Briefe,* 4:87 (to Wittgenstein).

20. Count Hardegg performed under the pseudonym "Jules Egghard." Both he and Hellmesberger were advocates of Liszt's music in Vienna.

21. Unpublished letter in the Deutsche Staatsbibliothek (Mus.ep.Fr.Liszt 18). The letter is transcribed complete in Rosenblatt, "The Concerto as Crucible," 442–443. Another example of Liszt's efforts to promote the work can be found in his letter of 24 May 1853 to the piano teacher Louis Köhler; see *Franz Liszt's Briefe*, 1:139.

22. See Hans von Bülow, *Briefe und Schriften*, ed. Marie von Bülow, 2d ed. (Leipzig: Breitkopf & Härtel, 1899–1907), 1:501 (27 January 1853).

23. Quoted in Walker, *Franz Liszt: The Weimar Years, 1848–1861* (New York: Knopf, 1989), 2:178; see Bülow, *Briefe und Schriften*, 2:53–54.

24. *Briefwechsel zwischen Franz Liszt und Hans von Bülow*, ed. La Mara [Marie Lipsius] (Leipzig: Breitkopf & Härtel, 1898), 23. The piano solo version was no. 14 of the second series of these works (see the discussion of the publication history below).

25. *Briefwechsel Liszt-Bülow*, 318. Cosima was Liszt's second daughter and, at this time, Bülow's wife.

26. Berlin, Deutsche Staatsbibliothek, shelflist Mus. 10433.

27. Unpublished letter, Basel, Universitäts-Bibliothek.

28. *Briefwechsel Liszt-Bülow*, 323.

29. Helene Raff, "Franz Liszt und Joachim Raff im Spiegel ihrer Briefe," *Die Musik* 1 (1901–1902): 397.

30. See Raabe, *Die Entstehungsgeschichte der ersten Orchesterwerke Franz Liszts*, Inaugural Dissertation for the Doctor of Philosophy, University of Jena (Leipzig: Breitkopf & Härtel, 1916), 26–29; also idem, *Franz Liszt*, 2:71–74.

31. *Franz Liszt's Briefe*, 2:383. This score with some of Liszt's emendations is presently in the Library of Congress.

32. See ibid., 384–385 (November 1885).

33. See ibid., 393 (22 June 1886, to Reuss).

34. See Franz Liszt, *Music for Piano and Orchestra*, Complete Music for Solo Piano, vol. 53a (Hyperion CDA67401/2 [1998]).

35. The history of the *Hungarian Rhapsodies* is presented in greater detail, including the use of the shared themes between the two cycles, in Zoltán Gárdonyi, "Paralipomena zu den Ungarischen Rhapsodien Franz Liszts," in *Beiträge von ungarischen Autoren*, ed. Klára Hamburger (Budapest: Corvina Kiadó, 1978), 197–225. Note that *Hungarian Rhapsodies* nos. 16–19 are late works and date from the 1880s (see Chapter 6).

36. See the brief discussion in Walker, *Franz Liszt: The Weimar Years*, 2:381.

37. These emendations have been misinterpreted as revisions to the piano solo version, but they are more likely markings for Conradi, so that he could combine Raff's copy with Liszt's manuscript of the orchestral parts.

38. Comparison of Liszt's orchestral score in the Goethe- und Schiller-Archiv in Weimar and Conradi's copy in the Library of Congress reveals that Liszt's shorthand evidently confused Conradi at this point. Nevertheless, the music appears to jump from the end of the first section (*Più animato*) to the *Allegretto à la Zingarese*.

39. *Franz Liszt's Briefe*, 1:104 (to Louis Köhler).

40. See *Briefwechsel Liszt-Bülow*, 281 (5 December 1859).

41. *Franz Liszt's Briefe*, 1:346 (to Eduard Liszt). Although the first two marches are not mentioned by key, they must be nos. 1 and 3 of the final set, as nos. 2 and 4 are noted in the next letter. Liszt never completed a set of six.

42. Ibid., 1:348–349 ([arrived 26 January 1860]). These transcriptions are discussed in Mária Eckhardt, "Liszts Bearbeitungen von Schuberts Märschen: Formale Analyse," *Studia Musicologica* 26 (1984): 133–146.

43. Ibid., 5:110 (18 December 1860, to the Princess Wittgenstein). These transcriptions were, of course, for voice and orchestra, as opposed to his earlier transcriptions of songs for solo piano.

44. See ibid., 1:382 (19 December 1860).

45. Ibid., 1:396 (27 August 1861).

46. Kahnt also published Liszt's three songs from Schiller's *Wilhelm Tell*, issuing them by 1872. Raabe notes that they may have been orchestrated in the 1850s, without providing a reference, and the only secure date is a letter of 10 October 1863, where Liszt hopes to send Kahnt the manuscript soon; see *Franz Liszt's Briefe*, 2:56 (to Dr. Franz Brendel).

47. Raabe, *Franz Liszt*, 2:356; see also Schnapp, "Verschollene Kompositionen Franz Liszts," 143–144 (item 64).

48. See Walker, *Franz Liszt: The Weimar Years*, 2:500–501.

49. See *Franz Liszt's Briefe*, 4:447 (27 February [1859], to the Princess Wittgenstein).

50. See ibid., 4:453 (2 March [1859], to the Princess Wittgenstein).

51. *Portrait of Liszt: By Himself and His Contemporaries*, ed. Adrian Williams (Oxford: Clarendon Press, 1990), 356.

52. See MW, vii/3: vi.

53. Dates are inscribed at the end of four of these manuscripts: in addition to no. 2 (noted above), his transcription of no. 14 is dated September 1859, no. 5 is dated 29 January 1860, and no. 9 is dated April 1860.

54. There is some confusion over the correct numbering of these transcriptions. Raabe in his worklist assigns the piano version of no. 12 to the orchestral version of no. 2 and the piano version of no. 2 to the orchestral version of no. 4, a numbering which was also taken up by Searle in the *New Grove*. Although this was the original ordering, as can be seen in the Library of Congress manuscript scores, by the time the arrangements were published in 1875, the well known no. 2 was made to agree in both versions.

55. See MW, vii/2: 23–30 and 68–75. Note that Raabe's *Mignon I* is the version of the song as published in 1856, and *Mignon II* is the transcription with Liszt's own piano reduction as found on the two lowest staves of the orchestral publication. These piano reductions are also found in the orchestral scores of *Die Loreley* and Schubert's *Lied der Mignon*, where in the latter a footnote reads: "Clavier-Arrangement bleibt natürlich bei Orchesterbegleitung weg." Note however that the piano part does not slavishly follow the orchestral texture and could serve for performance when an orchestra was not available.

56. See ibid., vi.

57. In his preface to the first published score, Schnapp argues that the orchestral version may be the original form; see Ferenc Liszt, *Légendes for Orchestra* (Budapest: Editio Musica, 1984), vi–vii. Without the manuscripts of the piano versions, it is difficult to be certain, however.

58. See Raabe, *Franz Liszt*, 2:310. Raabe does not offer a date for the transcriptions, but the original versions date from around 1862–1863 and were both published in 1865 along with other arrangements. The orchestral transcriptions remain unpublished, however.

59. See *Franz Liszt's Briefe*, 6:289 (24 February 1871).

60. Schubert's fragment has since been completed and published; see Franz Schubert, *Die Allmacht für gemischten Chor und Klavier D875A*, ergänzt von P. Reinhard Van Hooricks, ed. Harry Goldschmidt (Leipzig: VEB Deutscher Verlag für Musik, 1983).

61. On the Schubert marches and Liszt's revisions to them prior to publication, see A. W. Gottschalg, *Franz Liszt in Weimar und seine letzten Lebensjahre*, ed. Carl Alfred

René (Berlin: Arthur Glaue, 1910), 92–95 (letters of 16 September and 9 October 1870); see also the description of the manuscripts in Eckhardt, *Liszt's Music Manuscripts in the National Széchényi Library* (Budapest: Akadémiai Kiadó, 1986), 146–152 (items 48–50).

62. *Briefwechsel Liszt-Bülow,* 334–335 (3 November 1865).

63. See *Franz Liszt's Briefe,* 2:314 (4 December 1881).

64. Ibid., 7:379.

65. See Z[denko]. Nováček, "Der entscheidende Einfluss von Liszt auf die fortschrittliche Musikorientation in Pressburg," *Studia Musicologica* 5 (1963): 236.

66. See *Briefwechsel Liszt-Bülow,* 261.

67. Williams, *Portrait of Liszt,* 659.

68. "Es stand an kühler Stätte / Ein Sarg noch ungefüllt; / Den nahm er zum Ruhebette, / Zum Pfühle nahm er den Schild. / Die Hände tät er falten / Auf's Schwert und schlummerte ein; / Die Geisterlaute verhallten, / Da mocht es gar stille sein."

V

Vocal Music

13

Sacred Choral Works

Michael Saffle

Second only, perhaps, to his works for piano and for symphonic orchestra, Franz Liszt's sacred choral compositions hold the most important place within his compositional corpus:[1] In all Liszt completed two massive oratorios, five masses (including the *Requiem* for male voices and organ), several cantatas, six extant Psalm settings, a host of smaller-scale liturgical pieces, minor masterpieces like the *Hymne de l'enfant à son réveil*, and such experimental works as *Ossa arida* and *Via Crucis*. He also left fragments of a third oratorio devoted to the life of St. Stanislaus (S 688). Liszt only began composing songs at the end of the 1830s, his organ works are few in number, and his worldly choral works are rarely performed. But he produced church music throughout his entire career; moreover, many of his piano pieces (including some early works) and not a few of his symphonic poems also concern themselves with issues of transcendence and faith. Ours is a secular age, however, and comparatively few of Liszt's religious compositions can be heard today with any frequency in either churches or concert halls.

Liszt's first explicitly sacred work was a *Tantum ergo* (S 702), written when he was eleven or twelve years old and long ago discarded or lost. By the mid-1830s he had completed the independent piano piece known as *Harmonies poétiques et religieuses* (S 157) as well as the unfinished *De profundis* for piano and orchestra (S 691); these too are "religious," although by no means choral. By the mid-1840s at the latest he had drafted many of the numbers eventually included in the *Album d'un voyageur* (S 156) and the first volumes of his *Années de pèlerinage* (S 160–161), and in 1846 he published, in what today are rare editions, the first versions of his first *Pater noster* and *Ave Maria*. Portions of the keyboard pieces and collections mentioned above sound like transcriptions of choral works, and a few of them are; others bear such explicitly religious titles as *Psaume* (S 156/6), *Bénédiction de Dieu dans la solitude* (S 173/3), and

Miserere, d'après Palestrina (S 173/8). It was only in 1848, however, that Liszt proclaimed himself a full-fledged liturgical composer with the first version of his Mass for male voices, better known in its revised version of 1869 as the *Szekszárd Mass* (S 8). During the 1850s and early 1860s he completed or at least began his most important religious works for church and concert hall: the oratorios *Christus* and *Die Legende von der heiligen Elisabeth*, the *Gran* and *Hungarian Coronation* masses, and his settings of Psalms 13, 18, and 23 for various vocal and instrumental ensembles.

Liszt's sacred choral music, considered as a body of work, is remarkable—and remarkably uneven in style. Some of it is breathtaking, even virtuosic, in its more bravura passages; some of it is so drab that it can be difficult to listen to. Much of it is explicitly Catholic in text and sentiment, but some of it draws upon Protestant musical traditions and is suitable for performance in Lutheran, Congregational, Methodist, and even Baptist churches. Some of it expresses exaltation and aims at conversion by means of beautiful tunes, lush chromatic harmonies, and instrumental accompaniments that call to mind the more full-bodied symphonic poems. Some of it, on the other hand, mirrors in many of its musical gestures the works of Palestrina, Lassus, and other sixteenth- and early seventeenth-century masters of counterpoint. Put another way: it is difficult to generalize about Liszt's sacred choral works. Those inclined, as Peter Raabe was, to dismiss them out of hand miss the point: they cannot easily be dismissed, because they cannot easily be understood—at least not collectively.[2]

In the present chapter Liszt's sacred choral works will be considered first in chronological order, then under such subheadings as "Oratorios," "Masses," "Psalm Settings," and "Miscellaneous Pieces." Because many of the smaller-scale works are similar in style and liturgical appropriateness, only representative examples will be discussed in any detail.

VIRTUOSO YEARS, 1838–1847

1840s	Five Choruses. S 18.
1845–1874	*Hymne de l'enfant à son réveil.* S 19.
1845–1874	*Die heilige Cäcilia. Legend.* S 5.
1846–1848	*Pater noster* for unaccompanied male chorus. S 21/1–2.
1846–1852	*Ave Maria* for mixed chorus and organ. S 20/1–2.

Except, perhaps, for the first version of *Cäcilia*, which has been lost, and for the *Hymne* (Song of a Child Awakening)—a prettier piece in its original incarnation than in its revised versions of 1862 and 1874—the most interesting thing about the earliest surviving examples of Liszt's explicitly religious music is its similarity in spirit and style with many of his later compositions. Both the *Ave Maria* (Hail, Mary) and *Pater noster* (Our Father, better-known in English as the Lord's Prayer) are quiet, modest works; most of the part writing and harmony in them is conventionally functional as well as, in a few places, superficially modal. See Example 13.1: in this sequential passage from the revised 1852 version of the *Ave Maria*, the juxtaposition of G major and A minor chords in mm. 48–49, and of E-minor and F♯-major chords in mm. 50–51, suggests the Mixolydian scale.

Example 13.1
Liszt, *Ave Maria* (S 20/2), mm. 48–55

Like so many of his sacred works, Liszt's first *Pater Noster* and *Ave Maria* are meant not only for liturgical performance, but can be performed by comparatively unskilled musicians. The last comment also holds true for his equally modest, albeit non-liturgical choral settings of texts by Jean Racine and Vicomte François-Auguste-René de Chateaubriand; five choruses survive as manuscript copies in the collections of the Bibliothèque Nationale, Paris, although a sixth appears to have been lost.[3] Incidentally, keyboard transcriptions of the *Hymne*, *Pater noster*, and *Ave Maria* were incorporated into the multi-movement version of the *Harmonies poétiques et religieuses*, published in 1852; in this form they are today far better known than their vocal models. The *Hymne*, which features a lilting cantilena and arpeggiated accompanimental figures (see Example 13.2), is by no means stylistically unique among Liszt's sacred works; consider his setting of Psalm 23, discussed below. On the other hand, Liszt more often employed pretty tunes and "songful" accompaniments in his secular compositions, especially later in his career.

WEIMAR, 1848–1861

1848–1869	Mass for male voices and organ. S 8.
1850	*Pater noster* for mixed chorus and organ. S 22.
1853	*Domine salvum fac regem.* S 23.
1853	*Te Deum* for male chorus and organ. S 24.
1855–1858	*Missa solemnis zur Einweihung der Basilika in Gran.* S 9.
1855–1859	*Die Seligkeiten.* S 25 (later incorporated into *Christus*).
1855–1859	Psalm 13 ("Lord, How Long?"). S 13.
1857–1862	*Die Legende von der heiligen Elisabeth.* S 2.
1859	*Te Deum* for mixed chorus, organ, brass, and timpani. S 27.
1859–1862	Psalm 23 ("The Lord is My Shepherd"). S 15.
1859–1862	Psalm 137 ("By the Waters of Babylon"). S 17.

1860–1861	Psalm 18 ("The Heavens Tell God's Glory"). S 14.
1860	Responses and Antiphons. S 30.
1860–1874	*An die heiligen Franziskus von Paula. Gebet.* S 28.
c. 1861	*Pater noster* for mixed chorus and organ. S 29 (later incorporated into *Christus*).

Example 13.2

Liszt, *Hymne de l'enfant à son réveil*, revised version, mm. 19–24

The choral works Liszt completed, drafted, or conceived during his Weimar years are among his greatest artistic achievements. *Christus* (which incorporates settings of the Beatitudes and the *Pater noster* of the early 1860s); the setting of Psalm 18 for male chorus, organ, and orchestra; portions of *St. Elisabeth*; and especially the *Gran Mass*—all are splendid examples of Romantic religious music. In fact, with the sole exceptions of Beethoven's great Mass in D and Brahms's *Ein Deutsches Requiem,* Liszt's *Missa solemnis zur Einweihung der Basilika in Gran* deserves to be acknowledged as the greatest of all nineteenth-century European sacred choral compositions. This is not meant, however, to disparage such fine works as his settings of Psalms 13 and 23 or the less complex but effective *Te Deum* of 1859. Even these lesser works testify to their author's insight, skill, and sincere religious convictions. *Christus*, which was "begun" as an independent composition only in 1862, will be discussed later in the present chapter.

Oratorios

Die Legende von der heiligen Elisabeth (The Legend of St. Elizabeth), one of its composer's most intriguing works, is supposed to have been inspired by a visit Liszt paid in 1855 to the restored Wartburg Castle outside Eisenach, where he examined Moritz von Schwind's frescoes depicting important events in the life of Elizabeth of Hungary (1207–1231), herself a princess, outcast, and doer of good deeds. In point of fact, Liszt almost certainly began work on his oratorio only in 1858, when he met János Danielik, the author of a book about the saint, and asked for a copy. By 1859 Liszt cannot have made much progress. We can infer this from a letter written in May of that year, in which Wagner asks Liszt to visit him and bring his [Liszt's] "Crusader's Chorus" with him; this chorus, perhaps the weakest of the oratorio's numbers and certainly its least smoothly integrated, must have been composed separately, because the rest of *Elisabeth* is permeated by motives that appear nowhere in it. A draft of the complete score seems to have been finished by mid-1862, and the following November Liszt informed Grand Duke Carl Alexander that he hoped his composition would "contribute to the glorification of the 'dear Saint,' and . . . disseminate the celestial perfume of her piety, of her grace, of her sufferings, of her resignation to life, and of her gentle submission towards death."[4] Only in 1864, though, did Liszt surrender the full score for copying. *Elisabeth* was first performed in Budapest in August 1865 and quickly became a staple of the Central European repertory. Since the end of World War I, however, it has been performed only infrequently in Europe and the United States.

That Schwind's frescoes as well as Liszt's own religious convictions had something to do with the oratorio, however, cannot be doubted. To his mother the composer wrote in December 1862 about this work:

You know . . . how for several years on end during my youth I ceaselessly dreamt myself, so to speak, into the realm of the saints. . . . An extraordinary coincidence led me lovingly to St. Elizabeth. Born, like her, in Hungary, I spent twelve years—of decisive importance for my destiny—in Thuringia, not far from the Wartburg in which she dwelt. How eagerly I followed the restoration of the Castle. . . . (T)he Elisabeth-passageway leading to the chapel . . . was painted under my eyes by Schwind. His scenes . . . I adopted for my work.

And earlier in the same letter Liszt makes this confession: "When I now read the *Lives of the Saints* I feel as though after a long journey I am meeting old and venerable friends from whom I shall part no more."[5]

Organized in six principal sections or numbers divided between two "acts," and scored for solo singers, large chorus, and orchestra, *Elisabeth* presents us with several problems. The most obvious has to do with artistic integrity: the music shifts directions several times from the sublime orchestral introduction to the vulgar Crusader's Chorus of no. 3, then to the effective, quasi-operatic dialogue between Elisabeth and her husband, and later to the orchestral storm heard in no. 4—the last "scene" reminiscent of *Hunnenschlacht* and *Mazeppa*. As Robert Collet has written, Liszt does not seem in *Elisabeth* to have been "quite certain what kind of a work he was writing."[6] This problem is exacerbated by certain of the musical materials he borrowed from pre-existing sources and thoughtfully identified for his listeners in an afterword appended to the published score. Portions of a Gregorian hymn sung on the saint's day permeate many of the numbers and help hold the work together; another, much livelier tune—one with Hungarian associations; Franz Erkel also used it in his nationalist opera *Bank bán* of 1861—forms the basis for the chorus "Es herrsche lang und leb' in Ehren" (Long may she reign and live in honor), sung in no. 1 to Elisabeth by the Magnates upon her arrival at the Wartburg and in celebration of her marriage to Landgraf (Count) Ludwig.[7] Least appealing is the so-called "Crusader's Hymn" that appears in no. 3 as mentioned above; ostensibly a Medieval melody, it is actually a seventeenth-century forgery. The disparate musical character of these borrowings contributes to the erratic nature of the oratorio as a whole. Finally, there are the operatic aspects of *Elisabeth*. Nothing else Liszt ever wrote, not even the sketches he left us for his unfinished opera *Sardanapale* (S 687), sounds so theatrical. Yet Liszt forbade staged performances of his oratorio, nor would the whole of *Elisabeth* work on stage.

No. 2 is devoted in part to the story of the "Rose Miracle" (not in fact associated originally with this saint, but with Elizabeth of Portugal). Daily the young bride brings food to the poor; her husband, disliking the practice, catches her at it and demands to see what she has hidden in her clothing. God transforms the hidden bread into roses; realizing that something marvelous has taken place, Ludwig falls to his knees and acknowledges divine intervention. To illustrate the moment of enlightenment Liszt employs arpeggiated harp and string figures as well as an operatic cantilena sung by the penitent Count; the tune played by the first horn and cellos contains the Gregorian motif that represents Elisabeth throughout the oratorio (see Example 13.3).

Example 13.3
Liszt, *Elisabeth*, no. 2 ("The Miracle"), mm. 1–4

Example 13.4
Liszt, *Elisabeth*, no. 5 ("Chorus of the Poor"), mm. 21–40

Of the remaining numbers, perhaps the most effective—and certainly the most affecting—is no. 5, especially the scene that depicts the saint giving aid to the poor after having herself been abandoned by her husband's family following his death in the Holy Land. Example 13.4 reproduces part of the chorus sung by the poor: the understated, modally inflected harmonies employed in this passage, the use of unison vocal writing, the handsome ritornello at rehearsal letter T (the pizzicato strings suggest the furtive movements of the impoverished), and the emotional sincerity of the passage as a whole—Liszt was himself deeply moved by the saint's generosity and purity of heart—make this perhaps the finest moment in a massive composition that also contains some disappointments, uneven passages, and outright eccentricities.[8]

Contemporary critics, on the other hand, mostly applauded this example of Liszt's music-making; the *Leipziger Illustrirte*, a news magazine, observed that "the composer, whom we have been accustomed to seeing storming irrepressibly ahead with his symphonic poems, keeps the musical reins much more firmly under control in this oratorio."[9] Too, throughout the last half of the nineteenth century, *Elisabeth* was regularly performed in Europe as a stage work, although Liszt himself objected to this practice. Today it is little known and rarely performed even in abridged concert versions. This is most unfortunate: in spite of its weaknesses, it is a work every lover of Romantic music should have an opportunity to hear.

Masses

The *Missa quattuor vocum ad aequales concinente organo*, the title under which the Mass for male voices first appeared in print in 1848, is a skillful composition that includes some quotations from Gregorian chant and some effective if understated harmonic progressions. Revised for republication in 1869, it became known in its new form as the *Szekszárd Mass* because its first performance took place in the Hungarian town of that name. Significant even in its early version for what musicologist Paul Merrick identifies as "the quality of [its] choral writing" (especially for male voices, "a medium for which [Liszt] had a special predilection"),[10] this is a work that deserves to be heard more often.

Of enormously greater importance, however, is the *Gran Mass*, scored for four vocal soloists as well as mixed chorus and full-sized symphony orchestra. With the possible exception of the Sonata in B minor, this is—as Alan Walker writes, "by common accord"—one of Liszt's masterpieces.[11] Together with the original version of the *Harmonies poétiques*, the *Bénédiction* for piano mentioned above, some of the numbers from *Christus*, and perhaps the *Via Crucis*, it demonstrates a grasp of compositional technique and a depth of religious conviction unequalled by any other nineteenth-century composer.

It is impossible to summarize so complex and compelling a work as the *Gran Mass* in these few pages. Suffice it to say that the entire composition is held together by an intricate network of motifs, key relationships, and styles of expression that serve primarily to illuminate the words of the Holy Eucharist. Begun in 1855 for the ceremony held in Esztergom at the end of August 1856, then revised during the two years that followed and finally published in 1858, it was early recognized and applauded for its musical as well as its religious character. Liszt himself wrote Princess Sayn-Wittgenstein just before its first performance that local performers had already grown "passionately fond" of it, saying, *Das ist wohl ganz neue Musik, aber zum Niederknien* (That is entirely new music, but for kneeling to).[12] On the other hand, some people, among them Eduard Hanslick, criticized the Mass for "bringing the Venusberg into the church."[13] Even Hanslick, though, could not deny the music's sincerity: as Liszt himself wrote, the entire work was as much or more "prayed" than composed.[14] To Agnès Street-Klindworth Liszt also exulted, following the success of its first performance (and, I imagine, of the work's musical and religious grandeur), over its reception. He added that he could not "recover from my sickness. At certain moments it floods my every fibre, my every vein; I suffer from an unquenchable thirst, and prayer even increases its ardour. This feeling for the impossible becomes apparent, it seems, in my works, and on hearing my Mass one of my compatriots said: 'This music is religious to the point of converting Satan himself!' "[15]

Alone of Liszt's masses the *Gran* has been the subject of a book-length study, written by the composer's defender Leopold Alexander Zellner and published originally in serial form in that author's music magazine.[16] Merrick, too, has written most intelligently about its strengths and subtleties. Nevertheless, this is a work that deserves another or even several books; too often it has been slighted or misunderstood.[17] Moreover, the *Gran* deserves regular and repeated performances by great singers, conductors, and orchestral musicians. These, to date, it has not received for decades.

The Credo, the longest of its movements, is also the greatest and, as Merrick points out, "the most complex in construction."[18] This titanic composition begins and ends in C major but visits many other keys along the way, including B major and its dominant, F♯ major; it is full of topical shifts appropriate to the various portions of the text—the use of martial music to suggest the Last Judgement at m. 203 is merely one case in point; and it contains some wonderful examples of thematic transformation. Merrick discusses many (although not all) of these things, but one subject he does not address at any length is text-painting. Liszt was not only an innovator; he was also a master of musical traditions, and this one—the illustration in music of the meaning of single words and phrases by appropriate, not necessarily topical means—goes back in a few instances to Gregorian chant and was employed in literally thousands of works by Renaissance composers of masses, motets, and madrigals. Eighteenth-century English-language examples include rapidly alternating notes for words such as "shake" and sustained single notes accompanying words such as "plain" in numbers from Handel's *Messiah*.

In some portions of the Credo Liszt gives us more or less what previous composers have also given us, at least in terms of text-painting: thus the music descends in arpeggiated figures at m. 83 as the soloists sing the words "he descended from heaven" (*descendit de caelis*) and rises again by step at mm. 186–189 as the chorus sings "he ascended into heaven" (*et ascendit in caelum*). A less traditional kind of text-painting, and one that occurs in conjunction with a shift of topic from cantilena to a kind of instrumental restlessness found elsewhere in Liszt's late religious works, involves the words "and was made man" (*et homo factus est*) at mm. 121–131, sung as a unison descending chromatic line against a restless instrumental backdrop. This phrase was interpreted by earlier composers in light of the miracle of Christ physically entering our world; consequently, many of those composers had their soloists or choristers pause and solemnly intone these words to beautiful harmonies. Liszt's interpretation is quite different: it implies, instead, the sufferings all men are heir to. By entering into our world and our flesh Christ too enters into those sufferings. Nicely, as one might expect, Liszt's music (especially the repeated major seconds first presented by the violins in mm. 113–115), reappears later in the passages depicting Jesus' crucifixion and death. The music reminds us, through this and other forms of expression, that physical life leads to death for us all, Christ included; it also serves to link different sections of the movement together motivically and texturally. Only the appearance of a joyful, upward-leaping motif at m. 171 returns us to the heavenly realm with the words "he rose again" (*et resurrexit*).

Another example of text-painting occurs at mm. 344–346: after a tremendous contrapuntal passage celebrating the church and the sacrament of baptism (see below, too), everything stops; we hear the words "and we look forward to" or "we expect" (*et expecto*) sung hesitantly by the choir; only then does the full-blown glory of eternal life break upon us in a martial apotheosis similar to those found in several of the symphonic poems. The return of this "Last Judgment" music at m. 347 in the horns, trumpets, and trombones is not only theologically appropriate but links this portion of the movement musically with the original statement of this material (see Example 13.5).

Finally, the prolongation—in the fugue that leads the Credo toward its conclusion—of the words "and apostolic church" in the phrase "We acknowledge one Catholic and apostolic church" (*et unam sanctum catholicam et apostolicam ecclesiam*) that begins in m. 278. (See Example 13.6, reproduced from a keyboard-vocal score of the Mass published in the nineteenth-century by Schubert & Co. of Leipzig.) Fugue, of course—the "learned style"—is the appropriate and traditional topic for musical representations of the church as an institution, but the way in which Liszt lays out the syllables of his text emphasizes the *length* of the apostolic tradition and of that institution's authority over men. Walker, like Humphrey Searle, might be inclined to discredit these moments of specificity, especially because they involve the explicitly theological as well as the traditionally musical. Liszt himself certainly did not. There is much to be said for Liszt the innovator; I have just said some of it myself. But Liszt the traditionalist also deserves praise, especially in those passages—like the ones described above—in which he builds upon the familiar to create something that is both solid and novel.

Example 13.5
Liszt, *Gran Mass,* **Credo, mm. 344–348**

Example 13.6
Liszt, *Gran Mass*, Credo, mm. 275–292 (piano-vocal score)

Psalm Settings

Why Liszt's settings of psalm texts have so often been neglected does not altogether make sense. True, published versions of several of them are difficult to obtain even today, and at least one has never appeared in print. And, true, some of the published settings call for large numbers of skilled performers. Psalm 13 especially, scored for tenor, mixed chorus, and large orchestra, is simply too demanding to be presented in all but a handful of churches and even by some concert organizations. Its several beauties, including fine tunes and fugal passages, must often have been obscured by such practical considerations as "Will anybody pay to listen to this piece of music?" or even "Can we find enough people to sing and play it?"[19] Unfortunately, too, Psalm 18, a shorter and even more compelling composition, also requires large orchestra and organ as well as two-part men's chorus. This magnificent and ultimately jubilant work, which lasts only eight minutes in performance (Psalm 13 lasts twenty-five), exults concisely—an oxymoronic epitome and an accurate one, I believe, of the work's emotional and aesthetic impact.

Liszt's setting of Psalm 23, on the other hand, is scored modestly for tenor, harp (or piano), and organ (or harmonium). Furthermore, it is organized in straightforward ternary form, lasts no more than ten minutes, and is a delight to listen to.[20] Why, then, is it not performed more often? Could it be—I hope this is not a rhetorical question—because it includes a part for harp? Today, one would think, sophisticated music-lovers would be willing to forget increasingly outdated modernist prejudices against "the Victorian" and acknowledge, instead, that not all nineteenth-century harp music is saccharine. Liszt writes most effectively in this piece for that instrument; moreover, if necessary or considered desirable, the entire composition can be performed by tenor and piano. Also effective are the chromatic harmonies Liszt uses to accompany Herder's translation of the words "in the Valley of the Shadow of Death" (*im dunklen Thal*) and the dominant-ninth chords, reminiscent of Wagner, he employs in conjunction with its more rapturous passages. The tenor's melody, one of the most engaging its composer ever wrote—Merrick writes enthusiastically about its "long-breathed" phrases, a "rarity" in Liszt's overall output[21]—resembles that of Gounod's *Ave Maria* and rivals it in accessible beauty.

Psalm 137, a partial setting of the Vulgate text for solo voice (apparently mezzo-soprano), women's chorus, and an instrumental ensemble consisting of violin, harp, piano, and organ, possesses operatic moments of its own but is gentler and less fulsome than the Psalm 13 and 18 settings.

Miscellaneous Pieces

Whether Liszt's *Heilige Franziskus* actually dates from 1860 is uncertain; he mentions a work about St. Francis of Paola, scored for men's voices, in his Testament of that year.[22] The published composition, scored for trombones and timpani as well as solo male voices and male chorus, incorporates some text-painting in the wave-like rising and falling of the unison choral setting of the words "Over the ocean's waves thou stridest through the storm!" (*Ueber Meeres Fluten wandelst du im Sturm!*). Interestingly, material that appears in the concluding measures of this choral work also appears in the piano "legende" *St. François de Paule marchant sur les flots* (S 175/2) of 1863. As Merrick has it, the *Domine salvum fac regem*, scored for tenor solo, male chorus, and organ, exemplifies Liszt's "ceremonial style . . . at its best" and even concludes with "a short fugal peroration in the Handelian manner."[23] Of the remaining pieces, several are Palestrina-like in style; one—another *Pater noster* (S 29)—was incorporated into *Christus* during the early 1860s.

ROME AND AFTERWARD, 1861–1868

1862–1881	*Cantico del sol di Francesco d'Assisi.* S 4.
1863	*Christus ist geboren* (two settings). S 31–32.
1863–1868	*Christus.* S 2.
1865	*Missa choralis.* S 10.
1865–1869	*Ave maris stella* (two settings), *Crux!*, *Dall'alma Roma*, and other minor works. S 34–37.
1867–1868	*Requiem.* S 12.
1867–1869	*Hungarian Coronation Mass.* S 11.
1868	*Mihi autem adhaerere.* S 37.
1869	Psalm 116 ("Praise the Lord, All ye Nations!"). S 15a.

Although most of Liszt's best sacred compositions were finished or had been begun prior to his departure from Weimar in 1861, several fine works were composed entirely in and around Rome (where he spent most of the 1860s) or during his visits to other parts of Europe. The latter groups include the *Missa choralis*, the fine *Hungarian Coronation Mass*, and the first version of the *Cantico del sol*, another of Liszt's Franciscan pieces. Although part of what eventually appeared in *Christus* dates from the Weimar years, the oratorio as a whole is perhaps more appropriately considered a "Roman" work.

Oratorios

Christus is one of Liszt's masterpieces, second only among his sacred compositions to the *Gran Mass* in grandeur of conception, details of execution, and overall intellectual and emotional conviction. In one sense it is greater even than the *Gran* because it is far more stylistically and expressively variegated. And, of course, *Christus* is also outstanding in its choice of subject; Merrick calls it "the greatest musical composition of its time based upon the life of Christ."[24] Compositionally it runs the gamut of styles from extremely conservative to experimental. In the disposition of its vocal and instrumental forces it calls in some numbers for no more than a dozen performers, in others for several hundred—including piccolo, English horn, three trumpets, a large percussion battery, harp, organ or harmonium, six vocal soloists (soprano, mezzo-soprano, alto, tenor, baritone, and bass), and mixed chorus as well as Liszt's "standard" orchestral complement of woodwinds, brasses, timpani, and strings.

To some extent, as we have noted, *Christus* was assembled from pre-existing pieces completed during the Weimar years. *Die Seligkeiten*, Liszt's setting of the Beatitudes, for instance, was eventually incorporated into it—and renamed "Die Seligpreisungen" (although its text, like that of the rest of the oratorio, is in Latin). So was his *Pater noster* of 1861. Yet, although plans for the oratorio were in place as early as 1853, most of it was actually written during the mid-1860s. The "Shepherds' Song at the Manger," "Stabat mater speciosa," and other numbers date from 1863; the orchestral introduction, "Pastorale and Annunciation," and other numbers from 1864; and so on.[25] Liszt had some trouble deciding what text or texts he would use; eventually he decided not so much to tell the story of Jesus' life as to "illustrate" it in fourteen tableaux of various sizes and styles. The result is something of a jumble: a few numbers are entirely instrumental, others are based on Biblical passages, still others incorporate Gregorian melodies in an obvious way, and several sections resemble the symphonic poems in their use of topics and thematic transformation. Searle goes so far as to call *Christus* a "patchy" work,[26] and its long and complex history doubtless influenced its ultimate form. The entire composition may have been finished as early as 1868, but it was performed for the first time in its entirety only in May 1873, indicating that additional work on it may have taken place during the late 1860s and the early 1870s.

The tableaux that compose *Christus* are arranged in three sections: the first five constitute a "Christmas Oratorio" (*Weihnachts-Oratorium*) in their own right and are the most frequently performed, the next five are entitled "After Epiphany," and the final four are identified as pertaining to Christ's "Passion and Resurrection." In the present chapter we can consider only a few aspects of these sections in terms of representative passages. Consider, for instance, one portion of no. 9, "Das Wunder" (The Miracle), devoted to Jesus calming a storm on the Sea of Galilee (see Example 13.7). The dramatic intensity especially of mm. 58ff., which climaxes in mm. 159–169—the topic is *Sturm und Drang* (storm and stress), familiar to anyone who has ever heard the "Wolf's Glen" scene from Weber's *Der Freischütz* or the first movement of Beethoven's Fifth Symphony—is appropriate programmatically as an accompaniment to the apostles' frantic cries for help (*Domine, salvanos, perimos!*).

Nothing could be more different from these passages than the purity and innocence of no. 13, the Easter Hymn "O filii et filiae," scored throughout for at most eight or ten sopranos and altos (children's voices would be perfect here), accompanied either by a few wind instruments or by solo harmonium. See Example 13.8: the use of E♭-major and C-minor triads in an otherwise F-minor harmonic context replaces key with mode—in this case, transposed Dorian. The part writing, too, is extremely simple, and in many measures everyone sings in unison. A rather different simplicity is captured by the melody at mm. 45ff. of the "Papst-Hymnus" or "Papal Hymn" (no. 8, "The Establishment of the Church" [*Die Gründung der Kirche*]), an original melody Liszt arranged several

times during his career. Again the music has a "Protestant" flavor, although the
text is quintessentially Catholic.

Example 13.7
Liszt, *Christus* no. 9 ("Das Wunder"), mm. 156–163

Example 13.8
Liszt, *Christus* no. 13 ("O filii et filiae"), mm. 1–26

Example 13.9
Liszt, *Christus* no. 8 ("Tu es Petrus"), mm. 45–52

Example 13.10
Liszt, *Christus* no. 6 ("Beatitudes"), mm. 1–47

Example 13.11
Liszt, *Christus* no. 10 ("Entry into Jerusalem"), mm. 357–366

Two additional passages worth examining are the opening of no. 6, the "Beatitudes," and the climax of no. 10, the "Entry Into Jerusalem" (*Die Einzug in Jerusalem*). The former—see Example 13.10—illustrates a technique Liszt employed in many of his sacred works: that of recitative, often more or less unbarred, employed either in transitional passages or in anticipation of instrumental or choral responses. The organ solo that introduces this, the first of the blessings Jesus proclaims at the beginning of the Sermon on the Mount, is extremely simple in style. By contrast, the sheer power and rousing good nature of the "hosannah" passage from the "Entry" movement—see Example 13.11—is reinforced by sequential harmonic writing that takes us effortlessly first from Eb to E major, then from E to F major. In an unusual example of instrumental-vocal doubling in his works, Liszt here supports the alto solo with similar music in the upper woodwinds even as the brass instruments support the choral parts, thickening the sound and creating a texture unique in *Christus* as a whole. Portions of this movement anticipate the religious works of Holst and other early twentieth-century figures. Liszt, it seems, was forever bringing new moments of musical style into being.[27]

Masses

As early as 1865 Liszt expressed interest in composing a mass in honor of the coronation of Francis Joseph I, Emperor of Austria, as King of Hungary. This triumph of diplomacy, also known as the *Ausgleich* (or "Compromise")— an event that soothed Hungarian national longings without actually doing much for the citizens of what remained sovereign Austrian territory—took place in Budapest on 8 June 1867. Liszt's commission was confirmed officially only a few months before the coronation took place, and he not only had to work quickly but tailor his music to rather demanding specifications: it had to be brief, easy to perform, and "appropriate" to both Austrian and Hungarian sensibilities. At its premiere the Mass lacked a gradual; this was added in the form of a fragmentary setting of Psalm 116 prior to the complete work's sumptuous publication at Austro-Hungarian national expense in 1869.

The *Coronation Mass* represents Liszt at his most diatonic and straight-forward. Each movement has a home key: Eb for the Kyrie, C for the Gloria and Gradual, E for the Sanctus, and so on. Several of the movements "bracket" other key areas: Gb major in the Kyrie, for example; and B major and Bb major, with brief references to A and E major, in the Gloria. Otherwise, though, the piece is far from "difficult": there are no experimental harmonies, no counterpoint to speak of, and few or no special or demanding orchestral effects. "National" touches include passages using the Hungarian minor scale, martial rhythms reminiscent of *verbunkos* music, and quotations from the *Rákóczy March*; the Offertory, scored exclusively for violin and orchestra, is full of these and other characteristic inflections. Interestingly enough, the Credo is not by Liszt at all; he took it, whole, from the *Messe royale* composed in the early seventeenth century by Henri Dumont. Given the solemn occasion for which the Mass was written, the Credo by Dumont is "correct" in its modesty and forthrightness; musically it is effective (even though it goes on for more than a few minutes).

The *Missa choralis* is a quite different kind of composition. Written during Liszt's short-lived involvement with the German Caecilianists—a group of Catholic composers, performers, and publishers who wished to return liturgical music to the purity it had enjoyed in Palestrina's day—the work is simple and straightforward to the point of austerity. Much of it is cast in what seems at first glance to be the *Palestrinastil* (Palestrina style) favored by Franz Xaver Witt, leader of the Caecilianists, and his followers. Nineteenth-century works that conformed to this style featured modal harmonies and cadences, "points of imitation" at the beginnings of new portions of text, an extremely discrete use of accidentals and anything smacking of "modulation," and other Renaissance gestures.[28]

But Liszt's *Missa choralis* blends sixteenth-century counterpoint with chromatic harmonies and some deft accompanimental touches for organ. In the Kyrie, for instance, a passage of almost faultless and thoroughly conventional imitative Renaissance counterpoint is interrupted at m. 25 by the organ playing diminished-seventh chords. In mm. 44–71 of the Credo the music slides effortlessly from A major through G to F major, then shifts suddenly and most effectively to B major in m. 72. In mm. 19–24 a lyrical arpeggiated organ accompaniment hovering between F major and E♭ major soothes us after a series of forceful cadences in A♭ major and F major in mm. 9–15. Finally—see Example 13.12—in mm. 22–53, Liszt moves from G major (introduced unequivocally at m. 19) through B♭ major to D♭ and even G♭ major. Here too, as in *Christus* (see Example 13.8), recitative-like passages link sequential choral statements. This was a texture Liszt employed with increasing frequency in his later, liturgically orientated religious compositions.

A slighter and, in certain passages, more astringent work, the *Requiem* for solo male voices, men's chorus, brass instruments, timpani, and organ was probably completed in 1868—completed, that is, except for the Libera me, which dates from 1871. Evidence survives that the work was composed in memoriam of Maximilian I of Mexico, that it commemorates the death(s) of Liszt's mother and/or the deaths of his children Blandine and Daniel, and that it was intended for Liszt's own funeral. Whatever the source of its inspiration, the *Requiem* is liturgical music through and through; in every passage it is modest enough, understated enough, and textually transparent enough for regular church use. Nevertheless, chromatic passages abound; harmonically it is anti-Caecilianist. One passage from the Dies irae, cited by Merrick, features an arpeggiated accompaniment that shifts unexpectedly from C major to A major at precisely the point at which the vocal line leaps upward from G to C♯.[29] In 1883, shortly before his own death, Liszt made an arrangement of the entire *Requiem* for organ. Did he play it to himself, one wonders, during his more somber musings? Keyboard masses were commonplace in seventeenth-century Europe and were often intended for meditative circumstances.

Example 13.12

Liszt, *Missa choralis* (Benedictus), mm. 22–54

THE FINAL YEARS, 1869–1886

1869–1875	*Ave Maria* (several settings), *Pater noster* (two settings), *Tantum ergo* (two settings), *O salutaris hostia*, and other minor works. S 38–48.
1874	*Die Glocken des Strassburger Münsters*. S 6.
1874	*Die heilige Cäcilia. Legende*. S 5.
1874	*Sankt Christoph. Legend*. S 47.
1878	*Septem sacramenta*. S 52.
1878–1879	*Via Crucis*. S 53.
1878–1879	Twelve chorale settings for unaccompanied chorus or for chorus and organ. S 50.
1879	*Cantantibus organis* (Antiphon). S 7.
1879	*O Roma nobilis, Ossa arida,* and *Rosario*. S 54–56.
1881	Psalm 129 ("Out of the Depths"). S 16.
1883–1885	*Pro Papa, Pax vobiscum!*, and other shorter works. S 57–66.

Liszt's last years as a composer witnessed the production of a large number of individual sacred choral compositions and collections. Few of these pieces conform to what radio announcers today call "easy listening," but none of them is as unrelentingly harsh and grim as the remarkable *Via Crucis*. Scored for solo voices, mixed chorus, and organ or piano, the collection consists of a setting of the Gregorian melody *Vexilla Regis*, an introductory passage for the four soloists on the words *O crux, ave, spes unica* based on the so-called "Cross motif" or Liszt's "musical fingerprint" (in C major: C–D–F).[30] This is followed by fourteen short pieces, some fragmentary in style, associated with the fourteen Stations of the Cross depicted in many Catholic churches and mostly derived from scripture. The scorings of these pieces are quite different: no. 10 and others, for example, are keyboard solos; no. 2 calls only for solo baritone voice and organ; no. 3 calls only for men's voices and organ; while no. 14 calls for mezzo-soprano solo, chorus, and organ.

The styles and sources vary too: several numbers draw upon chant tunes, but no. 6, "St. Veronica Wipes Jesus' Face with Her Veil," includes a choral harmonization of the Lutheran hymn *O Haupt voll Blut und Wunden*. In no. 11—see Example 13.13—we hear in the organ (or piano) the nails being driven into the cross as the crowd chants "Crucify him!" (*Crucifige*); the sound is deliberately ugly and utterly appropriate to its subject. Searle is correct: this is music that attains its expressiveness "not by organic development or contrapuntal complexity, but by a forthright 'primitivity' remarkably attuned to the twentieth-century spirit and ideal."[31] As is so often the case, Liszt employs a short instrumental recitative in mm. 11–14 of this movement to link it with the music that follows—and also, perhaps, to suggest the crowd dispersing after the awful entertainment has ended.

Example 13.13
Liszt, *Via Crucis*, **Station XI complete, mm. 1–15**

Largely experimental in its harmonic language and internal musical organization, *Via Crucis* nevertheless might be appropriate for liturgical use were there a Catholic ceremony into which it could be integrated.[32] Today the work is performed with increasing frequency in concert settings. Striking and highly effective, its newfound popularity has unfortunately eclipsed some of Liszt's other, less unconventional religious compositions.

Example 13.14
Liszt, *Ossa arida*, mm. 15–27

Of the remaining pieces, Psalm 129 deserves to be mentioned. Simpler and less genial in style than many of the earlier settings, this setting of the Latin text *De profundis* (Out of the Depths) is largely taken up with unison passages for male voices and with a lengthy organ prelude that recalls stylistically some of the late piano pieces. A fragmentary psalm setting is the *Qui seminant in lacrimis* (S 63) for mixed chorus and organ; the text comes from Psalm 125, and the simple, somewhat harsh music rises to an effective climax at *in exultatione*

metent. Other works are more obviously Caecilian in style: these include two settings of the *Tantum ergo*, one for women's voices with organ and one for men's. Although Palestrina would have shunned certain details of voice-leading, these remarkably conservative pieces are said to recall, in Liszt's own words, the mood of the long-lost *Tantum ergo* he set to music in 1822. *Ossa arida* (Dry Bones), on the other hand, opens with a striking anticipation of twentieth-century harmonic experimentation: a slowly arpeggiated half-diminished diatonic "fifteenth" chord built on B (i.e., B–D–F–A–C–E–G–B). See Example 13.14. Merrick praises the "directness and simplicity" of *Ossa arida* as a whole and points out that "only a performance reveals the visionary element not apparent from the score, a tribute to the quality of Liszt's aural imagination."[33]

The twelve chorale harmonizations, on the other hand, contain some striking modulations but will probably never replace those of Bach and other Baroque masters. Four of them were incorporated into the *Via Crucis*. Of the *Salve regina* of 1885 Merrick points out, correctly, that "there is not the marked [stylistic] difference in this late work" so characteristic of the composer's last pieces for piano and orchestra.[34] A fascination during the 1950s and 1960s for the "modern," especially in Liszt's late piano works, served indirectly, and perhaps inadvertently, to draw attention away from his religious music as a whole. Thus Searle—himself a composer of consequence—wrote of the later choral works, that "on they whole they do not show [Liszt] at his most original." In his brief discussions of particular pieces Searle paid closest attention to *Ossa arida* and the *Via Crucis* as well as the *Qui seminant in lacrimis* mentioned above—the last of which, as he points out, contains "some curious harmony."[35] The second of the two numbers in *Pro Papa* (S 59/2) is an arrangement for male chorus and organ of the "Tu es Petrus" tune from *Christus*; see Example 13.9 above.

NOTES

1. Surprisingly little has been written about Liszt's sacred choral music as a whole. Perhaps the best broader studies—besides that of Paul Merrick, *Revolution and Religion in the Music of Liszt* (Cambridge and London: Cambridge University Press, 1987)—are Paul Allen Munson, "The Oratorios of Franz Liszt" (Ph.D. diss., University of Michigan, 1996); Ralph Woodward, "The Large Sacred Choral Works of Franz Liszt" (Ph.D. diss., University of Illinois, 1964); and Charles White, "The Masses of Franz Liszt" (Ph.D. diss., Bryn Mawr University, 1973). A pamphlet, now hard to find—Eugen Segnitz, *Franz Liszts Kirchenmusik* (Langensalza, Switzerland: H. Beyer, 1911)—may be useful for scholars. Of unfortunately little use is Anselm Hartmann, *Kunst und Kirche: Studien zum Messenschafffen von Franz Liszt* (Regensburg: Gustav Bosse, 1991).

2. See Peter Raabe, *Franz Liszt*, 2 vols., ed. Felix Raabe (Tutzing; Hans Schneider, 1968), especially 2: "Liszts Schaffen," passim.

3. See Michael Saffle, "Liszt Manuscripts in the Bibliothèque Nationale, Paris: A Preliminary Catalog," in *Analecta Lisztiana I: Proceedings of the "Liszt and His World" Conference Held at Virginia Polytechnic Institute and State University, 20–23 May 1993*, ed. Saffle (Stuyvesant, NY: Pendragon, 1998), 128. A new study of these documents, prepared by Michael Short, will appear in print in the near future.

4. Quoted in Franz Liszt, *Selected Letters*, ed. Adrian Williams (Oxford: Clarendon Press, 1998), 589.

5. Ibid., 593.

6. Robert Collet, "Choral and Organ Music," in *Franz Liszt: The Man and His Music*, ed. Alan Walker (New York: Taplinger, 1970), 320–321.

7. Collet provides a useful "synopsis" or "plot summary" for *Elisabeth*; see "Choral and Organ Music," 323–327.

8. The best survey of *Elisabeth* as a whole is Michael Palotai's "Liszt's Concept of Oratorio as Reflected in his Writings and in 'Die Legende von der heiligen Elisabeth' " (Ph.D. diss., University of Southern California, 1977).

9. Quoted in Walker, *Franz Liszt: The Final Years, 1861–1886* (New York: Alfred A. Knopf, 1996), 3:91.

10. Merrick, *Revolution and Religion in the Music of Liszt*, 107. See also James Thompson Fudge, "The Male Chorus Music of Franz Liszt" (Ph.D. diss., University of Iowa, 1972), which discusses such other sacred works as *Ossa arida* and Liszt's setting of Psalm 129.

11. Walker, *Franz Liszt: The Weimar Years, 1848–1861* (New York: Knopf, 1989), 2:403.

12. Franz Liszt, *Selected Letters*, 414.

13. Liszt himself quotes this observation in his letter of 5 September 1856 to the Princess; see Franz Liszt, *Selected Letters*, 417. The "Venusberg" reference links Liszt and Wagner through the latter's *Tannhäuser*—which had, at that time, yet to receive its scandalous Paris performance.

14. See Walker, *Franz Liszt: The Weimar Years*, 2:403.

15. Franz Liszt, *Selected Letters*, 457.

16. See L. A. Zellner, *Ueber Franz Liszts Graner Festmesse und ihre Stellung zur geschichtlichen Entwicklung der Kirchenmusik* (Vienna: F. Manz, 1858).

17. Collet ("Choral and Organ Works," 335), for example, describes the "more dogmatic" portions of the work merely as "relatively conventional."

18. Merrick, *Revolution and Religion in the Music of Liszt*, 119.

19. Collet disagrees; see "Choral and Organ Works," 338.

20. I include this solo-vocal composition in a chapter otherwise devoted to choral or solo-vocal/choral works primarily because Raabe and Humphrey Searle have also done so. Liszt did, in fact, write several songs (alternately, chansons or Lieder) on religious texts; moreover, Raabe and Searle cataloged them as songs, i.e., as secular solo-vocal (rather than sacred) choral compositions; among these, interestingly enough, is an *Ave Maria* for solo voice and organ (S 341). Liszt's works can be difficult to classify by categories and genres, and new thematic catalogues scheduled to appear in print in the immediate future may well firm up sectional divisions in favor of emphasizing the histories of and interrelationships among the pieces themselves. On this last point, see Leslie Howard and Michael Short, "A New Catalogue of Liszt's Music," *Analecta Lisztiana I*, 75–100.

21. Merrick, *Revolution and Religion in the Music of Liszt*, 152.

22. Information about Liszt's will may be found in Walker, *Franz Liszt: The Weimar Years*, 2:555–565 (Appendix I).

23. Merrick, *Revolution and Religion in the Music of Liszt*, 218.

24. Ibid., 184. See also Friedrich Riedel, "Die Bedeutung des 'Christus' von Franz Liszt in der Geschichte des Messias-Oratoriums," in *Liszt-Studien 2*, ed. Serge Gut (Munich and Salzburg: Emil Katzbichler, 1981), 153–162.

25. Merrick, *Revolution and Religion in the Music of Liszt*, 183.

26. Searle, *The Music of Liszt* (New York: Dover, 1966), 107.

27. For additional information about *Christus*, see N. Lee Orr, "Liszt's 'Christus' and Its Significance for Nineteenth-Century Oratorio" (Ph.D. diss., University of North Carolina, 1979); and especially Lina Ramann, *Franz Liszt's Oratorium Christus. Eine Studie als Beitrag zur zeit- und musikgeschichtlichen Stellung desselben*, 3d ed. (Leipzig: C. F. Kahnt, 1880). Material from Orr's dissertation also appeared in *JALS* 9 (1981): 4–18.

28. For additional information about Liszt and the Caecilianists, see Saffle, "Liszt and Cecilianism: The Evidence of Documents and Scores," in *Der Caecilianismus: Anfange—Grundlagen—Wirkungen,* ed. Hubert Unverricht (Tutzing: Hans Schneider, 1988), 203–213.

29. See Merrick, *Revolution and Religion in the Music of Liszt*, 141 (Example 44).

30. Collet ("Choral and Organ Works," 323) uses the phrase "musical fingerprint" for this motif.

31. Searle, *The Music of Liszt*, 120. Searle quotes the passage in question from an unidentified London newspaper of 1952. See also Roland Moser, "Unitonie—Pluritonie—Omnitonie: Zur harmonischen Gedankenwelt in der 'Via Crucis' von Franz Liszt," in *Basler Jahrbuch für historische Musikpraxis* 21 (1997): 129–142.

32. Ceremonies do take place in Catholic churches in which the various stations depicted on those churches' walls are visited and "celebrated." There is no "stations" ceremony, however, equal in importance to such sacramental ceremonies as baptism and marriage.

33. Merrick, *Revolution and Religion in the Music of Liszt*, 231.

34. Ibid., 232.

35. Searle, *The Music of Liszt*, 118.

14

Secular Choral Works

Kristin Wendland

Although Liszt's reputation primarily rests on his piano and orchestral works, vocal music figures prominently into his musical oeuvre, including solo songs and choral music. The catalog of Liszt's choral works attests to the composer's love for the medium, and the establishment of the Liszt Society Choir in the mid-1870s demonstrates the firm foothold his choral music had with choral singers. While his sacred music has received some attention from music scholars and performers,[1] Liszt's secular choral music remains mostly unknown. Many of the pieces received few or no performances during the composer's lifetime, and, since his death, most have fallen into obscurity. The scores are difficult to locate now, and only a few appear in modern editions. Those scores that survived from early editions in the twentieth century are located in rare book collections in libraries or on microfilm, and some of the pieces are still in manuscript in various Liszt collections (see Table 14.1).

Recordings are difficult to find, too. The Hungarian label Hungaroton recorded a six-volume set of LPs entitled *Liszt Choral Works* in the 1970s. Now long out of print, the set includes two records of the secular works. Hungaroton issued a compact disc in 1991 that included two cantatas, *Hungaria 1848* and *An die Künstler*, as well as one patriotic song, *Magyar király-dal* (Hungarian Royal Anthem).

Liszt's secular choral music warrants close attention because a detailed investigation of this body of repertory yields some undiscovered jewels. From short patriotic songs, to more refined part-songs and full-length cantatas, the secular choral works portray a little-known side of Liszt—a side that helps illuminate the entire psyche of the composer.

Some of the works discussed below mark as drastic a departure from the mold of classical forms and tonal techniques as Liszt's late music. Indeed, the "prophetic music of Liszt's old age has, paradoxically, obscured for us the originality of [the] pieces of the earlier Weimar period, which in their way contain music as bold and uncompromising as anything he wrote in later life."[2] The *Prometheus Cantata* and *An die Künstler*, for example, contain music that is especially innovative, as well as some of the earlier short works for men's voices, such as *Der Gang um Mitternacht*.

Most of Liszt's secular choral music dates from the 1840s and 1850s, and within those two decades he composed many of the pieces before and during the years he served as Kapellmeister in Weimar (1848–1861). With few exceptions, his thirty secular choral works fall into two general categories— works for men's voice (*Männerchor*) and cantata-type pieces for mixed voices and orchestra.

Table 14.1
Location/Citation Of Secular Choral Scores[3]

Library Sigla

LC   Library of Congress, Washington D.C.
NYPL   Music Division of the New York Public Library, New York City
UCB   University of California at Berkeley

A lelkesedés dala (Das Lied der Begeisterung). Pest: Táborszky es Parsch, 1871. LC
An die Künstler. Weimar: Schlesinger, 1854. LC; Weimar: n.d. [1856 or 1857]. UCB
Chöre zu Herders Entfesseltem Prometheus (Prometheus Cantata). Leipzig, C. F. Kahnt, 1876 [?]. UCB
Das deutsche Vaterland. Second version at Curtis Institute of Music, Rare Manuscript of Liszt (1969), title page and five pages.[4]
Drei vierstimmige Männerchöre. Basel: Ernst Knop, n.d. [1845]. UCB
   1. *Trost*
   2. *Trost*
   3. *Nicht gezagt!*
Es war einmal ein König. Weimar: Nationale Forschungs-und Gedenkstätten der klassischen deutschen Literatur, 1986. Facsimile copy with commentary by Hans Rudolf Jung on this and other Goethe settings by Liszt.
Festalbum zur Säkularfeier von Goethes Geburtstag. Leipzig: Schuberth, 1849. LC
   I. *Introduction*
   II. *Licht mehr Licht!"**
   III. *Weimars Todten*
   IV. *Über allen Gipfeln ist Ruh!**
   V. *Chor der Engel. aus Goethe's Faust* for mixed and women's voices (also version for women's chorus)
Festgesang zur Eröffnung der zehnten allgemeinen deutschen Lehrerversammlung. Liszt Complete Works Series 5/VI, reprinted from the original Breitkopf & Härtel edition, Farnborough Hants., England: Gregg Press, 1966.
Festkantate zur Enthüllung des Beethoven-Denkmals in Bonn. Reconstructed and edited by Günther Massenkeil, Frankfurt: C. F. Peters, 1989.
Für Männergesang. Leipzig: C. F. Kahnt, n.d. [1861]. LC
   1. *Vereinslied**
   2. *Ständchen**
   3. *Wir sind Mumien**

Geharnischte Lieder
4. *Vor der Schlacht*
5. *Nicht gezagt**
6. *Es rufet Gott*
7. *Soldatenlied**
8. *Die alten Sagen kunden*
9. *Saatengrün**
10. *Der Gang um Mitternacht*
11. *Festlied zu Schiller's Jubelfeier*
12. *Gottes ist der Orient*
Gaudeamus igitur, humoresque. Leipzig: Schuberth, n.d [1871]. LC
Grüss. Leipzig: Licht & Meyer, n.d. [1885?]. LC
Hungaria 1848. Modern ed. with a foreword by István Szelényi, Budapest: Zeneműkaidó Vállalat, 1961.
Zur Säkularfeier Beethovens (2nd Beethoven Cantata). Leipzig: C. F. Kahnt, 1870. LC.
Le forgeron. Modern edition with a foreword by István Szelényi, Budapest: Zeneműkaidó Vállalat, 1962.
Vierstimmige Männergesang. Mainz: Schott, n.d. [1841].
   1. *Rheinweinlied* (NYPL, LC; also published with Hungarian text under the title *Rajna-bordal* as no. 94 in the third part of an anthology for male choruses titled *Apollo* in 1892)[5]
   2. *Studentenlied.** LC
   3. *Reiterlied*, 1st version. LC, missing pages 3–6
   4. *Reiterlied*, 2nd version.* NYPL, LC
Weimars Volkslied. * Weimar: Kühn, n.d. [1858]. LC
Zwei Festgesang zur Enthüllung der Carl-August Denkmals in Weimar am 3 September 1875. Leipzig: Fr. Kistner, 1875. LC
   I.   *Karl August weilt mit uns*
   II. *Psalmenverse Der Herr bewahret dei Seelen seiner Heiligen* (sacred)

*also in *Liszt Ferenc Männerchöre*, ed. by Forrai Miklós. Budapest: Zeneműkaidó, 1959.

WORKS FOR MEN'S VOICES

1839	*Das deutsche Vaterland.* S 74.
	Les quatre élémens, no. 2 (*Les aquilons*). S 80.
1841	*Vierstimmige Männergesänge.* S 72.
	1. *Rheinweinlied*
	2. *Studentenlied*
	3. *Reiterlied*, 1st version
	4. *Reiterlied*, 2nd version
1842	*Über allen Gipfeln ist Ruh* (1st version). S 75/1.
	Das düstre Meer umrauscht mich. S 76.
	Titan (rev. 1845 and 1847). S 79.
1843	*Trinkspruch.* S 78.
1845	*Les quatre élémens*, nos. 1 (*La terre*), 3 (*Les flots*), and 4 (*Les astres*). S 80.
	Es war einmal ein König, baritone solo. S 73.
	Le forgeron, tenor and bass solos, piano. S 81.

Drei vierstimmige Männerchöre (rev. and pub. as *Geharnischte Lieder* in 1859). S 90.

1. *Trost*
2. *Trost*
3. *Nicht gezagt!*

1846   *Die lustige Legion.* S 77.

A patakhoz [To the Brook]. S 81a.

1848   *Hungaria 1848*, soprano, tenor, and bass solos, orchestra. S 83.

Arbeiterchor, baritone solo, piano. S 82.

1849   *Festalbum zur Säkularfeier von Goethes Geburtstag*

II. *Licht, mehr Licht.* S 84.

IV. *Über allen Gipfeln ist Ruh!* (2nd version), solo men's quartet. S 75/2.

1850   *Festchor zur Enthüllung des Herder-Denkmals in Weimar.* S 86.

1853   *An die Künstler*, orchestra. S 70.

1842–1859   *Für Männergesang* (entire collection published by C. F. Kahnt, Leipzig, 1861). S 90.

1. *Vereinslied* (1856)
2. *Ständchen* (before 1858)
3. *Wir sind nicht Mumien* (1842)

Geharnischte Lieder (1859)

4. *Vor der Schlacht*
5. *Nicht gezagt*
6. *Es rufet Gott*
7. *Soldatenlied* (1844)
8. *Die alten Sagen kunden* (c.1845)
9. *Saatengrün* (c. 1845?)
10. *Der Gang um Mitternacht* (c. 1845?)
11. *Festlied zu Schillers Jubelfeier* (1859)
12. *Gottes ist der Orient* (1842)

1857   *Weimars Volkslied.* S 87.

1858   *Festgesang zur Eröffnung der zehnten allgemeinen deutschen Lehrerversammlung.* S 26.

1871   *A lelkesedés dala* (*Das Lied der Begeisterung*). S 91.

1875   *Zwei Festgesang zur Enthüllung der Carl-August Denkmals in Weimar*

I. *Karl August weilt mit uns*, soprano and alto ad libitum, brass, and timpani. S 92.

1883   *Magyar király-dal* (*Ungarisches Königslied*) (male voices or mixed voices), piano/orchestra. S 93.

1885?   *Grüss.* S 94.

About two-thirds of Liszt's entire output of secular choral music is for *Männerchor*. Bombing raids destroyed many of the original scores during World War II.[6] Those that remain are difficult to find, and only a few are in modern editions. The Library of Congress holds a number of Liszt's male secular choral works in first-edition performance folios, both on microfilm and in the special collections case (see Table 14.1).

Liszt contributed his share of cantatas, patriotic ballads, sacred music, and merry drinking songs to the popular repertory of men's choral music. The *Männerchor* movement was at its height between the years 1840 and 1871 (the year of German unification). The surge of nineteenth-century German nationalism and the movement towards political unity created a fertile climate for the men's chorus movement to grow. Choral organizations sprang up in German-speaking countries where groups sang for social camaraderie and patriotic zeal.

Liszt wrote many of his choruses for specific functions or groups. The earliest of these is *Das deutsche Vaterland* written for the King of Prussia, Friedrich Wilhelm IV, who in return on 16 June 1842 decorated Liszt with the highest honor given to a citizen, the Order of Merit.[7] Other early occasional works for men's voices include *Vierstimmige Männergesang* (1841–1842), which contains four part-songs written for the benefit of the Mozart Foundation, and *Trinkspruch* (1843), written for the Munich *Stubenvollgesellschaft* in return for a *Festabend* in Liszt's honor on 31 October 1843.[8]

Other works for male chorus grew out of the political turmoil of the 1840s, when the Industrial Revolution created poverty among the urban masses who began to revolt. Singing groups brought workers together and helped unite them in their cause for freedom and equality. Liszt created *Le forgeron* (The Blacksmith, 1845), *Hungaria 1848*, and *Arbeiterchor* (Workers Chorus, 1848) with such groups in mind.

In the 1850s Liszt wrote *An die Künstler*, a longer and more substantial work for solo male quartet, men's chorus, and orchestra set to Schiller's poetry, as well as a number of smaller pieces for ceremonial occasions. Some of these smaller works include *Festchor zur Enthüllung des Herder-Denkmals in Weimar*, a fanfare for the unveiling of the Herder monument in Weimar on 25 August 1850, and two short works for men's voices written for occasions honoring the prince of Weimar, Karl August. Liszt composed the first, *Weimars Volkslied* (1857), expressly to be a national anthem for the house of Sachsen-Weimar,[9] and entitled the second *Karl August weilt mit uns*. Other short pieces written for specific occasions include *A lelkesedés dala* (*Das Lied der Begeisterung*, 1871), dedicated to the Hungarian Choral Society; *Magyar király-dal* (*Ungarisches Königslied*, 1883), commissioned for the opening of the Budapest Opera in 1883; and *Grüss*, a miniature welcome piece dedicated to the Riga *Liedertafel*.

In addition to the independent works for male chorus, it is important to mention the two symphonic works that include male voices. The *Schlusschor aus Eine Faust Symphonie* (1857) dramatically concludes the Symphony. *Les morts*, after the poem by Lamennais, is the first of the *Trois odes funèbres* for orchestra written in direct response to Liszt's grief over the death of his son Daniel in 1860.

Shorter Works for Male Chorus

Liszt's shorter works for Männerchor reveal a miniaturist side to his complex persona. Most of this music belongs to the genre of romantic part-songs, and he contributed to this category of vocal composition alongside other great composers such as Franz Schubert, Felix Mendelssohn, Robert Schumann, and

Johannes Brahms. His choral writing in these early part-songs is at times practical and straightforward, clearly with an amateur chorus in mind, yet at other times harmonically adventurous, illustrating his romantic taste for chromaticism and new modulations that may challenge the intonation of amateur choruses. General style characteristics emerge from the early pieces, however, such as harmonic preference for chromatic third relationships, a propensity for motivic variation (an early manifestation of his concept of "thematic transformation"), expressive use of dynamics, and idiomatic writing for the voice. In general, Liszt's shorter Männerchor pieces emphasize harmony over counterpoint, with modest structures in mostly strophic form.

The music may not be of the highest artistic standard since he wrote many of the pieces for social or political reasons, or for the pleasure of the singers and the public. The texts range from traditional poetic verses of love, spring, fun, and patriotism, such as *Ständchen, Saatengrün, Studentenlied*, and *Rheinwein-lied*, to more radical political and social themes, such as *Wir sind nicht Mumien* and *Der Gang um Mitternacht*. Liszt draws at times on the greatest of German poets, such as Goethe and Schiller, to lesser-known writers, such as Georg Herwegh (1817–1875), and even pedestrian authors of third-rate verses.

Vierstimmige Männergesang. Liszt composed his early part-songs for men's voices, *Rheinweinlied, Studentenlied*, and the two versions of *Reiterlied* in 1841 and 1842. Schott published them in 1843 as *Vierstimmige Männergesang* for the benefit of the Mozart Foundation in Frankfurt. Prior to this publication, though, the composer had already shown his support for the newly formed Mozart Foundation by giving a benefit piano performance in Frankfurt on 25 September 1841. Liszt held a strong affinity for fraternal orders, and he was involved with Freemasonry and other German Masonic Lodges throughout his entire life.[10] These fraternal orders and societies provided a social and spiritual environment for their members, and his involvement with them must have inspired him to compose music for their singing groups.

Interesting connections exist between Liszt's association with the Freemasons in Frankfurt, his induction into the Mozart Society, and the appearance of *Vierstimmige Männergesang* four part-songs for the Mozart Foundation. Liszt spent the summer of 1841 (as well as the summers of 1842 and 1843) on the remote island Nonnenwerth on the Rhine, near Bonn. He composed his song *Die Loreley* to Heine's poem that summer, and perhaps the Rhine inspired him to produce *Rheinweinlied*. In any case, Liszt visited nearby Frankfurt-am-Main in the early fall of 1841 and was inducted into the Freemason's Lodge there on 18 September. His sponsor, the businessman Wilhelm Speyer (or Speier) (1790–1878), was a lesser-known composer and violinist who had founded the local Mozart *Stiftung* and also ran a series of *Liederkranz* evenings for the performance of male-choral music. Liszt most likely composed his part-songs *Rheinweinlied, Studentenlied*, and *Reiterlied* for performances on Speyer's *Liederkranz* evenings. Each part-song bears an inscription. Liszt dedicated *Rheinweinlied* to his friend Joseph Lefebvre[11] and *Studentenlied* to W. Speyer. Both versions of *Reiterlied* are dedicated to Herr

Grafen Alexander Teleky von Szék. Liszt continued the association with his fellow mason Speyer for the next few years. On 4 October 1843 Liszt played, and even sang, at a private matinée that Speyer hosted.[12]

Although Liszt published these four part-songs as a group, their performance history verifies he did not compose them as a set. They were mostly performed independently, and in the early 1840s he occasionally included them to "flesh out his German programs."[13] *Rheinweinlied* seems to have been a particular favorite, probably owing to its rousing patriotic text. Between 1841 and 1843, it received seven performances in Jena, Leipzig (where the *Neue Zeitschrift* praised it), Berlin, Breslau (with Liszt conducting), and Paris (Liszt conducting, along with a performance of *Reiterlied*). The Berlin *Männergesang* performed *Reiterlied* in Berlin in 1843 with Liszt conducting, and *Studentenlied* was heard in both Leipzig and Paris in 1841.

Liszt revised two of these early part-songs later in his life. He had further thoughts of improving the *Studentenlied* after fifteen intervening years of practical experience from the date of composition. In a letter to Johann Herbeck, the director of the *Musikverein* in Vienna, Liszt expressed his thanks for the careful reading of the work and mentioned other successful performances in Cologne, Berlin, and Paris. He also wrote, "When I published it fifteen years ago, I did not think much of making allowances for any possible laxity in the intonation of the singers: but today when my experience has taught me better, I should probably write the somewhat steep and slippery passage as follows."[14] Here Liszt simplified the dotted rhythms of the original into steady eighth notes and also smoothed out the voice leading in all the parts in mm. 10–13. He then suggests a change in the third strophe, mm. 105–107 "in honor of prosody."[15]

Liszt made several changes to *Rheinweinlied* in June 1884. He wrote a note on the first edition score giving permission to Carl Huber, the new director of the Hungarian Music and Song Festival in Miskolcz who was also a violinist and composer at the Budapest Academy of Music, to use and orchestrate *Rheinweinlied* for the Festival.[16] The combined choruses participating in the festival performed the piece at the national song festival on 9 and 10 August 1884.[17] Huber's orchestration never appeared in print, and there has been no documentation of subsequent performances of this version after the song festival in Miskolcz.[18]

All four pieces of the *Vierstimmige Männergesang* are set to German romantic texts. *Rheinweinlied* and *Reiterlied* are by Herwegh, a contemporary of Liszt's with a revolutionary spirit and lyric sensitivity, and they have themes of patriotism and love of freedom, respectively. *Studentenlied*, from Goethe's *Faust*, is a light-hearted song about the ill fate of a rat. Liszt paints each text in a uniquely dramatic way. The introduction to *Rheinweinlied* begins with a fanfare motive to portray the hearty German spirit, juxtaposed with a flowing pentatonic melody to express the element of nature. The first version of *Reiterlied* uses a steady running eighth-note scalar pattern in a minor key to create the atmosphere of the mysterious night ride of a horseman who will perish at dawn in his fight for freedom: *O Reiterlust, am frühen Tag/ Zu sterben, zu sterben!* (O rider's joy, early in the day/ To die, to die!). *Studentenlied* is full of joyous laughter in the voices. Each part-song is in strophic form with three stanzas, although both versions of *Reiterlied* are in a more sophisticated modified strophic form. *Rheinweinlied* and the first version of *Reiterlied* are for piano accompaniment, while the other two, *Studentenlied* and the second version of *Reiterlied*, are *a cappella*.

Liszt's choral writing in these short pieces is predominantly four-part homophonic style, although brief passages of staggered entrances and imitative writing occur. One particular favorite cadential figure in *Vierstimmige Männergesang* (and in many of the *Männerchor* works) is a linear 6̂–5̂, either prepared or unprepared, in the first tenor over dominant harmony.

Example 14.1
Liszt, *Vierstimmige Männergesang*, illustrating typical cadential figure

(a) *Rheinweinlied*, mm. 21–22   **(b) *Reiterlied*, 2nd Version, mm. 14–15**

The melodic lines of these part-songs are generally given to the first tenors as the top-line of the four-part chordal texture, and they tend to follow scalar patterns and arpeggio figures. Rhythms are mostly straightforward and in agreement with the text. Dotted rhythms, a preference of Liszt's, add excitement and drive to the music. The harmony at times is quite adventurous, including chromatic third relationships, enharmonic spellings, and his signature augmented triad.

To illustrate some of these general observations about Liszt's *Vierstimmige Männergesang*, as well as many of his other works for *Männerchor*, let us take a closer look at the composer's rousing setting of the patriotic poem *Rheinweinlied*. Herwegh's poem extols the virtues of the German Rhinewine as a symbol of the German spirit: *Wo solch ein Feuer noch gedeiht, und solch ein Wein noch Flammen speit/ da lassen wir in Ewigkeit uns nimmer mehr vertreiben/ Stosst an, stosst an, Der Rhein, der Rhein, und nur um den Wein, der Rhein soll deutsch, der Rhein soll deutsch verbleiben!* (Where such a fire still flourishes, and such a wine still spews flames/ thence we will never in all eternity allow ourselves to be expelled/ Let's toast, let's toast, the Rhine, the Rhine, and only for the wine, the Rhine should remain German, remain German!)

The introduction establishes the harmonic structure of the work, while it also exposes the primary motivic ideas (see Example 14.2).

Example 14.2
Liszt, *Rheinweinlied*, mm. 1–19

RHEINWEINLIED

Gedicht von HERWEGH. Musik von FRANZ LISZT.

Liszt circles around the tonic B♭ by emphasizing first the mediant, D. The opening fanfare staccato motive in eighth notes first sounds in octaves oscillating between D and A. Liszt immediately contrasts this motive in the second measure with the legato pentatonic melody on B♭. He repeats the juxtaposition of these two motives twice in expanded form by first harmonizing the octaves in D major and the pentatonic melody with B♭ major, and then repeating that harmonization again an octave higher. The fanfare motive starts a fourth time, but takes a different turn harmonically when the flowing motive follows. A series of descending fifths follows: D–G–C–F–B♭. A third motive, which is integral to the work and foreshadows the choral entrance, sounds with the arrival of B♭ in dotted eighth followed by sixteenth notes, and the bass-line descends yet another fifth to E♭ by step. At this point Liszt departs on a seemingly unrelated harmonic path of F♯ major leading to a B major sixth-chord—really nothing more than a chromatically embellished 5-6 linear progression over the bass-note E♭, respelled as D♯. The B major sixth-chord is then respelled as C♭ major in m. 13, a notation that clarifies the chord's harmonic function as the Neapolitan. A cadential dominant follows, expanded by yet another important motivic idea of the piece—a descending scalar figure in octaves—paving the way for the expected tonic. The voices enter in a homophonic texture in dotted rhythms. An augmented triad appears at the end of the work in the coda at m. 107, as the bass line descends from tonic to dominant (B♭ to F) via a G♭ (see Example 14.3). The piece concludes with a hymn-like reverential setting of the text *Der Rhein soll deutsch verbleiben!* on a descending third diatonic progression (B♭–G–E♭–C), ending with a final descending step to the tonic B♭ *bleiben.*

Drei vierstimmige Männerchöre. After his tour of Spain ended in April 1845, Liszt gave concerts in France and Switzerland as he made his way toward Bonn for the upcoming Beethoven Festival in August. He stayed in Switzerland during June and July, traveling back and forth between Zurich and Basel. As thanks for the special torchlight procession dedicated to him after his second concert in Basel, Liszt composed *Drei vierstimmige Männerchöre* for the Basel Männerchor to texts by the Swiss physician and writer Theodor Meyer-Merian. The compositions are still in the Basel Männerchor Archives, and Ernst Knop published them in Basel in 1845.[19]

As with *Vierstimmige Männergesang,* each part-song in *Drei vierstimmige Männerchöre* carries a dedication to someone associated with the creation of the music. No. 1, *Trost* is dedicated to Herr Carl Brenner, the president of the Basel Männerchor; no. 2, *Trost* (same text, different setting) is dedicated to Herr Heimlicher, Architect in Basel who was also a member of the Basel Männerchor and the secretary of the society; and no. 3 *Nicht gezagt* is dedicated to Herr Müller, Musikdirektor in Zurich.

Example 14. 3
Liszt, *Rheinweinlied*, mm. 104–117

Drei vierstimmige Männerchöre stylistically resembles the earlier four *Vierstimmige Männergesang*. All are strophic in form, contain predominantly homophonic writing, and consistently employ Liszt's harmonic preferences for chromatic third and enharmonic relationships. Comparison of the two settings of *Trost* yields interesting compositional differences. The text setting of the second follows even quarter-note rhythms more frequently than the first, yet the second is more chromatic than the first. Liszt's characteristic cadence with suspension figure illustrated above in Example 14.1 also appears in both settings.

Liszt later reworked these three choral works, and they appeared as nos. 4, 5, and 6 in the collection of twelve *Für Männergesang* that Kahnt published in 1861 in Leipzig under the title *Geharnischte Lieder* (Armored Songs). The two settings of *Trost* were renamed, reordered, and revised from their original form. Both are *a cappella*, omitting the piano accompaniment from the original. *Trost* no. 1 from the original Basel version appears as *Vor der Schlacht*, and it remains the first of the group. Both versions are in E♭ major, 3/4 time, and strophic form. While the overall harmonic plan is the same in each, Liszt makes changes in the voicings and text setting in the revised version. *Trost* no. 2 from the original Basel version appears under the title *Es rufet Gott*, taken from the opening line of text, and it is third in the revised group. Both versions are in the key of C with same opening unison setting, but Liszt substantially shortened the revised version by omitting transitions between strophes and an extension after the third strophe. The harmonic plan is substantially altered, too, such as moving to E major rather than E♭ major in the second strophe. In addition, the text in these two revised arrangements of *Trost* is mysteriously attributed to Carl Götze rather than to Meyer, and the dedications are omitted. *Nicht gezagt*, the third in the original set, appears in the middle of the revised set. It is note-for-note the same, including the piano accompaniment. The same title appears in the modern collection of Liszt's *Männerchöre* edited by Forrai Miklós and published in Budapest by Zeneműkaidó in 1959. It is in the key of G major, rather than the original A♭ major, with some changes in the text setting as well as omissions of musical transitions between strophes. Furthermore, in this version the text is also attributed to Götze, although in the Raabe catalog printed in the back of the Miklós edition, Meyer's name appears first with a question mark, followed by Götze's name. The changes in the Miklos edition are puzzling, since the source for the music is the 1861 Kahnt edition.

Für Männergesang. Written between 1842 and 1859, *Für Männergesang* is a collection of twelve short pieces varying in style from playful drinking songs to intimate part-songs. Kahnt published the group in 1861, adding it to the house's substantial catalog of *Lieder für Männerchor* where Liszt had a corner in this popular market. A list of some of his contemporaries in this medium, many of whom have since fallen into obscurity, appear below (see Example 14.4).

Example 14.4
Copy of a back advertisement page from *Für Männergesang* for other *Lieder für Männerchor* published by Kahnt

Lieder für Männerchor

aus dem Verlage von **C. F. Kahnt Nachfolger, Leipzig.**

	Part. Mk.	à St. Pf.
Adam, C. F., Op. 10. No. 5. **(Bismarcks Leiblied:)**		
„Wie könnt' ich dein vergessen".	—.40	15
Becker, R., Op. 122. Der Tod des Kolumbus. Mit Baritonsolo	—.60	15
Breitung, F., Op. 16. Der kluge Peter	—.60	15
Clarus, M., Op. 33 a. Der Matrose	—.40	15
— „ 33 b. Herzenskönigin	—.40	15
Harder, E., Drei Lieder. No. 1. Allgemeines Wandern. No. 2. Frühlingslied.		
No. 3. Zwiegesang.	—.60	30
Hartung, H., Op. 3. Vier Gesänge:		
No. 1. Wanderlied	—.40	15
„ 2. Schenkenlied	—.60	20
„ 3. Lieder und Wein	—.40	15
„ 4. Heimkehr	—.60	20
Heinz, P., Op. 46. a) Lieblingsplätzchen. b) Ständchen	—.40	15
— Op. 60. Strampelchen	—.40	15
— „ 69. Aufforderung zum Tanz. (Mit Klavierbegleitung ad. lib.)	1.20	25
— „ 70. Eh' das Jahr vergeht	—.40	15
— „ 86. Waldesrauschen	—.40	15
— „ 100. Mein Regenschirm	—.60	30
— „ 101. No. 1. Ungarisches Trinklied	—.40	13
„ 2. Nacht am Meer	—.40	15
— „ 111. Frauenlob	—.60	20
— „ 114. Ich grüße dich, du mein goldlockiges Kind	—.40	15
— „ 115. Mein Heimatland	—.40	15
— „ 117. Über Tag und Nacht	—.40	15
— „ 118. Warnung	—.40	15
— „ 120. Deutsches Männerlied	—.40	15
— „ 121. Im Frühling	—.40	15
Hesse, F., Op. 30. No. 1. Liebesbitte	—.40	15
„ 2. Wandermut	—.60	15
Höhne, W., Blau Blümelein	—.40	15
— Anhalt-Hymne	—.40	15
Ketschau, W., Op. 6. Zwei Lieder:		
No. 1. Es steht eine Lind' im tiefen Tal	—.60	15
„ 2. Abendlied im Frühling	—.60	15
Krug, Arnold, Op. 128. Pilgergesang der Kreuzfahrer	—.60	30
Möskes, H., Op. 18. Drei Gesänge:		
No. 1. Abendgruß	—.60	15
„ 2. Der sterbende Soldat	—.60	15
„ 3. Es fuhr ein Fischer wohl über den See	—.60	15
Parlow, E., Op. 58. Der Teufel und der Spielmann	—.30	20
Perfall, K. v., Noch sind die Tage der Rosen	—.40	10
Petschke, H. T., Neuer Frühling	—.60	15
Rietz, Jul., Morgenlied „Kein Stimmlein noch schallt"	—.60	30
— Maienzeit „Und wenn die Primel"	—.60	30
Robert-Hansen, E., Der Mai. Mit Sopran- oder Tenorsolo	3.—	30
Solostimme		30
Schmidt-Wetzlar, W., Kaiserhymne	—.40	15
Schumann, C., Op. 19. No. 1. Weihnachtslied	—.60	20
„ 2. Abendgebet	—.60	20
Spielter, H., Op. 65. 's Röslein (Preislied)	—.60	15
Stange, Max, Op. 97. Vier Lieder:		
No. 1. Hoch das Banner, deutsches Lied	—.60	30
„ 2. Im Mai	—.40	15
„ 3. In der Mondnacht	—.40	15
„ 4. Im Walde	—.60	30
Wenzel, Max, Op. 28. Das Vöglein	—.40	15
Wiedermann, F., Op. 13. Grüße aus dem Liedergarten des deutschen Volkes. 15 Volkslieder.		
Heft I: No. 1. Der grausame Bruder. No. 2. Abschied und Heimkehr. No. 3. Der Ritter und die Königstochter. No. 4. Die Wäscherin. No. 5. Herzlieb im Grabe. No. 6. Mondscheinlied. No. 7. Nachtfahrt.	1.—	30
Heft II: No. 8. Der verwundete Knabe. No. 9. Lebewohl. No. 10. Feines Mägdelein. No. 11. Einladung. No. 12. Die Nachtigall als Bote. No. 13. Soldatenlied aus dem 7jähr. Kriege. No. 14. Vom bayr. Erbfolgkriege. No. 15. Liebeswechsel.	1.—	30
Zak, J., Op. 1. Heimweh	—.40	15

The autograph manuscripts of most of the *Für Männergesang* pieces, including nos. 1–8, 10, and 11, are in the Liszt Museum in Weimar. The autograph manuscript of no. 9, *Saatengrün*, is in the Országos (National) Széchényi Library in Budapest. Raabe's Liszt catalog also lists a version of this part-song with piano accompaniment, which has not been printed, in the Liszt Museum.[20] A beautiful setting of Ludwig Uhland's poem *Lob des Frühlings*, *Saatengrün* is also known under the titles *Lied des Frühlings* and *Frühlingstag*. Its exact date of composition is unknown, although the imprint of the music paper for the manuscript in Budapest "Cöln, bei Eck & Comp." suggests a date in the first half of the 1840s, the period during which Liszt kept in close touch with the music publisher Eck & Lefebvre of Cologne.[21] *Saatengrün*, a title taken from the first word of the poem, first appeared in print in the 1861 Kahnt collection.

Nos. 3 and 12, *Wir sind nicht Mumien* and *Gottes ist der Orient*, were published prior to the Kahnt edition. According to Searle in his catalog for the *New Grove Dictionary*, Eck published both in 1844 in Cologne. Raabe, however, indicates *Wir sind nicht Mumien* first appeared in 1842, together with the independent pieces *Über allen Gipfeln ist Ruh* (first version) and *Das düstre Meer umrauscht mich*.

Liszt composed two of the pieces in *Für Männergesang* for specific occasions or groups. No. 1, *Vereinslied*, is a jovial song of camaraderie written for the *Neu-Weimarverein*, whose membership must have been sympathetic to the *Zukunftsmusik* "despite the Philistine's cry" (*trotz Philistergeschrei*). With text praising both Schiller and Germany, *Festlied zu Schillers Jubelfeier* was probably written for the Schiller centenary celebration in Weimar on 9 and 10 November 1859. Apparently Liszt was absent from participating in the celebrations, but the *Festlied* was published in the *Leipziger illustrierte Zeitung*, 12 November 1859.[22]

The compositional style of these part-songs is similar to the other pieces for *Männerchöre* discussed above, although some of them move into a deeper, more expressive realm. For texts, Liszt chose poems by German romantic poets, including Goethe (*Soldatenlied* from *Faust* and *Gottes ist der Orient*), Hoffmann von Fallersleben (*Wir sind Mumien* and *Vereinslied*, Friedrich Rückert (*Ständchen*), Uhland (*Saatengrün*), Herwegh (*Der Gang um Mitternacht*), and Franz von Dingelstedt (*Festlied zu Schillers Jubelfeier*). The twelve part-songs cover a wide range of the themes—from festive praises for the great poet Schiller (*Festlied zu Schillers Jubelfeier*), to political/social issues (*Wir sind nicht Mumien* and *Der Gang um Mitternacht*) and expressions of religious faith (*Gottes ist der Orient*).

Liszt portrays the words with exquisite text painting and special instrumentation in some of these pieces. The intimate setting of *Ständchen*, for example, poignantly expresses the word *einwiegen* (to rock to sleep) in the third strophe as the tenor solo rocks between D and C♯ in mm. 77–80.[23] Liszt musically portrays the martial text of *Soldatenlied* with a marching homophonic style and instrumental parts for two trumpets and timpani.

All but *Nicht gezagt* in *Für Männergesang* are *a cappella*, and most of the pieces are in strophic form. Some notable exceptions, however, occur in Liszt's standard part-song form. *Die alten Sagen kunden* opens with an introduction followed by two large parts, each with sections alternating between solo quartet on the verses. The voice parts in the verses are quite independent, where Tenors I and II tend to move together in thirds against a faster moving Bass II and a more lyrical Bass I line. *Saatengrün*, the shortest piece of the twelve, divides its forty-three measures into two sections of slow-fast. The tenors and basses move in a lead-follow relationship in the slow section. In the second section the texture turns more homophonic with basses divided mostly into a drone on A–E, with the baritones singing the melody and the tenors echoing in thirds. *Gottes ist der Orient*, a slow and expressive hymn, is another short piece in simple two-part form. It contains an abundance of unison writing. Liszt repeats and varies the second section at the end to include the reverential "Amen"—a fitting end to the set of twelve pieces.

Liszt's preference for chromatic-third relationships governs many of the harmonic progressions in the twelve *Für Männergesang*. *Ständchen*, for example, employs this relationship between first and second sub-sections, in G major and Bb major respectively. *Wir sind nicht Mumien* contains exciting chromatic modulations as well as harmonic motion by thirds. *Festlied zu Schillers Jubelfeier* also captures the interest harmonically with chromatic third relationships between the first strophe in A major and the second strophe in C major. The third strophe moves into the ♮VI (F major, a chromatic third down from the home-key of A) and then progresses to the Neapolitan area of Bb.

In *Der Gang um Mitternacht*, the most expressive and complex of the twelve short pieces in *Für Männergesang*, Liszt expertly expresses Herwegh's poignant text in an extended two-part form. The first section in C minor creates an air of mystery as the basses sing in unison, *Ich schreite mit dem Geist der Mitternacht, die weite stille Strasse auf und nieder* (I paced with the ghost of midnight, up and down the wide still streets). The section fades away with the full chorus on the line, *die Welt is müde, o lasst sie träumen!* (The world is tired, o let it dream), which the basses alone eerily echo on *träumen!* The second section contrasts a slower hymn-like texture in C major, *O Gott der Armuth, lass die Armen träumen* (O God of poverty, let the poor dream). A tenor solo draws out the final line, *lass uns alle träumen* (let us all dream), in a twenty-seven-measure-long chromatic and melismatic melody, supported by the chorus on sustained, slow-moving harmonies. The piece concludes with a coda at an even slower tempo on those final words, with a bass line reminiscent of the opening music on the last line of the first section, *die Welt ist müde, lasst sie träumen.*

Männerchor pieces in the Goethe Festival Album (1849). Liszt composed his *Festalbum zur Säkularfeier von Goethes Geburtstag* for a great festival in Weimar celebrating the 100th anniversary of Goethe's birth. The *Festalbum* contains five pieces, two of which are for male chorus. No. 2, *Licht! Mehr Licht*, cites Goethe's last words with an elaboration by Franz von Schober (1798–1882). A $\hat{6}-\hat{5}-\hat{1}$ melodic motive in the low-brass accompanies the opening text set for the chorus in unison and returns at the end of the piece. The formal structure consists of five varied strophes, with a primarily homophonic texture. No. 4, *Über allen Gipfeln ist Ruh!*, from Goethe's *Wanderers Nachtlied*, appears in this *Fest Album* in a second version for solo male quartet from the earlier 1842 version. It serves here as a prelude to the final *Chor der Engel* from *Faust*, Part II. Liszt's setting of the text is slow and expressive, featuring the baritone section in a leader role answered by the full chorus. The other three numbers of Liszt's *Festalbum* include an instrumental introduction titled *Fest Marsch*, a middle solo song called *Weimars Todten* for baritone, and the final *Chor der Engel* arranged for mixed voices.[24]

Miscellaneous Patriotic and Ceremonial Songs. Other *Männerchor* works that Liszt wrote include short patriotic, festive, and ceremonial songs. The earliest of the patriotic songs, *Das deutsche Vaterland*, is the simplest of all Liszt's works for the medium, yet it displays many of the characteristics discussed above. It is strophic in form and essentially straightforward in the part writing with scale and arpeggio figures, yet is harmonically adventurous, utilizing chromatic third relationships. Liszt performed the short piece numerous times on his German performances in the early 1840s, along with *Rheinweinlied* as noted above, and even played a virtuoso piano arrangement of the piece for a private audience at a hotel in Bonn on 1 November 1841.[25] Although the *Allgemeine musikalische Zeitung* criticized it as being too operatic and complex for a "popular" (*volkstümlich*) composition,[26] Liszt intended *Das deutsche Vaterland* to be a moneymaker. His handwritten note to the publisher Schlesinger on the final page of the manuscript illustrates his intentions: "F. Liszt requests, in a friendly manner, H. Schlesinger to obtain, through his influence and work, the greatest possible dissemination in Germany through performances, sending out copy, sufficient advertisement (perhaps it would be useful later on if the song appeared printed in the *Illustrierte Leipziger Zeitung*). For this the author would be especially grateful to him."[27]

Another short patriotic piece, *Es war einmal ein König* (1845), is for baritone solo and men's voices to the text of *Mephisto's Lied* from Goethe's *Faust*. The work exists only in manuscript in the Liszt Museum, but a facsimile copy with extensive commentary on Liszt's textual and dramatic settings of Goethe was printed in 1988 (see Table 14.1).

Prince Karl Alexander commissioned *Weimars Volkslied* (1857), to a text by Peter Cornelius, for celebrations honoring his father Karl August. The prince hoped the piece would replace *God Save the Queen* as the national anthem of Weimar. Liszt made a number of versions for various performing forces, including women's voices and children's voices. The first version, however, written for the big centennial celebration concert and published by Kühn in Leipzig, is for men's voices, winds, brass, and timpani. It consists of five varied strophes plus a short coda, where the first three strophes are more or less exact musical repetitions. The fourth strophe changes key from E major to G major—yet another chromatic third relationship—and varies the harmonic plan as it moves up yet another third to B♭. The fifth strophe returns to E major with the full instrumental forces and the chorus singing *fortissimo* in octaves until the majestic ending, where the voices divide back into parts. Even though Liszt made a modified popular version for men's voices *a cappella* with only three strophes, the piece never fulfilled the prince's hope of being a new national anthem for Weimar. Perhaps a more straightforward piece like *Das deutsche Vaterland* would have better served the purpose.[28]

Another short ceremonial piece is *Festgesang zur Eröffnung der zehnten allgemeinen deutschen Lehrerversammlung* (1858) for men's voices and organ. The only secular choral piece included in the Liszt *Complete Works*,[29] *Festgesang* was written for the opening of the Tenth Universal German Teacher's Meeting. It is in varied strophic form, where Liszt saves most of his variation for the third and final strophe, to texts by the Weimar Court poet Hofmann von Fallersleben.

Eighteen years later in 1875, Liszt again had the occasion to write ceremonial music in honor of Carl August when the prince's statue was unveiled in the Fürstenplatz. The first of the two *Festgesang*, *Karl August weilt mit uns* (Karl August stay with us to the honor, glory, and blessing of Weimar's princedom) is a short but festive fanfare for men's voices, brass, and percussion, with soprano and alto parts *ad libitum*. Its simple harmonic structure centers around C major and the choral writing is primarily in unisons and triads.

In addition to these miscellaneous German pieces, Liszt also produced two Hungarian patriotic ceremonial songs: *A lelkesedés dala* (*Das Lied der Begeisterung/Song of Enthusiasm*, 1871), and *Magyar király-dal* (*Ungarisches Königslied*, 1883) both set to texts by Kornél Ábrányi. The first is an exciting *a cappella* setting, exhibiting Liszt's intricate late harmonic practices and his use of disguised repetition between the three strophes. The second, written for the opening of the Budapest Opera House on 27 September 1884 in honor of the Emperor Franz Joseph, "King of Hungaria," was withdrawn ten days before the festivities. The veiled disguise of the old *Rákóczy Tune* (not the March discussed below) in *Magyar király-dal*, and its links to Hungarian nationalism, unnerved the festival organizers. Although the work was not performed for the celebration in honor of the opening of the opera house, Liszt published it in six different versions. The manuscript for *Magyar király-dal* is lost, but the work survived in its various published versions. The manuscript for another Hungarian piece composed a year earlier, *A Magyarok Istene* (Hungarian God), has also been lost. Upon the publication of *Liszt's Hungarian Letters* by Margit Prahács in 1966, the existence of this work, which is for baritone solo and male chorus with piano accompaniment, was discovered. Liszt described the piece in a letter dated 23 June 1882 to Ábrányi, and also sent the instrumental setting. He stated he wrote it for the Debrecener Musikfest, which took place the summer of 1882.[30]

Finally, *Grüss* (1885?) composed for the Riga *Liedertafel* is a miniature welcome song of only fifteen measures. Liszt's *a cappella* setting of the text, *Glück auf*, places all four voices in their upper registers as the music rushes by with excitement and anticipation.

The Longer "Workers' Choruses"

Liszt composed three large-scale dramatic works for men's voices that confront the mid-nineteenth century social and class issues of the "workers' question." In these pieces, he clearly sympathizes with the workers and the 1848–1849 revolution in Hungary. Owing to their radical and therefore politically risky texts, none of these three works were performed during Liszt's lifetime. The first, *Le forgeron*, to text by the priest and leftist politician Félicité de Lamennais (1782–1854), describes the struggle of the working class. *Hungaria 1848*, to text by von Schober, was written as a passionate tribute to the Hungarian revolution. *Arbeiterchor*, whose author of the text is unknown, urges the workers to march forward to freedom.

Le forgeron (1845). Approximately ten minutes in duration, *Le forgeron* is the earliest of the three works for men's voices inspired by the political unrest of the 1840s. The unpublished manuscript that Conradi prepared in 1848 is in Weimar, but the work is accessible in a modern piano edition.[31] Liszt finished the work on 12 February 1845 in Lisbon, during his six-month tour of the Iberian peninsula from October 1844 to April 1845. After completing the manuscript, the composer discussed the work in a letter to the author of the poem, Lamennais. He thanked the author for the texts, but anticipated musical problems mounting a performance in Paris. He wrote, "I wouldn't even attempt it without being there to conduct the rehearsals myself. While I wait for some such favorable occasion, allow me to tell you that I have enjoyed the task and I hope I haven't entirely mistaken the solution."[32]

Apparently Liszt had hoped to collaborate further with Lamennais on a set of workers' choruses because in that same letter he also asked Lamennais for a complete series of poems about farmhands, sailors, and soldiers, (*les Laboureurs, les Matelots et les Soldats*).[33] The idea never came to fruition, and no "favorable occasion" appeared during Liszt's lifetime for a performance of *Le forgeron*. The first performance took place 116 years after its composition in Budapest on 22 April 1961 by a steel-workers' chorus under the direction of Lajas Voss.

The text of *Le forgeron* depicts the struggle and hopelessness of the workers. Liszt usually features the tenor and bass soloists in the role of the leader/narrator, with the chorus mostly in the role of the laborers. Only towards the end, in the final three sections of the piece (mm. 185ff.), do the soloists drop out. Here the chorus/workers have the final word as they rally to battle with courage.

Liszt portrays Lamennais' opening text *Le fer est dur, frappons, frappons!* (Hard is the iron! Strike it, strike it!) with driving dotted rhythms. The hammering effect is so convincing that, according to the late Austrian Liszt scholar August Göllerich (1859–1923), Wagner got the idea for Siegfried's "Forging Song" from this chorus.[34] This recurring line, always sung by the chorus, serves as the refrain that holds the work together.

Example 14.5
Liszt, *Le forgeron*, opening choral refrain, mm. 28–31

Example 14.6
Liszt, *Le forgeron*, comparison of the closing of first refrain to final refrain
a. mm. 38–41

b. mm. 269–272

Cast in a loose refrain structure, *Le forgeron* is more similar in form to Liszt's symphonic poems than to the smaller works for *Männerchor* discussed above. Two main contrasting sections, both of which recur, alternate with the repeated refrain. The first contrasting section has a lyrical melody in two phrases for the tenor solo, accompanied by arpeggio figures in the piano, that describes the beauty of the light as the sun rises over the hills and the lake. The chorus then answers in a musical transition that leads back to the refrain, *Mais non pour nous, serfs de las faim! Le fer est dur, frappons, frappons!* (But what awaits us, servile fate! Hard is the iron! Strike it, strike it!). The next contrasting section features the men's chorus alone in a flowing, chordal passage in the key of C major. Here the workers experience a moment's relief from their toil, and the style is more similar to the short *Männerchor* pieces. The rejoicing is short-lived, however, as the persistent hammering refrain returns after the repeat of the serene phrase. Liszt incorporates another contrasting section (mm. 119–158) into the work, where tenor and bass soloists alternate recitative passages with the recurring A theme in the chorus. In each solo passage, the singer narrates a tale of sorrow and distress about the deprivation of his family and the fear of winter. The A theme frames each short section, creating a further sense of hopelessness for escape (see Example 14.5).

Liszt's adventurous harmonic language in *Le forgeron* even foreshadows some of his experimental late works. The original harmonic progression that closes the refrain idea moves by a chromatic third in its final transformation from the E-minor tonic chord to a C-minor chord before continuing on to the dominant-tonic cadence. Yet in the final statement of the refrain, now in E major, Liszt moves to an augmented triad built on the lowered root C♮ rather than the diatonic C♯-minor chord (see Example 14.6).

Hungaria 1848. A cantata for bass, tenor, and soprano soloists with men's voices and piano accompaniment, *Hungaria 1848* is a setting of von Schober's text that may have been written at Liszt's special request.[35] The work dates from April 1848, just one month after the "March Revolution" in Hungary, where the people first broke their bonds from the Austrian emperor Ferdinand V and began the great but ill-fated Hungarian revolution of 1848–1849. Liszt had just arrived in Weimar in February to assume his post as Kapellmeister. Two months later he traveled to Kryzanowicz outside of Gräz to meet his Russian lover, Princess Carolyne von Sayn-Wittgenstein and escort her back to Weimar to live with him. While on that trip Liszt wrote his friend Schober to thank him for the poem and briefly described his composition.

Schloss Gräz, 22 April 1848
Dearest, honored friend,
    Your lovely letter brought me even closer to you during the crisis of poetic creativity, which the "Hungaria" brought forth in me. As thanks for your good influence I hope that you will not be displeased with the composition.
    Since my Beethoven Cantata I have written nothing so pronounced and so suddenly poured forth as this. Within the next days the instrumentation should be completed, and when we have the opportunity we can have it performed in Weimar in your honor, alongside *Weimar's Todten.*[36]

Although the work was not performed in Weimar as Liszt had hoped, the piano arrangement came back into his hands years later in 1865 while living in Rome. He made a note on the score that the work should be kept, but it needed many changes. He added corrections to the manuscript, along with the date "1848," perhaps to distinguish it from the Symphonic Poem *Hungaria* composed in 1854. The work was first heard on 21 May 1912 in Weimar under the direction of Peter Raabe, and Raabe led a second performance on 21 October 1912 in Budapest. The music remained in manuscript at the Liszt Museum in Weimar, along with Conradi's orchestrated version, until István Szelényi's Hungarian edition appeared in 1961.

Liszt's setting of Schober's patriotic text, a passionate and rousing tribute to the efforts of the Hungarian people to gain their freedom, is a musical call to arms. Liszt's musical interpretation of the patriotic text is truly in a Hungarian style because he directly uses a folk march-tune that in turn becomes the source for all the melodic and rhythmic ideas.

Liszt casts the cantata in a loose three-part structure of fast-slow-fast, where the sections are interspersed with orchestral interludes. The first large section, divided into two subsections, portrays a great processional march. Dotted rhythms predominate, and the bass soloist plays a major role in expressing the drama. The slower and more lyrical middle section still in mostly dotted rhythms, features first the tenor and then the soprano solo. The text wistfully expresses a yearning for Hungary to once again blossom as the garden of Europe, even as the beauty lives in the *Ungarn Blut* (Hungarian blood). Only the second part of the A section returns in the reprise, where the soprano solo soars above the chorus and brings the work to a rousing finish. The final *Alla Marcia* coda inspires the listener to strive for even greater heights of freedom, and here Liszt adds the Hungarian cry *Eljen!* to the closing melody of Schober's original text.

Liszt unifies the three sections of *Hungaria 1848* with a basic motive and its subsequent transformations. The result of such thematic unity creates a sense of one large "through-composed" work—a compositional form Liszt is well known for in his later symphonic poems. The primary "call to battle" motive of the rising fourth A to D is first heard in the eight-bar introduction, which in turn is sung by the bass soloist and immediately expanded by an upper neighbor-note figure A to B♭ in the opening text, *Das Osten*. This motive is elaborated and varied to become the first theme proper, and at the end of the first part of the A section, the bass soloist and chorus join together with the opening motive and the upper neighbor figure in augmentation with a descending fourth.

Part Two of the first large section again transforms the opening rising fourth motive into an exuberant march theme in the relative major. Here Liszt reveals his source of the basic motive, as he makes a direct quote from the famous *Rákóczy March*, named after Prince Rákóczy who led a Hungarian revolt against Austrian rule in the first decade of the eighteenth century. The following example illustrates the basic motive and the quote from the *Rákóczy March*.

Example 14.7
Liszt, *Hungaria 1848*
a. Opening rising fourth motive, mm.7–8

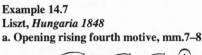

b. March theme, mm. 78–81

Arbeiterchor (1848?). Although the exact date of composition in unknown, *Arbeiterchor* was probably composed before *Hungaria 1848*. The only reference Liszt made to the work was in a hand-written note to his publisher Karl Haslinger on the corrected proof in the spring of 1848.

Example 14.8
Liszt's hand-written note on the proof of *Arbeiterchor* [37]

"Dear Karl, Since events have served us with a quite extraordinary commentary on the workers' question, it would seem more expedient perhaps to postpone the publication of this workers' chorus. I leave the decision entirely with you. F. Liszt"[38]

It seems certain Haslinger destroyed the plates, but the corrected proofs, which bear neither date nor title, are in the Weimar Liszt Museum.[39] Given the time involved in the printing process, however, it is highly likely that Liszt actually composed the piece in 1847 or even earlier.[40]

In any case, the first performance of *Arbeiterchor* did not take place until 1930, when the Austrian Association of Workers' Choirs sang Anton Webern's arrangement for mixed chorus and orchestra. In 1931 the Hungarian Association of Workers Choirs took over the same arrangement and performed it in 1932 for a laborer's celebration.

The text of *Arbeiterchor* calls for unity among all workers:[41] *Herbei, den Spath und Schaufel ziert,/ Herbei, wer Schwerdt un Feder führt,/ Herbei, wer Fleiss und Muth und Kraft,/ Wer Grosses oder Kleines schafft.* (Let us have the adorned spades and scoops,/ Come along all, who wield a sword or pen,/ Come here ye, industrious, brave and strong,/ All who create things great or small.) The text is arranged in eight four-line stanzas, and Liszt arranges the music in three varied strophes. The first two strophes include two main themes encompassing three stanzas each, and the second strophe is an exact musical repetition of the first. The first theme uses steady marching quarter notes and dotted rhythms, while the second theme begins with a rising quarter-note figure followed by martial double-dotted chords. Liszt quoted his own *Arbeiterchor* first theme in the finale of his symphonic poem *Mazeppa*. Here the theme is used to portray "Mazeppa's freedom and his new position as leader."[42] The following example compares the two themes, the first in E♭ major and the second in D major.

Example 14.9
Comparison of the first theme of *Arbeiterchor* and its quote in *Mazeppa*
a. Arbeiterchor, first theme, mm. 8–11

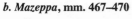

b. Mazeppa, mm. 467–470

The third and final strophe sets the least amount of text, yet it is the longest of the three. Liszt varies the music from the first two strophes both melodically in the bass solos and harmonically in the second part of the first theme. (Compare mm. 20–38 with mm. 141–159. The goal of each passage is a half cadence on B♭, approached by a C♭ major (♭VI) chord, but the harmonic paths are quite different.) Between the first and second themes, the composer inserts a beautiful interlude for the bass solo and four solo voices *a cappella*, punctuated briefly by two bars of chordal accompaniment. Here the men sing to brotherhood in a stirring *Männerchor* style: *D'rum schliess den grosse Bruderbund,/ Und Herz an Herz, und Mund an Mund,/ Ein Vater sieht vom Himmel d'rein,/ Wir mussen alle Brüder sein.* (Therefore rally to the great brotherhood,/ Heart to heart, lips to lips,/ The Father sees us from Heaven/ We must all be brothers.) The full chorus repeats the final stanza to the music of the interrupted second theme, and the chorus concludes with a rousing coda based on the music from the first theme.

Arbeiterchor bears some striking similarities to both *Le forgeron* and *Hungaria 1848*. All three pieces use dotted rhythms extensively to create the sense of urgent marching or rallying to freedom. *Arbeiterchor* and *Le forgeron* feature the soloists in the role of a leader/narrator, while the chorus mostly assumes the role of the people. The three "workers' choruses" also share some striking motivic similarities, such as the half-step upper neighbor figure discussed in *Hungaria 1848* and the motive of the rising fourth. On the whole, though, *Arbeiterchor* is the least impressive of the three, both musically and dramatically, and perhaps is another reason Liszt desired to suppress its publication.

An die Künstler (1853). Among Liszt's secular choral works, *An die Künstler* (*To the Artists*) belongs to a class by itself. Although a cantata for male voices, it is more sophisticated than any of Liszt's earlier *Männerchor* pieces and more refined and symphonic in scope than the "workers' choruses." Liszt conducted the premier performance at the fall music festival in Karlsruhe, where he served as music director, on 3 October 1853. The composer later revised the score and conducted a second performance for the unveiling of the Goethe-Schiller Monument in Weimar on 5 September 1857 during the Carl August centennial concert.[43] Numerous other performances of the work were given, including two in November 1859 for the Schiller centenary celebrations in Jena and Berlin, although the composer attended neither performance. Schlesinger first printed the score in 1854 in Berlin (a reproduction of a manuscript copy), and Kühn and Kahnt brought out subsequent editions of the piece in Weimar and Leipzig, respectively.[44] For the following discussion of the music, I refer to the Kühn edition, which possibly dates from 1856 or 1857 (see Table 14.1).

Schiller's text describes the duty of the artist as a spiritual task, and Liszt's lyrical music, juxtaposed with rousing fanfare passages, portrays this task with the same reverence and awe for art that his sacred choral works portray for the Divine. The first stanza sums up the challenge:

> Der Menschheit Würde ist in eure hand gegeben
> bewahret sie!
> Sie sinkt mit euch, wird sie sich heben!
> Der Dichkunst heilige Magie?
> dient einem weisen Weltenplanen.
> Still lenke wie zum Ozeane
> der grossen Harmonie.

> The dignity of humanity is placed in your hand
> Preserve it!
> It sinks with you, it will rise (with you)!
> The holy magic of poetry serves wise world plans.
> Quietly guide as to the ocean
> of the great harmony.

The composer carefully informs the prospective performers and listeners about the true nature of his work. The first page of the score bears the inscription, *Was schöne Seelen schön empfunden, Muss trefflich und vollkommen sein.* (When beautiful souls experience beauty, it must be excellent and perfect.) In addition, Liszt wrote a foreword to the score, in which he states his intention to give Schiller's lines a musical rendering to their noble character, and warns that only those who can judge success can suitably capture and empathize with this character. This could exclude, he warns, those who are used to the usual standards of the cheerful *Liedertafel* compositions or to the popular demands of singers and listeners who desire lavish praise over deep artistic substance. He further instructs the performers on specific interpretative techniques, requesting them to put meaningful and poetic emphasis on the words, as well as to observe carefully the subtle nuances of the soft dynamics.[45]

With four stanzas of text, Liszt casts the form of *An die Künstler* in a loose ternary structure, where the A section comprises the first stanza, the B section the second, an extended transition section the third, and a varied return of the A section the fourth. The formal divisions are blurred, however, by his extraordinary use of thematic transformation.

The opening theme begins with a broad four-note motive with the brass prevailing, reminiscent of the opening of *Licht! Mehr Licht!*, which spins out to end on the tonic pitch B. A gentle, lyrical descending scalar figure in the woodwinds answers this fanfare call. The four soloists present the second theme, and the unison chorus then elaborates. The first section concludes with a descending third bass progression in a hymn-like texture, an important musical idea of the work reminiscent of the "Dresden Amen" and Wagner's "Grail" motive from *Parsifal*. Liszt uses not only traditional third relationships such as this in *An die Künstler*, but also highly chromatic ones. The overall harmonic progression in mm. 12–20, for example, moves from B major to D major.

The middle section transforms motives and themes heard in the A section. For example, the exciting tenor solo opens the middle section with a melody that combines elements of both the first and second themes on which the four soloists immediately elaborate. This section surges to a climax with the entrance of the chorus, first in an antiphonal effect with the soloists in mm. 125–131, then together with the soloists and the full orchestra in mm. 133–140. A transformation of the opening four-note motive follows as the music begins the transition back to the A section to round out the form.

WORKS FOR MIXED VOICES

1845   *Festkantate zur Enthüllung des Beethoven-Denkmals in Bonn*, 2 soprano, tenor, and bass solos, piano/orchestra. S 67.

1849   *Festalbum zur Säkularfeier von Goethes Geburtstag*
        V. *Chor der Engel.* S 85.

1850   *Chöre zu Herders Entfesseltem Prometheus*, soprano, alto, men's quartet solos, orchestra. S 69.

1869   *Gaudeamus igitur, humoresque*, soprano, alto, tenor, and bass solos (arr. for piano four-hands 1870). S 71.

1870   *Zur Säkularfeier Beethovens* (2nd Beethoven cantata) soprano, alto, baritone, and bass solos, orchestra. S 68.

In addition to his pieces for *Männerchor*, Liszt produced five secular choral works for mixed voices: three large-scale cantatas and *Humoreske* for soloists, mixed voices, and orchestra, and a version of the *Chor der Engel aus Goethe's Faust* for mixed and women's voices. He composed all five works for specific concert celebrations. All but the *Humoreske* celebrate great German artists, and two of the three large-scale cantatas honor Beethoven.

Liszt wrote the first Beethoven Cantata for the inauguration of the Beethoven Monument in Bonn in 1845 and the second, *Zur Säkularfeier Beethovens*, in 1870 for the Beethoven centenary celebration in Weimar. His third large-scale cantata, *Chöre zu Herders Entfesseltem Prometheus* (Prometheus Cantata), was written for the celebrations honoring the great German writer Johann Gottfried Herder (1744–1803) and the unveiling of the Herder monument in Weimar in 1850. He published the short *Chor der Engel aus Goethe's Faust* for mixed and women's voices as the fifth and final part of the *Festalbum zur Säkularfeier von Goethes Geburtstag* celebrating Goethe's birthday in 1849. Shorter than the cantatas, *Gaudeamus igitur, humoresque* celebrated the 100th anniversary of the Jena Concert Academy in 1869.

The Beethoven Cantatas

Festkantate zur Enthüllung des Beethoven-Denkmals in Bonn. In August 1845 Liszt composed the *Festkantate*, his earliest work for mixed chorus and orchestra, for the Beethoven Festival in Bonn. Upon the encouragement of Heinrich Carl Breidenstein, who initiated the Beethoven Monument, Liszt wrote the *Festkantate* for the seventy-fifth anniversary celebration of Beethoven's birth and the unveiling of the great Beethoven statue. The festival was somewhat of a fiasco, poorly planned from the beginning by an incompetent committee and poorly executed when it took place.[46] The festival probably would have never happened if Liszt had not come to the rescue of the committee. He not only raised large amounts of money to contribute towards the cost of the statue and the building of the concert hall by his series of "Beethoven concerts" in Vienna beginning in 1839, he also took over as director of the Festival. Liszt conducted the premier of his cantata on 13 August. The work was received coolly, as was its subsequent performance in Paris the following January.

The full score and parts used for the performance that Joachim Raff wrote out have been lost, and the score was never published. Liszt's own manuscript score, now in the Liszt Museum in Weimar, contains sketchy performance indications, as well as sparsely-written text in the vocal parts.[47] B. Schott's Söhne in Mainz published a piano four-hand version with underlaid text in 1846. Günther Massenkeil used this early printed version, along with Liszt's piano reduction written below the orchestral parts in the autograph manuscript, to reconstruct his modern piano-vocal score. The resulting performance edition makes this early work of Liszt's accessible.

The text to Liszt's first *Beethoven Cantata* appeared in a festival booklet that Breidenstein compiled, containing programs and other information about the Beethoven celebration.[48] Written by Bernhard Wolff (1799–1851), the text extols Beethoven's genius and virtues with all the pomp due such a festive celebration. In the final section, for example, the chorus exclaims *Heilig des Genius* and *Heil Beethoven* in reverence and awe for the musical hero.

The choral voices in the cantata include soprano I and II (no alto), tenor, and bass, while the solo voices are soprano, tenor, and bass. At times Liszt utilizes his vocal forces by alternating between the full chorus and all the soloists, but he mostly features the chorus over the soloists. The textures are predominantly homophonic, although he includes some instances of contrapuntal writing. The harmony is consistent with those of other choral pieces discussed thus far, that is, full of chromatic relationships and modulations. Liszt often uses dotted rhythms for the festive march music, and in the slower movements steady running eighth- and sixteenth-note patterns are often heard in the accompaniment. The opening motive of a descending fourth, rising step, and rising third generates many of the melodic ideas in the cantata and unifies the entire work as it appears in many guises.

Example 14.10
Liszt, *Beethoven Cantata* (1845), primary motive, mm. 1–2

A work of over thirty minutes in length, the first *Beethoven Cantata* is in four parts. Part I begins with a long orchestral introduction (*Maestoso*) as a fanfare call to the festival. The first choral section establishes the celebratory purpose of the day. The pastoral middle section features the four soloists in a repeated triplet pattern as it develops the main musical ideas from the first section, and the final section reaffirms the themes of the opening section.

The soloists rest in Part II *Allegro deciso,* and the movement includes some of the most exciting choral writing of the entire cantata. The chorus begins in unison—*Gleich den Wogen des Meeres rauschen die Völker alle vorüber im Zeiten strom* (Like the waves of the seas they all rush by in the flow of time)—over a running sixteenth-note pattern in the accompaniment and a slower-moving bass line that descends two fourths by step. In the next section Liszt divides the chorus and uses the men and women's voices antiphonally: *Aber unter ihnen in unablässig kreisendem Werde die unaufwechselnde Erd!* (But under them in incessantly circling development, the unchanging earth!). The final section contrasts this thick texture, first with fewer voices, then with a lead-and-follow phrase between the tenors and the combined sopranos. The basses join in, followed by the divided sopranos and tenors, and the parts finally come back together for the phrase, *nur im Tod ist Fortbestehn* (only in death is endured).

The harmonic plan of this movement is as exciting as the choral writing. Beginning in A minor, the music modulates to F♯ minor for the double-chorus section, then moves to D minor via a strong A pedal point, when the voices return to a single chorus and the opening music returns transformed at m. 55. Then in the lead-follow section, Liszt moves chromatically through E♭, E♮, F, and F♯ to D major of the closing phrase. D major, however, moves up a chromatic third to F♯ major, which concludes the movement.

The F♯-major harmony at the end of Part II leads convincingly to Part III, which begins *Andante mesto* in the key of B minor. The movement opens mysteriously with a long melodic line of three gestures hovering around the pitch F♯. Curiously, the tonic pitch B never appears in the opening, but rather is saved for the arrival of the B-minor chord in m. 8. As in Part II, the bass line descends a fourth by step in the opening progression B–A–G–F♯ (mm. 8–11). In fact, this fourth motive, both ascending and descending, permeates the movement in the instrumental part. The chorus enters in steady quarter and half-note rhythms—*Die Völker, die vorüberzogen, versanken in die Nacht der Nächte.* (The people, who marched on, were engulfed in the night of nights.)—where the bass repeats the descending step-progression from the opening of the movement.

The key changes to B major, and the tempo quickens to a majestic march *Allegro maestoso*, where Liszt alternates between soloists, chorus, and instrumental sections. One particularly striking section is the long soprano solo recitative: *Aber soll der Menschheit Streben auch entfluten mit dem Leben?* (But should mankind's striving also fly away with life?). The chorus has the final word, though, as it returns to the main motive from the opening of the cantata in mm. 154–161 on the text, *Der Genius, der Genius! In seinem Wirken ewig wahr und groß!* (The genius, the genius! In his work ever true and great!). An instrumental link transforms the main motive once again (mm. 162), which leads into the final section of Part III. Here the chorus further elaborates the motive and text, and the music gets so carried away as to take the sopranos and tenors up to high Bs (m. 193 and 197). The movement comes to a triumphant close with an instrumental march based on the main motive in E major.

The *Festkantate* could have ended with this grand flourish, yet Liszt included a fourth part as a spiritual tribute to Beethoven. He quotes nearly note-for-note the piano part that begins the third movement (mm. 1–56) of the "Archduke" Trio, op. 97. He transposed this passage from D major to C major and even changes Beethoven's tempo marking *Andante cantabile ma pero con moto* to *Andante religioso*. Above Beethoven's music, Liszt adds first a tenor solo—*Er, den keine Nacht umfing, den nicht irrt des Alltags Spott* (He, whom no night enclosed, [who] erred not of the everyday mockery)—followed by a gentle choral phrase—*Er, dem Gott die Stirne krönet, ist's der das Geschick versöhnet* (He, whose brow God crowns, is reconciled to fate)—and a return of the tenor solo joined by the soprano and bass—*er verleiht der Spanne Zeit Abglanz hellster Ewigkeit* (he endows the span of time with the reflection of brightest eternity). While some of the vocal entrances correspond to those of the violin and cello parts of Beethoven's trio, the melody is Liszt's own.

The middle section of Part IV combines the soloists and the chorus. Here the chorus repeats in a varied form the first tenor solo melody, while the soloists elaborate on a new text to bring the section to a heroic climax: *a nimmer beugt ihn Wucht der Jahre, er bezwingt, ein Held, den Tod* (but the weight of years never bent him; a hero, he conquered death). Liszt brings the quiet opening music back briefly before launching into the final section, where chorus and soloists join forces again: *Heilig! Heilig! Des Genius Walten auf Erden.* (Holy!

Holy! The genius's reign on earth!). The texture diminishes for a solo passage on the same text, then the chorus returns with the worshipful *Heil Beethoven!* Liszt rhythmically sets "Beethoven" as "Beet-" an eighth note, "-ho" a half note, and "-ven" a quarter note (♪ ♩ ♩). The chorus carries the movement to a close, finally returning to the opening motive of the work in the *Allegro con brio*, *Solch' ein Fest hat uns verbunden* (Such a festival has bound us). As in Part III, the music in this final section builds to such great heights that the sopranos and tenors reach high Bs. The main motto returns one last time at the close of the work through a reverential "Amen" cadence, where the vocal range drops into a lower register even while maintaining the *forte* dynamic.

Zur Säkularfeier Beethovens (2nd Beethoven Cantata). In 1870, twenty-five years after the Beethoven Festival in Bonn, Liszt planned the centenary Beethoven Festival in Weimar. He was not invited to return to Bonn for the festivities there, and he declined an invitation to participate in the Beethoven celebration in Vienna. Instead, he transformed the usual May Tonkünstler-Versammlung organized by the Allgemeiner Deutscher Musikverein in Weimar into an all-out Beethoven celebration. The final concert on 29 May was a triumph in the Hoftheater, where Liszt conducted Beethoven's *Emperor Concerto* (featuring Carl Tausig, the great virtuoso and former student of Liszt's, as the piano soloist) and Ninth Symphony. Liszt's second Beethoven Cantata, dedicated to the Grand Duchess Sophie of Weimar, was also featured on this final concert conducted by Müller-Hartnung. Later that year on 16 December, the actual date of Beethoven's birthday, Liszt organized another Beethoven concert in Pest Vigadó, Hungary. Again Liszt featured Beethoven's Ninth Symphony as well as the Violin Concerto (Eduard Reményi as soloist), and his second Beethoven Cantata with the text translated into Hungarian by Ábrányi. Kahnt published both a full score and a vocal score in Leipzig the same year as the premier performance at the jubilee concert in Weimar. Fragments of the manuscript may be found in the National Schéchényi Library in Budapest and in the British Museum.[49]

Liszt's second Beethoven Cantata is much more than a revised version of the 1845 Bonn Cantata.[50] Although they bear some striking similarities, the two cantatas are different pieces altogether. Whereas the Bonn cantata is organized into four clearly divided and distinct parts, Liszt divided the Weimar cantata into two main sections. As in the Bonn cantata, he quotes the third movement of Beethoven's "Archduke" Trio in the Weimar cantata, but he uses the material in an entirely different way. Liszt based the first part, a lengthy orchestral *Einleitung*, completely on Beethoven's music. The second part, a continuous movement for chorus, soloists, and orchestra, carefully works out the opening stepwise descending third motive of Beethoven's opening theme. Although the texts of both cantatas follow similar themes of deification of Beethoven, including *Heil Beethoven* in the final sections, Adolf Stern wrote the text for the second cantata.

Scored for winds in pairs, four horns, and strings, the *Einleitung* retains Beethoven's original key of D major from the "Archduke" Trio, and the harmony never roams far from that key. The transition to the long section for chorus and soloist, however, moves in typical Lisztian fashion, that is, by a chromatic third from D major down to B♭ major. This long section flows through no less than twenty tempo fluctuations, ranging from *Allegro* to *Sehr langsam*, and varies the moods from *Ruhig* to *Maestoso trionfante*. In addition to the chromatic modulations and adventurous key relationships, the music also briefly moves twice into the unusual meter signature of 7/4 (at mm. 197–202 and mm. 290–293), each time dividing into 3 + 4.

Unlike the 1845 Beethoven Cantata, the 1870 cantata employs the full four-part vocal forces of SATB chorus, and the solo voices include soprano, alto, baritone, and bass. The choral sections generally favor homophony over counterpoint. Whereas Liszt highlighted the tenor soloist in the Bonn cantata, especially in the lyrical Part IV, he omits a tenor soloist altogether in the Weimar cantata. The composer particularly favors the bass soloist in his second cantata and, in general, prominently features the solo voices either alone or with one or more sections of the chorus. One favorite arrangement employs the alto solo with the women's choral voices alone, such as in mm. 62 ff. and mm. 863 ff., or the women's voices alone in quiet passages, such as mm. 156 ff.

One especially exciting passage in the Weimar cantata occurs just beyond the midpoint of the work. The solo bass sings the text *des Menschen tiefste Klage den Zweifel seiner Brust, in Symphoniren sagen und seine reinste Lust* (Man's deepest lament, the doubt in his breast, in symphonies say and his purest pleasure), with a metrically free chromatic setting—a recurring idea in the solo bass. Liszt then quotes directly from the first theme of Beethoven's Symphony no. 3 (the "Eroica"), transposed from E♭ major to G major. The theme returns soon again in C major at the beginning of the *Allegro ma non troppo* section (m. 616). This time, Liszt's reference to the opening of the "Eroica" is even more explicit, since the composer states the theme in the low strings as Beethoven does in the opening of the Third Symphony. The "Eroica" quote returns one last time in the *Maestoso trionfante* section (*Heil Beethoven*), now in E major, as the second cantata concludes in the same key as the first.

Chöre zu Herders Entfesseltem Prometheus (*Prometheus Cantata*) 1850

Liszt's *Prometheus* choruses are settings of texts from *Prometheus Unbound* by von Herder written for the celebrations surrounding the unveiling of the Herder monument in Weimar. Liszt conducted the premier performance on 24 August 1850. Raff orchestrated the overture, which later became the symphonic poem *Prometheus*, and the instrumental accompaniment to the choruses in their original versions. Liszt later revised the score and choruses, and also added texts written by Richard Pohl (1826–1896) to link the choruses. The orchestration varies between numbers, but overall it draws upon winds, two horns, brass, strings, and timpani. In addition, the full score includes a piano reduction below the orchestral parts. This revised version was first heard in 1857 in Weimar, and Kahnt later published it in Leipzig. Subsequent performances of the *Prometheus*

Cantata took place in 1860 in Vienna, a "débâcle" conducted by Johann Herbeck;[51] on 7 August 1861 during the second festival of the Tonkünstler-Versammlung (Congress of Musical Artists), of which Liszt was a founder and the first president; and during the Lower Rhine Music Festival in early May, 1876, along with Liszt's *Gran Mass*. That same year on 20 March the Liszt Society Choir presented the "Chorus of the Harvesters" from the *Prometheus Cantata* in between selections of Liszt's benefit piano recital in Budapest for the victims of the terrible flood in February.

Liszt aptly describes his romantic reading of the struggles and ultimate triumph of the great Titan hero *Prometheus*: "Suffering and Apotheosis! Thus compressed, the fundamental thought of this all too truthful fable demanded a stormy and blazing mode of expression. Desolation triumphing through the perseverance of untamed energy constitutes the musical character of the present work."[52]

Like Berlioz's *Damnation of Faust* (1846), Liszt's *Prometheus Cantata* depicts a dramatic legend through musical narrative, which describes the struggling, suffering, and apotheosis of Prometheus. Liszt illuminates Herder's romantic text by dividing it into eight individual scenes or tableaux, each with its own program. The narrator sets each scene with a brief prologue, and, in the sixth and seventh numbers, even makes a dramatic reading while the orchestra plays. Unlike his other large-scale cantatas, Liszt lets the chorus carry the dramatic weight throughout the *Prometheus Cantata* while minimizing the role of the soloists. The eight choruses vary between women's voices, men's voices, and mixed voices. Nos. 1 and 3 are for women's chorus, nos. 2, 4, and 8 are for mixed voices, and nos. 5, 6, and 7 are for men's voices.

The main musical themes in the original overture, which later became the symphonic poem *Prometheus*, appear throughout the cantata. Appearing in different guises, these thematic ideas unify the individual choral numbers as they are developed and transformed. For example, the *Andante* (Recitative) section immediately following the introduction in the tone poem *Prometheus* (mm. 27 ff.) appears as the half-step setting of *Weh dir* (Woe to you) in both the first and third choral numbers of the cantata. In the tone poem, the English horn and bassoon present the recitative theme itself, which centers around the diminished-seventh chord, and this theme is transformed into the dramatic alto solo recitative in no. 3 of the cantata. The soaring cello theme in the following section of the tone poem (mm. 129 ff.) becomes the "Prayer to Themis" sung by the men's solo quartet in no.7. Finally, the subject of the fugue section in the tone poem (mm. 161 ff.), which is really a transformation of the earlier recitative, becomes the broad descending third opening theme in the closing chorus, no. 8. In general, this descending third pattern unifies the entire cantata as it appears in various shapes.

The opening prologue sets the grim stage of the cantata—a desolate land where a vulture tears at the liver of the bound Prometheus. In the first chorus, *Chor der Oceaniden* (Chorus of the Ocean People), the women's voices respond to the suffering of the Titan exclaiming, *Weh, dir! Prometheus!* (Woe to you, Prometheus!) accompanied by intensely chromatic harmonies in the orchestra.

The Ocean People bring curses upon him, though, for disturbing the peace of the sea. The second chorus, *Chor der Tritonen* (Chorus of the Tritons), contrasts the dark mood of the first chorus with a bright, full chorus praising the Titan. It forms a three-part structure, where the men's voices begin with marching music, followed by the women's voices and an alto solo, and then finally the mixed voices. No. 3, *Chor der Dryaden* (Chorus of the Dryads [Wood Nymphs]), is another lament for women's chorus, full of woeful diminished arpeggios in the strings. One of the more eloquent numbers in the cantata, the "Chorus of the Dryads" includes an expressive alto solo with a performance indication, *declamirt, mit tragischen pathos* (declaim with tragic pathos), accompanied by strings and winds.

Nos. 4 and 5 provide relief from the intensity of the "Chorus of the Dryades." No. 4, C*hor der Schnitter* (Chorus of the Harvesters) for mixed chorus, reminiscent of peasant music, uses folk-like syncopated dance rhythms in 3/4 meter over drone fifths in the bass. The English horn and the oboe carry the initial tune, and their reedy sounds further portray the pastoral scene. No. 5, *Chor der Winzer* (Chorus of the Vine-Growers), continues the lighter mood in 3/4 meter with the men's voices alone. Liszt casts the longest of the eight movements, *Chor der Winzer,* in ABA form. After the quiet solo quartet passage, the vintagers build to an all-out bacchanal that rivals Tannhäuser at the Venusberg.

The men's voices continue alone in nos. 6 and 7. In the *Chor der Unterirdischen* (Chorus of the Subterraneans), Liszt opens the door to the Netherworld with the narrator's *melodramatisch* recitation, *Die Erde spaltet, dumpfer Donner kündet, Dass in der Unterwelt ein Kampf begann* (The earth splits, dull thunder announces that in the underworld a struggle has begun). The men's voices moan an answer *weh* with a chromatic setting similar to the earlier laments of the women's voices. Whirling chromatic scales punctuated by brass *fortissimo* chords aptly portray the ominous inferno of the underworld, while the voices sing entirely in octaves and unisons. A transformation occurs at the end of the number where the narrator declaims, *Die Schatten flieh! Vollendet is der Kampf! Empor zum Licht steigt Herkules, als Sieger!* (Flee the shadows! The battle is finished! Upward to the light Hercules ascends as the victor!), and the orchestra breaks into a triumphant fanfare theme highlighted in the brass. No. 7, *Chor der Unsichtbaren* (Chorus of the Invisibles), begins with a divine transformation in the winds of this same fanfare theme. The heavenly music supports the melodramatic recitation of the narrator, *Und ein Ölbaum spriesst aus starrem Felsen,* (And an olive tree sprouts out of fixed rock), and the men's solo quartet voices enter with a reverential prayer to the goddess Themis to save the afflicted. The final chorus for mixed voices, *Schluss-Chor/Chor der Musen* (Closing Chorus/Chorus of the Muses), brings the cantata to a triumphant close, praising Prometheus and all of humanity.

Chor der Engel aus Goethe's Faust (1849) and *Gaudeamus igitur, humoresque* (1869)

The first of the two shorter works for mixed voices, *Chor der Engel aus Goethe's Faust*, appeared as the concluding number in Liszt's *Goethes Festalbum* of 1849.[53] He illustrates the heavenly angels with harp arpeggios in the introduction and throughout the first section. Formally rather elaborate, the chorus consists of four varied strophes of two subsections each and an elaborate coda. The women sing the first two strophes of the opening angelic music in imitative texture, then the men take over in the martial third strophe in a *forte* homophonic texture. The women's voices join the men's at the end of the strophe, bringing the music to a great climax.[54] A twenty-one measure instrumental interlude follows, which leads into the fourth, greatly disguised and varied strophe. Here the women's parts divide so that the texture expands to seven parts. The voices march in note-against-note fashion in the coda, and the chorus concludes with a mighty salute to the spirit: *Alle vereinigt hebt euch und preist, Luft ist gereinigt, athme der Geist* (All united, rise up and praise, air is cleanses, let the spirit breath).

Liszt wrote *Gaudeamus igitur, humoresque* (Therefore Rejoice), a setting of the traditional Latin university song for either mixed chorus or men's chorus, soloists, and orchestra, for the 100th celebration of the Academy Concerts in Jena. An arrangement published for piano four-hands appeared the following year in 1870. Liszt composed the work to include cuts and an alternate ending so that, in the event a chorus is not present, the piece could be performed with the orchestra alone. Indeed, *Gaudeamus igitur* is primarily an orchestral piece with a choral section, rather than a work that centers around a chorus. After a lengthy orchestral introduction the chorus proclaims, *Vivat Academia, Vivat haec Musarum sede!* (Long live learning, long live this seat of the muses!). A contrasting section from the straightforward passage in C major moves to A♭ major and then passes through various chromatic harmonies before returning to the opening choral music back in C major. In the middle section, Liszt also inserts new text in honor of Saint Cecelia, the patron saint of music, for four solo voices and half the chorus. After the return of the main theme with the full chorus, the music makes a momentary aside into an *Adagio* before moving to a full-force rousing close.

WORKS FOR FEMALE AND CHILDREN'S VOICES

1849   *Festalbum zur Säkularfeier von Goethes Geburtstag*: V. *Chor der Engel*. S 86.
1859   *Morgenlied*, female voices. S 88.
          Mit klingendem Spiel, children's voices. S 89.

In addition to the two main groups of his secular choral music, Liszt wrote two pieces for women's voices and one for children's voices. He arranged *Chor der Engel* from the 1849 *Goethes Festalbum* for female voices. In 1859 in Weimar he wrote another work for female voices, *Morgenlied*, published in a collection entitled *Mädchenlieder* in Weimar in 1861, and *Mit klingendem Spiel* for children's voices, published in *Vaterländisches Liederbuch* in Weimar in 1860.[55]

Liszt's secular choral music constitutes a small percentage of his output, but the music deserves close attention from both performers and scholars. Although the thirty works display varying strengths and weaknesses, many of the pieces are accessible for both amateur and well-trained choruses to perform. Some of them exhibit a depth of expression and construction to entice the music analyst.

Liszt was a functional composer in the genre of secular choral music. He not only wrote in the popular *Männerchor* tradition, he also wrote many of his secular choral pieces for specific celebratory occasions. The results yield a variety of pieces, which range from crowd-pleasing fanfares to gentle lyrical part-songs. His texts range from patriotic and political verses to lyrical poetry. The relationship between text and music is usually strong in the choral pieces, and some of them exhibit expressive text painting. The three rousing "Workers' Chorus" and some of the tender part-songs are especially noteworthy.

While Liszt's secular works for men's voices far outnumber those for mixed voices, the five works in the latter category consistently reach greater artistic heights. Yet, there are jewels in each category. Some of them should be heard and studied today so new light could be shed on this little-known side of Liszt in both the concert hall and in print.

NOTES

1. See Chapter 13, "Sacred Choral Works," in this volume.

2. Alan Walker, *Franz Liszt: The Weimar Years 1848–1861* (New York: Alfred A. Knopf, 1989), 2:308.

3. Many thanks to Stephen Soderberg in the Music Division of the Library of Congress for help locating many of these scores.

4. Cited in James Thompson Fudge, "The Male Chorus Music of Franz Liszt" (Ph.D. diss., University of Iowa, 1972), 51, n. 17.

5. Mária Eckhardt, *Franz Liszt's Music Manuscripts in the National Széchényi Library, Budapest.* Studies in Central and Eastern European Music 2, ed. Zoltán Falvy (Budapest: Akadémiaikiadó Kiadó, 1986), 66.

6. Fudge, "The Male Chorus Music of Franz Liszt," 41.

7. Ibid., 43.

8. Ibid., 44.

9. Walker, *Franz Liszt: The Weimar Years*, 2:481.

10. The lodges in which Liszt was inducted or honored include the Masonic Lodge *Zur Einigkeit* in Frankfurt-am-Main, 18 September 1841; *Zur Eintracht* Lodge in Berlin, 22 February 1842; the Freemasons Lodge in Iserlohn, 23 September 1843; and the Lodge *St. Johannes Modestia cum Liberate* in Zurich, 15 July 1845. He was elected a master of the *Zur Einigkeit* Lodge in Budapest in 1870, and after his death the *Freemason's Journal* published his obituary. Liszt's associations with other fraternal orders include honorary membership in both the Mozart Society and the Albrecht Dürer Society in Nuremberg, October 1843, and honorary membership in the *Männergesang-Verein* (Men's Choral Society) in Berlin, 1842. Liszt had further associations with that society in

March 1844 when he was made honorary director and was serenaded by the group. See also Walker, *Franz Liszt: The Virtuoso Years, 1811–1847* (New York: Alfred A. Knopf, 1983), 1:368, n.17, and Saffle, *Liszt in Germany*, 170–171, n. 253.

11. Joseph Maria Lefebre of the Eck & Lefebre Music Publishers of Cologne, with whom Liszt kept in close touch between 1840–1845 when he toured through towns along the Rhine.

12. Saffle, *Liszt in Germany*, 157.

13. Ibid., 128.

14. Fudge, "The Male Chorus Music of Franz Liszt," 48, trans. from *Letters of Franz Liszt*, 2 vols., ed. La Mara [Marie Lipsius], trans. Constance Bache (New York: Haskell House, 1968), 1:314.

15. Ibid., 49.

16. Eckhardt, *Franz Liszt's Music Manuscripts in the National Széchényi Library*, 66. See 66–67 for a list of changes in the revised score and a facsimile of the printed copy with autograph corrections.

17. Ibid., 68. The author further notes in n. 95, "The Hungarian Choral Society functioning since 1867 was regularly organizing national song festivals in which several choruses participated. On these occasions there were always joint choral performances for which Liszt's compositions were frequently chosen."

18. Ibid., 193.

19. See Edgar Refardt, "Die Basler Männerchöre von Franz Liszt," *Schweizerische Musikzeitung* (1942), in *Musik in der Schweiz* (Bern: Verlag Paul Haupt, 1952), 99–102, for more historic details surrounding the compositions.

20. Eckhardt, *Franz Liszt's Music Manuscripts in the National Széchényi Library*, 74, n. 108.

21. Ibid., 74.

22. Walker, *Franz Liszt: The Weimar Years*, 2:513.

23. Fudge, "The Male Chorus Music of Franz Liszt," 149.

24. This work also exists in a version for women's voices. See Table 14.1.

25. Saffle, *Liszt in Germany*, 121 and 238, (item 64).

26. Ibid., 84, n. 117.

27. Fudge, "The Male Chorus Music of Franz Liszt," 53.

28. Ibid., 140–141.

29. MW, v/6: 61–68.

30. Fudge, The Male Chorus Music of Franz Liszt," 294.

31. Liszt, *Le Forgeron*, ed. István Szelényi (Budapest: Zeneműkaidó Vállalat, 1962)₂2. *Franz Liszts Briefe*, ed. La Mara [Marie Lipsius] (Leipzig: Breitkopf & Härtel, 1893) 1:54–55, trans. János Mátyás, *Liszt Choral Works: Secular Male Choruses*, 6 (Hungaroton LP, SLPX 11765 [n.d.])

33. *Franz Liszts Briefe*, 1:55.

34. Walker, *Franz Liszt: The Virtuoso Years*, 1:414, n. 74.

35. Mátyás, *Liszt Ferenc, Choral Works* (Hungaroton SLPD 12748 [1991]), 5.

36. Franz Liszt, *Hungaria 1848*, rev. and ed. István Szelényi (Budapest: Zeneműkaidó Vállalat, 1961), Foreword.

"Theuerer, verehrter Freund,

Dein lieber Brief hat mich in der Crisis des Estro poetico, welche die 'Hungaria' in mir hervorgebracht, noch mehr Dir genähert, und diesem guten Einfluss zu Danke, hoffe ich, dass Du mit der Composition nicht unzufrieden sein wirst. Seit meiner Beethoven-Cantate habe ich nichts so Ausgeprägtes, und aus einem Guss Dahingestelltes geschrieben. Dieser Tage soll die Instrumenetierung beendigt sein, und gelegentlich können wir es in Weimar Dir zu Ehren, nebst 'Weimar's Todten' aufführen lassen."

Liszt's reference to *Weimar's Todten* refers to his song *Weimar's Todten* for baritone or bass to text by Schober, which appeared in the *Festalbum zur Säcular-Feier von Goethe's Geburtstag*, August 1849.

37. Liszt, *Arbeiterchor*, ed. Lajos Bárdos with an Introduction by Dénes Bartha (Budapest: Zeneműkaidó Vállalat, 1954).

38. "Lieber Karl, Da die Zeitumstände einen ganz abnormen Commentar zur Arbeiter-Frage liefern, so könnte es zweckmässiger erscheinen, die Publication dieses Arbeiter Chors aufzuschieben. Darüber gebe ich Ihnen die Entscheidung anheim. F. Liszt."

39. Dénes Bartha, Introduction to *Arbeiterchor*.

40. There is a discrepancy between Raabe and Walker in dating this work. In his Liszt biography, Raabe indicates the work was written before 1848. See Bartha, Introduction to *Arbeiterchor*. Walker indicates the piece was written in the spring of 1848 after Liszt's visit to Vienna and his contact with the rebels there. See Walker, *Franz Liszt: The Weimar Years*, 2:69.

41. See Saffle, *Liszt Guide to Research*, 125, item 302, where the summary of "Zum Autograph des 'Arbeiterchors' von Franz Liszt" by Hans Rudolf Jung (*Burgenländische Heimatblätter* 50 (1988), 111–117), indicates the words are by Johann Philipp Kaufmann. The summary also indicates Jung used an autograph manuscript as a source for his article, owned by the Stadt-und Landesbibliothek, Vienna.

42. Humphrey Searle, "Foreword" to *Mazeppa* by Franz Liszt, (London: Eulenburg, 1976), viii.

43. See Walker, *Franz Liszt: The Weimar Years*, 2:291 for a list of pieces performed in this concert and 483 for a facsimile of the concert bill. Other works performed for male voices by Liszt included *Über allen Gipfeln is Ruh* and a work entitled *Schwager Kronos* (for which I have found no other citation), as well as the first complete performance of *A Faust Symphonie* with the closing chorus for male voices, and *Weimars Volkslied*.

44. See Fudge, "The Male Chorus Music of Franz Liszt," 166–183 for a comparison of the first Schlesinger edition of 1854 and a subsequent edition by Kahnt, which the author presumes to date from 1865.

45. Liszt, *An die Künstler* (Weimar: Schlesinger, 1854), Vorwort.

"Der Componist hat es versucht den Strophen, aus dem Schillerschen Gedicht 'An die Künstler' entnommen, ihren erhabenen, erhebenden Character, musikalishe zu verleihen. Ob es ihm gelungen oder nicht, ist nur denen zur Beurtheilung überlassen, welche diesen Character geziemend auffasen und mitempfinden. Gegen den gewöhnlichen Maasssab [sic] aber, den man an erheiternde Liedertafelcompositionen zu legen pflegt, sowie gegen die beliebigen Anforderungen der zu jedem Preis vergnügungs– und zerstreuungslustigen Sänger und Zuhörer, muss er sich leider zum voraus bescheidenst verwahren.

Bei etwaiger Aufführung wird gebeten um möglichst deutliche und poetische Beton-nung der Worte, sowie um genaue Beobachtung der musikalischen Vorzeichnungen, mit der Bemerkung, dass die geringeren crescendo's (durch bezeichnet) besonders im piano und pianissimo, nicht zu laut und grell hervortreten dürfen. Zu Erleichterung des Einstudirens ist eine Clavierbegleitung der Partitur beigefügt; diese Clavierbegleitung fällt bei einer Gesammtaufführung natürlich weg."

46. See Walker, *Franz Liszt: The Virtuoso Years*, 1:417–425 for a detailed account of the Festival.

47. Günther Massenkeil, Preface to Liszt, *Kantate zur Inauguration des Beethoven-Monumnets zu Bonn*, reconstructed and ed. Massenkeil (Frankfurt: C. F. Peters, 1989).

48. Copies of the *Festgabe* are scarce, but a facsimile edition was published in Bonn in 1983.

49. See Eckhardt, *Franz Liszt's Music Manuscripts in the National Széchényi Library*, 62–65 for a description of the incomplete autograph manuscript of the piano reduction.

50. See Alan Walker, *Franz Liszt: The Final Years 1861–1886* (New York: Alfred A. Knopf, 1996), 3:209, n. 36 and 226, where the author refers to the second Beethoven cantata as a revision of the first.

51. Walker, *Franz Liszt: The Final Years*, 3:204.

52. Liszt, "Preface" to *Prometheus*, trans. Searle (London: Eulenburg, 1975).

53. As mentioned above, the work also appeared in a revised form for four-part *Frauenchor*, which retains the overall texture and essence of the original but makes considerable musical and textual changes.

54. This passage marks the end of the women's version.

55. Unfortunately I have been unable to locate the music for both pieces.

15

Songs and Melodramas

Ben Arnold

Throughout his adult life Liszt composed songs—the first in 1839, the last shortly before his death in 1886.[1] During these forty-seven years he set at least eighty-six different texts to music for voice and piano and made forty-one separate revisions, amounting to at least 127 songs (not including the three solo songs from the *Wartburg-Lieder* or *A magyarok Istene–Ungarns Gott* which concludes with a chorus).[2] While his songs are frequently mentioned in Lisztian studies, no book-length study about them has ever been written in English and serious studies of his songs rarely appear in general histories of song.[3] The only large-scale study of Liszt's songs is in French: Suzanne Montu-Berthon's "Un Liszt Méconnu: Mélodies et Lieder."[4] As late as 1991 Michael Saffle wrote: "No comparable portion of Liszt's compositional output has received less attention from scholars than his songs and recitations for solo voice, some of which rank among the finest works of their kind."[5]

Liszt's songs are under programmed in recitals in comparison with the Lieder of Franz Schubert, Robert Schumann, Johannes Brahms, Hugo Wolf, and Richard Strauss—the only composers who wrote as much solo vocal music of first-rate quality as Liszt. Many of Liszt's best songs clearly rank with those of the recognized masters of the nineteenth century. Martin Cooper suggested that Liszt would come out well in comparison to other composers: "It would be interesting to compare in the concert hall settings of the same poems (those of Heine, for instance) by Schubert, Schumann[,] and Liszt. In not a few cases Liszt would, I believe, suffer less in the comparison than many musicians imagine."[6] Cooper continued, "The intrinsic tenderness and chastity of Schumann's setting [of *Du bist wie eine Blume*] may be a nobler emotion than Liszt's; but Liszt understood Heine the better of the two and his setting is truer, if it is less beautiful."[7] Cooper summed up Liszt's settings of Heine's *Vergiftet sind meine Lieder, Im Rhein, Du bist wie eine Blume,* and *Anfangs wollt' ich fast verzagen*: "The beauty of these settings lies in their complete aptness, in their catching and heightening every shade of the poem's emotion. In this, though not in his prosody, Liszt was as scrupulous as Wolf—sometimes indeed so scrupulous that the wealth of detail obscures the homogeneity of the poem and the song."[8] Elaine Brody and Robert Fowke claimed that "Liszt's Heine songs . . . are among the finest devoted to this poet's work."[9]

While Liszt had written a few songs in the 1830s and 1840s, he turned with renewed interest to the genre after 1848. Rena Mueller wrote, "With a vocal ensemble that included the fine baritone and soprano combination Feodor and Rosa von Milde, Liszt embarked upon a spate of song composition [in Weimar] that can only be likened to Schumann's glorious outpouring of Lieder in 1840."[10] Liszt himself found great delight in his songs and made efforts to have them performed. As early as September 1842 and February 1844 he performed his first song *Angiolin dal biondo crin* in concert with Signor Pantaleoni and Franz Carl Götze respectively.[11] In 1870 La Mara [Marie Lipsius] witnessed Liszt perform the accompaniment to *Mignons Lied* and recorded the event, "He himself played the accompaniment, the song under his hands becoming a complete drama. The capable, vivacious singer he lifted far above her usual level."[12] After he heard Liszt accompany Emilie Genast in his *Die Loreley* in 1859, Alexander Serov described the Lied as "supremely beautiful."[13] Wendelin Weissheimer discussed a performance of Liszt's *Die Loreley*, "It will be difficult for any of those present ever to forget that performance: Liszt at the piano, and in front of him, interpreting the *Loreley*, Emilie Genast, one of the finest Lieder singers of the time!"[14] Liszt accompanied *Die Loreley* again in 1882 at the Tonkünstler-Versammlung of the Allgemeine Deutsche Musikverein.[15]

Liszt's interests led him to publish over a hundred different songs during his lifetime, including their various versions. In December 1859 he wrote to Franz Brendel:

It is of great consequence to me not to delay any longer the publication of my 'Gesammelte Lieder'. . . . The songs can hold their ground in their present form (regardless of the criticism of our choking and quarrelling opponents which will infallibly follow!); and if a few singers could be found, not of the *raw* and superficial kind, who would boldly venture to sing songs by the notorious *non-composer*, Franz Liszt, they would probably find a public for them.[16]

He added almost as an afterthought: "A couple of them made a *furore* in certain salons which are very much set against me, as *posthumous songs of Schubert*—and were encored! Of course I have begged the singer to carry the joke on further."[17]

From his letters it appears Liszt often improvised accompaniments or composed portions of whole songs at the piano before notating them. He remarked, for instance, in November 1841 to Marie d'Agoult, "I believe, also, to have finished the *Loreley*, but it will not be written until the day after tomorrow."[18] Nearly two decades later he outlined a similar compositional process with his setting of Nikolaus Lenau's *Die drei Zigeuner:* "Incidentally, the fancy seized me . . . to set Lenau's *Zigeuner*—and I found the whole contour very quickly at the piano. If that can be done in such a manner itself, without encountering, in the middle, one of those ferocious and tenacious resistances which are the hardest trials that the artist has to submit to—I will put it in writing."[19]

Liszt could upon occasion toss off a song quickly, which was the case of Oskar von Redwitz's *Es muß ein Wunderbares sein* (How wondrous it must be). Liszt explained the origins of the setting to Princess Carolyne on 8 July 1852: "The Princess [of Prussia] had given me a *romance* to compose, between dinner and the soirée. Wishing to write it without delay, I was not able to go to tea until almost 9 o'clock."[20] He appeared, as well, to struggle with certain texts. About his many versions of *Ich scheide*, he lamented: "I have done little this last week, while tormenting myself to work for 6 or 7 hours through the day. Hoffmann's Lied, *Scheiden*, has singularly made me fidgety. I have made 3 or 4 different versions [of the Lied], torn them up one after the other—and, for the sake of peace and quiet, I completed it yesterday evening."[21] In a similar vein Liszt admitted that setting *Ihr Glocken von Marling* gave him more trouble than he would have thought, having to write it nearly three times in order to have an appropriate accompaniment for the text.[22]

Upon occasion he wrote of his satisfaction with his songs in his letters. He mentioned both the vocal and piano transcriptions of his *Tre sonetti di Petrarca* to Marie d'Agoult on 8 October 1846: "I hold them to be singularly successful and more finished in form than any of the other things I have published."[23] As well, he seemed pleased with the revision of *Du bist wie eine Blume*. On 7 February 1851 he described to Princess Carolyne a performance of it and *Schlummerlied* for the Grand Duchess: "Götze sang my two *Lieder* delightfully and full of soul—the first of which, *Du bist wie eine Blume*, the Grand Duchess immediately asked for again."[24]

Furthermore, Liszt often identified strongly with the texts that he set. He told Princess Carolyne on 12 April 1851: "My poor *Hingehn*! . . . At the top of the first page I wrote these words . . . This *Lied* is my testament of youth. I would hardly ever doubt that there would be *someone* to listen to it this way—because how could I have imagined that I would encounter such a woman—and that this woman would want to become mine!"[25]

Yet Liszt's songs met criticism in his own day, and critics have, in general, continued to be overly severe. They frequently indicate one or two incorrect stresses on certain syllables and generalize that he was always careless with his text setting. William Dart generalized, "One weakness often encountered in Liszt's Lieder is that of poor word-setting, especially of the German poems."[26] In the first version of *Schwebe, schwebe, blaues Auge* Liszt has text-setting problems on *in* (m. 36) and *und* on high ab^2s (m. 37). He also uses too much text repetition in some of his early settings and even changes the text at one point in *Der du von dem Himmel bist* to *Der du im Himmel bist,* as Raabe pointed out.[27] In *Der Hirt* Liszt pads the first version with a highly effective musical gesture on the syllable "Ah!" in mm. 64–69. Yet he corrects these excesses in his revisions.

Critics also point out Liszt's misunderstanding of the subtleties of certain poems. Charles Osborne wrote, "If Liszt has one consistent fault as a composer of songs, it is that he sometimes tends to be over-emphatic, over-elaborate and unsubtle in his response to a poem."[28] Alfred Einstein, with few examples, made a ridiculous assertion, stating emphatically: "With Liszt, song lost its form. . . . One need only compare his setting of Goethe's Night-Song ('Über allen Gipfeln ist Ruh') with Schubert's to see how, with him, form runs off into sentimental ariosos."[29] Cooper took issues with some of these criticisms:

> Liszt offends many people by the exuberance and shamelessness of his emotion more than by faults of construction and occasional insincerities and it is a pity to reject some very fine lyrics for what is at worst only a fault of manner. Brahms's songs have equally unfortunate mannerisms, but they are pardoned for the intrinsic merit of the music, and the same is true of Richard Strauss and even, to a certain extent, of Wolf.[30]

Critics also condemn Liszt's songs because of the poetry he set to music. Einstein wrote that Liszt "is literary-minded, even if out of kindness he frequently set to music verse that was very poor and definitely of a drawing room variety. Folk song meant nothing to him."[31] Cooper, on the other hand, declared that Liszt's best songs are those set to the best poets, chiefly Goethe, Heine, Schiller, and Hugo. Of second rank Cooper included Lenau, Hoffmann von Fallersleben, Hebbel, and de Musset. The others, he indicated, are "literary nonentities, occasional friends."[32] Then he claimed, "the settings of worthless poems being on the whole worthless and the settings of fine poems fine music."[33] Brahms, who too was criticized for his choice of poets, set several of the same minor poets as Liszt: Hoffman von Fallersleben, Friedrich Bodenstedt, Emanuel Geibel, Johann Herder, Friedrich Rückert, and Ludwig Uhland. Liszt, though, did set numerous songs to the same noted texts as Schubert, Schumann, and Wolf. He even went so far as to set each of these songs more than once, and several three and four times (see Table 15.1).

German and French were the two languages in which Liszt was most fluent and consequently the languages he most often selected to set his songs. Nearly three-fourths of the songs he wrote and revised are based on German texts of over thirty different poets. Frequently, he set music to the poems of Goethe and Heine, with six and seven settings respectively. He also set numerous other poets, ranging from Hoffman von Fallersleben, Bodenstedt, Geibel, Herder, Rückert, and Uhland (mentioned above) to Schiller, Ludwig Rellstab, Peter Cornelius, Ferdinand Freiligrath, Friedrich Hebbel, Georg Herwegh, and Lenau. Thus Liszt set sixty-three different texts and revised these texts twenty-nine times to bring the total German settings to ninety-two. Of these songs he composed fifty-one initially before 1860 and only twelve from 1871 to the end of his life.[34] He also set thirteen different French texts from seven poets, ranging from major literary figures—Victor Hugo, Alexandre Dumas (père), and Alfred de Musset—to minor poets—Pierre Jean de Béranger, Delphine de Gerardin, Étienne Monnier, and Mme. Pavloff. Liszt revised six of these, bringing his total French output to nineteen songs. He wrote all but *Tristesse* during the 1840s. With only a few exceptions, his revisions took place before the 1860s. Liszt's

revisions and multiple settings of several of these songs illustrate the meaning
they had for him and the care he took in rethinking his settings.

Table 15.1
Liszt songs that Schubert, Schumann, and Wolf also set

Schubert	Schumann	Wolf
Es rauschen die Winde	Anfangs wollt' ich fast ver-zagen	Der du von dem Himmel bist
Der du von dem Himmel bist	Der Hirt	Du bist wie eine Blume
Kennst du das Land?	Du bist wie eine Blume	Kennst du das Land?
Wer nie sein Brot mit Tränen aß	Im Rhein	Wer nie sein Brot mit Tränen aß
	Kennst du das Land?	
	Morgens steh' ich auf und frage	
	Wanderers Nachtlied	
	Wer nie sein Brot mit Tränen aß	

Frits Noske claimed Liszt's songs on French texts "reveal no essentially
French traits . . . [and] that the point of departure for Liszt was the German
Lied. . . . Liszt's *mélodies* nevertheless agree perfectly with their French words
and this may be explained by his choice of texts."[35] David Cox agreed, stating:
"Nor are Liszt's settings of French poems . . . French in style, but directly
influenced by German *Lieder*."[36] On the other hand Osborne viewed at least one
of the songs quite differently. "One of the best of them [Hugo's settings] is *Oh!
quand je dors* with its langourous romantic melody which, even without the
words, sounds completely French in style and sentiment."[37]

The most important of Liszt's French songs are his settings of texts by Hugo.
Four of the seven Hugo poems Liszt set are frequently performed and are among
his most recorded songs: *Oh! quand je dors; Comment, disaient-ils; Enfant, si
j'étais roi;* and *S'il est un charmant gazon.* All are passionate love poems of
romantic excess. Liszt composed them in the early 1840s, published first
versions in 1844, and revised them extensively before publishing the second
versions in Berlin in 1859. Today performers almost uniformly select the
revisions for concerts and recordings. In each case Liszt shortened the second
versions, from 104 measures to 93 in *Oh! quand je dors;* 90 to 87 in *Comment,
disaient-ils;* 70 to 58 in *S'il est un charmant gazon;* and 84 to 66 in *Enfant, si
j'étais roi.*

During his travels throughout Europe Liszt became acquainted with
numerous languages and authors. Consequently, he wrote a few songs based on
languages for which he had less command: five in Italian; three in Hungarian;

and one each in English and Russian. Except for the *Petrarch Sonnets*, none of these songs is performed often today. Liszt revised each of his Italian songs, which include some of his earliest efforts at song writing. The *Petrarch Sonnets* are among his most popular in their first version, although Liszt revised them and curtailed them dramatically in the 1880s.

Liszt's songs and melodramas deal with universal topics, primarily love and death, farewell and sadness, and beauty and despair. A few are based on religious texts, such as *Sei still* and *Und sprich*. *Hohe Liebe* deals with a "higher" or religious love, far more valuable than the physical love on earth. *Le vieux vagabond* (The old Vagabond), based on a Béranger poem, exhibits Liszt's interest in writing political music (even if it is one of his weakest efforts in song). The text itself is an angry social commentary, which prompted Rey Longyear to call it "Liszt's most 'revolutionary' composition . . . which was as much an attack on the established order of the 1840s as *Lyon* was for the 1830s."[38] Most common are songs dealing with love and death. *Ich möchte hingehn* is a poignant longing for death—a longing of someone so weary of life that death is the only answer. *Die Vätergruft* is a macabre setting of a soldier dying in his ancestral crypt. *Die Loreley, Der Fischerknabe*, and *Die Fischerstochter* have their protagonists drowned by the Loreley in the Rhein, the mermaids in a lake, or a storm. *Es war ein König in Thule* and *Die Fischerstochter* are love stories ending in death. Liszt's most passionate outburst of love is *In Liebeslust* (In Love's Delight), which ends with the last three stanzas unabashedly proclaiming *Ich liebe dich*. Although its title sounds like a lament, *Gestorben war ich* (I was dead) is a love song depicting a man so in love that he feels nearly dead. *O lieb, so lang du lieben kannst, Was Liebe sei, Wieder möcht ich dir begegnen, Kling leise, Der Glückliche, Wo weilt er?*, and the *Petrarch Sonnets* are all based on themes of love.

CHARACTERISTICS

Liszt's songs range from twelve measures in length (*Nimm einen Strahl der Sonne*) to over 300 (*Die Macht der Musik*). Almost all of them are independent of each other, but his *Lieder aus Schillers 'Wilhelm Tell'* flow one into another without breaks, making them a true song cycle. The three *Petrarch Sonnets* are often performed together as a cycle, as are four of the Hugo songs. Some are of the simplest kind with little requisite virtuosity (e.g., *Es muß ein Wunderbares sein*) while others tend to be dramatic scenes or ballads (e.g., *Jeanne d'Arc au bûcher* or *Die Loreley*). In one of Liszt's most peaceful and beautiful songs *Lasst mich ruhen* (Let me Rest), for example, little flamboyant virtuosity is required of the singer or pianist, but the song remains one of his most difficult in sustaining the lyrical nuances required by playing and singing so softly.

Liszt's innovations in his songs range from their operatic nature, advanced harmonic language, formal experimentation, and virtuosic vocal and piano writing to the declamatory style of his late songs and his pioneering efforts in orchestral song. Brody and Fowkes suggested Liszt has been overlooked in his role of innovator in the genre: "Liszt, greatly underestimated as a composer of instrumental music, was also, never properly acknowledged for his innovations in Lieder composition."[39]

Several writers discuss how operatic Liszt sometimes is in his settings. Cooper wrote, "He was dramatic to the core and his songs bear the mark of a personality which delighted in violent contrast, brilliant colour and short, unsustained bursts of ecstatic emotion."[40] Brody and Fowkes further suggested, "Often Liszt's dramatic handling of the material resembles the approach of an operatic composer rather than that of a *Lied* specialist."[41] Edwin Hughes summarized Liszt's songs: "To the almost purely lyrical character of the *Lied* up to that time, Liszt added a new note, the dramatic, which had previously put in its appearance only in the ballad, and which Liszt now introduced on appropriate occasion and with remarkable effect in the musical settings of poems of this character as well."[42]

Liszt's music was harmonically advanced even in his early songs, and he is certainly the most innovative before Wolf, rivaling him years earlier in expanded tonality. Liszt often modulates by thirds and uses a large number of augmented and diminished-seventh chords, particularly in his later settings. The augmented triad appears frequently for different reasons. As Liszt turns to the theme of God in the second setting of Elim Metschersky's *Bist du!*, he uses an augmented triad to introduce this idea. The second version of *Vergiftet sind meine Lieder* also displays prominent use of the augmented triad and other dissonances as R. Larry Todd elaborated:

But most gripping of all is the bitter climax of the song, 'und dich, Geliebte mein!' At least one critic, Louis Köhler, commented on this extraordinary passage, focusing his attention, understandably enough, on its dissonant suspension chord, which, he maintained, might well cause musicians to faint. But Köhler did not notice how Liszt outlined the augmented triad in the vocal line (A–F♮–C♯), and injected it into the piano postlude, including the final cadence (C♯–E♯–A).[43]

Liszt's intense use of dissonance in *Anfangs wollt' ich fast verzagen* includes many unresolved half-diminished-seventh chords flowing directly to fully-diminished sevenths and on to dominant sevenths and ninths; his rich harmonic palette includes a broken major-ninth chord for the opening five measures of *Wie singt die Lerche schön. Ich scheide* utilizes a large number of dissonant suspensions in the piano, and its highly chromatic accompaniment often masks clear key centers (although each B section ends on an F-major chord). In the last line of *Wer nie sein Brot mit Tränen aß*, Liszt leaps a diminished seventh in the voice from *Schuld* to *rächt* and lands on a French augmented-sixth chord which has been preceded by a half-diminished-seventh chord and an augmented triad in the piano. The voice meanders to a final descent on a^1, a tritone away from the $d\sharp^1$ of *rächt*. To illustrate the darker and defiant change of mood in the last two stanzas of *Ich möchte hingehn*, Liszt alters not only the sternness of the music but also includes reference to Wagner's *Tristan und Isolde* in the famous measure (m. 125) following the word *versinken* that contains the so-called

"Tristan chord."[44] Yet, when the text requires it, Liszt can write blandly consonant and even remain within a key throughout, as he does throughout *Das Veilchen.*

Although Brahms set nearly one-fourth of his songs in "simple strophic settings,"[45] Liszt rarely relies on such set musical patterns; instead, he looks afresh at each verse and searches for new possibilities of meaning. His purely strophic sections are largely limited to the first version of *Angiolin* (mm. 6–14), *Le vieux vagabond* (mm. 34–63), *Oh pourquoi donc,* and *Das Veilchen,* although several others appear in a modified strophic structure. Liszt also composed through-composed songs, often unified through motivic transformations, as well as the more traditional ternary and, upon occasion, rondo forms. He rarely recalls entire sections without substantial changes, using some type of melodic, harmonic, or textural variant of the previously heard material.

Liszt's writing for the voice includes attractive melodies with occasional ornamentation, particularly in his early and middle songs. He generally gives the vocal part considerable independence in later versions, but some doublings occur throughout his music, particularly in the first version of *Morgens steh' ich auf und frage, Ich möchte hingehn, Das Veilchen,* and the second version of *Petrarch Sonnet* no. 47. The range in some of the early works is nearly operatic in scope, particularly the first versions of the Petrarch and Schiller songs. He specifically designates recitatives in *O lieb* (mm. 60, 63) and *Hohe Liebe* (m. 26); more frequently he employs unmarked recitatives, indicating *fast gesprochen* (almost spoken) or *gesprochen* (spoken) in *Die stille Wasserrose, Die Zigeuner,* and *Die Vätergruft,* the first version of *Wer nie sein Brot mit Tränen aß,* the second versions of *Kling leise* and *Die Loreley,* and the first two versions of *Was Liebe sei.* He uses the Italian designation *parlando* (speaking) in the second version of *Angiolin, declamando* (declaiming) in *Le vieux vagabond,* and *declamato* (declaimed) in the first version of the first *Petrarch Sonnet. La tombe et la rose* is reminiscent of Wolf with its repeated-note vocal line and declaimed texts. Brody and Fowkes claimed that Liszt's Lieder, "with their frequent use of recitation and declamation . . . anticipate the later songs of Hugo Wolf and Alban Berg."[46] Liszt notates the vast majority of his vocal parts in the treble clef, saving the bass clef for the second version of *Petrarch Sonnet* no. 104, *Ungarns Gott, Ungarisches Königslied, Die Vätergruft, Le vieux vagabond, Gastibelza, Weimars Toten,* and three songs from the *Wartburg-Lieder: Wolfram von Eschenbach, Der tugendhafte Schreiber,* and *Biterolf und der Schmied von Ruhla.*

Liszt's use of the piano ranges from the simple and sparse to the formidably virtuosic. In some of the early songs—*Gastibelza* and *Lieder aus Schillers 'Wilhelm Tell,'* for example—the piano is a virtual orchestra with brilliant thirty-second-note arpeggios, *fortissimo* open octaves, or tremolos. In contrast to his pianistic virtuosic style, Liszt often writes simple arpeggiated or block-chord accompaniments in many of his love songs, in particular *Hohe Liebe, O lieb, so lang du lieben kannst, Ich liebe dich, Du bist wie eine Blume, Es muß ein Wunderbares sein,* and *Blume und Duft.* Some songs may have only broken-chord accompaniments, but the piano plays a vital role, either musically or programmatically, in nearly every song. Many songs have extensive keyboard introductions, interludes, and codas, and frequently contain essential melodic material.

Montu-Berthon described interesting ways that Liszt employs the piano, including its ability to establish psychological elements of characters, evoke particular ambiences, serve as commentator on events in texts, and illustrate individual events or words.[47] Occasionally Liszt employs the piano to imitate other instruments, such as the guitar (in the second version of *Comment, disaient-ils*), the horn (in the first version of *Der Hirt*), and particularly the harp in *Die Macht der Musik, Ich möchte hingehn, Wer nie sein Brot mit Tränen aß*, and *Heinrich von Ofterdingen*. The piano also sometimes illustrates specific words in the narrative. On a repeated d^2 in *Und wir dachten der Toten*, for example, the music moves from *fortissimo* to *piano* in one measure to accentuate the word *Toten*, only to return in the next measure to *fortissimo*. Liszt represents the swallows musically in *Die Fischerstochter*, the nightingale in both versions of *Die tote Nachtigall* and *Schwebe, schwebe, blaues Auge*, and the larks in *Jugendglück*. In *Lasst mich ruhen*, for example, he supplies trills for the nightingale (m. 10) and triplet arpeggios to indicate the flow of the brook in the second stanza. In *Die drei Zigeuner* he uses wonderful little treble figurations for the second gypsy who smokes and watches the smoke rise (mm. 51–63). The tempo slows down as the third gypsy sleeps, while the treble-clef tremolos depict the wind blowing over the strings of his *cymbalon* hanging on a tree (mm. 63–83). In *Wer nie sein Brot mit Tränen aß, Ihr Glocken von Marling*, and *Bist du!*, Liszt often uses repeated-chord textures in setting text about the power of heaven (see Example 15.10). In the first version of Schiller's *Der Fischerknabe* he employs continuous thirty-second-note runs (chiefly in the left hand) to set the stage for the mermaids swimming in the music. This along with both versions of *Im Rhein, im schönen Strome, Die Loreley*, and *Die Fischerstochter* represent examples of Liszt's power to depict water music.

One of Liszt's most conspicuous piano figurations is his use of tremolos (see Example 15.11). He uses them to aid in his depiction of the sinking of the boats in *Die Fischerstochter* and *Die Loreley* as well as in *Wer nie sein Brot mit Tränen aß* at the words *Dann überlaßt ihr ihn der Pein* (Then you abandon him in pain). In his late years he uses tremolos occasionally for less dramatic purposes in *Und wir dachten der Toten, Magyar király-dal* (Ungarisches Königslied), *A magyarok Istene—Ungarns Gott, Go not, Happy Day*, and his revision of *Der Alpenjäger*. In *J'ai perdu ma force et ma vie* he includes upper-register tremolos between mm. 42 and 59. Further use of tremolos is found in two of his melodramas: *Der traurige Mönch* and *Des toten Dichters Liebe*. In *Der traurige Mönch* tremolos symbolize the fear and sadness the horse and rider face during their journey before the horse finally jumps into the lake. Liszt enhances the drama of *Des toten Dichters Liebe* by placing tremolos at the point where the soldier is killed in battle.

As a rule Liszt's late songs, composed after 1870, become darker and more despairing, allowing for a greater degree of dissonance. Often the later songs are shorter (*Einst* is only fourteen measures long) and less virtuosic for both voice and piano. Songs such as *Go not, Happy Day, Einst,* and *An Edlitam,* require almost no virtuosity from the performers. *Einst* has one of his most restricted vocal ranges—that of a fifth (f$\sharp^1$–c$\sharp^2$)—and often the melodic lines are almost exclusively declamatory as in *Und sprich.*

One of the most immediate and striking characteristics of many of Liszt's late works is the way the voice and piano interact with one another. Not only is the piano part often linear in conception, but the voice and piano rarely sound together in some of these works (see Example 15.12). During the last forty-seven measures of *Go not, Happy Day,* the piano and voice sound together in only five measures, each being almost independent of the other. Nearly a third of the text in *Und sprich* remains unaccompanied, and the sparse piano part consists of middle-to-upper register blocked chords and contains almost no melodic content. *Heinrich von Ofterdingen* opens with an extended recitative; the voice and piano do not coincide until m. 16. *Reimar der Alte,* a through-composed song that is almost all recitative, opens with solo voice only, and the piano does not enter until the fourth measure; fifteen of the thirty-two measures containing the voice are unaccompanied, meaning that the piano and voice rarely perform together. In *Verlassen* (1880) Liszt employs an extremely thin accompaniment, and the right hand of the pianist does not play for over fifteen measures of the fifty-four-measure song. Silence plays an increasingly important role in the late songs *Gebet, Reimar der Alte,* and the revision of *Petrarch Sonnet* no. 104.

As in his late piano music, Liszt often uses the tritone and augmented triad in addition to general dissonance in his late songs. The single-note opening of *Verlassen* in the piano consists first of a tritone which becomes a motive sung at mm. 18, 33, and 49. The last phrase in m. 49 begins and ends with this tritone on c^2–f$\sharp^1$. In *Gebet* Liszt uses unresolved augmented chords in mm. 25–26 and a melodic tritone leading to the word *Zweifel* (Doubt) in m. 36. Rarely do the works cadence on root position, and often they conclude on dissonances and in un-resolved ways. *Einst* ends with the piano holding a fully-diminished-seventh chord, and *Verlassen* ends on a diminished-seventh chord in a piano part containing tritones in each hand.

Amidst these dissonances, surprisingly, some of the songs (*Verlassen, Go not, Happy Day, Und sprich,* and *Einst*) are heavily diatonic and contain chiefly consonant sonorities. Of all Liszt's late songs *Der Glückliche* contains the highest proportion of major triads, and, because of its jubilant nature, includes *ff* markings in mm. 1, 26, and 34 and specifies a faster tempo. Almost alone among his late songs, *Der Glückliche* is happy, with its impassioned text of love and singing.

Liszt often employs optional (*ossia*) passages in both piano and voice parts. He includes optional endings for both voice and piano in *Die Zigeuner* (fourteen measures) and *Ich liebe dich* (three measures). He provides optional piano parts in the last two measures of *S'il charmant gazon* and *Jugendglück* (m. 55, second version) as well as an entirely different accompaniment in the first version of *Im Rhein*; he also includes an extensive *ossia* in the first version of *Es war ein König in Thule* (mm. 71–79) and an optional cut in the second version of *Die*

Loreley (beginning at m. 110). He even includes optional parts for additional instruments in two of his songs: an optional trumpet part in *Wolfram von Eschenbach* and optional *Tromba* and violin parts in *Weimars Toten*. He supplies *ossia* passages for the voice in nearly a third of his total song output, as indicated in Table 15.2.

Table 15.2
Optional Voice Parts in Liszt's Songs

Song	Version	Measure number
Anfangs wollt' ich fast verzagen		23–25
Angiolin	1	35
Bist du!	2	82–84, 96–100
Comment disaient-ils	1	66–80
Comment disaient-ils	2	87–88
Der du von dem Himmel bist	2	42–43
Der Glückliche		35–36
Die Loreley	1	70–76, 89
Die Loreley	2	46–48, 83–84, 119, 127–131
Die Macht der Musik		185–186, 189–190, 221–222, 278–280, 282–284
Die stille Wasserrose		58–60
Die tote Nachtigall	1	10–11, 45–56, 81–82
Die tote Nachtigall	2	17, 45–55
Die Zigeuner		91, 93
Élégie: En ces lieux	1	74–81
Es war ein König von Thule	1	44, 52–53
Freudvoll und leidvoll	3	31–32
Gastibelza		92, 110–111, 222–225
Gestorben war ich		6, 20–24
Ich liebe dich		57–58
Ich möchte hingehn		21, 137, 158
Im Rhein	2	32–36
Istén veled!	1	16–17
Istén veled!	2	16–17
Jeanne d'Arc au bûcher	1	37, 74, 101, 106, 115, 117–123
Jeanne d'Arc au bûcher	2	104–107, 115–118, 145–147
Kennst du das Land	3	109–110
Morgens steh' ich auf und frage		12
Petrarch: Benedetto sia'l giorno	1	73–74, 84–85, 91
Petrarch: Pace non trovo	1	76–78, 90, 100, 104–105
Schiller: Der Alpenjäger	1	97–100
Schiller: Der Alpenjäger	2	21–22, 36
Schiller: Der Fischerknabe	1	80–92
Schiller: Der Hirt	1	31
Ungarisches Königslied		36–42, 50–60
Weimars Toten		44
Wer nie sein Brot mit Tränen aß	1	58–59

One famous example is in the first version of *Comment, disaient-ils.* Liszt wrote a cadenza on the last word that many performers (Kathleen Battle and Kiri Te Kanawa, for example) restore in the second version, even though Liszt omitted it in his revision. Set to the text "You must love! the girls replied," the cadenza seems most appropriate. Furthermore, in 1885 Liszt suggested that a singer might add a cadenza. Lillie de Hegermann-Lindencrone wrote, "He had the music of *Comment, disaient-ils* in the same book and begged me to sing it. 'Do you think,' he said 'you could add this little cadenza at the end?' And he played it for me."[48]

REVISIONS

Liszt revised nearly a fourth of his songs. On several occasions he set previously used texts to completely new music, creating independent settings. These songs, which consequently offer a different interpretation of the text, include the second version of *Freudvoll und leidvoll,* the second versions of *Ein Fichtenbaum steht einsam, Schwebe, schwebe, blaues Auge,* and *Wer nie sein Brot mit Tränen aß,* and the second and third versions of *Was Liebe sei.* Instead of *Quasi Allegretto* or *Andantino* indicated in versions one and three of *Freudvoll und leidvoll,* for example, Liszt writes *Allegro agitato, appassionata assai* in his second version. The piano opens and closes with energetic, pulsating triplet chords in alternation—a series of diminished triads. Except for fermatas on the words *Tode* and *Seele,* the piece is nearly in perpetual motion. Over half the song is devoted to the single line of text *glücklich allein ist die Seele, die liebt.* The mood is completely different from the other versions, and the nuances between joyful and sorrowful, even with the diminished chords and tritone on the word *leidvoll,* are missing compared to the more sensitive writing in the first and third versions. It is the most buoyant and euphoric version of the three.

In his revisions Liszt often changes the tempo, slowing down the second versions of *Wer nie sein Brot mit Tränen aß* and *Die tote Nachtigall,* and speeding up *Kling leise* and the 1848? version of *Freudvoll und leidvoll.* Upon occasion he changes the meter from triple to duple, as in the third version of *Der du von dem Himmel bist;* he also removes the seventeen meter changes alternating between 3/4 and 4/4 in the first version of *Schwebe, schwebe, blaues Auge.* In the second version of *Morgens steh' ich auf und frage* he begins the vocal entry on beat four instead of starting at the downbeat, making the song much less square than the first version.

Liszt dramatically shortens the second versions of *Wer nie sein Brot mit Tränen aß* (from 82 to 29 measures), *Lieder aus Schillers 'Wilhelm Tell'* (from 353 to 228), and *Kling leise, mein Lied* (from 159 to 130). He likewise shortens the third version of *Freudvoll und leidvoll* (from 84 to 37) from his original conception. At least on one occasion he lengthened the revision—the second version of *Morgens steh' ich auf und frage* is seven measures longer than the first.

Often Liszt's revisions retain their original vocal lines, but he makes adjustments to them, changing a phrase here or there as in *Der du von dem Himmel bist, Die Loreley,* and *Im Rhein.* More often he reduces vocal ranges and simplifies virtuoso passages. He substantially lowers the range, for example, in the second version of *Der du von dem Himmel bist, Der Fischerknabe,* and the *Petrarch Sonnets.* At times, however, he increases difficulties; the vocal part, if anything, is more difficult in the revision of *Oh! quand je dors.* He reduces or removes text repetitions in *S'il est un charmant gazon, Oh! quand je dors, Wer nie sein Brot mit Tränen aß,* and *Der du von dem Himmel bist,* but adds considerable text repetition at the end of the second version of *Kling leise, mein Lied* to turn it into a more conventional ABA' form. Liszt also corrects text-setting problems in almost all of his revisions as noted above. In the second version of *Morgens steh' ich auf und frage* he also pays greater detail to the words, adding a descending tritone on the word *klage* (to complain) in m. 11.

Liszt usually reduces the texture and simplifies the role of the piano in his revisions. The first version of *Im Rhein,* for example, has an optional piano part running throughout that, in effect, creates two different versions. The pianist can elect to play triplet sixteenths or the more difficult sixteenth-note constant arpeggio and scale figurations. The piano tends to dominate too much in the first setting and is too involved with the depiction of the Rhine to reflect the subtleties of the poem. Liszt refines the accompaniment considerably in its revision. He acknowledged the trend toward simplification in a letter to Joseph Dessauer in the 1850s: "My earlier songs are mostly too ultra sentimental, and frequently too full in the accompaniment."[49] He made a similar remark in a letter to Louis Köhler in 1853 where he mentioned simplifying the accompaniments in his revisions.[50] More than two decades later he praised simplicity in songs again, stating that they "should have a simple accompaniment and avoid any unnecessary modulation."[51] In 1879 Albert Gutmann recalled Liszt praising *Es muß ein Wunderbares sein,* among the simplest of his songs, "holding it up as a model of song writing."[52] In the first version of *Es war ein König in Thule,* on the other hand, Liszt pulls out all the virtuoso stops in the piano part to depict the goblet sinking in the sea in the return of the first section. The simplified *ossia* in this version becomes the only choice of performance in the second, making the revision simpler, calmer, and less virtuosic.

Liszt greatly lightens the piano texture in several songs, particularly the Hugo songs, in effect making them better resemble French *mélodies.* The first version of *Oh! quand je dors* with its thick texture and more aggressive accompaniment can not compete with the subtle and refined setting found in the revision. In the second version of *S'il est un charmant gazon* Liszt adds to the original *Allegretto* marking the words *con moto et grazioso.* He rewrites the piano part, pruning the texture to create the graceful delicacy necessary to convey a peaceful landscape of blooming flowers and dreams of roses. In the first version (1844) the piano part never stops; it almost becomes a broken-chord etude, with both hands sawing away sixteenth notes. In the second version Liszt replaces the sixteenth notes in the left hand with simple eighths in a slightly higher register and gives the singer a couple of measures without accompaniment for a calming effect.

Liszt's revisions generally improve earlier versions, but in many cases revisions diminish the spirit and genuineness of earlier compositions. Several performers and scholars prefer the first versions of the *Petrarch Sonnets,* the songs from *William Tell, Ein Fichtenbaum steht einsam, Wer nie sein Brot mit Tränen aß, Freudvoll und leidvoll, Der du von dem Himmel bist, Schwebe, schwebe, blaues Auge,* and *Kling leise, mein Lied.* I have argued elsewhere that "while there uniformly may be significant improvements in text setting in the latter versions, the first versions show a musical originality and an overall spirit that are often lacking in the latter stripped-down versions."[53] In his revision of Schiller's *Der Alpenjäger* Liszt cuts the heart out of the earlier, fascinating song, stripping it to the barest outline in comparison to the first version. He retains the opening mood with his *Allegro con strepito* and frequent tremolos but undercuts its energy at m. 37 with tremolos, and especially at m. 43 with its unaccompanied recitative on *das grünende Feld.* To listeners familiar with the earlier version, the song sounds emaciated and not nearly long enough.

Liszt's *Tre sonetti di Petrarca* provide the best examples of revisions less effective than the original compositions. Liszt published the original versions between 1842 and 1846, but he revised the sonnets extensively and dramatically changed their character between 1864 and 1882.[54] In writing to Giuseppe Ferrazzi in May 1880, Liszt stated: "I hesitate to publish the second original version [of the *Petrarch Sonnets*] (very modified and more subtle) for voice, because to express the sentiment that I tried to breathe into the musical notation of these Sonnets, it would be necessary for some poetic singer [to be] in love with an ideal of love. . . *rarae aves in terris.*"[55]

Liszt's own comments show the high esteem in which he held the revisions, but in actuality they appear to be weaker than the originals. First, he reverses the order of the first two songs in the cycle and changes his setting of no. 104 to bass clef, scoring it for baritone instead of tenor. In the second version of the sonnets he improves some text-setting errors, but he also reduces the melodic variety, waters down the previously brilliant pianism, and removes much of the torrid passion that made the first versions so wonderful.[56] In each of the revisions he throws in unaccompanied recitatives that disrupt the lyrical mood so prevalent in the early versions.

Liszt opens the original sonnets with *Pace non trovo* (no. 104). Petrarch's text (a highly dramatic poem which deals with a man so in love that he can find no peace within himself) offers an array of tumultuous metaphors, including those of a soul that is burning but turning to ice, soaring yet stationary, free yet imprisoned. Not surprisingly, this song is one of Liszt's most virtuosic pieces; it resembles an operatic scene with its recitative and aria format and extended range. Liszt sets Petrarch's text in a key he often associated with love, A♭ major, and begins with a forceful five-measure piano introduction, *Agitato assai.* In effect, the first twenty-seven measures are recitative-like with full "orchestral" writing in the accompaniment (see Example 15.1).

Example 15.1
Liszt, *Petrarch Sonnet* no. 104, first version, mm. 1–11

These measures, with their subterfuge of pre-tonality, fail to establish the A♭ tonality until the *cantabile* melody begins at m. 37—a technique Liszt uses in several of his large-scale works. The crescendo at m. 12 builds with repeated chords and arrives at dramatic tremolos for the text *e volo sopr'l cielo, e giaccio in terra,* reaching a g♭² on *cielo* (heaven) and drops an octave lower on *terra* (earth). When the poet "embraces all the world" (mm. 24–27), Liszt employs an elaborate melisma in a high tessitura. At m. 37, when the subject of love is introduced, the piano presents the sublime first theme in single notes and octaves in the right hand accompanied by florid patterns in the left hand. After the eight-measure interlude, the voice restates the piano melody, adding an octave leap on an eighth note (m. 46). Liszt varies the sublime theme (m. 62) in setting the third stanza of the poem, transforming this melody into a stunning climax at mm. 76–78 with the voice soaring for four beats on a high c♭³. The florid music continues throughout the fourth section of the poem until m. 90, where the voice breaks into a cadenza, with an optional d♭^{3} in the *ossia*. Even after the cadenza the operatic writing continues *con somma passione,* and the voice soars again on a high a♭^{2}. Liszt carries himself away in this ecstasy with several repetitions of the last line of text and even goes so far as to insert the lady's name into Petrarch's text; an elaborate *ossia* on "Laura" reaches d♭^{3} in m. 104.

The second version of *Pace non trovo* differs so greatly from the first that it indicates how different Liszt himself was as a person when he revised the earlier song. The trials and tribulations he had suffered are clearly present in the bowdlerized second version. He designates the revision *Molto agitato e presto* and omits the recitative section from the first version entirely (see Example 15.2).

Example 15.2
Liszt, *Petrarch Sonnet* **no. 104, revised version, mm. 1–17**

The new voice line is completely different, and the revision is much more limited in expression and range. The florid high notes in the first version are nowhere to be found. The piano accompaniment is simpler, with extended use of tremolos (mm. 26–37 and mm. 56–73). In the middle of the revision, he sets the text beginning with *Pascomi di dolor piangendo io rido* without accompaniment (mm. 75–77); from there the voice and piano alternate in a type of disunion. The piano has half-note and whole-note chords or single-line patterns. Furthermore, there are several occasions in this last section where silences last for three or four beats. The work ends with a nine-measure coda of slow, instrumental recitative, concluding on a single note—almost an exact repeat of the introduction beginning at the *Andante* (mm. 7–13).

Liszt's first version of Sonnet no. 47, *Benedetto sia'l giorno*, is more lyrical than his first version of *Pace non trovo*. Petrarch's *Benedetto* does not have the dramatic contrasts of the previous sonnet; in setting *Benedetto* to music Liszt concentrates on the outpouring of love and how blessed the time has been since Petrarch first set eyes on Laura. The ten-measure introduction establishes the warm, romantic tone for the poem in the undulating syncopation of the accompaniment, but there is little virtuosity compared to no. 104. The second half of the introduction (mm. 5–9) reappears in the coda. The first part of Liszt's melody is largely diatonic but becomes increasingly chromatic in the second quatrain, where the text deals with the pang of love. He employs rather blatant tone painting on *lagrime* (mm. 57–59) where the music descends chromatically from ab^2 to cb^2. The song briefly modulates to B major before slipping back to the tonic (m. 69). The tessitura of the vocal line is quite high, frequently venturing above the staff, particularly in the optional *ossia* where several b^2s and even a sustained db^3 (m. 92) appear. Material from the introduction returns at m. 86 to help unify the work.

In revising Sonnet no. 47 Liszt made the music comparatively less fluent, more austere, and, in some ways, hollow. The second version in Db major begins with a descending eight-measure introduction in the middle register of the keyboard. This is in stark opposition to the opening that so warmly ascends in the first version. The revised A section consists largely of a triplet quarter-note/eighth-note pattern that occurs repeatedly in the right-hand piano part. piano using alternating chords in the right hand. In places the accompaniment even doubles the voice in octaves (mm. 62–69), and the melody, diatonic for the most part, remains throughout within the range of a tenth (c^1–e^2). After a brief, single-line interlude (mm. 39–40), the B section begins with a new melodic vocal pattern, but the alternating, syncopated pattern from the A section returns. After the climax of this section, Liszt launches into a brief unaccompanied recitative for the voice (mm. 54–57). After the B section repeats, the song concludes with another unaccompanied vocal phrase based on the opening piano introduction and followed by restating a variant of this theme before launching into soft half-note and whole-note chords concluding in Db major.

Liszt's first version of Sonnet no. 123 *I vidi in terra angelici costumi* opens with the most exquisite introduction of the three sonnets and closes with his most refined postlude. The simplest of the three in structure and technique, it retains the sweetness touched with longing of the poem itself. The opening vocal line with its triplet patterns and ascending lines exudes lyricism over the simple, arpeggiated accompaniment. Its dramatic climax occurs in the last stanza that deals with heaven's harmony (mm. 54–69) and is depicted through its diatonicism and *dolcissimo* character.

Liszt's revision of no. 123, in F major instead of A♭, begins with a reduced, eight-measure introduction of flowing eighth-note triplets under a piano melody in octaves based on the first section of the original. The A section consists of two similar phrases separated by a brief two-measure piano interlude. This section climaxes in mm. 28–31. The second section, *Un poco meno lento,* is soft, accompanied by the piano in the upper register of the keyboard. This section also builds with repeated chords and octave melodies in the piano before suddenly changing dramatically. As in the second version of no. 104, Liszt breaks up the song with an extended vocal recitative at m. 64. The beginning tempo, *Molto lento,* returns and the song continues softly with the introduction theme in the voice to end in F major. Of the three revisions, Sonnet no. 123 is the most successful. While not as sensuous or melodically inventive as its predecessor, it succeeds in its poignancy and serenity.

Liszt's revisions of the sonnets remove the luster of the previous versions. While they are valid in their own ways, the later songs are a product of a different intellect who could no longer unabashedly believe in the exhilaration of love as he could a quarter of a century before his revisions.

SELECTED SONGS

The twelve songs discussed below represent some of Liszt's most outstanding examples of German and French songs. The *Petrarch Sonnets,* examined above, may be considered distinguished examples of his Italian songs. Together, these fifteen songs illustrate the breadth and scope of his efforts in the genre, including three of his enigmatic late works.

The most important of Liszt's French songs are his settings of texts by Hugo. Four of the seven Hugo poems Liszt set— passionate love poems of romantic excess—are frequently performed in their revised versions and are among his most recorded songs: *Oh! quand je dors; Comment, disaient-ils; Enfant, si j'étais roi;* and *S'il est un charmant gazon.*

Oh! quand je dors is the most famous of these and remains Liszt's most beloved French song. In a letter to Marie d'Agoult on 25 January 1842 Liszt wrote, "In these last two weeks I have written two new songs, one for me and the other for you, dear Marie."[57] According to Adrian Williams the one for Liszt was *Titan* and the "other" for Marie was *Oh! quand je dors.*[58] Noske highly praised this song: "*Oh! Quand je dors* is certainly the masterpiece of Liszt's French songs and may even be described as one of the most beautiful *mélodies* written before Duparc. Hugo's language, so rich in imagery, has only rarely found such a worthy musical equivalent."[59]

The second version of *Oh! quand je dors,* dating from 1849, is among the most exquisite and polished of all Liszt's songs. He retains the three-stanza format Hugo creates and organizes it in an ABA' form. The text is ecstatic, with each stanza ending with an exclamation mark. In the first stanza the narrator urges his lover to come to his bedside "as Laura appeared to Petrarch," and each successive stanza intensifies this desire. With great sensitivity Liszt captures the nuances of Hugo's text.

The song opens with a seven-measure piano introduction in the middle-and-upper register of the keyboard that sets the mood throughout with its pregnant pauses and general dignity. Although the introduction gives little hint of tonic, an E-major broken triad in m. 8 prepares for the vocal entry that restates the opening four notes of the piano introduction with a different harmony. The vocal melody is almost exclusively diatonic in its first extended ten-measure phrase that soars to a g^2 for a whole-note duration. After a two-measure interlude, the initial phrase repeats as an eight-measure melody cadencing on C♯ minor. The brief interlude alternates a treble melody (which imitated with a slight change the last motive of the voice) with a bass statement of the opening four-note motive. The B section (second stanza), in contrast, contains more chromaticism and modulates through F major to its climax on the dominant of E. Liszt builds this climax with a variant of the opening four-note motive, soaring to an a^2 over which he writes a fermata before the short cadenza descends down one and a half octaves.

Example 15.3
Liszt, *Oh! quand je dors,* conclusion (revised version)

The A' section returns immediately for the third stanza in E major, and the piano accompaniment consists of single-note, ascending arpeggios. In his first version Liszt wrote much thicker, full triads for the arpeggiated accompaniment, not nearly as impressionable as in his revision. In the brief coda Liszt continues to employ another variant of the four-note motive before the voice restates the text *Oh viens! comme à Pétrarque appraissait Laura.* Liszt's handling of this phrase is the culmination of the song with its two long notes on "Oh come" and his ascending stepwise setting of the last phrase. Liszt arrives on a g$\sharp^2$ and sustains the note over four measures while the accompaniment changes the harmony from C$\sharp$ major to C$\sharp$ minor before closing on two *ppp* E-major triads (see Example 15.3).

All seven of Heine's songs are major works: *Anfangs wollt' ich fast verzagen, Die Loreley, Du bist wie eine Blume, Ein Fichtenbaum steht einsam* (most successful in its earlier version), *Im Rhein, Morgens steh' ich auf und frage,* and *Vergiftet sind meine Lieder.* I have chosen three of these songs to show Liszt's ability to deal with different subjects.

Liszt's revised setting of *Im Rhein, im schönen Strome* illustrates in its three stanzas the river Rhine and a picture within the Cologne cathedral that is suggestive of the narrator's beloved. The triplet sixteenth notes establish the Rhine from the beginning but also refers to the *Wildnis* (wilderness) of the narrator's life. The tuneful melody mellows strikingly as the narrator explains how the picture shone friendly upon him. When the text turns to flowers and angels, the piano figuration becomes softer, higher, and more delicate. The sixteenth-note figurations in the piano stop at m. 34 as the text turns to the narrator's acknowledgement that the woman in the picture has eyes, lips, and cheeks that resemble his own beloved's features. In the brief coda that follows, Liszt overlays the text, describing his lover with the opening Rhine motive to unify the end of the song. This piece ranks as one of Liszt's most performed songs because of how masterfully he portrays Heine's elegant poem.

Both Liszt's versions of *Vergiftet sind meine Lieder* (Poisoned are my Songs) are about a minute long and largely *forte.* Instead of specifying a tempo, Liszt gives the opening direction as *Heftig deklamiert* (omitting the *Quasi Andante* of the first version). Both open without introduction or any piano pitch—the only Liszt songs that begin without the piano (see Example 15.4). Raabe pointed out, however, that a French edition opens with four *fortissimo* chords in the left hand.[60] The two versions are extraordinarily different from one another, with an opening triplet phrase in the original that is not included in the revision. In the second version the piano accompaniment has no melodic interest whatsoever when the voice is singing. Liszt also removes the slight ornamen-tation from the first version (mm. 4, 17, and 22) to strip the second down to the bare minimum. In the second version Liszt adds a brief six-measure interlude which builds in intensity to set up the text *Ich trag' im Herzen viel Schlangen* and ends with a clever musical depiction of the serpents at the end in the piano part that was not present in the first. The ending of the first version is reminiscent of Liszt's concluding measures to his *Vallée d'Obermann* and is harmonically simpler than the sinister, bass, chromatic scales, and diminished-seventh and augmented sonorities of the second version. The revised version is one of the finest settings of anger and ranks on par with Wolf's greatest songs. Gerald Abraham wrote, "But when Liszt is obliged to concentrate, as in the scathing 'Vergiftet sind meine Lieder' (1844), he achieves a masterpiece, one of the most terrible hate-songs ever written."[61] Cooper, too, applauded Liszt's setting of *Vergiftet sind meine Lieder*: "The feeling of suddenly 'seeing red,' the loss of all control for a moment is perfectly caught."[62]

Example 15.4
Liszt, *Vergiftet sind meine Lieder*, revised version, mm. 1–13

Die Loreley was Liszt's first song set to Heine's texts and one of his best ballads. Singers today almost exclusively perform the revision that he reworked between 1854 and 1859 primarily because of its dramatic setting of the poem as a ballad. Liszt arranges the song with a narration in the form of a recitative to begin and describes the story through music and action, ending with the return of the narrator to complete the commentary (see Example 15.5).

Example 15.5
Liszt, *Die Loreley*, revised version, mm. 1–17

The second version differs from the first in a number of ways. The opening piano introduction did not appear at all in the earliest version, and the lovely E-major melody that unfolds in m. 31 *(Sehr ruhig aber nicht schleppend)* is not nearly as beautiful as in the revision. The piano writing depicting the sinking of the boat is much more difficult and denser in texture in the earlier version. Liszt replaces the widespread arpeggiated figures of the first version with tremolos and single-note passages in the second version. The concluding g^2 in the voice that so effectively closes the later version was not in the first, which ends with the voice on a g^1 followed by a rather conventional eight-measure piano coda. Liszt includes an optional cut of ten measures beginning at m. 110 in the second version that does not seem necessary, and most performers tend not to take it. Although *Die Loreley* surpasses Liszt's other ballads, Einstein chose this setting to criticize Liszt: "One need only compare his setting of Heine's 'Loreley' with any ballad by Schubert, Schumann or Loewe, to see how everything resolves itself into details—often very clear details—and is held together only by a single melodic idea. This is a product of the Romantic, Parisian salon."[63]

On par with the Heine settings are those Liszt made on poems of Goethe. From the six settings of Goethe (*Der du von dem Himmel bist, Es war ein König in Thule, Freudvoll und leidvoll, Mignons Lied: Kennst du das Land, Wanderers Nachtlied: Über allen Gipfeln ist Ruh,* and *Wer nie sein Brot mit Tränen aß*), I have selected two of his most well-known songs to examine.

The second version of Liszt's three settings of *Mignons Lied: Kennst du das Land* is perhaps the most performed and one of his loveliest songs. Based on *Wilhelm Meister*, this Lied sets Mignon's longing to return to Italy after her years of abduction in Germany. Each of the three stanzas, which contain two sections in modified strophic form, begins with (A) *Kennst du* (Do you know?) and ends with (B) her desire to return to Italy with Wilhelm. Set in F♯ major, each of the A sections begins in tonic but closes respectively on D major, D minor, or, deceptively, E♭-major chords (Enharmonically spelled D♯–G–B♭). The directionless melodic line is accompanied by numerous rolled chords in the opening A section. The B section which begins each time *Kennst du es wohl* or, in the last case, *ihn wohl,* starts out tentatively with alternating voice and piano, followed by the faster *Dahin! Dahin!* The third A section is more impassioned with its more restless accompaniment, but the last *Dahin!* section is slower and somewhat more plaintive. Osborne wrote, "The second version, published in 1856, is the finest setting of this text to have been composed before Wolf's great song."[64] Cooper concurred, "This is as good as anything Liszt ever did, and the setting as a whole has been fine enough to remain in a few singers' regular repertories."[65] Liszt himself seemed pleased with the song years later as he described to Princess Carolyne on 28 September 1876:

To tell the truth, I have never keenly felt for Italy, its lemon trees and oranges, the *Sehnsucht* of Goethe's Mignon. Nevertheless, when I composed the song *Kennst du das Land?* in Berlin in February 1842, after 50 other musicians [had already set it], I identified myself somehow or other with the dreamy sentiments of a young girl. Several of Goethe's friends, in particular Chancellor Müller, told me that I had succeeded passably—even that the stress on *dahin! dahin!* would not have displeased the great poet![66]

Liszt's second version of his last Goethe setting, *Über allen Gipfeln ist Ruh* (*Wanderers Nachtlied*), composed in 1859, is one of his calm masterpieces. The text evokes the peace and quiet over the mountain peaks, and the contentment that a person feels when the struggles of life are over. The work opens *pianissimo* with simple blocked chords, alternating major and minor sonorities that rise to indicate the mountain peaks (see Example 15.6). The voice enters with four repeated notes and a melody of restricted motion and range, resting on the word *Ruh* as the tonic E-major sonority establishes the emotional and musical feeling of rest. Liszt is as effective in the next phrases where he depicts "scarcely a breath" (*kaum einen Hauch*) and silent birds in the woods. The work rises to a climatic *forte* moment on the text "only wait, soon you will also be at rest" (mm. 24–30) before returning to *pp* by the end of the phrase. Liszt turns the eight-line poem into a larger three-part structure, returning musically to the opening chords and utilizing considerable text repetition of the last two lines. The return of the opening chords creates a stillness that is breathtaking. The song ends exquisitely with an irregular resolution of a V_7 going to a G-major chord (♭III) before resolving to tonic. Before it resolves, though, the voice drops surprisingly an octave to low small bs as a reminder, *du auch!* (you also!). Watson claimed that the final version mirrors "exactly the enchantment and simplicity of the poetry, with unhurried, pictorially effective chords."[67]

Example 15.6
Liszt, *Über allen Gipfeln ist Ruh*, revised version, mm. 1–15

Rounding out Liszt's major German songs from his early and middle periods are three Lieder by other poets: von Redwitz, Rellstab, and Uhland. Liszt's setting of von Redwitz's *Es muß ein Wunderbares sein* is one of the composer's simplest love songs and most frequently recorded Lieder. Cast in Eb major and labeled *Schwebend* (suspended or floating), it displays a restricted vocal line (c^1–eb^2) with a bare chordal accompaniment (see Example 15.7).

Example 15.7
Liszt, *Es muß ein Wunderbares sein*, mm. 1–16

In only thirty-two non-virtuosic measures Liszt is able to capture that wondrous love that "lasts from the first kiss until death" (*Vom ersten Kuß bis in den Tod*). Brody and Fowkes suggested, "With its simple, unobtrusive accompanimental figure, *Es muß ein Wunderbares sein* represents the closest example of an

intimate lied in the manner of Schumann and Brahms."[68] Liszt heard Eduard
Hanslick's wife perform it in 1878, and even Hanslick, the anti-Wagner and
New German School critic, called *Es muß ein Wunderbares sein* Liszt's
"simplest, and for that reason the best, of his songs."[69]

Liszt composed his brilliant, Wolf-like setting of Rellstab's *Wo weilt er?*
(Where does he live?) in 1844. Rellstab poses three questions in the poem: the
restless woman wonders where her beloved is, what he's doing, and what he's
thinking. Liszt remains true to the poem and effectively evokes a feeling of the
questions through an ascending motivic introduction (see Example 15.8).

Example 15.8
Liszt, *Wo weilt er?*, mm. 1–3

Liszt sets each question in a slower tempo with a rising motive, and on two
occasions asks the question unaccompanied. The answer is always faster and
lower. Because of its structure and setting, the song contains more than a dozen
tempo-related indications and three key signature changes in only forty-two
measures.

Wo weilt er? opens with a key signature of A♭ major (in which the work
ends) but avoids the tonic key throughout the ten measures within that key
signature. The questioning introduction hangs on a $V_{6/5}$ chord from which the
voice immediately imitates the last three notes in the piano. It is not until the
final cadence in the voice part that A♭ major is established as the protagonist
calls her beloved home, *Heimat zurück*: Liszt blatantly includes a V_7–I cadence
that he has scrupulously avoided throughout the work. With tonic firmly
established, a brief piano postlude follows; the soprano line, however, ascends in
the final cadence keeping the question unanswered: "Will he come home?"
Cooper wrote that this Lied "is a good dramatic lyric on a small scale, and the
piano accompaniment has something of the beauty of Wolf's 'Verschwiegene
Liebe', which it resembles."[70]

Liszt set Uhland's *Die Vätergruft* first in 1844 but returned to it during the
final days of his life. It is another gloomy masterpiece, and Liszt creatively
establishes a classic tone to this poem about coffins and death with a stark,
ominous beginning. Written in bass clef for bass or baritone, the song opens
Mäßig langsam with a single-line piano introduction on a CC. He further

intensifies the drama by doubling the voice with the piano in open octaves with no filled-in harmonies (see Example 15.9).

Example 15.9
Liszt, *Die Vätergruft*, mm. 1–14

The song contains numerous diminished chords and several augmented sonorities, first sounding on the word *Waffengeschmeide* in m. 9. Liszt also displays his fondness for the melodic augmented second that first occurs in the first measure between d♭ and e. He sets the "wonderful song" of the third verse as the B section (mm. 34–51) in a full-bodied, heroic manner, thrice repeating *Heil mir! Ich bin es wert!* Beginning at m. 76 Liszt slows down the Lied dramatically and ends on two low octaves at the text *Die Geisterlaute verhallten, da mocht es gar stille sein* (The ghostly sounds became quiet, as it became entirely still). Hughes wrote that this work "must be placed side by side with the most powerful ballads of German musical literature. Indeed it is difficult to say who after Löwe has written anything which can be ranked with it."[71]

Liszt's most important late songs include the impressionistic *Ihr Glocken von Marling,* the dark setting *Und wir dachten der Toten,* and his greatest French setting after his Hugo settings, Alfred de Musset's *J'ai perdu ma force et ma vie* (*'Tristesse'*). Composed on 14 July 1874, Liszt based his conception of Emil Kuh's *Ihr Glocken von Marling* on the tolling bells that he depicts throughout with repeated chords in the right hand. The blocked seventh and ninth chords are almost impressionistic in their nature because they do not resolve according to proper harmonic functions. Furthermore, the entire piano part sounds in the treble clef. The lowest note to sound in the piano is a small f♯ in mm. 35–39 (see Example 15.10).

Example 15.10
Liszt, *Ihr Glocken von Marling,* mm. 1–18

Ihr Glocken von Marling is arguably Liszt's greatest song written after 1870 and certainly represents a shift in compositional style from his earlier song settings. Brody and Fowkes wrote, "The delicate, ethereal sound of the bells (the persistent eighths) reveals a completely different facet of Liszt's style."[72]

Liszt composed *Und wir dachten der Toten* around 1871, based on a brief twenty-five word text dealing with thoughts of death while on a horse ride in the night-time rain. Marked *Langsam* it contains only twenty-three measures, over half of which are for piano alone (see Example 15.11).

Example 15.11
Liszt, *Und wir dachten der Toten***, complete**

This nearly fragmentary work opens with a nine-measure introduction consisting of two long pauses and a single-line, descending figure (mm. 3–8). The voice enters in a recitative-like manner and the piano drops out for a measure before returning with four measures of tremolos beginning *pianissimo* and increasing to *fortissimo*. On a repeated d^2 the music moves from *fortissimo* to *piano* in one measure to accentuate the word *Toten* only to return in the next measure to *fortissimo*. The short coda ends with a similar figuration to the introduction. Christopher Headington wrote, *"Und wir dachten der Toten* is completely convincing structurally; this last verse of a poem by Ferdinand Freiligrath has received a setting which is both massively expressive and durationally small."[73]

Composed on 28 May 1872, Liszt's *J'ai perdu ma force et ma vie* (*'Tristesse'*) opens with a seven-measure piano introduction and a series of unresolved dissonances, including augmented and fully-diminished-seventh chords. The voice opens unaccompanied in a recitative-like manner, and, as Noske points out, Liszt's songs are often set in a declamatory style.

Example 15.12
Liszt, *J'ai perdu ma force et ma vie* (*'Tristesse'*), mm. 1–14

Liszt accompanies the voice so little that Noske suggested that *J'ai perdu ma force et ma vie* is not a song at all. He wrote that it is "endowed with features of unusual beauty [and] is no longer either a *mélodie* or a Lied; it is a musically declaimed poem sustained by chords almost no longer obeying musical laws"[74] (see Example 15.12). Over a fourth of the song is unaccompanied and the piano rarely adds melodic content. Liszt includes upper-register tremolos between mm. 42 and 59, bringing in the opening chords beneath them in m. 54. The song ends with a series of dissonant chords, including augmented and diminished triads, and a major-seventh chord that moves in an unresolved manner to an incomplete diminished-seventh chord. Watson summed up this song "as a symbol of Liszt's last period: it is a sad, affecting reflection on the weariness and resignation of an old man."[75]

ORCHESTRAL SONGS

Liszt's orchestral songs are also an important part of his vocal output.[76] As early as 1848 and as late as the last year of his life, Liszt arranged a few of his songs for voice and orchestra,[77] making him a pioneer in this genre. Tünde Szitha suggested that, at Liszt's request, Conradi arranged *Le juif errant* for baritone and orchestra around 1848, and that Liszt evidently made an arrangement for voice and orchestra of the 1845 variant of *Jeanne d'Arc au bûcher* (S 373).[78] Szitha further stated that Liszt re-orchestrated *Jeanne d'Arc au bûcher* "26 years later, but he then took as his basis not the 1845 version of the song but a reformulated version of 1874, and he never returned to the versions Conradi had done."[79] Szitha concluded, "Though *Le juif errant* was never published and *Jeanne d'Arc* only in a late 1874 variant, the two pieces bear out that back in the latter half of the 1840s Liszt was already experimenting with the genre of the orchestral song."[80]

Of his orchestral songs *Jeanne d'Arc* received several performances as a dramatic scene for voice and orchestra. In addition to this song, Liszt set the *Lieder aus Schillers 'Wilhelm Tell'* in 1855, *Die Loreley*, *Mignons Lied*, and *Die drei Zigeuner* in 1860, and *Die Vätergruft* before his death in 1886. Liszt also arranged several Schubert songs (S 375) in 1860 and vocal works by Francis Korbay and Zichy for voice and orchestra (S 368 and S 377) in the 1880s.

The orchestral songs are literal orchestrations of Liszt's Lieder. The most effective are the three Schiller songs that profit noticeably with the availability of orchestral color. These songs, in particular, anticipate the nature writing found in the orchestral songs of Mahler, and the orchestration itself sounds strikingly Mahleresque at times. Few major composers other than Berlioz, Wagner, and Liszt wrote orchestral songs in the mid-nineteenth century, and these songs, other than the *Wesendonck Lieder* (which were also originally written with piano accompaniment), are almost never performed. It was left to Mahler and Strauss to popularize the voice-and-orchestra genre. Liszt's orchestral versions, based on poems by Schiller, Goethe, and Heine, nevertheless, are all worthy of repeated performances.

MELODRAMAS

Liszt composed four melodramas—a genre for narrator and piano popular at times in the nineteenth century—between 1857 and 1877. He also penned a melodrama with orchestral accompaniment entitled *Vor hundert Jahren* that remains unpublished. He arranged another brief melodrama by Felix Draeseke, known as *Helge's Treue*.

Liszt composed his first melodrama *Lenore* between 1857 and 1858, and revised it in 1860. Based on a text of Gottfried August Bürger, it is the longest of Liszt's melodramas, and music plays a greater percentage of the whole than in the other compositions in this style. The gothic story tells of a young woman in such despair because her lover has not returned from war that she pleads with God to let her die. In the middle of the night her lover returns and takes her to their marriage bed. When they arrive, the rider turns immediately into a skeleton and the young woman dies. Liszt's depiction includes marching soldiers and a galloping horse of the dead rider and young woman, using syncopated broken chords in the right hand and triplet left-hand scales and arpeggios to represent their journey. Liszt also writes some of his Mephisto-like music in the treble register of the keyboard, with plenty of staccato and grace-note passages to portray the dancing dead *(Sehr schnell)*.[81]

Liszt's 1862 music to Lenau's *Der traurige Mönch* (The Sad Monk)—his shortest melodrama for narrator and piano—contains fewer than one hundred measures and lasts approximately seven minutes (shorter than some of his Lieder). From a purely musical point of view, *Der traurige Mönch* is the most famous because of its whole-tone ostinato that occurs fourteen times, its use of the augmented triad, and its general dissonance.[82] It opens with repeated syncopated chords in the right hand, consisting of a major third and tritone over the whole-tone scale in octaves in the bass. This opening evolves into an augmented sonority that repeats fifteen times and continues over the ascending scales. Nearly half of the seventy-two lines of text are narrated without accompanying music.

Liszt's remaining melodramas are not as important. His only Hungarian melodrama, written in February 1874, is based on the Hungarian poet Mór Jókai's *A holt költő szerelme (Des toten Dichters Liebe* or The Dead Poet's Love)—which, in turn, Jókai based on the life of Sándor Petőfi. Liszt includes Hungarian references and direct allusion to Petőfi in the work. Composed between 1875 and 1877, Liszt's last melodrama, *Der blinde Sänger,* on a text by Alexey Tolstoy, contains large blocks of unaccompanied material, making it chiefly narration with incidental music. Liszt leaves nearly half of the thirty stanzas unaccompanied, often interspersing short musical fragments after significant portions of text.

Liszt, as a songwriter of significant stature in the nineteenth century, increased the role of the accompanist, adding considerable virtuosity and nearly orchestral effects to the keyboard as well as arranging a number of songs for orchestral accompaniment. At the same time he, more than any other composer of the century, also wrote a few songs that approached the idea of operatic arias, with higher notes and greater than usual vocal virtuosity. He was an innovator as well, particularly in his late songs with their restricted accompaniments and austere and dissonant harmonic language. Dietrich Fischer-Dieskau suggested that Liszt and the New German School had a significant influence on the German Lied:

This assault [by Liszt and the New German School] with new instrumentation, new programme music and many other kinds of sensory stimulus found an echo in the new German song. The piano part became virtuoso and orchestral, music became vastly more literary, the Lied became theatrical. With its newly acquired occasional orchestral accompaniment, it resembled a scene from an opera, and led via Mahler and the early Schoenberg straight into expressionistic atonality. Liszt was among the first who were prepared to welcome each innovation without reserve, as a result bring about amazing progress—a breed which up to the present day has suffered no lack of progeny.[83]

T. S. Eliot once wrote that "no poetic reputation ever remains exactly in the same place: it is a stock market in constant fluctuation."[84] Liszt's songs, so long undervalued, will one day receive the scholarly and popular attention they warrant. Hans Richter once remarked in Bayreuth, " 'You will see,' he said with conviction, 'we will *have* to come back to Liszt.' "[85] The excellence imbedded within Liszt's songs will find their rightful place among the major songs of Schubert, Schumann, and Wolf in the twenty-first century.

NOTES

1. Indeed, August Stradal recorded: "The last piece on which he [Liszt] worked was the orchestration of the accompaniment to his setting of Uhland's ballad *Die Vätergruft*. Knowing him to be engaged on such a work had a most melancholy effect upon me: the feeling came to me that he himself would now be 'descending to the coffins of his forefathers.' " Quoted in Adrian Williams, *Portrait of Liszt: By Himself and His Contemporaries* (Oxford: Clarendon Press, 1990), 659.

2. Included in this number are six songs added to the catalog in the work list of the *New Grove Dictionary*, 2d ed. (London: Macmillan, 2001). None of these is available in a modern edition and four remain unpublished: *Barcarole vénitienne de Pantaleoni*, 1840 (LW:N2); *Dem Felsengipfel stieg ich einst hinan*, 1843? (LW:N15); *Über die Aeolsharfe*, 1846 (LW:N38); *Göttliche Gedanken, selige Gefühle*, 1848 (LW:N41); *Es hat geflammt die ganze Nacht (Lied der Grossherzogin Marie Pavlovna)*, 1849–1854 (LW:N47); and *Serbisches Lied (Ein Mädchen sitzt am Meeresstrand)*, 1858? (LW:N57).

3. Jack M. Stein ignored Liszt in his *Poem and Music in the German Lied from Gluck to Hugo Wolf* (Cambridge: Harvard University Press, 1971), as did Pierre Bernac in his *The Interpretation of French Song* (New York and London: W. W. Norton, 1978). Dennis Stevens devoted only two paragraphs to Liszt's songs in *A History of Song*, rev. ed. (New York and London: W. W. Norton, 1970), 248–249.

4. Suzanne Montu-Berthon, "Un Liszt Méconnu: Mélodies et Lieder," *La Revue musicale* 342–346 (1981): entire issues.

5. Michael Saffle, *Franz Liszt: A Guide to Research* (New York: Garland, 1991), 307.

6. Martin Cooper, "Liszt as a Song Writer," *Music & Letters* 19 (1938): 181.

7. Ibid., 175.

8. Ibid., 176.

9. Elaine Brody and Robert A. Fowkes, *The German Lied and Its Poetry* (New York: New York University Press, 1971), 207.

10. Rena Charnin Mueller, "Liszt's 'Tasso' Sketchbook: Studies in Sources and Revisions" (Ph.D. diss., New York University, 1986), 100.

11. See Saffle, *Liszt in Germany, 1840–1845: A Study in Sources, Documents, and The History of Reception*. Franz Liszt Studies Series no. 2 (Stuyvesant, NY: Pendragon, 1994), 143, 165.

12. Quoted in Williams, *Portrait of Liszt*, 460.

13. Ibid., 349.

14. Ibid., 356.

15. Ibid., 607.

16. *The Letters of Franz Liszt*, ed. La Mara [Marie Lipsius], trans. Constance Bache (New York: Scribner's, 1894; New York: Greenwood, 1969), 1:413–414.

17. Ibid., 1:414.

18. *Correspondance de Liszt et de la comtesse d'Agoult*, ed. Daniel Ollivier (Paris: Grasset, 1933–1934), 2:179. ["Je crois aussi avoir terminé la *Lorelei*, mais elle ne sera écrite qu'après-demain."]

19. *Franz Liszt's Briefe*, ed. La Mara [Marie Lipsius], 8 vols. (Leipzig: Breitkopf & Härtel, 1893–1905), 5:8–9. ["*Nebenbei* la fantaisie m'a pris . . . de composer les *Zigeuner* de Lenau—et j'en ai trouvé très vite au piano tout le contour. Si cela se fait en quelque manière de soi, sans qu'il se rencontre au beau milieu une de ces féroces et tenaces résistances, qui sont la plus dure des épreuves que l'artiste ait à subir—je me mettrai à les écrire."]

20. Ibid., 4:38–39. ["La Princesse m'avait donné une romance à composer, entre le dîner et la soirée. Voulant l'écrire sans retard, je n'ai pu me rendre que vers 9 heures au thé."]

21. Ibid., 5:8. ["J'ai fait peu de chose cette dernière semaine, tout en me tourmentant 6 ou 7 heures par jour à travailler. Le *Lied* de Hoffmann, *Scheiden*, m'a singulièrement crispé les nerfs. J'en ai fait 3 ou 4 versions différentes, déchirées l'une après l'autre—et de guerre lasse, je l'ai achevé hier soir."]

22. Ibid., 7: 77.

23. *Correspondance de Liszt et de la comtesse d'Agoult*, 2:368. ["Je les tiens pour singulièrement réussis et plus achevés de forme qu'aucune des choses que j'ai publiées."]

24. *Franz Liszt's Briefe*, 4:64. ["Götze a chanté délicieusement et avec tout plein d'âme mes deux *Lieder*—dont le premier *Du bist wie eine Blume*, a été redemandé de suite par Mme la Grande-duchesse."]

25. Ibid., 4:89. ["Mon pauvre *Hingehn* . . . Au haut de la première page, j'écrivis ces mots. . . . Ce *Lied* est mon testament de jeunesse. Je ne me doutais guère alors qu'il se trouverait quelqu'un pour l'écouter de la sorte—car comment aurais-je imaginé que je rencontrerais une femme pareille—et que cette femme voudrait devenir la mienne!"]

26. William J. Dart, "Revisions and Reworkings in the Lieder of Franz Liszt," *Studies in Music* [Australia] 9 (1975): 43.

27. Peter Raabe, *Franz Liszt: Leben und Schaffen*. 2 vols. (Stuttgart: J. G. Cotta, 1931; Tutzing: Hans Schneider, 1968), 2:113.

28. Charles Osborne, *The Concert Song Companion: A Guide to the Classical Repertoire* (London: Victor Gollancz, 1974), 59.

29. Alfred Einstein, *Music in the Romantic Era* (New York and London: W. W. Norton, 1947), 195.

30. Cooper, "Liszt as a Song Writer," 181.

31. Einstein, *Music in the Romantic Era*, 195.

32. Cooper, "Liszt as a Song Writer," 173.

33. Ibid.

34. Liszt did not begin any new song settings in German between 1861 and 1870.

35. Frits Noske, *French Song from Berlioz to Duparc*, trans. Rita Benton (New York: Dover, 1970), 126.

36. David Cox, "France," in *A History of Song*, 202.

37. Osborne, *The Concert Song Companion*, 59.

38. Rey M. Longyear, "Review," Walker, *Franz Liszt: The Weimar Years 1848–1861* (New York: Knopf, 1989) in *JALS* 26 (1989): 69.

39. Brody and Fowkes, *The German Lied and Its Poetry*, 207.

40. Cooper, "Liszt as a Song Writer," 173.

41. Brody and Fowkes, *The German Lied and Its Poetry*, 208.

42. Edwin Hughes, "Liszt as Lieder Composer," *Musical Quarterly* 3 (1917): 395.

43. R. Larry Todd, "The 'Unwelcome Guest' Regaled: Franz Liszt and the Augmented Triad," *19th-Century Music* 12 (1988): 103.

44. It appears that Liszt altered the measure sometime after Wagner had written *Tristan und Isolde*. See Mueller, "Liszt's 'Tasso' Sketchbook," 119–127.

45. Lucien Stark, *A Guide to the Songs of Johannes Brahms* (Bloomington and Indianapolis: Indiana University Press, 1995), 1.

46. Brody and Fowkes, *The German Lied and Its Poetry*, 208.

47. See Montu-Berthon, "Un Liszt Méconnu: Mélodies et Lieder," 101–113.

48. Quoted in Williams, *Portrait of Liszt*, 644.

49. *The Letters of Franz Liszt*, 2:502.

50. Ibid., 1:172.

51. Quoted in Williams, *Portrait of Liszt*, 568.

52. Ibid.

53. See Arnold, "Visions and Revisions: Looking into Liszt's 'Lieder,' " in *Liszt and the Birth of Modern Europe: Music as a Mirror of Political, Religious, Social, and Aesthetic Transformations,"* ed. Saffle and Rossana Dalmonte (Hillsdale, NY: Pendragon; forthcoming).

54. Mueller, "Liszt's 'Tasso' Sketchbook," 114.

55. *Franz Liszt's Briefe*, 8:368. ["J'hésite à en publier la seconde version originale (très modifiée et subtilisée) pour chant, car pour exprimer le sentiment que j'ai tâché d'inhaler à la notation musicale de ces Sonnets, il faudrait quelque chanteur poétique, amoureux d'un idéal d'amour . . . *rarae aves in terris*."]

56. Derek Watson wrote, "In the first version of the Petrarch sonnet *I vidi in terra* the word *soglia* is mistakenly set as three syllables, corrected in the later version." See Watson, *Liszt* (New York: Schirmer, 1989), 306.

57. *Correspondance de Liszt et de la comtesse d'Agoult*, 2:199–200. ["Dans cette dernière quinzaine, j'ai écrit deux nouveaux lieder, un pour moi et l'autre pour toi, chère Marie."]

58. See Franz Liszt, *Selected Letters*, ed. and trans. Adrian Williams (Oxford: Clarendon Press, 1998), 178.

59. Noske, *French Song from Berlioz to Duparc*, 132.

60. See Raabe's notes in NLE vii/2: xiii. Thomas Hampson and Geoffrey Parsons perform this version on their compact disk (EMI Classics CDC 5 55047 2 [1994]).

61. Gerald Abraham, *The Concise Oxford History of Music* (New York and Oxford: Oxford University Press, 1979), 771–772.

62. Cooper, "Liszt as a Song Writer," 175.

63. Einstein, *Music in the Romantic Era*, 195.

64. Osborne, *The Concert Song Companion,* 59.

65. Cooper, "Liszt as a Song Writer," 177.

66. *Franz Liszt's Briefe,* 7:157–158. ["A la vérité, je n'ai jamais ressenti pour l'Italie, ses citronniers et ses oranges la *Sehnsucht* de la Mignon de Goethe. Néanmoins, en composant à Berlin au mois de Février 1842, après 50 autres musiciens, le *Lied: Kennst du das Land?* je me suis identifié tant bien que mal au sentiment rêveur de la jeune fille. Plusieurs amis de Goethe, en particulier le chancelier Müller, me dirent que j'y avais passablement réussi—même que l'accent du *dahin, dahin!* n'aurait pas déplu au grand poète!"]

67. Watson, *Liszt,* 308.

68. Brody and Fowkes, *The German Lied and Its Poetry,* 218.

69. Quoted in Williams, *Portrait of Liszt,* 558.

70. Cooper, "Liszt as a Song Writer," 180.

71. Hughes, "Liszt as Lieder Composer," 400.

72. Christopher Headington, "The Songs," in *Franz Liszt: The Man & His Music,* ed. Walker (New York: Taplinger, 1970), 245.

73. Brody and Fowkes, 224.

74. Noske, *French Song from Berlioz to Duparc,* 135.

75. Watson, *Liszt,* 309.

76. See Chapter 12 for additional discussion of Liszt's transcriptions for voice and orchestra.

77. See Liszt, *Orchestral Songs* (Hungaroton SLPD 12105).

78. Tünde Szitha, "Liszt's 'Unknown' French Songs," *Studia musicologica* 29 (1987): 262–263.

79. Ibid., 263.

80. Ibid., 265.

81. See Gerhard J. Winkler, " 'Tradition' and 'Progress': Liszt's first Melodrama *Lenore,*" in *Liszt the Progressive,* ed. Hans Kagebeck and Johan Lagerfelt (Lewiston, MA: Edwin Mellen, 2001), 223–237.

82. See Winkler, " 'Der traurige Mönch' (1860): Considéra-tions archéologiques sur les oeuvres tardives de Liszt." *La Revue musicale* 405–407 (1987): 105–118.

83. Dietrich Fischer-Dieskau, *The Fischer-Dieskau Book of Lieder* (New York: Knopf, 1980), 22–23.

84. T. S. Eliot, "What is Minor Poetry?" in *On Poetry and Poets* (New York: Farrar, Straus & Cudahy, 1957), 46.

85. Hughes, "Liszt as Lieder Composer," 408.

Selected Bibliography

LISZT'S CORRESPONDENCE

Autour de Mme d'Agoult et de Liszt. Ed. Daniel Ollivier. Paris: Grasset, 1941.

Briefe hervorragender Zeitgenossen an Franz Liszt. Ed. La Mara [Marie Lipsius]. 3 vols. Leipzig: Breitkopf & Härtel, 1895, 1904.

Briefwechsel zwischen Franz Liszt und Carl Alexander, Grossherzog von Sachsen. Ed. La Mara [Marie Lipsius]. Leipzig: Breitkopf & Härtel, 1909.

Briefwechsel zwischen Franz Liszt und Hans von Bülow. Ed. La Mara [Marie Lipsius]. Leipzig: Breitkopf & Härtel, 1898.

Briefwechsel zwischen Wagner und Liszt. Ed. Erich Kloss. 3d ed. Leipzig: Breitkopf & Härtel, 1910.

Correspondance de Liszt et de la comtesse d'Agoult. Ed. M. Daniel Ollivier. 2 vols. Paris: Grasset, 1933–1934.

Correspondance de Liszt et de sa fille Madame Émile Ollivier, 1842–1862. Ed. Daniel Ollivier. Paris: Grasset, 1936.

Correspondence of Wagner and Liszt. Trans. Francis Hueffer. Ed. W. Ashton Ellis. 2d ed. New York: Scribner's, 1897. Reprint, 1973.

Franz Liszt and Agnès Street-Klindworth: A Correspondence 1854–1886. Ed. and trans. Pauline Pocknell. Stuyvesant, NY: Pendragon, 2000.

Franz Liszt in seinen Briefen. Eine Auswahl. Ed. Hans Rudolf Jung. Berlin: Henschelverlag, 1987.

Franz Liszt und sein Kreis in Briefen und Dokumenten. Ed. Mária P. Eckhardt and Cornelia Knotik. Wissenschaftliche Arbeiten aus dem Burgenland no. 66. Eisenstadt: Burgenländisches Landesmuseum, 1983.

Franz Liszt. Correspondance. Ed. Pierre-Antoine Huré and Claude Knepper. Paris: Lattès, 1987.

Franz Liszt. L'artiste—Le Clerc. Documents inédits. Ed. Jacques Vier. Paris: Les Éditions du Cèdre, 1950.

Franz Liszt: Unbekannte Presse und Briefe aus Wien 1822–1886. Ed. Dezső Legány. Budapest: Corvina Kiadó, 1984.

Franz Liszt's Briefe an Baron Anton Augusz, 1846–1878. Ed. Wilhelm von Csapó. Budapest: Franklin, 1911.

Franz Liszt's Briefe. Ed. La Mara [Marie Lipsius]. 8 vols. Leipzig: Breitkopf & Härtel, 1893–1905.

Franz Liszt: Briefwechsel mit seiner Mutter. Ed. Klára Hamburger. Eisenstadt: Amt Burgenländisches Landesregierung, 2000.

Franz Liszt—Richard Wagner Briefwechsel. Ed. Hanjo Keating. Frankfurt a. M.: Insel, 1988.

Franz Liszts Briefe an Carl Gille. Ed. Adolf Stern. Leipzig: Breitkopf & Härtel, 1903.

Franz Liszts Briefe an seine Mutter. Ed. and trans. La Mara [Marie Lipsius]. Leipzig: Breitkopf & Härtel, 1918.

Hamburger, Klára. "Liszt, Father and Grandfather: Unpublished Letters to Cosima and Daniela von Bülow." *New Hungarian Quarterly* 32/121 (1991): 118–131.

The Letters of Franz Liszt. Ed. La Mara [Marie Lipsius]. Trans. Constance Bache. New York: Scribner's, 1894; New York: Greenwood Press, 1969. Vols. 1 and 2 of *Franz Liszt's Briefe.*

The Letters of Franz Liszt to Marie zu Sayn-Wittgenstein. Ed. and trans. Howard E. Hugo. Cambridge: Harvard University Press, 1953.

The Letters of Franz Liszt to Olga von Meyendorff, 1871–1886. Trans. William R. Tyler. Introduction and notes Edward N. Waters. Washington, D.C.: Dumbarton Oaks, 1979.

Liszt, Franz. *Briefe aus ungarischen Sammlungen, 1835–1886.* Ed. Margit Prahács. Budapest: Akadémiai Kiadó, 1966.

Liszt, Franz. *Lettres à Cosima et à Daniela.* Ed. Klára Hamburger. Sprimont: Mardaga, 1996.

Liszt, Franz. *Selected Letters.* Ed. and trans. Adrian Williams. Oxford: Clarendon Press, 1998.

Suttoni, Charles. "Liszt Correspondence in Print: A Supplementary Bibliography." *JALS* 46 (1999).

———. "Liszt Correspondence in Print: An Expanded, Annotated Bibliography." *JALS* 25 (1989): entire issue.

Une Correspondance romantique: Madame d'Agoult, Liszt, Henri Lehmann. Ed. Solange Joubert. Paris: Flammarion, 1947.

LISZT'S WRITINGS

Liszt, Franz. *An Artist's Journey: Lettres d'un bachelier ès musique 1835–1841.* Trans. and annotated Charles Suttoni. Chicago: University of Chicago Press, 1989.

———. "Berlioz and his Harold Symphony." *Source Readings in Music History.* Ed. Oliver Strunk. New York: Norton, 1950: 846–873.

———. *De la Fondation Goethe à Weimar.* Ed. Otto Goldhammer. Weimar: Nationalen Forchungs-und Gedenkstätten der klassischen deutschen Literatur, 1961.

———. *Frederic Chopin.* Trans. Edward N. Waters. New York: The Free Press, 1963.

———. *Gesammelte Schriften.* Ed. and trans. Lina Ramann. 6 vols. Leipzig: Breitkopf & Härtel, 1880–1883; Wiesbaden, 1978.

———. *Gesammelte Schriften.* [Ed. Julius Kapp.] 4 vols. Leipzig: Breitkopf & Härtel, 1910. Volksausgabe.

———. *The Gypsies and their Music in Hungary.* Trans. Edwin Evans. 2 vols. London: Reeves, n.d.

————. *Pages romantiques.* Ed. Jean Chantavoine. Paris: F. Alcan, 1912; Paris, 1985.

————. *Sämtliche Schriften.* Ed. Detlef Altenburg. Wiesbaden: Breitkopf & Härtel, 1989–. 9 vols. planned: 1. *Frühe Schriften*; 2. *Frédéric Chopin*; 3. *Die Goethe-Stiftung*; 4. *Lohengrin und Tannhäuser von Richard Wagner*; 5. *Dramaturgische Blätter*; 6. *Aus den Annalen des Fortschritts*; 7 and 8. *Die Zigeuner und ihre Musik in Ungarn.* 9. *Programme und vermischte Schriften/Register.*

————. "Wagner's *Tannhäuser.*" *Dwight's Journal of Music* (19 November–17 December 1853). 5 installments.

GENERAL BIBLIOGRAPHY

Abraham, Gerald. *A Hundred Years of Music.* London: Duckworth, 1938.

————. *The Concise Oxford History of Music.* New York and Oxford: Oxford University Press, 1979.

Agawu, Kofi. *Playing With Signs: A Semiotic Interpretation of Classic Music.* Princeton, NJ: Princeton University Press, 1991.

Allen, Melinda Moody. "Historical Background for a Hermeneutic Interpretation of the Liszt B Minor Piano Sonata as the Metaphysical Embodiment of His Spirit." D.M.A. diss., University of Texas, Austin, 1997.

Altenburg, Detlef. "Die Schriften von Franz Liszt: Bemerkungen zu einem zentralen Problem der Liszt-Forschung." *Festschrift Arno Forchert zum 60. Geburtstag am 29. Dezember 1985.* Kassel and New York: Bärenreiter, 1986.

————. "Liszts Schriften: Zur Konzeption und zu Problemen der historisch-kritischen Ausgabe." *Die Projekte der Liszt-Forschung.* Ed. Detlef Altenburg and Gerhard J. Winkler. Wissenschaftliche Arbeiten aus dem Burgenland no. 87. Eisenstadt: Burgenländisches Landesmuseum, 1991.

————, ed. *Liszt und die Weimarer Klassik.* Laaber: Laaber-Verlag, 1997.

Anderson, Lyle John. "Motivic and Thematic Transformation in Selected Works of Liszt." Ph.D. diss., Ohio State University, 1977.

Arnold, Ben. "Franz Liszt: the Reader, the Intellectual, and the Musician." In *Analecta Lisztiana I: Proceedings of the "Liszt and His World" Conference Held at Virginia Polytechnic Institute and State University, 20–23 May 1993*, Michael Saffle. Franz Liszt Studies Series no. 5, 37–60. Stuyvesant, NY: Pendragon, 1998.

————. "Liszt and the Music of Revolution and War." In *Analecta Lisztiana II: New Light on Liszt and His Music*, ed. Michael Saffle and James Deaville. Franz Liszt Studies Series no. 6, 225–238. Stuyvesant, NY: Pendragon, 1997.

————. "Recitative in Liszt's Solo Piano Music." *JALS* 24 (1988): 3–22.

Arnold, J. von. "Concertmusik: Franz Liszt, 'Todtentanz.' " *Neue Zeitschrift für Musik* 61 (6 October 1865): 353–355.

Arrau, Claudio. "Conversation with Claudio Arrau on Liszt." *Piano Quarterly* 23 (Spring 1975): 7–11.

Augustini, Folke. *Die Klavieretüde im 19. Jahrhundert. Studien zu ihrer Entwicklung und Bedeutung.* Duisburg: Gilles a Francke, 1986.

Backus, Joan. "Aspects of Form in the Music of Liszt: The Principle of Developing Idea." Ph.D. diss., University of Victoria, 1985.

————. "Liszt's *Sposalizio*: A Study in Musical Perspective." *19th-Century Music* 12/2 (Fall 1998): 173–183.

Baker, James M. "The Limits of Tonality in the Late Music of Franz Liszt." *Journal of Music Theory* 34/2 (1990): 145–173.

Bakken, Howard. "Liszt and the Organ." *Diapason* (May 1969): 27–29.

Banowetz, Joseph. "A Liszt Sonetto: Sonnet 47 of Petrarch." *Clavier* (March 1978): 12–15.

———, ed. *Franz Liszt: An Introduction to the Composer and His Music.* Park Ridge, IL: General Words & Music, 1973.

Bárdos, Lajos. "Ferenc Liszt, the Innovator." *Studia musicologica* 17 (1975): 3–38.

Baron, Michael David. "The Songs of Franz Liszt." D.M.A. diss., Ohio State University, 1993.

Barricelli, Jean-Pierre. "Liszt's Journey through Dante's Hereafter." *Bucknell Review* 26 (1982): 149–166. Reprint *JALS* 14 (1983): 3–15.

Bartók, Béla. "Liszt's Music and Today's Public." In *Béla Bartók Essays*, selected and ed. Benjamin Suchoff. No. 8 in the New York Bartók Archive Studies in Musicology. New York: St. Martin's Press, 1976.

Bates, William. "The Haselböck Edition of Liszt's Organ Works." *JALS* 28 (1990): 42–68.

Becker, Ralf-Walter. "Formprobleme in Liszts h-moll Sonata: Untersuchungen zu Liszts Klaviermusik um 1850." Diss., University of Marburg, 1979.

Berlioz, Hector. *Correspondance générale*, ed. Pierre Citron et al. Paris: Flammarion, 1972–1999.

Bernstein, Susan. *Virtuosity of the Nineteenth Century: Performing Music and Language in Heine, Liszt, and Baudelaire.* Stanford: Stanford University Press, 1998.

Bertagnolli, Paul. "From Overture to Symphonic Poem, From Melodrama to Choral Cantata: Studies of the Sources for Franz Liszt's *Prometheus* and his *Chöre zu Herder's 'Entfesseltem Prometheus.'* " Ph.D. diss., Washington University, 1998.

Biget, Michelle. "Liszt: La *Vallée d'Obermann*—Ecriture(s) instrumentale(s)." *Analyse musicale* 21 (1990): 85–95.

Block, Joseph. "Liszt's 'Die Zelle in Nonnenwerth.' " *Piano Quarterly* 81 (1973): 4–11.

Bonner, Andrew. "Liszt's *Les Préludes* and *Les Quatre Élémens*: A Reinvestigation." *19th-Century Music* 10 (Fall 1986): 96–101.

Bory, Robert. "Diverses lettres inédites de Liszt." *Schweizerisches Jahrbuch für Musikwissenschaft* 3 (1928).

———. *Une retraite romantique en Suisse. Liszt et la Comtesse d'Agoult.* A Lausanne, SPES edition, 1930.

Brendel, Alfred. *Music Sounded Out: Essays, Lectures, Interviews, Afterthoughts.* New York: Farrar Strauss Giroux, 1990.

———. *Musical Thoughts and Afterthoughts.* Princeton: Princeton University Press, 1976.

Brendel, Franz. *Franz Liszt als Symphoniker.* Leipzig: C. Merseburg, 1859.

Brody, Elaine, and Robert A. Fowkes. *The German Lied and Its Poetry.* New York: New York University Press, 1971.

Broeckx, Jan L., and Walter Landrieu. "Comparative Computer Study of Style, Based on Five Lied Melodies." *Interface* 1/1 (1972): 29–92.

Bülow, Hans von. *Briefe und Schriften.* Ed. Marie von Bülow. 2d ed. Leipzig: Breitkopf & Härtel, 1899–1907.

Burger, Ernst. *Franz Liszt: Eine Lebenschronik in Bildern und Dokumenten.* Munich: Paul List Verlag, 1986.

———. *Franz Liszt: A Chronicle of His Life in Pictures.* Trans. Stewart Spencer. Princeton: Princeton University Press, 1989.

Burke, Richard. N. "The Marche funèbre from Beethoven to Mahler." Ph.D. diss., City University of New York, 1991.

Busoni, Ferruccio. *The Essence of Music and other Papers.* Trans. R. Ley. London: Rockliff, 1957.

Cannata, David Butler. "Perception & Apperception in Liszt's Late Piano Music." *The Journal of Musicology* 15/2 (1997): 178–207.

Chop, Max. *Franz Liszts symphonische Werke, geschichtlich und musikalisch analysiert*, 2 vols. Leipzig: Reclam, 1924–1925.

Cinnamon, Howard. "Chromaticism and Tonal Coherence in Liszt's Sonetto 104 del Petrarca." *In Theory Only* 7 (1983): 3–19.

———. "Third-related Harmonies as Elements of Contrapuntal Prolongation in Some Works by Franz Liszt." *In Theory Only* 12/ 5–6 (1992): 1–30.

———. "Third-relations as Structural Elements in Book II of Liszt's *Années de pèlerinage* and Three Later Works." Ph.D. diss., University of Michigan, 1984.

———. "Tonal Structure and Voice-leading in Liszt's *Blume und Duft*." *In Theory Only* 6/3 (1981–1983): 12–24.

Claus, Linda W. "An Aspect of Liszt's Late Style: The Composer's Revisions for *Historische, Ungarische Portraits*." *JALS* 3 (1978): 3–18.

Collet, Robert. "Choral and Organ Music." In *Franz Liszt: The Man & His Music*, ed. Alan Walker, 318–349. New York: Taplinger, 1970.

Cook, Nicholas. "Liszt's Second Thoughts: 'Liebestraum' No 2 and Its Relatives." *19th-Century Music* 12/2 (1988): 163–172.

Cooper, Martin, "Liszt as a Song Writer." *Music & Letters* 19 (1938): 171–181.

Cornette, Arthur Jakob Hendrik. *Liszt und zijne "Années de Pèlerinage."* Antwerp: L. Opdebeek, 1971.

Dahlhaus, Carl. "Liszts *Bergsymphonie* und die Idee der Symphonischen Dichtung." In *Jahrbuch des Staatlichen Instituts fur Musikforschung Preussischer Kulturbesitz, Germany 1976*, 96–130. Berlin: n.p., 1976.

———. "Liszts 'Faust-Symphonie' und die Krise der symphonischen Form." In *Über Symphonien. Beiträge zu einer musikalischen Gattung: Festschrift Walter Wiora zum 70. Geburtstag*, 129–139. Tutzing: Hans Schneider, 1979.

———. "Liszts Idee des Symphonischen." In *Liszt Studien 2*, ed. Serge Gut, 36–42. Munich and Salzburg: Emil Katzbichler, 1981.

———. "Liszt: Mazeppa." In *Analyse und Werturteil*. Musikpädagogik no. 8. Mainz: Schott, 1970.

———. *Nineteenth-Century Music*. Trans. J. Bradford Robinson. Berkeley and Los Angeles: University of California Press, 1989.

Dale, Kathleen. *Nineteenth-Century Piano Music: A Handbook for Pianists*. London, New York, and Toronto: Oxford University Press, 1954.

Dalmonte, Rossana. "Liszt's Lieder: An Essay in Formalization." In *Analecta Lisztiana I: Proceedings of the "Liszt and His World" Conference Held at Virginia Polytechnic Institute and State University, 20–23 May 1993*, ed. Michael Saffle. Franz Liszt Studies Series no. 5, 271–294. Stuyvesant, NY: Pendragon, 1998.

———. "Liszts und Wagners Lieder nach Gedichten Goethes." In *Franz Liszt und Richard Wagner. Musikalische und geistesegeschichtliche Grundlagen der neudeutschen Schule. Referate des 3. Europäischen Liszt-Symposions. Eisenstadt 1983. Liszt Studien 3*, ed. Serge Gut. 28–35. Munich and Salzburg: Emil Katzbichler, 1986.

Damschroder, David Allen. "Liszt's Composition Lessons from Beethoven (Florence, 1838–1839): *Il penseroso*." *JALS* 28 (1990): 3–19.

Danuser, Hermann. "Der Orchestergesang des Fin de Siècle," *Die Musikforschung* 4 (1977): 425–452.

Dart, William J. "Revisions and Reworkings in the Lieder of Franz Liszt." *Studies in Music* [Australia] 9 (1975): 41–53.

Deaville, James. "A Checklist of Liszt's Writings 1849–1879." *JALS* 24 (1988): 86–90.

————. "Liszts Orientalismus: Die Gestaltung des Andersseins in der Musik." In *Liszt und die Nationalitäten*, ed. Gerhard J. Winkler, 163–195. Eisenstadt: Burgenländisches Landesmuseum, 1996.

————. "Liszt's Virtuosity and His Audience: Gender, Class and Power in the Concert Hall of the Early 19th Century." In *Das Andere: Eine Spurensuche in der Musikgeschichte des 19. und 20. Jahrhunderts*, ed. Annette Kreutziger-Herr, 281–300. Frankfurt: Peter Lang, 1998.

————. "The Making of a Myth: Liszt, the Press, and Virtuosity." In *Analecta Lisztiana II: New Light on Liszt and His Music*, ed. Michael Saffle and James Deaville. Franz Liszt Studies Series no. 6, 181–195. Stuyvesant, NY: Pendragon, 1997.

————. "The New-German School and the *Euterpe* Concerts, 1860–1862: A Trojan Horse in Leipzig." In *Festschrift Christoph-Hellmut Mahling zum 65. Geburtstag*, ed. Axel Beer, Kristina Pfarr, and Wolfgang Ruf, 253–270. Tutzing: Hans Schneider, 1997.

Debussy, Claude. *Monsieur Croche the Dilettante Hater*. Trans. B. N. Langdon Davies. New York: Viking, 1928. Reprinted in *Three Classics in the Aesthetic of Music*. New York: Dover, 1962.

Decarsin, François. "Liszt's *Nuages Gris* and Kagel's *Unguis Incarnatus est*: A Model and Its Issue." Trans. Jonathan Dunsby. *Music Analysis* 4/3 (1985): 259–263.

Diercks, John. "The *Consolations*: 'delightful things hidden away.' " *JALS* 3 (1978): 19–24.

Döhring, Sieghart. "Réminiscences. Liszts Konzeption der Klavierparaphrase." *Festschrift Heinz Becker*. Ed. J. Schläder and R. Quandt. Laaber: Laaber-Verlag, 1982.

Dömling, Wolfgang. "The Unknown Liszt—The World of his Songs with Piano." In *Franz Liszt Lieder*. Deutsche Grammaphon 447–508–2GX3.

Douglas, John. "Franz Liszt as a Song Composer." *NATS Journal* 43/4 (1987): 4–15.

Eckhardt, Mária. "Die Handschriften des Rákóczi-Marsches von Franz Liszt in der Széchényi Nationalbibliothek, Budapest." *Studia musicologica* 27 (1975): 347–405.

————. *Franz Liszt's Music Manuscripts in the National Széchényi Library, Budapest*. Studies in Central and Eastern European Music 2, ed. Zoltán Falvy. Budapest: Akadémiai Kiadó, 1986.

————. "Liszt à Marseille." *Studia musicologica* 24 (1982): 192.

————. "Liszt on Opera." *New Hungarian Quarterly* 116 (1989): 115–118.

————. "Liszts Bearbeitungen von Schuberts Märschen: Formale Analyse." *Studia musicologica* 26 (1984): 133–146.

————. "New Documents on Liszt as Author." *New Hungarian Quarterly* 95 (1984): 181–194. Also, *JALS* 18 (1985): 52–66.

Edel, Theodore. "Liszt's La Notte: Piano Music as Self-Portrait." *JALS* 42 (1997): 43–59.

Egert, Paul. "Die Klaviersonate in H-moll von Franz Liszt." *Die Musik* 28/2 (1936): 673–682.

Eigeldinger, Jean-Jacques. "Les Années de Pèlerinage de Liszt: Notes sur la genèse et l'esthétique." *Revue Musicale de Suisse Romande* 33 (1980): 147–172.

Einstein, Alfred. *Music in the Romantic Era*. New York and London: W. W. Norton, 1947.

Ellis, Katharine. *Music Criticism in Nineteenth-Century France: La Revue et Gazette musicale de Paris, 1834–80*. Cambridge: Cambridge University Press, 1995.

Eösze, László, ed. *119 Római Liszt-Dokumentum*. Budapest: Zeneműkaidó, 1980.

Fauser, Annegret. *Der Orchestergesang in Frankreich zwischen 1870 und 1920*. Laaber: Laaber-Verlag, 1994.

Feofanov, Dmitry. "How to Transcribe the Mephisto Waltz for Piano." *JALS* 11 (1982): 18–27.

Fetsch, Ulrich Wolfgang. "Liszt's B-Minor Sonata: A Structural Analysis." Part two of D.M.A. thesis, Indiana University, 1958.

Fischer-Dieskau, Dietrich. *The Fischer-Dieskau Book of Lieder.* New York: Knopf, 1980.

Floros, Constantin. "Die Faust-Symphonie von Franz Liszt. Eine semantische Analyse." In *Franz Liszt,* ed. Heinz-Klaus Metzger and Reiner Riehn. *Musik-Konzepte* 12 (1980): 42–87.

Forte, Allen. "Liszt's Experimental Idiom and Music of the Early Twentieth Century." *19th-Century Music* 10 (1987): 209–228.

Fowler, Andrew. "Franz Liszt's *Années de Pèlerinage* as Megacycle." *JALS* 40 (1996): 113–129.

―――. "Franz Liszt's *Petrarch Sonnets*: The Persistent Poetic Problem." *Indiana Theory Review* 7 (1986): 48–68.

―――. "Motive and Program in Liszt's *Vallée d'Obermann.*" *JALS* 29 (1991): 3–11.

―――. "Multilevel Motivic Projection in Selected Piano Works of Liszt." *JALS* 16 (1984) 20–34.

François-Sappey, Brigitte. "Sonates d'Alkan et de Liszt: operas latents." In *D'un opera l'autre: Hommage a Jean Mongredien,* 55–66. Paris: Presses de l'Université de Paris-Sorbonne, 1996.

Friedheim, Arthur. *Life and Liszt: The Recollections of a Concert Pianist.* Ed. Theodore L. Bullock. New York: Taplinger, 1961.

Friedheim, Philip. "First Version, Second Version, Alternative Version: Some Remarks on the Music of Liszt." *Music Review* 44 (1983): 194–202.

Fudge, James Thompson. "The Male Chorus Music of Franz Liszt." Ph.D. diss., University of Iowa, 1972.

Fukuda, Wataru. "An Unknown Version of Liszt's *Cantico di San Francesco.*" *LSJ* 23 (1998): 17–26.

Gárdonyi, Zoltán. "Neue Tonleiter- und Sequenztypen in Liszts Frühwerken (Zur Frage der 'Lisztschen Sequenzen')." *Studia musicologica* 11 (1969): 169–199.

―――. "Paralipomena zu den Ungarischen Rhapsodien Franz Liszts." In *Franz Liszt: Beiträge von ungarischen Autoren,* ed. Klára Hamburger, 197–225. Budapest: Corvina, 1978.

―――. *Le Style hongrois de François Liszt.* Budapest: Az Orsz. Széchényi könyvtár kiadása, 1936.

Gárdonyi, Zsolt, and Siegfried Mauser, eds. *Virtuosität und Avantgarde. Untersuchungen zum Klavierwerk Franz Liszts.* Mainz: Schott, 1988.

Geck, Martin. "Architektonische, psychologische oder rhetorische Form? Franz Liszts Klaviersonate h-moll." In *Festschrift Klaus Hortschansky zum 60. Geburtstag,* 425–433. Tutzing: Schneider, 1995.

Gerling, Cristina Capparelli. "Franz Schubert and Franz Liszt: A Posthumous Partnership." In *Nineteenth-Century Piano Music: Essays in Performance and Analysis,* ed. David Witten. Perspectives in Music Criticism and Theory. Vol. 3, 204–232. New York and London: Garland, 1997.

Gifford, David E. "Religious Elements Implicit and Explicit in the Solo Piano Works of Franz Liszt." D.M.A. diss., University of Missouri-Kansas City, 1984.

Goebel, Albrecht. "Franz Liszt: 'Die drei Zigeuner' (Ein Beitrag zum Balladenschaffen im 19. Jahrhundert)." *Music* 35 (1981): 241–245.

Göllerich, August. *Franz Liszt.* Berlin: Marquardt, 1908.

Goode, William M. "The Late Piano Works of Franz Liszt and Their Influence on some Aspects of Modern Piano Composition." Ph.D. diss., Indiana University, 1965.

Gottschalg, Alexander Wilhelm. *Franz Liszt in Weimar und sein letzten Lebensjahre: Erinnerungen und Tagebuchnotizen.* Ed. Carl Alfred René. Berlin: A. Glaue, 1910.

Grabócz, Márta. "Die Wirkung des Programms auf die Entwicklung der instrumentalen Formen in Liszts Klavierwerken." *Studia musicologica* 22 (1980): 299–325.

———. *Morphologie des oeuvres pour piano de Liszt: Influence du programme sur l'évolution des formes instrumentales.* Budapest: MTA Zenetudományi Intézet, 1986.

———. "Renaissance de la forme énumérative, sous l'influence du modèle épique, dans les oeuvres pour piano de Liszt; facteurs de l'analyse structurale et sémantique." *Studia musicologica* 26 (1984): 199–218.

Gut, Serge. *Franz Liszt.* Paris: Editions de Fallois, 1989.

———. "Franz Liszt: *Années de Pèlerinage. Première Année: Suisse.*" *L'Education musicale* (1986–1987) 333: 11–16; 334: 5–9; 335: 19–24; and 336: 14–18.

———. "Nouvelle approche des premières oeuvres de Franz Liszt d'après la correspondance Liszt-d'Agoult." *Studia musicologica* 28/1–4 (1986): 237–248.

———. "Swiss influences on the compositions of Franz Liszt." Trans. Michael Short. *JALS* 38 (1995): 1–22.

———, ed. *Franz Liszt und Richard Wagner. Musikalische und geistesegeschichtliche Grundlagen der neudeutschen Schule. Referate des 3. Europäischen Liszt-Symposions. Eisenstadt 1983. Liszt Studien 3.* Munich and Salzburg: Katzbichler, 1986.

———, ed. *Liszt Studien 2. Referate des 2. Europäischen Liszt-Symposions Eisenstadt 1978.* Munich and Salzburg: Emil Katzbichler, 1981.

Hall, James Husst. *The Art of Song.* Norman: University of Oklahoma Press, 1953.

Hallmark, Rufus, ed. *German Lieder in the Nineteenth Century.* New York: Schirmer Books, 1996.

Hamburger, Klára. *Liszt.* Trans. Gyula Gulyás. Budapest: Corvina, 1987.

———. "Musicien Humanitaire." *New Hungarian Quarterly* 27 (Autumn 1986): 85–92.

———. "Program and Hungarian Idiom in the Sacred Music of Liszt." In *Analecta Lisztiana II: New Light on Liszt and His Music,* ed. Michael Saffle and James Deaville. Franz Liszt Studies Series no. 6, 239–251. Stuyvesant, NY: Pendragon, 1997.

———, ed. *Franz Liszt: Beiträge von ungarischen Autoren.* Budapest: Corvina, 1978.

———, ed. *Liszt 2000: Selected Lectures Given at the International Liszt Conference in Budapest, May 18–20, 1999.* Budapest: Liszt Ferenc Társaság, 2000.

Hamilton, Kenneth. "Liszt Fantasises—Busoni Excises: The Liszt-Busoni 'Figaro Fantasy.'" *JALS* 30 (1991): 21–27.

———. *Liszt: Sonata in B Minor.* Cambridge Music Handbooks. Cambridge: Cambridge University Press, 1996.

———. "The Operatic Fantasies and Transcriptions of Franz Liszt: A Critical Study." Ph.D. diss., Oxford University (Balliol College), 1989.

Hankiss, Jean. "Liszt écrivain et la littérature europénne." *Revue de la Littérature comparée* 17 (1937): 299–323.

Hansen, Bernard. "'Nonnenwerth': Ein Beitrag zu Franz Liszts Liederkomposition." *Neue Zeitschrift für Musik* 122 (1961): 391–394.

Hanslick, Eduard. "Liszt's Symphonic Poems." In *Music Criticisms 1846–99,* trans. Henry Pleasants, 53–57. Baltimore: Penguin Books, 1963.

Hantz, Edwin. "Motivic and Structural Unity in Liszt's Blume und Duft." *In Theory Only* 6/3 (1981–1983): 3–11.

Haraszti, Emile. "Franz Liszt: Author Despite Himself." *Musical Quarterly* 33/4 (October 1947): 490–516.

———. "Le problème Liszt." *Acta Musicologica* 9 (1937): 123–136.

Harich, Johann. "Franz Liszt—Vorfahren und Kinderjahre." *Österreichische Musik-zeitschrift* 26 (1971): 503–514.

Harrison, Vernon. "Liszt's Faust Symphony: A Psychological Interpretation." *LSJ* 4 (1979): 2–5.

Haselböck, Martin. "Liszt's Organ Works." *American Organist* 20/7 (1986): 56–63.

———, ed. *Franz Liszt: The Complete Works for Organ.* 10 vols. Vienna: Universal Edition A.G, 1985–.

Headington, Christopher. "The Songs." In *Franz Liszt: The Man and His Music*, ed. Alan Walker, 221–247. New York: Taplinger, 1971.

Heinemann, Ernst-Günter. "Liszts *Angelus*—Beobachtungen zum kompositorischen Entstehungsprozess." In *Henle Festschrift*, ed. Martin Bente, 213–217. Munich: Henle, 1980.

Helm, Everett. "A Newly Discovered Liszt Manuscript." *Studia musicologica* 5 (1963): 101–106.

Hersh, A. B. "A Consideration of Programmatic Associations in the Piano Music of Liszt." D.M. diss., Indiana University, 1971.

Heuss, Alfred. *Erläuterungen zu Franz Liszts Sinfonien und sinfonischen Dichtungen.* Leipzig: Breitkopf & Härtel, 1912.

Hinson, Maurice. "The Long Lost Liszt Concerto." *JALS* 13 (1983): 53–58.

Hirschmann, Ursula. "Die Wagner Bearbeitung Franz Liszts." In *Richard Wagner und die Musikhochschule München.* Schriften der Hochschule für Musik München 4. Regensburg: Bosse, 1983.

Howard, Leslie, ed. *Ferenc Liszt: The Complete Music for Violoncello and Pianoforte.* The Liszt Society Publications 10. Edinburgh: The Hardie Press, 1992.

———. *Ferenc Liszt: The Complete Music for Pianoforte, Violin and Violoncello.* Liszt Society Publications 11. Edinburgh: The Hardie Press, 1996.

Howard, Leslie, and Michael Short. "A New Catalogue of Liszt's Music." In *Analecta Lisztiana I: Proceedings of the "Liszt and His World" Conference Held at Virginia Polytechnic Institute and State University, 20–23 May 1993*, ed. Michael Saffle. Franz Liszt Studies Series no. 5, 75–100. Stuyvesant, NY: Pendragon, 1998.

Huckvale, David. "Massive Reductions: Wagnerian Piano and Vocal Scores." *Wagner* (London) 13 (1992): 60–82.

Hudson, Richard. *Stolen Time: The History of Tempo Rubato.* Oxford and New York: Clarendon Press, 1994.

Hughes, Edwin. "Liszt as Lieder Composer." *Musical Quarterly* 3 (1917): 390–409.

Hughes, William H., Jr. "Liszt's *Première Année de Pèlerinage: Suisse:* A Comparative Study of Early and Revised Versions." D.M.A. diss., Eastman School of Music, 1985.

Hunkemoller, Jürgen. "Perfektion und Perspektivenwechsel: Studien zu den drei Fassungen der Etudes d'exécution transcendante von Franz Liszt." *Archiv fur Musikwissenschaft* 51/4 (1994): 294–314.

Hunt, Mary Angela. "Franz Liszt: The 'Mephisto Waltzes.' " D.M.A. diss., University of Wisconsin, 1979.

Hur, Chunghwa. "Schubert's Wanderer Fantasie: A Creative Springboard to Liszt's Sonata in B Minor." D.M.A. diss., University of Arizona, 1997.

Huré, Pierre-Antoine, and Claude Knepper, eds. *Liszt en son temps.* Paris: Hachette, 1987.

Huschke, Wolfram. "'Sammlung und Arbeit in Weimar' und 'offener Kompositions-prozess': Anmerkungen zur Bearbeitungsproblematik bei Franz Liszt." In *Das Weimarer Schaffen Franz Liszts*, 71–78. Weimar: n.p., 1987.

Hutcheson, Ernest. *The Literature of the Piano: A Guide for Amateur and Student.* New York: Alfred A. Knopf, 1948.

Irwin, Stanley. "The Songs of Franz Liszt: A Survey and Catalogue." *NATS Journal* 4949/34 (1993): 10–17 and 14–23.

Jankélévitch, Vladimir. *Liszt et la rhapsodie: Essai sur la virtuosité*. Paris: Plon, 1979.

Janina, Olga. *Souvenirs d'une cosaque*. Paris: C. Marpon et E. Flammarion, 1874.

Johns, Keith T. *"De Profundis, Psaume instrumental*; an Abandoned Concerto for Piano and Orchestra by Franz Liszt." *JALS* 15 (1984): 96–104.

———. *"Malédiction*: The Concerto's History, Programme and Some Notes on Harmonic Organization." *JALS* 18 (1985): 29–35.

———. *The Symphonic Poems of Franz Liszt*. Stuyvesant, NY: Pendragon, 1998.

Jung-Kaiser, Ute. "Liszts Raffael-Interpretation—oder die Frage nach der 'verborgenen Verwandtschaft der Werke des Genies.' " *Zeitschrift fur Musikpädagogik* 14/52 (1989): 19–24.

Kabisch, Thomas. "Struktur und Form im Spätwerk Franz Liszts: Das Klavierstück 'Unstern' (1886)." *Archiv für Musikwissenschaft* 42 (1985): 178–199.

Kaczmarczyk, Adrienne. "Liszt: *Marie, Pòeme* (A Planned Piano Cycle)." *JALS* 41 (1997): 88–101.

Kagebeck, Hans, and Johan Lagerfelt, eds. *Liszt the Progressive*. Lewiston, MA: Edwin Mellen, 2001.

Kaiser, Manfred. "Anmerkungen zur Kompositionstechnik Franz Liszts: Am Beispiel der 'Hunnenschlacht.' " In *Liszt Studien 1. Kongress-Bericht Eisenstadt 1975*, ed. Wolfgang Suppan, 125–129. Graz: Akademische Druck- u. Verlagsanstalt, 1977.

Kánski, Jósef. "The Problem of Form in Franz Liszt's Sonata in B minor." *JALS* 5 (1979): 4–15.

Kecskeméti, István. "Two Liszt Discoveries: 1. An Unknown Piano Piece; 2. An Unknown Song." *Musical Times* 115 (1974): 646–648 and 743–744.

Keeling, Geraldine. "Liszt's Appearances in Parisian Concerts, 1824–1844," *LSJ* 11 (1986): 22–34; and 12 (1987): 8–22.

Kelkel, Manfred. "Wege zur 'Berg-Symphonie' Liszts." In *Franz Liszt und Richard Wagner. Musikalische und geistesgeschichtliche Grundlagen der neudeutschen Schule. Referate des 3. Europäischen Liszt-Symposions. Eisenstadt 1983. Liszt Studien 3*, ed. Serge Gut, 71–89. Munich and Salzburg: Emil Katzbichler, 1986.

Kielniarz, Marilyn. "The Organ Works of Franz Liszt." D.M.A. diss., Northwestern University, 1984.

Kinsky, Georg. *Musikhistorisches Museum von Wilhelm Heyer in Cöln: Kleiner Katalog der Sammlung alter Musikinstrumente*. Vol. 4, Leipzig: Breitkopf & Härtel, 1916.

Kirby, F. E. "Liszt's Pilgrimage." *Piano Quarterly* 23/89 (1975) 17–21.

Kókai, Rudolf. *Franz Liszt in seinen frühen Klavierwerken*. Freiburg, 1933. Reprint. Kassel: Bärenreiter, 1968.

Kramer, Lawrence. "The Mirror of Tonality: Transitional Features of Nineteenth-Century Harmony." *19th-Century Music* 4 (1981): 191–208.

Krauklis, Georgii Vilgelmovich. *Simfoncheskie poemy F. Lista*. Moscow: "Muzyka," 1974.

Kravitt, Edward F. *The Lied: Mirror of Late Romanticism*. New Haven and London: Yale University Press, 1996.

Kroó, György. *"Années de pèlerinage—Premiere année*: Versions and Variants. A Challenge to the Thematic Catalogue." *Studia musicologica* 34/3–4 (1992): 405–426.

La Mara [Marie Lipsius]. *Liszt und die Frauen*. 2d ed. Leipzig: Breitkopf & Härtel, 1919.

———, ed. *Klassisches und Romantisches aus der Tonwelt*. Leipzig: Breitkopf & Härtel, 1892.

Lang, Paul Henry. *Music in Western Civilization*. New York: W. W. Norton, 1941.

Lee, Robert Charles. "Some Little-known Late Piano Works of Liszt (1869–1886): A Miscellany." Ph.D. diss., University of Washington, 1970.

Legány, Dezső. "Egyuttmukodesi tavlatok a magyar es osztrak Liszt-kutatasban." *Magyar zene* 36/1 1995): 22–25.

———. *Franz Liszt: Unbekannte Presse und Briefe aus Wien 1822–1886.* Vienna: Böhlaus Verlag, 1984.

———. "Hungarian Historical Portraits." *Studia musicologica* 28 (1986): 79–88.

———. *Liszt and His Country, 1874–1886.* Budapest: Occidental Press, 1992.

———. *Liszt Ferenc and His Country, 1869–1873.* Trans. Gyula Gulyás. Budapest: Editio Musica, 1983.

Lemoine, Bernard C. "Tonal Organization in Selected Late Piano Works of Franz Liszt." In *Liszt Studien 2. Referate des 2. Europäischen Liszt-Symposions Eisenstadt 1978,* ed. Serge Gut, 123–131. Munich and Salzburg: Emil Katzbichler, 1981.

Leppert, Richard. "Cultural Contradiction, Idolatry, and the Piano Virtuoso: Franz Liszt." In *Piano Roles: Three Hundred Years of Life with the Piano,* ed. James Parakilas. New Haven: Yale University Press, 1999.

Levy, Norma. "Multiple Settings in the Solo Songs of Franz Liszt." M.A. thesis, University of Oregon, 1983.

Lipke, William Alan. *Liszt's Dante fantasia: An historical and musical study.* D.M.A. diss., University of Cincinnati, 1990.

Liszt, Franz. *An die Künstler für Männergesang.* Weimar: Kühn, n.d. (c. 1858).

———. *Arbeiterchor.* Ed. Lajos Bárdos with an Introduction by Dénes Bártha. Budapest: Zeneműkaidó Vállalat, 1954.

———. *Balladen.* Ed. Rena Charnin Mueller and Ernst-Günter Heinemann. Munich: G. Henle, 1996.

———. *Complete Transcriptions from Wagner's Operas.* Introduction Charles Suttoni. New York: Dover, 1981.

———. *Consolations.* Ed. Maria Eckhardt and Ernst-Günter Heinemann. Munich: G. Henle, 1992.

———. *Grande Fantaisie symphonique über Themen aus Hector Berlioz' "Lélio" (Lélio-Fantasie).* Ed. Reiner Zimmermann. Leipzig: Breitkopf & Härtel, 1981.

———. *Harmonies Poétiques et Religieuses* (1847 Version). Ed. Albert Brussee. 2 vols. Huizen, Holland: B.V. Muziekuitgeverij XYZ, 1997.

———. *Hungaria 1848.* Ed. with a Foreword by István Szelényi. Budapest: Zeneműkaidó Vállalat, 1961.

———. *Kantate zur Inauguration des Beethoven-Monuments zu Bonn.* Reconstructed and ed. Günther Massenkeil. Frankfurt: C. F. Peters, 1989.

———. *Klaviersonate H-moll: Faksimile nach dem im Eigentum von Mr. Robert Owen Lehman befindlichen Autograph.* Munich: G. Henle, 1973.

———. *Le Forgeron.* Ed. with a Foreword by István Szelényi. Budapest: Zeneműkaidó Vállalat, 1962.

———. *Légendes for Orchestra.* Budapest: Editio Musica, 1984.

———. *Mazeppa,* Symphonic Poem No. 6, with a Foreword by Humphrey Searle. London: Eulenburg, 1976.

———. *Pages romantiques.* Ed. Jean Chantavoine. Paris: F. Alcan, 1912.

———. *Piano Piece No. 1 in A Flat.* Liszt Society Publications. Aylesbury: Bardic Edition, 1988.

———. *Piano Transcriptions from French and Italian Operas.* Introduction Charles Suttoni. New York: Dover, 1982.

———. "Preface" to *Prometheus.* Trans. Humphrey Searle. London: Eulenberg, 1975.

———. *Sonata in B Minor and Other Works for Piano.* From the Franz Liszt-Stiftung edition, ed. José Vianna da Motta. New York: Dover, 1990.

————. *Zwei Konzertsetüden*. Ed. Maria Eckhardt and Wiltrud Haug-Freienstein. Munich: G. Henle, 1994.

Longyear, Rey M. "Liszt's B Minor Sonata: Precedents for a Structural Analysis." *Music Review* 34 (1973): 198–209.

————. *Nineteenth-Century Romanticism in Music*. 3d ed. Englewood Cliffs, NJ: Prentice Hall, 1988.

————. Review of *Franz Liszt*. Vol. 2. *The Weimar Years, 1848–1861* by Alan Walker. *JALS* 26 (1989): 67–72.

————. "Structural Issues in Liszt's Philosophical Symphonic Poems." In *Analecta Lisztiana I: Proceedings of the "Liszt and His World" Conference Held at Virginia Polytechnic Institute and State University, 20–23 May 1993*, ed. Michael Saffle. Franz Liszt Studies Series no. 5, 247–270. Stuyvesant, NY: Pendragon, 1998.

————. "The Text of Liszt's B minor Sonata." *The Musical Quarterly* 60 (1974): 435–450.

Lozza, Giuseppe. "La doppia versione del Lied di Liszt 'Der Fichtenbaum.' " *Nuova rivista musicale italiana* 20 (1986): 387–399.

Macklenburg. "Liszt und seine Ideale." *Bayreuther Blätter* (1926): 153–169.

Main, Alexander. "Franz Liszt the Author, 1834–47: An old Question Answered Anew." *Actes du XIIIe Congrès de la Société Internationale de Musicologie, Strasbourg 1982* (1986). 2: 637–656.

————. "Liszt after Lamartine: 'Les Préludes.' " *Music & Letters* 60 (1979): 133–148.

————. "Liszt's *Lyon:* Music and the Social Conscience." *19th-Century Music* 4 (1981): 228–243.

Manwarren, Matthew. "The Influence of Liszt's Sonata in B Minor on Julius Reubke: A Study of Reubke's Sonata in B-flat Minor for Piano and the Sonata on the Ninety-fourth Psalm for Organ." D.M.A. diss., University of Cincinnati, 1993.

Marget, Arthur W. "Liszt and *Parsifal*." *Music Review* 14 (1953): 107–124.

Marggraf, Wolfgang. "Eine Bearbeitung des *Vallée d'Obermann* aus Liszts Spätzeit." *Studia musicologica* 28 (1986): 295–302.

Margittay, Sándor, ed. *Franz Liszt: Összes orgonzmuve. Sämtliche Orgelwerke*. 4 vols. Budapest: Editio Musica Budapest, 1970–1973.

Massenkeil, Günther. "Die Bonner Beethoven-Kantata von Franz Liszt (1845)." In *Die Sprache der Musik Festschrift Klaus W. Niemöller zum 60 Geburtstag*, 381–400. Regensburg: Bosse, 1989.

Mastroianni, Thomas. "The Italian Aspect of Franz Liszt," *JALS* 16 (1984): 6–19.

Merrick, Paul. "Original or Doubtful? Liszt's Use of Key in Support of his Authorship of 'Don Sanche.' " *Studia musicologica* 34/3–4 (1992): 427–434.

————. *Revolution and Religion in the Music of Liszt*. Cambridge: Cambridge University Press, 1987.

Micznik, Vera. "The Absolute Limitations of Programme Music: The Case of Liszt's 'Die Ideale.' " *Music & Letters* 82 (1999): 207–240.

Montu-Berthon, Suzanne. "Un Liszt Méconnu: Mélodies et Lieder." *La Revue musicale* 342–346 (1981): entire issues.

Moser, Roland. "Unitonie—Pluritonie—Omnitonie: Zur harmonischen Gedankenwelt in der 'Via Crucis' von Franz Liszt." *Basler Jahrbuch für historische Musikpraxis* 21 (1997): 129–142.

Mueller, Rena Charnin. "Liszt's Catalogues and Inventories of His Works." *Studia musicologica* 34 (1992): 231–250.

————. "Liszt's 'Tasso' Sketchbook: Studies in Sources and Revisions." Ph.D. diss., New York University, 1986.

————. "Reevaluating the Liszt Chronology: The Case of 'Anfangs wollt ich fast verzagen.' " *19th-Century Music* 12/2 (1988): 132–147.

Munson, Paul. "Les Morts as a Paradigm of Liszt's Religious Music." *JALS* 41 (1997): 102–110.

————. "The Oratorios of Franz Liszt." Ph.D. diss., University of Michigan, 1996.

Murphy, Edward. "A Detailed Program for Liszt's 'Hamlet.' " *JALS* 29 (1990): 47–60.

Neumeyer, David. "Liszt's *Sonetto 104 del Petrarca:* The Romantic Spirit and Voiceleading." *Indiana Theory Review* 2 (1979): 2–22.

Newman, Ernest. *The Man Liszt.* New York: Scribner's, 1935.

Newman, William S. *The Sonata Since Beethoven.* 3d ed. New York: W. W. Norton, 1983.

Niemöller, Klaus Wolfgang. "Zur night-tonalen Thema-Struktur von Liszts 'Faust-Symphonie.' " *Die Musikforschung* 22 (1969): 69–72.

Noske, Frits. *French Song from Berlioz to Duparc.* Trans. Rita Benton. New York: Dover, 1970.

Oh, Young Ran. "The Eternal Paradox in Franz Liszt's Persona: Good and Evil as Illustrated in his Piano Sonatas." D.M.A. diss., University of Washington, 1996.

Orga, Ates. "Rediscovered Liszt." *Music and Musicians* (December 1967): 34–36, 62.

Orr, N. Lee. "Liszt's 'Christus' and Its Significance for Nineteenth-Century Oratorio." Ph.D. diss., University of North Carolina, 1979. Material from Orr's dissertation also appeared in *JALS* 9 (1981): 4–18.

d'Ortigue, Joseph. "Etudes biographiques: Frantz Listz [sic]." *Gazette musicale de Paris* 2 (14 June 1835).

Osborne, Charles. *The Concert Song Companion: A Guide to the Classical Repertoire.* London: Victor Gollancz, 1974.

Ott, Bertrand. "An Interpretation of Liszt's Sonata in B minor." Trans. Sida Roberts and P. Vaugelle. *JALS* 10 (1981): 30–38 and 11 (1982): 40–41.

Palotai, Michael. "Liszt's Concept of Oratorio as Reflected in his Writings and in 'Die Legende von der heiligen Elisabeth.' " Ph.D. diss., University of Southern California, 1977.

Parakilas, James. *Ballads Without Words: Chopin and the Tradition of the Instrumental Ballade.* Portland, OR: Amadeus, 1992.

Perahia, Murray. "Reflection & Comments." In *Horowitz: The Last Recording.* New York: CBS Records and Sony Classical, 1990.

Perényi, Eleanor. *Liszt: The Artist as Romantic Hero.* Boston and Toronto: Little, Brown, & Co., 1974.

Pesce, Dolores. "Expressive Resonance in Liszt's Piano Music." In *Nineteenth-Century Piano Music*, ed. R. Larry Todd, 355–411. New York: Schirmer, 1990.

————. "Liszt's *Années de Pèlerinage*, Book 3: A "Hungarian" Cycle?" *19th-Century Music* 13/3 (1990) 207–229.

————. "MacDowell's Eroica Sonata and its Lisztian Legacy." *Music Review* 49/3 (1988): 169–189.

Pohl, Richard. "Liszts symphonische Dichtungen: Ihre Entstehung, Wirkung und Gegnerschaft." In *Franz Liszt: Studien und Erinnerungen, Gesammelte Schriften über Musik und Musiker* 2. Leipzig: Bernhard Schlicke [Bathasar Elischer], 1883.

Popovic, Linda. "Liszt's Harmonic Polymorphism: Tonal and Non-tonal Aspects in 'Héroïde funèbre.' " *Music Analysis* 15/1 (March 1996): 41–55.

Prahács, Margit. "Liszts letztes Klavierkonzert." *Studia musicologica* 4 (1963): 195–200.

Presser, Dieter. "Die Opernbearbeitung des 19. Jahrhunderts." *Archiv für Musikwissenschaft* 12 (1955): 228–238.

————. "Liszt's *Années de Pèlerinage. Première Année: Suisse'* als Dokument der Romantic." In *Liszt Studien 1. Kongress-Bericht Eisenstadt 1975,* ed. Wolfgang Suppan, 137–154. Graz: Akademische Druck- u. Verlagsanstalt, 1977.

Raabe, Peter. *Die Entstehungsgeschichte der ersten Orchesterwerke Franz Liszts.* Leipzig: Breitkopf & Härtel, 1916.

————. "Die Lieder." In *Liszts Schaffen.* 2:112–131. Tutzing: Hans Schneider, 1968.

————. *Franz Liszt: Leben und Schaffen.* 2 vols. Stuttgart: J. G. Cotta, 1931; Tutzing: Hans Schneider, 1968.

Raff, Helene. "Franz Liszt und Joachim Raff im Spiegel ihrer Briefe," *Die Musik* 1 (1901–1902).

Ramann, Lina. *Franz Liszt als Künstler und Mensch.* 3 vols. Leipzig: Breitkopf & Härtel, 1880–1894.

————. *Franz Liszt's Oratorium Christus. Eine Studie als Beitrag zur zeit- und musikgeschichtlichen Stellung desselben.* 3d ed. Leipzig: C. F. Kahnt, 1880.

————. *Lisztiana: Erinnerungen an Franz Liszt in Tagebuchblättern, Briefen und Dokumenten aus den Jahren 1873–1886/1887.* Ed. Arthur Seidl and Friedrich Schnapp. Mainz and New York: B. Schott's Sons, 1983.

Ratner, Leonard. *Romantic Music: Sound and Syntax.* New York: Schirmer, 1992.

Rea, John Rocco. "Franz Liszt's 'New Path of Composition': The Sonata in B Minor as Cultural Paradigm." Ph.D. diss., Princeton University, 1978.

Redepenning, Dorothea. *Das Spätwerk Franz Liszts: Bearbeitungen eigener Kompositionen.* Hamburg: Verlag der Musikalienhandlung Karl Dieter Wagner, 1984.

————. "Erinnerung und Vergessen: Bemerkungen zu einigen Spätwerken Franz Liszts." In *Franz Liszt und Richard Wagner. Musikalische und geistesgeschichtliche Grundlagen der neudeutschen Schule. Referate des 3. Europäischen Liszt-Symposions. Eisenstadt 1983. Liszt Studien 3,* ed. Serge Gut, 119–127. Munich and Salzburg: Emil Katzbichler, 1986.

————. "'Zu eig'nem Wort und eig'ner Weis' . . . Liszts Wagner-Transkriptionen." *Die Musikforschung* 39 (1986): 305–317.

Refardt, Edgar. "Die Basler Männerchöre von Franz Liszt." *Schweizerische Musikzeitung* 82 (1942): 289–291. Reprinted in *Musik in der Schweiz,* 99–102. Bern: Verlag Paul Haupt, 1952.

Rexroth, Dieter. "Zum Spätwerk Franz Liszts—Material und Form in dem Klavierstück 'Unstern.'" In *Bericht über den internationalen musikwissenschaftlichen Kongress Bonn 1970,* ed. Carl Dahlhaus et al., 544–547. Kassel: Bärenreiter, 1971.

Riedel, Friedrich. "A propos de l'Héroïde funèbre: Quelques caractéristiques stylistiques des musiques de Liszt, de ses prédécesseurs et de ses contemporains." *La Revue musicale* 405–407 (1987): 29–35.

————. "Die Bedeutung des 'Christus' von Franz Liszt in der Geschichte des Messias-Oratoriums." In *Liszt Studien 2,* ed. Serge Gut, 153–162. Munich and Salzburg: Emil Katzbichler, 1981.

Riethmüller, Albrecht. "Franz Liszts 'Réminiscences de Don Juan.'" *Analysen: Festschrift für Hans Heinrich Eggebrecht.* Ed. W. Breig et. al. Beihefte zum Archiv für Musikwissenschaft 23, 276–291. Stuttgart: Steiner, 1984.

Rosado, Sara. "Liszt, Lenau, and the Four Mephisto Waltzes." *JALS* 45 (1999): 34–45

Rosen, Charles. *The Romantic Generation.* Cambridge: Harvard University Press, 1995.

Rosenblatt, Jay. "A Recently Recovered Liszt Concerto." *JALS* 26 (1989): 64–66.

————. "The Concerto as Crucible: Franz Liszt's Early Works for Piano and Orchestra." Ph.D. diss., University of Chicago, 1995.

————. "New Wine in Old Wineskins: Franz Liszt's Concerto in E-flat major, Op. Posth." *The Pendragon Review* 1/1 (Spring 2001): 7–31.

Saffle, Michael. *Franz Liszt: A Guide to Research*. New York: Garland Publishing, 1991.
———. "Liszt and Cecilianism: The Evidence of Documents and Scores." In *Der Caecilianismus: Anfange—Grundlagen—Wirkungen*, ed. Hubert Unverricht, 203–213. Tutzing: Hans Schneider, 1988.
———. "Liszt and the Traditions of the Keyboard Fantasy." In *Liszt the Progressive*, ed. Hans Kagebeck and Johan Lagerfelt, 151–185. Lewiston, MA: Edwin Mellen, 2001.
———. *Liszt in Germany 1840–1845: A Study in Sources, Documents, and the History of Reception*. Franz Liszt Studies Series no. 2. Stuyvesant, NY: Pendragon, 1994.
———. "Liszt Music Manuscripts in Paris: A Preliminary Survey." In *Analecta Lisztiana I: Proceedings of the "Liszt and His World" Conference Held at Virginia Polytechnic Institute and State University, 20–23 May 1993*, ed. Michael Saffle. Franz Liszt Studies Series no. 5, 101–135. Stuyvesant, NY: Pendragon, 1998.
———. "Liszt's Sonata in B minor: Another Look at the 'Double Function Question.' " *JALS* 11 (1982): 28–39.
———. "Liszt's Uses of Sonata Form: The Case of 'Festklänge.' " In *Liszt 2000: Selected Lectures Given at the International Liszt Conference in Budapest, May 18–20, 1999*, ed. Klára Hamburger. 201–216. Budapest: Liszt Ferenc Társaság, 2000.
———. "New Light on Liszt's Prelude and Fugue on B–A–C–H." *The American Organist* (November 1982): 44–49.
———, ed. *Analecta Lisztiana I: Proceedings of the "Liszt and His World" Conference Held at Virginia Polytechnic Institute and State University, 20–23 May 1993*. Franz Liszt Studies Series no. 5. Stuyvesant, NY: Pendragon, 1998.
Saffle, Michael, and James Deaville, eds. *Analecta Lisztiana II: New Light on Liszt and His Music*. Franz Liszt Studies Series no. 6. Stuyvesant, NY: Pendragon, 1998.
Saint-Félix, Raymond de. "Concerts Listz [sic] et Berlioz." *L'artiste* 12 (1836).
Samson, Jim. "East Central Europe: the Struggle for National Identity." In *Music and Society: The Late Romantic Era From the mid-19th century to World War I*, ed. Jim Samson. Englewood Cliffs, NJ: Prentice Hall, 1991.
———. *Music in Transition*. New York: Norton, 1977.
Sandresky, Margaret V. "Tonal Design in Liszt's Sonata in B Minor." *JALS* 10 (1981): 15–29.
Schaeffner, André. "Liszt transcripteur d'Opéras italiens." *La Revue musicale* 9 (1928): 89–100.
Schibli, Siegfried. "Franz Liszt: 'Orpheus.' " *Neue Zeitschrift fur Musik* 147/7–8 (1986): 54–56.
———. "Sonate für Klavier h-Moll." *Neue Zeitschrift für Musik* 145/11 (1984): 29–32.
Schläder, Jürgen. "Der schöne Traum vom Ideal. Die künstlerische Konzeption in Franz Liszts letzter Symphonischen Dichtung." *Hamburger Jahrbuch für Musikwissenschaft* 6 (1983): 47–62
———. "Zur Funktion der Variantentechnik in der Klaviersonaten F-Moll von Johannes Brahms und H-Moll von Franz Liszt." *Hamburger Jahrbuch für Musikwissenschaft* 7 (1984): 171–199.
Schnapp, Friedrich. "Verschollene Kompositionen von Franz Liszt." In *Von Deutscher Tonkunst: Festschrift zu Peter Raabes 70. Geburtstag*, ed. Alfred Morgenroth, 119–152. Leipzig: C. F. Peters, 1942.
Scholz, Gottfried, ed. *Der junge Liszt. Referate des 4. Europäischen Liszt-Symposions Wien 1991. Liszt Studien 4*. Munich and Salzburg: Emil Katzbichler, 1993.
Schütz, Georg. "Form, Satz- und Klaviertechnik in den drei Fassungen der 'Grossen Etüden' von Franz Liszt." In *Virtuosität und Avantgarde: Untersuchungen zum Klavierwerk Franz Liszts*, 71–115. Mainz: Schott, 1988.

Schwarz, Boris. *French Instrumental Music Between the Revolutions 1789–1830*. New York: Da Capo, 1987.

Schwarz, Peter. *Studien zur Orgelmusik Franz Liszts. Ein Beitrag zur Geschichte der Orgelkomposition im 19. Jahrhundert*. Berliner musikwissenschaftliche Arbeiten 3. Munich: Emil Katzbichler, 1973.

Searle, Humphrey. "Franz Liszt." In *The New Grove: Early Romantic Masters: Chopin, Schumann, Liszt*, rev. Sharon Winklhofer. Vol. 1. London: Papermac, 1985.

———. "Liszt and the Twentieth Century." *Piano Quarterly* 89 (1975): 38–40.

———. "Liszt's Organ Music," *Musical Times* (June 1971): 596–598.

———. "The Orchestral Works." In *Franz Liszt: The Man & His Music*, ed. Alan Walker, 279–317. London: Macmillan, 1971.

———. *The Music of Liszt*. 2d rev. ed. New York: Dover, 1966.

Sebestyén, Albert. "Franz Liszts Originalkompositionen für Violine und Klavier." In *Liszt-Studien I*, 163–178. Graz: Akademische Druck- u. Verlagsanstalt, 1977.

Sebestyén, Ede. *Liszt Ferenc hangversenyei Budapesten. Hat évized krónikája*. Budapest: Liszt Ferenc Társaság Kiadása, 1944.

Segnitz, Eugen. *Franz Liszts Kirchenmusik*. Langensalza, Switzerland: H. Beyer, 1911.

Shipwright, Edward Ralph. "A Stylistic and Interpretive Analysis of Selected Compositions from the Late Piano Works of Franz Liszt." Ed.D. diss., Columbia University, 1977.

Short, Michael. "The Doubtful, Missing, and Unobtainable Works of Ferenc Liszt (1811–1886)." *LSJ* 24 (1999): 28–39.

Simoni, Dario. *Un soggiorno di Francesco Liszt a San Rossore*. Pisa: Nistri-Lischi, [1936].

Sitwell, Sacheverell. *Liszt*. Rev. ed. London: Faber and Faber, 1955.

Smeed, John W. *German Song and Its Poetry 1740–1900*. London: Croom Helm, 1987.

Smith, M.W.A. Virtuoso "Pianism from the QWERTY Keyboard: The Electronic Realization of Liszt's Scores." *Computers and the Humanities* 29/4 (1995): 285–296.

Somfai, László. "Die Gestaltwandlungen der 'Faust-Symphonie' von Liszt." In *Franz Liszt: Beiträge von ungarischen Authoren*, ed. Klára Hamburger, 292–324. Budapest: Corvina Kiadó, 1978.

Stein, Jack M. *Poem and Music in the German Lied from Gluck to Hugo Wolf*. Cambridge: Harvard University Press, 1971.

Steinbeck, Wolfram. "Musik nach Bildern: Zu Franz Liszt's *Hunnenschlacht*." In *Töne, Farben, Formen: Über Musik und die bildenden Künste: Festschrift Elmar Budde zum 60. Geburtstag*. 17–38. Laaber: Laaber-Verlag, 1995.

Stengel, Theophil. *Die Entwicklung des Klavierkonzerts von Liszt bis zur Gegenwart*. Berlin: Graphisches Institut P. Funk, 1931.

Stenzl, Jürg. "L'énigme Franz Liszt: Prophéties et conventions dans les oeuvres tardives: 'R.W.—Venezia' (1883)." *La Revue musicale* 405–407 (1987): 127–135.

Stevens, Dennis, ed. *A History of Song*. Rev. ed. New York and London: W. W. Norton, 1970.

Stradal, August. "Liszts Mazeppa-Werke." *Neue Zeitschrift für Musik* 78 (1911): 577–583 and 597–601.

Strunk, Oliver. *Source Readings in Music History*. New York: Norton, 1950.

Sulyok, Imre. "Liszt Ferenc es Michelangelo ciprusai." *Muzsika*, Hungary 18/9 (1975): 36–37.

Suppan, Wolfgang, ed. *Liszt Studien 1. Kongress-Bericht Eisenstadt 1975*. Graz: Akademische Druck- u. Verlagsanstalt, 1977.

Sutter, Milton. "Liszt and His Role in the Development of 19th Century Organ Music," *Music/American Guild of Organists* (January 1975): 35–39.

―――. "Liszt and the Weimar Organist-Composers." In *Liszt Studien 1. Kongress-Bericht Eisenstadt 1975*, ed. Wolfgang Suppan, 203–213. Graz: Akademische Druck-u. Verlagsanstalt, 1977.

Suttoni, Charles. "Liszt the Writer." In *Liszt & the Arts: A Collection of Papers Presented at a Liszt Centennial Celebration in 1986*, ed. Steven Marcus, 64–74. New York: Heyman Center for the Humanities, Columbia University, 1996.

―――. "Liszt's Letters: Réminiscences of Norma." *JALS* 8 (1980): 77–79.

―――. "Piano and Opera: A Study of the Piano Fantasies Written on Opera Themes in the Romantic Era." Ph.D. diss., New York University, 1973.

Szabolcsi, Bence. *A Concise History of Hungarian Music*. 2d ed. Ed. and trans. Sára Karig and Fred Macnicol. Budapest: Corvina, 1974.

―――. *The Twilight of Ferenc Liszt*. Trans. András Deák. Budapest: Akadémiai Kiadó, 1959.

Szász, Tibor. "Liszt's Symbols for the Divine and Diabolical: Their Revelation of a Program in the B Minor Sonata." *JALS* 15 (1984): 39–95.

Szelényi, István. "Der unbekannte Liszt." *Studia musicologica* 5 (1963): 311–331.

Szitha, Tünde. "Liszt's 'Unknown' French Songs." *Studia musicologica* 29 (1987): 259–265.

Tagliavini, Luigi Ferdinando. "La prima versione d'un lied di Liszt in una fonte sinora sconosciuta. L'album musicale della poetessa russa Evdokija Rostopčina." *Rivista musicale italiana* 19 (1984): 277–297.

Tannenbaum, Michele. *"Variations on a Motive of Bach."* *JALS* 41 (1997): 49–87.

Todd, R. Larry. "Liszt, Fantasy and Fugue for Organ on 'Ad nos, ad salutarem undam.' " *19th-Century Music* 4 (1981): 250–261.

―――. "The 'Unwelcome Guest' Regaled: Franz Liszt and the Augmented Triad." *19th-Century Music* 12/2 (1988): 93–115.

Tommasini, Anthony. "The Portraits for Piano by Virgil Thomson." D.M.A. diss., Boston University, 1982.

Tse, Benita Wan-Kuen. "Piano Variations Inspired by Paganini's Twenty-Fourth Caprice from op. 1." D.M.A. diss., University of Cincinnati, 1992.

Tubeuf, André. *Le Lied Allemande: Poètes et paysages*. Paris: Éditions François Bourin, 1993.

Turner, Ronald. "A Comparison of Two Sets of Liszt-Hugo Songs." *JALS* 5 (1979): 16–31.

Voronova, Marina. "Simfoniceskaja poema Lista v ee svjazjah s literaturnoj Romanticeskoj poemoj." In *Pamjati N. S. Nikolaevoj*, 36–41. Moscow: Moscow Conservatory, 1996.

Wagner, Günther. *Die Klavierballade um die Mitte des 19. Jahrhunderts*. Munich and Salzburg: Emil Katzbichler, 1976.

Walker, Alan. *Franz Liszt*. Vol. 1, *The Virtuoso Years 1811–1847*. New York: Alfred A. Knopf, 1983. Rev. ed. Ithaca: Cornell University Press, 1987.

―――. *Franz Liszt*. Vol. 2, *The Weimar Years 1848–1861*. New York: Alfred A. Knopf, 1989. Reprint. Ithaca: Cornell University Press, 1989.

―――. *Franz Liszt*. Vol. 3, *The Final Years 1861–1886*. New York: Alfred A. Knopf, 1996. Reprint. Ithaca: Cornell University Press, 1997.

―――. "Liszt and the Schubert Song Transcriptions." *Musical Quarterly* 67 (1981): 50–63.

―――. *Liszt, Carolyne, and the Vatican. The Story of a thwarted Marriage as it emerges from the original Church Documents*. American Liszt Society Studies Series no. 1. Stuyvesant, NY: Pendragon, 1991.

―――, ed. *Franz Liszt: The Man & His Music*. New York: Taplinger, 1970.

————, ed. *Living with Liszt from the Diary of Carl Lachmund: An American Pupil of Liszt 1882–1884*. Franz Liszt Studies Series no. 4. Stuyvesant, NY: Pendragon, 1995.

Watson, Derek. *Liszt*. New York: Schirmer, 1989.

————. "Liszt and Goethe: The Songs." *LSJ* 10 (1985): 2–5.

Way, Elizabeth. "Raphael as a Musical Model: Liszt's *Sposalizio*." *JALS* 40 (1996): 103–112.

Weinmann, Alexander. *Beiträge zur Geschichtes des Alt-Wiener Musikverlages*, Reihe 2, Folge 14. *Verzeichnis der Musikalien des Verlages Maisch-Sprenger-Artaria*. Vienna: Universal Editions, 1970.

Wellings, Joy. "Liszt's Christmas Tree." *LSJ* 13 (1988): 4–28.

————. "Liszt's 'Hungarian Historical Portraits.' " *LSJ* 11 (1986): 88–92 and 12 (1987): 48–53.

————. "The Csárdás macabre': A Study of Motivic Unity." *LSJ* 7 (1982): 2–6.

Werba, Eric. "Franz Liszt und das Lied." *Österreichische Musikzeitschrift* 16 (1961): 412–415.

Westerby, Herbert. *Liszt, Composer, and His Piano Works*. London: Reeves, [1936].

White, Charles. "The Masses of Franz Liszt." Ph.D. diss., Bryn Mawr University, 1973.

Whitton, Kenneth. *Lieder: An Introduction to German Songs*. London: Julia MacRae Books, 1984.

Wilde, David. "Liszt's Sonata: Some Jungian Reflections." In *Analecta Lisztiana II: New Light on Liszt and His Music*, ed. Michael Saffle and James Deaville. Franz Liszt Studies Series no. 6, 197–224. Stuyvesant, NY: Pendragon, 1997.

Williams, Adrian, ed. and trans. *Portrait of Liszt: By Himself and His Contemporaries*. Oxford: Clarendon Press, 1990.

Williams, Graham. *Liszt Sonata in B Minor*. Mayflower study guides 14. Leeds: Mayflower Enterprises, 1991.

Wilson, Karen Sue. "A Historical Study and Stylistic Analysis of Franz Liszt's *Années de pèlerinage*." Ph.D. diss., University of North Carolina, Chapel Hill, 1977.

Winkler, Gerhard J. "'Der traurige Mönch' (1860). Considérations archéologiques sur les oeuvres tardives de Liszt." *La Revue musicale* 405–407 (1987): 105–118.

————. "Ein' feste Burg ist unser Gott.' Meyerbeers Hugenotten in den Paraphrasen Thalbergs und Liszts." In *Der junge Liszt. Referate des 4. Europäischen Liszt-Symposions Wien 1991. Liszt Studien 4*, ed. Gottfried Scholz, 100–134. Munich and Salzburg: Emil Katzbichler, 1993.

————. "Liszt contra Wagner. Wagnerkritik in den späten Klavierstücken Franz Liszts." In *Franz Liszt und Richard Wagner. Musikalische und geistesegeschichtliche Grundlagen der neudeutschen Schule. Referate des 3. Europäischen Liszt-Symposions. Eisenstadt 1983. Liszt Studien 3*, ed. Serge Gut, 189–210. Munich and Salzburg: Emil Katzbichler, 1986.

————. " 'Tradition' and 'Progress': Liszt's first Melodrama *Lenore*." In *Liszt the Progressive*, ed. Hans Kagebeck and Johan Lagerfelt, 223–237. Lewiston, MA: Edwin Mellen, 2001.

Winklhofer, Sharon. "Liszt, Marie d'Agoult, and the Dante Sonata." *19th-Century Music* 1/1 (1977): 15–32.

————. *Liszt's Sonata in B minor: A Study of Autograph Sources and Documents*. Ann Arbor, MI: UMI Research Press, 1980.

————. Review of "Liszt, Franz [Ferenc]." In *The New Grove Dictionary of Music and Musicians. 19th-Century Music* 5 (Spring 1982): 257–262.

Woodward, Ralph. "The Large Sacred Choral Works of Franz Liszt." Ph.D. diss., University of Illinois, 1964.

Wright, William. "Liszt's London Appearances in 1827." *LSJ* 16 (1991): 9.

————. "The Transcriptions for Cello and Piano of Works by Liszt." *JALS* 35 (1994): 30–58.

Wuellner, Guy S. "Franz Liszt's Prelude on 'Chopsticks.' " *JALS* 4 (1978): 37–44.

Yang, Ching Ling. "The Development of the Piano Etude from Muzio Clementi to Anton Rubinstein: A Study of Selected Works from 1801 to 1870." D.M.A. diss., University of North Carolina, Greensboro, 1998.

Yeagley, David Anthony. "Franz Liszt's Dante Sonata: The Origins, the Criticism, a Selective Musical Analysis, and Commentary." D.M.A. diss., University of Arizona, 1994.

————. "Liszt's Dante Sonata: Origins and Criticism." *JALS* 37 (1995): 1–12.

Zellner, L. A. *Ueber Franz Liszts Graner Festmesse und ihre Stellung zur geschichtlichen Entwicklung der Kirchenmusik.* Vienna: F. Manz, 1858.

Index of Works

Index of Names and Subjects

Contributors

BEN ARNOLD has published numerous articles on Liszt in the *Journal of the American Liszt Society* and *Analecta Lisztiana I* and *II*. His interest in music and its relationship to war led to his book *Music and War* (1993) and related articles in *The Musical Quarterly, International Review of the Aesthetics and Sociology of Music, Holocaust and Genocide Studies, The Oxford Companion to American Military History,* and *Handbook of the Literature and Research of World War Two*. Arnold is an Associate Professor of Music at Emory University in Atlanta.

JAMES DEAVILLE is an Associate Professor in the School of the Arts, McMaster University. He has published extensively about Liszt, in particular about issues of reception. Other research topics include Wagner, Peter Cornelius, women and music, and film music.

KLÁRA HAMBURGER was born in Budapest. She studied musicology at the F. Liszt Music Academy, Budapest where she received her diploma in 1961. She received her "candidate of musicological sciences" from the Hungarian Academy of Sciences in 1981, and "dr. Phil." from the F. Liszt Music Academy in 1982. She has served as the Librarian at the Hungarian Academy of Sciences and at the Music Department of National Széchényi Library, Budapest. Between 1966 and 1990 she was editor of music books of the publishing house Gondolat, and has served as the Secretary General of the Hungarian Liszt Society since 1999. Her book *Liszt* (1966) has been published in Hungarian, German, and English, and she is also author of a handbook of Liszt's works, *Liszt Kalauz* (1986). She has edited two collections of Liszt's letters, *Franz Liszt. Lettres à Cosima et à Daniela* (1996) and *Franz Liszt: Briefwechsel mit seiner Mutter* (2000), as well as the collection, *Franz Liszt: Beiträge von ungarischen Autoren* (1978).

MARILYN KIELNIARZ earned three degrees in organ performance at Northwestern University (Evanston, IL), and a Certificate in Dalcroze Eurhythmics from Carnegie Mellon University (Pittsburgh, PA). Active in many different areas of music, she has concertized and successfully competed in various organ competitions throughout North America and Europe, and is a keyboardist for the Omaha Symphony. She is an Associate Professor at Omaha's Creighton University, where she serves as Chair for the Department of Fine and Performing Arts. Dr. Kielniarz is also the director of Creighton's Javanese Gamelan ensemble, reflecting her annual summers abroad in Indonesia where she studies and performs. She is a recording artist as well as a published author of writings on Dalcroze Eurhythmics, music theory, and church music.

JAY ROSENBLATT is an assistant professor of music history at the University of Arizona. His research has focused on the works for piano and orchestra of Franz Liszt, and his editions include "De Profundis (psaume instrumental)" and the Concerto in E-flat Major, Op. Posth., both of which have been recorded several times. He has also published articles in the *Journal of the American Liszt Society* and the *Pendragon Review*.

MICHAEL SAFFLE, Professor of Music and Humanities with the Center for Interdisciplinary Studies at Virginia Tech, has specialized in the careers and compositions of Franz Liszt and Richard Wagner, American music of the late nineteenth and early twentieth centuries, and interdisciplinary topics involving music, literature, gender, and popular entertainment. His *Richard Wagner: A Guide to Research* (New York: Routledge) is scheduled to appear in print in 2002; he has also published articles and reviews in the *Journal of the American Musicological Society*, *Notes*, *Acta Musicologica*, and the *Programmhefte der Bayreuther Festspiele*, and edited several collections of essays dealing with musical and cultural subjects. He serves as a contributing editor for American entries in the new edition of *Die Musik in Geschichte und Gegenwart* and spent the 2000-2001 academic year as Bicentennial Fulbright Professor of American Studies at the University of Helsinki.

CHARLES SUTTONI (Ph.D., New York University, 1973) is the translator of Liszt, *An Artist's Journey: Lettres d'un bachelier ès musique* (University of Chicago Press, 1989) and has compiled two volumes of Liszt's opera paraphrases (Dover Publications, 1981 and 1982). He also compiled an extensive bibliography of "Liszt Correspondence in Print" (*JALS* 25, January-June 1989) together with a "Supplement" (*JALS* 46, Fall 1999). Suttoni served on the Board of Directors of the American Liszt Society for several years and was the 1995 recipient of the Society's Medal for Excellence.

KRISTIN WENDLAND teaches music theory and aural/keyboard skills at Emory University. She was a contributor to the *International Dictionary of Black Composers* and is editor of the *GAMUT* (Georgia Association of Music Theorists) *Journal*. She has served GAMUT as president and secretary and is past-chair of the Society for Music Theory's Committee on Diversity. Her current research interests center around Argentine tango music and dance.

WILLIAM WRIGHT is a pianist, scholar, and former Council Member of the Liszt Society. Since giving the world premiere of Liszt's piano piece in A♭ S189 in a B. B. C. Scotland broadcast recital in 1987 he has been engaged in intensive Liszt research, presenting papers and performing in American, British, and Canadian universities and on two occasions lecturing at the Liszt Academy in Budapest. He has written several articles including "The Transcriptions for Cello and Piano of Works by Liszt" for the *Journal of the American Liszt Society*.